sports skills

sports skills

a conceptual approach to meaningful movement

second edition

Beverly L. Seidel, *Kent State University*
Fay R. Biles, *Kent State University*
Grace E. Figley, *Kent State University*
Bonnie J. Neuman, *Hood College*

Foreword:

Dr. Glenn A. Olds, President
Alaska Pacific University

ᴡᴄᴃ

Wm. C. Brown Company Publishers
Dubuque, Iowa

PHYSICAL EDUCATION
CONSULTING EDITOR

Aileene Lockhart
Texas Woman's University

HEALTH
CONSULTING EDITOR

Robert Kaplan
The Ohio State University

PARKS AND RECREATION
CONSULTING EDITOR

David Gray
California State University, Long Beach

Cover photo courtesy of University of Connecticut

Copyright © 1975, 1980 by Wm. C. Brown Company Publishers
Library of Congress Catalog Card Number: 79-54090
ISBN 0-697-07168-5

Printed in the United States of America
10   9   8   7   6   5   4

*To those outstanding teachers
who showed us a concern
for students as individuals,*

Ruth L. Carroll □ **Elizabeth Bookhout** □ **Ruth Brunton** □ **Hazael Taylor**

and

*to those students
at Kent State University who
through the years have taught us
the value of caring, this book is
respectfully and affectionately
dedicated.*

CONTENTS

FOREWORD

Most of human life is lived in the tension and polarity of our amphibian nature as body-mind, soma-psyche. The tragedy of our time, if not all time, is to seek to ignore or to crown one or another aspect of our nature. Whatever else may be said about the contemporary crisis in education, this much is clear. We are suffering from an education and a culture that has sundered soma and psyche, the body with its natural, organic intelligence and immediate experience, and the mind with its verbal abstract intelligence and reflective experience. Ours is an age of the split personality. With all of our pampering, protecting, and preening the body, we do not seriously seek to understand its wisdom and ways, or what is more important, to relate this wisdom to the mind and its search for meaning.

At the same time, the attention and interest of education is drawn increasingly to the mind, and its verbal, abstract intelligence. We know that something is wrong; that all of our abstract intelligence has not been able to produce character; that all of our knowledge has not been able to stay the breakdown of mind and body; that our post-Sputnik panic to return to a classical curriculum but recalls an earlier sterility in American education with its aristocracy of the abstract intellect; that I.Q. tests do not insure personal or collegiate success; that it is questionable whether information substantially alters attitudes; in short, that something is wrong with contemporary education, basically, and at the core.

The emphasis on the almost exclusive education of the mind is easy to understand. It reflects the major triumph of the West in developing the tools of the mind, language and mathematics, for the simplification, measurement and mastery of the external world and communication of that knowledge. Indeed, the classical liberal arts curriculum is modeled after this primacy of the languages of measurement, mathematics, and communication. Such is the view of persons who assume that if you fill a person's mind, his knowledge will filter through his muscles, and eventually change the way he behaves. It is psychosomatic in nature.

Many of us deeply involved in education in a period of swift change and critical challenge believe a reversal in this priority is in order. It is offered in the introduction of this thoughtful volume because the spokesmen for this reversal of emphasis, even in physical education, are so few. One would expect that educators concerned primarily with the soma, with the human body, its form, function and movement, would smell brimstone in the almost exclusive attention to the mind in contemporary education. Physical educators are the ones who understand man's and woman's natural intelligence, this organic nonverbal wisdom which is the secret to health, clue to responsible action, and the inner artistry that relates body and mind, energy and meaning in every human act. They are those who understand what Aristotle called man's vegetative soul, in charge of such simple mysteries as breathing, heartbeat, digestion, and healing. They are those who should shed light on other nonverbal aspects of a being's experience—inspiration, morale, vision, and spiritual self-transcendence. They are those who should know how to educate this delicate dimension of the individual, the nonverbal, somatic humanity, in the kinesthetic and other senses, memory, the autonomic nervous system, and spiritual insight. These lie at the root of somatopsychic education, able to heal the split in modern humanity's nature.

But, unhappily, physical educators too have been caught in the alchemy of the mind and its mathematical and verbal successes. The tools of the mind have trapped the interpreters of the body into a superficial imitation through measurement, mechanical analysis, and formal functions, and the physical educators have turned their art into a science, their philosophy into a skill, and their education into training. They have forgotten Nietszche's warning: "A man who lives from a *why* can handle any *how*. But he who knows how, but not why, cannot even live as a man."

This volume addresses this larger question. What is the why of a person, somatopsychic unity in function and difference in structure? What light does the *soma* shed on the *psyche*? How does their partnership provide a clue to the promise of the person and the meaning of education? What special contributions do the science and art of physical education shed on the contemporary crises of education? It would take volumes to spell this out in detail. This introductory note permits only the hint at an outline of an educational philosophy which derives from the natural primacy of the body, and in its wisdom a contribution to four basic maladies of our time: (1) impersonality; (2) emptiness and boredom of work; (3) sterility of the spectator with his mentality and morality of the viewer, not doer; and (4) the erosion of egotism in all our service. For each, somatopsychic education makes a major contribution in its accent on: (1) the primacy of the personal; (2) the integrity and innocence of play; (3) the discipline of total participation; and (4) the grace of self-transcendence.

The principles of such education drawn on in this volume can be swiftly stated, although it would take a lifetime to substantiate their rich content. They may be put as follows: (1) The personal is primary in the discovery of the self, the learning of meaning, and the making of people. (2) The integrity and innocence of play is the most valid theatre for the rehearsal and recreation of the emerging self and the expansion of sense, the self's contact with the other. (3) The discipline of total participation insures the wholeness of learning, the healing of the split between thought, affection, and action, and the character of the maturing person. (4) The grace of self-transcendence informs all heroic action, and mirrors in time, our human destiny.

THE PRIMACY OF THE PERSONAL

Most educators have forgotten that the uniqueness of the person and the integrity of the individual is rooted in a primitive somatic fact—the primacy and privacy of the kinesthetic sense, man's basic bodily awareness. We vulgarly think of this fact as bodily and of preschool significance, beneath the sophistication of our verbally self-conscious education. Yet this much-neglected kinesthetic sense carries the inward clue to the emergence of the sense of self, the inner authenticity of the presence of the person. It is the main line of communication between our autonomic animal intelligence and our conscious self. It is not deceived by the accident of color, birth, station, or circumstance—its knowledge is more inward and personal than that. Its domain is the immediate sense: its security is firsthand, individual, unique. To ignore, corrupt, or debauch this sense, as contemporary culture and education have done, is to flirt with inner chaos, loss of personal identity, preoccupation with peripheral clues, and not the primacy of the person. It is amazing, if not amusing, that in a culture stressing the primacy of the person, verbally and intellectually, we become more impersonal, less certain of self, more deeply and inwardly confused about who we are and why. The reason is not hard to find. We have not tended the soil in which the self can grow, the privacy and primacy of the bodily sense

that is uniquely "mine." This must be educated into a secure sense of self, in power, promise, and mastery. Such is our task.

THE INTEGRITY AND INNOCENCE OF PLAY

Most educators have forgotten that the self is not a finished fact—a blank page, an empty receptacle to be filled with information from without, but is rather an act, creating and recreating itself from within. Education may midwife and mend—it cannot produce from without save what is given in promise from within. This creation and recreation from within is the stuff of play—spontaneous, natural, and innocent. Play is primary in the architecture of the authentic self. In play the person is open, uncomplicated, self-forgetful. In play we rehearse roles of promise from deep within our nature. In a synthetic culture with its sham morality and substitute selves, play is the enemy of all self-deception, "other-directedness," and cold calculation. Through the spontaneous self-expression of play, the kinesthetic sense is transformed into imaginative action, prophecy of the self to be. In such action, we externalize ourselves, mirror ourselves in time, test our power, and create a stable framework within which to paint the portrait of the promise of the self. Next to prayer, play is the mirroring of the authentic self.

THE DISCIPLINE OF TOTAL PARTICIPATION

Most educators have forgotten that the discipline which remakes the self is never imposed from without. It is always self-imposed. Such discipline is not of the mind alone, holding in focus ideas in proper relationship, but rather of the total self in which thought, affection, and action complete a cycle and style of life. Unlike the discipline of the mind, in which ideas may be organized and harmonized without altering the basic nature of the self, organic discipline of the body involves a total participation in which the self is changed from within. The disciplined completion of an act involves a delicate harmony of idea, affection, intention, and execution. This cycle forms and transforms the self, personally and permanently. Bodily discipline can never be achieved as spectator—the posture of so much of our academic learning—but only as participant. Competence is not merely a matter of skill, it is a blend of the why and how, the feeling and forging of intention and action into a whole. It heals the split between mind and body, meaning and movement that haunts contemporary education.

THE GRACE OF SELF-TRANSCENDENCE

Most educators have forgotten that the highest learning of persons lies not in self-conscious grasping for meaning, but in moments of self-forgetfulness when we are grasped by a meaning which transcends ourselves. Indeed, in most movements of the self that remake us, we transcend ourselves through the inspiration of that Spirit which carries us beyond ourselves. This is the root fact which turns work into service, action into responsibility, and as every coach knows, sport into the occasion for character. In self-transcending action, we go beyond ourselves, trace an immortal image in this vessel of clay, reveal kinship to that Spirit who inspires heroic action on behalf of others. Too little is known of this inner drama of heroic action, which through inspiration and expectation transcends our normal powers and natural reach in meaning and vitality. Too little is known of this somatic sanity which releases new possibilities in the face of imaginative demands.

In this meeting place of body-mind where motive, muscle and meaning blend into human action of heroic self-giving we have the surest clue and largest promise of the evolution of persons. Here is the prophecy of the Spirit in whose image we are made to use body and mind to fulfill its promise. Here is an invitation to a new kind of education and educator.

Persons are many-splendored. So are they who tend and teach them. People in these modern times have lost their way, but not their souls. They have driven a wedge between mind and body; they have left the latter to shift for itself while devoting all their energies to the cultivation of the former. The imbalance has made them dizzy and disturbed, as reflected in the illnesses of mind and body. Their deep need is for an education toward wholeness, recovery of the primacy of the education of the body, apart from which they can never know the primacy and privacy of their person, the delight and discovery of self through play, the discipline of integrity of total participation in learning and life, or the grace of self-transcendence in heroic self-giving.

Those who are custodians of such a mystery and mission were never more needed, however inhospitable the present climate of education. Let such educators, then, enact this heroic action which gives that others might find themselves, their authentic selfhood, and the meaning of a man.

The authors of this book, whom I know personally and who happily practice what they preach, suggest an approach that should be an exciting help and incentive to all future physical educators for whom the whole person and the whole life is one grand "movement with meaning."

GLENN A. OLDS
President
ALASKA PACIFIC UNIVERSITY

PREFACE

"Back to basics!" This is the cry of many critics of the educational system today, critics from both within and without the profession. At the same time, no matter how paradoxical it may seem, accountability, individualization, personalization and humanization are key words in educational theory.

"Back to the basics" may mean to some people only a return to an emphasis on the three R's; to others, it portends the value of stressing the basics in every phase of the educational process. A child must learn to walk before he can run, albeit some educators seem not to subscribe to this tenet of learning. If a learner is missing a foundation skill upon which to build, failure along with a dislike for the subject area is apt to occur.

The problem of basics inheres in physical education as well. The effects of Title IX and the concurrent swing to an emphasis on interschool athletic programs, often to the detriment of a physical education program for *all* students, can only be self-defeating. We must somehow ensure that we do not end with a minority of students exceptionally well-educated physically while the majority ae hopelessly neglected.

This book is an attempt to make practical the theoretical concepts discussed by presenting a conceptual approach to the teaching of physical education which, if followed, will do much to ameliorate the problems referred to above since it takes cognizance of the learner and his individual needs and thus better achieve the purposes of education in a humanistic fashion. The focus of this suggested approach is on *movement* and on *what moves.* Bodies, objects, and bodies controlling objects move through *space* and *time* with *force* and *flow.* Additionally, this approach divorces itself from the traditional approach to teaching with its emphasis on conformity and imposed discipline, and stresses instead a more personalized methodology with an emphasis on self-discipline, creativity and the joy of discovery. Physical educators, in their attention to the development of motor skill, traditionally have overlooked the meaning inherent in movement. Often complex skills and competitive situations are introduced before basic skills are mastered. The learners themselves have objected; yet another example of the idea that "a child shall lead them." Movement sense, as discussed in Chapter Two, is a basis for meaning. The moving person needs to understand the elements of movement (space, force, time and flow), and he needs to be able to incorporate them into movement patterns and thus become "aware" of his body. Body awareness, then, becomes the key to perceptual meaning "from inside-out." Meaning, understanding, feeling, movement . . . all are basic to the moving human "becoming."

The motivation to write this book was threefold: (1) to help those teachers who are attempting to teach conceptually by attending to all the domains of learning with a discussion of new methodology, commonalities among sports, and techniques by which instruction can be individualized, and by sharing sample unit and lesson plans; (2) to analyze and synthesize the relationships between physical education and the latest educational theory; and (3) to introduce students of physical education to movement and pedagogical terminology as early as possible in their professional lives.

The present work is different from other books of this nature in the area of physical education in that it integrates the educational objectives in the cognitive, affective, and psychomotor domains, and it presents unique activity skills in a form which should be helpful in planning for such integration. In addition, this book emphasizes the *indirect method of teaching.* Other methods are not presented for two reasons: (1) the authors firmly believe that the indirect method is the most conducive to results in the three domains of learning; and (2) the mechanics of the more traditional, more direct approaches are already well-known.

For those to whom this approach is new or perplexing, a model, "development of the total individual through volleyball," pages 339–353, presents a progression of movement experiences which includes attention to all three domains of learning as specific skills are taught. The amount of space required to present such a progression for each activity is monetarily prohibitive. However, the teacher can use the volleyball chart as a model for other activities. The chapter on volleyball also includes a sample lesson plan using the indirect method of teaching; this, too, can serve as a model.

Only the simpler movement combinations which are fundamental to specific activities are addressed. *More advanced skills, typically reserved for a coaching situation, are not within the purview of this volume.*

This second edition is reorganized into six parts. Part I, Foundations, which is expanded and updated, presents background information on the conceptual approach, its methodology, and on the mechanical principles which underlie efficient movement.

Part II, Concept Commonalities, is also revised and it focuses on those movement concepts which are common to several activities as well as on common strategy and safety concepts. **The necessity for the user of this book to become thoroughly familiar with the contents of Part II cannot be stressed too strongly. A real and workable understanding of Part II is requisite to an effective use of the total book.**

The various sports activities analyzed are grouped according to the authors' taxonomy, as shown on page 84, with an introduction to each group. Part III, Goal-Oriented Sports, focuses on the activities of basketball, field hockey, and soccer. Part IV, Field Sports, deals only with softball. Badminton, tennis, and volleyball are included in Part V, Net Sports, while Part VI, Individual Sports, examines archery, golf, gymnastics, track and field, and swimming.

Each of the parts which deals with specific activities concentrates on their distinctive skills, as well as on their common and unique concepts. In addition, suggestions for individualizing instruction are given for each activity.

Sports Skills: A Conceptual Approach to Meaningful Movement should prove to be a basic and invaluable reference for professional students and for dedicated teachers who are interested in furthering the concept of phys-ical education as an academic discipline as well as in teaching the total human being to become meaningfully physically educated. Although the generic "he" is used throughout, the book is for both sexes, and illustrations are approximately equally divided between male and female performances. In addition, greater attention is paid to the male performer in this revised edition; for example, events for men are added to the chapter on Gymnastics.

Special thanks are due Judy Devine, Laurel Wartluft, Heidie Mitchell, Tod Boyle, Marilyn Cerny, Chris Hirsch, Sherri Kemp, Phyllis Hilburn, Sally Ramsburg and Sue Lyngaas. Grateful acknowledgement is extended as well to Dr. Glenn A. Olds, President of Alaska Pacific University, for permission to re-use his most perceptive Foreword.

PART I. □ FOUNDATIONS

We shall not cease from
exploration
And the end of all our
exploring
Will be to arrive where
we started
And know the place for
the first time.

T. S. Eliot

1

Introduction

Current Emphases in Education
Objectives in Physical Education
Terminology
Why the Conceptual Approach?

I should not like my writing to spare other people the trouble of thinking. But, if possible, to stimulate someone to thoughts of his own.

Wittgenstein

There is strong evidence that physical education is making strides toward becoming accepted as an academic discipline as dedicated scholars formulate a theoretical framework for it that is, at the same time, functional and capable of application. As the phenomena of persons, movement and meaning are explored, the body of knowledge which makes physical education an academic discipline is growing both in amount and in stature. Indeed, the primary concern of the Scholarly Directions Committee of the American Alliance for Health, Physical Education, and Recreation is to encourage scholars to extend the "horizons, boundaries, and dimensions" of basic knowledge in physical education as well as to organize such knowledge in a way that will serve to generate new knowledge.[1]

The study of human movement with all of its congruent aspects has become generally accepted as the nucleus around which the academic discipline of physical education is built. As a part of this discipline, movement education, however defined and taught in the U.S., is no longer accorded the tenuous position which characterized it only a few years ago. Although there is still disagreement and misunderstanding about the *process* of movement education, the *concept* seems somewhat firmly established. Almost every author who writes about movement education stresses the conceptual learnings which can accrue from properly presented

1. W. R. Morford, "New Frontiers in Physical Education: The Need for Scholarship." (Paper presented at the National Conference of the AAHPER, Seattle, April 1970).

subject matter, understandings basic to the development of effective, efficient human movement. While the authors of this book agree that such learnings *can* result, they believe that a subject-matter approach which overlooks the *subject of the approach*, the learner, is not nearly as productive as it might be. Therefore, close attention to the learner in the learning process is advocated. It is felt that recognition of the importance of individual internalization more nearly ensures that the learner who *understands* the basic principles of movement (cognitive domain) will *use* effective, efficient movement (psychomotor domain) simply because he realizes the *value* of such movement (affective domain).[2] These three domains are discussed in greater detail later in this chapter.

Generally, movement education seems to be considered as an exclusive function of physical education at the elementary school level; however, elements of it—particularly aspects such as problem-solving and guided discovery which characterize its methodology—are just as apropos at the secondary school and college level. Since professional students of physical education in our teacher-training institutions tend to teach their future students in approximately the same manner as they were taught, it becomes evident that the somewhat traditional approach to the teaching of sports skills (i.e., verbal discussion by the teacher of how a skill should be performed, and a demonstration by the teacher of how it is done, followed by a practice session in which the learners attempt to emulate the teacher's demonstration) must be supplemented if not supplanted if physical education is to keep pace with educational philosophy based on the latest research in the area of the behavioral sciences.[3]

CURRENT EMPHASES IN EDUCATION

The knowledge explosion, along with an increased insight into how learning best takes place, has led philosophers of education and curriculum makers to scrutinize rather severely not only those objectives which have been traditionally espoused for education but also the curricular content which allegedly served as a vehicle to those objectives. Pioneer attempts at classifying the goals of education resulted in a taxonomy consisting of three major domains: cognitive, affective and psychomotor.

The *cognitive domain* focuses upon intellectual objectives, including those dealing with recall or recognition of knowledge and the development of intellectual abilities and skills.[4]

The *affective domain* focuses upon a concept of internalization or a ". . . continuous modification of behavior from the individual's being aware of a phenomenon to a pervasive outlook on life that influences all his actions." Hence objectives in this domain emphasize feelings, emotions, values and attitudes which contribute to the individual's

2. For a more complete description of the process of internalization, see David R. Kratwohl, Benjamin S. Bloom, and Masia Bertram, *Taxonomy of Educational Objectives, Handbook II: Affective Domain* (New York: David McKay Co., 1964), pp. 29–30.
3. See Eleanor Metheny, *Movement and Meaning* (New York: McGraw-Hill Book Co., 1968); W. R. Morford, "Toward a Profession, Not a Craft," *Quest* 18 (May 1972):88–93; Thomas J. Sheehan and William L. Alsop, "Educational Sport," *Journal of Health, Physical Education and Recreation* 45 (May 1972):41–45; Daryl Siedentop, "On Tilting at Windmills while Rome Burns," *Quest* 18 (May 1972)94–97.
4. See Benjamin S. Bloom, ed., *Taxonomy of Educational Objectives, Handbook I: Cognitive Domain* (New York: David McKay Co., 1956); also, Thomas J. Sheehan, "The Cognitive Domain and the Teaching of Physical Education," *Seventy-fifth Proceedings of the National College Physical Education Association for Men*, 1972, 141–147.

life style.[5] (For examples of desired outcomes in this domain, see Table 3.1, page 32.)

The *psychomotor domain* focuses upon manipulation of material and objects, and neuromuscular and motor skill.[6] In this book, the terms psychomotor and motor domains are used interchangeably.

Sometimes the attainment of an objective in one domain serves as a means to the attainment of an objective in another domain. It would seem, however, that too many teachers view this as some kind of an automatic outcome. For example, they assume that the learner will continue in activities that make him physically fit simply because he knows the medical value of fitness. That this does not occur is attested to in part by the number of overweight, physically unfit adults in our population. However, the discerning teacher who understands the psychological principles of learning as well as the complexities of the learner can *plan* so that behavioral outcomes occur in all three domains.

Most teachers realize that motivation is critical to learning; however, many of them do not seem aware that motivation results more often than not from attention to the affective domain. Methodology which encourages the "act of discovery" seems indicated if we are to build an interest in learning.[7]

Physical education has lagged behind many other subject areas in a critical self-examination of philosophy, curriculum, and methodology. It is an undisputed fact that little in the way of new and innovative material has been introduced into the physical education curriculum in the past fifty years. (The trend toward movement education seems to be a significant exception.) Thus, American physical education, with its traditional emphasis centered largely on specific games, dance, sports and tumbling skills (psychomotor domain), has had literally to fight for its existence as an integral part of the total educational curriculum. The current emphasis in educational programs on creative and innovative teaching with stress on such objectives as intellectual understandings and creativity (cognitive domain), attitudes and interests, self-actualization, self-direction, self-discipline, and democratic involvement (affective domain) calls for curriculum designers in physical education to reexamine and reevaluate the subject matter of the field as well as the methodology commonly employed.[8] Inattention by the experts to the public's increasing demand for accountability in education may result in a drastically altered physical education program, according to the whims of a particularly vocal segment of society, or in the complete elimination of the program from the school system.

OBJECTIVES IN PHYSICAL EDUCATION

If physical education is to be a vital part of the entire educational spectrum, it would seem that many changes—some of them rather sweeping in nature—must be made. Objectives, stated in terms of behavioral out-

5. See Don R. Kirkendall, "Physical Education Effects in the Affective Domain," *Seventy-fifth Proceedings of the National College Physical Education Association for Men,* 1972, 147–151; also, Kratwohl et al., *Educational Objectives: Affective Domain.*
6. Anita J. Harrow, *A Taxonomy of the Psychomotor Domain* (New York: David McKay Co., 1972).
7. Jerome S. Bruner, "The Act of Discovery," *Harvard Educational Review* 31 (Winter 1961):21–32.
8. See Committee on Understandings and Knowledge in Physical Eduction, *Knowledge and Understanding in Physical Education* (Washington, D.C.: American Association for Health, Physical Education & Recreation, 1969); also, Marlin M. Mackenzie, *Toward a New Curriculum in Physical Education* (New York: McGraw-Hill Book Co., 1969); also, Celeste Ulrich and John Nixon, *Tones of Theory* (Washington, D.C.: American Association for Health, Physical Education & Recreation, 1972).

comes (see Table 3.1, p. 32, for examples of how objectives can be stated in such terms), should be redefined. Such objectives are further clarified in the section, "Why the Conceptual Approach?" One of the major objectives of such outcomes is a student who is motivated, perhaps because of self-perception of ungraceful or awkward movement patterns, to seek to understand (cognitive domain) the bases of effective movement and thus ultimately to develop his skill potential.

The Committee on Understandings and Knowledge in Physical Education of the American Association for Health, Physical Education & Recreation listed objectives of physical education in each of the following categories: physiological, motor skills, aesthetic, social, and intellectual, and it further clarified its position by saying:

> Although the intellectual objectives are listed in parallel order to the four other categories, they actually undergird the entire structure. They provide the "how" and the "why" of the skill learning process and the activity which results. They are also important because they have value in themselves as adjuncts to the physically educated person.[9]

Thus, intellectualization of physical education is a necessity.

Personalization of physical education, or attention to the affective domain, is also a necessity. Nearly all learning theorists today agree that concept formation or cognitive learning is the basis for all learning. However, if the teacher ignores the learner as an individual with unique basic drives and emotions, he will no doubt be unable to motivate interest in learning to any significant extent. Therefore, the teacher must realize the need to use cognitive learnings in rewarding (affective domain) situations. Rewarding situations, in turn, somewhat guarantee interest, and interest usually guarantees greater learning.

The academic discipline of physical education deals uniquely with human movement (motor domain); for that reason perhaps, most physical educators pay greater attention to the motor than to the other domains of learning as they attempt to increase the learner's skill in movement. However, emphasis on the motor domain ought not preclude attention to the intellectualization (cognitive domain) and personalization (affective domain) so necessary if physical education is to take its rightful place as a respected and vital part of the total curriculum. And, if the cognitive and affective domains are to be internalized, careful attention must be paid to an holistic concept of the learner as a *total person.*

TERMINOLOGY

Although it may seem that a section on terminology is misplaced at this point, the necessity to learn the vocabulary and then to internalize it cannot be over-emphasized. Therefore, several terms are defined here as they are used in this book. Attention to these definitions is essential since, in some cases, no one meaning of a term is so universally accepted as to ensure communication. Without a comprehension of these terms, the material that follows it will be much less meaningful.

Basic movement is a content area unit in the physical education program which has for its objective to teach the student the capacities and limitations of his body based on principles and laws of human movement. It is the foundation stone of physical education. Stress is placed on *what* moves (an awareness of the various body parts and how they move in relation to each other), *where* it moves (in space, in relation to self

9. Committee on Understandings and Knowledge in Physical Education, *Knowledge and Understanding in Physical Education,* p. viii.

and others, with and without equipment), and *how* it moves (with force and with flow, in time).

The *elements of movement* are force, flow, time and space. These are the basic elements of all movement. Students must be helped to realize that *time* describes a movement in terms of speed (slow, fast; accelerate, decelerate), *force* describes the effort required in movement (weak, strong; explosive, sustained; production, absorption), *flow* describes the connection of moving body parts in a sequential, effective manner (free, bound), and *space* describes the area in which the movement occurs (self-space, general space; forward, backward; up, down).

Body awareness is a kinesthetic recognition of one's own body parts and how each moves in relation to the other.

Fundamental movement skills are such skills as walking, twisting and turning, and striking an object. Fundamental skills can be classified into three groups: locomotor, nonlocomotor and manipulative.

Basic sports skills are a combination of fundamental movement skills, such as a volleyball serve or the approach to a vault in gymnastics.

Movement education is the descriptive term for the physical education program which aims to accomplish the goal of having each child control his body in movement. It starts with the content area of basic movement and builds upon this until efficient, effective movement, whether in the realm of fundamental movement skill or highly sophisticated specific skill, is achieved.

The *methodology of movement education* is largely that of exploration, centered around two main approaches: *problem solving*, in which the teacher attempts to design a problem in such a manner that the learner, through experimentation, discovers for himself the best and most efficient movement pattern; and *guided discovery*, in which the teacher plays a more direct role in that he poses the problem in such a manner that certain desired outcomes are somewhat ensured. In both of these approaches, the teacher is more than an interested observer. He actively teaches throughout the lesson. Although he does not usually demonstrate how particular movements should be performed, he helps the learner evaluate, he aids him in understanding why certain movements feel more comfortable, and he can suggest possible changes.

Perception is the term applied to that recognition of a stimulus which is necessary before one can conceptualize appropriately. Both the recognition and the response are learned.

Self-perception or *self-image* is how the learner perceives himself. Basically, self-perception is a part of the affective domain.

A *concept* is a broad and abstract generalization which conduces to an organization of related ideas, facts, and experiences.[10] Such a categorization represents a synthesis of the cognitive, affective and psychomotor domains with an end toward simplifying understanding and thus internalizing the concept.

The conceptual approach to the teaching of physical education, the method of teaching advocated by the authors of this book, is an approach which is a *planned* arrangement of all three domains of learning. This approach, which most nearly ensures that the learner will internalize concepts, is more fully explained in the following section.

10. Marion B. Pollock, "Speaking of Concepts," *Journal of School Health* 41 (June 1971):284.

WHY THE CONCEPTUAL APPROACH?

The major purpose of this book is to present what the authors term a conceptual approach to the teaching of sports skills—an approach which, because it pays attention to the three domains of learning, shows promise of producing skilled performers who move with meaning and understanding.

As suggested earlier, physical education has largely been concerned in its teaching with only those educational objectives which are within the realm of the motor domain. This is true in spite of the fact that physical educators have given lip service to such objectives as the mental ability necessary to react quickly and decisively (cognitive domain) as well as to such traits as sportsmanship and teamwork (affective domain). The result of all this, seemingly, has been a minority of the student body superbly trained to execute fine neuromuscular skills while, generally, the majority of the learners are woefully inadequate in behavior representative of the motor domain; and, specifically at the high school and college level, the majority neither understand the bases for effective movement nor do they see any real need to improve their movement skills.

The kind of teaching alluded to in the preceding paragraph is often referred to as "traditional." It is traditional not only in the sense described (i.e., attention basically to only the motor domain) but also in that the teacher generally uses a direct, even command, style of teaching in which demonstration and practice of a skill follow a brief verbal explanation of it. The teacher who uses the conceptual approach, on the other hand, is a "facilitator;" that is, he focuses on the learners and their needs as he prepares objectives stated in terms of behavioral outcomes.

Stating objectives in terms of behavioral outcomes is at first quite difficult. However as one focuses on what the learner is to *do,* to what *extent,* and under what *conditions* the description of such objectives becomes easier. The objective "to inculcate desirable social values" is nebulous at best; the objective "to have each student demonstrate a willingness to share equipment and facilities," although less nebulous is still difficult to evaluate; while the objective "to have each learner cooperate in the decision-making process about how gymnastic equipment is to be shared and to show consistently through his actions that he accepts the decision" is a measurable redefinition of the original objective regarding "social values," and it describes a behavioral outcome.

In sum, the proposed conceptual approach, then, is an attempt to combine content and method in such a way as to insure that the objectives in all three domains are better met through purposeful planning of the following:

CONTENT +	METHOD	= OUTCOME	
Knowledges and understandings	Personalization, attention to individual	Efficient, effective movement	The *total* thinking, feeling, moving individual
(Cognitive Domain)	(Affective Domain)	(Psychomotor Domain)	

This approach in no way refutes the fact that the study of human movement is largely through an activity program. Nor does it deny that physical education is more concerned with the motor domain than are other subject areas. Instead it recognizes that attention to the individual learner, his emotions and feelings, as well as attention to the necessary intellectual understandings, will, in the end, be productive of the best result: a meaningfully physically educated individual rather than a physically trained one.

REFERENCES

Bell, Virginia Lee. *Sensorimotor Learning.* Pacific Palisades, Calif.: Goodyear Publishing Co., 1970.

Bloom, Benjamin S., ed. *Taxonomy of Educational Objectives, Handbook I: Cognitive Domain.* New York: David McKay Co., 1956.

Bruner, Jerome S. "The Act of Discovery." *Harvard Educational Review* 31 (Winter 1961):21–32.

Committee on Understandings and Knowledge in Physical Education. *Knowledge and Understanding in Physical Education.* Washington, D.C.: American Association for Health, Physical Education & Recreation, 1969.

Gates, Alice A. *A New Look at Movement.* Minneapolis, Minn.: Burgess Publishing Co., 1968.

Hanson, Margie. "Physical Education '73." *Instructor* 82 (January 1973):45–53.

Harrow, Anita J. *A Taxonomy of the Psychomotor Domain.* New York: David McKay Co., 1972.

Kirchner, Glenn; Cunningham, Jean; and Warrell, Eileen. *Introduction to Movement Education.* Dubuque, Iowa: Wm. C. Brown Company Publishers, 1978.

Kirkendall, Don R. "Physical Education Effects in the Affective Domain." *Seventy-fifth Proceedings of the National College Physical Education Association for Men,* 1972, 147–151.

Kratwohl, David R.; Bloom, Benjamin S.; and Masia, Bertram. *Taxonomy of Educational Objectives, Handbook II: Affective Domain.* New York: David McKay Co., 1964.

Lawther, John D. *The Learning of Physical Skills.* Englewood Cliffs, N.J.: Prentice-Hall, 1977.

Leonard, George. *The Ultimate Athlete.* New York: Viking Press, 1975.

Mackenzie, Marlin M. *Toward a New Curriculum in Physical Education.* New York: McGraw-Hill Book Co., 1969.

Metheny, Eleanor. *Movement and Meaning.* New York: McGraw-Hill Book Co., 1968.

Morford, W. R. "Toward a Profession, Not a Craft." *Quest* 18 (May 1972):88–93.

Mosston, Muska. *Teaching Physical Education.* Columbus, Ohio: Charles E. Merrill, 1966.

Novak, Michael. *The Joy of Sports.* New York: Basic Books, 1976.

Pollock, Marion B. "Speaking of Concepts." *Journal of School Health* (June 1971):283–286.

Seidel, Beverly L. and M. C. Resick. *Physical Education: An Overview.* Reading, Ma.: Addison-Wesley Co., 1978.

Sheehan, Thomas J. "The Cognitive Domain and the Teaching of Physical Education." *Seventy-fifth Proceedings of the National College Physical Education Association for Men,* 1972, 141–147.

Sheehan, Thomas J., and Alsop, William L. "Educational Sport." *Journal of Health, Physical Education and Recreation* 43:5 (May 1972):41–45.

Siedentop, Daryl. "On Tilting at Windmills while Rome Burns." *Quest* 18 (May 1972):94–97.

———. *Physical Education: Introductory Analysis.* Dubuque: W.C. Brown Co., 1976.

Singer, Robert N. *Physical Education: Foundations.* New York: Holt, Rinehart, Winston, 1976.

Sweeney, Robert T., ed. *Selected Readings in Movement Education.* Reading, Mass.: Addison-Wesley Publishing Co., 1970.

Travers, John F. *Learning: Analysis and Application.* New York: David McKay Co., 1965.

Ulrich, Celeste, and Nixon, John. *Tones of Theory.* Washington, D.C.: American Association for Health, Physical Education & Recreation, 1972.

Wickstrom, Ralph L. *Fundamental Motor Patterns.* Philadelphia: Lea & Febiger, 1977.

2

Movement Sense

A CONCEPTUAL MOVEMENT APPROACH

The humanistic goal of education is for a person to become the best that he can become. Maslow refers to that goal as the process to self-actualization.[1] Physical education contributes to that goal in a personal, immediate, and meaningful way, for it is the personal self that experiences satisfaction, delight, and joy in movement. Joy emanates from the innermost emotional and mental domains as well as the physical. The self strives to become a total thinking, feeling, moving human being. Human movement exists as the very basis of life necessary to cope and communicate with others and our environment.

Children who have been introduced to movement education during the elementary years have more than likely experienced fundamental movements such as those connected with locomotion, simple manipulation of objects, and the use of their bodies to express their feelings. They have been exposed to experiences that call for sensitivity and awareness of space, force, objects and persons in the immediate environment. Through exploration and discovery, these individuals have begun to mold movement patterns that form the basis for the acquisition of specific skills as well as a basis for expression of personality. Such experiences provide the child with a good background as an introduction to human movement. What direction will his physical education take during high school and college years? The purpose of the conceptual movement approach in teaching sports is to help students continue to achieve movement with meaning.

1. Abraham H. Maslow, *The Farthest Reaches of Human Nature* (New York: Viking Press, 1971), p. 168.

CONCEPT. Movement sense is acquired when motor sensitivity, motor knowledge, and motor competency are combined into a holistic, personal, meaningful experience.

Movement sense implies a *feeling* for movement based on the person's kinetic experience and the *perception* of himself and his environment as he is experiencing movement (fig. 2.1). Movement here refers to any physical activity that is based on the informed observation of others as they move. *Movement sense* implies, too, that the individual is capable of performing skills which ultimately depend on the knowledge he has obtained and the favorable attitudes and appreciation he has developed toward the skill. Movement acquiring such meaning helps enrich a person's daily life as well as helping him to build a valid concept of himself (self-concept) and his relationship with the world.

The comprehension of the individual as a thinking, feeling, moving human being dictates relevant learning experiences in each of the three domains, cognitive, affective, and psychomotor. The ultimate goal of an individual who moves with meaning should be the conceptualization of his personal style of movement based on how he uses force, the form the movement takes in space, and the time it takes. The perceptual process enables him to form concepts that identify and integrate environmental forces. He then moves within a model of movement behavior that reflects a gestalt view, coordinating all three domains.

Movement sense, then, while depending on the natural psychomotor endowments of the individual, may be developed and encouraged through:

1. providing movement experiences that result in self perception, kinesthetic awareness and feelings, positive attitudes, values, and enjoyment. (affective)
2. applying principles of movement and other knowledge concepts that are involved in movement. (cognitive)
3. emphasizing effective, efficient skilled performance through sound teaching-learning situations. (psychomotor)

In progressing from a stage of basic awareness to one of skillful performance, the learner moves from the perceptual process (percepts) to a conceptual process (concepts). If content is presented within the perceptual-conceptual process, the learner will be able to acquire more readily true movement sense.

FEELING AND PERCEPTION

Preparing teachers who are fully aware of the implications and relationships of the affective, cognitive and psychomotor domains becomes an important task for physical education. Each individual moves in his own unique way, and every movement pattern performed in a sport becomes an intimate part of his physical personality. Learning motor skills that will become integrated into highly skilled sports patterns is a *personal* experience that must relate to an individual's body structure, his thought processes and his emotional adjustments. The objective is not to make movement so automatic that we are moving like machines or robots, for it is within each movement endeavor (to approach a "perfect swing" or a "grooved" swing) that meaning and challenge lie.

CONCEPT. Kinesthetic awareness and other sensory perceptions form the basis for motor sensitivity as manifested in feelings, attitudes, and values that give meaning to movement.

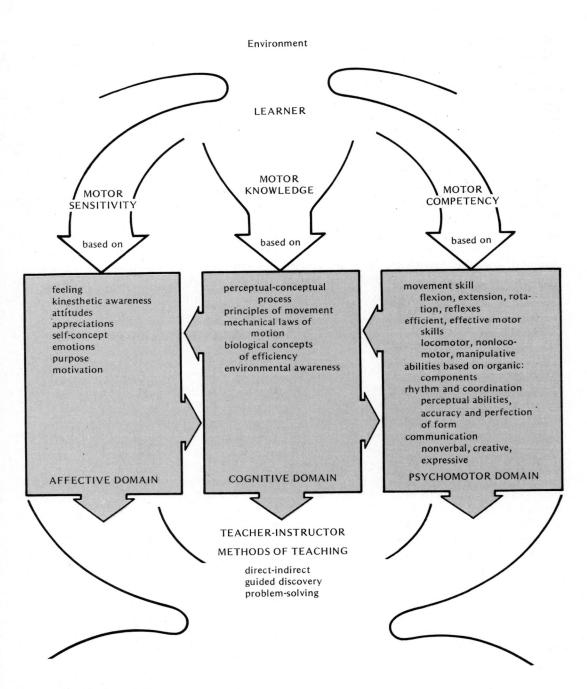

Figure 2.1. **Movement sense**

Movement experience involves the way an individual feels while he is performing a particular skill. The student-centered approach to teaching motor skills places emphasis on a complete understanding of *how, where* and *why* the individual is moving the way he is. The *understanding* of the complexities of human movement is not a simple task, for it involves *recognizing* the psychological, emotional and social needs of the individual as well as *satisfying* psychological, neurophysiological, and perceptual-motor needs.

The human body can move in many different ways and in countless combinations of patterns. Movement patterns are combined into fundamental skills and these are used for a great many purposes, some necessary to carry out daily tasks, others to be used for play, communication, or coping with environmental changes. All human movement takes time, requires force and uses space. Within each of the temporal, spatial and force factors there are dimensions that provide a variety of movement possibilities. The human body expresses its needs through hundreds of space-time-force combinations, each unique to the individual who is moving. The more complex the movement patterns become, the more introspection is required, which in turn requires a more thorough understanding of the biomechanical principles of movement. Balance, the systems of levers, Newton's laws of motion—all can assume a personal identification with the learner who is moving.

With self-actualization as the goal, teachers can cater to individual differences while staying within the realm of efficient mechanical potential. It is necessary to provide an environment in which students feel free, open and anxious to seek satisfying movement experiences. The epitome of performance is to feel enjoyment, even a moment of ecstasy when a skill is performed correctly. With that feeling and satisfaction, movement experiences become more personal and thus more meaningful.

Experiencing satisfaction while performing a sport skill belongs to a larger awareness, that of perceiving the wholeness or totality of the sport. It is possible for the individual to equate sport with feelings. In fact, many persons have known a peak experience within the realm of sports. During a peak experience when the performer surrenders himself completely to the movement of pure joy, or pure pain in some cases, he is moving toward expressing and feeling his own being as near to perfection as he can get. *Feeling* can help make the sport have *meaning* for the performer. Maslow lists fourteen values that are perceived as feelings during a peak experience: wholeness, perfection, completion or fulfillment, justice, aliveness, richness, simplicity, beauty, goodness, uniqueness, effortlessness, playfulness, truth and honesty, and self-sufficiency.[2]

Persons involved in intense activities report creative breakthroughs or flashes of insight that they cannot explain later. The mind-body relationship is better understood with new knowledge gained regarding the activities of the brain. The left hemisphere of the brain is believed to be the center of rational, intellectual, productive part of the mind while the right hemisphere is believed to control the intuitive, psychic, creative flow. If the natural rhythm and flow of body movment during a vigorous sport are satisfying and exhibit beautiful performance, chances are that the performer has tuned out the rigorous, inflexible thinking hemis-

2. Abraham H. M. Maslow, *Toward a Psychology of Being* (Princeton, N.J.: Van Nostrand Reinhold Co., 1968).

phere. The flow of movement has allowed a whole new consciousness to take over.

Gallwey explains in *The Inner Game of Tennis* that the mind can actually get in the way and exhibit body achievement.[3] When the overpowering mind is given a task on which to concentrate, the body is free to pursue its natural movement patterns. It could be referred to as relaxed concentration. Heightened awareness, changed perceptions and relaxed concentration, could lead to discovery of a new level of human potentiality through sports, and/or other physical activities.

In order to be free to feel the sport experience, the performer should not feel inhibited because of inadequacies. It is the teacher's role within the conceptual movement approach to equip the student with experiences, knowledges and skills as a background upon which to build adequacy.

The student needs knowledge in the realm of perception. He should develop an awareness of cues both from within the body and from outside stimuli that will help him use mechanical principles more adequately. Kinesthetic awareness is perceptual awareness and relies on internal cues such as balance or positioning of body parts (see figure 2.2). Perception in this case is internal and is felt. The more highly skilled an individual becomes, the more receptive he becomes in picking up external stimuli or cues (such as spatial and temporal relationships) from the environmental setting. Part of his skill, then, is the ability to become selective in choosing or perceiving the appropriate cues to perform the skill efficiently.

Each individual as a unique performer should understand that his skill repetoire is based on such variables as speed, time, accuracy, form, and adaptability. All skills are performed within a time limitation, and they must be mechanically accurate within a range if they are to be successful. Satisfactory form results when the movement is efficient and effective and expends a minimal amount of energy. Adaptability *allows* the individual to perform under various conditions and environments.

In summary, then, to move with understanding in sport skills it is necessary to experience movement as a *change in position in time-space resulting from force developed from the individual's expenditure of energy while interacting with the environment.* All movement has purpose and in order to achieve the desired purpose, the individual has to move within an environment. Desired purposes that an individual might be motivated to achieve include: nonverbal communication, self-expression, developmental skills, human performance, or coping behavior. In coping with his environment, an individual uses himself as an instrument to effect changes. He can extend his physical self through the use of an implement such as a tennis racket, golf club or softball bat. While he is moving within an environment, he should consider all the elements and factors that affect him as a performer. Human movement, then, should be understood in terms of how it is a function of the individual in his environment.

It has been fairly well accepted now that a basic movement approach helps children to build a foundation for an understanding of sport skills at a later time. Students at all grade levels should review and relate the common movement elements (space, time, force, flow) to their own learning of movement patterns. Then, building on the basic knowledge of what moves, how it moves, where it moves, and why it moves, principles of movement based on mechanical prin-

3. Timothy Gallwey. *The Inner Game of Tennis,* New York: Random House, 1974.

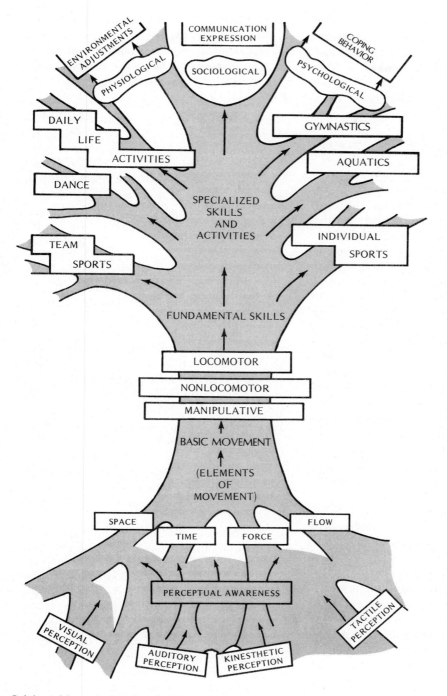

Originated by and reproduced with the permission of Margie R. Hanson, Ph.D.
Figure 2.2. **The beginnings and evolution of efficient movement**

ciples should be thoroughly understood. Based on the understanding of cognitive knowledges and skills the learner is free to experience feeling and meaning. It is when the whole individual is feeling, thinking and moving that he is tuned in and ready to experience movement with meaning.

WHY THE MOVEMENT APPROACH

As movement education became accepted as the background for elementary physical education, it became evident that the progress gained should be continued through the secondary level and into adulthood.

Understanding movement as *learning why* remains just as important as *learning how*. And then the entire realm of perceiving the joy, kinesthetic feelings, and satisfaction through movement joined the motor and cognitive aspects. With the emphasis on self during the 60's, human movements in all types of activities, demonstrated its value in building confidence, a more positive body image, the very core of a positive self concept.

The British, through the ideas and principles of Rudolph Laban, have considered the broader values of meaningful human movement at all age levels. Movement education has embraced much of Laban's work in this country.

Within the last few decades the idea of movement as a means of education has been explored, accepted and developed as a major emphasis in the United States. The English have for a long time considered the broader values of movement. They have realized that the intellectual, emotional and intuitive aspects of the personality are involved and reflected during movement. It is this concept of wholeness or activity of the whole person that we too wish to foster.

CONCEPT. The personal self is the focus in the movement approach to teaching sport skills with emphasis on exploration, perception, and experience in order to acquire movement sense, a basis for self actualization.

Laban, extremely aware of the quality of movement, and of the individual and nature of the personality, analyzed movement not only in terms of *what* moves, but also *how* it moves and *where* it moves. His analysis is easily understood and has relationship to everyday concepts, such as rolling, stretching, twisting in space and time. This very factor of simplicity and ease in communication has given rise to an entirely new approach to human movement.

Besides the impact of Laban's philosophy and analysis of movement on the teaching of physical education, other factors have also contributed to the acceptance of his ideas. Over the years, there has been an ever-increasing awareness of the individual differences of children in relation to growth and development and an awareness of the necessity of fostering and catering to these individual differences. A program geared almost entirely toward the acquisition of specific skills, where the *product* became almost more important than the *process*, where students were rated against set standards of progress, did very little toward achieving the concept of the whole person and self-actualization.

In Laban's movement philosophy, the selection of the activity can be the choice of the student within the limits which the teacher sets for the student. The content (force, space, time, flow) is thus student-centered and is pursued by the method and principles of movement exploration, discovery and selection. This method of setting the task is known as problem solving. The student can progress according to his own ability and make some contribution to the lesson in terms of his particular ingenuity. The student can thus experience satisfaction and enjoyment of movement. Self-motivation can become an outgrowth of this confidence. The self-direction and self-discipline that accrue will help each student to make the maximum progress within his own limits of ability.[4]

There are some individuals who are able to perform sport skills naturally and well without an identifiable technical knowledge or recognized feelings for movement. A great majority of individuals do not manage so well and for them the tools leading to good movement are important and should be made available.

> CONCEPT. *Basic movement content provides the background for development of fundamental skills which in turn lead to more specialized motor skills.*

A complete discussion of basic movement content and fundamental skills is beyond the scope of this book, but an outline provides a review of content. For a detailed analysis, see Gilliom's book, *Basic Movement Education:* Rational and *Teaching Units;* for implementation within a program see Figley, Mitchell, and Wright's book, *Elementary School Physical Education.*

WHAT MOVES

The body is the instrument that moves in reaction to internal and external stimuli emanating from the environment. (see figure 2.2, page 15). Kinesthetic sense leads to a feeling for movement. The sense of vision, audition, and touch pick up stimuli.

Body parts that move (head, neck, shoulder, etc.)
Body surfaces (front, back, sides)

Body shapes
    long and narrow (see page 110)—basketball jump shot
    wide and flat (see page 464)—straddle roll
    round and circular (see page 462, 466)—forward and backward rolls
    twisted (see page 547)—shot put
How does it move?
    Transfer of weight from one body part to another, as a unit, in flight, rocking, rolling.
    Balancing weight on different body parts.
Where does it move?
    In space—personal, general, range, direction, level, patterns, height and distance, planes.
When does it move?
    In time—speed, rhythm
With what *force?*
    Degrees of force or weight
With what type of *flow?*
    Sequential, free, bound.
Space, time, force, and flow will be covered in more detail under the heading Motion Factors later in the chapter. Because each sport skill in the book is analyzed in terms of space, time, force, flow and body awareness, those factors should be thoroughly understood. (see figure 5.1, p. 70)
Fundamental skills:
    In describing how the body moves, weight transfer was mentioned. The skills which serve as a basis for more specialized skills and move the body through space or in space follow. An awareness of symmetry and asymmetry in movements should be noted. Three general patterns exist: one side of the body is active (moving), alternate sides move, (walking) both sides move together (jumping).
    Locomotor skills—walk, run, leap, hop, jump, skip, slide, gallop

4. Rudolf Laban, *Modern Educational Dance,* (London: Macdonald & Evans, LTD., 1963).

Non-locomotor skills—bend, stretch, twist, turn (basis for flexion, extension, and rotation), swing, sway

Manipulative skills—those which carry, propel or receive objects, throw, catch, strike, kick

The common elements described emphasize kinesthetic awareness of movement. They denote the quality of movement as an individual matter based on personal attitudes; the way the individual feels about any movement influences and perhaps determines the way he moves while completing the movement. It is understood that the movement must be performed within the correct structure dictated by principles of movement. Although the individual must obey the fundamentals of mechanical laws, each person is unique and therefore has some personal movement preferences to movement within the parameters of the laws. Because each person moves differently, we say there are many different styles of movement. What feels right to one person may not feel equally effective to another person. It is the blending of the two domains, cognitive and affective, that dictates a successful movement pattern. Brown refers to the flowing together of the two domains as confluent education.[5]

MOTION FACTORS

There are quantitative aspects which must be considered in learning sport skills, and these elements are fused together for control and precision of movement. These elements are referred to by Laban as motion factors and have to do with factors of space, time, force, flow and rhythm, or where, how and with what we move. The motion factors that are common to all sport skills are:

1. spatial elements of movement (space)
2. temporal elements (time)
3. energy factors (force, weight)
4. rhythm and flow of movement

Spatial Elements

Just as water is the swimmer's medium, space belongs to the moving individual. A keen awareness of space is important in learning about *where* the body is, *where* it can move and *what* it can do in the space surrounding it. Conscious awareness develops when the individual is freed to move with versatility, with less inhibition, with more concentration and attention. A beginning tennis player who hits a ball at mid-court with the same amount of force as he did deep at the baseline has yet to develop court consciousness. Has he perceived a change of cues or does he possess a sense of spatial awareness?

Space can have tangible as well as intangible qualities if one is perceptually aware of what is in the space—air, smog, dew, mist, wind, rain, hail, snow, etc. Movement is influenced not only by the mentioned spatial substances, but also by objects, things and people in space to which one must relate. The moving person perceives and understands space through sensory experiences. A perceptual awareness or feeling of one's self moving in relation to space is enhanced by kinesthetic awareness.

Personal space

Immediately surrounding the body is personal space. It includes everywhere that can be reached without changing the stance.

5. George Brown, *Human Teaching for Human Learning: An Introduction to Confluent Education* 2nd ed. (New York: Viking Press, 1977).

This sphere of movement has as its center the center of the body; within this sphere, movements can be made away from or towards the center of the body, or movement can go out from and into this point, around the center, at all levels and in all directions. The arms and legs can move around the center of the body and still remain within the individual's personal space. (see Tennis, p. 295).

A person's psychological makeup often affects the awareness he has of personal space. In many cases an individual's body image and self-concept determine how he responds to personal space. Some persons feel inhibited when another object or person invades their personal space, and this inhibition tends to be reflected in movement patterns. Some individuals experience embarrassment when others watch them performing in their personal space; they would prefer to strike objects away from their personal space into general space, thus taking attention away from themselves instead of directing it toward themselves.

General space

As soon as the body begins to travel, it moves into the unlimited space around the person. In general space, any form of movement is possible. (see Running Long Jump, p. 540) One can move quickly, slowly, stop, start, advance, retreat, whirl, reach. In all games and sports the players should be helped to develop an awareness of general space and shared space whether on a field, court, gym floor, golf course, trampoline, or in a swimming pool. At times a player scores a goal when he never seemingly looks up or toward the goal. His perceptual awareness tells him exactly where he is within the playing area, what the angle of his shot should be and what space is occupied by other players.

Range of movement

Whether a movement is small, wide, large, narrow, close to the body or extended depends on the purpose and intent of the movement and whether the movement is performed consciously or automatically as habit.

Direction

One can change direction forward, backward, sidewards, upward, downward, diagonally and in all combinations. A player can move by facing and moving forwards or backwards or he can move in those directions but face the opposite throughout. Sensory perception helps us to determine in which direction we are moving.

Level

Moving in space close to the ground, high in the air or in the space between denotes the movement level of the body or limb.

Pattern

When the pathway of movement can be traced, it forms a pattern through space. A pathway can be either direct (————) or flexible (⌒ ⌇ ⌇). Combinations of direct and flexible pathways form patterns such as △ ▢ ○ ⟋ ▭ ⌒ ▯ or any other forms of creative design. Spatial patterns tend to become "grooved," as in a golf swing or a tennis drive.

Height and distance

An awareness of general space helps the performer to judge the height, distance, width, size of objects, size of space to be negotiated, and angles of approach. This awareness will enable the individual to judge accurately and concisely his position in space in relation to people or objects around him (near, far, behind, in front, at the side and alongside). A feeling for objects in general space can become the basis for highly coordinated movement patterns so necessary for the development of highly skilled sport patterns.

All sport skills are performed in relationship to other people or to objects in space. Every object is related to every other object but not in any absolute manner; the relationship is relative to the observer.

To judge "out there" in general space, the individual uses sensory perceptions related to vision and audition. To judge "in here" in personal space and within the body, one uses perception related to tactual and kinesthetic senses.

If movement is static, the perceptual mechanisms adapt and no further information goes to the brain; when movement is dynamic, perceptual information is fed constantly to the brain. Movement provides *perceptual information.* Vision, for example, can be distorted as to size of objects near and far away, but when movement has occurred, there is a matching of visual information to motor information. One should relate vision to movement, not movement to vision. For example, when an object is seen at a distance, it appears small, but as one moves closer, the object is seen in its correct proportion. (see Tennis, p. 287)

This principle is extremely important when learning motor skills. In sports, the individual must develop form constancy in space. He must constantly be perceiving moving objects in an environment that is also moving. Through experimentation with basic movement patterns, the individual becomes more skilled at removing the distortion from perceptual data. The performer strives to make objects "out there" as stable and consistent as "in close." Spatial judgment becomes *the* key element in sports where hitting a moving target is the major objective of the game.

Temporal Elements

Time, like space, is relative. Today becomes yesterday and tomorrow becomes today. The unit of the temporal dimension is rhythm and some movement theorists say that time is the fourth dimension of space. Rhythm originates in movement and we could say that a movement pattern is motor rhythm. Rhythm in movement has been described as the right proportions or the balanced relationships between factors of space, time and energy. There are infinite numbers of ways that these factors interrelate.

The time factor is concerned with speed in motion and the amount of time used in an action. Movements can be lightning fast or infinitely slow or exist on a continuum between the two extremes. Movement patterns evolve from the use of varying speeds. The action and purpose of the movement determines the speed needed for effective and economical performance.

Sport skills are dependent on the concept of temporal rhythm. The ability to accelerate and decelerate and to start and stop suddenly or gradually are absolute necessities for controlled movement. Certain sport skills demand great speed; others are dependent on slower speeds.

There is a personal quality of feeling in the temporal system that causes important effects, referred to as "time stress in movement." Pyschologically, the speed of movement has its effects on the human being and can be used therapeutically.

Quick movement is exciting and stimulating and it encourages vitality and alertness. It demands quick, decisive thinking and both mind and body are stirred by having to think and react quickly. Slow movement is calming and induces control; it holds the attention and helps to develop concentration and can do much to give poise and balance to nervous or fussy children.[6]

The possibility that certain personalities prefer to move at certain speeds in movement patterns is manifested in specific sports. The teacher should attempt to understand why and attempt to plan accordingly for individualized teaching.

Energy Factors (Force)

The body has potential power built into it and the energy factor is concerned with that power in movement, with tension in the muscles and with a feeling of control in the body. The control of energy output produces different intensities of strength and lightness in movement.

In moving, we have to resist constantly the pull of gravity. We must control downward movements. Control of upward movement occurs when power is gathered towards the center of the body as preparation for the strong release of movement outward and away from the center.

Flow of Movement

The ability of the body to be aware of and to feel movement traveling through the body gives greater control and a knowledge of what type of movement it is. Flow of movement refers to the active aspect of movement; movement flow fluctuates from moment to moment, depending on the task which is being performed. Movement flows from one part of the body to another part at the peak of its speed so that the flow is rhythmic and efficient for the continuation or completion of the action pattern. If the flow dissipates in one part of the body before it gets to the next part, the movement results in a jerky, awkward flow. The quality of smooth flow produces grace and economy of effort—thus a harmony of movement. Flow of movement brings about the union or joining of separate parts of a movement pattern, giving wholeness, rhythm and fluency. Movement can be, then, a successive type or it can be simultaneous movement in which all moving parts are affected at the same time.

The flow of movement may be *bound,* restrained and controlled so it can be stopped on command. If there is a *free flow,* there is no restraint. Flow of movement can be *continuous*—which is smooth—or it can be *broken,* stopped and held in check.

When equilibrium is threatened by the release of balance, there is a rapid flow of movement through space. Weight is transferred quickly, but it is stabilized when balance is restored; thus the flow of movement following a precarious position in any sport skill is necessarily very rapid and is very forceful.

In teaching sports by the movement approach it is necessary to conceptualize movement. Knowledge must serve as a foundation for skilled movement patterns. At the same time a feeling and perception of self accompany the experience. It is the combination of the cognitive, affective and psychomotor domains that truly frees an individual to become self-actualized.

MOTOR QUALITIES

The elements that deal with what is moving, how it is moving and where it is moving are qualitative in nature. The elements that deal with time, space, force, and flow are quantitative in nature. The quantitative elements have more to do with the cognitive

6. Ruth Morison, *Educational Gymnastics for Secondary Schools* (Liverpool, England: I. M. Marsh College of Physical Education, 1965), p. 20.

domain (knowledge). The qualitative elements have more to do with the affective domain (feeling).

CONCEPT. Motor competency (skill) depends on the level achieved in consideration of physiological fitness, motor fitness, motor ability and motor capacity.

No matter how knowledgeable or how perceptive the person is, he should also possess basic components such as strength, flexibility, endurance, coordination and other physical fitness traits so that he will have the basis upon which to build a highly skilled performance.

The capability to move effectively and efficiently in sports, in daily life activities and ultimately to participate in the more holistic aspects of life depends also on the individual's general motor ability, his motor fitness, his motor potential, his motor skills. The motor qualities mentioned are outgrowths of one's basic organic or physiological state; for example, if a tennis player does not possess basic strength to hold the racket firmly at the moment of impact with the ball, all the movement skill in the world will not enable that player to become highly skilled. Singer has defined motor qualities in terms of the following:

Motor ability indicates present athletic ability. It denotes the immediate state of the individual to perform a wide range of motor skills. Ability is general and enduring.

Motor skill is specific to a given task and is attained with experience. Because it is task-oriented, skill usually refers to a highly developed specific sequence of responses.

Motor fitness implies the ability to perform a given task having those physical qualities developed to the extent demanded by the task.

Motor capacity depicts the maximum potential of an individual to succeed in motor-skilled performance. Ultimate motor potential is a sort of motor intelligence test.[7]

For excellent performance, body control is necessary and requires a building of motor qualities (fig. 2.3).

Motor learning principles underlie the applications of concepts within the three domains, cognitive, affective and psychomotor. Concepts relating to learning and performance, motivation, massed and distributed practice sessions, transfer, memory, and all other motor learning parameters should be considered. More and more superior teachers and coaches at all levels are becoming very much concerned with various facets of human behavior. Response characteristics of the performances dealing with reaction time, activation-arousal, group interaction, and motivation should be studied in order to learn more about all levels of performances.

For a student to become a truly physically-educated individual, it is necessary for him to acquire knowledge and experience in all the aspects of human movement (fig. 2.1, p. 12). Only then can we say that this person has acquired movement sense.

When a person acquires movement sense, there is a feeling that accompanies a complete harmony of movement described as the "fun in fun."[8]

APPLICATION OF CONCEPTS TO A SPECIFIC SPORT—TENNIS

Movement sense is acquired when motor sensitivity, motor knowledge, and motor competency are combined into a holistic personal meaningful experience. Examples of application:

Motor sensitivity—The tennis player experiences success in developing a positive at-

7. Robert N. Singer, *Motor Learning and Human Performance: An Application to Physical Skills* (New York: Macmillan Co., 1975), p. 108.
8. William Barry Furlong. "The 'Fun in Fun'," *Psychology Today*, June, 1976, p. 35.

titude toward the game, enjoys the feeling of swinging a tennis racket, hitting the ball, placing shots, winning points. The level of self confidence increases as personal success is achieved and as the player is motivated to improve.

Perceptively, the player is able to make judgments on tracking a moving ball and adjusting by changing body positions and deciding on the speed and force in execution of strokes. (see page 296–305 under headings space, time, force, flow)

Motor knowledge—The tennis player should study and use the basic principles related to levers. (see page 288 for concepts) Basic concepts related to force should be applied to tennis in order to understand racket face angle, amount of backswing, and follow-through. (see pages 289, 297)

Perceptions regarding the weather, court condition, wind factors, light intensity form concepts to determine any changes necessary to continue play.

Motor competency—Basic movement content provides the background for development of fundamental skills which in turn lead to more specialized motor skills.

The *body* is the instrument that moves. (see pages 298, 301, 302, 304) The body moves by transfering weight from one part to another or as a total unit. (see page 298)

The body moves in *space*. (see pages 296, 299, 302, 303)

The body moves in relation to *time*. (see pages 296, 299, 302, 304)

The body moves with degrees of *force* or weight (page 297, 299, 302, 304)

Fundamental skills are basis for more specialized skills and serve as means of moving the body from one place to another. (see page 17—running, sliding, stop, start, change direction)

Manipulative skills—propelling body (see page 18).

CONCEPT. Motor competency (skill) depends on the level achieved in consideration of physiological fitness, motor, fitness, motor ability, and motor capacity.

The tennis player must have enough strength to hold a tennis racket and deliver forces through maintaining a firm racket face at moment of impact. The speed of the racket head depends on the length of the lever which depends on the range of motion of the swinging arm and the use of the whole body.

Cardio-respiratory endurance determines the amount of energy and how long the player can endure play.

Agility and coordination are necessary for the tennis player to move quickly and efficiently forward, backward, sideways, while moving the racket in relation to body position.

Hand-eye coordination determines the ability to track the ball and meet it with the racket at just the right moment.

The basic specialized skill pertinent to tennis is striking.

Motor ability indicates the natural endowment the player has in relation to motor skill performance.

At the secondary and adult levels a physical education teacher should be able to assume that much of the learning about basic movement content, fundamental skills, and motor behavior had taken place at the elementary level. Teachers cannot put adults through "what children delight in." Movement education must be appropriate to the specific age level, but the teacher can provide activities related to the basic content needed.

For a student to develop movement sense, an awareness on the teacher's part must also be developed. Greenburg, in a book entitled

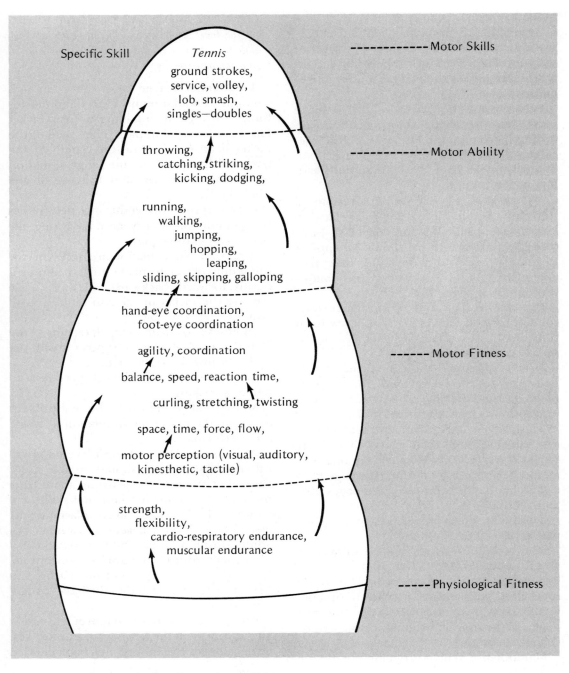

Specific Skill   *Tennis*
ground strokes,
service, volley,
lob, smash,
singles—doubles
------------ Motor Skills

------------ Motor Ability

throwing,
catching, striking,
kicking, dodging,

running,
walking,
jumping,
hopping,
leaping,
sliding, skipping, galloping

hand-eye coordination,
foot-eye coordination

agility, coordination

------ Motor Fitness

balance, speed, reaction time,

curling, stretching, twisting

space, time, force, flow,

motor perception (visual, auditory,
kinesthetic, tactile)

strength,
flexibility,
cardio-respiratory endurance,
muscular endurance

----- Physiological Fitness

Figure 2.3. **Body control related to motor qualities**

Teaching with Feeling, identifies the humanistic challenge for all students and teachers:

No matter how much emphasis is placed on such other qualities in teaching as educational techniques, technology, equipment, or buildings, the humanity of the teacher is the vital ingredient if children are to learn.[9]

Physical education should focus on the humanistic concept of learning, which is truly a confluent education (a flowing together of the cognitive and affective domains with the psychomotor domain). This concept focuses on the being and the becoming of the whole person—the totality of the human being. The delight waiting for the individual who becomes a total person—alive, thinking, feeling, moving, experiencing—is in the realm beyond the ordinary, the ultimate, but isn't that what education is all about?

REFERENCES

Brown, George. *Human Teaching for Human Learning: An Introduction to Confluent Education.* New York: Viking Press, (Second Ed.) 1977.

Furlong, Wm. Barry. "The Fun in Fun," *Psychology Today,* June, 1976.

Gallwey, Timothy. *The Inner Game of Tennis,* New York: Random House, 1974.

Greenburg, M. Herbert. *Teaching with Feeling.* New York: Macmillan Co., 1969.

Laban, Rudolf. *Modern Educational Dance.* London: Macdonald & Evans, LTD., 1963.

Maslow, Abraham H. *The Farthest Reaches of Human Nature.* New York: Viking Press, 1971.

————. *Toward a Psychology of Being.* 2d ed. Princeton, N.J.: Van Nostrand Co., 1968.

————. *A Movement Approach to Educational Gymnastics,* London: J. M. Dent and Sons, Ltd., 1975.

Morrison, Ruth. *Educational Gymnastics for Secondary Schools.* Liverpool, England: I. M. Marsh College of Physical Education, 1965.

Singer, Robert N. *Motor Learning and Human Performance: An Application to Physical Skills.* New York: Macmillan Co., 1975.

9. M. Herbert Greenburg, *Teaching with Feeling* (New York: Macmillan Co., 1969), p. 10.

3

The Role of Methodology

INTRODUCTION

The term *methods* is interpreted quite often to encompass all of the procedures and techniques used by the teacher to present content to the learner. Thus, procedures generally include planning objectives, ordering content, organizing students and equipment, and finally, evaluating student progress. The success of a lesson is dependent upon careful planning in each of these important phases; however, this chapter concentrates only on an overview of methods as they influence the role of the teacher, alter the organization of students and facilities and enhance or diminish specific outcomes. A detailed analysis of the role of methodology is beyond the scope of this chapter; rather, the purpose is to cite the many different techniques possible and to suggest that certain techniques lend themselves to a greater involvement of the student in the learning process. Included are suggestions for enhancing the learning climate for every individual through methods of organization as well as instruction. These suggestions are applicable to typical classes in physical education in which the teacher is confronted with a need to provide for individuals. It is hoped that the reader will be stimulated to go beyond this chapter to peruse techniques of teaching that will enable him to make physical education a meaningful movement experience for all students.

METHODS OF INSTRUCTION

Many different terms are used to describe and classify methods of teaching. A lack of uniformity in the use of terminology, however, makes it difficult to interpret the literature. Some authors categorize all methods of teaching physical education as either direct or indirect. Others speak in terms of the teacher-centered approach and the student-centered approach. Still others describe or classify methods as being either traditional or problem-solving.

The adage that "teachers teach as they have been taught" is probably true more often than not. Too often teachers do not choose a method for a particular lesson because their background is void of a study of methods and/or their learning experiences have been lacking in a variety of teaching techniques. Thus, they continue in a pattern of instruction unaware that other possibilities exist.

CONCEPT. The role the teacher assumes alters both the behavior and the verbalization of the teacher and can be identified as characteristic of a specific method of teaching.

Direct Methods

Historically and traditionally, physical education has been taught by a direct method. The pattern is very teacher-centered in that the teacher explains and demonstrates, the student imitates and participates, and the teacher evaluates. Mosston calls the most extreme teacher-centered method the command method, a throwback to the old German gymnastics (calisthenics) where the students performed all movements to the voice command of the teacher. He describes less rigidly structured teacher-centered methods as task, reciprocal, small group and individual.[1] Although the teacher directs through explanation and demonstration, the student is free to make some decisions in these methods. To facilitate communication in this chapter, those methods of instruction which involve the teacher in demonstration and explanation are referred to as direct methods of instruction. The role the teacher assumes in direct methods is quite often that of an expert, a model and an instructional manager or pro-

cessor of information. Verbalization tends to be explanatory in the initial introduction of material while corrective comments predominate during student practice.

Indirect Methods

Problem solving, guided exploration, free exploration and guided discovery are found at the student-centered end of a continuum of methods. A study of these methods reveals a common characteristic, the act of discovery or the opportunity for students to explore. Those who propose exploration as a method of teaching quite often give isolated samples of lessons, but do little to clarify the guidelines for implementing such methods. Some interpret exploration as meaning that the teacher does very little and the student does as he pleases. The lack of conformity and the flexibility of structure in an indirect lesson tend to intensify this impression. A method very much like exploration is described by Mosston as *guided discovery*.[2] The teacher decides on the goal—that which is to be discovered—and then, with planned progression, he leads the student through a series of problems (many times posed as questions), allowing the student to explore alternatives through movement and cognition and thus to discover the best solution. Hence, the title "guided discovery" better describes the process of exploration in education.

The format of *problem solving* is very much like that of guided discovery with one exception. Rather than the possibility of only one best answer, the problems are structured to allow for multiple solutions. The intellect is involved to a greater degree by providing opportunities for students to be creative; however, the student is still active physically.

1. Muska Mosston, *Teaching Physical Education* (Columbus, Ohio: Charles E. Merrill Publishing Co., 1966), p. 19–30.
2. Mosston, *Teaching Physical Education*, pp. 143–80.

Godfrey and Kephart summarize movement problem solving as "completing a task through physical-mental and muscular-activity."[3] Future reference in this chapter to indirect methods of instruction includes those methods that allow the student to explore alternative solutions. The role the teacher assumes in indirect methods is that of a guide, facilitator and counselor. Once the goal and/or task is clearly defined the verbalization of the teacher tends to be questioning and suggesting.

CONCEPT. *Although content somewhat dictates the method to be used, it is not as limiting as it initially appears.*

Many teachers in the secondary school believe that the indirect method of teaching can be used successfully only at the elementary school level. The content at the secondary school level, according to them, is too structured. Skills are specific to the sport, the dance and other content areas. While it is true that one cannot learn to participate in a sport without actually experiencing the game, the student can be led to discover the concepts of movement based on the mechanical principles that apply to the sport skills. The student can discover how to achieve the desired direction and how to impart the appropriate amount of force to the ball. Broer, in a study involving seventh graders in the sports of basketball, volleyball, and softball, concluded that instruction using a problem-solving method with emphasis on the mechanical principles underlying the skill produced more effective learning.[4]

Since movement principles are governed by the laws of physics, the discovery of these principles leads to very specific facts. The indirect method of arriving at the exact answer takes the form of *guided discovery*. The teacher decides on the fact to be discovered and then leads the student through the process of discovering this fact. However, students can also be led to discover specific sport skills through a carefully planned progression of problems during which they explore alternatives.[5] Quite logically, the understanding of the principles of movement and the learning of movement skills go hand in hand and should be taught simultaneously.

The opportunities for *problem solving* at the secondary level are also quite numerous. The content in gymnastics and dance lends itself well to multiple solutions. A student can be led to discover that there are many ways to mount a balance beam, and even many ways given the limitation of a right angle approach.[6] In dance the students can be challenged to create their own sequences of movement or vary specific technique according to individual preference or style. The possibilities are unlimited. In games (sports), offensive and defensive strategies can be learned through problem solving. Students learn to think and react to an ever-changing environment. The process of identifying the problem, exploring alternatives, finding solutions and making decisions helps prepare students for living in a democratic society. If physical education is taught using indirect methods, the possibility of producing thinking-moving individuals is considerably enhanced.

CONCEPT. *The teaching method employed in instruction influences the learning outcomes (objectives and goals) of the lesson.*

3. Barbara B. Godfrey and Newell C. Kephart, *Movement Patterns and Motor Education* (New York: Appleton-Century-Crofts, 1969), p. 188.
4. Marion R. Broer, "Effectiveness of a General Basic Skills Curriculum for Junior High School Girls," *Research Quarterly* 29 (December 1958):379–88.
5. Sample problems are included in the soccer chapter, pp. 201–204.
6. Sample problems are included in the gymnastic chapter, pp. 486–487.

With the variety of direct and indirect methods possible, the teacher is faced with the choice of which method or methods to use. Is one method better for developing movement skills, for developing the components of fitness, for imparting related knowledges, for gearing to individual differences, or for developing the whole student? The objectives of education and physical education are very broad and deal with the development of the total individual. The unique contributions of physical education, however, deal with the physical development of the individual and research in the area of methodology, scant as it may be, generally contrasts methods in relation to developing motor skills. Although the methods studied vary slightly in technique, the trend is to compare the traditional teacher-directed methods with the indirect or problem-solving methods. The findings are by no means conclusive. Most often no significant difference is found between the two types of methods; each is equally effective in developing motor skills.[7, 8, 9] Broer and Graylee, however, found problem solving to be more effective; while Ziegler, who found the traditional method to be superior in one instance suggested the need to review the merits of problem solving.[10, 11, 12] Do the proponents of problem solving and indirect methods claim that these methods will develop the physical to a greater degree or do they speak in terms of gearing to individuals, developing the whole individual and fostering creativity? Possibly the components being measured are not the objectives that are being affected by the extremes in methods.

When considering broad educational objectives it appears that the indirect methods or student-centered methods of teaching are more likely to attain those objectives. The traditional methods, where the teacher commands and the student responds, places emphasis on external discipline and conformity. This procedure does little for the development of self-direction, self-discipline, or gearing to individual differences. Conversely, indirect methods provide an opportunity for the learner to be active in the learning process rather than a passive recipient. In addition to acquiring content, students tend also to learn the process being used in instruction. Thus, through indirect methods, students develop cognitive skills in exploring alternatives and solving problems. As Brunner indicates, "Knowing is a process, not a product."[13]

Although the attainment of specific instructional objectives is enhanced most often by specific methods, progress toward broader goals is not precluded by a majority of methods. Nevertheless, certain methods tend to emphasize specific outcomes while diminishing others. Thus a teacher who understands methods and who is competent in using a variety of teaching styles is better able to plan intelligently for the achievement of desirable outcomes.

7. Carol Ann Berensen, "The Relative Effectiveness of Descriptive Teaching and Structural Problem Solving in Learning Basic Tennis Skills" (An unpublished Master of Science thesis, University of Washington), 1967.
8. Marilyn La Plante, "A Study of the Problem Solving Method of Teaching Bowling" (Master of Science thesis, University of North Carolina at Greensboro), 1965.
9. Robert S. Scott, "A Comparison of Teaching Two Methods of Physical Education with Grade One Pupils" (Master of Science thesis, Wisconsin State University at LaCrosse), 1965.
10. Broer, "Basic Skills Curriculum."
11. Gayle Gravlee, "A Comparison of the Effectiveness of Two Methods of Teaching a Four Week Unit on Selected Motor Skills to First Grade Children" (An unpublished Master of Science thesis, University of North Carolina at Greensboro), 1965.
12. Yvonne P. Ziegler, "A Comparison of Two Methods of Teaching Gymnastics" (Master of Science thesis, University of Wisconsin), 1965.
13. Jerome S. Bruner, *Toward a Theory of Instruction* (Cambridge, Mass.: Harvard University Press, 1966), p. 72.

PLANNING EDUCATIONAL OBJECTIVES IN THREE DOMAINS

CONCEPT. Learning outcomes are specific to the experiences one has in a lesson and can be classified according to domains: cognitive, motor or affective.

Regardless of planning, something does occur in each of the domains during the instructional period. The intent of planning outcomes is to assure, if possible, that those outcomes are positive and desirable. Objectives of physical education have always included goals relating to all facets of individual development. However, the nature of the content of physical education (activity) and the connotation of the word education (knowledge) have led traditionally to a greater emphasis of the motor and cognitive domains than has been given to the objectives of the affective domain. The assumption has been that with strides made in the cognitive and motor domains, the objectives of the affective domain naturally would follow. Although this assumption is not totally unfounded, careful planning in the affective domain ensures greater progress in the attainment of its objectives.

The objectives of the motor domain are developed through carefully planned movement experiences in which the student progresses in the ability to control his body while performing purposeful movements. Because the movement skills in this text are specific to the content of each sport, specific skill analysis is contained in each sport chapter. Although a variety of methods of teaching bring about the desired outcomes in the motor domain the choice of method also can enhance or diminish the attainment of desirable outcomes in the other two domains.

The related knowledges or cognitive objectives that are common to many sport skills are compiled in chapter five. Specific appli-

cation and unique application of concepts are then included in each sport chapter when necessary for clarification. Included in these knowledges are the laws of motion and their application to sport skills. Again a variety of methods of teaching are adequate for acquiring factual content. The teacher can behave as an information processor and convey the necessary information through lecture. However, the students not only acquire the information, hopefully, but also tend to learn the process by which the information is acquired. Thus, a careful choice of process can enhance the development of desirable cognitive skills. Certainly the ability to gather information, select alternatives, explore solutions and draw conclusions is a desirable cognitive goal in education. If physical education is to assist in attaining current broad educational goals, the student must be involved other than as a passive recipient. And if the student is to become truly involved in the learning process he must be given the opportunity to explore alternatives.[14] The methods that enhance the development of problem solving skills are the more indirect methods. Several examples of indirect lessons are contained in the chapters on specific sports (Archery, pp. 382–391, Soccer, pp. 201–204, Volleyball, pp. 348–353).

The objectives of the affective domain are concerned with the development of desirable attitudes, feelings, appreciations and values related to self and others. In addition to learning the cognitive process employed in instruction, students also tend to learn the social structure of the classroom experience. Thus, specific techniques of organization and teaching enhance certain affective goals while they diminish others. Although the attainment of certain goals is immediate, the complete internalization of other concepts

14. Bruner, *Toward a Theory of Instruction*, p. 43.

may take a much longer time. Student-centered methods of organization which allow students to interact socially fosters development in relation to working with others. Methods of instruction and organization which allow students to be involved in making decisions foster self-direction and self-discipline. If the teacher provides for various levels of achievement, all students can be successful which in turn fosters a positive self-concept. These are but a few of the many outcomes of the affective domain. Direct methods of teaching most often are accompanied by rigid teacher-centered methods of organization while the indirect methods generally are associated with less rigid organizational patterns. This tendency is not irreversible; however, tradition has intensified the pattern. Physical education, with its open space in the gymnasium, courts and fields and its many chances to group students, has a unique opportunity to foster desirable behavior in the affective domain. Teachers of physical education need to be more cognizant of the relationship of classroom experiences to the development of attitudes, feelings, appreciations and values.

Unlike the other two domains, the techniques of organization and the desired outcomes of the affective domain are dealt with in more detail in this chapter, Table 3.1, and only mentioned briefly in the sport chapters. Again, specific techniques do not always foster specific outcomes; instead they may influence the development of several or many objectives. Therefore, the numbers grouped in parentheses under "Desired Outcomes" (Table 3.1) show a relationship to the techniques of the same number in the left-hand column, "Teacher Behavior." Note that the teacher behavior described in the chart tends to be that of a teacher playing the role of a guide and/or counselor.

DEVELOPING LESSONS USING AN INDIRECT METHOD

CONCEPT. Developing competence in a variety of methods of teaching requires careful planning and considerable practice.

Convincing teachers of the merits of indirect teaching does not suddenly transform them into expert teachers capable of using the techniques of this method. Nor do all students become automatic problem solvers when presented with a problem. Many times the outcome is tragic when a traditional teacher, poorly versed in the techniques of problem solving, presents his first lesson to students who likewise have few skills in problem solving. The lesson lacks direction or purpose and is thus frustrating for all involved. Both students and teacher must practice if they are to become proficient in the techniques of problem solving. Thus, some general guidelines are offered for developing an indirect lesson. These guidelines are intended as an aid for the teacher unfamiliar with indirect teaching.

1. The teacher *decides on the focus* or major idea of the lesson in relation to the content and abilities of the students. The focus of the lesson can take a variety of forms. The main focus might be a specific skill pattern (p. 487) or team strategy (p. 189). The lesson may focus on one or several principles of movement as utilized in skill development or the principle(s) of movement may be the main focus with a variety of movement responses (p. 439). If the focus is narrow and leads to specific outcomes, the indirect method is guided discovery. If the focus allows for multiple solutions, the process becomes that of problem solving.

2. The second step is to *list specific concepts and skills* the student should acquire through

AFFECTIVE DOMAIN

TABLE 3.1

Teacher Behavior	Desired Outcomes
1. Allow the student to assume the responsibility for his own conditioning in relation to his own needs.	(1,3,4,12) The student progresses in the ability to estimate his own needs and to look at himself realistically.
2. Allow the student to make the decision of where in the space of the teaching station he will work.	(1,2,3,4,7,9,11,12) The student develops a feeling of importance when given the opportunity to make a decision. (His self-image is enhanced.)
3. Allow the student to decide on which individual skill he needs to work.	
4. Provide the opportunity for the student to set his own goals in individual skill development.	(1,2,3,4,6,11,12) The student progresses in the ability to be self-directed when given the opportunity to decide where, what, and how intense his involvement will be.
5. Analyze the progress of each individual in relation to his own previous record rather than the progress of other students in the class.	(1,3,4,5,12,13,19,20) The student feels the course is meeting his individual needs for skill development as he works at his own level. The individual becomes more important than the content.
6. Provide the opportunity for students to begin working immediately upon entering the gymnasium rather than waiting for the total class to assemble to begin work.	(1,3,4,6,8,12) The student develops the ability to be both self-directed and self-disciplined when given the responsibility for his own skill development.
7. Allow students to choose their own partners with whom they wish to work, and their own combinations of partners for small groups and teams.	(7) The student progresses in the ability to associate freely with his peers when given the opportunity to choose his own partner and group associates.
8. Provide opportunities for reciprocal interaction of partners in evaluation of skill progress and development.	(8,9,11) The student develops in the ability to interact with his peers in a give-and-take process. The student questions and accepts the ideas of others. He also learns to accept the fact that his own ideas will be tried and tested, accepted or rejected.
9. Provide the opportunity for partners and small groups to solve problems and make decisions together.	
10. Allow small groups to identify themselves by name or number and provide for the permanency of the group for a period of time.	(8,9,11) The student develops in the ability to interact with a peer or peers to make a decision and/or to find a solution.
11. Allow the groups to set their own goals for specific team tactics developed in the group.	(10) The student develops a feeling of security by belonging to a group over a period of time.
12. Allow the student to decide (at the termination of a unit of study, whenever feasible) whether he will participate in competitive play, continue to work on individual skill development, or progress into some other phase of that unit of study.	(11) The student progresses in the ability to work with a group toward a common goal.
13. Adapt rules, standards, and/or motor skills to provide success for each individual, especially during the initial encounter with new content material.	(12) The student progresses in the ability to make a decision—to be self-directed.
14. Bring students into a close group for analysis and discussion.	(14) The student feels that the teacher recognizes him as an individual, since the teacher talks to students grouped close enough for good eye contact.
15. Involve students in a discussion and analysis of the content being studied.	(15) The student progresses in the ability to become a contributing member of the group.
16. Explore all ideas and contributions made by individuals.	(16, 17) The student feels that his contributions are worthy when his ideas are explored. (This enhances his self-image.)
17. Accept individual styles in solving movement problems; i.e., if the individual movement response is efficient and effective, accept it, even though it appears unorthodox.	
18. Provide a relaxed atmosphere during class with dialogue in a conversational tone.	(12,19,20) The student feels that he is important when the teacher relates to him as an individual in personal interaction.
19. Move throughout the teaching station giving individual help as students work on their own.	
20. Check individual skill cards periodically and make specific written comments or recommendations to the individual.	

participation in the lesson.[15] The cognitive understandings are the essentials one would tell the student if the lesson were taught by a direct method. There is generally a progressive order for these concepts and skills.

3. The teacher should then *outline main problems* or major questions in relation to the concepts and skills determined in step two. These problems should be stated in such a manner as to elicit both cognitive and physical activity (p. 188 and p. 201).

4. Being cognizant of the expected movement responses to the main problem, the teacher *formulates the subproblems* next. If the lesson is one of guided discovery, the subproblems lead the student to explore alternatives, reject certain responses while accepting others, and to arrive at a specific solution (p. 202). If the intent is to find new ways or multiple solutions, the subproblems should promote variety. Due to unexpected movement responses the teacher may need to add to, alter, or change the planned subproblems during the lesson. The teacher takes his cues for developing relevant subproblems by observing the movement responses of the students (p. 485 and p. 439).

5. Solving problems may be done individually, with a partner, or in a small group. The content of each main problem will determine the *grouping of students*. Groups should be kept small so that the individuals within the group are actively participating both physically and mentally.

6. The teacher may *present the lesson orally* (p. 309) or put the *problems on mimeographed sheets* (p. 382 and p. 386) to hand to the students. It is difficult to conform to the speed of each individual in solving problems when teaching orally. A mimeographed sheet of problems will allow individuals to progress at their own speed. However, students inexperienced in indirect lessons will sometimes flounder with written problems; thus they may need more oral direction from the teacher. As the students progress in their ability to solve problems and to be more self-directed, written problems can be introduced.

7. *Demonstrations and analyses* of movement skills are incorporated into the lesson as needed. One student may demonstrate, or several students may demonstrate to show the variety of possible solutions. The teacher involves the remaining students in an analysis of the appropriate movement techniques and in an application of movement principles to these techniques. In addition, the teacher, while planning the lesson, must be constantly searching for opportunities to develop the objectives of the affective domain. This domain is discussed in greater detail on pages 30–32 of this chapter.

When introducing indirect methods to students, the teacher should proceed slowly at first, giving more freedom of choice as the students progress in the ability to make decisions. He must also learn to guide the student to discovery by questioning rather than by "teaching by telling." Probably the greatest hurdle the traditional teacher has to leap in using the indirect approach is to restrain himself from interfering and correcting faults rather than guiding the student to find these for himself. The teacher should, by all means, share with the students what he is trying to do. With carefully planned progression, the physical education classroom comes alive with the excitement of discovery.

The ultimate in individualizing physical education is to have a series of problems with varying degrees of difficulty. The student then selects the problem that challenges him according to his ability. This procedure is especially applicable to the in-

---

15. These are the specific instructional objectives in the cognitive and motor domains. See objectives, p. 440.

dividual sports—gymnastics, golf, archery, etc.

The following sample problems, lessons, units, contract, checklists, etc. are included throughout the sports chapters. They are not intended as master lessons but merely examples of the many ways the teacher can individualize and personalize the learning experience. Fourteen examples of indirect teaching are included. For ease of reference, the examples are categorized by type of technique or tool and identified by sport, content and location.

Skill Checklists
(individual and partner)

Archery (Form, Accuracy)—pp. 381–382
Badminton (Basic Skills, Game Play)—pp. 282 and 285
Basketball (Individual and Game Skills)—pp. 131 and 133
Gymnastics (Rolls, Balances)—pp. 481 and 489
Softball (Diagnostic Checklist)—p. 255
Volleyball (Basic Skills)—p. 338

Methods

GUIDED DISCOVERY

Archery (Use of Bow Sight)—p. 382
Archery (Force Production . . . Flight)—p. 386
Badminton (Force . . . Clear)—p. 281
Field Hockey (Choice of Pass)—p. 188
Gymnastics (Principles of Stability)—p. 439
Gymnastics (Cartwheel)—p. 487
Soccer (Foot Surface for Ball Control)—p. 201
Swimming (Bouyancy and Propulsion)—p. 513
Tennis (Tracking . . . Forehand Drive)—p. 308
Volleyball (Overhand Volley)—p. 348

PROBLEM SOLVING

Gymnastics (Balancing, Partners to Pyramids)—p. 439
Gymnastics (Balance Beam Mounts)—p. 486
Gymnastics (Variations for Rolling)—p. 485

Other Examples

Gymnastics (Lesson in Rolling Utilizing Three Teaching Methods)—p. 483
Gymnastics (Culminating Routines for Various Proficiencies)—p. 491
Track and Field (Contract)—p. 555
Volleyball (Sample Unit Plan)—p. 339

Learning takes place with a variety of techniques and teachers should be competent in more than one method of teaching. Teachers also need to view their methods critically in light of current educational objectives and to provide opportunities for the development of the student in three domains: affective, motor, and cognitive. This involves a careful selection of methods of instruction and organizational techniques in order to foster the development of desirable outcomes. It is hoped that physical education teachers will become more adept in using a variety of methods in order to be able to choose and use those methods or combinations of methods that best meet the objectives for each particular situation. Certainly if teachers intend to use a method unfamiliar to them they should study the mechanics of that specific method in more detail. Currently Muska Mosston's book, *Teaching Physical Education,* is one of the most comprehensive books available on teaching methods for secondary school physical education.[16]

16. Mosston, *Teaching Physical Education,* pp. 19–30.

PROVIDING FOR THE INDIVIDUAL THROUGH ORGANIZATIONAL TECHNIQUES

CONCEPT. The method of teaching employed with the related role played by the teacher is reflected also in the manner in which the learning environment is organized (space, students and equipment).

Quite often the direct methods of instruction are accompanied by inflexible techniques of organization of students and equipment. This bond is not inseparable. Although the learning climate created by indirect methods of instruction is negated with rigid organizational patterns, the climate of a direct lesson can only be enhanced by using flexible methods of organization. The following portion of this chapter deals with a contrast of methods of organization and affirms that innovative and flexible techniques of organizing students and equipment attends to the needs of individual students.

The exposure of the student to appropriate methods and the acquisition of movement concepts, however important, do not make him proficient in movement skills. If one of the objectives of physical education is to develop the physical potential of the individual through participation in a sport, the student must be given the opportunity to develop his skills. It becomes the job of the teacher to provide each individual with an optimal learning climate and many opportunities to practice. To do this he must utilize available space, equipment and time to the fullest extent.

Development of Individual and Game Skills

Frequently the first portion of a class period is spent on the practice of individual and game skills in organizational patterns which traditionally are termed drills. In volleyball, for example, everyone might work on the underhand serve in the first five minutes, the second five minutes is devoted to the overhand volley, and in the third five possibly the forearm bump pass is practiced. Although these mass drills facilitate the teacher's job, they do little or nothing toward allowing for individual student differences. There is a time for togetherness during the initial exposure to a new skill, but learning is individual and each individual progresses at his own rate; therefore, practice should be geared to individual needs. Individual practice stations with skill cards can meet these needs. After students have been exposed to the basic skills, practice stations involving different skills can be set up in various places of the teaching area. Reciprocal and small group interactions at these stations and recording the results of individual progress are excellent ways to get immediate feedback during practice. Students can even be given the opportunity to choose the station at which to work—an opportunity for self-direction. The teacher is then able to individualize instruction as he moves among the students, giving help and encouragement. However, teachers do need to review the skill cards periodically to guide and advise students in their skill development.

A sample skill card is included in the volleyball chapter, page 338. Although the score is recorded and can eventually be used as some portion of the skill grade, the main purpose of recording the score is to provide feedback to students concerning progress in their skill development. Work on the skill card can be an actual part of various class periods and/or can be used as a warmup at the beginning of each class period. The skills listed on this sample card are a few examples of the many possibilities. The procedure at each station may be varied to become more difficult as students progress in their ability to handle the ball. The idea of the skill card can be adapted to all sports. A similar device which provides for students to progress individually is included in the chapter on gymnastics, pages 481 and 489.

The final application of individual skills is in the culminating activity—the game. The amount of class time devoted to practice as opposed to game play depends upon the needs of the class. Logically there is a greater need for skill development at the beginning of the unit, with more attention being given to game play at the end. An early exposure to the game, however, is quite desirable. This early exposure might take the form of a modified game (what is commonly known as a lead-up game). The students then, with the guidance of the teacher, can analyze their weaknesses and plan ways to improve their skills. The practice sessions which follow will have greater meaning as a result.

Individual and small group work should be closely related to the game situation and should become increasingly complex as the students become more proficient. Practice involving strategy approached through the problem-solving method contributes to the development of the students' ability to cope with the ever-changing environment in game-like situations.

The game itself, however desirable, does not provide the opportunity for the development of specific skills. Since a person learns by doing, the more opportunities he has to practice, the better are his chances to improve. The game quite often limits participation because it is highly structured and usually many people are interacting using one set of equipment; this is especially true in the team sports. As the number of interacting members increases, the chances of interaction and improvement for the more poorly skilled player decreases. This does not mean to imply that the game should be abandoned, for it plays a vital role in the curriculum. It provides the necessary opportunity to blend the parts into the whole. Nevertheless, a unit of instruction in which a majority of the class time is spent in game play does little toward the development of individual skills. Thus, class sessions which provide students with opportunities to become proficient in individual skills and to extend this proficiency through small group interaction (possibly games) keep students involved and motivated. The purpose in using an activity (sport) as a vehicle for learning is to teach the student and not just the activity. Activities (sports) are the organization of skills which develop from concepts into recognizable, purposeful movement.

Grouping Students

There are as many ways to group students as there are needs to group students. The need may be for as simple a task as taking roll to as complex a task as homogeneous grouping. The job of the teacher concerning grouping is two-fold: (1) to enhance the learning climate by the types of groups he utilizes; and (2) to do this as efficiently as possible using a minimum of class time.

There are many efficient ways of completing required administrative chores (checking attendance, appropriate attire, etc.). One way that has proven effective in saving time is to provide the opportunity for students to begin working immediately upon entering the gymnasium. The teacher can complete necessary administrative chores while the students are working. In the course of a year many hours of valuable class time can be saved. In addition to providing privacy for the student who may need to confer with the teacher a few minutes, this procedure also fosters the development of an independent student, able to discipline himself and direct his own activities.

There are instances when lines and organizational patterns must be very specific for reasons of safety, such as in archery and golf. However, in many activities a scattered formation is adequate and less time-consuming. Students can learn to find a space on the floor quickly and begin to work. If there is a need for partner work, the students can choose a partner, or form groups of three if necessary. One pair of partners may join with another pair to make a group of four. Two groups of four may join together to form a group of eight. Once students learn to function in this student-centered method of organization it is much less time-consuming than the traditional line where students count off by two's or four's etc., and then form groups. It is quite interesting to group informally and watch leadership emerge rather than assigning groups and leaders. Furthermore, a person arbitrarily assigned to be a captain or squad leader does not automatically become a leader.[17]

Teams for competition within the class should grow out of the existing organizational structure of the class. This is both functional and beneficial in that those students who have been working together on skills and combinations now have an opportunity to work together in the game situation. There are circumstances, however, when there is a need for the teacher to control team membership. It may be necessary to balance teams according to ability or to group homogeneously. When these procedures are desirable, the actual mechanics of grouping should be completed prior to the class period. Regardless of how the teacher arranges students on teams, he will find each system has certain merits and certain flaws. There is one way, however, which should be discarded. That is the practice of choosing captains and then having the captains "choose up sides" from the class members during the class period. This practice is not only very time-consuming, but it is also extremely demoralizing for those students who are chosen last.

To summarize, one might conclude, then, that the organization of students within the class should be both efficient and effective—efficient in terms of time and ease of moving from a simple organization to a more complex organization; effective in that it conforms to the needs of the students, meets the objectives of the unit and is appropriate to the content area.

Utilizing and Improvising Facilities

Changing techniques of organization creates very little difficulty. Once convinced of the merits of student-centered methods the teacher needs only to begin to accustom students to working within this structure. The facilities and equipment needed to implement a program geared to individuals pose more of a problem. The number of balls, for example, needed for individual and small group skill practice far exceeds the number of necessary balls for large group, line-oriented drills. If the budget is such that the necessary number of balls cannot be acquired, then one should look for ways to improvise. One might look to the other sports to see if the balls they use can be borrowed to supplement the existing inadequate supply. Students can use a volleyball or soccer ball to pass and shoot in basketball. Basketballs cannot be used in volleyball because of possible injury to the fingers, but large, lightweight balls used in the primary grades or beach balls can be used. A second source of additional equipment is to check into purchasing seconds. Without a doubt, quality equipment is desirable, if there is a choice; however, a less-than-perfect ball is better than no ball at all. Another

17. Joseph B. Oxendine, *Psychology of Motor Learning* (New York: Appleton-Century-Crofts, 1968), pp. 41–42.

possibility for expanding equipment, many times overlooked, is to have athletics and physical education share equipment. With a little cooperative planning to avoid conflicts, equipment supplies can possibly be doubled.

If an adequate quantity of equipment cannot be secured, other ways of organizing students and content must be found. One possibility is the overflow plan. Either by interest or rotation, one squad could be instructed in tennis outdoors while others work on skills taught in a previous unit. For example, several groups could work on softball or track and field events while the teacher instructs a group in tennis. If necessary, the teacher could divide his time between the groups. Another possibility is to have a unit on recreational games indoors (table tennis, shuffleboard, modified handball, etc.) with tennis instruction outdoors. Still another combination might be a unit in gymnastics overlapping the end of a volleyball unit in which the students supervise and officiate their own volleyball games. The use of individual skill cards with the overflow plan can help to guide the students in their activity when working on their own. There are many possible combinations in the overflow plan. Probably the most limiting factor is available space.

If both space and equipment are limited, and there is a real need to include that specific sport in the curriculum, the teacher must take a closer look at the sport and search for those skills that can be practiced without equipment. If the sport involves starting and stopping, a change of direction and dodging, a station could be set up to practice moving in space and using these skills in relation to other people. The sport of basketball involves the fundamental skill of jumping, both for rebounds and jump balls. Some students could work at a station that might look like a jump-and-reach test. Although practicing manipulative skills for

sports involving those actions is surely necessary, one must not lose sight of the fact that the body controls the ball and that developing better body control can lead to better ball control.

Mechanical aids and/or improvisations can also expand the available facilities and provide more opportunity for individual practice. These aids may be as sophisticated as the Ball Boy or as simple as a blank wall, as expensive as an indoor putting green or as inexpensive as a paper cup held by a partner. One need only review the equipment catalogues to find that there are many mechanical aids available. Unfortunately, budgets are limited and purchasing mechanical aids is often not feasible. However, with a minimum of resources and a little ingenuity, many aids can be improvised.

Often a means to expand facilities is so obvious and simple that it is overlooked. A blank wall, for example, can be used as a rebounding surface for many sports involving striking skills. All the basic skills of volleyball can be practiced with the wall as a rebounding surface. The wall can be a very consistent opponent for the beginning student in tennis. In soccer or speedball one can kick the ball against the wall for accuracy and then react to the rebound with a trap, another kick, a block or a lift. In basketball, tape can be used on the wall at the appropriate height to simulate the basket and students can shoot at the tape as a target while waiting to rotate to the regulation basket. With the addition of each improvised basket, the number of opportunities to shoot is multiplied. These are just a few of the many possibilities for using a blank wall.

There are many other means of expanding equipment and facilities. The lines on the floor may be used for balancing in gymnastics. A stage or sturdy desk can be used as a vaulting station for practicing the approach and take off. In track and field inflated inner tubes placed under a tumbling mat can serve as the landing pit for an indoor high jump station. Using ingenuity and imagination, the teacher with limited space and equipment can provide meaningful experiences for his students.

Although adapting facilities to provide more opportunities is of great importance, adapting facilities to provide successful experiences for the students is of prime importance. If a student continually fails in his attempts to master movement skills, he soon loses interest and stops trying. Therefore, success must be encountered early in a unit of study. Adapting facilities may not be enough to provide success. The teacher may also need to adapt the content or alter the rules to provide successful experiences. Examples of these adaptations are lowering the beam, the buck, and possibly the uneven bars to provide for the less capable student in gymnastics. The net in volleyball can be lowered in the early stages of practice for the hit over the net or spike. Allowing the less competent student to serve from a spot closer to the net than the baseline provides success in the volleyball serve for some students. Target areas should be large during initial practice of skills involving accuracy. The teacher should adapt the rules and skills of the activity to suit the competence level of the students. One should remember that nothing succeeds like success. Success can be our greatest motivating tool.

SUMMARY

The purpose of examining methods of teaching and techniques of organization is to arrive at some conclusion as to which methods and techniques enhance the attainment of desirable outcomes for secondary school physical education. One might list the characteristics of a good lesson and then choose methods that enable the lesson to meet those characteristics. A more interesting way is to list those items a student should experience in a lesson. Although the list might become unwieldy, it can be condensed into three words: activity, involvement, and success. If the student is active, the mechanics of organization are efficient. If the student is involved, the lesson is meeting the needs and interests of the total individual. If the student is successful, learning is taking place. Finally, if all these criteria are met, a sense of achievement and satisfaction should carry over beyond the school day as well as beyond the school years.

REFERENCES

Barrett, Kate R. *Exploration—A Method for Teaching Movement.* Madison, Wisc.: College Printing and Typing Co., 1965.

Berensen, Carol A. "The Relative Effectiveness of Descriptive Teaching and Structured Problem Solving in Learning Basic Tennis Skills." Master of Science thesis, University of Washington, 1967.

Broer, Marion R. "Effectiveness of a General Basic Skills Curriculum for Junior High School Girls." *Research Quarterly* 29 (December 1958):379–88.

———. *Efficiency of Human Movement.* 3d ed. Philadelphia: W. B. Saunders Co., 1973.

Bruner, Jerome S. *Toward a Theory of Instruction.* Cambridge, Mass.: Harvard University Press, 1966.

Figley, Grace E.; Mitchell, Heidie C.; and Wright, Barbara L. *Elementary School Physical Education: An Educational Experience.* Dubuque, Iowa: Kendall/Hunt Publishing Company, 1977.

Godfrey, Barbara B., and Kephart, Newell C. *Movement Patterns and Motor Education.* New York: Appleton-Century-Crofts, 1969.

Gravlee, Gayle. "A Comparison of the Effectiveness of Two Methods of Teaching a

Four Week Unit on Selected Motor Skills to First Grade Children." Master of Science thesis, University of North Carolina at Greensboro, 1965.

Gronlund, Norman E. *Stating Objectives for Classroom Instruction.* New York: Macmillan Co., 1978.

Joyce, Bruce R. *Selecting Learning Experiences: Linking Theory and Practice,* Washington, D.C.: Association for Supervision and Curriculum Development, 1978.

La Plante, Marilyn. "A Study of the Problem Solving Method of Teaching Bowling." Master of Science thesis, University of North Carolina at Greensboro, 1965.

Leeper, Robert R., ed. *Humanizing Education: The Person in the Process.* Washington, D.C.: Association for Supervision and Curriculum Development, National Education Association, 1967.

Mager, Robert F. *Preparing Instructional Objectives.* Belmont, Calif.: Fearon-Pitman Publishers, 1975.

Mosston, Muska. *Teaching Physical Education.* Columbus, Ohio: Charles E. Merrill Publishing Co., 1966.

Oxendine, Joseph B. *Psychology of Motor Learning.* New York: Appleton-Century-Crofts, 1968.

Scott, Robert S. "A Comparison of Teaching Two Methods of Physical Education with Grade One Pupils." Master of Science thesis, Wisconsin State University at La Crosse, 1965.

Singer, Robert N. *Motor Learning and Human Performance: An Application in Physical Education Skills.* New York: Macmillan Co., 1975.

Ziegler, Yvonne P. "A Comparison of Two Methods of Teaching Gymnastics." Master of Science thesis, University of Wisconsin, 1965.

4

Mechanical Principles of Movement

The performer utilizes the elements of movement—space, force, time and flow—in his attempt to move effectively and efficiently. As he walks, runs, leaps, jumps, starts, stops, bends, stretches, twists, turns, throws, catches, and strikes, he endeavors to use his body in the most efficient manner. In order to do this he must understand how to use space to his advantage and how to move with a light or strong force, at a fast or slow speed, with free or bound flow. In addition, he must understand the principles that govern all movement. These basic, underlying principles are referred to as the mechanical principles of movement because they have evolved from the phase of physics known as mechanics.

This chapter is an introduction to the mechanical principles of movement. Its purpose is to be functional rather than technical. For a more comprehensive treatment the resources listed at the end of the chapter should prove helpful. Discussion within this chapter focuses upon (1) motion; (2) stability; (3) force; (4) spin and rebound; and (5) projectiles.

MOTION

Motion and Factors Affecting Motion

Motion is movement produced by a force that is exerted as a push or a pull. The amount of motion produced is dependent upon the amount of force exerted in relation to the amount of resistance present. In the human body movement is produced by muscular contractions. Gravity, air resistance, water resistance, and friction exist as forces which often resist motion. These forces can either aid or retard movement. It is important that the performer utilize these forces when they contribute to the intended movement and minimize them when they impede the movement.

Gravity is a natural force in the universe which pulls everything towards the center of the earth. It acts on all objects by pulling through the weight center of the object. This weight center is referred to as the center of gravity. If it were not for the force of gravity, a ball that is thrown would not return to the ground. An individual executing a jump would remain in space rather than land again on the earth.

The strength of gravity's pull depends upon the mass or quantity of matter comprising the object upon which it is acting. The greater the mass of an object, the greater is the pull of gravity. A measurement of the strength of the pull of gravity upon an object is referred to as the weight of the object. Two objects can have a different shape but the same mass; therefore, they weigh the same. Two objects may be the same size and shape but different in mass. The object with the greater mass effects a greater pull of gravity which results in its having a greater weight. For example, compare a volleyball with a medicine ball of the same circumference. In lifting the two balls, one notices that the medicine ball is heavier than the volleyball. The medicine ball has the greater quantity of matter, causing a greater pull of gravity as measured in pounds; thus, the medicine ball has the greater weight.

Friction is the force produced when one object moves across another. Friction assists the motion of a body exerting force diagonally backward against a supporting surface but hinders the motion of an object that is pushed, pulled, or rolled. Movement is facilitated when it occurs on a supporting surface that allows sufficient friction to exist. The performance of an individual running on ice, a wooden floor, and sand differs due to friction. Movement is difficult on ice, as little friction exists between the feet and the ice. On the other hand, movement is difficult on sand due to the great friction existing between the performer's feet and the sand. Movement is easiest on the wooden floor, as this surface provides sufficient friction for movement to occur but does not retard movement due to an excess of friction.

The motion of an object that is pushed, pulled, or rolled is hampered due to sliding and rolling friction. The speed and distance achieved by a field hockey drive on a well-kept, close-cropped field is different than the same drive in a field of taller grass. The ball will not travel as far nor as fast on the second field because of the additional friction produced by the taller grass.

It is the responsibility of the performer to utilize friction when it assists in his movement and to minimize friction when it retards movement. A sprinter wears track shoes to produce friction against the track. Golf greens are kept well-groomed to reduce the friction that retards the forward motion of the golf ball. The effect of friction increases as the size of the object increases, as the surface exposed becomes greater or more irregular, as the speed of the object increases, and as the weight of the object increases.

Air resistance is the force that is active upon objects moving through atmospheric space. Air resistance is desirable in an activity such as sailing but is undesirable in an activity in which it impedes the progress of a performer or the flight of an object. In archery, a wind blowing from the side of the archer alters the path of an arrow. In badminton air resistance changes the flight of the shuttlecock.

The effect of air resistance increases as the speed, size, and surface area exposed to the resistance increase and as the weight of the object decreases. The effect of air resistance is greater upon a ball moving with great speed than upon a slower ball. A ball thrown with twice the speed of another ball of the same mass will travel farther, but it will not travel twice as far due to the air resistance that is interfering with its flight. As the size of the object receiving force increases, the effect of air resistance also increases. If the same force is exerted in throwing a basketball and a softball, air resistance is more active upon the basketball due to its greater size. Likewise, as the surface area of an object becomes rougher or more irregular and as the weight of the object decreases the effect of air resistance also increases. A cut in a golf ball or a softball causes air resistance to be more active upon the ball. A plastic practice golf ball does not achieve the distance of a regulation golf ball due to air resistance. The effect of air resistance is greater upon the practice ball because of its more irregular surface and its lighter weight.

In many sport activities, performers attempt to reduce air resistance by reducing the surface area exposed to it. Experienced archers fletch their arrows with small, smooth plastic vanes rather than larger, rougher feathers to reduce the air resistance that is active upon the arrows. Many badminton players prefer to use feather rather than plastic shuttlecocks due to the difference in surface areas and the resulting reduction of air resistance.

Water resistance is the force exerted by water against an object. It can assist movement by pushing an object forward or it can retard movement by opposing the object's forward motion. As with friction and air resistance, the effect of water resistance varies in relation to the size, shape, surface, and speed of an object. The effect of water resistance increases as the object increases in size, has more surface area exposed to the water, and is moving at a faster speed.

A swimmer utilizes water resistance to propel him forward. In the breast stroke, the surface of the hand acts against the water to create a forward impetus. To gain full advantage of the glide phase of the breast stroke, it is necessary for the swimmer to reduce the water resistance active upon his body. The arms are extended forward to streamline the surface area exposed to the water.

Momentum

Momentum is the product of an object's mass times its velocity. *Velocity* is the rate of movement or the distance an object moves in a given period of time. *Acceleration* is an increase in velocity, while *deceleration* is a decrease in velocity. The greater the velocity or the greater the mass of an object, the greater is the momentum of that object. A tennis ball traveling twice as fast (velocity) as a second tennis ball has greater momentum than the second ball. A solid rubber ball traveling at the same speed as a tennis ball has greater momentum due to its greater mass. Greater momentum means that the object will remain in motion for a longer period of time.

Velocity and momentum are both important concepts in sport skills. In a throw for distance, momentum is dependent upon the velocity imparted to the object at the time of its release. Since the mass of the thrown object does not change, the velocity of the object becomes the determining factor in the amount of momentum achieved, or in the length of time that the object remains in motion.

In striking activities, both mass and velocity can change to produce greater momentum to allow the object to continue in motion longer. Selection of a heavier striking implement increases the mass of the object imparting force. A heavier softball bat has greater mass than a lighter bat and therefore allows for greater momentum to be produced. Velocity relates to the speed of the object as it leaves the striking surface. Greater velocity of the approaching object or greater velocity of the striking implement produces greater velocity in the object struck.

Newton's Laws of Motion

Newton's laws of motion provide a foundation for the principles of motion.

1. *Law of Inertia: A body at rest will remain at rest and a body in motion will remain in motion at the same velocity unless acted upon by an external force.* The resistance of a body to a change in its present state of motion is known as *inertia*. The inertia of an object at rest resists the initiation of motion in the object. The inertia of an object in motion resists a change in its state of motion. Inertia is directly proportional to the mass of an object and its velocity. The greater the mass and the greater the velocity, the more difficult it is to effect a change in the motion of an object because of its greater inertia. Due to inertia, less force is required to maintain a constant rate of motion than to either begin or change the motion.

Inertia as it affects movement is a significant factor in the selection of playing positions for participants in some sports. For example, the responsibilities of a blocker in football dictate that the blocker be a player whose position can not be easily changed by an opposing player. Generally, a player who is heavy in terms of body weight is selected to become a blocker in preference to a lighter player. Due to the greater weight (mass) of the heavier player, his inertia or resistance to a change in motion is greater, and thus it becomes harder for the opposing players to alter his position.

The law of inertia applies to the motion frequently seen in a ball. A ball will not begin moving until it receives an external force, whether the force be the result of contact with a striking implement, such as a bat, or contact with a body part, such as the hand. A ball in motion will continue in motion until it is acted upon by an outside force. A thrown ball would continue in motion forever if it were not for air resistance, the force of gravity, or the action of a player catching the ball.

The law of inertia is also apparent in the motion of a swimmer as he executes a glide in several strokes (crawl, breaststroke, side stroke, etc.). The initial movement of the swimmer's body counteracts inertia, the glide maintains his motion, and the subsequent actions propel him forward. However, if the glide phase of the stroke is too long, inertia will again have to be overcome, resulting in greater energy expended by the swimmer. In activities which require several actions in the same direction, movement from one to another should be continuous so that inertia does not have to be overcome with each action.

2. *Law of Acceleration: The acceleration of an object that is acted upon by a force is directly proportional to the force and inversely proportional to the mass of the object.* A tennis player executes a lob on one stroke and a smash on the next. The tennis ball receives the greater acceleration on the smash as greater force is imparted to the ball by the tennis racket. Acceleration is directly proportional to force. A player who compares a serve in tennis with a serve in volleyball when both have been executed with the same force notes that the tennis ball receives the greater acceleration. The mass of the tennis ball is much less than the mass of the volleyball and acceleration is inversely proportional to mass.

The law of acceleration is also applicable in archery. In archery, an arrow receives impetus from the bow. As the bow is bent to a greater degree, greater force is produced. If an archer releases an arrow before coming to full draw, the arrow will not have the velocity of an arrow that is released from the fulldraw position. The velocity of the arrow is directly proportional to the force imparted by the bow. In selecting equipment, the archer must be aware that acceleration is inversely proportional to mass. If he is consistent in his draw and imparts equal force in shooting two different arrows, one a very light aluminum arrow and one a heavier wooden arrow, greater velocity and distance are achieved by the aluminum arrow. Since the mass of the aluminum arrow is less than the mass of the wooden arrow, it achieves greater velocity.

3. *Law of Action-Reaction: For every action there is an equal and opposite reaction.* As an object imparts force upon a surface, the surface imparts an equal and opposite force upon the object. In running, the feet push diagonally backward against the ground. The reaction force provided by the ground propels the runner forward. The force the feet exert against the ground is not apparent in the movement of the ground as its mass is so much greater than the mass of the runner.

To receive maximum reaction force, the surface against which the force is exerted must be stable. If one attempts to run on sand or in mud, much of the reaction force is dissipated due to the nature of the surface. As the foot contacts the sand or mud, the surface gives and moves, thus decreasing the force which propels the runner forward.

Types of Motion

There are two basic types of motion, linear and rotary. Other forms of motion are a variation of these or a combination of the two.

Rotary motion (also called angular or rotatory motion) is movement in an arc or a circle about an axis or a fixed point. A spin on a ball causes rotational movement of the ball.

In rotary movement, as the radius of the circle decreases, rotary speed increases. An ice skater applies this principle as he executes a twirl. To increase his rotary speed his arms are kept close to the body; to decrease the speed the arms are extended. In executing a roll in tumbling the performer also utilizes this principle by keeping his arms and legs well tucked to increase the speed of the roll and by straightening the body to stop the roll.

Linear motion (translatory motion) occurs when the body or object as a whole moves uniformly in a straight line with all parts moving at the same speed and in the same direction. Linear motion usually occurs when the body is transported by another object, such as in skiing, horseback riding, or riding in a car. The body may move in a linear pathway in walking or running, but it does so through the rotary movements of the legs. If one end of an object is fixed and not free to move, rotary movement will occur. The leg is inserted into the hip joint. As force is applied, the leg rotates about the axis of this joint. Through the rotary action of the leg, the body is able to move forward in a straight or linear pathway. Most movements of the body are a combination of linear and rotary motion.

A variation of linear motion is curvilinear motion. An object begins motion in a linear pathway but due to gravity, air resistance, or friction, its motion becomes a curved pathway. Resistance causes the linear motion to become curvilinear. The curvilinear motion that results differs from rotary motion in that its pathway is curved but does not necessarily describe a circle or an arc of a

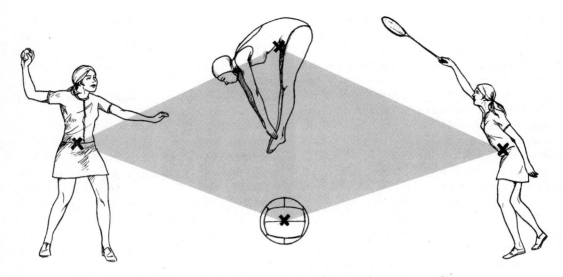

Figure 4.1. **The center of gravity in a symmetrical object and in a performer executing various movements**

circle. All projectiles move in a curved pathway.[1]

STABILITY

In considering the stability of an object, one must consider the object's center of gravity, line of gravity, and base of support. The *center of gravity* of an object or a body is an imaginary point about which its weight is equally distributed or balanced. It may fall within or outside of the body, depending upon the position assumed. The center of gravity of a symmetrical object such as a basketball is the geometric center, whereas the center of gravity of a performer in the pike position falls outside of the body (fig. 4.1).

The position of the center of gravity in the body is generally in the pelvic region, provided a normal stance is assumed with weight distributed on both feet and arms hanging at sides. This position may vary with body proportions and the posture as-

sumed. Concentration of weight in the upper portion of the body raises the center of gravity, which is valuable to a gymnast performing a handstand but is a disadvantage to an individual performing in an upright position. A high center of gravity decreases the stability of a lineman in football. A performer should be cognizant of the greater stability that is possible as his center of gravity moves closer to his base of support. Bending the knees lowers the center of gravity and affords greater stability than a position of stretching overhead, which raises the center of gravity.

The location of the center of gravity changes as a body part moves away from the body and as an additional weight is added to the body. The center of gravity moves in the direction of the additional weight or the movement of the body part unless compensatory measures are taken. Extending one leg straight to the side moves the center of

1. Additional discussion of linear and rotary motion is included under "Application of Force," page 56.

gravity in that direction. The body compensates for this change by leaning slightly to the opposite side so that balance is maintained. Lifting a bowling ball in one hand causes the center of gravity to shift to that side of the body. The opposite arm is extended slightly to counteract this movement of the center of gravity. Reaching overhead to execute a clear in badminton raises the player's center of gravity.

An individual's *base of support* consists of the body parts that are in contact with the supporting surface and the area between these parts (fig. 4.2). If the center of gravity moves outside of the base of support, the body must compensate for this movement or stability will be lost. To maintain balance, another body part may compensate by moving to relocate the center of gravity over the base of support or a new base of support can be established under the center of gravity.

The *line of gravity* refers to the imaginary line which extends through the center of gravity straight down toward the center of the earth. A stable or unstable position becomes obvious when one determines the position of the line of gravity in relation to the base of support. Greatest stability results when the line of gravity passes through the center of the base (fig. 4.3). Within limits, the wider an individual's base of support, the greater the stability achieved. A wide base of support will allow greater movement of the center of gravity and line of gravity before the location of each moves outside of the base and equilibrium is disturbed. Likewise, greater stability results as the center of gravity is nearer to the center of the base of support.

Directions for performance often indicate that weight should be evenly distributed. This is an indication that the performer should keep his center of gravity over the center of the base of support.

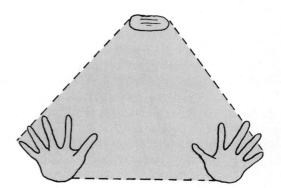

Base of support in a headstand: two hands, head, and area between.

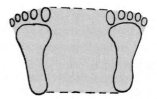

Base of support: two feet and area between.

Figure 4.2. **Base of support**

Broer refers to a desirable base of support as being not larger than the width of the hips.[2] A wider stance introduces a second component of force—an outward component in addition to the downward component. The outward component makes stability difficult on a surface (such as ice) which provides little friction.

In activities in which force is to be exerted or received, or in which movement is to be initiated or stopped, stability can be increased by increasing the size of the base of support in the same direction as the force or movement. Sports activities utilize two basic stances (bases of support) or combinations of the two (fig. 4.4). When force is to be

2. Marion R. Broer, *Efficiency of Human Movement*, 3d ed. (Philadelphia: W. B. Saunders Co., 1973), p. 52.

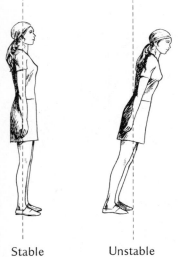

| Stable | Unstable |
| Position | Position |

Figure 4.3. **In a stable position the line of gravity is centered over the base of support. In an unstable position the individual would fall forward or a new base of support would be established to maintain balance.**

exerted in a forward direction or when forward or backward movement is to occur, the performer utilizes a forward-back stride position. One foot is placed diagonally ahead of the other. When movement to the side is to occur, a side stride position is assumed. The feet are placed in a parallel position, approximately shoulder-distance apart.

In adjusting the position of the base of support, the performer should adhere to the *principle of opposition*. Body parts usually move in opposition. In walking, the natural movement is for the right foot and left arm to swing forward simultaneously. One does not usually find that the right foot and right arm swing forward at the same time. As a performer throws a softball with his right arm, he steps forward with his left leg. This movement enlarges his base of support in

the direction of the force, allows greater forward movement of his center of gravity before it moves beyond the base, and utilizes the principle of opposition. Opposition of body parts is important in maintaining balance as it assists in keeping the center of gravity over the base of support.

Stability is increased as a force is received close to the peformer's center of gravity, causing little change in the position of the center of gravity in relation to the base of support. A volleyball player's stability is decreased if he plays the ball to his right or left rather than directly in front of his body. Reaching to the right or left moves the center of gravity closer to the edge of the base of support. Less movement then becomes possible before the center of gravity moves outside of the base and stability is lost.

The friction offered by the supporting surface is important in tasks demanding stability. Sufficient friction must exist between the surface and the individual's base of support or the individual will slip or fall. Leather-soled shoes provide little friction when walking or running on a surface such as ice. A rubber-soled shoe such as a boot with tread provides greater friction and thus the admonition to wear boots on a snowy or icy day. In the gymnasium the tennis shoe is selected in preference to a more smoothly soled shoe to increase the friction (traction) between the individual and the gymnasium floor. Socks provide little friction and thus running in stocking feet is discouraged. The performer should select his footwear according to the activity and the surface utilized.

The degree of stability desired is dependent upon the nature of the movement to be performed. If the body is to initiate movement quickly, a relatively unstable position is desired. The ready position for those sports demanding quick movement places the weight forward on the balls of the feet with the upper trunk inclined slightly forward, thereby moving the performer's center of gravity closer to the edge of his base of support. Such a position allows for balance to be lost quickly in order to initiate movement. The weight is moved to the edge of the base that is nearest the line of intended movement.

When movement is no longer desired, the performer should enlarge his base of support and lower his center of gravity so that stability may be maintained as he stops moving. A basketball player moving forward stops his forward motion with his feet in a forward-back stride position to enlarge his base of support in the direction of the force. His front knee is bent to lower his center of gravity.

Several sensory organs are important to stability. The eyes, the organs of the inner ear, and the proprioceptors of the skin, tendons, and joints play significant roles in stability. A performer is told to focus his eyes straight ahead rather than to focus near the feet. According to Schurr, focusing on the feet moves the head forward and down, causing forward movement of the center of gravity and a more precarious position with respect to balance.[3] Focusing the eyes on a point that is directly ahead provides a reference point for the eyes. However, when performing on a piece of equipment such as a trampoline or a balance beam, the performer focuses on the frame of the trampoline or the end of the beam in order to maintain orientation with the surface he is contacting.

Stability is important to performance because it aids in efficient movement. Stability is needed to execute a movement, to prepare the body for subsequent movements, and to produce force. However, the degree of stability that is desired is dictated by the movement to be performed. Activities such

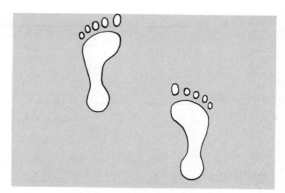

Forward-back Stride Position

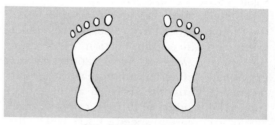

Side Stride Position

Figure 4.4. **Basic stances for sport activities**

as performing on a balance beam require a high degree of stability, while activities demanding quick movements or quick changes of direction require a relatively low degree of stability.

FORCE

Force can be defined as a push or pull that produces motion. Force that moves the human body can be classified into two categories: internal force, the force produced by muscular contraction; and external force,

3. Evelyn L. Schurr, *Movement Experiences for Children: A Humanistic Approach to Elementary School Physical Education*, 2nd ed. (Englewood Cliffs, N.J.: Prentice Hall, Inc. 1975), p. 179.

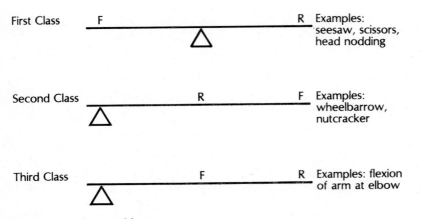

First Class   F   R   Examples:
                                                        seesaw, scissors,
                                                        head nodding

Second Class   R   F   Examples:
                                                        wheelbarrow,
                                                        nutcracker

Third Class   F   R   Examples: flexion
                                                        of arm at elbow

Figure 4.5. **Classes of levers**

the force produced by gravity, air resistance, water resistance, and friction. *Force equals mass times acceleration.* Acceleration has been previously defined as an increase in velocity or speed. Thus, the force of an object becomes the product of its mass times its acceleration (increase in speed). Force will be discussed according to: (1) levers; (2) internal force and the effects of mass and speed upon it; (3) external force; (4) force achieved in striking activities; (5) application of force; and (6) absorption of force.

It should be remembered that maximum force is not always desired in sports activities. The amount of force utilized is often varied to allow for placement and the deception of an opponent. The magnitude of the force desired is dependent upon the nature of the movement to be performed. Some actions, such as the smash in badminton, call for maximum production of force; other actions, such as the drop shot in badminton, call for less force. However, in all instances sufficient force must be exerted to overcome inertia if movement is to result.

Levers

Basic to an understanding of force is an understanding of levers. A lever is a rigid bar that rotates about an axis. A force applied to the lever is used to move a resistance or weight. Levers produce a mechanical advantage in terms of either speed or force.

There are three classes of levers (fig. 4.5). The class is determined by the location of the fulcrum (the axis about which the lever rotates) in relation to the force and the resistance. The distance from the resistance to the fulcrum is referred to as the resistance arm (RA). The distance from the force to the fulcrum is known as the force arm (FA).

The mechanical advantage produced by a lever depends upon the ratio of the length of its force arm to the length of its resistance arm. A longer force arm produces an advantage in terms of force; a longer resistance arm produces an advantage in terms of speed and range of movement. A first-class lever can produce an advantage in either speed or force, depending upon the location of its fulcrum and the resulting lengths of the force arm and the resistance arm. A second-class lever has a longer force arm than resistance arm and produces an advantage in force at the expense of speed and range of movement. Therefore, with a longer force arm, it takes less force to move a certain resistance. A third-class lever has a longer resistance arm than force arm and produces an advantage in speed and range of motion at the expense of force. As a lever moves about its fulcrum, the distance each point on the lever moves is proportional to its distance from the fulcrum.[4] The point farthest from the fulcrum will move the greatest distance, and will move this distance in the same time that a point closer to the fulcrum moves a shorter distance. Thus, its speed is greater. A longer resistance arm increases the distance that its distal end moves in a given period of time, thus producing an advantage in terms of speed and range of movement.

Movement in the body occurs through a system of levers. The bones act as the lever; the joint where movement occurs becomes the fulcrum; the force is supplied by contraction of muscles; and the resistance becomes the body segment to be moved and any weight that is added to that segment.

Most levers in the body are third-class levers (fig. 4.6). Muscles (the source of force) are inserted close to joints. The resistance is applied farther from the joint than the force. Thus, levers in the body have a shorter force arm than resistance arm and an advantage is gained in tasks demanding speed and range of movement rather than in tasks demanding force. Additional discussion of the levers of the body is included as it pertains to internal force production.

Internal Force

Force is dependent upon both mass and speed ($F = M \times A$). Through the action of muscles, the body is able to effect an increase in mass utilized and/or speed to increase force. Sports activities utilize the internal force originating with the contraction of muscles to produce the force that moves a body part or moves an implement. A closer examination of both mass and

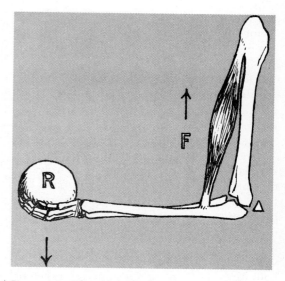

Figure 4.6. **Example of the arm as a third-class lever**

speed as each relates to force will assist the sports performer in understanding how to produce the force that is most efficient for his particular activity. However, to utilize both mass and speed effectively in force production the body segments involved in a motion must be stabilized. Discussion of internal force is therefore divided into: (1) stabilizing body segments to increase force; (2) increasing speed to increase force; and (3) increasing mass to increase force.

STABILIZING BODY SEGMENTS TO INCREASE FORCE

Stabilizing the body segments involved in a motion increases the force that may be achieved. The previous discussion of stability (p 46) emphasized the importance of a stable base of support and sufficient friction existing between the supporting surface and the feet if a balanced position is to be obtained. A stable base of support is essential if the application of force is to be effective. To achieve a

4. Refer to figure 4.7, page 53.

stable base it is often necessary for the performer to keep his feet in contact with the ground. The badminton player should move his feet and get into proper position to execute a stroke rather than jump to hit the shuttlecock, since in jumping the body does not have a stable base from which to operate. When throwing, it is possible to achieve greater distance when the feet have established a firm base with the supporting surface. A player who jumps and releases the ball at the height of his jump imparts less force to the ball because the body segments involved in throwing are not operating from as stable a base. However, the feet do not remain in contact with the ground in actions such as the volleyball spike and the basketball jump shot. In such instances it is essential that the trunk provide stability for the movement of the arms and shoulders.

INCREASING SPEED TO INCREASE FORCE

Speed is increased by increasing the range of movement of the body segment imparting the force. An increase in range of motion allows for the speed of the segment involved to be developed through a greater distance. Range of movement may be increased through a backswing, utilizing the longest lever that is efficient for the activity; rotation of the trunk; and transfer of body weight.

The length of the body's levers can be altered by extension or flexion of joints. Flexion shortens the resistance arm, thereby increasing the force advantage of the lever. A person lifting a heavy object utilizes a shorter resistance arm by keeping the object close to his body as it is lifted. Extension at a joint increases the length of the lever, which allows for greater range of movement and greater speed at the distal end of the lever.

In many sports activities an implement is held in the hand to increase the length of the lever (fig. 4.7). It is apparent that the longer lever resulting from the use of a tennis racket moves a greater distance than the shorter lever, the hand. The distal end of the lever (racket head) moves this greater distance (to point *B,* fig. 4.7) in the same time that the hand moves to point *A*. Hence, it must move faster.

To achieve the longest lever possible, a tennis player should grip the racket as close to its end as possible, rather than choking up on the racket handle. However, the advantage gained by the use of the longer lever can be negated if the player does not have sufficient strength to control the longer lever. An increase in the resistance arm such as is afforded by the use of an implement increases the range of movement and speed at the expense of strength. Greater strength is required of a player who does not choke up on the implement. Also, the impact received upon striking a moving object is greater when received at the end of a long lever. In executing a volley in tennis, a player may need to choke up on the racket or shorten the lever arm to reduce the impact of the ball and to allow for greater control.

Many performers select heavy implements to use since a heavier implement has a greater mass. A softball player may select a heavier bat, a tennis player a heavier racket. As mass is increased, force can also be increased, since F = M × A. Again, it should be recognized that the heavier implement demands greater strength of the performer. In all activities utilizing a paddle, racket, bat, or another implement, selection of the implement should be in accord with the performer's strength and ability to control the implement.

Trunk rotation also increases the range of movement of the lever arm. As a player prepares to execute a forehand drive in tennis, he rotates his body so that the shoulder of the non-racket arm points towards

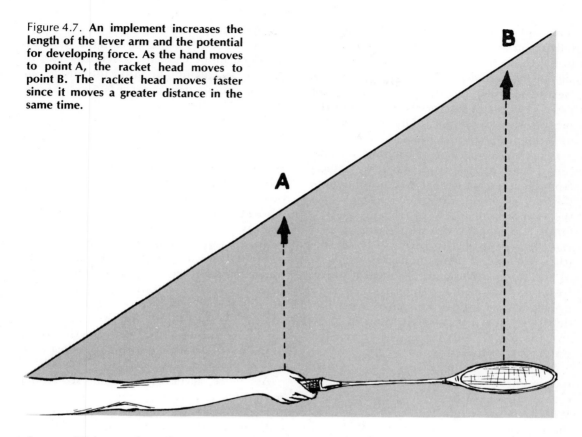

Figure 4.7. **An implement increases the length of the lever arm and the potential for developing force. As the hand moves to point A, the racket head moves to point B. The racket head moves faster since it moves a greater distance in the same time.**

the net. This rotation allows for the execution of a longer backswing and a greater distance in which to accelerate the tennis racket.

To achieve the greatest rotation that is efficient, the performer should utilize the principle of opposition. The tennis player steps forward with the foot opposite of the shoulder which is rotated away from the net. A right-handed player places his left foot forward as he rotates his right shoulder and the racket away from the net. Using opposition is important in that it enables the player to rotate his body to a greater extent while preventing strain on any joint. If a right-handed player stepped forward with the right foot while rotating the right shoulder

away from the net, strain would be placed upon the right hip and this hip would limit the rotation that was possible. As discussed under stability, the principle of opposition also assists the player in maintaining a stable position.

Rotation is also important in that it calls more muscles into use, increases the number of levers used, and thus increases the mass producing the force. Greater mass produces greater force. Therefore, rotation of the trunk is important to force production because it increases both the mass supplying the force and the speed with which a body part moves.

The effect of rotation upon force production is apparent when comparing the throws of two performers, one who uses trunk rotation, and one who doesn't. If one relies totally upon arm action in throwing and fails to rotate his body to produce force, the result is an inefficient throw from the elbow lacking in force and distance. The greater force and greater distance is achieved by the performer using trunk rotation as a means of force production.

In activities which propel an object, transfer of body weight from the foot farthest from the intended direction of movement to the foot closest to the direction allows for the lever arm to move through a greater distance. A performer throwing a ball with the right arm shifts his weight to the back foot (the right foot) during the backswing phase of the throw. As the throwing arm moves forward toward the point of release, he transfers his weight onto the forward foot (left foot). For such a weight transfer to occur, the player must have his feet in a forward-back stride position.

In addition to increasing the range of movement, a transfer of body weight increases the mass used to produce force. With a shift of weight onto the forward foot more muscles are called into use. Skills such as the underhand serve in volleyball, the overhead clear in badminton, and the forehand drive in tennis utilize this weight transfer to increase both range of movement and mass.

Speed is increased by increasing the speed of contraction of muscles. A faster contraction of muscles causes a faster movement at the distal end of a lever. In throwing and striking activities, the force developed in the body is transferred to the hand, leg, or an implement to in turn be imparted to the object that is struck or thrown. The object moves at the speed the body part or implement is moving when force is applied. A faster contraction of muscles increases the speed of the body part or implement, and thus, increases the speed of the object. In executing a serve in volleyball, quick extension of the serving arm increases the speed imparted to the ball. In kicking, the faster the muscles of the leg operate, the easier it becomes to impart speed to the ball.

Speed is increased by the sequential movement of the levers of the body. The body functions as a system of levers to produce movement. Seldom, if ever, is only one lever active in a sports movement. Maximum speed can be produced if the levers of the body operate in sequence, each lever being utilized before it reaches its peak in speed. The lever at an extremity is the last to operate, receiving the combined speed of all the other levers and imparting this speed to the movement to be performed. Release of the ball in throwing is the end product of the work of many levers in sequence, beginning with the levers of the leg and continuing until reaching the levers of the wrist and the imparting of force to the ball.

As more levers are used, sequential movement is increased and the speed imparted to an object is correspondingly increased. In addition, the use of a greater number of levers means that a greater mass is being employed to produce the force. Thus, sequential movement can increase the force produced because of an increase in both speed and mass.

In tasks demanding greater strength than speed, such as in pushing a heavy object, the levers utilized in the task function simultaneously rather than in sequence to produce the greatest strength possible.

Force is increased by the utilization of a follow-through. A follow-through is the motion of a body segment that occurs after the release of an object. Use of a follow-through prevents the lever arm from decreasing its speed prior to release of the object. For example, in executing a drive in tennis, if the player stops the movement of his racket (lever arm) as he contacts the ball, the speed of the racket has already begun to decrease before it contacts the ball. For greatest speed of the racket, the player should hit through the ball, utilizing a follow-through to assure the greatest possible speed of the lever arm at moment of impact. A follow-through also assures a smooth motion and the prevention of strain on any joint. The lever arm needs the time provided by a follow-through to decelerate its speed gradually. Thus, a follow-through is important to force production and safety. It does not influence the direction of the propelled object, since it occurs after the release of the object.

A preliminary movement that stretches a muscle prior to its use increases the force that may be produced by that muscle. A muscle that is stretched slightly is able to exert greater force than a muscle that is shortened. A pitcher uses a wind-up and a tennis player uses a backswing to initially stretch the muscles involved in the respective movements.

An increase in the distance through which force is applied increases the effectiveness of the force. In throwing a ball, the ball remains in contact with the hand during the backswing. As the length of the backswing is increased, the distance through which force is applied is increased. Therefore, the time of application of the force is increased and the force is more effective. However, as the backswing is lengthened, the opportunity for errors in accuracy is also increased.

The distance that force is applied can also be increased by using a running approach or a hop. This movement prior to the throw places the object to be thrown in motion before the throw and assists in producing greater speed in the object.

INCREASING MASS TO INCREASE FORCE

An increase in the mass used to produce force will increase the force produced. As previously described, mass may be increased through rotation of the trunk, transfer of weight, and sequential movement. Each of these movements calls more muscle groups into action, thus increasing the mass used to produce force.

Mass is also increased by using the strongest muscles available for a task and using as many muscle groups as are efficient in the performance of the task. The muscle groups used must work together in the same direction and in proper sequence for an advantage in mass to be gained. In executing an overhand volley in volleyball, the player assumes a crouched position prior to contacting the ball in order to enable him to utilize the muscles of the legs as well as the arms in the production of force. The use of the stronger and larger muscles of the legs in addition to the muscles of the arms increases the number of muscle groups in operation and increases the potential for sequential movement. The mass used to produce force has been increased, thus increasing the resulting force.

It must be remembered that an increase in the number of muscle groups used assists in force production only when the muscles contribute to the action to be performed. The utilization of muscle groups that do not contribute to the movement does not increase the force produced. The action of these muscles produces wasted energy and inefficient movement.

External Force

Gravity, air resistance, water resistance, and friction are external forces which affect motion. They can either assist or resist motion and should be utilized when they aid in performance and reduced when they retard performance. Each of these forces has been previously discussed under "Motion and Factors Affecting Motion," (p. 41).

Force Achieved in Striking Activities

In striking activities, the momentum (force) imparted to a moving ball struck by a moving implement is slightly less than the sum of the momenta of the ball and the implement. Slight momentum is lost due to force absorption by the striking implement and friction. The ball will move in the direction of the greater momentum. The momentum of the implement must be greater than that of the object struck in order to change the object's direction. The momentum imparted by a softball bat to a pitched ball is an example of this principle. As the ball is contacted, its direction is changed because of the greater momentum of the bat. The momentum imparted to the ball is slightly less than the sum of the momenta of the bat and the ball.

If maximum momentum is to be produced by an implement, a firm grip must be utilized to minimize the absorption of force by the implement. A loose grip such as used in a bunt allows force to be absorbed and results in less rebound of the object. In tennis if the racket is gripped firmly enough at impact to return maximum momentum to the ball, less striking force is needed to return the ball. The momentum imparted to the ball as it is struck by the racket is slightly less than the sum of the momenta of the ball and the racket. Thus, if the ball is approaching with great speed, less momentum is required of the racket. If the ball is approaching with less speed, greater momentum is required of the racket to achieve the same distance.

Application of Force

Force should be applied in the direction of the desired movement. Discounting the effects of gravity, air resistance, water resistance, and friction, the nearer the force is applied through the center of an object, the more likely the object will travel in a straight line in the desired direction. Force applied away from an object's center of gravity will cause rotary motion and alter the pathway of the object. A volleyball that is contacted through its center of gravity will be free to achieve the direction desired and to travel in a linear pathway. A volleyball contacted away from its center of gravity will spin and travel in a curved pathway. However, gravity, air resistance, water resistance and friction will alter the pathway of an object regardless of the point at which force was applied. In soccer, a ball may be kicked through the center of gravity and begin moving in a linear pathway. Due to the friction of the ground against the ball as it rolls, both linear and rotary motion results.

An object receiving force will continue moving in the direction it was moving at its moment of release until acted upon by gravity, air resistance, or friction. The movement of the hand or implement in throwing and striking describes an arc. The object struck or thrown moves in a line that is tangent to the point of release in this arc (fig. 4.8). When throwing an object, a release that occurs too early in the arc causes the ball to go high. A release that is too late causes the ball to go low. A right-handed batter who hits the ball too early in his swing causes the ball to go to the right. If it is hit too late in the swing, it will go to the left. The direction in which the ball moves is a line that is tangent to the point of contact in the batter's swing.

As the arc of the implement or the hand is flattened, greater accuracy is achieved because there is less deviation in the line tangent to the arc at the various points of release (fig. 4.9). A flatter arc also allows greater speed to be achieved. According to Broer, the arc of motion may be flattened by rotating the body, transferring weight to a

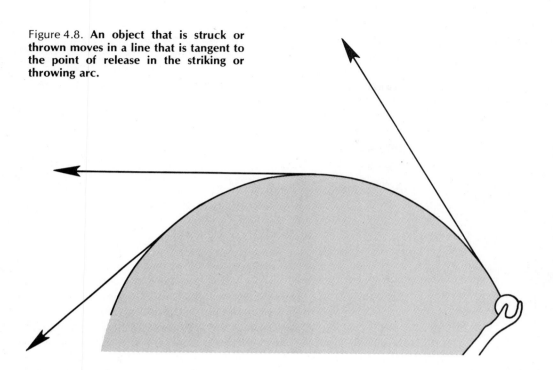

Figure 4.8. **An object that is struck or thrown moves in a line that is tangent to the point of release in the striking or throwing arc.**

forward bent leg, and utilizing a follow-through.[5]

Absorption of Force

As the body receives a force, the momentum of the force at impact determines the degree of body adjustments which must be made to assure a gradual reduction of the impact. The greater the momentum, the greater the impact will be and the greater the necessity to reduce momentum gradually. A gradual reduction prevents injury or rebound and prepares the body for any suceeding motion. The impact of the force can be reduced by increasing the surface area and the distance or time over which it is received. The larger the surface used to receive the force, the less the force that is received by any one area of that surface. In catching a ball, the impact of the ball should not be received on the tips of the fingers because injury to the fingers may result. The

surface area receiving the ball can be increased by using the palm of the hand, using a glove, or using two hands rather than just one.

Distance and time can be increased by giving as the ball contacts the receiving surface and pulling the ball in towards the body. If a greater force is being received, it may be desirable to also shift the body weight backward away from the line of flight of the ball as it is caught. This allows a greater distance through which momentum of the ball is reduced.

Giving with the ball is important if a rebound from the receiving surface is to be prevented. A player who tries to catch a ball with stiff, flat hands is presenting a rigid surface and is inviting a rebound. Newton's third law (action-reaction) provides an explanation for the rebound. The surface receiving the ball, in this case the surface of

5. Broer, *Efficiency of Human Movement,* p. 213.

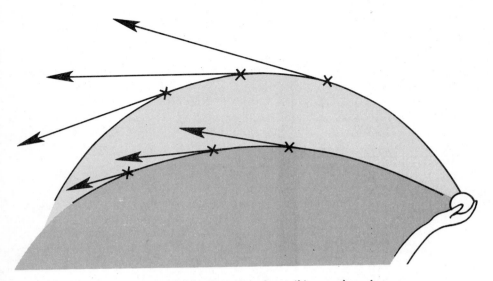

Figure 4.9. **Accuracy is increased by flattening the striking or throwing arc.**

the rigid hands, will allow for the return of some of the force to the ball.[6] When a ball is bounced on the ground, it rebounds back into the air because the rigidity of the ground allows for force to be returned to the ball (action-reaction). However, when a ball is bounced on sand, it does not rebound, as the sand gives and dissipates the force of the ball. Likewise, in catching a ball, the hands must give to dissipate the force of the ball and to prevent a rebound.

The body should receive force in a position that insures maximum stability. The center of gravity of the body should be kept over the base of support. The base of support should be enlarged in the direction of the force to allow body weight to shift backwards away from the flight of the ball while still maintaining the center of gravity over the base. The backwards shift of weight increases the distance and time over which the force is received. The force should be received close to the body's center of gravity so that it does not displace the center of gravity beyond the base of support. If a forward-

back stride position is utilized, the player must be in line with the force and receive it in front of his body rather than to the right or left of his body; otherwise, his center of gravity will be moved beyond his base.

SPIN

In the discussion of force it was mentioned that an object's flight is determined by the point at which force is applied in relation to the object's center of gravity and the amount of resistance that is active upon the object. The effect of an off-center application of force and the resulting air resistance upon the flight of an object is clearly demonstrated in the concept of spin.

Spin is rotary movement of an object about an axis. For ease of understanding, the discussion which follows will be focused upon spin as it relates to the movement of a ball. Top spin and backspin cause a ball to

6. J. Tillman Hall et al., *Fundamentals of Physical Education* (Pacific Palisades, Calif.: Goodyear Publishing Co., 1969), p. 39.

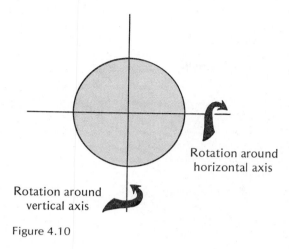

Figure 4.10

Rotation around horizontal axis

Rotation around vertical axis

rotate about its horizontal axis. Left spin and right spin cause a ball to rotate about its vertical axis (fig. 4.10).

To facilitate an understanding of the concept of spin, it is recommended that the reader use a ball and perform the actions as they are described in the following paragraphs.

Top spin causes the top of the ball as it faces the direction of flight to move forward and down, resulting in the bottom of the ball moving backward and up. To create top spin, the ball should be contacted above its center of gravity. The hand or implement imparting force moves upward across the

Figure 4.11. **Top spin**

Back of Ball

back of the ball (the side away from the direction of flight).

Backspin causes the bottom of the ball as it faces the direction of flight to move forward and up. The top of the ball moves backward and down. Backspin is created as the ball is contacted below its center of gravity or as the hand or implement imparting the force moves downward across the back of the ball.

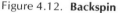

Figure 4.12. **Backspin**

Back of Ball

Right spin (a clockwise spin) causes the front of the ball as it faces the direction of flight to move to the right. The back of the ball should be contacted to the left of its center of gravity to initiate a right spin. Right spin can be produced when a hand placed on the right side of the ball is pulled back away from the direction of the flight, or when a hand placed on the left side of the ball is pushed forward towards the direction of the flight.

Left spin (a counterclockwise spin) causes the front of the ball to move to the left. The back of the ball moves to the right. Left spin is produced by contacting a ball to the right of its center of gravity. It is also produced when the hand is placed on the left side of the ball and is pulled back quickly, or when the hand is placed on the right side of the ball and pushed forward quickly.

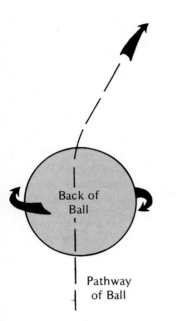

Figure 4.13. **Right spin**

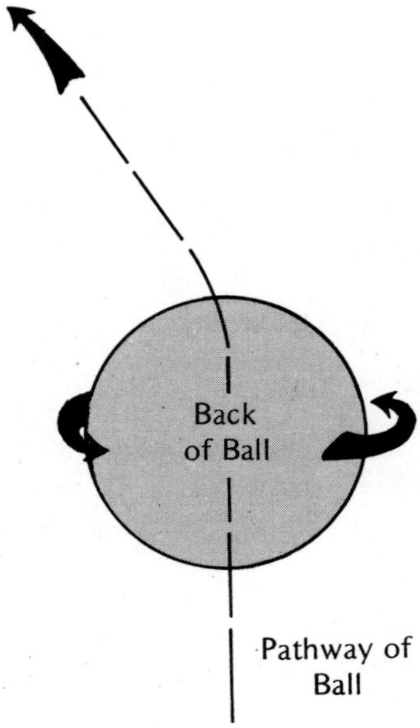

Figure 4.14. **Left spin**

Spin is the result of uneven air pressure. The ball moves in the pathway of least resistance or in the direction of the lesser air pressure (fig. 4.15). For example, as the back of a ball is contacted above its center of gravity, the top of the ball is moving forward into a wall of air pressure. The bottom of the ball moves backward as less air resistance is present behind the ball. The result is top spin. Backspin is the reverse of top spin, with the greatest resistance meeting the bottom of the ball; the top of the ball moves backward in the direction of least resistance.

As a ball is contacted to the left of its center of gravity, the left front side of the ball moves into a wall of air pressure. Less air pressure exists on the right side of the ball. The ball moves in the pathway of least resistance towards the right, producing a curved trajectory to the right (a right spin). Left spin is the opposite of right spin, with the ball moving to the left, the direction of least resistance. For both right spin and left spin the ball curves in the direction of the spin.

Spin affects the length of time that the ball remains in the air as well as the flight of the ball. In top spin, the greatest resistance is on the top of the ball. The least resistance is on the bottom of the ball, causing the ball to drop faster or not remain in the air as long as would a ball without spin. Backspin results in greater resistance on the bottom of the ball and less resistance on the top of the ball, causing the ball to remain in the air longer than usual.

Spin can be beneficial or detrimental in sports activities. Top spin is utilized on a drive in tennis. Since the ball does not remain in the air as long, it assists the player in keeping the ball in bounds. When projecting an object for distance, backspin may be applied to keep the object in the air longer and to achieve greater distance.

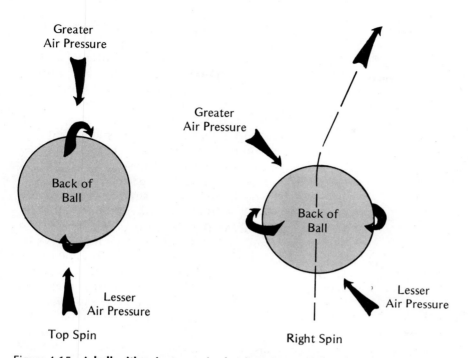

Greater
Air Pressure

Back of
Ball

Lesser
Air Pressure

Top Spin

Greater
Air Pressure

Back of
Ball

Lesser
Air Pressure

Right Spin

Figure 4.15. **A ball with spin moves in the direction of lesser air pressure.**

Jensen and Schultz state that:

An object propelled without spin tends to waver because of air resistance against the object's irregular surface. . . . A small amount of spin on an object produces a stabilizing effect which tends to hold it on its line of flight.[7]

In applying this to a volleyball serve they state:

A volleyball served with slight spin follows a true course of flight determined by the propelling force, but if the ball is contacted decidedly off center, the resulting increase in spin will produce a curve. If the ball is hit directly through its center of gravity, the ball receives no rotary motion, and it tends to waver.[8]

This explanation applies to the effect achieved in a floater serve in volleyball.

Spin makes an object more difficult to control. A volleyball player has difficulty executing an overhand volley on a ball that is spinning. The result is often an illegal hit. The player usually has to utilize a forearm pass rather than an overhand volley when great spin is present on the ball. A discussion of the effects of spin on the angle of rebound is included under the discussion of rebound.

REBOUND

Rebound is the return of an object from a surface that provides a resistance greater than the momentum of the object. Generally, the angle of incidence (the angle at which an object strikes a surface) is equal to

7. From *Applied Kinesiology*, 2nd ed. by Clayne R. Jensen and Gordon W. Schultz, p. 249, copyright 1977, New York: McGraw-Hill Book Company. Used with permission of McGraw-Hill Book Company.
8. Jensen and Schultz, *Applied Kinesiology*, 2nd ed. p. 249.

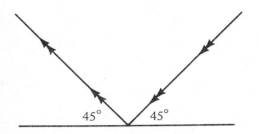

Figure 4.16. **The angle of incidence equals the angle of reflection.**

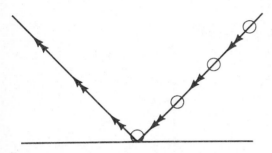

Figure 4.17. **The portion of a ball that contacts a hard surface is flattened or compressed.**

the angle of reflection (angle of rebound). A ball will rebound from a surface at an angle equal to that at which it contacted the surface, unless the rebound is altered by the elasticity of the ball, the firmness of the surface, or spin.

Elasticity of an object refers to its ability to return to its original shape after being compressed. A highly elastic ball will return quickly; a less elastic ball will take longer to resume its initial shape. As a ball contacts a hard surface such as a wooden floor, the portion of the ball that contacts the floor will be compressed or flattened (fig. 4.17). If the ball is highly elastic, it will return to its original shape quickly and its rebound will not be affected. However, a ball of lesser elasticity does not resume its shape quickly, absorbs some of the reaction force from the floor, and as a result, rebounds lower. A new ten-

nis ball has greater elasticity than a dead tennis ball and therefore rebounds or bounces higher. A properly inflated basketball will bounce higher than an under-inflated basketball because its elasticity is greater. A medicine ball has only a very slight rebound because its elasticity is very low and most of the force is absorbed. On the other hand, a rubber playground ball properly inflated will have a high rebound because its elasticity is great.

The nature of the surface receiving the impact of the ball also influences the rebound. As the firmness of the surface increases, the rebound becomes higher. A surface that is not firm will absorb some of the force of the ball and not return as much force to the ball. The rebound is therefore lower. A ball dropped on dry sand will not rebound because the force of the ball is absorbed by the sand and not returned to the ball. A ball dropped on wet, packed sand (creating a firmer surface) will rebound to the extent that the sand is firm enough to return some of the force to the ball. The wet sand does not give as much on impact as the drier sand. A tennis racket with loose strings decreases the speed of the rebound of the ball. The strings give, causing less force to be returned to the ball.

Spin also affects the rebound of a ball. When striking a horizontal surface such as the floor, a ball with top spin will have a lower angle of rebound than a ball with no spin. It will bounce longer, and will achieve greater roll. A ball with backspin will have a higher angle of rebound, a shorter bounce, and less roll (fig. 4.18).

Right and left spin change in relation to their angle of incidence with the horizontal surface. The smaller the angle of incidence, the greater is the effect of the spin in the direction of the spin. As the angle of incidence becomes larger and approaches

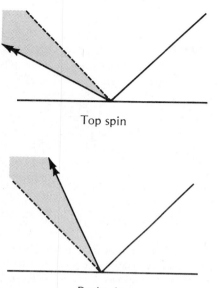

Top spin

Backspin

Figure 4.18. **Spin affects the rebound of a ball from a horizontal surface. In top spin, the angle of reflection is less than the angle of incidence. In backspin the angle of reflection is greater than the angle of incidence.**

ninety degrees, spin has less of an effect. A ninety-degree angle of incidence will eliminate the effect of spin.

Spin also affects a ball rebounding from a vertical surface (such as a wall, a backboard, or a racket face held perpendicular to the ground). Top spin causes the rebound to be higher, while backspin causes it to be lower. Right and left spin hitting a vertical surface have an effect opposite to that which occurs when hitting a horizontal surface. A ball that has right spin rebounds to the left and one with left spin rebounds to the right when striking a vertical surface. An understanding of spin is important to the performer so he may adjust his actions according to the spin and utilize it to his advantage.

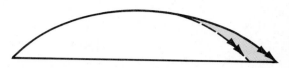

Figure 4.19. **Due to air resistance the path of a projectile deviates from a parabola.**

PROJECTILES

A *projectile* is an object that is propelled into space. The propelling force can be the result of throwing, striking, kicking, or moving another object which in turn imparts force to the object propelled. An archer draws a bow. The bow in turn imparts force to the arrow, a projectile. The body itself is a projectile when executing a broad jump or a dive.

The projecting force, gravity, and air resistance are the three forces active upon a projectile. A projectile begins moving in a linear pathway but due to the pull of gravity, its motion becomes curvilinear. Discounting air resistance, the path of a projectile would be a parabola. However, due to air resistance, the projectile does not move in a true parabola. As air resistance increases, the deviation from the path of a true parabola is greater (fig. 4.19).

Discounting air resistance, the angle at which an object returns to the ground is equal to the angle from which it is projected, provided the object is projected from ground level. However, in most sports activities, an object is projected by a performer standing above ground level. If a line were extended from the point of projection, the angle the returning projectile makes with this line would be equal to the angle of projection (fig. 4.20). The angle with the ground becomes slightly larger due to gravity.

The distance achieved by a projectile is dependent upon its initial speed and its

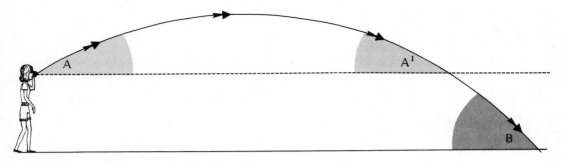

Figure 4.20. An object projected by a performer standing above ground level: angle A equals angle A′; angle B is greater than angle A.

angle of projection. There are two components to the force of a projectile, a horizontal component and a vertical component. The horizontal component allows the projectile to gain distance; the vertical component opposes gravity. With a small angle of projection, the horizontal force is greater than the vertical force. Since the vertical force is not great, gravity acts sooner on the projectile and it does not stay in the air long. Thus, the distance it travels is decreased. With a large angle of projection the vertical component of force is greater than the horizontal component. Gravity does not affect the flight of the projectile until it has overcome the vertical force. Thus, the projectile will remain in the air longer. However, since the horizontal component is not as great, neither is the forward movement or distance achieved as great. With a forty-five degree angle of projection, the horizontal component of force equals the vertical component of force, enabling the projectile to travel the greatest distance.

A performer should utilize the angle of projection that is best suited to the desired results. If he wants greater speed than distance, the angle of projection should be lowered appreciably from forty-five degrees. In executing a throw that demands speed rather than distance, the angle of projection

should be as low as possible, provided it still allows for the horizontal distance necessary to reach its target. If distance is desired in the throw, the angle of projection should be close to forty-five degrees. As air resistance increases, the angle of projection should be made smaller to allow for an increase in the horizontal component of force. When throwing into a head wind, the angle of projection should be less than forty-five degrees. The effect of air resistance upon an object has been previously discussed under "Motion and Factors Affecting Motion," (p. 41).

SUMMARY OF PRINCIPLES

Motion

1. Gravity, friction, air resistance, and water resistance are external forces which either assist or retard movement (pp. 41–43).
2. Momentum is the product of an object's mass times its velocity (p. 43).
3. Newton's Laws of Motion provide a foundation for the principles of motion.
   a. Law of Inertia: A body at rest will remain at rest and a body in motion will remain in motion at the

same velocity unless acted on by an external force (p. 44).

  b. Law of Acceleration: The acceleration of an object that is acted upon by a force is directly proportional to the force and inversely proportional to the mass of the object (p. 44).

  c. Law of Action-Reaction: For every action there is an equal and opposite reaction (p. 45).

4. Linear and rotary motion are the two basic types of motion (p. 45).

Stability

1. The center of gravity should be kept within the base of support to increase stability.

   a. The lower the center of gravity, the greater is the stability (p. 46).

   b. The closer the center of gravity is to the center of the base, the greater is the stability (p. 47).

2. A base of support enlarged in the direction of the force or movement increases stability (p. 47).

   a. Opposition of body parts is important in keeping the center of gravity over the base of support (p. 48).

3. A force should be received close to the center of gravity if greatest stability is to be maintained (p. 48).

4. Stability is dependent upon friction existing between the base of support and the supporting surface (p. 48).

Force

1. The force of an object is dependent upon its mass and the speed at which it is moving (p. 50).

2. Force may be increased by:

   a. stabilizing the body segments involved in a motion (p. 51);

   b. increasing the range of movement of the body segments imparting force (p. 52);

   c. increasing the speed of muscular contraction (p. 54);

   d. utilizing sequential movement of the muscles of the body (p. 54);

   e. utilizing a follow-through (p. 54);

   f. stretching a muscle prior to its use (p. 55);

   g. increasing the distance through which force is applied (p. 55);

   h. using the strongest muscles available for a task (p. 55);

   i. using as many muscles as will contribute to a task (p. 55).

3. Force should be applied in line with an object's center of gravity if linear movement is desired. It should be applied away from the center of gravity if rotary movement is desired (p. 56).

4. In throwing and striking activities, the direction in which an object moves is a line that is tangent to the point of release in the throwing or striking arc (p. 56).

5. Force can be reduced efficiently by increasing the surface area and the distance or time over which it is received (p. 57).

Spin and rebound

1. Spin is the result of force being applied away from an object's center of gravity. The object spins in the direction of least resistance (pp. 58–60).

2. A ball will rebound at an angle equal to that at which it strikes a surface unless the rebound is altered by the elasticity of the ball, the firmness of the surface, or spin (p. 62).

Direction and Trajectory
1. Point of application of force (linear or rotary movement)
2. Line tangent to striking arc
3. External forces present

Force
1. Leverage
2. Range of movement
3. Sequential movement
4. Speed of muscular contraction
5. Follow-through
6. Mass

Stability
1. Size of base of support
2. Direction base enlarged
3. Position of center of gravity
4. Friction with supporting surface

Figure 4.21

Projectiles

1. In the absence of air resistance, an object propelled at a forty-five-degree angle will achieve the greatest distance (p. 64).

REFERENCES

Broer, Marion R. *Efficiency of Human Movement.* 3d ed. Philadelphia: W. B. Saunders Co., 1973.

Dyson, Geoffrey. *The Mechanics of Athletics.* 7th ed. London: University of London Press, 1978.

Hall, J. Tillman; Melnick, Merril J.; Morash, Talmage W.; Lersten, Kenneth C.; Perry, Richard H.; Pestolesi, Robert A.; and Seidler, Burton. *Fundamentals of Physical Education.* Pacific Palisades, CA.: Goodyear Publishing Co., 1969.

Jensen, Clayne R., and Schultz, Gordon W. *Applied Kinesiology.* 2nd ed. New York: McGraw-Hill Book Co., 1977.

Read, Albert J. *Physics: A Descriptive Analysis.* Reading, MA.: Addison-Wesley Publishing Co., 1970.

Schurr, Evelyn L. *Movement Experiences for Children: A Humanistic Approach to Elementary School Physical Education.* 2nd ed. Englewood Cliffs, N.J.: Prentice Hall, Inc., 1975.

Wells, Katharine F. *Kinesiology.* 6th ed. Philadelphia: W. B. Saunders Co., 1976.

Williams, Marian, and Lissner, Herbert R. *Biomechanics of Human Motion.* Philadelphia: W. B. Saunders Co., 1962.

PART II. □ CONCEPT COMMONALITIES

The whole art of teaching is only the art of awakening the natural curiosity of young minds for the purpose of satisfying it.

Anatole France

5.   Common Concepts

5

Common Concepts

INTRODUCTION

In this chapter an attempt is made to conceptualize, via models, much of what has been discussed in chapters one to four, to chart common fundamental movement skills and the mechanical principles underlying them, and to list and discuss common concepts of movement, strategy and safety.

Figure 5.1, depicting the beginnings and evolution of efficient movement, focuses pictorially on the elements of movement (space, force, time and flow) as the basis for the fundamental locomotor, nonlocomotor and manipulative skills which eventuate into the specialized skills for efficient participation in motor activities—games, sports, dance or the motor patterns necessary in everyday living.

"Commonalities of Fundamental Movement Skills," Table 5.1, is a presentation of the various locomotor and manipulative movements common to skills in the several activities included in this book. If a reperusal of the various factors that affect such movement seems desirable, the reader should refer to chapters two and four.

Figure 5.1, illustrating the beginnings and evolution of efficient movement, is an adaptation of Hanson's model, and it elaborates upon perceptual awareness and its contiguous components which enable the learner more readily to comprehend the elements of movement and their relationship to the psychomotor skills necessary in efficient motor patterns. The learner thus experiences the resultant affective values in meaningful movement, which produces a truly self-actualizing individual able to adapt to changing environmental phenomena.

Finally, in order to avoid unnecessary duplication of material in specific chapters dealing with different activities, this chapter treats concepts of movement which are *common to several activities*. These common

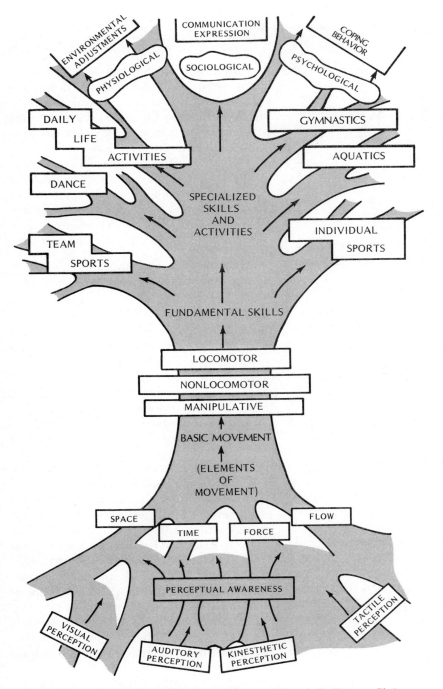

Originated by and reproduced with the permission of Margie R. Hanson, Ph.D.

Figure 5.1. **The beginnings and evolution of efficient movement**

TABLE 5.1
COMMONALITIES OF FUNDAMENTAL MOVEMENT SKILLS AND RELATED MECHANICAL PRINCIPLES

Moving the Body through Space	+	Moving an Object through Space	=	Moving the Body and an Object through Space
(Initiating Movement, Locomotion, Absorbing Momentum)		(Altering the Pathway, Sending, and Receiving)		

Activities	Locomotor Skills	Activities	Manipulative Movements	Activities	Manipulative Movements	Locomotor Skills
Badminton Basketball Field Hockey Gymnastics Soccer Softball Tennis Track and Field Volleyball	Starting (staying ready to move) Running Sliding Jumping Stopping Changing directions (flexible pathways)	Softball Field Hockey Badminton Tennis Golf Volleyball	Striking }	Basketball	Dribbling (hands)	Starting Running Stopping Changing directions Sliding
		Soccer	Kicking } Sending	Soccer	Dribbling (feet)	
Swimming	Landing Propulsion			Field Hockey	Dribbling (stick)	
		Softball Basketball Field Events	Throwing }	Basketball	Juggle (air dribble)	
		Archery	Projecting			
		Softball Basketball	Catching } Receiving			
		Soccer	Blocking and trapping }			

Control of Body	+	Control of Object	=	Control of Body and Object

movement concepts are divided into three main categories: moving the body through space, moving an object through space, and moving the body and an object through space. In addition, common concepts in strategy and in safety are discussed in the last part of the chapter.

For purposes of ready reference, the major concepts are identified by letter and the sub-concepts by number. **Subsequently, all references to them in the activities chapters are by the same letter-number designation.** Therefore, if in reading the chapter on basketball, a reference to sub-concept B-2 is made and if a more universal explanation of it than is given at that point is desired, referring to the original treatment of the concept in this chapter should suffice. (It should be noted that the activities chapters often contain concepts and sub-concepts which are particular to that chapter subject, and these concepts and sub-concepts do not carry identifying letter-number designations.)

MOVING THE BODY THROUGH SPACE

Moving the body through space occurs to some degree in all activities. This movement may be merely for the purpose of moving from place to place, as in golf, or it may be so intricately involved in the purpose of the activity that efficiency of the movement leads to success or failure.

When moving the body through space is the *major* goal, the movements are most often unique to that activity due to the medium in which the activity is performed or to the equipment used in the activity. Swimming, gymnastics, track and field fall into this category.

In yet another category the player moves in relation not only to an opponent, but also to a teammate(s) and/or an object being manipulated. Some combination of the movement relationships of this category is found in all dual and team activities. Thus, the locomotor skills of starting and stopping, running and sliding, jumping and landing are of prime importance.

In the following section, treatment is devoted to those locomotor skills which are common to the activities covered in this book (badminton, basketball, field hockey, soccer, softball, tennis and volleyball). Gymnastics, swimming, track and field are mentioned briefly; however, the more unique movements of these activities are discussed in the individual activities chapters.

CONCEPT A. Moving the body with control involves a conscious manipulation of the center of gravity in relation to the base of support, either to maintain stability or to initiate locomotor movement, as the situation demands.

Sub-concept A-1. Staying ready to move allows a player to get a faster start in order to outmaneuver the opponent, to gain possession of the ball, or to get into a desirable position to project an object.

In many activities a player quite often arrives too late to achieve his objective. Sometimes this is due to the fact that he is a slow starter. A position with weight centered directly over the base of support and knees locked results in a slow start. In order to initiate movement, the center of gravity must be moved beyond the base of support. Therefore, a position that keeps the center of gravity near the edge of the base of support in an unstable position, and the legs in a position to push diagonally downward against the ground, allows the player a faster start. The player should stand with feet comfortably apart in a forward-back stride position, facing the direction of the immediate objective. The weight or line of gravity should fall over the balls of the feet with hips, knees and ankles flexed and ready to push off in a forward direction. This position also allows the player to pivot quickly and push off in another direction, if necessary. This *ready position* is common to many sports (pp. 48–49).

Sub-concept A-2. Enlarging the base of support in the direction of the force allows a player to start, stop, and change directions quickly.

As previously stated, a good ready position enlarges the base of support in the direction of intended movement (i.e., in the direction force is to be applied). An efficient stop or change in direction or pathway employs the same principle. In order to absorb the momentum of a forward-moving body, one must widen the base in the direction of the force (with a forward-back stride) and lower the center of gravity by flexing the forward knee. The flexed forward leg pushes the center of gravity back over the now stationary base of support, the feet. A player actually stops, pivots, and starts again when making a sharp change in pathway. However, the motion is fluid; it must not be three separate movements. Force is applied and absorbed through the length of the foot in order to avoid lateral strain on the ankle and knee joints. Toes are positioned in line with the direction of the force.

Sub-concept A-3. Running in a forward direction is the quickest way to cover a distance of some magnitude.

Due to anatomical structure, the body moves through space more quickly when moving forward than when moving backward or sideward. Thus, while in a home position somewhat back of the exact center of the space to be covered, a ready position is assumed facing the immediate objective (the home position in badminton is a good example). However, the larger the space of the playing area, the more likely the player will need to use the skill of running. Moving in this space of the field or the court in relation to the object being propelled is a matter of short sprints. The run (sprint) should be on the balls of the feet with the body focused forward. The arms and legs move in opposition in a forward and backward motion with a minimum of lateral motion. Any deviation from this action is discussed as it applies in specific sports chapters. For example, such action is altered slightly if an implement is being carried in the hand(s), such as in field hockey. In addition, a more detailed analysis of the run is included in the chapter on track and field.

Sub-concept A-4. Sliding sideways or in a diagonally forward or backward direction is often a more efficient manner of moving the body through space if the distance to be covered is minimal and if the body needs to remain facing the immediate objective.

Sliding is most appropriate as a defensive technique as one attempts to cover the spaces and angles through which the offense might maneuver or send the ball.[1] Carrying the weight on the balls of the feet and transferring the weight with short,

quick steps allows the player to maneuver and change directions quickly. When sliding, the side of the body leads the movement, thus allowing the player to remain facing in the direction of the immediate action.

Sub-concept A-5. Recovering quickly after the execution of a skill involves reassuming the ready position and relocating oneself in space in the home position, or some other advantageous position, in order to stay alert and ready to react again.

Quite often a beginner becomes a spectator as he watches the results of his efforts from an immediate previous action. This usually leaves him standing flat-footed and in poor position to react. Examples of this are numerous and common to many sports (e.g., failure to follow a shot at the goal in basketball, hockey, or soccer; failure to get ready for the return of the serve in tennis, badminton and volleyball; and failure to anticipate play by relocating oneself after passing or blocking and spiking in volleyball, basketball, hockey and soccer). Beginners should be reminded frequently to recover quickly and to adjust their movements as play evolves. Then, too, a choice of action may leave the player in a poor position to recover quickly to resume play. For example, a lunge or reach as a defensive technique places the lunging player in a poor position to recover, since the body is extended in one direction with a wide base of support and the center of gravity moving rapidly in the direction of the lunge. The lunging action may be necessary in order to save the play if one is caught in a poor position in which to react to the play (e.g., the dig in volleyball). On the other hand, this

1. Sliding as it is used here is the step-close-step action of the feet with the side of the body leading.

technique may be a gamble if it is used in an attempt to steal the ball or spoil the play. Nevertheless, all players should develop the ability to recover quickly and reassume an active ready position in which to continue play.

Sub-concept A-6. Propelling the body through space requires a firm reacting surface and sufficient friction between the reacting surface and the base of support.

The firmer the reacting surface and the greater the friction, the more efficient the propelling movement. One needs only to have played on a wet, muddy field or to have tried to start, stop or change directions quickly with smooth-soled tennis shoes or in stocking feet on a wooden floor to realize the ramifications of this concept. Not only does the movement cause frustration, but the chances for injury are compounded. Thus, an outdoor playing field should be crowned to provide sufficient drainage and well sodded or seeded to eliminate bare spots which become muddy with a minimum of precipitation. Indoors, the playing surface should be free of grit and dust and finished with a durable nonskid surface. Whether indoors or outdoors, appropriate footwear lends itself to greater friction and thus greater reaction (p. 48).

CONCEPT B. Creating and absorbing force to control the movement of the body through space may involve all of the body or only parts of the body, in unison or in sequence; however, the relaxation of noncontributing muscle groups is imperative for smooth, efficient movement.

Sub-concept B-1. A smooth transfer of momentum from one part of the body to another part, or to the total body, results in sustained movement, while an explosive transfer of momentum increases the speed and/or magnitude of the resulting movement.

Transferring momentum from one part of the body to another may be sustained (smooth) or sudden (explosive). An example of smooth flow is the transfer of weight from the feet to the hands to the feet in the limber (gymnastics). Movement is initiated by the rotation of the arms and upper trunk downward toward the mat. Momentum is transferred to the lower trunk, and the legs contribute to the rotatory movement by one leg whipping while the other leg pushes off from the mat. As the legs pass overhead, gravity aids in the downward rotation. Then, as the feet touch down on the mat, momentum is transferred to the upper trunk to aid the body in righting itself as the hands push off the mat. If one stops the action at some balanced point within the sequence, momentum is lost and it becomes more difficult to complete the movement since inertia must again be overcome (chapter 15, fig. 15.33, p. 478). This same movement pattern, preceded by a run and an explosive takeoff results in a front handspring.

Possibly a more common example of transferring momentum, in this instance to the total body in an explosive manner, is the use of the arms to lift the body when jumping. The greater the range and speed of the contributing body part, whether arms or legs, the greater the momentum produced and transferred. The act of setting the total body in motion prior to takeoff (as in an approach run) produces even greater momentum to be transferred to the total body for the purpose of propulsion. The execution of some sports techniques dictates the amount of momentum it is possible to initiate and transfer. For example, a student executing the jump ball in basketball or the standing broad jump is limited to using mainly the arms to build and transfer momentum, whereas the running spike in volleyball or the running long jump or high jump in track and field allows for the total body to build momentum. Thus, the limitations of the technique and the desired outcome dictate the nature of the transfer of momentum.

Sub-concept B-2. Absorbing the force of a landing or fall over a greater time and distance increases stability and decreases the chance of injury.

Although landing after flight is unique to some sports activities, tripping or falling is possible in any activity in which the body moves through space. In all instances of landing or falling, one should attempt to touch down with the feet first. When dropping vertically, the feet should be positioned about hip-width apart to contribute to stability upon landing. If momentum carries the body other than straight downward, a step in the direction of the force helps dissipate the momentum over a greater time and distance. If the speed or momentum is of great magnitude and the body is well off-balance as it touches down, the hands may also be needed to extend the base and/or a roll-out may be necessary. If the feet or hands cannot touch down first, an attempt should be made to adjust the position of the body to land on the hip or shoulder, or another flat, large, padded area, with a subsequent roll-out. In all instances, the momentum should be reduced by a sequential flexion of joints to increase both the time and distance over which momentum is absorbed (p. 57).

Sub-concept B-3. Relaxing noncontributing muscle groups leads to smooth, efficient movement and thus to the proficiency of the performance.

Besides staying ready, one must also stay loose and relaxed. Although it is very necessary to keep muscles in a state of readiness to move, the relaxation of noncontributing muscle groups is of equal importance. The violation of this principle (the principle of reciprocal innervation or inhibition) quite often results in a fumbled ball, a stumble during a start, or an uncoordinated, jerky movement that destroys timing and wastes energy rather than contributing to the task at hand. A good example of this is the jerky movement of arms, head and upper trunk if one fails to relax when running. Probably the most evident violation of this principle is seen in the uncoordinated thrashing movements of a beginner in the water before he learns to relax and allow the water to support him. Proficiency of performance does not develop until the performer learns to relax the antagonistic muscle groups while contracting only those that contribute to the movement.

MOVING AN OBJECT THROUGH SPACE

Moving an object through space implies projection. The objects moved may be of a variety of sizes, shapes, and weights and include balls, shuttlecocks, arrows, javelins, or the discus. Prior to projection the object may be stationary, as in a golf drive or the place kick in soccer, or it may be moving, as in tennis, badminton, and volleyball. It may be projected by throwing, striking, kicking, or by using an implement such as a bow. Striking involves contact with a body part such as the hands or an implement such as a racket, bat, club, or stick. Kicking is distinguished from striking in that the body part used to project the object is the foot.

The concepts which follow are common to all activities involving moving an object through space. They are categorized either as sending an object through space, or receiving an object moving through space. Concepts basic to receiving an object are included since many of the activities which require projection of an object first require gaining control of the object by slowing or stopping its motion.

Sending an Object Through Space

CONCEPT C. A player must be in a desirable position in relation to the object to be projected.

Many times a poor hit or kick is due to poor positioning on the part of the performer. If he is too close or too far from the object, it becomes increasingly difficult to control its flight. In activities which involve striking with an implement (tennis, badminton, softball, golf, and field hockey) the participant must be a desirable distance from the object prior to contact if the movement is to be effective in terms of force production and direction. In badminton, contact with a shuttlecock which is overhead rather than in front of the body changes the angle of the racket face at contact and therefore changes the flight achieved.

In an activity in which striking with a body part occurs (such as in volleyball or soccer), a desirable spatial relationship with the object is essential for a successful hit. Kicking or striking a ball that is too close to the body decreases the length of the lever and restricts the range of motion possible. Contacting a ball that is too far away makes it difficult to apply force through its center of gravity. Such positioning also necessitates movement of the player's center of gravity to the edge of his base of support, thus reducing his stability.

Achievement of a desirable spatial relationship with the object requires good footwork, kinesthetic awareness of one's position, and practice. (One might wish to refer again to the concepts relating to footwork as mentioned in "Moving the Body with Control," page 72.)

CONCEPT D. Creating force: The production and transfer of force depend upon mass, speed, and the striking surface used.

Sub-concept D-1. Increasing the mass used to produce force increases the force produced.

Mass is dependent upon the number of body parts used in an action and/or the nature of the implement that is used. For an increase in mass, the strongest muscles available for the task as well as the largest number of muscle groups which contribute to the performance should be used. Such an increase in mass can be produced through trunk rotation, a forward transfer of body weight, and sequential movement (chapter 4, p. 55).

In striking activities which involve an implement, mass can be increased by increasing the weight of the implement used (chapter 4, p. 43). Thus, a softball player increases his potential for producing force as he increases the weight of the bat used.

Sub-concept D-2. Increasing the speed of the implement or the body segment imparting force increases the force produced.

In throwing and striking activities the force developed in the body is transferred to a body segment or to an implement which in turn imparts the force to the object that is struck or thrown (chapter 4, p. 54). Increasing the speed of contraction of the muscles utilized in the action increases the speed imparted to the object; thus a snap of the wrist or a quick extension of a body segment is often used. In badminton, wrist action is essential to move the racket rapidly prior to contacting the shuttlecock. In soccer, the knee is extended quickly to increase the speed imparted to the ball through kicking.

Sub-concept D-3. Increasing the range of movement of the body segment or the implement imparting force increases the distance through which speed can be developed, as well as the force imparted to the object.

An increase in the range of movement increases the distance through which speed can be developed and thus allows for greater speed to be produced. The range of movement is increased by utilizing the longest lever possible, i.e., using a backswing, rotating the trunk, and transferring body weight into the action (p. 52).

In order to utilize the longest possible lever when striking with an implement, the player's grip should be as near the end of the implement as possible; thus, choking up on a racket, bat, or club is discouraged. However, the length of the lever should not be increased to the extent that control is sacrificed (p. 52). When striking with an implement, a player uses the longest lever by contacting the object at full reach. Thus a tennis player reaches to contact the serve with an extended rather than a bent arm; the badminton player does the same on the clear or a smash. If maximum force is desired when striking with a body part, it is equally important that the player contact the object at the instant the arm or leg is extended. Thus, in a volleyball spike, the player contacts the ball at the highest level he can reach.

To gain maximum range of movement a backswing is utilized. As the force desired increases, the length of the backswing must increase correspondingly. Again, however, the player must be certain not to sacrifice

control for range of motion. Rotating the striking or throwing arm, or the arm holding the implement, away from the intended direction of flight allows for increased distance in which to produce speed. This rotation is extremely important for force production in a throwing or striking action. Thus one sees a softball player rotate his throwing arm away from the direction of flight when throwing, and a tennis player rotate the striking arm away from the net when executing a forehand drive. To facilitate trunk rotation, the player should assume a forward-back stride position, utilizing the principle of opposition (p. 48).

A forward transfer of body weight onto the foot closest to the intended direction of flight assists force production in throwing and striking activities since it effects an increase in both mass and range of motion. The outfielder throwing to home, the player serving in tennis, the hockey player executing a drive, and the individual clearing in badminton all shift their weight forward as the object is thrown or struck. A soccer player transfers his weight forward over the supporting foot and onto the kicking foot. Again, a forward-back stride position is needed to allow for this transfer of weight.

Sub-concept D-4. Setting the body in motion prior to contact with an object, or to the release of an object, builds greater force which in turn is transferred to the object. However, at the instant of contact or release, the body should be stabilized.

A preliminary movement used to increase force is evident in projecting a softball, shot, or discus; in the running spike in volleyball; and in the place kick in soccer. This preliminary movement aids in force production provided it places the individual in an advantageous position for the release or contact of the object and flows smoothly into the act of projecting. Thus, a preliminary run or sliding cross-step is used in a throw or kick for distance, or when maximum force is desired. However, at the moment of contact or release, the player's position must be stable to provide a firm foundation for the body parts used to impart force (see sub-concept D-6).

Sub-concept D-5. A follow-through allows for greater force to be transferred to an object.

When maximum force is desired, the throwing or striking action should be continued following the release or contact of the object. This action prevents deceleration of the lever arm prior to contact or release (p. 54). A follow-through is utilized in striking or throwing skills in which force or distance is the objective. However, when maximum force is not the primary focus, the follow-through can be shortened or eliminated. In a floater serve in volleyball, a follow-through is *not* used, in order that the floating action may be achieved. In the drop in badminton, the follow-through is limited, since force is not the objective. On occasion it is necessary to limit a follow-through to prevent violating a rule such as touching the net. For this reason, a complete follow-through is not always possible in a volleyball spike or a badminton smash.

Sub-concept D-6. Stabilizing the body segments involved in an action allows for greater force to be imparted to the object.

If a player is to have a firm base on which to create force, he must be in a stable position at the instant of contact or he must utilize other body parts to stabilize the action. For this reason, players are directed to move quickly to establish their position prior to contacting an object. Likewise, many skills are executed with one or both feet on the ground to provide a stable base of support and to allow all a player's efforts to be directed to producing force rather than to maintaining stability. In skills which are executed from a position in the air, such as a jump shot in basketball or a running spike in volleyball, the trunk is used to stabilize the body parts used in the throwing or striking motion (p. 51).

Sub-concept D-7. A firm striking surface allows for greater force to be imparted to the object.

Whether striking a moving or a stationary object a firm striking surface is needed to prevent force absorption and to allow for greater force to be imparted. A firm grip is needed when using an implement such as a racket, club, or stick in order to minimize force absorption. The firmness needed depends on the object struck and whether it is stationary or moving. As the mass and speed of a moving object increase, a firmer grip is needed to effect a firm hitting surface. Due to the difference in the mass of a tennis ball and a badminton shuttlecock, a much firmer grip is needed to hold the tennis racket. In addition, in tennis the wrist is stabilized or firm to prevent force absorption when striking the moving tennis ball.

When striking or kicking with a body part, the body part must be stabilized to provide a firm hitting surface. The ankle joint is firm to stabilize the foot when kicking in soccer. For a forearm pass in volleyball the forearms are stabilized by straightening the elbows and clasping the hands together.

In some activities a stable striking surface is important not only for imparting force but also to prevent an illegal hit. For example, holding or pushing is called in volleyball when the ball is allowed to rest momentarily in the hands.

CONCEPT E. Directing Force: The direction in which an object moves is determined by the point at which force is applied in relation to the object's center of gravity.

Sub-concept E-1. Applying force directly through the center of gravity of an object results in a straight trajectory; an off-center application of force produces a curved trajectory.

Applying force directly through the center of gravity of an object assists the performer in achieving the desired direction. To achieve an upward trajectory, force is applied under and through the center of gravity; a downward direction is achieved by applying force down and through the center of gravity. To move an object to the left, force is applied to the right and through the center of gravity; force applied to the left and through the center of gravity moves the object to the right. If spin is desired, the object should be contacted away from its enter of gravity. The nature of the spin and direction achieved are dependent upon where the force is applied (p. 58).

In some instances, such as a pass to a teammate, a throw for speed or distance, or a drive in hockey, spin is not desired and force should be applied directly through the center of gravity. However, in other instances spin is desirable and force is intentionally applied away from the center of gravity. Thus, a tennis player may apply top spin to a drive to keep the ball from going out of bounds or a basketball player may utilize backspin to cause the ball to rebound from the backboard into the basket.

Sub-concept E-2. Keeping one's eyes on the object (i.e., objective focus or tracking) facilitates the application of force in line with the intended direction of flight

or the absorption of force when slowing or stopping an object. However, if the performer is throwing at a target, he must focus on the target rather than on the projectile.

When kicking or striking a moving or a stationary object, it is important that the performer watch the object to be projected as he contacts it. The golfer should keep his head down and eyes focused on the ball; the batter in softball must keep his eyes on the ball.

Likewise, when slowing or stopping an already moving object, such as when catching in basketball, fielding in softball or trapping in soccer, it is equally important that the performer watch the object. However, if the performer is to throw at a target, he must focus upon the target rather than the object projected. Thus, the infielder throwing to first base focuses upon first base rather than the ball. Likewise, the basketball player focuses upon the basket when shooting.

Sub-concept E-3. Contacting an object with a large, flat surface facilitates applying force directly through the center of gravity in the direction desired.

In some sports the size of the hitting surface is determined by the implement used. Hitting surfaces vary in size from the relatively small portion of the hockey stick or golf club used for contact to the larger area provided by a tennis or badminton racket. When body parts are used to strike, the performer should utilize the largest, flattest, and safest legal area. Since two hands provide a larger surface area than one, the volleyball player should strive to hit the overhand volley with all ten fingers. To avoid an unpredictable flight, the striking surface must also be flat. Thus, hitting with a closed fist is discouraged in volleyball as the knuckles create an uneven surface which could result in an uncontrolled hit.

Sub-concept E-4. External forces such as gravity, air resistance, and friction alter the flight of a projectile.

Due to gravity, an object projected through the air (such as an arrow, ball, or shuttlecock) moves in a curvilinear pathway. When distance is desired, an object should be projected at a forty-five-degree angle (in the absence of air resistance), so that the effect of gravity is not as immediate (p. 64). The same angle of projection is used in a softball throw for distance and clout shooting in archery. When speed is more desirable than distance, the angle should be reduced.

Air resistance also acts upon a projectile in either assisting or retarding motion. Due to the weight and irregular surface area of a badminton shuttlecock, air resistance alters its flight appreciably more than it would a heavier and smoother object such as a tennis ball. Air resistance causes the shuttlecock to travel more slowly and drop almost vertically. Air resistance can also be a negative influence on the flight of an arrow in archery. In the aiming procedure, the archer must compensate for this influence. The flight of a golf ball also is altered by air resistance. On occasion it is desirable to reduce the angle of projection to reduce the effect of air resistance.

Rolling friction alters the motion of an object moving on the ground (such as a hockey, soccer, or golf ball). As the conditions of the playing surface change, the friction present also changes. Long grass or wet playing conditions increase rolling friction and thus increase the resistance to the ball's progress.

CONCEPT F. Sending the ball to a receiver who is moving requires directing the ball to an open space ahead of him.

Passing is a skill used to send the ball through space from one player to another. It is a skill common to team sports which utilize striking (field hockey), throwing (basketball), or kicking (soccer). The skills of sending and receiving are both basic to passing. In addition to utilizing Concepts C, D, and E, as previously described, the sender must be aware that he may be passing to a moving target. If so, he must direct the ball ahead of the receiver so that the receiver's forward momentum can be continued. Beginners often fail to recognize that the receiver is moving and pass to where he is rather than to where he is going, thus retarding his forward progress. To allow for a running approach the set for a spike in volleyball must be directed to a space near the net rather than to the spiker. A pass to a basketball player executing a lay-up must be directed ahead of him so that his forward motion is not stopped when receiving the ball. Likewise, in field hockey and soccer, the ball is passed diagonally ahead so that the forward line may continue its progress down the field.

To receive the object passed, a player must first gain control by either slowing or stopping its motion. Concepts basic to receiving an object are included in the section which follows.

Receiving an Object Moving Through Space

CONCEPT G. To receive an object which is moving through space a performer must slow or stop its motion by absorbing all or part of its force.

The absorption of force is not desirable in all activities. In the racket sports, force should not be absorbed, but instead returned to the object. Likewise, force absorption is not desirable in golf and archery. However, in the team sports of softball, basketball, volleyball, soccer and field hockey, force must be absorbed to allow teammates to maneuver the ball within the space of their territory. Prior to striking or throwing the ball, its force must first be controlled by slowing or stopping it. Absorbing force correctly is essential in catching (softball, basketball), in fielding (softball, hockey), in a forearm pass in volleyball, and in blocking and trapping (soccer).

CONCEPT H. Three techniques help the performer to absorb force efficiently: (1) establishing a stable position; (2) utilizing the largest possible surface area; and (3) increasing the time or distance over which the force is received.

Sub-concept H-1. A stable position should be maintained as the force of an object is absorbed.

A forward-back-stride position is utilized to enlarge the base of support in the direction of the force to be received. The force should be received in line with the performer's center of gravity to prevent displacing the center of gravity and creating an unstable position. Thus a ball being caught, blocked, fielded or trapped should be received in front of the body rather than to the right or left. This often means that the player must move to get in line with the approaching ball. Utilization of a forward-back-stride position not only increases stability but also allows for weight to be transferred to the back foot, which aids in force absorption (Sub-concept H-3).

Sub-concept H-2. A large surface area reduces the force that is received by any one area of that surface.

To distribute the force over the largest area possible, a player must wisely select the receiving surface. The insides of the forearms are used in the volleyball forearm pass because they form a large padded surface. Likewise, the abdomen and thighs are used to block in soccer. A softball player uses a glove to increase the surface area over which the ball is received and to present a padded surface.

Sub-concept H-3. Moving the receiving surface with the ball upon contact (giving with the ball) allows force to be absorbed over a greater time and distance.

Increasing the time and distance over which force is absorbed allows for a gradual reduction of force and prevents injury or rebound. A gradual reduction can be accomplished by giving with a body part, with the entire body, or with an implement. In catching, the arm flexes at the elbow and wrist and moves with the ball at contact to absorb its force. When executing a forearm pass in volleyball, the arms move with the ball to reduce its force and to control the rebound. However, in blocking (as in soccer) the entire body moves backward in a jumping action. To facilitate the backward movement a forward-back-stride position must be used.

Using an implement such as a softball bat (in bunting) or a hockey stick (in fielding) to absorb force requires a loose grip and movement of the implement away from the approaching ball at contact. In hockey the handle of the stick is held ahead of the blade and the blade gives on impact to decrease the opportunity for rebound and to keep the ball on the ground.

MOVING THE BODY AND AN OBJECT THROUGH SPACE

The title of this section implies a combination of locomotor and manipulative movements (see Table 5.1). Dribbling is the term commonly assigned to a specific skill used as the body moves an object through space (notable exceptions are lacrosse, where the ball is cradled, and speed-a-way, in which the ball can be carried in the arms as the player runs down the field, neither of which is included in this book). However, dribbling involves different body parts in different activities (e.g., the feet in soccer, the hands in basketball) or the use of an implement (such as the stick in field hockey).

Commonly, too, the player moving through space should maintain the object being moved fairly close to the ground and/or to the moving body.

The concepts involved in moving the body through space and in moving an object through space, as dealt with in the two previous sections, also apply in this section. In addition, several concepts are unique when considering a combination of moving bodies and moving objects. The remainder of this section is devoted to a treatment of these unique concepts.

CONCEPT I. The purpose of the dribble is to maintain possession of the ball while moving through space; thus the amount and direction of force applied to the ball must be controlled.

In activities such as soccer and field hockey, it is necessary to use only a light force if the ball is to be kept close to the moving body. Keeping the ball close is mandatory not only for control but also for quick redirection of the ball when necessary, as when an opposing player moves in to tackle or when a space opens through which a quick pass should be made.

A basketball dribble necessitates greater force, even though the ball is maintained close to the body, since it is desirable normally to cause the ball to rebound at waist height. In addition, direction (the angle of rebound) must be controlled in order to

allow the body to move at the same speed as the ball.

For a complete review of the role that force plays, the reader is referred to chapter four.

CONCEPT J. The ability to dribble with either/or alternating hands or feet provides maximum flexibility in controlling the ball and its direction.

Ambidexterity is a relatively simple skill to master if taught early enough. However, even if dominance on one side seems to be ingrained, an attempt should be made to teach students how to dribble using alternating hands or feet. It is perhaps easiest to teach this in basketball since the ball is larger and hand skills are relatively easier to refine than foot skills. Nevertheless, it is important to foster this ability in most activities involving dribbling skills because: (1) alternating feet while dribbling in soccer allows for more immediately flexible pathways since the dribbler does not have to wait for the dominant foot to be in proper position; (2) such is also the case in basketball, with the exception that the hands are used rather than the feet. In addition, the necessity for a quick change of direction in order to avoid an opponent is perhaps more pronounced in basketball than in the other sports.

CONCEPT K. In order to reach the desired goal in the shortest possible time, the dribbler must move in a direct pathway; however, intervening opponents and other variables on occasion cause the dribbler to maneuver in flexible, nondirect pathways.

The shortest distance between two points is a straight line. Consequently, when the dribbler sees no obstruction between himself and the desired goal, he should increase his speed to the point where he can still control both his body and the ball and move in the straightest possible pathway toward the goal (for example, as in an unguarded lay-up shot in basketball).

If the defensive players are effective, however, the opportunity to move in a direct, unguarded pathway is limited. Therefore it becomes necessary for the dribbler to out-maneuver the opponent by opening spaces and using flexible pathways. Such ability is dependent upon several factors.

1. The dribbler must be able to change directions quickly. This involves all the points discussed in Concepts I and J.

2. The dribbler must master the *feint*—a pretense to move in one direction followed by a quick move in the opposite direction. Since ball control is a bit easier in basketball, the feint is probably used most often in this activity. Feinting, as a specific skill, is discussed in the chapter on basketball.

3. When the dribbler sees that an opponent is moving in to guard him, he can protect the ball by keeping his body between it and the opponent (except in field hockey, where such a maneuver is illegal). This involves, in addition to the other points discussed in this section, an awareness of space as discussed in Concept M.

CONCEPT L. Although there is a distinct rhythmic pattern involved in dribbling, the tempo may increase or decrease as a pattern of play evolves.

As mentioned in the last concept, when an unobstructed, direct pathway to the goal opens, the dribbler should increase speed to get through the open space before it again closes. This is true regardless of the activity being played.

Feinting may also involve a change in tempo. The change may be an accelerative one in order to outmaneuver the opponent by mere speed, or it may be decelerative in an attempt to deceive the opponent into thinking that the pace of action is being slowed. As soon as the opponent seems to be relaxing his guarding (marking) stance, the dribbler should quickly change direction and drive toward the goal.

CONCEPT M. Although the dribbler must focus his eyes on the ball during contact, he must also survey the playing area in order to be able to change tactics as the situation demands.

The smaller the ball and the more complicated the skill, the more it is necessary to keep one's eyes on the ball (objective focus or tracking). Dribbling in field hockey is a good example. However, focusing on the ball to the exclusion of attention to teammates, opponents and the playing area itself is productive of inefficient play in a game situation since the dribbler may run into teammates and/or opponents or fail to see open pathways. The answer to this problem lies in the principle of objective focus (attending to the immediate task at hand, e.g., driving for a goal in field hockey, without being distracted by extraneous factors). As the ball becomes larger and the skill becomes somewhat less complicated, peripheral vision can be used to good advantage. In fact, the skilled basketball dribbler need not focus on the ball at all. Instead, since the ball is large and the angle of rebound is controlled due to a firm, smooth surface (contrasted to an oftentimes bumpy surface in field hockey and soccer), kinesthetic awareness takes over and thus the dribbler is freed to survey the playing area.

STRATEGY

Because each sport is unique in certain aspects, it is impossible to discuss common strategy concepts that apply to all of them.

Thus, for the purposes of this book, all sports included are classified as follows:

ACTIVITIES	CLASSIFICATION
Basketball Field Hockey Soccer	Goal-oriented sports
Softball	Field sports
Badminton Tennis Volleyball	Net sports
Archery Golf Gymnastics Swimming Track and Field	Individual sports

In the *goal-oriented sports,* basketball, field hockey and soccer, both teams intermingle and move over the same space as they progress toward an area called a goal. The one *field-sport,* softball, differs from the other team sports in that the two teams occupy different spaces; the runner (offensive player) invades the opponents' (defensive team) space. There are, however, basic and common concepts that are naturally inherent when more than two people occupy the same field or court of play. The term *front-line player* or *back-line player* is a general one and may be applied to all sports but using a different nomenclature; for example, front-line players in softball may be the infield players while back-line players may be the outfield players. Therefore, common concepts for both goal-oriented and field sports are addressed as one.

The games played over a net, badminton, tennis and volleyball are termed *net sports.* Concepts which pertain specifically to them begin on page 87.

Sports such as archery, golf, gymnastics, swimming, and track and field are so individualized in their special strategies that they are described in conjunction with the skills involved.

Strategy differs according to the immediate needs of the game. The team in possession of the ball attempts to score, and all efforts made to maintain possession and score are termed *offensive* strategies. The efforts of a team not in possession of the ball, directed toward retrieving the ball and preventing the opponents from scoring, are termed *defensive* strategies. Concepts are listed according to whether they relate to offensive play or defensive play for goal-oriented sports.

Goal-Oriented and Field Sports

PLAYERS' POSITIONS AND RESPONSIBILITIES

CONCEPT N. Proper use of personnel, based on each player's strengths and limitations, is of paramount importance when molding a team.

Sub-concept N-1. Each player on a team must assume specific responsibilities for the position he is playing.

Teamwork involves the combination of mastered skills from all players in all positions. Each individual should be able to relate the duties of his position to all other positions on the team. According to the sport, players are considered either totally offensive or totally defensive or they assume both offensive and defensive responsibilities at different times during the game.

Offensive players, sometimes referred to as forwards, front-line, or infield players, should be fast runners, skilled in moving the ball, and highly skilled shooters. Offensive players are required to move quickly and aggressively, using fast starts and stops.

Defensive players, sometimes referred to as backfield or outfield players, should be skilled in techniques used to recover or regain possession of the ball, as in tackling in hockey and soccer. They should be perceptive and be able to anticipate, intercept and restart an offensive drive by careful placement of passes and throws.

Interchanging of positions is often necessary and should occur automatically as a result of careful practice sessions. If a player with the ball loses his opponent, another defensive player should take over, since any player in possession of the ball is a potential threat. Shifts in spatial patterns occur when spaces or players must be adequately covered. For example, the softball outfield shifts according to the position of runners on bases.

Backing up a player affords a second line of attack and occurs when a back-line player or any other player stands or runs behind another player to gain possession of a ball that has passed through the first player. When a player loses possession of the ball, a backup player can start the offensive drive by returning the ball to the front-line player. Ideally, every player, except a goalkeeper, has a backup player.

OFFENSE

CONCEPT O. In goal-oriented and field sports a system of offense is essential if a team is to be successful. The prime purposes of an offensive system are to build upon the strengths of the players, to shift the balance of power away from the defense, and to capitalize on defensive weaknesses.

All sports are played within spatial boundaries and how movement occurs within that spatial area determines how successful a player or team is. In some cases a player sends the ball or object into space and the placement is strategic. In some cases the player must position himself strategically to send or receive the ball. Many times the player with the ball must maneuver into strategic positions to pass or shoot.

Sub-concept O-1. If and when a player decides that maintaining possession of the ball will gain ground more successfully, the player must be able to dribble, dodge, and feint effectively.

Moving oneself and the ball together demands particular skills in order to follow a determined strategy (see "Moving the Body and an Object through Space," in this chapter).

In order to get around an opponent, it is necessary to execute a successful *dodge*. In some sports, a short pass to one side of an opponent while the dodger runs to the other side enables the player to regain possession of the ball and continue on his way.

A *feint* is a pretended movement to one side followed by a quick maneuver to the other side. Feints become a necessary strategy for continued possession of the ball.

Sub-concept O-2. Effective passing involves spatial patterns based on positioning of teammates and opponents.

Passes directed to a space ahead of a teammate who is running can be picked up without inhibiting speed or direction. Passes are usually made at a forty-five degree angle. In many sports the angled passes complete a triangle pattern in order to bypass an opponent. There is no adequate defense against a well-executed triangular pattern.

Flat passes of less than forty-five degrees are effective when an opponent is out of position and the teammate can handle a ball in his present position. Sometimes the first pass in the triangular pattern is almost a flat pass.

In order to become free to receive a pass, it is often necessary to cut in front of an opponent. In most sports players cut toward the goal. Give-and-go is a common term used to describe a pass and cut for the goal.

Sub-concept O-3. Creating spaces is basic to sound team strategy.

While effective passing can create spaces, each offensive player can maneuver positioning so that spaces are opened. A player can pull away from the ball to deceive the defense. Fast cutting can create spaces. By moving into a space and drawing the opponent with him, a player can create an open space into which the ball can be sent. Creating spaces always involves movement either toward or away from the ball.

Sub-concept O-4. In order to score it is necessary to place the ball in a strategic position in relation to the goal.

Usually the goal is located at the center of the end line of the court or field. All efforts are made to move the ball toward the goal. This action is called *centering* the ball and is strategic when an attempt is to be made at scoring. Passing patterns or dribbling toward the goal usually occur prior to scoring.

Sub-concept O-5. Shooting for a goal involves individual and team strategy.

If a player is alone and far ahead of his teammates he should dribble in close and shoot. If he encounters an opponent, a pass or a dodge must be executed to bypass the opposition. A screen play is sometimes used when a player with the ball has passed to a teammate and then stands still to allow the teammate to shoot. The screen prevents the defense from getting close enough to guard effectively.

Sub-concept O-6. Rushing the goal insures follow-up to a shot at the goal.

A follow-up by the players making the goal attempt is imperative, and many goals are scored by the second attempt. All teammates whose positions allow their presence at the goal should move toward the goal for followup shots. Every angle in front or surrounding the goal should be covered by some player.

DEFENSE

CONCEPT P. Individual defensive techniques are for the purpose of closing spaces through which a ball can be passed or inhibiting the progress of a player or ball, thereby preventing the opponents from maintaining possession of the ball and/or scoring.

Sub-concept P-1. Defensive play depends on guarding techniques which enable the player to anticipate movement, to intercept passes, to tackle, or block.

Players who play defensive positions are assigned to *guard* or *mark* an offensive player on the opposing team. Marking is a technique of staying close enough to a player to intercept a pass coming to that player, or tackling if he receives the ball. The level of skill of the offensive player and of the defensive player determines how close to the opponent a guard plays. Staying too close encourages a fast break or dodge around the guard. Keen perceptive judgments are made quickly by highly skilled defensive players, and often the successful team's defense is based on the level of judgments made by the defensive players.

Sub-concept P-2. Covering is a technique for closing spaces through which long passes might be sent.

To facilitate the interception of long passes and to make sure all spaces are watched, defensive players may want to play back in a deeper defensive position. A player may move into a position on the opposite side of the field or court from the ball in order to guard a space through which a long pass might be directed. In goal-oriented and field sports, with the exception of basketball, all defensive players except the center halfback are assigned positions to cover spaces. Covering players must shift positions quickly according to the location of the ball. Constant movement of defensive players in all games forms the basis for good defensive coverage.

Sub-concept P-3. The defense should advance to tackle or guard immediately when the ball enters its territory.

In all team sports defensive strategy depends on being able to first intercept a ball or, failing that, to attempt to regain possession.

In goal-oriented sports, excluding basketball, tackling involves getting the ball away from an opponent or forcing the player to pass. In basketball, tackling involves stealing the ball. Tackling-back is a technique used by forwards who have lost the ball and immediately try to regain possession.

In a stick game, such as field hockey, tackles must be executed from straight on, the stick side and non-stick side. In soccer the legs and feet are involved in tackling the ball from the sides and from in front.

Sub-concept P-4. Clearing the ball involves a fast defensive maneuver because the ball must be moved quickly away from the goal.

The deeper the play in defensive territory, the more quickly the ball is moved to the sidelines. A rebound from the basketball backboard is moved directly toward the sidelines or passed long down the middle. Clearing the ball to the corner of the court

or field is sometimes the criterion for the direction of the pass. The ball is never passed in front of the goal.

CONCEPT Q. A system of defense is essential if a team is to be successful. The prime purposes of the defense are to prevent the opponents from scoring and to capitalize on offensive weaknesses.

Sub-concept Q-1. Team strategies follow a particular planned defensive pattern based on man-to-man defense or a spatial pattern (zone) defense.

The strategy selected depends on the skill level and endurance of the guards or defensive players. In a man-to-man defense each player is responsible for his own particular opponent, but another defensive player covers the opponent who has successfully evaded his own player.

Spatial patterns involve a set zone in which each defensive player has responsibility for a specific area of the court, or a shifting zone in which a defensive player moves to intercept a pass and his teammates cover the remaining zones.

Each sport becomes specialized in its defensive strategies. It is necessary to study carefully the intricate designs unique to each sport.

Net Sports

Volleyball, tennis and badminton are games played on a court with a net separating the opposing teams. The objective of net sports is to play the ball or shuttlecock in such a way that the opponents cannot return it successfully.

The concepts which follow are similar to those identified under Goal-Oriented and Field Sports (pp. 84–87). However, their application is unique to net sports since these sports are not goal-oriented and opponents do not share the same playing area.

Thus, these concepts have been identified separately.

CONCEPT R. The player should be aware of his position within the playing area.

Spatial perception, sometimes called court consciousness, is an attribute that beginners should develop early. Keen awareness of all boundary lines is imperative; likewise, awareness of one's position in relation to the boundary lines is essential if a player is to utilize space to his advantage. It is wasted effort to defend a space larger than that designated by the boundary lines. In essence, this is what a player does when he plays a ball or shuttlecock which would have fallen short, wide or outside the boundary lines. A quick point or an opponent's loss of service is often made possible by simply knowing which hits will land in bounds, and thus should be played, and which should be allowed to pass since they will fall outside the boundary lines.

In addition, the performer must be aware of his distance from the net as well as the height of the ball or shuttlecock in relation to the net. This height and distance determines the trajectory needed to clear the net to achieve the desired results. Also, awareness of distance from the net is essential since tennis, badminton, and volleyball rules all stipulate that the performer (and racket) cannot touch the net.

CONCEPT S. Individual, partner, or team play is based on a particular plan of spatial arrangement.

The space of one's court may be covered alone, as in singles; with another, as in doubles; or shared with several other players, as in the team game of volleyball. An awareness of the territory one is to cover as well as how the space is to be shared with other players is necessary for successful court coverage. Good strategy in net games dictates that between shots one returns to a position on the court which allows him to reach almost any shot. The actual location of this home position is dependent upon the activity and the system of court coverage used. For example, in badminton singles the player returns to a position midway between the sidelines and slightly behind the center of the court. As his opponent places the shuttlecock to various corners of the court, the player moves to contact the shuttlecock. Following contact he quickly returns to home position to assure maximum court coverage.

Beginning tennis and badminton players often establish a home position which favors either their racket or non-racket side. One stroke (either the forehand or backhand) is sometimes weaker than the other. To compensate, the beginner shifts his court position to protect the weaker side. It is wiser strategy to develop strength on both sides, thus eliminating the need for protective positioning.

When sharing the space of a court with one or more players, careful planning and constant communication are needed to assure that all space is covered. A system of court coverage must be selected which: (1) covers the space of the entire court; (2) defines the playing territories of individual players; and (3) allows all players to have a clear, unobstructed view of the net and the opponent. Parallel play in which players play side by side is one example of a spatial relationship which may be used in badminton and tennis. In volleyball, the W and crescent formations are two of the many systems possible.

CONCEPT T. Creating spaces and sending the ball (or shuttlecock) to open spaces of the court or to weaknesses in

the opponent's defense are basic to scoring.

Offensive strategy may range from the very simple to the very complex, depending upon the ability of the player. However, basic to any strategy is the ability to hit to the most vulnerable area of the opponent's court, to focus upon weaknesses in the opponent's game and to disguise the force and placement of the hit.

In order to score points the successful player capitalizes upon his opponent's positioning. He utilizes a variety of techniques to hit to an undefended area of the court or to force his opponent to move and create open spaces. Regardless of the techniques used, the pattern should be varied to catch the opponent unaware.

A player should be quick to detect any weakness in the opponent's play. After a few minutes of play he should be able to identify the side of the body and level in space which causes the opponent the greatest difficulty and then capitalize upon this weakness in the ensuing play.

The use of similar preliminary movements for a variety of hits prevents the opponent from anticipating the force and placement to be used. Sound strategy requires that the opponent should be kept guessing. Disguising one's intentions, as well as varying the force and placement of each hit, are requisite to keeping the opponent off guard.

SAFETY

The necessity to develop safety consciousness in both students and teachers cannot be emphasized too strongly. Too often, unfortunately, such an attitude is motivated only after an accident or near accident. It is hoped that serious attention to the development of safety skills will preclude most, if not all, injuries.

CONCEPT U. An affective attitude based on a cognitive understanding of the dangers inherent in an activity is necessary if one is to perform safely.

Sub-concept U-1. Providing a safe environment for participation contributes to the development of desirable affective attitudes toward the activity.

The teacher, as the expert in charge of the activity, is directly responsible for a safe environment. First, he must secure the space and equipment necessary to participate safely in the activity. A safe environment includes appropriate space (field, court, pool, etc.) with an adequate surface which is free from extraneous objects and debris that might threaten the safety of the participants. Appropriate spacing of equipment and participants throughout the available space must also be taken into consideration. Equipment necessary for safe participation is unique to each activity and includes such things as face guards, guards for glasses, padding, etc. In addition, the equipment and/or apparatus needed for the activity must be sound and in good repair. In swimming, the cleanliness of the water and the assurance that it is free of bacteria enhances the desire of the participants to take part in the activity, and protects their health.

Sub-concept U-2. Educating the participants to use the environment wisely contributes not only to personal safety but enhances the total climate of the classroom.

Students must be cognizant of the dangers inherent in certain activities such as swimming, archery, and trampolining. In addition, students must realize their own capabilities and limitations and choose their involvement accordingly. This is especially important if students are free to decide their own rate of advancement. An awareness and consideration of the location of others and sharing the available space is of prime importance. This awareness involves safety in the manipulation of objects as well as the ability to manipulate the body in space to avoid collisions. A student is more eager to play if he is relatively certain he will not be battered and bruised by teammates and opponents in the execution of the activity. The development of individual skill in handling the body, hand apparatus and projectiles contributes to a safe environment for all participants. The teacher must be firm in enforcing all safety rules.

PART III. □ GOAL-ORIENTED SPORTS

Not too young, not too old,
Not too timid, not too bold,
Just the kind for sport . . .

Henry J. Sayers

6. Basketball
7. Field Hockey
8. Soccer

INTRODUCTION

Scoring goals reflects the objective and the excitement of a group of team sports commonly associated because they are goal-oriented. The sports in this group involve skills necessary to move the body and an object through space. Doing both at one time constitutes the most complex actions in the world of sports. The skills become even more demanding because the players are dependent on each other for receiving and sending the object (ball) in a manner that makes progress toward a specific area designated as the goal. In goal-oriented sports both teams occupy the same playing space. They are not separated as in net sports and are not assigned to one specific part of a playing area.

Basketball, field hockey, and soccer require proficiency in the locomotor skills of running, starting, stopping, and constant changing of directions. Manipulative movement patterns form the basic skills in goal-oriented sports. In basketball throwing, catching and shooting are essential; in field hockey skills involved with sending and receiving an object are essential; soccer demands kicking, volleying, blocking and tackling as well as trapping. All of them have in common the basic skill in dribbling whether it be by the hands, feet or with a stick. Individually skills must be strong; the team's success will depend on the expertise exhibited by the teamwork of individual players.

Teamwork is the key element in all goal-oriented sports from both an offensive and defensive viewpoint. Tactics and strategy provide the system upon which creative ideas are based. Creative ideas are implemented through the efforts of many persons and therein lies the challenge of coordinating teaching skills and playing the game. Patterns of line-ups, back-ups, shifts, and interchanges as well as out of bound plays become possibilities for outwitting and out-maneuvering the opposition.

Common concepts involve the utilization of the elements of space, time, force and flow; once all four are combined into a smoothly operating team plan, the game is played skillfully. Perceptual awareness of all four elements is essential throughout the entire duration of playing time. A keen perception of space, for example, is basic; sports are played within spatial limitations. Knowing precisely where one is on the playing field in relation to the goal determines what particular techniques or strategy or tactics will be used. There are certain maneuvers that are almost never employed such as a defensive player passing in front of the opposition's goal deep in his own territory. There must be awareness of spatial elements when passing to a teammate at the proper angle or when cutting at a proper angle. Creating spaces, blocking spaces, covering spaces are important to goal sports. Basic systems of defense and offense are built strictly on spatial boundaries. Shifts occurring in goal-oriented sports both in the backfield and on the forward line usually become so automatic that players are not even aware that movement has taken place. Beginners must be helped to perceive the importance of space, but, as skill increases, spatial awareness becomes almost unconscious on the part of the players.

Force is determined by the requirement of the particular situation. Sometimes a hard driving pass is needed; at other times a soft push pass or even a hand-off is better. Even though much effort has been spent in individual practice, the heat and emotion of competition can distort the amount of force a player imparts to the object being moved. Control is gained through experience. A basketball player knows just the right amount of force required for a soft lay-up shot. The force used in passing and receiving with either the hands or the feet or the head must be judged and executed effectively in goal-oriented sports.

Timing is extremely important in goal-oriented sports, and entire patterns of play are predicated on exactness. A pass, cut, shot, shift or interchange can spell the difference between success and failure. Superb timing brings space and force together in the most effective implementation possible.

Flow usually refers to the smooth sequential movement from one lever to another within the individual player; in team sports it refers to the flow of play from one player to another. An entire team can experience the feeling of flow. Flow can be smooth or jerky in its implementation. In recent years players themselves have given a new connotation to the word "flow." When a team is so completely absorbed in what they are doing that the movements become automatic, perfectly timed, with just the right amount of force, using just the correct space requirements, the results are perfection.

Flow occurs when all players are "up" on the ball, anticipate almost every movement, execute all movements with a sensation that binds all the players into a closely coordinated unit.

Systems of defense and offense share commonalities whether the pattern is simple or complex and whether it is a man-to-man or a complicated zone. Ingenuity and creativity are keys to effective patterns, and the traditional practices are changing to incorporate newer ideas of line-ups, shifts, guarding and covering.

Before teams can build perfection in play, individuals should be proficient in skills that must be practiced and performed over and over. Weak links in a line-up can be spotted very quickly. Attention should be paid to the skill suggestions in each chapter and the commonalities should be noted.

6

Basketball

INTRODUCTION

Basketball, a team game, is played in a general space of approximately ninety-four feet by fifty feet, and involves almost continuous movement among the five players on each team as they attempt to score by putting the ball through the basket on their respective end of the court. (See figure 6.1 for the official court markings.) Since no great degree of physical contact is permitted, it is a constant challenge to the players to control their bodies regardless of the speed or force of the movement.

The game begins with a center jump between two opposing players who try to tap the ball to one of their teammates. From this point on, the team in possession of the ball maneuvers it toward its goal by means of dribbling or passing. When the person with the ball considers himself near enough to the basket to be successful, he uses one of a variety of shots in an attempt to score. Meanwhile the opposing team is defending against a goal being scored by trying to intercept passes, by forcing turnovers, and by guarding shots and open players. After a goal is scored, the team scored against is awarded the ball out of bounds under the opponent's basket and now it is its turn to attempt to score.

The game is divided into periods (either two or four) of a set number of minutes (ranging from eight to twenty). Goals scored from the field count two points. Free throws for the goal are awarded for violation of some rules and successful conversions count one point each.

The official rules for the game have undergone many revisions to the point that today there is very little difference between the men's and the women's game. For the latest rules, the current *Basketball Guide* as published by an official agency (National Association for Girls and Women in Sport,

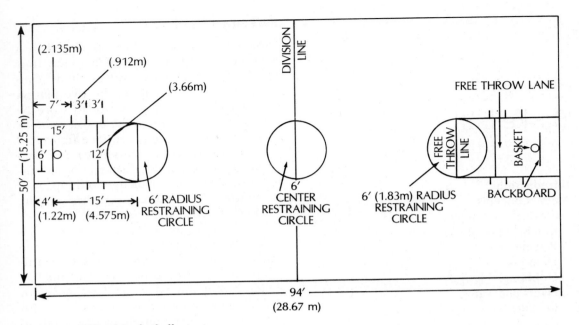

Figure 6.1. **Official basketball court**

National Collegiate Athletic Association, National Federation of High School Athletic Associations, or the Amateur Athletic Union) should be consulted.

VALUES

The game of basketball has universal appeal. In the United States it is probably the single most popular spectator sport; in addition, hundreds of thousands of people of both sexes participate in some form of the game. Dr. James Naismith, the man who is generally credited with having invented the game, would undoubtedly be amazed at the ubiquity of backboards and baskets. Although the game as played today bears little resemblance to that which was played at Springfield College in 1891, the values which Naismith attributed to it at that time are still inherent in the activity. Others have been added as well.

As a recreational activity for all but the aged, basketball has few peers. Recreation departments even sponsor slow-break basketball leagues with modified rules for older players. School-age children of both sexes attest to its popularity by engaging in pickup games at every opportunity. No park or recreation area is complete without basketball courts. Recreational values run the gamut from satisfying a need for physical activity, to catharsis, to emotional release.

The need for vigorous activity is genuinely fulfilled in basketball. The skills of running, stopping, throwing, catching, jumping, and landing are among those most often used. Cardiorespiratory endurance is probably the greatest specific physical value of participation in basketball, but playing the game also contributes to muscle strength and coordination. Participation in basketball, as in any fairly strenuous physical activity, also contributes generally to maintaining a healthy, more youthful body.

Social and ethical values are inherent in any team activity, but these values are particularly manifested in basketball because of its adaptability to modified game situations. For example, although the rules state that there are five players on a team, many games are played with a fewer or greater number of participants, on full courts or half-courts, or even on no court at all, so long as a basket is available. More often than not in such games, there are no officials and the players readily admit violations of the rules.

ELEMENTS OF MOVEMENT

The elements of movement—space, force, time and flow—as discussed in part one of this book are paramount in any activity requiring continuous, vigorous movement. Basketball is no exception.

Basketball is a spatial game. As indicated earlier, the general space in which basketball is played is dictated by the rules. Likewise, the rules dictate personal or self-space to the extent that contact with another player is not allowed. Therefore, the necessity to learn to control one's body in a defined space is of prime importance.

Basketball is a game of force. Varying degrees of force are required in the skills fundamental to basketball. The long pass downcourt to a teammate demands great force, while a successful hook shot necessitates a soft touch using little force. Dribbling the ball while driving for the basket requires greater force than dribbling in place while waiting for a teammate to cut to an open space.

Basketball is a temporal game. Not only do the rules of basketball dictate attention to time (e.g., five seconds are allowed to put the ball in play from an out-of-bounds position), but the skills themselves are inextricably woven around the time element. For example, as one attempts to fake his guard

out of position, he must accelerate quickly to drive past his opponent. Or, in passing, one must judge the speed with which his teammate is moving if he is to get the ball to the open space at exactly the right time.

Basketball is a game of flow. Smoothly flowing sequential movements such as screen in a driving lay-up shot are basic to success in basketball. So, too, a relatively uncomplicated skill such as a chest pass requires continuity of movement, with each isolated aspect of the total skill interdependent on every other part of the holistic totality.

SAFETY FACTORS

Since basketball is a constantly moving, vigorous activity, attention to conditioning factors is significant. Cardiorespiratory and muscular endurance are an absolute necessity if one is to be able to play a complete game at maximum effort with no congruent ill effects.

Provision of a safe playing area is dependent upon a smooth, nonslippery surface free from obstacles close to the sideline which might cause injuries if one were to run into them. In those cases where the boundaries of the court are quite close to the walls, the walls should be padded.

Personal playing equipment includes well-fitting, rubber-soled shoes and garments which allow freedom of movement. If it is necessary for a player to wear glasses, safety lenses or glass guards should be required. Finally, it is most essential that players learn to control their bodies effectively in movement.

Other safety factors and concepts which apply to basketball are discussed in chapter five and later in this chapter.

TERMINOLOGY

The more basic terms in basketball are defined here. On occasion, two or more terms mean virtually the same thing (e.g., pick, block, screen); in addition, certain skills are variously named in different parts of the country (e.g., give-and-go and pass-and-cut). Nevertheless, the list given here is undoubtedly a representative one.

Backboard: the surface to which the basket is attached. It is most often made of fiberglass.

Backcourt: that half of the court which contains the opponent's basket or that part of the frontcourt near the centerline.

Blocking-out: a maneuver by the defense to control rebounding by positioning themselves in such a way that offensive players cannot get near the backboard.

Block-and-roll (pick-and-roll): a maneuver in which an offensive player blocks (picks) his teammate's guard from moving. If the blocker's opponent then switches to pick up the unguarded player, the blocker rolls (breaks) toward the basket as a potential pass receiver.

Cut: a quick movement, often following a feint, into an unguarded area.

Defense: the team not in possession of the ball.

Drive: a player with the ball dribbles rapidly toward the basket, hoping to score.

Fake or feint: a pretense of moving in one direction followed by a quick movement in another direction.

Fast break: an attempt to gain an offensive advantage by beating the defense to the offensive end of the floor. A fast break usually follows a defensive rebound or an opponent's score.

Foul: an infraction of the rules for which the opposite team receives one or more free throws.

Free-lance offense: a term describing no set pattern of offensive play.

Frontcourt: that half of the court which contains the offensive team's basket. Also that portion of the offensive half-court near the end line.

Give and go (pass-and-cut): an offensive maneuver in which a player, after passing the ball to a teammate, moves into an open space to receive a return pass.

Hand off: to simply hand the ball to a teammate.

Offense: the team in possession of the ball.

One-on-one: an even ratio describing a pattern of one offensive player against one defensive player. Similarly, there could be a two-on-two, three-on-three etc., ratio. When the ratio is uneven, it becomes two-on-one, three-on-two, etc.

Outlet pass: the pass that starts a fast break. An outlet pass usually follows a defensive rebound and is thrown toward the nearest sideline or long up the middle.

Pass-and-cut: see "Give-and-Go."

Pattern play: a system of preplanned offensive play.

Pick: see "Screen."

Pick-and-roll: see "Block-and-Roll."

Post (or pivot) player: an offensive player stationed at a designated spot near the free throw lane. Can be low (near the basket) or high (away from basket). There can be a single (one) post player or double (two) post players.

Press: a very aggressive style of defensive play in which all offensive players are constantly harassed in an attempt to force a turnover.

Screen (pick or block): an offensive maneuver wherein a player momentarily blocks a defensive man from moving, thus freeing a teammate for a shot or a cut into an open space.

Stall: an offensive maneuver to slow down the pace of the game. A stall is usually used late in the game in order to protect a slim lead.

Strong side: the side of the court where the ball is in play.

Switch: a defensive maneuver in which assigned guarding responsibilities are temporarily exchanged because one of the guards is out of position.

Turnover: in a turnover the offense loses possession of the ball because of an error such as a bad pass or a violation such as traveling.

Violation: an infraction of the rules for which the opposite team receives the ball out of bounds.

Weak side: the side away from the ball.

MAJOR CONCEPTS

A great many of the major concepts discussed in chapter five are pertinent to basketball. However, those most apropos, together with any unique applications, are briefly reviewed in this section. For ease of reference, the concepts cited are subdivided into the same categories, and in the same order, as in chapter five.

MOVING THE BODY THROUGH SPACE

Most of the activities included in this book require the body to move through space. Basketball is no exception. Sine personal space in basketball is often quite delimited, the importance of controlling the body as it moves through space cannot be overemphasized.

CONCEPT A. Moving the body with control involves a conscious manipulation of the center of gravity in relation to the base of support, either to maintain stability or to initiate locomotor movement, as the situation demands.

Sub-concept A-1. Staying ready to move allows a player to get a faster start in order to outmaneuver the opponent, to gain possession of the ball, or to get into a desirable position to project an object.

Sub-concept A-2. Enlarging the base of support in the direction of the force allows a player to start, stop, and change directions quickly.

Sub-concept A-3. Running in a forward direction is the quickest way to cover a distance of some magnitude.

Sub-concept A-4. Sliding sideways or in a diagonally forward or backward direction is often a more efficient manner of moving the body through space if the distance to be covered is minimal and if the body needs to remain facing the immediate object.

Sub-concept A-5. Recovering quickly after the execution of a skill involves reassuming the ready position and relocating oneself in space in the home position, or some other advantageous position, in order to stay alert and ready to react again.

Sub-concept A-6. Propelling the body through space requires a firm reacting surface and sufficient friction between the reacting surface and the base of support.

The importance of being ready to move, with the body constantly under control, is essential to effective play in basketball. Shooting and dribbling, two basic skills, are good examples of the importance of readiness and control. The jump shot, for instance, demands body control lest the shooter jump into a defensive player and thus commit a foul. Dribbling is an intricate skill and its successful execution, particularly when trying to outmaneuver an opponent, requires the center of gravity to be well balanced over the feet and legs. Pivots, feints and turns nearly always require a wide base of support, particularly when such a maneuver follows a dribbling drive. If a player does not stay ready to move, there is little chance for him to intercept an opponent's pass or cause a turnover. The good player's weight is always on the toes, ready to go.

A nutshell description of the individual defensive skill of guarding is contained within sub-concept A-4. Since the defensive player should keep both his opponent and the ball in his vision at all times, the necessity to slide forward, backward, and laterally is apparent. A defensive player's back should never be turned to the ball until after a shot is airborne. Also, a shooter, to be effective, must not fail to follow his shot for a possible rebound. The area assigned to a defensive player, such as in a particular zone, or to an offensive player, such as a high post, is termed his home position.

CONCEPT B. Creating and absorbing force to control the movement of the body through space may involve all of the body or only parts of the body, in unison or in sequence; however, the relaxation of noncontributing muscle groups is imperative for smooth, efficient movement.

Sub-concept B-1. A smooth transfer of momentum from one part of the body to another part, or to the total body, results in sustained movement, while an explosive transfer of momentum increases the speed and/or magnitude of the resulting movement.

Sub-concept B-2. Absorbing the force of a landing or fall over a greater time and distance increases stability and decreases the chance of injury.

Sub-concept B-3. Relaxing noncontributing muscle groups leads to smooth, efficient movement and thus to the proficiency of the performance.

Jumping and its companion basketball skill, rebounding, are prime examples of the necessity to transfer momentum from one part of the body to others as well as of the absorption of force in landing. To be effective in securing the greatest height possible, the jumper flexes his knees, thereby lowering the center of gravity. As he uncoils, the push off the floor originates in the feet and travels vertically up the body as the momentum passes from the feet to the hands. As the jumper or rebounder again contacts the floor, the shock of landing should be absorbed by bending the knees and ankles and flexing slightly at the hips.

The principle of reciprocal inhibition (relaxing noncontributing muscles) is often violated by the learner simply because he is not relaxed. In basketball, this is evidenced by the shot that hits the backboard with such force that it has no possible chance to go into the basket or by the fumbled catch of an easy pass. Learning to relax while playing is not as simple as it may sound. Generally, this ability increases commensurate with general playing abilities.

MOVING AN OBJECT THROUGH SPACE

As discussed in chapter five, moving an object through space implies some type of projection. In addition, quite often the object projected must be caught or at least slowed down prior to the execution of another skill. Both passing and catching the ball are fundamental in basketball.

CONCEPT C. A player must be in a desirable position in relation to the object to be projected.

CONCEPT D. Creating force: the production and transfer of force depend upon mass speed, and the striking surface used.

Sub-concept D-1. Increasing the mass used to produce force increases the force produced.

Sub-concept D-2. Increasing the speed of the implement or the body segment imparting force increases the force produced.

Sub-concept D-3. Increasing the range of movement of the body segment or the implement imparting force increases the distance through which speed can be developed, as well as the force imparted to the object.

Sub-concept D-4. Setting the body in motion prior to contact with an object, or to the relese of an object, builds greater force which in turn is transferred to the object. However at the instant of contact or release, the body should be stabilized.

Sub-concept D-5. A follow-through allows for greater force to be transferred to an object.

Sub-concept D-6. Stabilizing the body segments involved in an action allows for greater force to be imparted to the object.

CONCEPT E. Directing force: the direction in which an object moves is determined by the point at which force is applied in relation to the object's center of gravity.

Sub-concept E-1. Applying force directly through the center of gravity of an object results in a straight trajectory; an off-center application of force produces a curved trajectory.

Sub-concept E-2. Keeping one's eyes on the object (i.e., objective focus or tracking) facilitates the application of force in line with the intended direction of flight or the absorption of force when slowing or stopping an object. However, if the performer is throwing at a target, he must focus on the target rather than on the projectile.

Sub-concept E-4. External forces such as gravity, air resistance, and friction alter the flight of a projectile.

CONCEPT F. Sending the ball to a receiver who is moving requires directing the ball to an open space ahead of him.

All of these concepts are inextricably woven into the skills of passing and, to a lesser degree, shooting. Such skills are discussed in detail in the next section of this chapter and the unique application of each of these concepts underlies the description of each one. Although it is possible to take any one of the skills (for example, the hook pass) and cite specific relationships to nearly every concept listed here, to do so would be redundant. If there is some doubt as to how a certain concept applies to a specific skill, a rereading of chapter four, "Mechanical Principles of Movement," should prove worthwhile.

CONCEPT G. To receive an object which is moving through space a performer must slow or stop its motion by absorbing all or part of its force.

CONCEPT H. Three techniques help the performer to absorb force efficiently: (1) establishing a stable position; (2) utilizing the largest possible surface area; and (3) increasing the time or distance over which the force is received.

Sub-concept H-1. A stable position should be maintained as the force of an object is absorbed.

Sub-concept H-3. Moving the receiving surface with the ball upon contact (giving with the ball) allows force to be absorbed over a greater time and distance.

These concepts apply primarily to catching and, again, a consideration of them underlies the specific discussion of catching in the next section. In addition, such ideas as passing ahead of a moving player and bringing a ball under control before shooting at the completion of a dribble must take into account the same concepts to be successful.

MOVING THE BODY AND AN OBJECT THROUGH SPACE

As discussed in chapter five, this section is primarily concerned with a combination of manipulative and locomotor movements. The skill of dribbling is the most frequently used technique in this category.

CONCEPT 1. Since the purpose of the dribble is to maintain possession of the ball while moving through space, the amount and direction of force applied to the ball must be controlled.

CONCEPT J. The ability to dribble with alternating hands or feet provides maximum flexibility in controlling the ball and its direction.

CONCEPT K. In order to reach the desired goal in the shortest possible time, the dribbler must move in a direct pathway; however, intervening opponents and other variables on occasion cause the dribbler to maneuver in flexible, non-direct pathways.

CONCEPT L. Although there is a distinct rhythmic pattern involved in dribbling, the tempo may increase or decrease as a pattern of play evolves.

CONCEPT M. Although the dribbler must focus his eyes on the ball during contact, he must also survey the playing

area in order to be able to change tactics as the situation demands.

The dribble is a fundamental skill in basketball and it differs in many ways from dribbling in other activities. It is probably easier to become a skilled dribbler in basketball than it is in any other activity which uses the technique. In the first place, since the hands are used to contact the ball, the amount and direction of force is more easily controlled than if the feet or an implement were used. Secondly, ambidexterity with the hands is a relatively easy trait to acquire in basketball. Thirdly, it is perhaps easier to change direction and alter pathways in basketball, due to the larger ball and the smoother playing surface. Fourthly, since it is easier to control the force of a dribble in basketball, it stands to reason that controlling the tempo is likewise not too difficult. Last, as explained on page 113, once the dribbler in basketball has control of the ball it is usually no longer necessary to look at it. Therefore, objective focus can be completely directed to the playing court and the position of the players on it while one's kinesthetic sense controls the dribble.

STRATEGY

Basketball is a team game and all the perfected individual skills are worthless if the individuals do not play together as a team. Such teamwork is based on a plan of action, called a strategy.

CONCEPT N. Proper use of personnel, based on each player's strengths and limitations, is of paramount importance when molding a team.

Sub-concept N-1. Each player on a team must assume specific responsibilities for the position he is playing.

As with any team sport, basketball strategy is based upon the physical attributes and skill levels demanded in certain positions. The ideal attributes of centers, forwards, and guards are discussed elsewhere in this chapter.

CONCEPT O. In goal-oriented and field sports a system of offense is essential if a team is to be successful. The prime purposes of an offensive system are to build upon the strengths of the players, to shift the balance of power away from the defense, and to capitalize on defensive weaknesses.

Sub-concept O-1. If and when a player decides that maintaining possession of the ball will gain ground more successfully, the player must be able to dribble, dodge and feint effectively.

Sub-concept O-2. Effective passing involves spatial patterns based on positioning of teammates and opponents.

Sub-concept O-3. Creating spaces is basic to sound team strategy.

Sub-concept O-4. In order to score it is necessary to place the ball in a strategic position in relation to the goal.

Sub-concept O-5. Shooting for a goal involves individual and team strategy.

Sub-concept O-6. Rushing the goal insures follow-up to a shot at the goal.

The implications of these concepts to basketball are readily apparent. No basketball team can perform successfully without a system of offense, and any such system is built upon a foundation of solid individual offensive skills. The individual offensive skills are discussed in the next section of this chapter; the team offenses, under "Team Techniques."

CONCEPT P. Individual defensive techniques are for the purpose of closing spaces through which a ball can be passed or inhibiting the progress of a player or ball, thereby preventing the opponents from maintaining possession of the ball and/or scoring.

Sub-concept P-1. Defensive play depends on guarding techniques which enable the player to anticipate movement, to intercept passes, to tackle, or block.

Sub-concept P-2. Covering is a technique for closing spaces through which long passes might be sent.

Sub-concept P-3. The defense should advance to tackle or guard immediately when the ball enters its territory.

Sub-concept P-4. Clearing the ball involves a fast defensive maneuver because the ball must be moved quickly away from the goal.

Concept Q. A system of defense is essential if a team is to be successful. The prime purposes of the defense are to prevent the opponents from scoring and to capitalize on offensive weaknesses.

Sub-concept Q-1. Team strategies follow a particular planned defensive pattern based on a man-to-man defense or a spatial pattern (zone) defense.

As with the offense, a defensive system is based upon the ability of the players to execute individual defensive skills. Although the terminology changes from sport to sport (e.g., "marking" in field hockey, "guarding" in basketball), essentially the theories behind the skills are basic to many activities. Defensive basketball skills, both individual and team, are presented later in this chapter.

SAFETY

The dangers inherent in basketball are not as great as those in some other activities, such as swimming and gymnastics. However, if a student is truly to develop a safety-consciousness, each activity instructor needs to emphasize the concept of safety as well as to repeat it over and over.

CONCEPT U. An affective attitude based on a cognitive understanding of the dangers inherent in an activity is necessary if one is to perform safely.

Sub-concept U-1. Providing a safe environment for participation contributes to the development of desirable affective attitudes toward the activity.

Sub-concept U-2. Educating the participants to use the environment wisely contributes not only to personal safety but enhances the total climate of the classroom.

In addition to those safety aspects specific to basketball discussed on page 97 of this chapter, attention is called to the necessity to be aware of the boundaries of personal and general space. Collisions with teammates and opponents are always dangerous; additionally, in basketball, the latter is a foul.

INDIVIDUAL TECHNIQUES

CONCEPT. Any system of offensive or defensive play is only as good as the ability of the individual players to execute properly the fundamental skills involved.

In order for a team to play successfully, team members must master the fundamental individual techniques. For the purposes of this chapter, such techniques are divided into categories. Each of these categories is analyzed according to the parts of the body used (body awareness) and the elements of movement (space, force, time, and flow).

Catching and Receiving

Since basketball is a game of ball handling, the importance of catching the ball correctly cannot be overemphasized. (Refer again to "Moving the Body through Space," chapter five, for major concepts pertinent to catching and receiving.)

In a fast game the receiver of the ball often has to pass or shoot almost in the same motion that the catch is made. If the catch is performed poorly due to the wrong body mechanics and/or ill timing, the movements which follow are almost invariably imperfectly executed also.

Body Awareness

1. The hands point upward to receive balls coming above waist level: they point downward for balls coming below waist level.
2. Preparatory to the catch, the hands are kept parallel and slightly cupped.
3. The ball should be caught with the fingers spread and relaxed.
4. If the force of the oncoming ball is judged to be great, the feet and legs should be in a forward-backward stride position with knees slightly bent.
5. If receiving the ball on the run, as often occurs, one should face toward the ball as much as possible while at the same time trying not to break stride.

Space

1. There is a great variation in space while waiting to receive the ball. This is dictated by the position of teammates, opponents, and boundary lines.
2. As soon as the ball is caught, it is usually brought close into the body for protection.
3. Variations to number two come into play when it is desirable to execute another technique, such as passing or shooting, at almost the same instant the catch is made.

Force

1. It is necessary to absorb force with the catch in order to prevent fumbling the ball and injuring the fingers.

2. Such absorption is usually described as giving with the ball. In other words, upon contact, the hands are pulled back toward the body with a resultant bend of the arms and elbows.

3. If possible, the body is placed squarely in front of the oncoming ball in order to increase stability by absorbing the force near the center of gravity.

Time

1. The absorption of force can be increased temporally by increasing the size of the base of support, by stepping back on one foot and assuming a forward-backward stride position. One foot, however, must remain stationary in order to avoid a violation of traveling.

Flow

1. The flow of movements involved in catching consists of giving with the hands and arms and possibly with the knees and legs.

2. If another skill is executed almost simultaneously with the catch, the flow into the succeeding motion should be continuous with the absorption of force required in the catch.

Passing

Basketball is a passing game, particularly in a fast-break offense. In fact, many coaches temporarily legislate against the dribble in order to stress the importance of passing. Every player must be able to pass accurately and quickly. Otherwise, scoring opportunities occur infrequently. Generally speaking, passes are aimed "at the letters" (i.e., at the receiver's chest level) and the speed of the ball is dictated by the speed of the player who is moving to receive the pass. Knowing which kind of pass to use under varying conditions is obviously just as important as mastering the techniques involved in each pass. Quickness in passing is essential since, in a well-played game, catching and passing are often part of one continuous, flowing motion and thus there is not time to think about which pass to use.

The three basic throwing patterns, overhand, underhand, and sidearm, are discussed in detail in chapter nine, "Softball," and the many passes used in basketball are simply variations of them. Because of this, it may be well to read the analyses of throwing patterns in chapter nine before proceeding further. In addition, the major concepts relative to throwing in chapter five should be reviewed.

CHEST PASS

The chest pass is the most basic pass in basketball. It is primarily used when the play at the moment requires a short, quick pass. As such, proficiency in its execution, including accuracy, is a requisite of a good basketball player. Variations of the chest pass are numerous (e.g., chest shot, drive for the basket, bounce pass), and its basic pattern can be used in an attempt to deceive an opponent.

Body Awareness

1. Fingers should be well spread on the ball with only the fleshy pads of the fingertips touching it.

2. The ball should be close to the body with arms bent and elbows near the sides.

3. The body should be balanced with the knees bent. Feet can be either parallel or in a forward stride position.

Figure 6.2. **Chest pass**

Space

1. As with all passes, personal space is somewhat dictated by the position of one's opponent. Therefore, the necessity to be able to move quickly and deceptively is paramount.

2. The passer must be able to detect open spaces or possible open spaces quickly and pass to them if a teammate seems to be moving in their direction.

Force

1. Force is generated by a quick movement of the arms, initiated by a circular down-and-up motion of the wrists, into a fully extended position in the direction of the pass.

2. Unless the pass is a very short one that can be made from a parallel stance, a step forward should be taken and the weight should be transferred to the forward foot as the arms are extended.

3. The follow-through is in the direction of the pass and the passer must move immediately in order to position himself for succeeding play.

4. The amount of follow-through is dependent upon the distance the ball must travel.

Time

1. As with all passes, the passer must time the release of the ball in relation to the pass receiver.

2. In many instances, a player catches and releases the ball in almost the same instant.

Flow

1. Often the sequence of movement flows almost instantaneously from the catch to the pass.

2. The sequence of movement after reception of the ball involves pulling the ball in close to the body with the elbows at the side (see "Body Awareness"), selecting a person or space as the target and timing the release of the ball in relation to it, and then following through as far and as forcefully as the distance of the pass demands.

BOUNCE PASS

The bounce pass is a variation of the chest pass. As such, everything previously discussed applies here as well. In addition, the following points should be stressed.

1. Since the ball is thrown to the floor, the angle of rebound becomes a significant factor (see chapter four).

2. For deception, the passer should look straight ahead rather than at the direction in which the ball is to be sent.

3. Spin should be used sparingly, since excessive spin is apt to make the receiver fumble the ball.

OVERHAND PASS

Overhand passes are primarily used by taller players for obvious reasons. However, they can be used to advantage by the shorter player who receives a high ball and passes it on in an almost simultaneous motion. This pass can also be used to advantage when attempting to get the ball to a teammate playing the pivot position and when being very closely guarded by an opponent.

Body Awareness

1. One or both arms should be raised above the head with the ball resting on the fleshy pads of the fingers.

2. The elbows should be slightly bent so that a more direct follow-through is possible.

3. The eyes should be on the receiver as well as on the open spaces.

Space

1. The personal space of the passer is delimited according to how closely he is guarded.

2. Although prior to passing the feet may be parallel, it is desirable to step forward on one foot as the pass is made. Whether or not this is mandatory is dictated by the distance the ball must travel as well as the power in the wrist snap.

Force

1. Force comes primarily from the wrist snap.

2. Unless a long pass is desired, the arms remain fairly straight.

Time

The player must time the release of the ball in relation to the position of the potential receiver.

Flow

The sequence of movements involves raising the ball over the head, selecting a receiver or open space as a target, releasing the ball with sufficient force to reach the target, and then moving on the court so as to be in an advantageous position for further play.

PUSH PASS

The one-hand push pass, sometimes called a "flip," is increasingly used as the popularity of the jump shot and the one-hand set shot continues. Often a player is in the air ready to shoot when he sees an open teammate who is in a more advantageous shooting position. It is relatively simple, then, merely to flip the ball to the teammate. Or, the player can pretend that he is going to use a one-hand set shot in an attempt to lure a guard into jumping to block the shot and then he can push the ball off to a teammate.

Body Awareness

1. The body is in the air with the eyes focused on the basket.

2. Or, the body is balanced in a forward stride position, knees bent, center of gravity slightly lowered, and eyes focused on target.

Space

1. Personal space is delimited by opponents, especially as one gets closer to the basket.

2. Peripheral vision should be employed to ascertain which teammates are open for a pass and possible shot.

Force

1. Relatively little force is necessary, since this is usually a short pass.

2. If speed is essential, greater force is employed to ensure greater velocity.

Time

1. The timing of the jump (if used) and the pass must be consistent with the receiver's movements.

2. If the one-hand push pass is used after an attempt to deceive a guard into jumping to block a possible shot, the passer must not make his move until after the guard has jumped into the air.

Flow

1. The push pass, if used with a jump, is a continuous flow of motion from the jump into the air, to the cradling of the ball in one hand while the other hand lightly supports it, to a lateral turn of the hand supporting the ball, to a release using the fingers and wrist.

2. The amount and direction of follow-through is dictated by the path and the distance the ball must travel.

HOOK PASS

The hook pass, although difficult to master, is a necessary part of a good player's repertoire since it is invaluable when one is being very closely guarded. In such an instance, the player steps *away* from the defensive player, jumps into the air and hooks the ball sharply downward to a teammate.

Body Awareness

1. The body should be pivoted away from the defensive player so that the non-throwing arm is between the passer and his guard.

2. As the pivot is made, the ball is transferred across the body and cradled in the throwing hand. The other hand supports it lightly.

3. With the weight entirely on the pivot foot, a step is taken in the direction the body is now facing and a jump into the air is made off that foot.

4. As the jump is made, the passing arm, with fingers spread, is raised in an arc to a fully extended position directly over the head. The non-throwing hand remains in contact with the ball as long as possible, or the ball can be cupped against the forearm.

Space

1. Space is limited by the defensive player and by the height of the jump.

2. The passer must focus on the space into which the ball is to be passed.

Force

1. The force of the release of the ball depends upon the distance the ball must travel plus its trajectory.

2. Usually a considerable amount of force is desirable, but if too much is applied the receiver may fumble the ball.

Time

The timing of the hook pass is extremely important and depends primarily upon the position of one's guard, the position of the potential receiver, the height of the jump, and the force that should be applied to the ball.

Flow

The sequence of movements involves quickly pivoting the body away from the defensive player, shifting the ball to the passing hand, stepping out and jumping into the air as the throwing hand is raised above the head, and releasing the ball sharply downward.

Shooting

Obviously, it is important for a player to work on all facets of the game, but the ability to shoot successfully is probably the most important skill in basketball. Likewise, the most outstanding developments in skill level have occurred in shooting, not only because of the innovation of new shots and shooting techniques but also because this is the most frequently practiced component of the entire game. Shooting baskets seem to be a universally popular activity.

Coaches refer to the necessity to develop touch and a shooting eye, traits which players develop through arduous practice and good coaching. One of the most important attributes of a good shooter is knowing when to shoot, or take the percentage shot. A player cannot know which are the percentage shots if he does not understand the target area and where to aim, the advantages of using the backboard for angle shots, and the angles of rebound from the board. These points are discussed in chapter four, "Mechanical Principles of Movement." One of the most comprehensive and analytical treatments of shooting is that by Sharman, and a perusal of it should prove beneficial to the coach or player who wishes a greater in-depth discussion.[1]

ONE–HAND SET OR PUSH SHOT

The one-hand set or push shot, generally attributed to be the innovation of Hank Luisetti in the 1930s, has become so popular that the two-hand shot is practically obsolete except when the distance the ball has to travel is very great. The advantages of this shot over the two-hand set are both a quicker release and the variety of positions from which the shot can be made. Once the one-hand set is mastered, the next logical step is the jump shot.

Body Awareness

1. The body should be balanced over the center of gravity with the knees flexed. The right foot should be slightly ahead of the left. (This seems to violate the principle of opposition, but all leading coaches agree that the right-handed shooter should lead with his right foot in this shot.)
2. The ball should be held on the fingertips of the shooting hand with the thumb and fingers well spread. The fingers of the nonshooting hand rest underneath the ball to help balance it.
3. The elbow of the shooting arm should be under the ball and close to the body.
4. The ball should be held shoulder high and *slightly* to the right.
5. The eyes should be focused on the point of aim. (There is not universal agreement among coaches on what should be the

Figure 6.3. **One-hand set shot**

point of aim if the backboard is not used. The majority seem to emphasize the front edge of the rim; some, the middle of the basket; still others, the back edge of the rim. If the backboard is to be used, the angle of rebound must be considered.)

Space

There must be enough personal space for the shooter to follow through without contacting the defensive player, since this shot often requires a slight jump off the floor.

Force

1. The initial force comes from extending the flexed knees.
2. The force thus generated should travel vertically up the body so that the power comes from the body and legs rather than from the arms.
3. The release of the ball is started by dropping (cocking) the wrist. This brings the elbow in front of the ball pointing directly at the basket. As the arm unwinds and

1. Bill Sharman, *Sharman on Basketball Shooting* (Englewood Cliffs, N.J.: Prentice-Hall), 1965.

Figure 6.4. **Jump shot**

JUMP SHOT

The jump shot, because of its great flexibility, is probably the most commonly used shot in basketball today. It evolved quite naturally from the one-hand set or push shot, since often the one-hand set ends in a slight jump from the floor in order to achieve greater body extension. Flexibility is achieved since the shot most often comes on the heels of some form of body motion—a turnaround, a dribble, a pivot, catching a pass, or merely a head feint. This flexibility leaves the defensive man at a distinct disadvantage and thus the jump shot is the shot most responsible for today's high scoring games.

Body Awareness

1. The body should be balanced over flexed knees with the feet parallel to the basket and about shoulder-width apart.

2. The position of the hands and arms, the handling and release of the ball, and the follow-through are similar to the one-hand set shot discussed previously, with the main exception being that the ball is generally held a bit higher, somewhere between the shoulders and the eyes or even a bit above the head.

3. The eyes are focused on the target.

Space

Personal space is generally limited unless the shooter has completely outmaneuvered the defense. Thus the importance of jumping straight up is evident.

Force

1. After directly facing the basket, with the feet in a parallel position and the body balanced over flexed knees, the spring should be made straight up by extending

starts toward the basket, the wrist is uncocked and the ball rolls off the fingertips, thus imparting backspin to it.

4. The follow-through is downward with the wrist and fingers pointing toward the target.

Time

1. The length of time which the shooter may take is dictated by the defense.

2. The release of the ball should be timed to come at the fullest extension of the body but before the arm is completely extended.

Flow

The sequence of movement is from the balanced body over flexed knees, through an extension of the body by straightening the knees and raising the center of gravity, the knees. The shooter should try to feel the extension run vertically up his body. His head should remain directly above his feet and not be allowed to move forward or laterally.

2. If the shooter is relatively close to the basket, not as much force is required on the release and the arm does not need to be completely extended.

Time

1. The release of the ball should occur at the highest point of the jump.

2. The time available for the complete shot is dictated by the defense.

Flow

The flow is the same as for the one-hand set shot with the exception that the jump generally follows a preparatory movement of some kind.

LAY–UP SHOT

The lay-up shot is basic in basketball, especially in a fast-break offense. Fortunately it is rather easy to learn and, once learned, it is one of the most accurate shots. Players should be able to execute this shot with either hand and from either side of the basket. They should also be able to cross under the basket and do a reverse lay-up. In the latter case, all the techniques of the regular lay-up are used except that, after the takeoff, the body is twisted back toward the basket.

Body Awareness

1. Since the shot is the culmination of a drive for the basket, the player should be able to execute the shot without breaking his stride.

2. If the player shoots right-handed, the takeoff is from the left foot and vice versa.

3. The takeoff should be straight up, not forward (it should be a high jump rather than a broad jump) and the opposite knee should be raised as high as possible in order to increase the height of the jump.

4. In order to better perform step number three, the step onto the take-off foot should be a short one.

5. The ball is raised high on the side of the body from which the shot is to be taken, but with both hands close to the body.

6. The eyes should focus on the target.

7. The release comes at the highest point of the jump. The ball may be released either with a push of the hand behind the ball or from an underhand position. In either case, the backboard should be used for greater accuracy unless the shooter is approaching the basket head-on from mid-court.

Space

Both personal and general space must be quite large for this shot if the player is to avoid the foul of charging.

Force

1. The primary force for extending the body high in the air comes from landing on the takeoff foot from a short stride and then jumping straight up into the air by extending the entire body from a flexed-knee position. Height can be increased by forcibly raising the opposite knee as high as possible.

2. Little force is required to release the ball since, if properly executed, the jump brings the ball hand very close to the basket. The farther the hand is away from the basket, the greater the necessary force.

Time

1. Speed is essential, since the shot follows a drive for the basket, unless the defense has been left far behind.

2. The release of the ball should be timed so that it comes at the height of the jump.

Figure 6.5. **Hook shot**

Flow

The sequence of movements is from a dribble, to a jump, to a raise and release of the ball, to a landing in a balanced position.

HOOK SHOT

The hook shot is probably the most difficult shot to master because, among other reasons, it is virtually impossible to aim for the basket until the last second. However, it is undoubtedly the hardest shot to defend against and therefore the time and effort spent practicing it may pay great dividends. The hook shot is usually associated with the taller players in the pivot or post position, but shorter players can use it to advantage as well, particularly as they drive across the top of the lane in front of the basket.

Body Awareness

1. The technique is very similar to the hook pass (p. 108). The greatest difference between the pass and the shot is in the release of the ball and the movement of the arm immediately prior to the release.

2. The ball is held in the shooting hand, lightly cradled on the fingertips. The arm moves upward in an arc until the elbow is almost fully extended. The release of the ball occurs sooner than in the hook pass, usually before the arm reaches its highest point, in order to provide a soft shot.

3. The eyes should be focused on the target area, if possible, prior to the ball release. Because of the nature of the shot, this is often impossible. Players can compensate for this by shooting from a spot on the floor which they know is a certain distance and direction from the basket; or, in other words, by using kinesthesis.

4. The shooting hand, by necessity, is under the ball; therefore, a somewhat high arc is required for this shot.

5. As with the hook pass, the non-shooting arm is used to protect the ball from the defender.

Space

Sufficient personal space is obtained by stepping away from the defender as the non-shooting side of the body is turned toward him.

Force

The force necessary for the hook shot is somewhat similar to that for the hook pass. The greatest variation is during the release of the ball. The shot requires little force; the pass, a considerable amount.

Time

The timing of the hook shot and the hook pass are also similiar, with the exception that the ball is released sooner in the shot.

Flow

There is a similarity, again, in the flow of the pass and the shot. The arm portion of the shot, however, is a much smoother and somewhat slower movement than in the pass.

FREE THROWS

Free throws are shots awarded to players against whom fouls have been committed. Such shots are unguarded and the distance from the free throw line to the basket is a constant one. Therefore, it is only natural that the shooter should use his most accurate shot. Although at one time the two-handed uderhand shot was considered the easiest to make, most players today use the one-hand set shot. Games are often won at the free throw line, and it is essential that such shots be practiced. This is precisely why the two-hand underhand free throw shot has become virtually obsolete. Since the shot is ineffective in a game situation because it is so easily guarded, coaches decry the time spent on practicing it. They prefer instead to have the player use a regular shot and thus receive extra benefit from practicing it.

Dribbling

The skill of dribbling is an important one in basketball, although it is often overused. Every player should be able to dribble well with either hand while making quick stops and starts, and changing direction. If used properly, the dribble provides great maneuverability. (Refer again to "Moving the Body and an Object through Space," chapter five.)

The dribble can be used to advance the ball down the court, to wait for a teammate to get into position, to stall, to break through a press, to clear the ball to the side after a rebound, and to drive for lay-up shots.

However used, the dribble can never be as fast as a pass. Therefore, players should be discouraged from needless dribbling. In some situations it often seems as if a player is impressed with his ability to dribble and he therefore monopolizes the ball. Likewise, many shooters have a bad habit of bouncing the ball before taking a shot. This, too, should be discouraged in most instances.

Body Awareness

1. Body weight should be balanced over the center of gravity and carried low.
2. The knees should be flexed.
3. The head should be up with the eyes focused on the court and on the players, never on the ball.
4. The ball should be in front of the body but slightly toward the dribbling hand side.
5. The ball should be controlled by the fingertips and by wrist action.
6. If necessary, the dribbler's body should be kept between the ball and the opponent.

Space

Personal and general space vary tremendously, depending upon what transpires on the court. If the space is great, the dribbler can maintain an upright position and advance the ball at some distance from the body; if small, the dribbler must crouch and keep the ball low and close to the body.

Force

1. The amount of force required depends upon the distance the ball can rebound from the floor without danger of interception.
2. If it is necessary to keep the ball close to the body, the angle of rebound is approximately ninety degrees and little force is required.
3. If the dribbler can cover a large space, the angle of rebound can be much more acute; thus, the necessary force would be greater.

Time

1. Timing of the dribble depends, again, upon conditions on the court.

2. If great distance is to be covered, or if the dribbler is attempting to outmaneuver an opponent, a rapid impetus can be used.

3. If using the dribble as a stall, it can be executed very slowly.

Flow

The sequence of movements after reception of the ball is a push of the ball to the floor with the dribbling hand while keeping the body weight balanced over the feet, head up and eyes forward. The speed of the running body, the angle of rebound, and the force imparted to the ball vary according to the purpose for which the dribble is being used. Regardless of the purpose, the movement should be continuous and smooth.

Pivots and Turns

Successful feinting, faking and dodging—with or without the ball—depend on the ability to employ the pivot or turn strategically. Although many coaches teach the pivot and front or rear turns separately, the mechanics of all of them are very similar. Perhaps the term "pivot" is most often associated with a player in possession of the ball while "turn" refers to a maneuver without the ball. However, it would seem that such differentiation is unnecessary; therefore, the two terms are used interchangeably in this chapter. Newell and Bennington state that a pivot is the sum total of a reverse turn, a front turn, and a rear turn. They also state that the basic difference between a front turn and a rear turn is that the moving foot is carried forward in the front turn and vice versa in the rear turn.[2]

REVERSE PIVOT OR TURN

This maneuver is most often used as a tactic to enable the offensive player to place his body between the ball and his opponent. As

such, it is most often used as the dribble terminates.

Body Awareness

1. The body is in a crouched position, legs in a forward stride position, knees flexed, and body balanced over the center of gravity.

2. From the stride stop, the rear foot becomes the pivot foot and the front foot can be moved in any direction around it. However, the turn is usually made in the direction of the forward foot (i.e., left foot forward, left turn).

3. The pivot foot may not be moved.

Space

Personal space is limited; therefore, care must be taken not to contact the opponent.

Force

The amount of force required is determined by the magnitude of the turn.

Time

Speed is essential lest the opponent tie the ball.

Flow

From a running stride stop, the rear foot is firmly planted and the front foot starts the entire body moving toward the rear foot. (If the rear foot is the right foot, the body moves to the right and vice versa.) To be most effective, the movement must be a smooth and continuous one.

FRONT PIVOT OR TURN

The primary purpose of this technique is to pivot toward the sideline and thus outmaneuver a guard coming in from the side of the dribbler. It is also used as a dodge or

2. Pete Newell and John Bennington, *Basketball Methods* (New York: Ronald Press Co., 1962), p. 72.

feint when the player is not in possession of the ball.

The analysis of the rear pivot or turn is also correct for the front pivot or turn *with one exception*. In the front pivot or turn, the forward foot is the pivot foot and the rear foot swings forward. Generally a ninety-degree forward turn is sufficient to block out an oncoming guard.

Jumping and Rebounding

The ability to jump obviously underlies effective rebounding. However, rebounding is a sophisticated skill that requires more jumping ability. For this reason the two skills are discussed separately.

JUMPING

Tipping the ball to a teammate in a jump ball situation is a technique that all players should practice, since tie balls occur frequently in a game. Height is an obvious advantage to the jumper, but height alone does not insure skill. (Before proceeding, it is well to review "Moving the Body through Space," chapter 00).

Body Awareness

1. The body is in a low crouched position, with the center of gravity directly over the balls of the feet and the feet in a forward-stride position.
2. The arms hang loosely at the sides with the elbows bent.
3. The head is up so that the eyes can focus on the ball as it is tossed.

Space

Personal space is very limited since, theoretically, no contact with a jumping opponent is allowed. Therefore, the jumper should attempt to jump straight up, thus eliminating any forward or lateral movement.

Force

1. Force is produced by the rapid extension of the legs. The deeper the crouch, the greater the force produced *if the leg muscles are strong.*
2. Extending the arms forcibly upward at the same time as the legs extend adds considerable force to the jump.
3. Only the fingertips should contact the ball; the amount of force of the tip is dependent upon the distance the ball is to travel.

Time

The jump must be timed so that its highest point is reached at the same time the ball reaches its zenith.

Flow

The sequence of movement is from the crouched position to a vertical jump, to a landing on both feet with a flexion of leg joints in order to absorb the shock of contact with the floor.

REBOUNDING

In addition to jumping ability, effective rebounding requires proper positioning and timing.

As soon as a teammate shoots for the basket, the *offensive rebounder* must strive for a position near the backboard which not only takes into account the probable angle of rebound should the shot miss but which also allows him to jump slightly forward as he goes high in the air. The ball should be controlled with the fingertips on an offensive rebound; a player adept at this can often tip the ball directly into the basket.

Timing of the jump is an art which can be developed with consistent, conscientious practice. There is no way to tell a player exactly when to jump.

On a *defensive rebound,* the player should position himself under the board so that he blocks out other offensive players. He, too, should jump slightly forward as well as upward and it is desirable that he place one hand completely over the ball and bring it forcibly down to meet the other hand. If the rebounder, because of a lack of height or the size of his hands, is unable to control the ball in this manner, he should place both hands firmly around the sides of the ball. In either case, he more nearly ensures the inability of opponents to steal the ball or to force a jump ball. The analysis of the skill of rebounding, with the exceptions noted, is the same as that for jumping.

Other Offensive Techniques

In addition to the fundamental skills already discussed, several tactics are basic to almost any offensive system. For the purpose of explaining all of the diagrams which follow, a legend is used.

Offensive players	O^1, O^2
Defensive players	D^1, D^2
Path of ball	- - -▶
Path of player	——▶
Dribble	∿∿∿▸
Screen	——▸
Pivot or feint	⊌ ₢
Line of sight	••••••••
Offensive player with ball	$O^1_\bullet$
Defensive player with ball	$D^1_\bullet$

SCREEN

The screen is a legal move by an offensive player to deter a defensive player's progress in which the offensive player positions himself between his teammate and the defensive player guarding that teammate. Body contact may not occur. Screens may be stationary or moving, inside (toward the lane) or outside (toward the sideline). Because of normal playing positions on the court (fig. 6.6), the simplest screens occur between a forward and a guard playing on the same side of the court. However, screens can become very complex and occur at any place on the court.

Figure 6.7 depicts an outside screen in which O^1 passes to O^2 and then cuts between O^2 and his guard. O^1 then stations himself in such a position that O^2 should be able to roll to the outside of O^1 and perhaps drive for the basket while his guard is left momentarily out of play.

Figure 6.8 depicts a screen by a pass receiver which should allow the original passer (O^1) an unguarded set shot. In this particular case, O^2 pivots and sets a screen against O^1's trailing guard.

Figure 6.9 shows a possibility for a moving screen. O^1 passes to O^2 and then cuts behind O^2's guard. Assuming O^1 and O^2 are fast and adroit ball handlers, they can both roll to the outside (O^1 with his back to the basket) and pass the ball back and forth until O^2 takes a shot.

PICK

A pick is an intentional barrier set against a teammate's guard. This allows the teammate wth the ball to drive around his blocked-out guard or to shoot. In actuality, it is difficult to distinguish between a pick and a screen. The former is usually set up by a player who is not directly involved with the

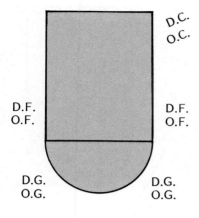

Figure 6.6 **General playing positions: F, forward; G, guard; C, center; O, offense; D, defense.**

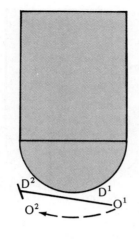

Figure 6.7. **Outside screen**   Figure 6.8. **Screen by receiver**

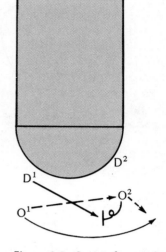

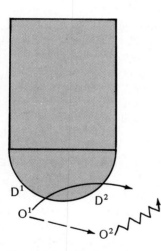

Figure 6.9. **Moving screen**

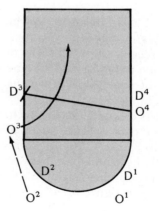

Figure 6.10. **Pick and drive**

ball; the latter, by a player who handles the ball in the process.

Figure 6.10 shows O⁴ setting a pick as O² passes the ball to O³. This should allow O³ to drive to the basket since his guard is temporarily out of the play.

GIVE–AND–GO

The give-and-go is one of the most basic tactics in basketball. A time-honored stratagem, it still works beautifully when players execute it well. It consists simply of a pass to a teammate followed by a cut into an open space for a return pass. Often it takes the pattern of passing to a teammate, follow-

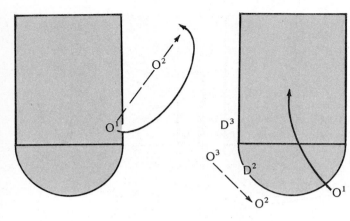

Figure 6.11. **Give-and-go**   Figure 6.12. **Cut**

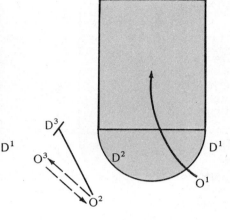

Figure 6.13. **Cut and screen**

ing the pass by going *behind* the teammate, and receiving the ball back from him via a handoff (as diagrammed in figure 6.11).

CUTTING

A cut is employed as an offensive player without the ball suddenly moves into an open space, hoping to receive the ball from a teammate. A cut often follows a fake of some kind, the purpose of which is to leave the defensive player behind.

Figure 6.12 depicts a simple cut in which, as O^3 passes to O^2, O^1 cuts the lane. O^2 has as one of his options to pass to O^1. If for some reason he does not, he could pass back to O^3 and set a screen for an inside roll by O^3. This option is shown in figure 6.13.

FEINT OR FAKE

A feint or fake is a pretense to move in one direction followed by a quick move in another direction. Its purpose is to make the defensive player react and commit himself first. It can be done in conjunction with a pivot, or it can be as simple as a quick shift of body weight, shoulder leading, to one side.

Individual Defensive Skills

Although many of these skills can be employed defensively as well as offensively, some specific individual defensive skills should be explained. The cliché that the best defense is a good offense, although often repeated, is debatable. All other things being equal, a team plays defensively fifty percent of the time; thus it would seem that the development of defensive skills should not be left to chance.

GUARDING AN OPPONENT WITH THE BALL

If an opponent has the ball, the guard must maintain a position between the ball and the basket. How closely the defensive player guards the opponent is dictated primarily by the opponent's position on the floor. If the opponent is in a potential scoring position, he should be guarded closely; if not, the defensive player can play more loosely unless he is pressing for an interception or trying to force a turnover. Other factors, such as the speed and shooting ability of the opponent, are also decisive.

Body Awareness

1. The body is slightly crouched, knees flexed, with the weight over the balls of the feet. One foot is slightly ahead of the other.

2. Sliding steps should be used to move. However, when an opponent starts a drive, the first step should be backward in the same direction.

3. The head should be up with eyes focused on the opponent's face.

4. One hand and arm is generally raised over the ball off the forward foot. The other hand and arm is carried somewhat low on the opposite side of the body. This is the best position for deflecting a shot or stopping an opponent who tries to drive. If the opponent is driving, the defensive player should drop both hands and try for an interception.

Space

Both pesonal and general space are obviously dictated by the position of the other players on the court.

Force

The force required of a defensive player is also dictated, this time primarily by the player he is guarding.

Time

A defensive player must never lose position if he is to be effective. Required speed and the length of time available for maneuvering are dependent upon the individual opponent.

Flow

Whatever sequence of movement is demanded by the situation, it should be smoothly flowing and continuous.

GUARDING AN OPPONENT WITHOUT THE BALL

In a man-to-man defense, a player must be aware of the position of his opponent as well

Figure 6.14. **Defensive stance**

as the position of the ball at all times. If he loses sight of either, his effectiveness is diminished if not entirely lost. Generally, he should stay between the opponent and the basket. An exception to this can occur when guarding a low post player. In this case, it is often desirable for the defensive player to keep the post player directly behind himself in the hopes of preventing a successful pass to the post position.

Basically the elements of movement are the same as those described for guarding an opponent with the ball.

MAJOR CONCEPTS RELATED TO STRATEGY

Mastery of all the individual techniques outlined in this chapter is for naught if the individuals who master them cannot play together as a team. Teamwork requires dedication, sacrifice, selflessness, pride, humility, and a host of other traits which are, if not nonhuman, at least somewhat uncommon. The teacher/coach's most important task is to mold a team from an assortment of individuals.

Player Positions and Responsibilities

CONCEPT N. Proper use of personnel, based on each player's strengths and limitations, is of paramount importance when molding a team.

Sub-Concept N-1. Each player on a team must assume specific responsibilities for the position he is playing.

The five players that make up a basketball team consist of two forwards, two guards, and a center. Generally they are stationed on the offensive court, as shown in figure 6.6, page 117.

THE CENTER

The center is usually, but not necessarily, the tallest player on the team. He should be the best jumper on the team since he is normally the player who jumps center at the beginning of each period.

The center also plays the post or pivot position when his team has the ball. He can play a high (away from the basket) or low (near the basket) post; in addition, he can be joined by a teammate so that there is a double post: both high, both low, or a combination.

The center should master the offensive skills of the hook shot, tip-ins, and push passes; he should be adept at stationing himself in such a way that he can assist in offensive rebounding.

On defense, the center should be an excellent jumper so that he can block shots; he should be fast so that he can get downcourt in time to set up his defense ahead of the offensive center; and he should be able to rebound off the defensive board and quickly throw the outlet pass to one of his teammates. He

needs quick, sure hands. Because of the importance of board play, he should be aggressive and possess good physical strength.

THE FORWARDS

Forwards also should be tall, since they play nearest the basket on offense. They must be adroit ball handlers, speedy, sure-handed, and aggressive. They must master a variety of shots, the dribble, and various tactics to outmaneuver their guards, such as the feint and pivot. They should also possess rebounding ability so that they can help clear the boards at both ends of the court. They must *master* a variety of shots since, normally, the offensive game revolves around them. Because of their vital role in board play they, too, need to possess physical strength.

THE GUARDS

The shortest men on the team are usually the guards and at least one of them is considered the quarterback of the team. He is the one who controls offensive patterns and the offensive tempo.

Guards should be good outside shooters since their shots are generally taken from beyond the free throw lane area. They should be both very fast and good dribblers since they usually lead a fast-break offense.

Defensively, guards should be quick; they should bother the offense and attempt to cause turnovers. Good jumping ability is essential.

Defensive Systems

CONCEPT Q. A system of defense is essential if a team is to be successful. The prime purpose of the defense are to prevent the opponent from scoring and to capitalize on offensive weaknesses.

Sub-Concept Q-1. Team strategies follow a particular planned defensive pattern

based on man-to-man defense or a spatial pattern (zone) defense.

Strategy in basketball can become extremely complex, so intricate that only the most highly skilled can become proficient. However, since this book is geared toward the general teacher and professional student of physical education, only simple strategies are covered. There is no attempt to analyze every conceivable strategical situation which might arise during a game. The section on commonalities in strategy, chapter five, should be reviewed.

Generally, offensive strategies are built around the system of defense employed by the opponents. For this reason, defensive strategy is discussed first.

There are two basic systems of defensive strategy, man-to-man and zone. Variations within each of them are numerous, with each variation requiring different kinds and degrees of abilities. Obviously, then, the skill level of the personnel dictates the particular system to be used in any given circumstance.

MAN–TO–MAN DEFENSE

The pattern of play in a man-to-man defense has evolved in a cycle from a strict type (where a player is assigned an offensive player to guard under all circumstances) to a switching type (where, if circumstances warrant it, defensive players change assignments), back to an assigned man-to-man which is currently probably the most popular defensive system.

Strict man-to-man defense

In this type of defense, players are usually placed according to ability. The most effective defensive player is assigned to guard the highest scoring player on the opposite team. On occasion other factors, such as height and speed, should be considered as well. The primary task of the teacher-coach is to equate abilities as closely as possible.

Each defensive player must keep the person he is assigned to guard, as well as the ball, in his sight. Although this is not always possible, the defensive player who uses open spaces intelligently can usually fulfill this responsibility. The defensive player who turns his back on the ball, even momentarily, is unable accurately to anticipate succeeding moves. If the defensive player's opponent does not have possession of the ball, the defense can guard loosely; the moment the offensive player receives the ball, the guard must play him closely. Any time the offensive player is in a potential scoring position he should be guarded closely, regardless of whether or not he has the ball. As a team, the defensive players on the weak side of the court should converge near the basket to assist the defense on the strong side in case a shot is attempted. Despite the convergence, a defensive player should not lose sight of his assigned man. Figures 6.15 and 6.16 diagram these relationships.

The biggest disadvantage of the strict man-to-man defense is that if the offensive player outmaneuvers the defensive player, there is little chance to prevent scoring. The convergence tactic assists in overcoming this disadvantage since the defensive player's teammates are in a position to assist him.[3]

Switching man-to-man defense

The switching man-to-man defense is also a system in which defensive players are assigned specific offensive players to guard. However, as positions change on the playing floor it sometimes becomes advantageous for defensive players to switch assignments. After a switch is made, the defensive player continues to guard the player to whom he switched until there is an opportunity to re-

3. Newell and Bennington, *Basketball Methods*, pp. 274–276.

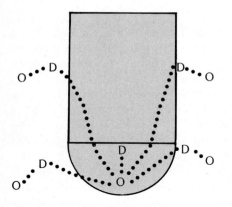

Figure 6.15. **Strict man-to-man defense**

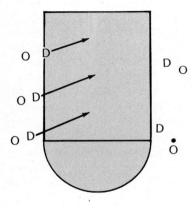

Figure 6.16. **Weak side convergence**

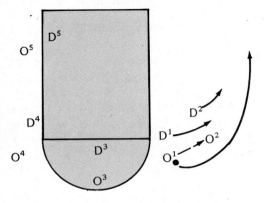

Figure 6.17. **Switching man-to-man defense**

turn to his originally assigned player without fear of an offensive breakthrough.

Generally, such offensive tactics as picks and screens are conducive to defensive switching, as shown in figure 6.17. As O^1 passes to O^2 he follows the pass and goes behind him. It is relatively simple for D^2 to slide to his left and pick up O^1. D^1 then switches to O^2.

Teamwork is essential in any system of defense, and vocal assistance is imperative in switching. Defensive players must talk to each other throughout the entire defensive effort. For example, the defensive player must call for a teammate to switch when it is apparent that he is going to be the victim of an offensive maneuver which takes him temporarily out of play.

ZONE DEFENSES

Although not employed as much as man-to-man defense, systems of zone defense are also very popular. It is undoubtedly possible to build a more effective defense with players of lesser ability if a zone is used since, theoretically, there are always teammates to cover for a player who is outmaneuvered. In addition, players can be placed on the floor in order to take advantage of their specific abilities. For example, the tall, strong rebounder can be assigned the zone closest to the goal, while the speediest guard with quick, sure hands can be assigned the point (the front or top) of the zone.

The particular system of a zone defense varies with the defensive philosophy of the coach, the personnel available, and the offensive pattern of play. A few of the more popular ones are described in the material following.

Two-one-two zone

This is perhaps one of the most popular defenses because it protects the lane, it sets the defensive players in good rebound positions, and it is relatively simple to adjust from this defensive position to a fast-break offense. Its biggest weakness is in its ineffectiveness against good outside shooters. Figure 6.18 shows the area (zone) assigned to each defensive player in this sytem.

Two-two zone with chaser

This zone defense attempts to overcome the basic weakness of the two-one-two while yet maintaining its strong points. Basically the setup is a two-two or box zone with a chaser, the best all-around defensive player, assigned to cover the best offensive player regardless of his movement on the court (fig. 6.19). Thus when the star offensive player enters a particular area in the zone, he is double-teamed. Another advantage of this defense is that the chaser can play his man very aggressively since he is assured of backup assistance.

One-three-one zone

This defense (see figure 6.20) is designed to overcome an offensive pattern which overloads the free throw area, particularly when a high post is employed. It also protects the baseline when the offense deploys players in that area. Its disadvantages are that it spreads the defense so that rebounding effectiveness is minimized, and it tends to be somewhat ineffective against corner shooters.

COMPARING DEFENSES

The type of defense employed depends basically upon the personnel available and the strength of the offense. All other things being equal, most coaches seem to prefer an assigned man-to-man defense around which necessary adjustments are made.

When comparing a man-to-man defense to a zone defense, the following prime differences are apparent.

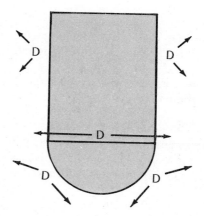

Figure 6.18. **Two-one-two zone**

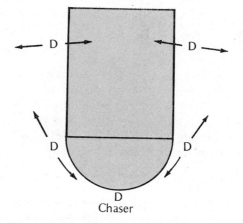

Figure 6.19. **Two-two zone with chaser**

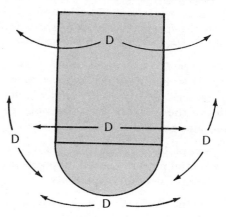
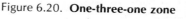

Figure 6.20. **One-three-one zone**

Vision

In a man-to-man defense, visual contact is divided between the ball and an assigned player.

In a zone defense, vision is concentrated primarily on the ball.

Movement and position

In a man-to-man defense, the defensive player moves not only every time his assigned man moves, but also in relation to the ball.

In a zone defense, movement occurs only with the ball; no particular player is watched. If the ball penetrates a specific zone, the defensive player in that zone guards it closely.

Responsibility

In a man-to-man defense, the responsibility is largely centered on an individual.

In a zone defense, even though an area is assigned to a specific individual, it is easier for a teammate to cover for a defensive player who is outmaneuvered.

Offensive Systems

CONCEPT O. In goal-oriented sports a system of offense is essential if a team is to be successful. The prime purposes of an offensive system are to build upon the strengths of the players and to shift the balance of power away from the defense.

Sub-Concept O-1. If and when a player decides that maintaining possession of the ball will gain ground more successfully, the player must be able to dribble, dodge, and feint effectively.

Sub-Concept O-2. Effective passing involves spatial patterns based on positioning of teammates and opponents.

Sub-Concept O-3. Creating spaces is basic to sound team strategy.

Sub-Concept O-4. In order to score it is necessary to place the ball in a strategic position in relation to the goal.

Sub-Concept O-5. Shooting for a goal involves individual and team strategy.

Sub-Concept O-6. Rushing the goal insures follow-up to a shot at the goal.

As stated earlier, the system of offense used is more often than not predicated upon defensive maneuvers. Therefore, various offenses that are successful against specific defenses are analyzed in this section.

OFFENSES AGAINST MAN–TO–MAN DEFENSES

Since the purpose of an assigned man-to-man defense is to keep each offensive player guarded at all times, the offense must attempt to outmaneuver the defense. This can best be done by using screens or picks, by splitting the post, and by employing weaves. Fakes or feints are integral in all these maneuvers.

Screens

As defined on page 116, a screen is a legal move which takes a defensive man momentarily out of play. A screen can be set on the player guarding the forward with the ball or on any defensive player. Screens can be stationary or moving; they can be inside, outside, or rolling.

The *outside screen* is perhaps the easiest one to learn since it involves only passing the ball to a teammate, following the pass toward the outside of the court, going behind the teammate in anticipation of a handoff, and then cutting sharply toward the basket (see figure 6.21). As the teammate O^2 pivots for the handoff to O^1, he screens D^1. In addition, other offensive players can set screens or picks on guards not involved with the ball; in this case, O^3 is screening D^3.

An *inside screen,* as the name implies, is merely a pick (block) which allows the offensive player to move toward the center of the court or inside. As is true with all screens, timing is extremely important. The offensive player who plans to move off the screen must time his movement with the set of the screen. In figure 6.22 O^2 passes to O^3 and then screens on D^3. O^3 can then drive the lane for a possible shot or he can pass to O^1.

Splitting the post

The technique known as splitting the post or rolling around the post is effective only if a high post position is being played. The post player must be adept at faking hand-offs and he should be a good shooter from that position as well, since a shot by him is one of the options. As shown in figure 6.23, O^4 passes to O^2, who has established a high post position. As the pass is thrown, O^1 feints to the outside and then moves directly toward O^2 and cuts inside. O^4 follows the pass and goes outside the post. The post player, O^2, can hand off to either O^1 or O^4, or he can turn around and drive the lane. In this particular situation, O^3 also cuts toward the basket for a possible rebound.

Weave

Another very effective maneuver against a man-to-man defense is the weave, a tactic which incorporates a series of moving screens. Weaves can be done by three, four or five playes. Four-man weaves are probably most often employed, as portrayed in figure 6.24. The weave looks deceptively simple but in reality it is a difficult skill to master. If it is to be successful, the players must:

1. practice the timing of the play so that there is a constant lateral spread and so that the handoff occurs at the side of the lane;

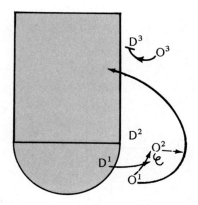

Figure 6.21. **Outside screen**

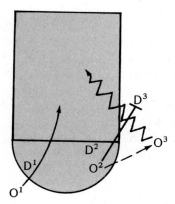

Figure 6.22. **Inside screen**

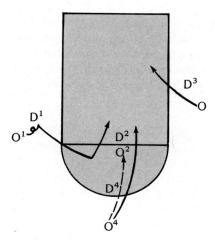

Figure 6.23. **Post split**

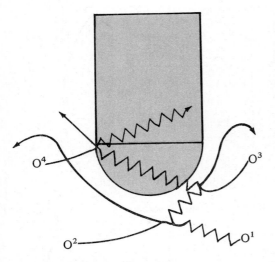

Figure 6.24. **Four-man weave**

2. hand the ball off to the receiver rather than pass it;

3. cut inside the player who receives the ball;

4. follow the inside cut to the side of the court before coming back toward the center for another reception;

5. penetrate on each dribble prior to handing off;

6. shoot as soon as a good opportunity presents itself.

Figure 6.24 shows O^1 dribbling toward O^2, handing the ball off to him, and continuing toward the sideline. O^2 then dribbles toward O^3, hands the ball off and continues toward the sideline. O^3 then repeats the process with O^4, etc.

OFFENSES AGAINST ZONE DEFENSES

The old cliché, "Patience is a virtue," is undeniably true when playing against a zone defense. The offensive players should use short, quick passes hoping that eventually the zone will react late and thus leave the offense open for a shot or at least for a drive. Dribbling and bounce passes should be

avoided in such a situation. In addition, the offense can overload a zone, thus forcing a guard to be concerned with more than one offensive player in his area.

Another very effective weapon against a zone defense is penetration[4]. As defensive players are forced into lateral movement, open spaces develop and offensive cuts can be made into these spaces. The zone is more apt to spread if there is at least one good outside shooter.

Playing the weak side of the zone is another potent offensive weapon. This simply means that two or three offensive players pass the ball back and forth on one side of the court (i.e., an overload). The defense, to be effective, must concentrate on that side of the floor also. If a pass can be quickly thrown to the other side of the floor, the defense may react too slowly to block an open shot or a drive.

Overloading a zone

There are various ways to overload a zone and quite often more than one maneuver is combined for maximal offensive pressure (e.g., an overload plus weak side play).

Figures 6.25 and 6.26 are examples of overload. Figure 6.25 depicts an extreme overload to the right. As O^3 passes to O^4, he runs deep to the baseline. O^2 moves to the same side of the court and O^1 can cut through the lane toward the right. O^5 can move to a low post position. The options available to O^4 are several: he can hand off to O^3 as he goes around; he can pass quickly to O^5 who can, in turn, pass to O^4 and screen for him; or he can pass to the cutting O^1.

Figure 6.26 is another example of an overload setup. As O^2 passes to O^1, O^2 runs to a low post position, O^5 comes across to a high post position, O^3 can start a cut hoping for a

4. Newell and Bennington, *Basketball Methods*, pp. 185–186.

handoff from O^5, and O^4 may or may not cut through the lane. It is probably best for O^4 to stay on the right side of the court so that, should a turnover occur, that side of the court is not completely defenseless.

Playing the weak side of zone

Figure 6.27 is essentially the same pattern as figure 6.25. However, in this case, O^2 penetrates only a very short distance and then quickly retreats and O^1 stays in his original position on the left side of the court. If O^4 can hit O^2 with a quick pass and if O^2 can, in turn, get the ball quickly off to O^1, O^1 should be able to penetrate toward the baseline for an open shot.

Penetrating a zone

Many players seem to be content to stay outside the zone and wait for spaces to open. However, if the defense is really proficient, this may be a long wait. In order, then, to spread the zone, cuts (penetrations) must be made. Figure 6.28 is one example of penetration which features three possible cuts. In this situation, O^3 passes to O^2 and cuts through the lane to the opposite baseline; O^4 penetrates a bit and receives a quick pass back from O^2; O^2 may cut through the lane; O^4 passes quickly to O^5 who, in turn passes to O^3. In addition O^1 can pivot and cut low through the lane as a possible screen for O^5.

Special Game Strategies

Many times during a game specific situations occur which are unique insofar as strategy is concerned. Basically these fall into three categories: jump ball situations, out-of-bounds plays, and free throws.

JUMP BALL SITUATIONS

Every period commences with a jump ball situation. In addition, tie balls, calling for a jump, occur throughout the game. A jump

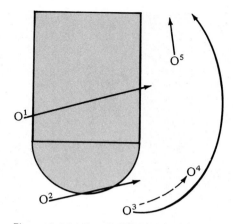

Figure 6.25. **Overloading a zone**

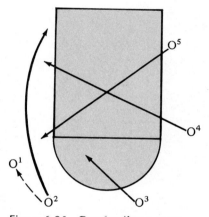

Figure 6.26. **Overloading a zone**

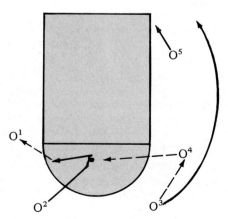

Figure 6.27. **Playing weak side of zone**

BASKETBALL/**127**

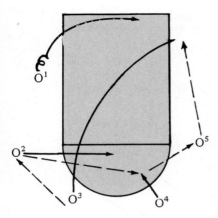

Figure 6.28. **Zone penetration**

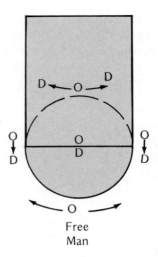

Figure 6.30. **Jump ball, expected defensive tip**

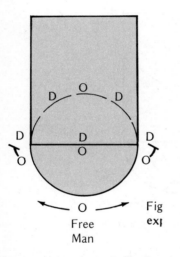

Figure 6.29. **Jump ball, expected offensive tip**

Preferably a team's jumper is able to tip the ball to one of his teammates. However, even though its jumper is outclassed, the team should always consider that the jump is an opportunity to control the ball. Many coaches teach their players to line up one way if they think they can control the tip; another way, if they are in doubt. It is probably best for most teams to use just one alignment with one player free to try to force a hurried turnover, or even retie the ball, if the opponents control the tip. If the opponents do not control the tip, the free man immediately becomes an integral part of the offense.

The unassigned or free player is aided by the knowledge that right-handed jumpers generally tip forward or to their left and vice versa, and that his movements are not directly visible to the opponent's jumper. As shown in figure 6.29, the free man generally stations himself behind his jumping teammate for an offensive tip. If he expects his opponents to control the tip (defensive tip), the opposing jumper's back is to him (fig. 6.30). This basic jump ball pattern can be used for center jumps as well as for tie ball situations.

ball is always taken in one of the restraining circles. Generally, in center jump situations, the best jumper from each team vies for the tip. In tie ball situations, the two players who tied the ball must jump unless one of them was injured and had to leave the game. In both situations, the non-jumpers are entitled to alternate positions around the restraining circle. However, players do not always choose this option.

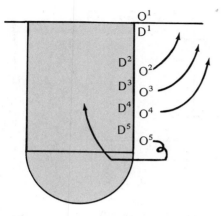

Figure 6.31. Out-of-bounds play

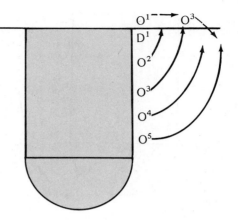

Figure 6.32. Out-of-bounds play

OUT–OF–BOUNDS PLAY

Normally, playing the ball in bounds from the defensive end of the court or from the sidelines is not a particular problem. The prime exception to this occurs with a full court press, a type of defense not covered in this book.

Out-of-bounds play from the offensive end of the court requires attention to specific floor patterns or plays. Again, it is probably best not to try to incorporate several such plays into a team's repertoire. One or two such patterns, with options from them, should be sufficient.

In figure 6.31 the basic pattern is one of four players lining up, one behind the other, just outside the free throw lane. The options for O[1] are several; he may throw to O[2], O[3], or O[4], or even to O[5] if O[5] is successful in getting behind the defense in the lane.

Figure 6.32 depicts an option that can be used when D[1] pressures O[1] to the extent that O[1] cannot pass in bounds. In this case O[3] quickly goes behind the end line to receive an unguarded pass from O[1]; O[3] in turn can pass to O[4] or O[5].

Regardless of the type of pattern play involved in an out-of-bounds ball, the majority of offensive players are usually stacked, either as shown in the diagrams, or across the free throw line, or parallel to the end line. The proximity of the offensive players serves to keep the defense at a disadvantage.

FREE THROW SITUATIONS

The free throw is, of course, an offensive weapon. However, if the free throw is missed, the offense is at a disadvantage since the defensive team's two best rebounders are probably closest to the basket. (The rules dictate that the two spots nearest the basket, one on each side of the lane, belong to the defensive team.) For this reason, all players should attempt to become proficient free throw shooters.

If the free throw is missed, probably the best offensive procedure is for the first line offensive man to attempt to tip the ball back or out and thus try to insure ball possession. It is not too realistic to attempt a goal by tipping the ball in the basket following a missed free throw, since the defensive players are nearer the basket. The logical person to receive a tip-back is the free throw shooter who, after his shot, should step forward. The other two offensive players must play somewhat back for defensive purposes, but

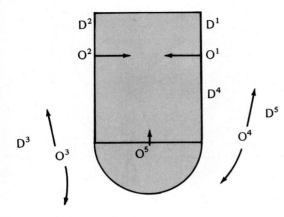

Figure 6.33. **Offense, free throw**

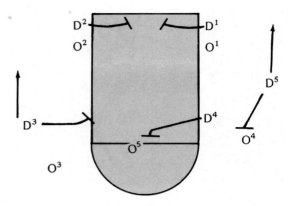

Figure 6.34. **Defense, free throw**

they are available for possible tip-outs to the side. Figure 6.33 depicts these offensive possibilities.

The defensive team should also be prepared for some type of patterned play if a free throw is missed. Basically this involves securing the rebound and throwing an outlet pass to start an offensive effort. In case the rebound is not secured, the defensive team should be ready to attempt to intercept a tip-back. This kind of setup is diagrammed in figure 6.34. D^1 and D^2 position themselves for a rebound while at the same time blocking out O^1 and O^2; D^4 positions himself in front of the shooter in case of a tip-back; D^3 and D^5 can move to the sides for a tip to the side or to block out O^3 and O^4.

INDIVIDUALIZING INSTRUCTION

In addition to following suggestions for indirect, individualized instruction as discussed in chapter three, and using as a model the total development chart and the sample indirect lesson plan in "Volleyball," chapter twelve, as well as the sample exploration problems in "Soccer," chapter eight, perhaps one of the better ways to in-

dividualize instruction is by self-evaluation, peer evaluation and instructor evaluation. Such evaluations can take many forms and can result in written comments and solid statistical information. The worth of any of these techniques is directly proportional to the seriousness with which they are done. Therefore, it is up to the instructor to attempt to teach students how to evaluate themselves and others effectively.

SELF–EVALUATION

Self-evaluation is effective to the degree that the individual is motivated to improve. Although motivation is multifaceted, the instructor plays a large role in the ultimate degree of personal involvement the student feels. The approach to this entire book is predicated upon the instructor's desire to help each sudent to achieve, among other traits, a positive self-image; therefore, it is assumed that self-evaluative tools are looked upon as meaningful and consequently used wisely, well, and often.

The following tests can be self-administered or administered with the assistance of just one other person. Frequent opportunities to engage in this type of testing arise during the teaching of a unit in basketball

| NAME | WEEK I | | | | WEEK II | | | | WEEK VI | | | |
	Free Throw	Jump	Lay-Up	One-Hand Set	Free Throw	Jump	Lay-Up	One-Hand Set	Free Throw	Jump	Lay-Up	One-Hand Set

SHOT CHART
(SELF-EVALUATION)

Figure 6.35

and students should be urged to take advantage of them. It is recommended that markings, such as the target for the wall pass test, be made more or less permanent.

Tests of shooting ability can be very simple and they can be completely self-administered, including scoring and recording. In the example shown (fig. 6.35), students are told to test themselves each week by attempting ten each of the shots listed. They do not all have to be done the same day. If the instructor wishes to include regulations (e.g., each one-hand shot must be taken beyond the top of the free throw lane) he can post a sheet of regulations on the bulletin board next to the tally sheet. This type of instruction should lead to self-direction as well.

Another simple test of shooting ability is a timed one and therefore requires the assistance of one other class member. In this *thirty-second shooting test*, the student may position himself anywhere on the floor and he may use any shot he likes. On the signal "Go" he starts shooting and continues until the timer says "Stop" at the end of the thirty seconds. His score is the total number of goals he makes.

The *wall pass test* measures speed and accuracy of passing (the specific pass can be dictated—e.g., chest pass) as well as eye-hand coordination.[5] The student must stand behind a restraining line drawn ten feet from the wall on which a target is drawn as shown. This test also requires the assistance of another person since it is timed (thirty seconds). On the signal "Go" the student, from behind the restraining line, throws the ball to

5. Harold M. Barrow and Rosemary McGee, *A Practical Approach to Measurement in Physical Education* (Philadelphia: Lea and Febiger, 1971), p. 283.

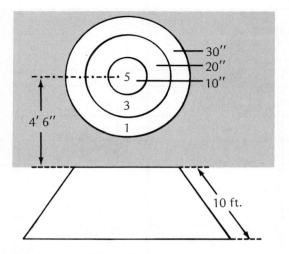

Figure 6.36. **Wall pass test**

INSTRUCTOR EVALUATION

There are many evaluative techniques available for the instructor which, if properly shared with the student, should result in the individualization of teaching. Some of those which result in statistical data are especially helpful in showing an individual how he is performing in relation to the team. Most books on coaching of basketball depict a variety of statistical charts.

Two rather basic charts are shown on page 134. Figure 6.38 is a sample of a single game chart, by individuals, of two skills: shooting and rebounding. Figure 6.39 is a sample accumulative chart, by individuals, of a variety of skills.

the target. He may step over the restraining line to retrieve the ball but he must always be behind the restraining line before another throw is made. At the end of thirty seconds, his score is the accumulation of points he hit on the target.

In addition to passing and shotting self-testing activities, the instructor can set up other tests which measure skills essential in basketball. For example, speed and agility, two highly desirable traits, are measured by standardized tests (such as the A.A.H.P.E.R. Youth Fitness Test) that can be found in many test manuals.

PEER EVALUATION

The example in figure 6.37 is a form of peer evaluation which has been found to be workable, especially with professional physical education students. As can be noted, one evaluator can rate more than one person at a time. If an attempt is made to rate four players simultaneously, it is well to pick two offensive players and two defensive players who are working against each other.

REFERENCES

Barrow, Harold M., and McGee, Rosemary. *A Practical Approach to Measurement in Physical Education.* Philadelphia: Lea & Febiger, 1971.

Cousey, Robert J. and Power, Frank Jr. *Basketball Concepts and Techniques.* Boston, Mass.: Allyn & Bacon, 1970.

Editors of the Basketball Clinic. *A Coaching Treasury from the Basketball Clinic.* West Nyack, N.Y.: Parker Pub. Co., 1974.

Ellis, Cliff. *Zone Press Variations for Winning Basketball.* West Nyack, N.Y.: Parker Pub. Co., 1975.

Haskins, Mary Jane. *Evaluation in Physical Education.* Dubuque, Iowa: Wm. C. Brown Company, Publishers, 1971.

Miller, Kenneth, and Horky, Rita. *Modern Basketball for Women.* Columbus, Ohio: Charles E. Merrill Publishing Co., 1970.

National Association for Girls and Women in Sport, *Basketball Guide.* Washington, D.C.: A.A.H.P.E.R. Press. (Current Edition).

Diagnostic Checklist—Basketball Skills

Date _____ Rater _____

Skill	G — Good F — Fair P — Poor	Player:			Player:			Player:			Player:		
		G	F	P	G	F	P	G	F	P	G	F	P
A. BALL HANDLING													
1. Handles ball lightly and easily													
2. Fingers spread on ball													
3. "Gives" when catching ball													
4. Avoids turnovers													
B. BOUNCING													
1. Keeps head up													
2. Controls ball with fingertips													
3. Bounces only when necessary													
C. PASSING													
1. Uses short, quick passes													
2. Uses a variety of passes													
3. Fakes effectively													
4. Passes to space ahead of receiver													
5. Follows through after pass													
D. SHOOTING													
1. Focuses on target													
2. Follows through with arms and fingers													
3. Arc is high enough													
4. Avoids bad shots													
5. Shoots on opportunity													
E. GUARDING													
1. Uses sliding steps—all directions													
2. Shifts with each pass													
3. Low stride position—hands up													
4. Not easily faked out of position													
5. Maintains correct position in defensive pattern													
6. Covers for teammates													
F. EVADING OPPONENT													
1. Uses feints to advantage													
2. Pivots effectively													
3. Moves into space to receive pass													
4. Breaks off cuts at right time													
5. Pulls opponent out, then breaks													
G. THINKS BASKETBALL!													

COMMENTS:

Adapted from M. C. Resick, B. L. Seidel, J. A. Mason, *Modern Administrative Practices in Physical Education and Athletics* (Reading, Mass.: Addison-Wesley Publishing Co., Third Edition, 1979). Reprinted courtesy of Addison-Wesley Publishing Co.

Figure 6.37. **Diagnostic checklist**

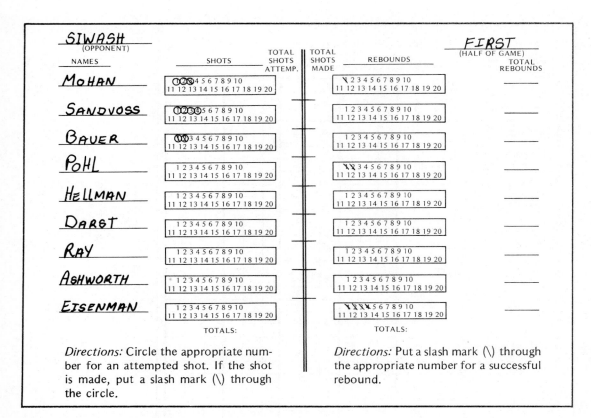

Figure 6.38. **Shots and rebounds chart**

NAME __J. BROWN__

GAME	TIME PLAYED	SHOTS			FREE THROWS			REBOUNDS		P.F.	"MARKS" AGAINST			"MARKS" FOR		
		S.A.	S.M.	PCT.	S.A.	S.M.	PCT.	OFF.	DEF.		BAD PASS	VIOL.	FUM.	HELD BALL	RECOV.	ASSIST
SIWASH	5:30	12	8	66	3	1	33	0	2	2	1	0	0	1	1	2
	8:00	4	1	25	0	—	—	4	2	2	0	2	1	0	0	4
BONNE																

Figure 6.39. **Accumulative skill chart**

National Collegiate Athletic Association. *Official Basketball Rules and Interpretation.* Shawnee Mission, Kansas: N.C.A.A. Publishing Department. (Current Edition).

Neal, Patsy, *Basketball Techniques for Women.* New York: The Ronald Press Co., 1966.

Newell, Pete, and Bennington, John. *Basketball Methods.* New York: The Ronald Press Co., 1962.

Richards, Jack. *Treasury of Basketball Drills from Top Coaches.* West Nyack, N.Y.: Parker Pub. Co., 1971.

Resick, M. C., Seidel, B. L. and Mason, J. *Modern Administrative Practices in Physical Education and Athletics.* Reading, Mass.: Addison-Wesley, 1979.

Schaafsma, Frances. *Basketball for Women.* Dubuque, Iowa: Wm. C. Brown Company, Publishers, 1977.

Severson, Marlowe and Erickson, Terrill. *Let's Teach Defense, "Read the Offense."* St. Cloud, Mn.: May Printing Co., 1976.

————. *Let's Teach Offense,* "Read the Defense." St. Cloud, Mn.: May Printing Co., 1976.

Sharman, Bill. *Sharman on Basketball Shooting.* Englewood Cliffs, N.J.: Prentice-Hall, 1965.

Stutts, Ann. *Women's Basketball.* Pacific Palisades, Calif.: Goodyear Publishing Co., 1973.

Vannier, Maryhelen, and Poindexter, Hally Beth. *Physical Activities for College Women.* Philadelphia: W. B. Saunders Co., 1964.

West, Jerry. *Basketball My Way.* Englewood Cliffs, N.J.: Prentice-Hall, 1973.

Wilkes, Glenn. *Basketball for Men.* Dubuque, Iowa: Wm. C. Brown Company, Publishers 1967.

Wooden, John. *Practical Modern Basketball.* New York: Word Books, 1973.

7

Field Hockey

INTRODUCTION

Field hockey is a space game. The space of a large, outdoor turf field is shared by two teams of eleven players each. The purpose of the game is for each team to make efficient use of the field space in attempting to outwit, outmanuever, and outscore the opposing team. The playing field measures 100 yards long and 60 yards wide (91.4 meters × 55 meters). Field markings are shown in figure 7.1.

Of the eleven players on each team, five are forwards, three are halfbacks, two are fullbacks and one is the goalkeeper. The forwards' responsibility is to attempt to score goals. The forwards are the left wing (LW), left inner (LI), center forward (CF), right inner (RI), and right wing (RW). The halfbacks and fullbacks have two basic responsibilities: to prevent the opposing forwards from scoring, and to assist their own forwards in scoring. The halfbacks and fullbacks are the left halfback (LH), center halfback (CH), right halfback (RH), left fullback (LFB), and right fullback (RFB). The goalkeeper (G) has primary responsibility for the defense of her goal, making every possible effort to prohibit any opponent from scoring. The spatial relationship of these players to one another is also shown in figure 7.1.

Field hockey is a goal-oriented game. Each player on the two teams wields a stick with a curved distal end, which is used to propel a small, hard ball downfield and into the opponent's goal. A goal is scored each time the ball passes over the goal line into the goal cage after being touched by an attacking player within the striking circle. The team with the higher number of goals at the conclusion of playing time is the winner.

Field hockey is a game of time. An official game of field hockey is seventy minutes in duration, divided into two equal playing

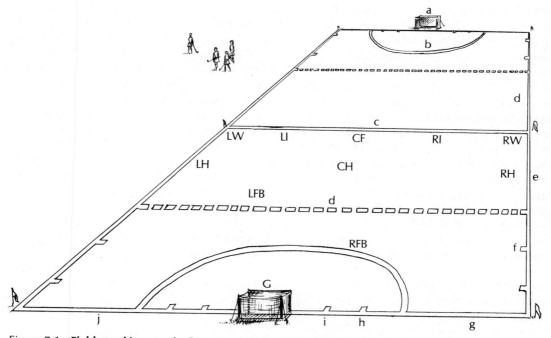

Figure 7.1. **Field markings and player positions: (a) goal cage, (b) striking circle, (c) centerline, (d) twenty-five-yard line, (e) sideline, (f) sixteen-yard mark, (g) five-yard line for long corner, (h) ten-yard mark for penalty corner, (i) five-yard mark, (j) goal line. Player positions are initialed accordingly.**

halves. The game is unique in that time-outs and substitutions are not permitted except in the case of incapacitating injury.[1]

In addition to a regulated playing time, a personal awareness of proper timing is essential in the successful execution of individual skills and team plays.

Field hockey is a game of force. Successful play in field hockey requires knowledge and application of the concepts of force production and force absorption. The degree of force desired in sending the ball varies with the purpose of the hit. Maximum force is desired when passing to a distant teammate, clearing the ball away from the defending goal, or shooting at the attacking goal. A lesser degree of force is desired when executing evasive maneuvers around defenders, passing to nearby teammates, or

propelling the ball downfield by dribbling. Absorption of force is important as a player attempts to field or control a ball coming toward her. Better players are able to field balls hit with varying degrees of force, and can field balls approaching from any direction.

Field hockey is a smoothly flowing, running game. Seldom is play stopped during the game, and rarely do players stop moving. Whether on offense or defense, near the attacking or defending goal, all players constantly must reposition in relation to teammates, opponents and the ball. It is in this continual movement of all players that the

1. Note exception in the "Rules, Changes, Notes and Modifications" section of current N.A.G.W.S. rules.

uninterrupted flow of the game is evidenced.

Field hockey offers personal challenge, camaraderie, and opportunity for the highly skilled player to progress into advanced play. Each participant in field hockey faces three major challenges: (1) the acquisition and mastery of specific individual skills; (2) the requisite for physical stamina; and (3) an understanding of the strategy of the game. The degree to which each of these challenges is met determines the effectiveness of one's contributions to the evolvement of comprehensive patterns of offensive and defensive team play. At its finest, field hockey is an artistic blend of eleven players in harmonious teamwork interspersed with individual initiative.

One of the strong points in women's field hockey organization throughout the world is maintenance of the club philosophy. In the United States, local clubs are affiliated with the United States Field Hockey Association and welcome all field hockey participants age eighteen or over, regardless of skill or previous experience. Opportunities for game play and participation in various social activities are offered by all clubs to all members. Clubs throughout the world seek to promote sportsmanship, enjoyment, and recreation through field hockey.

Opportunities are provided for all highly skilled players to progress into higher levels of competition. Players may be selected to represent their club on an association team, their association on a sectional team, or their section on a national team. Those who are selected to play on the United States first or second teams have a further opportunity to compete in international play supervised by the International Federation of Women's Field Hockey Associations, and to represent the U.S.A. in the Olympic Games.

The organizational structure of the United States Field Hockey Association has made provision for all hockey enthusiasts, whether their goal is to represent the United States in international play, or to simply enjoy the challenge, exercise, friendship and competition offered by a weekend club match. It is this enjoyment which makes the game an endearing one to its participants.

To reap maximum enjoyment from the game, certain understandings are necessary. The following discussion of common concepts related to field hockey, basic skill techniques, strategy, and safety is designed to aid the beginning student. The section on teaching field hockey is designed to aid the teacher in planning a meaningful learning experience through an indirect approach.

The following explanation of symbols will be useful in understanding the various diagrams used throughout the chapter.

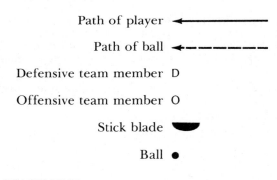

Path of player	←
Path of ball	←- - - -
Defensive team member	D
Offensive team member	O
Stick blade	◗
Ball	●

EQUIPMENT
Field hockey is a game which utilizes unique equipment.

Ball

An official field hockey ball is composed of cork and twine covered with white leather. Plastic-covered balls or composition balls are popular for practice sessions, while soft rubber pudding balls are available for indoor use.

Stick

Hockey sticks commonly range in length from thirty-five inches to thirty-seven inches. They are usually made of ash or mulberry and have a rubber or towel grip on the non-curved end. All hockey sticks have a flat left blade surface and a rounded right blade surface. Only the flat side of the stick may be used legally in contacting the ball.

Two styles of hockey sticks are currently in use. The English-head stick has a long blade; the Indian-head stick has a shorter, more compact blade which facilitates maneuverability, and thus is the more popular of the two (fig. 7.2).

Teachers and coaches should be more cognizant of the important relationship between proper stick length and performance, and make every possible effort to equip each player correctly. Two important considerations in choosing a stick for play are: the stick should afford a player the longest reach possible, thereby allowing greater territorial coverage and increasing the force potential of the lever arm; and a stick of proper length should allow a player to hit through the ball without striking the ground behind or topping the ball.

Shin guards

Beginning players, especially, should be required to wear shin guards. They provide both physical and psychological protection to the player whose inadequate stickwork permits a ball to hit her legs or ankles. It is unfortunate, but understandable, that some players develop a dislike for the game when they are not provided with the equipment to make participation safe and enjoyable.

Goalkeeper's equipment

Goalkeepers wear full-length leg pads with the addition of reinforced boots or kickers for the feet. A padded goalie glove for

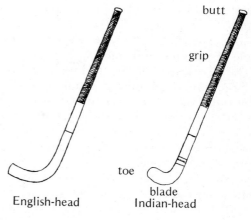

Figure 7.2

use in hand stops should also be made available.

Uniform

A typical uniform for the competing player is composed of a kilt and blouse, knee socks and cleated shoes. Goalkeepers most often wear warm-up pants rather than kilts for warmth and protection from the buckles and straps of the leg pads. Warm clothing should be kept handy for all players, as cold weather seldom stops the hockey enthusiast.

Tunics, shorts or any items of clothing which allow freedom of movement are suitable for participation in field hockey.

MAJOR CONCEPTS

A mechanical analysis of the total game of field hockey could prove to be a lengthy one. It is a game influenced by the external forces of gravity, air resistance and friction. All three of Newton's laws have specific application to various aspects of the game, and linear, rotary and curvilinear forms of motion are evidenced. All the factors of stability are utilized. Field hockey is a game of force calling for adherence to the principles of force production and force absorption; likewise, the instances of rebound require an understanding of ideas related to the angle of rebound and spin.

The locomotor skills of starting, running, sliding, jumping, stopping, changing directions and landing, the manipulative movements of striking, kicking, projecting and receiving, and a combination of various locomotor and manipulative movements are essential in field hockey.

General information concerning these factors has been conceptualized in chapter five. The discussion which follows further defines and relates the common concepts of chapter five to field hockey.

CONCEPT A. Moving the body with control involves a conscious manipulation of the center of gravity in relation to the base of support, either to maintain stability or to initiate locomotor movement, as the situation demands.

Sub-concept A-1. Staying ready to move allows a player to get a faster start in order to outmaneuver the opponent, to gain possession of the ball, or to get into a desirable position to project an object.

Sub-concept A-2. Enlarging the base of support in the direction of the force allows a player to start, stop, and change directions quickly.

Sub-concept A-3. Running in a forward direction is the quickest way to cover a distance of some magnitude.

Sub-concept A-4. Sliding sideways or in a diagonally forward or backward direction is often a more efficient manner of moving the body through space if the distance to be covered is minimal and if the body needs to remain facing the immediate objective.

Sub-concept A-5. Recovering quickly after the execution of a skill involves reassuming the ready position and relocating oneself in space in the home position, or some other advantageous position, in order to stay alert and ready to react again.

Sub-concept A-6. Propelling the body through space requires a firm reacting surface and sufficient friction between the reacting surface and the base of support.

Good body control in field hockey is necessary not only for efficient and successful performance, but it is required by the rules. The mere task of running downfield at top speed requires a certain degree of body control in itself; however, the addition of a striking implement, the required use of that implement in fielding and projecting a small object, and the congestion caused by opponents necessitates an even greater degree of control. The rules do not allow body contact of any kind (pushing, tripping, shoving, etc.), disallow any body part from contacting the ball except the hand (advancing), and deny a player the right to come between her opponent and the ball (obstruction). See figure 7.3.[2]

Seldom should a field hockey player establish a stationary position. From the beginning bully to the final whistle, she is constantly in motion, covering or creating spaces, drawing or outmaneuvering opponents, repositioning for every play. One of the most frequent errors committed by beginners is the tendency to reposition the ball in relation to the "too stable" body. By keeping the feet in constant motion and taking

2. Official rules are printed in the National Association for Girls and Women in Sport, *Field Hockey-Lacrosse Guide* (Washington, D.C.: Alliance Association for Health, Physical Education & Recreation). Published every two years.

very quick, small steps, one is able to reposition the body in relation to the ball, thereby gaining an invaluable time advantage over the player with lazy feet. A player in constant motion also gains a mechanical advantage over her stationary counterpart since she has already overcome the inertia of the stationary position.

A forward who is trying to gain a one-step advantage on her defender can most easily do so by keeping her feet pointing in the direction of the attacking goal. By maintaining this foot position, she can dart forward and continue in motion while her defender must stop and pivot before she can start after her. A forward who pays little attention to her intended direction gains no advantage as she, too, must turn goalward before progressing.

All players are required continually to relocate their positions with each change in ball position. The home position in field hockey does not refer to a particular spot on the field; instead it refers to a relative position in relation to the ball, the player's position on the field and location of both teammates and opponents. Whether recovering from the execution of an individual skill or from the results of a team play, the action must be immediate.

Part of the challenge of field hockey is one's ability to adapt to the differences in playing surfaces. While the condition of most fields cannot be guaranteed, a player may choose the most appropriate footwear for the given conditions and thereby increase the friction, reactive force and safety. Hard rubber or plastic cleats best penetrate the field's grassy cover, thereby making the ground underneath the actual contacting surface.

CONCEPT B. Creating and absorbing force to control the movement of the

Figure 7.3. **Obstruction foul**

body through space may involve all of the body or only parts of the body, in unison or in sequence; however, the relaxation of noncontributing muscle groups is imperative for smooth, efficient movement.

Sub-concept B-1. A smooth transfer of momentum from one part of the body to another part, or to the total body, results in sustained movement, while an explosive transfer of momentum increases the speed and/or magnitude of the resulting movement.

Sub-concept B-2. Absorbing the force of a landing or fall over a greater time and distance increases stability and decreases the chance of injury.

Sub-concept B-3. Relaxing noncontributing muscle groups leads to smooth, efficient movement and thus to the proficiency of the performance.

CONCEPT C. A player must be in a desirable position in relation to the object to be projected.

Few sports require the use of an implement as long as a field hockey stick. As an integral part of an individual's total movement pattern, the stick provides an extended reach, thereby allowing the ball to be played some distance from the body.

Since all sticks are right-handed, they are more comfortably and more efficiently positioned for play slightly to the right side of the body. The ball is contacted ahead of the feet and slightly to the right. Most ball contacts occur as both body and ball are in motion, thus increasing the degree of difficulty and calling for a keen sense of kinesthetic and spatial awareness. Teachers and students should note that practice of the drive, push pass or flick is of greatest benefit when executed from a moving, rather than stationary, position.

Poor ball-stick-body relationships during the dribble may be the result of a misunderstanding concerning the intent or purpose of the skill. Many beginners like to think of the dribble as a hit-and-run stroke, but since its purpose is to propel the ball with control, while at the same time protecting it from opponents, the ball-stick-body relationship must be a close one. Although the ball is kept in close proximity, it is imperative to keep it well away from the feet so that a smooth, forward running stride is maintained.

Proper footwork allows the player to maneuver her stick in presenting the legal flat side to the ball and permits her to reposition in relation to the opponent and ball in preventing obstruction. Head placement over the ball prevents lofting.

CONCEPT D. Creating force: The production and transfer of force depend upon mass, speed, and the striking surface used.

Sub-concept D-1. Increasing the mass used to produce force increases the force produced.

Sub-concept D-2. Increasing the speed of the implement or the body segment imparting force increases the force produced.

Sub-concept D-3. Increasing the range of movement of the body segment or the implement imparting force increases the distance through which speed can be developed, as well as the force imparted to the object.

Sub-concept D-4. Setting the body in motion prior to contact with an object, or to the release of an object, builds greater force which in turn is transferred to the object. However, at the instant of contact or release, the body should be stabilized.

Sub-concept D-5. A follow-through allows for greater force to be transferred to an object.

Sub-concept D-6. Stabilizing the body segments involved in an action allows for greater force to be imparted to the object.

Sub-concept D-7. A firm striking surface allows for greater force to be imparted to the object.

When maximum force production is required, such as for a shot at goal, a wing-to-wing pass, or a clearing drive from fullback to wing, a combination of all force-producing elements is utilized. The body is moving prior to contact; the full legal backswing is taken (the stick may not be raised above shoulder level); the trunk and arm rotation occurs in sequential order, increasing the force potential and speed of the implement; the arms are extended, increasing the lever arm; the wrists snap at contact and further increase the speed of the implement; the hands, wrists and elbows are firm, allowing minimum force absorption at contact; the weight is shifted onto the forward foot as the hit is made to continue the force potential created by the buildup of momentum; and a follow-through is utilized to prohibit the lever arm from decelerating prior to contact (the stick may not be raised above shoulder level).

When less force is required, the player has the option of eliminating some of the force-producing elements while still using the drive or choosing a stroke of less potential force. The push pass, flick and drive are arranged in order from least forceful to most forceful, and from least time-consuming to most time-consuming in execution. The problem for players then becomes not so much how to produce force, but how to produce the degree of force desired. Many beginning players have a tendency to overuse the drive, when other strokes could be executed more quickly and effectively.

CONCEPT E. Directing force: The direction in which an object moves is determined by the point at which force is applied in relation to the object's center of gravity.

Sub-concept E-1. Applying force directly through the center of gravity of an object results in a straight trajectory; an off-center application of force produces a curved trajectory.

Sub-concept E-2. Keeping one's eyes on the object (i.e., objective focus or tracking) facilitates the application of force in line with the intended direction of flight or the absorption of force when slowing or stopping an object. However, if the performer is throwing or striking at a target, he must focus on the target rather than on the projectile.

Sub-concept E-3. Contacting an object with a large, flat surface facilitates ap-
plying force directly through the center of gravity in the direction desired.**

Sub-concept E-4. External forces such as gravity, air resistance, and friction alter the flight of a projectile.

The relative length of the blade of a hockey stick decreases the possibility of hitting the ball to the right or left of the center of gravity. Improper positioning of the ball in relation to the body and stick or poor choice of stick length may cause the player to top the ball or hit the ground behind it. By not hitting directly through the center of gravity, both force and direction may be affected. To obtain optimal force for a hit in the desired direction the flat portion of the blade should face in the direction of the hit at impact.

To control a ball moving over the irregular surface of a hockey field at tremendous speed demands concentration and adherence to the principle of objective focus. Because the body is pulled into a forward position when the stick is in playing position, the player is deprived of the advantages of peripheral vision as she fields the ball. This fact necessitates that the player look up after controlling the ball in order to analyze the positions of teammates and opponents, choose an appropriate target, and then redirect her focus on the ball as contact is made.

Another challenge facing the field hockey player is her ability to adapt to the various external forces affecting the motion of the ball. While gravity and air resistance are relatively constant factors, the difference in friction of various playing surfaces is a problem with which players must contend. The irregularity of the playing surface, length of grass and dampness of the soil are the usual factors related to friction. With the advent of artificial playing surfaces these factors are minimized. Weather conditions are a major factor affecting the frictional relationships between ground and ball and ground and player. Wet or muddy fields offer greater resistance to the motion of the ball, thus slowing the ball down. A hard, frozen field offers little resistance to the ball's motion, allowing the ball to travel at great speed. In contrast, a player's efficient movement is dependent upon a firm, reactive surface. Water, mud, or ice on a field alter the nature of the reactive surface and slow the player's movement.

CONCEPT F. Sending the ball to a receiver who is moving requires directing the ball to an open space ahead of him.

CONCEPT G. To receive an object which is moving through space a performer must slow or stop its motion by absorbing all or part of its force.

Beginners must be carefully instructed to control the ball before redirecting it to another target. While the rules mandate this action in some instances (e.g., in receiving a corner hit), it is a matter of safety whenever a ball approaches a player. To prevent dangerous and forceful lofting of the ball back in the direction from whence it came, an attempt must be made to absorb its force.

CONCEPT H. Three techniques help the performer to absorb force efficiently: (1) establishing a stable position; (2) utilizing the largest possible surface area; and (3) increasing the time or distance over which the force is received.

Sub-concept H-1. A stable position should be maintained as the force of an object is absorbed.

Sub-concept H-2. A large surface area reduces the force that is received by any one area of that surface.

Sub-concept H-3. Moving the receiving surface with the ball upon contact (giving with the ball) allows force to be absorbed over a greater time and distance.

CONCEPT I. Since the purpose of the dribble is to maintain possession of the ball while moving through space, the amount and direction of force applied to the ball must be controlled.

CONCEPT K. In order to reach the desired goal in the shortest possible time, the dribbler must move in a direct pathway; however, intervening opponents and other variables on occasion cause the dribbler to maneuver in flexible, nondirect pathways.

CONCEPT L. Although there is a distinct rhythmic pattern involved in dribbling, the tempo may increase or decrease as a pattern of play evolves.

CONCEPT M. Although the dribbler must focus his eyes on the ball during contact, he must also survey the playing area in order to be able to change tactics as the situation demands.

BASIC SKILL TECHNIQUES IN FIELD HOCKEY

THE GRIP

A proper grip on the field hockey stick aids a performer in executing all of the basic skills correctly. Once correctly attained, the position of the left hand seldom changes on the stick; the right hand may slide up or down the stick, depending upon the particular skill being attempted.

To achieve the proper grip, the right hand holds the stick in front of the body, parallel to the ground, with the flat side of the blade facing left and the toe of the stick facing up. From this position, the left hand grasps the butt end of the stick with a firm but comfortable "handshake" hold. The thumb and fingers wrap around the stick and the butt end of the stick rests in or near the palm of the left hand (fig. 7.4). While maintaining this left-hand position the stick is lowered so that it is perpendicular to the ground, and the blade is rotated one-quarter turn clockwise so that it faces forward. The right hand is now placed on the grip. A low position of the right hand improves control of the stick, but restricts vision and ease of movement because the head and upper trunk are inclined so far forward. A high position of the right hand on the stick provides maximum vision and efficiency of movement while running, but reduces the control of the blade end of the stick. Each player must choose a position of the right hand which is most comfortable and efficient for her. Again, the thumb and fingers wrap around the stick.

If the grip is correct, the palms of both hands face each other, the left palm facing the body, the right palm facing forward, away from the body. The grip is firm but not tight (fig. 7.5).

The most common error in the grip is allowing the left hand to rotate counterclockwise, which in turn causes the palm to face either to the player's right or forward. This error ultimately affects the player's ability to produce and absorb force efficiently.

Force-Producing Skills

The dribble, drive, push pass, scoop and flick are force-producing skills which propel the ball varying distances away from the player. The initial body position, grip and body-stick-ball relationships are similar for each, which aids in the deceptiveness in executing each different stroke.

The purpose of the stroke determines the degree of force desired and where that

Figure 7.4. **Left-hand grip**

force is applied to the ball. The dribble, push pass, and flick, for example, are very similar except that the dribble utilizes fewer force-producing elements than the push pass and the flick uses more force-producing elements than the push pass. The scoop differs only in the point of application of force, and the drive differs appreciably only in the degree of force desired.

The timing of each stroke is crucial in that the body must be in proper position to apply the desired force, and stability must be maintained; however, the actual moment of contact can be varied to deceive the defense.

Each stroke is usually performed while a player is moving, thus continuing the flow of the game. It is when a player stops to execute a skill that the defense has time to position for the interception. After a stroke has been completed, it is important that the player reposition in relation to the new ball position, thus continuing the flow of movement.

Figure 7.5. **Correct placement of both hands on stick**

THE DRIBBLE

The dribble is a controlled means of propelling the ball at maximum speed along the ground with the field hockey stick.

Body Awareness

The trunk is inclined forward enough so that the blade of the stick just skims the grass. The head is in continual motion, first down while the player focuses on the ball during contact, then up to scrutinize the position of teammates and opponents. The

Figure 7.6. **Front view, dribble**

knees are flexed slightly and the weight is forward on the balls of the feet.

Space

The ball should be contacted in front and slightly to the right side of the body. The ball must be kept far enough away from the dribbler's feet so as not to interfere with the running stride, but it must also be kept close enough so that immediate control is possible when an opponent approaches. The proper distance can be established by reaching as far forward as possible with the left shoulder and arm while still keeping the stick perpendicular to the ground (fig. 7.6).

Time

It seems most natural to tap the ball with every other stride; however, this is a matter of individual preference. The irregularity of the playing surface, placement of opponents, and changes in the dribbler's tempo all affect the timing of each tap.

Force

The arms work in opposition in a pushing-pulling motion to provide force for the dribble. The left arm supplies most of the force while the right arm serves mainly to control the blade end of the stick. The left elbow is held high and away from the body,

Figure 7.7. **Side view, dribble action**

remaining relatively stable, and should not be allowed to collapse in toward the body. The left wrist is flexible, permitting increased motion at the blade end of the stick. As the left hand, wrist and forearm pull the butt end of the stick toward the body, the right arm may push the blade end of the stick forward slightly (fig. 7.7).

By allowing the left elbow to collapse in toward the body, the right arm becomes the major propelling force. The stick is no longer perpendicular to the ground, but rather inclined back toward the dribbler. This results in a scooping action of the ball and interferes with the running stride. The correct position of the left arm aids a player in reaching out for the ball, thus enabling her to keep it farther from her feet and increasing the speed of the dribble.

The ball should be tapped rather than hit. When a player breaks free, she may tap the ball harder, allowing it to travel farther from her feet, thus permitting her to move faster. This latter action is referred to as a loose dribble and control is sacrificed in favor of speed. While its use is limited, there are occasions where the loose dribble is valuable.

Flow

The dribble is a smooth, continuous series of taps. The movement flows from the arms and wrists to the stick to the ball.

DRIVES

A drive is a means of forcefully projecting the ball along the ground. It may be used for passing to distant teammates, for shooting at the goal, for free hits, corner hits, and defense hits. The terms, left, straight, and right drive, refer to the direction the ball is driven away from the player's body. (See figures 7.8, 7.9, 7.10).

Body Awareness

The right hand may remain low on the stick for a hands-apart drive or may slide up the stick to a position adjacent to the left hand. The head is kept over the ball at contact, and the left shoulder points in the direction of the hit.

Space

The ball is placed forward of the left foot for a drive to the left and slightly to the right of the right foot for a straight drive. In executing a right drive, the player overruns the ball to position it behind and to the right of her right heel.

Figure 7.8. **Hands-apart straight drive at moment of impact**

Time

The timing of the hit should correspond with the ball's placement about twelve inches in front of the left foot for a left drive, its parallel position to the right foot for a straight drive, and its position about twelve inches diagonally to the rear of the right foot for a right drive. A shorter backswing lessens the time of execution but sacrifices force.

Force

The hands slide together at the top of the stick, thus increasing the length of the lever. The upper trunk rotates to the right in the

Figure 7.9. **Left drive**

Figure 7.10. **Right drive**

backswing, increasing the time and distance over which momentum can be built. The degree of trunk rotation depends upon the drive being executed; the left drive requires minimal trunk rotation, the straight drive calls for an increase in trunk rotation, and the right drive requires maximum trunk rotation in order to hit the ball. The backswing cannot legally permit any part of the stick to be raised above shoulder level. Bending the right elbow and right wrist and maintaining a firm left wrist during the backswing help to prohibit the stick from being raised above shoulder level (fig. 7.11).

Figure 7.11. **Bending right elbow and wrist to help prevent "sticks"**

The weight of the body transfers from the back foot during the backswing to the forward foot at contact, thereby further increasing the range of motion and flattening the arc of the swing. This not only aids force production, but helps to ensure that the ball will travel along the ground after contact. Keeping the head over the ball at contact helps keep the body weight on the forward foot and aids in preventing lofted balls.

The follow-through is in the direction of the hit, with the wrists held firm to prevent raising the stick above shoulder height.

Flow

The action is continuous from the running motion during the dribble, to the drive, and back to a running motion. During the drive, movement flows from the upper trunk to the arms and wrists to the stick to the ball. Following ball contact a forward step is taken to maintain balance.

PUSH PASS

A push pass is a quick, deceptive means of passing the ball over short distances (fig. 7.12).

Body Awareness

Refer to the dribble.

Space

Refer to the dribble. The stick is placed in contact with the ball.

Time

A push pass is usually executed directly from the dribble. The deceptiveness of the

Figure 7.12. **Push pass**

Figure 7.13. **Scoop**

stroke is enhanced if the rhythmical tapping of the ball during the dribble is maintained until the push pass is attempted. No backswing is required, thus facilitating quickness and deception.

Force

The left forearm and wrist pull back toward the body while the right hand and arm extend away from the body, keeping the ball in contact with the stick as long as possible. The ball is not hit, but pushed or swept along the ground in the intended direction. The follow-through is low, with the arms extended away from the body as far as possible.

Flow

The push pass is a smooth, continuous movement. Movement flows from the arms and wrists to the stick to the ball.

SCOOP

The scoop is a stroke designed to loft the ball legally. The ball may be raised just high enough to clear an opponent's stick for a dodge, or high enough to be sent into the upper corners of the goal cage for a score. (fig. 7.13).

Body Awareness

The body is inclined forward, knees flexed, weight on the balls of the feet. The right hand may rotate slightly to the left on the stick.

Space

The ball is usually contacted off the right foot. The handle of the stick is inclined back toward the body prior to contact, and the stick is held diagonally across the body. The left hand is positioned close to the left knee and both elbows are fully extended downward. The flat side of the blade faces up. The blade is placed behind and under the ball.

Time

Timing is crucial in the success of the stroke and is difficult to master, since the scoop is usually attempted on a moving ball. The ball can be lifted only when the blade is diagonally under and behind the ball.

Force

The main force for the stroke comes from a lifting action of the right arm and is aided somewhat by the force of the legs in raising

Figure 7.14. **Flick**

the body. The action imitates a shoveling action without the extended follow-through.

Flow

The scoop is a smooth continuous movement. Movement flows from the legs to the arms to the stick to the ball.

FLICK

The flick is a combination of the scoop and push pass. It utilizes the deceptiveness and speed in execution of the push pass and the lofting potential of the scoop. The flick may be used for a shot at the goal, a pass, or as a clearing stroke (fig. 7.14).

Body Awareness

Refer to the dribble.

Space

The ball is usually contacted farther out in front of the body than in the dribble. Initially the stick begins in contact with the ball. The left arm inclines the butt end of the stick laterally to the left prior to contact. The left elbow remains high and well away from the body.

Time

Again, this stroke is usually attempted on a moving ball and, thus, critical attention to the moment when ball, feet and blade are in a desirable relationship to one another is required. The initial moment of force application occurs as the player begins the step into the stroke. The ball should remain in contact with the blade for as long as possible. Because a backswing is not necessary, execution time is minimal.

Force

The left elbow is drawn forcefully back toward the body while the right arm pushes forcefully away from the body. Body weight is transferred from the back to the forward foot as the player steps into the stroke during contact. By extending the upper body in the intended direction, the ball remains on the stick for a longer period of time. At the end of the stroke, the right wrist flicks to the left and the left wrist flicks to the right to add additional force and height to the ball. Maximum force and added height is achieved by lengthening the stride as a player steps into the stroke, thereby utilizing more mass-producing muscles and ultimately bringing the stick blade farther under the ball for additional lift. It is helpful for beginners who are having difficulty in force production for the flick to try sweeping the blade hard along the ground as far in front of them as possible. Most problems arise when the blade is lifted prematurely off the ground. The follow-through is low, with the upper trunk and arms fully extended in the intended direction. Because of the flicking action of the wrists, the flat side of the stick blade faces either to the player's left or down toward the ground at the completion of the stroke.

Flow

The flick is a smooth, continuous action. Movement flows from the back leg to the trunk as weight transfer begins. As the trunk begins moving in the direction of the hit, movement flows from the arms to the wrists to the stick to the ball.

Force-Absorbing Skills

Fielding with the stick or hand and tackling imply force absorption in controlling a moving ball. Regardless of which skill is used, similar execution is required. The contacting surface must be angled so that the ball will rebound with control into a playable position. The contacting surface gives at impact, allowing force to be absorbed over a greater time and distance. In attempting to control a ball, one must be aware of the ball's movement and time the placement of the contacting surface in the ball's pathway accordingly. It is imperative that a player continue moving after controlling the ball to prevent opponents from regaining possession of the ball.

FIELDING

Being able to field the ball is a vital skill that all players must master. A player must be equally proficient in receiving balls from all directions, in receiving ground balls or aerial balls, slow balls or fast balls. These factors make fielding skill acquisition an intriguing challenge.

Body Awareness

The feet face the attacking goal regardless of the direction of approach of the ball. The blade of the stick is held away from the feet, but close to the ground. The eyes focus on the ball during its approach. The weight of the body is held forward on the balls of the feet, enabling the player to move her feet quickly should the need arise. The degree of trunk rotation in fielding is dependent upon the angle of approach of the ball.

Space

1. Fielding a ball coming toward the player from the front: The ball is contacted in front and very slightly to the right of the body. The flat portion of the stick blade faces forward, allowing the ball to rebound into ideal position for the dribble (fig. 7.15).

2. Fielding a ball from the left: The ball is allowed to cross in front of the body. Contact is made in front and very slightly to the right of the body. The flat portion of the stick blade faces to the player's left, but at an angle which allows the ball to rebound into dribble position (figures 7.15, 7.16).

3. Fielding a ball from the right: The ball is contacted near the right foot, thereby not allowing it to cross in front of the body. The blade of the stick is rotated clockwise so that the flat side faces the oncoming ball. The toe of the stick faces diagonally to the right behind the player, allowing the ball to rebound forward into dribbling position (figures 7.15, 7.17).

4. Fielding a ball coming toward the player from behind: The player moves either to the right or left of the ball's pathway, thus fielding a ball from the right or left. By rotating the trunk to an extreme degree, the ball can be contacted behind or even with the body on the appropriate side. The blade of the stick should be angled to allow the ball to rebound into dribbling posi-

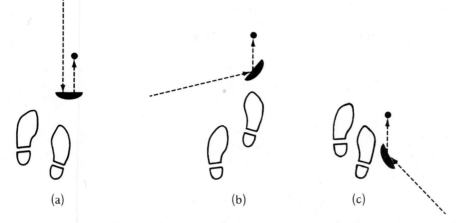

Figure 7.15. **Rebound angles: (a) angle of forward rebound; (b) angle of rebound fielding from left; (c) angle of rebound fielding from right.**

Figure 7.16. **Fielding from left**

tion in front and slightly to the right of the body.

Time

The ball is contacted at the time it is farthest from the body, while the stick is still perpendicular to the ground. When fielding a bouncing ball, the movements of the stick must be timed with the up-and-down motion of the ball if contact is to occur.

Force

The prime concern in fielding is force absorption. The butt end of the stick is inclined farther from the body than the blade, creating an angle which allows the ball to rebound downward and prevents it from rolling over the blade. The flat side of the blade contacts the ball squarely to prevent an uncontrolled, angular rebound. The body is directly in line with the oncoming ball to aid in maintaining body stability and to facilitate

Figure 7.17. **Fielding from right**

the alignment of the stick into the ball's pathway. The ball is contacted as far away from the body as possible, allowing a greater time and distance over which force is absorbed and decreasing the possibility of the feet illegally contacting the ball. At contact the left arm remains extended keeping the stick perpendicular, but the right arm draws back slightly toward the body, thus giving with the impact and preventing an uncontrolled rebound off the stick.

Flow

The movement may be either bound or continuous. Completely stopping the ball is seldom done; rather, the objective should be to control the ball while it is moving.

HAND STOP

While it is illegal to raise any part of the stick above shoulder level, an aerial ball may be fielded legally by the hand. The hand acts only as a rebound surface and the ball must drop in a perpendicular line to the ground.

Body Awareness

Hand stops are usually made with the right hand for players in the field, while the goalie usually uses the left hand. The palm is open facing the ball. The other hand maintains its grip on the stick, rendering it ready for immediate use as the ball hits the ground. The hand stop may be preceded by a jump if the ball is of sufficient height.

Space

The ball is contacted in front of the body so that it is in a playable position once it hits the ground.

Time

The ball rebounds from the hand immediately.

Force

The hand gives at contact to absorb the force of the ball.

Flow

The hand stop is a bound movement, but the bodily movement preceding and following the hand stop is continuous.

Figure 7.18. **Straight tackle**

TACKLES

When an opponent is in possession of the ball, a player may use one of a variety of tackles to retrieve the ball and start an offensive attack for her team. The more common tackles are the straight tackle, used when a player faces an opponent head-on; a left-hand lunge, used to tackle an opponent moving in the same direction but to the tackler's left; and a circular tackle, used on an opponent running in the same direction as the tackler but to the tackler's right. In all instances, the tackler should aim ahead of the ball, allowing for movement of the ball.

Straight tackle

Body Awareness

The blade of the stick is carried low to the ground. The player's concentration is focused upon the ball and the opponent's stick. Small, quick steps allowing for speed and ease of movement are taken (fig. 7.18).

Space

The ball is contacted ahead and to the right side of the tackler. This allows both opponent and tackler to play the ball on their stick sides, eliminating the possibility of body contact.

Time

The tackle is attempted when the ball is off the opponent's stick. Correct timing is dependent upon the speed of the ball, the speed of the tackler and the speed of the opponent.

Force

A tackle is a maneuver designed to absorb rather than to produce force. There should be no backswing! To absorb and control the force of the moving ball, the blade of the stick should be held perpendicular to the ground at contact and it should give with impact.

Flow

Movement in tackles should be well-planned and smoothly executed to avoid slashing or jerky tackling actions which can miss the ball and attack the opponent's legs or feet. Motion flows from the approach, to the tackle, to subsequent action after possession of the ball has been obtained.

1

2

3

4

5

Figure 7.19. **Left-hand lunge**

Left-hand lunge

Body Awareness

Refer to the straight tackle. The opponent is to the tackler's left (fig. 7.19).

Space

The ball is contacted ahead and to the left of the tackler, who is ahead to the right of the opponent. In this tackle the left leg lunges to the left and the left arm and stick extend to provide additional reach. The tackler must be aware of the spatial distance covered by her own lunge and allow sufficient distance for her extended reach.

Figure 7.20. **Circular tackle**

Time

Refer to the straight tackle.

Force

Refer to the straight tackle. From the dribble position the right hand pushes the stick to the left. The right hand then releases the stick as the left arm and hand continue the movement and control the direction of the stick.

Flow

Refer to the straight tackle. After contact the body pivots 180 degrees, the right hand is placed on the stick and the successful tackler is ready to dribble or drive toward her attacking goal.

Circular tackle

Body Awareness

Refer to the straight tackle. The opponent is to the tackler's right (fig. 7.20).

Space

To execute this tackle legally, the tackler moves ahead of the opponent, crosses in front of her from left to right, takes the ball, and completes a semicircular turn to face in the direction of her own goal. The ball is contacted ahead of the body off the right foot.

Time

Refer to the straight tackle. The tackler must be able to outrun her opponent in order to get ahead of her when attempting this tackle. Lack of proper timing often results in body contact, stick interference, or obstruction on the part of the tackler.

Force

The ball is contacted with a short dribble stroke, pushing it away from the opponent but not so far as to lose control.

Flow

The circular tackle is executed as a smooth, continuous motion from the running movement previous to contact, to obtaining possession of the ball, to running with the ball in the opposite direction after the tackle. After obtaining possession of the ball, very small, quick steps are taken which enable the body to turn sharply to the right and head in the direction of the attacking goal.

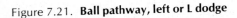

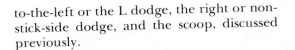

to-the-left or the L dodge, the right or non-stick-side dodge, and the scoop, discussed previously.

Pull-to-the-left or L dodge

Body Awareness
Refer to the dribble.

Space
The ball is moved at a ninety degree angle to the dodger's left, then sent forward at a ninety degree angle. The ball's pathway forms the letter L (See figure 7.21).

Time
The dodge should be attempted just as the tackler is about to tackle. If the dodge is attempted too soon, the tackler has time to intercept. If the dodge is attempted too late, a tackle cannot be avoided. The dodger must take into consideration the fact that she and her opponent are usually moving toward each other; therefore, the time allotted to execute the dodge is decreased.

Force
The ball is pulled rather than hit to the left. The ball remains in contact with the stick during the pull phase. The feet must move quickly to permit the best body position behind the ball. Once the ball has been pulled out of reach of the tackler's stick, a forward dribble is resumed.

Flow
Movement flows from the dribble preceding the dodge, to the evasive maneuver and quick acceleration around the defender, and back to the dribble.

Right or non-stick-side dodge

Body Awareness
Refer to the dribble.

Figure 7.21. **Ball pathway, left or L dodge**

Special Skills of Force Production or Absorption

Dodges, push-ins, bullies, and the goalkeeper's stop and clear are special game skills utilizing the mechanical principles of force production or force absorption. These are special skills in that the nature of the striking implement has been altered or the purpose of the skill is unique within the game setting. The feet and legs first absorb, then produce force in the goalkeeper's stop and clear. The dodge combines the elements of a push pass with an evasive maneuver around a defender. The bully combines intricate stickwork and footwork into an effective means of obtaining possession of the ball, then utilizes a push pass, flick, scoop, or drive to send the ball to a teammate. These special skills are described in greater detail in this section.

DODGES

A dodge is a means by which a player in possession of the ball evades a potential tackler. There are three main dodges: the pull-

Space

The ball is sent to the right of the dodger, which is to the left or non-stick side of the tackler. The obstruction rule prohibiting a player from coming between the opponent and the ball mandates that the player run around the opponent's right or stick side to retrieve the ball after dodging (fig. 7.22).

Time

Refer to the pull to the left dodge.

Force

A push pass provides the necessary force to place the ball behind the tackler. The backswing is eliminated to aid in the deceptiveness of the stroke.

Flow

Refer to the pull-to-the-left dodge. The dodger should accelerate quickly to retrieve the ball before the opponent has time to recover, turn, and tackle back.

PUSH–IN

A push-in is the technique used to put the ball back into play after the ball has been sent out of bounds over the side line. the player taking the push-in utilizes a push pass or low flick. The ball must be placed on the sideline where it crossed out of bounds, and all other players must be at least five yards away; however, the player taking the push-in may place feet and stick in any location (behind, on or over the sideline) while executing the stroke.

Body Awareness

Refer to the dribble.

Space

Refer to the push pass or flick. If a flick is used, it may not exceed knee height.

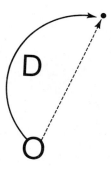

Figure 7.22. **Ball and player pathways, right dodge**

Time

The player should be in motion prior to contact using faking maneuvers in various directions. As the body changes position, the stick must remain in contact with the ball since no backswing is allowed. When an opponent has been lured into a position which creates a space for a teammate to enter, the ball should be pushed or flicked into that space.

Force

Refer to push pass or flick.

Flow

The faking action preceding the push-in should be abrupt, sharp, irregular and deceptive. Once the push pass or flick is begun, the action becomes smooth and continuous from force production through follow-through. The player must regain field position immediately after completing the push-in stroke.

BULLY

The bully is the method of starting the game at the beginning of each half or restarting the game after injury, score, interference, or a simultaneous hit out of bounds by opponents. To bully, two opponents face each other with left sides to the attacking goal

Figure 7.23. **Bully**

and the ball positioned between them. The bully procedure consists of hitting the ground to the right of the ball, then hitting the opponent's stick over the ball three times in succession.

Body Awareness

The feet are shoulder-width apart in a side-stride position. The knees are flexed with the weight of the body centered over the balls of the feet. The trunk is inclined forward. The left hand grasps the stick as if for dribbling while the right hand may slide lower down the stick than in normal dribbling position. The head is centered over the ball. (See figure 7.23).

Space

The ball is centered in front of the body. The flat side of the blade faces to the left toward the ball. The player should not reach for the ball but should be close enough so that stick and ball contact is easily made.

Time

The bully sequence is rhythmical and must coincide with the opponent's movements for successful completion. The bully sequence may be done slowly or quickly. After the last stick contact each player attempts to make ball contact before the opponent in order to gain control of the ball.

Force

Winning the bully is not the result of force but of proper timing. The ball is contacted with a push, pull or lift to gain control. (Refer to bully strategy, p. 179.)

Flow

The bully is a continuous action beginning with the ground-stick sequence and ending when one player has obtained possession of the ball and has passed it to a teammate.

GOALKEEPER'S STOP AND CLEAR

The goalkeeper's main method of stopping the ball is by using the large flat surface of her goal pads. For balls out of the reach of the legs or feet, a stick stop may be used (fig. 7.24). The main method of clearing the ball away from the goalmouth is with a kicking action.

Goalkeeper's stop

Body Awareness

The body is aligned with the oncoming ball. The knees are bent, weight is on the balls of the feet, and legs are held together. The right hand grips the stick at the middle of the handle, leaving the left hand free for hand stops. The arms are held out to the sides to aid in stabilizing the body. The eyes focus upon the oncoming ball (fig. 7.25).

Space

The goalkeeper aligns herself about three to four feet in front of the goal cage and at a point directly in line with the ball's approach to the goal.

Time

Timing is critical, since an error in judgment may result in a goal for the opponents. If the scoring attempt is a forceful hit, the

Figure 7.24. **Stick stop by goalkeeper**

Figure 7.25. **Goalkeeper in ready position**

goalkeeper must quickly move into the ball's intended pathway, stop the ball and still maintain sufficient balance to clear the ball away. If the shot at the goal is less forceful, the goalkeeper may wish to rush the ball rather than waiting for it to come to her.

Force

Force is absorbed by using the large, flat surface of the foot or lower portion of the goal pads and by bending the knees at such an angle as to force the ball to rebound down toward the ground directly in front of the goalkeeper's feet (fig. 7.26).

Figure 7.26. Goalkeeper stop showing desired angle of rebound

Flow

The goalkeeper takes small side-stride steps to get into position, stops the ball, then immediately clears it away. The actual stop is a bound movement.

Goalkeeper's clearing kick

Body Awareness

Refer to the goalkeeper's stop. The ball is in front of the goalkeeper after having been stopped.

Space

The goalkeeper must know her spatial orientation in relation to the goal. If she is positioned to the left of the goal at the time of the stop, the clearing kick is usually made in that direction. It is a dangerous move to clear the ball across the front of the goal cage.

Time

The timing of the clearing kick is again critical. A hard drive is followed by a rushing forward, thus cutting down on the time available. The goalkeeper's ability to execute an immediate clear is dependent upon her stability after stopping the ball, the distance the ball has rebounded from her pads and

Figure 7.27. Goalkeeper's clearing kick

the position of teammates and rushing opponents.

Force

The ball may be kicked with the toe or inside of either foot. The body rotation away from the ball and backswing aid in force production. A step into the kick is usually taken. The head is positioned over the ball at contact to help ensure a flattened arc of swing. The follow-through is low and in the intended direction. (See figure 7.27).

Flow

The clearing kick is part of a continuous action from the ready position, to the actual stop of the ball, to the clearing kick and back to ready position.

MAJOR CONCEPTS RELATED TO STRATEGY

The key to successful strategy in any sport is mastery of the fundamental skills of the sport. Once this has been accomplished, the task of blending individual talents into an efficient pattern of team play ensues. Planning and executing team strategy in field hockey becomes especially challenging when one considers the unique aspects of the game: The number of participants is large, thus the teacher or coach has less opportunity to give individual attention; the field area is large, thereby reducing the opportunity for communication between teammates, teachers, or coaches during play; the playing period is a continuous duration of time without time-outs being allowed, thereby eliminating opportunities for team discussions of problems that arise during play; and the large number of participants and the size of the playing area reduce a player's opportunities to handle the ball. These factors call upon the players of the game to assume more responsibility for analyzing play and initiating strategic moves during a game than is seen in many of the other team sports. Players are forced to become independent and creative in individual play while still contributing to the effectiveness of team play. The game of field hockey is player-oriented rather han teacher- or coach-oriented. By developing an understanding of the concepts which follow, students are aided in achieving such an orientation. The ultimate in strategy planning is evidenced by the creative, unexpected moves of the participants.

Player Positions and Responsibilities

CONCEPT N. Proper use of personnel, based on each player's strengths and limitations, is of paramount importance when molding a team.

Sub-concept N-1. Each player on a team must assume specific responsibilities for the position he is playing.

Of the eleven players on a field hockey team, the five forwards are generally considered to be offensive players (LW, LI, CF, RI, RW) and the five backs and the goalkeeper are generally considered to be defensive players (LH, GH, RH, LFB, RFB, G); however, the offensive unit assists the defense and the defensive unit assists the offense in certain situations. Students should select positions which match their capabilities so that the team as a whole is strengthened.

Forwards

It is the duty of the forwards to maneuver the ball through the opposing team's defense into the striking circle in order to score goals. Forwards must be fast, aggressive players with good stickwork and a good sense of spatial orientation. A forward who wanders across the field needlessly compresses the open spaces available to her teammates. Forwards should have the ability to dribble fast and well, to dodge an opponent when teammates are not available for passes, to pass quickly and accurately when the defense is in position and to field balls well, since there will be many opportunities for interception of defensive drives and goalie clears when on the attack. A forward should master a hard drive for scoring, and a quick accurate flick or push pass for follow-up shots. She should have a variety of deceptive moves in her repertoire in order to outmaneuver the defense, and she must be able to create open spaces in the opposing team's defense for offensive penetration. A forward must anticipate the moves of her teammates and of the defense in order to gain an advantage over the defender in reaching a ball, completing a pass or executing a successful dodge or shot for goal. Forwards must be courageous and innovative, for it is often the unexpected move that upsets the balance and timing of the opponent's defensive system. Most importantly, forwards must have an insatiable appetite for scoring, as persistence is the key to devouring the defense.

The general territory covered by each of the forwards is diagrammed in figure 7.28.

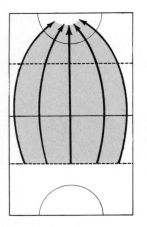

Figure 7.28. **Territory of forwards**

Forwards generally retreat no farther than their own twenty-five yard line and they advance to the opponent's goal line. It is important that players maintain their spatial relationship with teammates both horizontally (between forwards) and vertically (between forwards and halfbacks).

Halfbacks

It is the duty of the halfbacks to prevent their opponents from scoring while aiding their own forward line to obtain and retain possession of the ball. To accomplish this, halfbacks must have speed enough to match any forward line player on the field. They must have a keen sense of spatial awareness in order to execute appropriate passes in varying situations and to help maintain their position in relation to opponents and the ball. A halfback must anticipate all plays for, like her offensive counterpart, she needs to gain the advantage over her opponent. A defender is successful at this when she intercepts passes, completes successful tackles, and disrupts shots for the goal. Halfbacks must be adept tacklers with enough body control and stamina to finish the play by executing a well-placed drive to one of their own forward line players. Beginning halfbacks often pass only to the left, since the left drive is easiest to perform. A good halfback mixes her passes well, allowing all of her forward line players to handle the ball and forcing the opposing defense to shift continually. Halfbacks must also have the desire to score, for although they are a second line of offense, a well-positioned halfback will have many scoring opportunities.

The halfback position is perhaps the most challenging in field hockey, but it is also probably the most rewarding. Its responsibilities are endless, from the starting bully to the final whistle. A halfback must never give up and never quit moving, for once her defensive responsibilities end, her offensive contribution begins. By failing to perform either, she destroys the effectiveness of her team.

As evidenced in figure 7.29, halfbacks play from their own goal line to the edge of the opponent's striking circle.

Fullbacks

Fullbacks need many of the attributes of halfbacks. As a second line of defense, the quickness and good judgment of the fullback become increasingly important as the opponents near their attacking circle. Fullbacks should have the power and ability to make long, hard clearing drives in order to send the ball to teammates far away from the defending circle. Accuracy of passes and clears is paramount, for in the congestion and anxiety of the defensive circle, the slightest mistake can result in an opponent's score. Fullbacks need a great deal of patience also, for the temptations to be drawn out of position are many. Little assistance can be given the fullback who rushes out of the striking circle to tackle a lone oncoming forward. Fullbacks must be constantly aware of ball placement on the field in order to assume their proper tandem role in the up

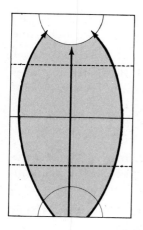

Figure 7.29. **Territory of halfbacks**

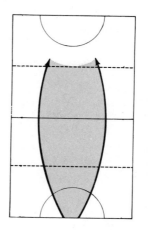

Figure 7.30. **Territory of fullbacks**

and back positions, and they must be capable of shifting quickly.[3] Fullbacks, too, can be an asset to the offensive threat of a team and should be encouraged to be so. The up fullback on the ball side of the field can play up as far as the halfback line if she is quick to recover should the ball shift to the other side of the field. Through courage and confidence, the fullback may be in position to take advantage of scoring opportunities.

Fullbacks play from their own goal line to approximately the twenty-five yard line of the opponents (fig. 7.30).

Goalkeeper

The goalkeeper must, above all, be a courageous individual willing to take chances and accept challenges. Quickness should be one of her foremost qualities, for there is never time to debate after an opposing forward has shot for goal. Agility is perhaps more important to the goalkeeper than to other players, for not only must she be able to move quickly, but the added burden of her protective equipment makes this more difficult. The goalkeeper should be an individual who does not readily become excited, either, for the situation before her in

her defensive circle is seldom calm and peaceful. Her composure under such pressure will often make the difference between a goal and a save.

The goalkeeping task, though physically and psychologically demanding, can be a most rewarding and enjoyable one. Too often teachers and students fill this position last, and usually with the least skilled player on the field. Once chosen the player is neglected in individual instruction and is left out of drills where all other players are involved. By choosing players wisely, by devoting some time to teaching the unique skills associated with the position, and by allowing the goalkeeper to participate in all team drills by using her feet instead of a stick, a high degree of necessary proficiency can be acquired. A good goalkeeper is invaluable in completing her team's defense and helping to make the goalmouth formidable to any foe.

The goalkeeper's area of coverage is seen in figure 7.31. While the goalie generally plays in the semicircular area three to four feet in front of the goal, she must occasion-

3. Fullback positioning is described in greater detail on pages 225–26.

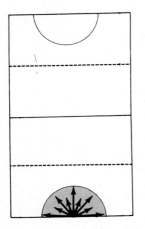

Figure 7.31. **Territory of goalkeeper**

ally rush out farther into the striking circle to intercept a lone, oncoming, opposing forward.

Beginning Play

To begin play each team lines up on its own half of the field. The two center forwards face each other and straddle the centerline in readiness for the center bully. The ball is placed on the centerline between the two center forwards. At the umpire's whistle, the center forwards strike the ground to the right of the ball, then strike their opponent's stick over the ball three times in succession. After the final stick contact, the two players have an equal opportunity to gain possession of the ball and pass it quickly to a teammate.

The team in possession of the ball is referred to as the offensive or attacking team, while the team not in possession of the ball is referred to as the defending team.

System of Offense

CONCEPT O. In goal oriented and field sports a system of offense is essential if a team is to be successful. The prime purposes of an offensive system are to build upon the strengths of the players, to shift the balance of power away from the defense, and to capitalize on defensive weaknesses.

Sub-concept O-1. If and when a player decides that maintaining possession of the ball will gain ground more successfully, the player must be able to dribble, dodge, and feint effectively.

Sub-concept O-2. Effective passing involves spatial patterns based on positioning of teammates and opponents.

Sub-concept O-3. Creating spaces is basic to sound team strategy.

Sub-concept O-4. In order to score it is necessary to place the ball in a strategic position in relation to the goal.

Sub-conept O-5. Shooting for a goal involves individual and team strategy.

Sub-concept O-6. Rushing the goal insures follow-up to a shot at the goal.

The moment a team gains possession of the ball, the offensive attack begins. The offensive goalkeeper, fullback, or halfback who gained possession of the ball initiates the attack by sending the ball quickly to one of her own forward line players. If all forwards are covered by the opposing defense, the pass may be sent first to a free, well-positioned halfback or fullback, but this is still to be considered an offensive move. Once the forwards have obtained the ball, they maneuver it down the field, through the opposing defense, always searching for the quickest, last congested path to the goal.

At the moment possession of the ball is obtained, all members of the offensive team should assume a ready position for ensuing action. Both hands should be kept on the stick, and the blade of the stick should be held low to the ground. Often beginning players hold the stick in carrying position rather than low and ready for play, and it is therefore rendered useless in attempting to field and control quick, unexpected passes. The weight should be forward on the balls of the feet to promote a quicker running start, and the player's feet should always face in the direction of the goal she is attacking.

A forward who has received the ball has many decisions to make as she begins her trek downfield. Should she keep the ball herself, dodge a defender, or pass to a teammate? Any one of these choices is appropriate in certain circumstances. Anytime a forward is free, she should maintain possession of the ball and dribble as fast as she possibly can in the direction of her attacking goal. More offensive players should be encouraged to go with the ball when they are free.

A player who encounters a lone defender while dribbling down the field ahead of her teammates has little choice but to attempt to dodge (pp. 158–159). Her choice of dodge will be based upon her knowledge of her own ability in performing each of the dodges, her assessment of the opponent's defensive ability, the proximity of other possible defenders, and her position in relation to her opponent, the sidelines, goal lines and the striking circle. Good judgment in choosing the right dodge at the right time comes from a thorough understanding of the strategy of a particular dodge, a keen awareness of spatial orientation on the field, and experience.

In the majority of instances the forwards should be horizontally in line with one another as one of them advances the ball downfield. This allows a much greater opportunity for a successful passing attack and places a greater burden on the opposing defense. By keeping well spread across the entire width of the field, the forwards spread the defense. This leaves large open spaces between the forwards, spaces which may be utilized as passing areas.

There are three types of passes common to field hockey. Students should understand each and be proficient in its execution, for passing is a much faster way of progressing downfield than dribbling. A flat or square pass is one which travels horizontally across the field between players and is used when a defender is some distance from a teammate, or when the defense has covered the angles for an angular or through pass. In figure 7.32 O^1 executes a flat pass to O^2. While the pass has value, it tends to slow the game down because the ball travels across the field rather than down the field.

A diagonal or angular pass is the one used most often. It is generally directed behind a defensive player who is defending a teammate closely. If the receiver darts quickly around the defender, she will be assured of receiving the pass. In figure 7.32, O^2, after receiving the flat pass from O^1, could now execute an angular pass behind D^1. Figure 7.33 shows this sequence.

The third type of pass seen in field hockey is the through pass. The direction of a through pass is vertically straight down the field. It may be used when a defender plays off to one side, leaving the area directly ahead of a player free (fig. 7.34), or by a side half or wing who is caught deep in her defensive end and does not want to send the ball into the middle of the field.

Through passes are always intended for a teammate, just as with the flat and angular passes. For the through pass, this necessitates a change in positions between the passer and the receiver, called an offensive interchange. In figure O^1 executes a through pass, O^2 sprints ahead and cuts into O^1's position to field the pass, and O^1 cuts over to O^2's position to maintain the offensive balance. The players continue playing

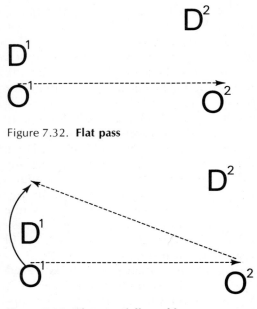

Figure 7.32. **Flat pass**

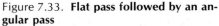

Figure 7.33. **Flat pass followed by an angular pass**

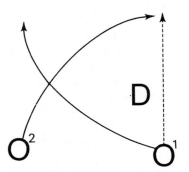

Figure 7.34. **Through pass**

Figure 7.35. **Offensive interchange**

in these positions until the play is over or until it is convenient for them to switch back to their original positions. Although the use of this pass is somewhat limited due to strong defensive covering systems, its occasional use can penetrate deep into the defense and cause havoic among defenders as they attempt to follow specific wandering forwards. An offensive line which is capable of interchanging often can be most confusing to an opposing defense. Students and players should also realize that while interchange usually occurs between neighbors on the forward line (LW and LI, LI and CF, RI and RW), it is even more baffling to the defense when a more exaggerated interchange occurs. If the LW and LI are caught deep in the defensive end, and the LW executes a through pass, the only logical receiver is the CF. If this occurs, the LI moves into the CF position, the LW becomes the LI and the CF

plays in the LW position untilit is convenient for all to switch back (fig. 7.36).

With twenty-two people involved in the game of field hockey, it becomes a matter of safety and strategy to keep them all well spread across the field. Until beginners understand the concept of maintaining spaces, the tendency is to play "gang ball," with players roaming needlessly and fruitlessly from sideline to sideline. Each of the forward line players has an approximate self-space of twelve yards in width, the halfbacks a self-space of approximately twenty yards in width, and the fullbacks a self-space of approximately twenty-five to thirty yards in width. If one were to imagine that each player on a team was enclosed in a large bubble (fig. 7.37), and that as the bubble moved it pushed the adjacent bubble a corresponding distance, the concept of spacing

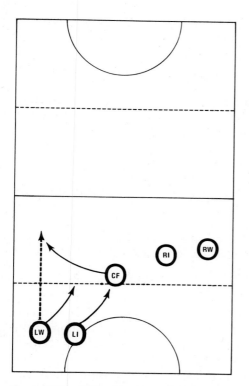

Figure 7.36. **Offensive interchange involving three forwards**

might be understood better. In figure 7.38 the spacing between the RI and CF has been maintained because both moved laterally to the left.

The importance of spacing becomes more evident as we look at the moves of the defense. If the CF had not moved in figure 7.38, the two forwards with their corresponding defenders would have been drawn closer together, compressing their self-space (fig. 7.39). The space between the two forwards has been eliminated as a passing area because of the proximity of the defenders. By maintaining spaces, each of the forwards has an area on either side of her into which passes might be sent and into which receivers may run to field such passes.

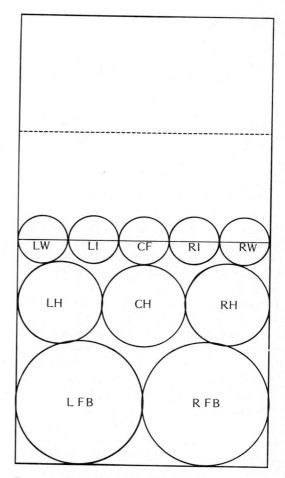

Figure 7.37. **Self-space bubble of each of the forwards, halfbacks, and fullbacks on a team**

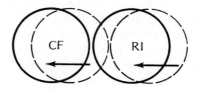

Figure 7.38. **Maintenance of self-space**

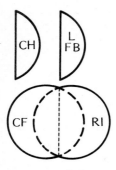

Figure 7.39. **Compressed self-space between two forwards**

In keeping with this idea, a player should not proceed in the direction of her pass, but should move in the opposite direction after execution of the pass. Again, by following a pass the passer and her defender are infringing upon the working self-space of the receiver and her defender.

Spacing must also be maintained between the forwards of a team and their own defense players. It is unfortunate to see a center forward and a center halfback from the same team fighting over the ball. As a halfback moves forward, the forwards should advance accordingly. If a forward reteats, the halfback should retreat, and as the halfback retreats, the fullback should retreat.

In any sport where a defensive unit faces an offensive unit, two competitive battles ensue. The more obvious is that battle between the teams—the team that plays better wins. The more subtle battle is that between each set of opposing individual players; in field hockey, each of the forwards against her opposing defender. It is in the success or failure of these competitive bouts that a team does or does not play well.

If an offensive player and a defensive player of equal abilities were matched, we would expect each to have a success/failure ratio of fifty/fifty. To increase that ratio in

favor of the offensive player, a variety of strategic methods might be employed.

1. An offensive player should maintain a constant surveillance of her teammates, the ball, her position on the field, and her spatial relationship to the goal. By anticipating that she might receive a pass, analyzing her options and preplanning her moves, a forward will be able to respond more quickly and execute the most appropriate play for the given situation. If players were more cognizant of these factors, there would be fewer passes sent directly to the opposition, fewer poorly aimed shots at the goal, and fewer well-intentioned passes skittering out of the reach of teammates and out of bounds.

2. An offensive player should be constantly on the move, repositioning herself in relation to the ball and maneuvering around her defender. This continual motion of the forward will keep her defender "entertained" and should force a one-to-one ratio between forwards and opposing defenders. It is when one offensive player remains relatively stationary on the field that her defender begins to roam across the field, helping other defensive players form a two-to-one ratio on other forwards. The stationary forward is not a threat in this case because by not constantly repositioning herself, she is unavailable to receive passes from teammates. Through the use of feints and cutting, an offensive player may be able to get in front of her defender to be in position to receive a direct pass, or she may draw the defender away from the ball, opening a space into which the ball may be passed. Only when all five forwards are moving is the spacing between them maintained as it should be. If the spacing is good it is the individual forward's responsibility to do what she can in seeing that she is free to receive passes.

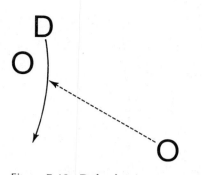

Figure 7.40. **Defender intercepting pass to a forward**

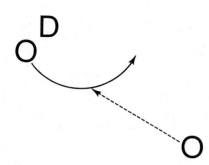

Figure 7.41. **Forward going to meet the ball**

Figure 7.42. **Forward positioned on the ball side of the defender**

3. One of the principal fundamentals that all players need to learn is that of going to meet the ball. She who waits for the pass to come shall also have the opportunity to watch her defender cut in front, intercept, and initiate an offensive attack for the opposing team (fig. 7.40). By going to receive the ball, whether it be a pass from behind, to the side, or in front of a player, that player gains an advantage over her defender (fig. 7.41). The advantage may be further increased if the offensive player initially positions herself on the ball side of the defender (fig. 7.42). This decreases the offensive player's distance to the ball while increasing the distance for the defender.

As an example of going to meet the ball and the action which may follow, let us assume that the CH attempts to pass to the LW. As soon as the LW has the slightest indication that the pass is hers to receive, she moves diagonally backward in the direction of the ball. The CH, not wishing to compress her space into which the LW is moving, shifts to her right. The LI cannot shift right without upsetting the balance of the forward line, but can move left into the vacated wing's position (fig. 7.43). In the process of going to meet the ball, an offensive interchange was incorporated.

4. Passes should be sympathetic. Unfortunately, many beginning students in field hockey obtain the false notion that all passes must be hard passes. The task is not to drive the ball through the opposing defenders, but rather to lure them from their defensive alignment, creating spaces for friendly passes.

Good strategy dictates that wings usually have the primary responsibility for advancing the ball downfield. After obtaining the ball in the defensive end, it should be cleared as far away from the opponent's circle as possible, to the wing position, where the defense is less congested than in the center of the field. Wings should be encouraged to stay well out, thereby spreading the opposing defense to its maximum. As the wing approaches the attacking twenty-five yard line, an action is needed to place the ball in a strategic position for a possible score. If the wing turns goalward at the twenty-five yard

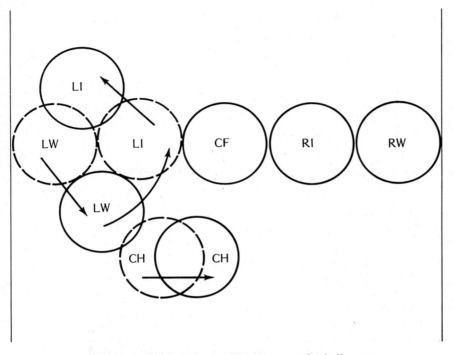

Figure 7.43. **Positioning of players as LW goes to meet the ball**

line and dribbles toward the circle, she unnecessarily congests the defense in the circle, making offensive passes and contrivances difficult, if not impossible, to execute. Better strategy suggests that the wing should usually stay out and attempt a flat or centering pass to any of the middle forwards.

As the spatial limitations of the field become more restrictive nearer the striking circle, less time is available for dribbling. Short, quick, sympathetic passes thread through the defense until the ball reaches the striking circle. At this point the proximity of defenders to forwards and the plethora of the circle leave little chance for unhindered dabbling with the ball. A shot at goal should be immediate!

Without hesitation all five forwards are now involved in an attempt to score on the follow-up shot if necessary. A rapid sprint

toward the goal should give the forward a desirable step advantage over her defender. Once behind the defensive line, a planned formation is generally used. Wings are positioned on the side edges of the circle and do not rush the goal itself. They move forward and back in relation to the ball, as does their forward line, but they maintain their position at the edge of the circle for the purpose of fielding goalie clears. The two inners rush toward their respective goal-posts on every attempted shot, hoping to intercept a goalie's clear and score, or to field the ball as it rebounds from the pads of the goalkeeper before the kick. The CF rushes directly toward the center of the goal in anticipation of a straight rebound or forward clear. This rushing alignment covers all angles of clears and

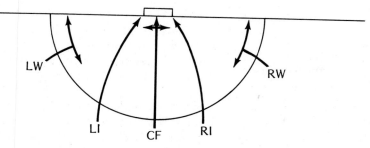

Figure 7.44. **Rushing alignment of forward line**

should result in some scoring follow-up shots (fig. 7.44).

Forwards should be prompted to advance and retreat quickly on successive attempts at goal: The continual pressure imposed upon the goalkeeper by an aggressive forward line can be devastating, forwards must keep moving to outmaneuver defenders, and the offsides rule mandates this movement. to prevent obstruction and to maintain the best position for attack, the forward's feet should always face the goal, both while advancing and retreating.

The halfbacks of the offensive team can provide invaluable assistance to their forwards in the attacking striking circle. While forwards are shooting and rushing, retreating, shooting and rushing, the offensive halfbacks should align themselves around the top of the attacking circle (fig. 7.45). Here, they attempt to retrieve the opposing goalkeeper's clears and intercept opposing defender's hits out of the circle. If successful, the ball is quickly passed back in to the forwards for another shot at goal. This action by the halfbacks, termed "backing up," allows the offensive forwards to remain concentrated in the scoring area and makes it extremely difficult for the opposing defense to clear the ball out of the circle.

Halfbacks who are backing up their forward line should also realize their own scoring potential. A halfback who intercepts a

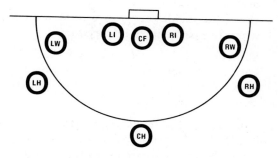

Figure 7.45. **Halfbacks backing up their forward line at the attacking circle**

defensive clear on the edge of the circle may have a beautiful, unmolested shot at goal. Forwards should move quickly to the sides, opening a space for the halfback shot. If an opposing defender intrudes in this situation, a forward line player is probably being neglected and would be open for a pass.

Halfbacks must be cautioned that should the opposing defense be successful in clearing the ball past them, a quick recovery to defensive alignment is in order. A moment's hesitation may produce drastic results.

Individual Defensive Techniques

CONCEPT P. Individual defensive techniques are for the purpose of closing spaces through which a ball can be passed or inhibiting the progress of a player or ball, thereby preventing the opponents

from maintaining possession of the ball and/or scoring.

Sub-concept P-1. Defensive play depends on guarding techniques which enable the player to anticipate movement, to intercept passes, to tackle, or block.

Sub-concept P-2. Covering is a technique for closing spaces through which long passes might be sent.

Sub-concept P-3. The defense should advance to tackle or guard immediately when the ball enters its territory.

Sub-concept P-4. Clearing the ball involves a fast defensive maneuver because the ball must be moved quickly away from the goal.

The moment a team loses possession of the ball, two objectives of defense become evident. The first is to prevent the opponents from scoring; the second is to regain possession of the ball. Each of the eleven members of the defensive team becomes involved individually and collectively in helping her team meet these two objectives.

At the instant a forward line player loses possession of the ball to an opposing defender, that forward line player's defensive responsibilities commence. The term "tackling back" refers to this particular maneuver. The forward quickly reverses direction and aggressively pursues the defender now in possession of the ball. It is hoped that the forward will be able to tackle back and regain possession of the ball herself; however, should this attempt fail, her impending presence may cause the defender to execute a hurried, poor pass.

Once the opposing offensive forward line gains control of the ball, specific responsibilities must be assumed by the members of the defensive team. The term "marking" refers to individual defensive coverage of

each of the opposing forward line players. To mark a player means to be in close enough spatial proximity to intercept a possible pass to that player or to tackle the player immediately should she receive a pass. Defensive halfbacks and fullbacks each mark a particular opposing forward: The left halfback marks the opposing right wing, the left fullback marks the opposing right inner, the center halfback marks the opposing center forward, the right fullback marks the opposing left inner, and the right halfback markes the opposing left wing (fig. 7.46). Each time one of these forwards receives the ball, the appropriate defender should be marking. To prevent bunching around the ball, beginners would benefit by understanding the concept of marking thoroughly before attempting game play.

A sequence of action might make this idea clearer. Let us assume that X-team (shaded) right inner is dribbling downfield (fig. 7.47a). She is tackled by the Y-team (non-shaded) left fullback, the appropriate defender (fig. 7.47b). Immediately, the X-team right inner reverses directions and pursues the Y left fullback to tackle back (fig. 7.47c). The inners' attempt is unsuccessful and a pass is sent from the Y-team left fullback to the Y right wing (fig. 7.47d). The wing dribbles downfield until meeting her appropriate defender, the X-team left halfback (fig. 7.47e).

In offensive strategy the most common pass to a teammate follows an angular or diagonal pathway. It would seem logical, then, defensively, to establish an alignment which would prohibit such passes by the opposing offense. By effecting a defensive maneuver called "covering" such passing options are expunged. Covering, as opposed to marking, denotes guarding a particular space rather than a particular player. Covering in field hockey means to position oneself in the space where a pass to a player will most logi-

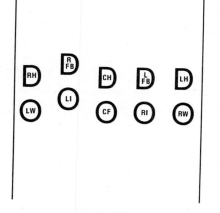

Figure 7.46. **Defenders marking appropriate opponents**

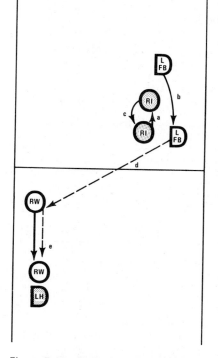

Figure 7.47. **(a) X-team R1 dribbles downfield; (b) X-team R1 tackled by Y-team LFB; (c) X-team R1 attempts to tackle back after losing possession of the ball; (d) Y-team LFB passes to Y-team RW; (e) X-team LH marking Y-team RW**

cally be sent. While one defender marks the opponent with the ball, the other defensive players cover their opponents, positioning themselves in the space where an angular pass would be directed to each of those opponents. In figure 7.48 the offensive RW has the ball. The defensive LH marks. The defensive LFB covers in the space where the RW would like to direct a pass to her RI. Correspondingly, the CH covers the space where an angular pass from the RW to the CF would be sent, the RFB covers the space of a pass from the RW to the LI, and the RH covers the pathway of a pass from the RW to the LW. The RH is considerably farther from her opponent than is the LFB, due to the increased distance and time of a pass traveling to the LW. It should also be noted in figure 7.48 that defenders also try to position themselves on the ball side of their opponent to increase the opportunity for successful interception of passes. Covering defenders must take care to maintain a sufficient distance between themselves and their individual opponent. A covering defender who crowds an opponent without the ball is

susceptible to a pass being directed behind her, thus initiating an offensive passing attack.

Just as the offense has a system of interchanging teammates into more advantageous positions, the defense uses a similar strategy. Of the five offensive forwards, the one with the ball must be considered the most dangerous for her offensive potential. The forwards in closest proximity to the ball must be considered highly dangerous, for they are most apt to receive a pass. The forward or forwards farthest from the ball are

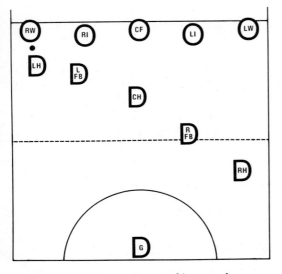

Figure 7.48. **Defense in marking and covering positions**

least dangerous. In figure 7.48 the opposing RW is the first priority of the defense. The RI is the most probable prospect for receipt of a pass; thus, she becomes the second area of concern for the defense. Progressing across the line of forwards, it is seen that the LW is the least dangerous as an offensive threat at the present time; therefore, she is the last concern for the defense. Since the scoring potential of the forward line is unbalanced to its right, it would seem logical to strengthen the defense to that side into a position to counteract this, to the defense's left.

A second line of defense positioned behind the first would be ideal. If a forward broke free from her first defender, she would meet a second before attempting a shot at goal. While it is not practical or legal to position ten halfbacks and fullbacks on the field, the concept of establishing a second line of defense is feasible.

The RH in figure 7.48 has the least to do at the moment. She is a likely candidate to

be pulled across the field and be positioned as a second line of defense behind her LH and LFB. To do this, however, she must run a distance of forty to sixty yards from her position to the opposite side of the field. In the quick action of a game, the forward who had broken free would be into the circle shooting before this halfback could travel the distance across the field and be of help.

The other player to be considered for this defensive maneuver is the RFB. Although she initially is guarding a more dangerous forward than the RH, the decreased distance she has to run to be in position behind her LH or LFB makes her a more likely candidate. The RH, who was guarding the least dangerous opposing LW, shifts to her left to guard the more dangerous opposing LI. The LW is not defended temporarily, but again, she poses the least offensive threat and the passing lanes toward her are covered.

The positioning of the player playing the second line of defense is vital to the success of this defensive tactic. The main purpose for a second line of defense is to prohibit an opposing forward who has broken away from her defender from taking an unhindered shot at the goal. The best position for the covering fullback, then, is at the edge of the striking circle. To advance into the field for a possible tackle leaves one as susceptible to a dodge as was the initial defender. The covering fullback must patiently wait for the oncoming forward, timing her tackle with the forward's commitment to a shot at goal (fig. 7.49).

Many beginning defense players cannot resist the temptation to leave their own forwards and attempt a tackle on a neighboring forward who has broken free. Without teamwork and a good communication system in the defense, the results can be hazardous. In figure 7.50 the RW has broken free from the LH. If the LFB drifts

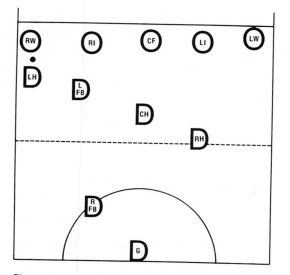

Figure 7.49. **Defense marking and covering with covering fullback in position**

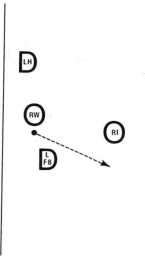

Figure 7.50. **LFB attempts to tackle free RW, leaving R1 available for a pass**

away from her RI and attempts a tackle on the RW, the RI is entirely open for a pass. Beginners should note that it is a defender's responsibility to recover immediately after being dodged and regain defensive positioning on the same forward. Other defenders guard their players closely, eliminating passing options to them. If a defender is unable to recover in time, the free forward will meet the covering fullback at the edge of the striking circle.

In figure 7.51 the defensive alignment is given when the RI or CF has possession of the ball.

In all defensive alignments, the tandem position of the fullbacks is apparent; the fullback on the ball side of the field guards her opponent while the other fullback positions herself on the ball side of the defensive striking circle. Should the forwards send a quick pass to the opposite side of the field, the back fullback sprints forward to resume her defensive obligation to her inner, and the up fullback sprints back to her position

on the ball side of the striking circle. Other defenders continually shift positions, either guarding opponents closely, or covering spaces into which passes might be sent.

For individual defense players, there are a variety of tactics which may be used to gain an advantage in time or movement over an opposing offensive forward.

1. The most vital asset a potential defense player can possess is the ability to anticipate. A defender who is expecting a pass at a certain angle, a dodge at a particular time, or a shot from one specific place always seems to be in the right place at the right time to spoil such offensive maneuvers.

2. A good defender aids her teammates in analyzing the opposing offense, capitalizing on evident weaknesses, and minimizing obvious strengths. She must be willing to verbally communicate pertinent information to her comrades, and heed information given her. The defense must work as a cohesive unit to overcome the offensive attack.

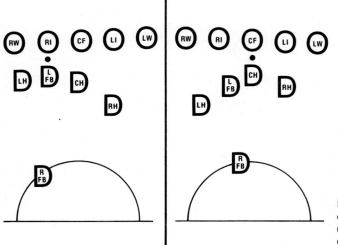

Figure 7.51. **(a) Defensive alignment when opposing inner has possession of the ball; (b) defensive alignment when opposing CF has possession of the ball**

3. Defenders should try to align themselves on the ball side of their opponent and should go to meet the ball rather than waiting for it to come to them.

4. After tackling or intercepting, the defender should dodge nearby opponents if necessary, look for an open forward of her own, and pass to her immediately. A defender who dabbles with the ball after tackling is liable to be tackled back by the opposing forward.

5. A ball obtained through tackling or interception on the right side of the field should usually be passed to the forwards on the left and vice versa. To return a pass into the area from which it came accommodates the opposing defense. A forward stationed away from the last play has a greater chance of being open, also.

6. Defenders playing close to or in their own striking circle must make every effort to clear the ball as quickly as possible and as far from that area as possible. Clearing passes should be directed to the near wing or inner, but never across the goal, for the

likelihood of interception and scoring by the opponents is too great.

7. Defenders in their own striking circle should mark their opponents closely. Any forward left free in the circle is highly dangerous. It is a challenging task to defend a forward who rushes, retreats and rushes again.

8. The goalkeeper should shift to the ball side of the cage so that the most direct route for a shot at goal is blocked. After stopping a ball, the ball should be cleared directly to the near sideline but away from the onrushing forwards.

Strategy for Special Situations

STARTING POSITIONS
Wings may prefer to begin the game standing wide and off the field. Many feel that this position gives them a better running start to cut in front of the defender and receive the pass from the center bully, and also widens the playing area, thereby further spreading the defense. Inners usually line up five yards from the bully in a ready

position to receive a pass. Side halfbacks cover the space of a possible pass to either of the wings, while the center halfback plays five yards from the bully in an attempt to spoil the opposing center forward's efforts to clear the ball to the wings should she win the bully. The left fullback usually begins the game in the up position protecting the center halfback's non-stick side. She plays between her left and center halfbacks but opposite her inner. The right fullback plays in the deep position, in this case in the middle of the defensive circle at the edge. The goalkeeper is positioned three to four feet in front of the center of the cage.

CENTER BULLY

Center forwards have four basic options in attempting to win the beginning center bully. The most frequently used suggests turning the toe of the stick counterclockwise at the completion of the bully, and pulling the ball toward the player while stepping back with the left foot. This is followed by a push pass to the left inner or a flick to the left inner or left wing. A second option suggests that the toe of the stick be turned clockwise after the bully, allowing a push pass between the opposing center forward's legs to the right inner. In the third option, the stick is left in the air following the last stick contact, allowing the opposing center forward to contact the ball. It is hoped that her hit in this situation would be directed to one's own center half or left fullback for a subsequent clearing pass to the wing. The fourth option proposes that the forward attempt to lift the ball over the opponent's stick by squeezing the ball against her stick, then recovering for a quick push pass or flick in either direction.

PENALTY STROKE

A penalty stroke is awarded to the offense when, by fouling, a defender stops a sure goal. The ball is placed seven yards in front of the goal and is directed by an offensive player from this spot toward the goal. The goalkeeper must remain on the goal line, and all other players must remain behind the near twenty-five yard line until completion of the penalty stroke.

The forward's objective in a penalty stroke is to score. After an indication from the official the ball may be directed toward the goal by means of a push pass, a flick, a scoop or an inverted hand flick (left hand low on stick, right hand high). The offensive player should attempt to exploit the goalkeeper's weak position by aiming for the high corners of the goal cage or by using enough force on the stroke that the goalkeeper will not have time to react to the shot. Since only one step is allowed in executing the stroke and since faking is forbidden, the tactics of deception are negated. A team would be wise in selecting the most competent individual to take the penalty stroke.

The defender is at an obvious disadvantage in the penalty stroke. She must be stationary at the time the stroke is started, then must abide by all normal regulations such as not raising her stick above shoulder height to stop or deflect a ball. A shot aimed high above her right shoulder mandates an attempt at a right hand stop, an unnatural maneuver. She must be prepared for a low, medium, or high shot, a shot wide to the edges, a soft or forceful stroke.

She must judge the angle, speed and height quickly, then decide whether it is more appropriate to use feet, pads, body, hands or stick to stop or deflect the ball. A positive and confident attitude, drills to develop quick reaction time, hours of practice and immediate focus upon the ball during the actual penalty stroke will aid the goalkeeper in more successful attempts at defending the goal.

If the offense is successful in scoring, or if the goalkeeper commits a violation such as "sticks," the goal counts and play resumes with a center bully. If the shot is wide or the goalkeeper prevents the goal from scoring, the game is resumed with a defense hit.

FREE HITS

Free hits, awarded at the spot of an opponent's infraction of the rules, are generally taken by halfbacks or fullbacks. Quickness in taking the hit is advantageous in that the opposing team has no time to position against the hit. In order to open spaces for passes to the forwards, the halfback or fullback should be as deceptive as possible while taking the hit. Focal aim and approach for a hit to the left will shift anticipating opponents in that direction. A quick pivot with rapid body rotation would then allow the player to hit to the right, perhaps to the surprise of the opposition. Halfbacks or fullbacks could also use the free hit opportunity to advantage in changing the field of play. A free hit taken by the left halfback need not be passed to the left wing or inner. If the ball has been played on this side of the field for any length of time, the opposing defense has shifted its strength to that side and the offensive forwards are probably tiring. In this instance, a hard free hit drive to the right inner or wing might be gainful. If all the forwards are covered, a flat or back pass may be sent to another halfback or fullback. This maneuver, it is hoped, will draw a defender, thus opening a space for a pass to a forward.

Offensive forwards must be constantly shifting prior to the free hit, trying to open spaces and evade their defenders. A successful free hit occurs only when an offensive forward receives the halfback's or fullback's pass.

Defensive forwards can be of assistance in preventing a successful free hit by the opponents through a maneuver termed "blocking up" the ball. In figure 7.52 the opposing RW, RI and CF have quickly positioned themselves in a small semicircle around the LH, who is taking the free hit. In so doing, most of the halfback's passing options have been nullified and pressure is put on the halfback to execute an almost perfect forceful drive or flick. The slightest miscue will result in a sure interception. Constant movement by the forwards who are blocking up will further detract the halfback. Sticks should be held low to the ground to at least deflect balls which cannot be controlled. Since the defensive forwards have blocked the passing spaces, the defensive halfbacks and fullbacks are free to mark their opponents closely.

PUSH–IN

Players to whom the push-in might be directed should keep the concept of creating spaces in mind. They should not wait in a stationary position for receipt of the ball, but should be moving into created spaces to meet the ball. One possible lineup utilizing this concept is illustrated in figure 7.53. The LW has aligned herself well ahead of the push-in and can utilize the space toward the sideline when the ball leaves the halfback's stick. The LI plays slightly ahead of the roll-in and has maintained a large space to her left, where she might likely receive the ball. The LFB plays a similar position but slightly behind the push-in. The CF and CH have drawn slightly to the left but have retained large open spaces into which they might cut should the ball be directed to either of them.

Those defending against the push-in should anticipate the angle of the pass by

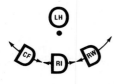

Figure 7.52. **Forwards blocking free hit attempt**

the position of the halfback's stick during contact with the ball. Such anticipation may give the defender a time advantage in reaching the ball ahead of the intended receiver. Defenders might also profit by positioning themselves in the spaces created by the opposing forwards, seriously hindering the halfback's choice of successful passing options.

CORNERS

Corners or penalty corners are awarded when the defense sends the ball out of bounds over the end line or when the defense fouls within the striking circle. Defensive halfbacks and fullbacks are positioned behind the goal line, while defensive forwards must remain beyond the center line. Offensive forwards are aligned around the edge of the striking circle as the offensive halfbacks and the up fullback back up their forward line (fig. 7.54).

Offensively, the wing's hit is usually directed to her near inner or center forward, thereby decreasing the distance of the hit and minimizing the time allotted the defense in rushing out to meet the forwards. Forwards should be in a ready position, sticks down, with feet moving, and should not, in this one instance, go to meet the ball. In so doing, they would advance toward the on-rushing defense. The ball should be contacted once for control, followed by an immediate drive and rush for goal. The wing taking the initial corner hit should be cautioned to return to an onsides position immediately following her hit.

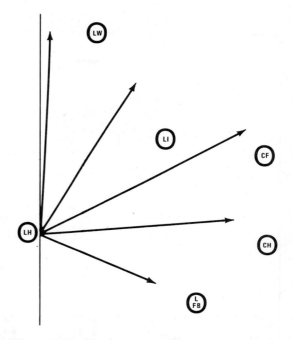

Figure 7.53. **Receivers creating spaces for the push-in**

Defensive halfbacks and fullbacks should align themselves directly opposite their respective forwards so the distance between the two will be as minimal as possible. The defense should be prepared for a sprint start and should synchronize that start with the wing's contact of the ball (fig. 7.55). The defenders should make every effort to intercept the ball before it reaches the forwards. If that is not possible, an attempt should be made to tackle the forward before she shoots, or to at least deflect her shot at goal. Defenders should rush to the stick side of their opposing forwards and keep their sticks down. A defender who rushes only halfway into the circle and stops endangers her defensive unit's effectiveness and her own personal well-being. By hesitating at mid-circle, the defender stands in the goalkeeper's way, puts no pressure on her op-

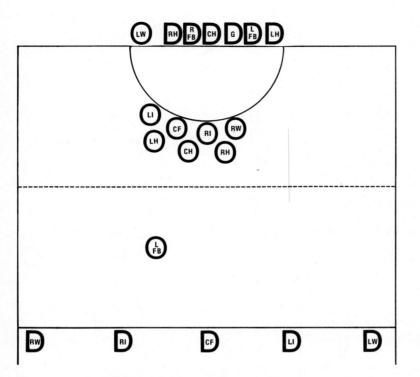

Figure 7.54. **Positioning of players for penalty corner**

Figure 7.55. **Defender sprinting from goal line at ball contact during corner hit**

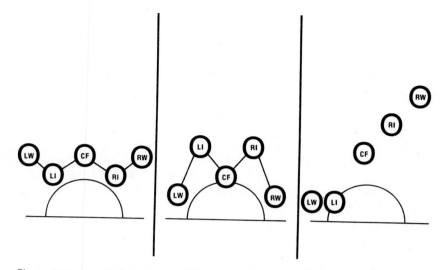

Figure 7.56. (a) **W formation**; (b) **M formation**; (c) **diagonal formation**

posing forward, and is liable to deflect balls into the goal, thereby scoring for the offense. Additionally, she is in personal danger by standing in front of a shooting forward. The mid-circle area should be considered a no-man's-land during the initial phases of the corner.

OFFENSIVE ALIGNMENT IN THE DEFENSIVE HALF OF THE FIELD

The ability of a team's halfbacks, fullbacks and goalkeeper to successfully gain possession of the ball and pass it to their forwards determines the offensive alignment in the defensive half of the field. If there is little problem in getting the ball to the forwards, the forward line players can remain on line with one another and closer to the center-line.

If halfbacks and fullbacks are having some trouble in advancing the ball to the forwards, various alignments may be used. The W formation suggests that the inners drop back toward their own defense players, field short clearing passes and send them immediately to the wing or center forward (fig. 7.56).

The M formation sends one additional player back to aid the defense in clearing the ball. The wings and center drop back and the ball is then passed ahead to the inners (fig. 7.56).

In instances where one side of the defense is having trouble clearing the ball, a diagonal formation may be used as forwards prepare to receive the clearing pass. The wing and inner from the troubled side drop back, field the clearing pass and execute an angular pass to the center forward or a through pass for which the center forward will interchange and receive. The center forward may then keep the ball if unguarded or pass to the right inner or right wing who are farther ahead (fig. 7.56).

DEFENSE HITS

A defense hit (a sixteen-yard hit) is awarded the defending team when the offense sends the ball over the goal line without scoring. The hit is taken sixteen yards from the goal line directly opposite the spot where the ball went out of bounds. All other players must be five yards away.

A fullback usually takes the defense hit. Goalkeepers can be helpful in retrieving out-of-bounds balls and returning them to the fullback for a quick hit away from the goal area. Once again, it would be advantageous to take the hit before the opponents could position against it. Since this is essentially a clearing hit from the goal area, the pathway desired would be diagonally to the wings or, perhaps, a long, through pass to the inners. Seldom, if ever, would the ball be played toward the center of the field, for the opposing team is clustered there, anxiously awaiting an interception and shot at goal.

If the fullback finds that the forwards on her side of the field are covered, she has yet another passing option. The side half is generally positioned only five yards away from the defense hit. The fullback might pass flat to the halfback, who could then clear the ball to a wing or an inner. This invaluable maneuver deserves more use in hockey today.

The forwards who are responsible for the out-of-bounds ball may rectify their mistake by blocking up the defense hit. Since the fullback will probably not use the passing option to her center forward and will certainly not pass across her own goal to a far inner or wing, the forwards can overplay to the sideline side of the fullback.

A System of Defense

CONCEPT Q. A system of defense is essential if a team is to be successful. The prime purposes of the defense are to prevent the opponents from scoring and to capitalize on offensive weaknesses.

Sub-concept Q-1. Team strategies follow a particular planned defensive pattern based on man-to-man defense of a spatial pattern (zone) defense.

There are basically two defensive systems used in field hockey, zone defense and man-to-man defense (in which each defender is responsible for one particular forward, regardless of where that forward roams on the field). The greatest advantage of the man-to-man defense system is that there is little confusion between defenders concerning responsibility for certain individuals. The greatest disadvantages for beginners are a lack of covering defense if one of the opposition breaks free; the tendency to bunch around the ball when forwards and their defenders come in close proximity to one another; the failure to cover spaces adequately while concentrating too hard on staying with the opponent; and possible confusion during offensive interchange.

Zone defense is the more widely used system today. In zone defense halfbacks and fullbacks defend against any player who passes through their specific area of responsibility. The zones are generally defined by the starting positions of a team's defense players (fig. 7.57). The advantages of zone defense are that the defensive unit's position is more stable, thereby allowing an effective system of aiding teammates; there is little confusion during an offensive interchange by the opponents; and players are better able to maintain marking and covering roles in relation to the position of the ball. The most obvious disadvantage of zone defense occurs when the offense puts two or more players in a particular zone, forcing a ratio of two offense players to one defender.

Most teams use a combination of the two defensive systems during play. Man-to-man defense is often used during play in the defensive circle, while a team switches to a zone and covering system of play outside the defensive circle.

SAFETY

As with all sport activities, safety considerations should be of prime importance when teaching field hockey. The instructor must possess a thorough understanding of the particular game situations in which danger may exist and be cognizant of the unique safety-related aspects of the game before she can successfully teach students to become safety conscious. Twenty-two participants moving at full speed over an uneven surface is a challenging safety aspect in itself, but when considering the addition of twenty-two force producing hockey sticks and one very firm and fast moving hockey ball, the need for stringent safety considerations is further manifested. Field hockey need not be a rough, slashing, bruising game. Through effective teaching methods, safety rather than danger becomes the inherent factor in the game. Field hockey can and should be a safe, enjoyable activity for *all* participants.

CONCEPT U. An affective attitude based on a cognitive understanding of the dangers inherent in an activity is necessary if one is to perform safely.

Sub-concept U-1. Providing a safe environment for participation contributes to the development of desirable affective attitudes toward the activity.

FIELD SAFETY

It is erroneous to assume that any large, open field is suitable for field hockey. One of the major factors to be considered in choosing an appropriate field space is its relative smoothness. Fields should be rolled periodically to level the sod and flatten the cleat imprints which often cause balls to bounce irregularly and unexpectedly. If possible, restrictions should be established regarding use of the field. Pathways en-

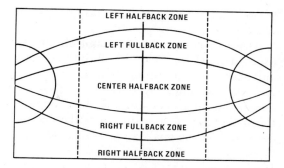

Figure 7.57. **Territory covered by each defender in zone defense**

trenched across the field create a dangerous, irregular surface, and cause bare or excessively worn spots in the field's grassy cover. While players should be able to adapt to the conditions found on different fields and adjust the speed of their game accordingly, bare spots cause increased, irregular rebound of balls, and, much to a player's surprise, may cause a significant difference in the rate of speed of balls passing over them.

Since players are not prohibited from playing in an out-of-bounds position during the game (i.e., wings often position themselves out-of-bounds on the sideline at the starting bully), the area immediately surrounding the playing field should be cleared of all obstacles. Benches should be placed well back from the field. In cases where fields are located adjacent to permanent obstacles, such as fences, tennis courts, poles, and goalposts, adequate measures should be taken to insure that collision with such an obstacle will not be injurious to the participant.

A relatively new hazard for players today is the slick surface of the artificial running track surrounding many multi-use artificial turfs. A quick turn on the track after dashing off the field to save a ball while wearing hard rubber or plastic cleats has given some players a surprising upset!

A non-burning lime or paint should be used in marking fields. Well-defined lines aid players in orienting themselves on the field at all times. A dangerous situation exists when players cannot find the edge of the striking circle and therefore dribble too close toward the goalkeeper before driving.

EQUIPMENT SAFETY

While the various aspects of equipment care are not within the realm of this book, the safe usage of such equiment is. One cannot condone the failure of teachers or coaches to ensure that any protective equipment designed for a particular sport is worn. Players should wear good field shoes and shin guards and goalkeepers must be outfitted in both pads *and* kickers. If the budget is tight, it would be far better to play without goalkeepers entirely rather than having a player participate unsafely.

A constant surveillance and immediate repair of all equipment is mandated if field hockey is to be a safe game. Cracked sticks should be destroyed immediately, splinters or gouges in the toes of sticks should be sanded smooth before play with them resumes, and broken straps or buckles should be replaced immediately. Students should understand the importance of keeping equipment in safe condition and they can help spot equipment needing repair. In some instances, students may be encouraged to learn field hockey equipment repair techniques and therefore, can help the instructor in maintenance.

Sub-concept U-2. Educating the participants to use the environment wisely contributes not only to personal safety but enhances the total climate of the classroom.

PLAYER SAFETY

To further ensure personal safety while participating, students must develop an understanding and appreciation for the safety-related elements of the game. Many of the rules in field hockey have been established for creation of a safer environment (i.e., sticks may not be raised above shoulder height, a forceful hit may not be lofted, the goalkeeper's clears must travel low along the ground, body contact is not allowed). Understanding and following the rules will permit safer play.

Good fundamentals and body control while executing various strokes or skills are probably the two most important aspects of safety in field hockey. A stronger insistence by teachers that skills be executed properly would do much to increase the safety of general play.

Field hockey, as one of the more vigorous and demanding sports for women, necessitates good conditioning. It is when players become overly tired that skills are executed poorly, positioning is poor and body control is lost. A well-conditioned player is vital to the welfare of all concerned.

INDIVIDUALIZING INSTRUCTION

Field hockey is one of the few team sports in which many women participate during the post-school years. The game has a proud history of respect and popularity, and strong bonds of tradition and friendship, making it an endearing activity for the game's participants. It becomes the challenge of the instructor of beginning field hockey players to provide a learning environment in which students may develop the psychomotor skills, cognitive understandings and affective appreciations which enable one to gain utmost satisfaction from the game.

This section is an extension of chapter three, "The Role of Methodology." The material outlined in the following pages provides suggestions for implementation of an indirect method of teaching field hockey.

PLANNING A SKILL PROGRESSION FOR TEACHING

It is suggested that skills be presented in a progression according to need, according to use as foundations for other skills, and according to degree of difficulty. The following is a sample progression for beginners:

a. Grip and carrying position
b. Dribble
c. Push pass
d. Fielding—straight, left, right, behind
e. Drives—left, straight, right
f. Tackles—straight, left-hand lunge, circular
g. Dodges—right and left
h. Scoop
i. Flick
j. Bully, push-in, goalkeeper skills

The rationale behind this skill progression may be helpful. The push pass is taught before the drives in order to aid students in realizing that hockey is a controlled-force game. When drives are taught first, students often find it difficult to grasp the idea of sympathetic passes at a later time. Fielding is taught next not only as a means of legally retrieving the push pass, but also so that fielding techniques can be learned and improved while receiving balls hit with minimal force, so that mistakes are not painful. Basic strategies of passing options and spacing may begin at this time and mini-games could be developed utilizing three or four players, without opponents, emphasizing the dribble, push pass, and fielding techniques learned to date. Rules and boundaries are not necessary at this point.

Drives are taught before tackles so that students appreciate the priority of passing over being tackled in game play. Dodges follow tackles because the successful execution of a dodge is dependent upon one's knowledge and familiarity with the various tackles and is intended as a means of evading tacklers. The scoop and flick are not vital in the early stages, but have enough commonality to allow them to be taught together when they are introduced. Bullies, push-ins and goalkeeper's skills are only important as players become prepared for game play.

It should be understood that this grouping does not refer to a daily progression. The tackles, for example, may be covered over a period of one or several lessons, depending upon the abilities of the individuals.

In the initial phase of skill presentation and development, it is suggested that students not be burdened with all the rules of play (other than those which affect performance of a skill), position play, or specific strategy. Presentation of such information should coincide with the student's ability to integrate that information into game play. This she cannot do until specific levels of skill have been reached. It would seem more valuable to present broad conceptual ideas which students could later apply to specific situations as their ability allows.

By creating many mini-games throughout the presentation of individual skills, the student learns to appreciate the use and value of specific skills, is motivated by modified game play, is afforded maximum practice opportunity due to the reduced number of participants and, most importantly, is internalizing concepts.

EVALUATING SKILL DEVELOPMENT

To state that all students will be able to learn skills at the same rate ignores individual differences and capabilities. In lieu of periodic class skill evaluations, provision should be made for students to progress at their own rate of skill development and have their progress checked accordingly. A chart for each student, listing the skills to be developed, is one suggestion. Whenever the student is ready, she may ask for evaluation of any skill from the instructor. The instructor checks off those skills which have been acquired and keeps the record for the student.

The chart may contain a simple listing of skills, or may combine skills into a more game-like performance task. Evaluation may be either subjective or objective, depending upon the design of the skill listing. Samples of possible performance tasks are included here. Evaluation is mainly objective, except for subjectivity in determining "sticks," or making subjective judgments of proper form used to execute a skill.

1. Start on the twenty-five yard line. Dribble forward toward the center line. Before reaching the center line, drive the ball across the field. To successfully complete this task, the player must execute the drive from a dribble, without stopping, must not commit "sticks," and the ball must at least reach the center of the field.
2. Dribble from the center line toward the goal. Upon reaching the striking circle, drive for goal. To successfully complete this task, the player must be able to dribble the distance without overrunning the ball, execute a legal drive from the *top* of the striking circle, and score a goal from the initial drive.
3. From any distance, dribble forward and execute a scoop stroke over any given line. To successfully complete this task, the player must execute this stroke while moving and the ball must cross the given line while still in the air. "Sticks" must not be committed.
4. Flick a stationary ball a distance of ten yards. to successfully complete this task, the ball must at some time be raised off the ground, a flicking arm motion must be visible, and the ball must travel a total distance of ten yards.
5. In three-on-three competition, demonstrate a successful straight tackle, left-hand lunge and circular tackle. To successfully complete this task, the player must obtain unquestionable possession of the ball.

INDIRECT LESSON

The following is an example of an indirect lesson in field hockey.

Focus

Passing—strategy and skill—is the focus.

Method

Guided discovery is the method used.

Grouping of students

Small groups, four students each, are organized.

Previous instruction

1. Students have learned and can demonstrate each of the four passing strokes: push pass, scoop, flick, and drive.
2. Students can exhibit cognitive understanding of the three passing options, flat, angular and through.

Objectives of lesson

1. The students should learn that the push pass is the most deceptive stroke.

2. The students should learn that the drive takes the longest time of execution.

3. The students should learn that the drive has the most force potential of the strokes.

4. The students should learn that an aerial pass (scoop or flick) is the most difficult for defenders to intercept.

5. The students should be able to demonstrate proper use of passing strokes and options after evaluating the position of teammates and opponents.

Method of presentation

Mimeographed sheets are distributed to students.

LESSON: PASSING

Passing is fundamental to successful team play in field hockey. The ability to execute passes properly and to choose the correct pass for different situations is the hallmark of a good player.

Directions: Form groups of four and find a space in which to work. Each group should have one ball.

1. This problem is designed to help you determine which passing stroke is most deceptive. Form a circle with one player in the middle.
   a. Use a push pass to pass the ball among the players on the circle as the center player attempts to intercept. Count the number of interceptions out of twenty passing attempts.
   b. Use a scoop to pass the ball among the players on the circle. Count the number of interceptions out of twenty passing attempts.
   c. Use a flick to pass the ball among the players on the circle. Count the number of interceptions out of twenty passing attempts.
   d. Use a drive to pass the ball among the players on the circle. Count the number of interceptions of twenty passing attempts.
   e. What reasons can you give for differences in the number of interceptions in these attempts?
   f. While you were in the center of the circle, what factors helped you to predict the direction in which the ball was to be sent?
   g. If you were attempting to pass the ball without interception, how could you disguise your intentions?
   h. Which stroke did you find most deceptive? Why?
2. This problem is designed to help you determine which stroke takes the longest time of execution. X^1, a tackler, stands on the sideline facing X^2, X^3, and X^4, who are standing midway between the sideline and center of the

field. X^3 begins dribbling toward the sideline. X^2 and X^4 move on line with her as possible pass receivers. When the ball touches the sideline, X^1 may move in to tackle. X^3 attempts to pass to X^2 or X^4.

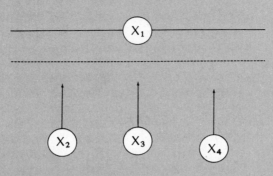

a. Try this problem using only push passes. Of ten attempts, how many were intercepted?
b. Try this problem using only flicks as passes. Of ten attempts, how many were intercepted?
c. Try this problem using only scoops as passes. Of ten attempts, how many were intercepted?
d. Try this problem using only drives as passes. Of ten attempts, how many were intercepted?
e. What reasons can you give for differences in the number of interceptions?
f. As a tackler, why were you more successful intercepting some passes more than others?
g. As a passer, what factors must you take into consideration before attempting to pass?
h. Which stroke did you find required the longest time of execution? Why?

3. This problem is designed to help you determine which stroke or strokes should be used for passes of different distances. Position players along the centerline in the right wing, right inner, center forward and left wing positions. The right wing should dribble forward and attempt a pass to each of her teammates, using the four different passing strokes.
a. Pass to each player using a push pass.
b. Pass to each player using a scoop.
c. Pass to each player using a flick.
d. Pass to each player using a drive.
e. Which passes reached the right inner?
f. Which passes reached the center forward?
g. Which passes reached the left wing?
h. Which stroke(s) would you recommend for passes of short distance? Why?

 i. Which stroke(s) would you recommend for passes of medium distance? Why?

 j. Which stroke(s) would you recommend for passes of great distance? Why?

4. This problem is designed to help you determine if some passing strokes are naturally more difficult to intercept than others. X^1 and X^3 are teammates attempting to keep the ball from X^2. X^4 is a recorder. The ball must remain within boundaries as defined by the sideline and a parallel five-yard line. X^1 begins with the ball.

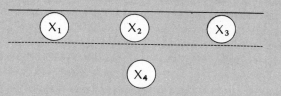

 a. Pass the ball to your teammate using a push pass. Of ten attempts, how many were intercepted?

 b. Pass the ball to your teammate using a scoop. Of ten attempts, how many were intercepted?

 c. Pass the ball to your teammate using a flick. Of ten attempts, how many were intercepted?

 d. Pass the ball to your teammate using a drive. Of ten attempts, how many were intercepted?

 e. What reasons can you give for differences in the number of interceptions?

 f. Which stroke or strokes are the most difficult to intercept? Why?

5. As a culminating activity, combine with another group of four. From this group, form two teams of four each. Play a four-against-four game using the passing strokes, passing options and strategy you have learned. After each interception, stop play and analyze the cause of the interception. Discuss the stroke or passing option which should have been used to prevent the interception. Boundaries, goals and additional rules are optional.

GENERAL COMMENTS ON TEACHING FIELD HOCKEY

1. The game should not be sacrificed for lack of equipment. The United States Field Hockey Association should be consulted for equipment on loan.

2. To ensure success and eliminate fear for beginners, larger or softer balls should be used (i.e., old basketballs, soccer balls, softballs, or tennis balls).

3. Rather than rushing into the confusion of game play, numerous mini-games may be used to focus on the game's components. Students will gain more from the active involvement and practice.

4. Almost all game play should be actively coached. It is difficult in field hockey to simulate many game situations and it is advantageous to all to have game play halted, the situation described and analyzed, then play resumed.

5. When players do become engaged in team play, the same positions should be

maintained over an extended period of time. Switching positions daily or weekly is too confusing for beginners.

6. The instructor should insist that the proper grip and dribble position be learned well. These are the basic components of most other skills.

7. The instructor should teach toward safety—and demand safe methods of skill execution. There should be no excuse for beginners not stopping the ball before redirecting it, or lofting the ball on drives.

REFERENCES

Barnes, Mildred J. *Field Hockey: The Coach and the Player.* Boston, Mass.: Allyn & Bacon, 1969.

Delano, Anne Lee. *Field Hockey.* Dubuque, Iowa: Wm. C. Brown Company Publishers, 1966.

National Association for Girls and Women in Sport. *Field Hockey-LaCrosse Guide.* Washington, D.C.: Alliance Association for Health, Physical Education & Recreation, (Current Edition).

Haussermann, Caroline. *Field Hockey.* Boston, Mass.: Allyn & Bacon, 1970.

Heyhoe, Rachael. *Just for Kicks: A Guide to Hockey Goalkeeping.* Oxford, England: Marjorie Pollard Publications, 1970.

Know the Game Coach Yourself Series: Women's Hockey. Oxford, England: Marjorie Pollard Publications, 1968.

Mackey, Helen. *Field Hockey: An International Team Sport.* Englewood Cliffs, N.J.: Prentice-Hall, 1963.

Mushier, Carole L. *Team Sports for Girls and Women.* Dubuque, Iowa: Wm. C. Brown Company Publishers, 1973.

Taylor, Eileen. *Coaching Hockey in Schools.* Oxford, England: Marjorie Pollard Publications.

8

Soccer

INTRODUCTION

The team sport of soccer is a space game. The space designated for an official game is 75 by 120 yards (maximum) and 60 by 90 yards (minimum). However, for class purposes the dimensions of the space may vary and still be adaptable to soccer-like games. The playing surface should be a smooth, well-sodded, level area free of debris and holes. The field markings needed for the game are shown in figure 8.1.

The *general space* or playing field is shared by twenty-two players, eleven on each team. Each team is lined up on its own half of the field for the kickoff. The lineup of the players for the kickoff is shown in figure 8.18. The purpose of the game is to maintain or obtain possession of the ball, propel it through or down the opponents' half of the field and send it into the opponents' goal, which is a space six yards wide and eight feet high. Each player must maneuver in space in relation to his teammates, the position of the ball, and the position of his opponents.

Soccer is a vigorous game, requiring players to have a great deal of speed and endurance. The official game for high school is played in four eighteen minute quarters with a two minute rest between quarters and a ten minute rest between halves. Players other than the goalkeeper should find themselves moving most of the time the ball is in play.

Soccer is a game of force. The objective may be to create force or to absorb force. Regardless, one must be able to control force. Sometimes the ball is contacted with a great deal of force, sending it toward the goal or clearing it away from the goal. A great deal of force might be needed to send the ball across in front of the goal in a position to score or to send it to a speedy wing when clearing it away from one's own goal. A

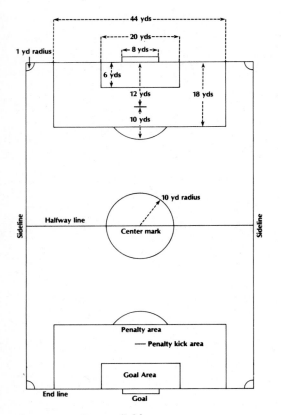

Figure 8.1. **Soccer field**

tripping, blocking and other body contact is illegal in girl's soccer and the team committing a body contact foul is penalized. In addition, controlling the ball in soccer involves more than just kicking with the feet. The head, shoulders, trunk or legs may be used to contact the ball. One may contact the ball near the ground, sending it away with a kick, or contact it above the level of the ground using the action identified as the volley. The progress of the ball may be impeded by a block with the trunk or thighs, or stopped completely by a trap with the lower legs and feet. Even the portion of the foot that contacts the ball in the kick varies with the task to be accomplished. Thus, the soccer player must be adept in using various body parts for controlling the ball both in direction and force if the game is to be safe and skillfully played.

The element of time is evident in the skills of soccer. The player moves quickly or deliberately (slowly), accelerates and decelerates, moves suddenly or with sustainment as the situation demands. He must judge the speed of the ball and the speed of his opponent if he is to maneuver into the right space at the right time. Some soccer skills have a distinct rhythmic pattern while in others the accent of execution is quite evident. Soccer is a game of timing and rhythm.

Soccer is a game involving flow and sequence of movements. A continuous sequence may be as simple as the continuous action of the leg in kicking a stationary ball, involving the backswing, the contact, and the follow-through. Or, the sequence may be as involved as moving to get into position, jumping to block, landing, passing the ball on and then moving to be in an advantageous position again. Smooth, coordinated, flowing movements are evident in a good soccer player.

lighter force is used to dribble and pass short distances. On the other hand, a player may need to absorb force as he attempts to impede the progress of the ball with a trap or a block, striving to gain possession of the ball in order to direct it to his team's advantage.

The main skills needed for soccer are running and kicking. However, the locomotor skill needed to maneuver in space in relation to other people and the ball involves more than just running. A player must be able to start, to stop, and to change directions quickly. The soccer player must learn to control the movement of his body in space to avoid contact with other players. Pushing,

Soccer is a challenging game. In no other game are the ball handling techniques restricted to parts of the body other than the hands. Although the feet and legs are predominantly used, the ball can also be contacted with the parts of the trunk, shoulder and head. The goalkeeper is the only player permitted to play the ball with the hands and then only while in the penalty area. Beginning students in soccer are challenged by the requirement of playing the ball with the feet and have a great deal of fun overcoming the urge to touch the ball with the hands.

SAFETY

CONCEPT U. An affective attitude based on a cognitive understanding of the dangers inherent in an activity is necessary if one is to perform safely.

Sub-concept U-1. Providing a safe environment for participation contributes to the development of desirable affective attitudes toward the activity.

Sub-concept U-2. Educating the participants to use the environment wisely contributes not only to personal safety but enhances the total climate of the classroom.

Students must feel that the game of soccer is safe if they are to participate fully and enthusiastically. Provisions for safety include appropriate personal equipment for individual players, a safe playing field or space, and the development of body and ball control.

Personal attire that allows freedom of movement is a necessity. Allowing students to wear slacks outdoors on cold days will increase the enthusiasm for going outdoors to play soccer. This added covering not only provides warmth but also helps to take the sting out of the contact with the ball when blocking with the legs. Shin guards of the hockey type are desirable. Glass guards or elastics to keep the glasses firmly in place are an important necessity. Appropriate shoes are probably the greatest problem. Although rubber-cleated shoes are most appropriate, they are seldom available. Tennis shoes with rough bottoms afford sufficient traction and are usually both available and appropriate. Bare feet or street shoes are taboo. Bare feet provide no protection to the feet of the player, while the stiff sole of street shoes could be dangerous to other players.

The field or playing space must be free of obstructions and debris. The outdoor turf should be closely cropped, reasonably level and void of holes or depressions. A dry field is also desirable since traction is decreased with an increase in wetness.

Sometimes, due to weather conditions, it becomes necessary to conduct the soccer class indoors. Again the space should be clear of obstacles. The arrangement of activities must be suitable to the space available and the lesson conducted accordingly. Deflating the balls will increase rolling friction and decrease the rebound, making the balls easier to control on the firm gymnasium floor.

The development of individual skill in ball handling and body control will also enhance the safety of the game for all players. A more detailed explanation of specific skill techniques which contribute to safe play is included in the discussion of body and ball control.

The remainder of the chapter expands the ideas expressed in the introduction. Major concepts, individual ball handling techniques, strategy, and specific game situations are explored as they relate to soccer.

MAJOR CONCEPTS

The initial experiences a beginning student in soccer has with the ball should develop the concepts of creating the appropriate amount of force, applying this force in the desired direction, and receiving or absorbing the force of the ball. An understanding of these concepts, along with many opportunities to practice, leads to better ball control. The organization of students, space and equipment should begin with the simplest combination of variables: moving the ball between students while keeping the students relatively stationary. Moving the ball and body through space, and in relation to other people, is introduced as the students develop ball control. The major concepts are common to many sports, as discussed in chapter five. The unique application of the major concepts to soccer skills is included in the following section. For ease of reference the concepts are grouped and lettered according to the same categories and letters designated in chapter five.

Moving an object through space

Striking can be defined as altering the state (momentum and trajectory) of an object by meeting it with a force greater than, less than, or equal to its initial force. The bulk of the skills in soccer fall into the category of striking. Moving the soccer ball with control involves movements of the body which create, direct, and/or absorb force as the body and ball come into contact. The concepts listed and discussed in the following material are related to controlling the ball by striking it with some part of the body or gaining control of the ball by allowing it to strike some part of the body.

CONCEPT E. Directing force: The direction in which an object moves is determined by the point at which force is applied in relation to the object's center of gravity.

Sub-concept E-1. Applying force directly through the center of gravity of an object results in a straight trajectory; an off-center application of force produces a curved trajectory.

Sub-concept E-3. Contacting an object with a large, flat surface facilitates applying force directly through the center of gravity in the direction desired.

The use of a large, flat striking surface increases a player's control of the ball. Since the use of the hands and arms is prohibited for all players except the goalkeeper, contact with the ball must be made with other parts of the body. All the surfaces of the foot (inside, outside, heel, toe, sole and instep) can be used to contact the ball.[1] For balls traveling at greater heights, the head or shoulder can be used. Although all body surfaces and all body parts, with the exception of arms and hands not held tightly to the body, can legally be used to contact the ball, certain characteristics make some parts more desirable than others. The larger and flatter the contacting surface, the more control one has of the ball. Those surfaces of the foot which present the most desirable contacting surface are the inside, outside and instep.

In addition, a large, flat surface provides more area for contacting the ball, thus increasing the chances of controlling the ball by contacting it in line with its center of gravity. Although spin may be desirable in advanced play, the beginner quite often has the problem of imparting uncontrolled spin to the ball. A spinning ball loses force and is difficult to receive and control. A game becomes hazardous when players kick indis-

1. The instep is that portion of the foot covered by the laces of the shoe.

criminately at the ball, causing it to spin and rebound in an uncontrolled manner.

Sub-concept E-2. Keeping one's eyes on the object (i.e., objective focus or tracking) facilitates the application of force in line with the intended direction of flight or the absorption of force when slowing or stopping an object. However, if the performer is throwing at a target, he must focus on the target rather than on the projectile.

The need for objective focus is quite evident; however, it is not unusual for a beginner to look to where he intends to project the ball rather than watch the ball. Although the field should be surveyed in order to determine where to kick, this should be done quickly and prior to contact with the ball. At the instant of contact, the eyes should be focused on the ball.

Sub-concept E-4. External forces such as gravity, air resistance, and friction alter the flight of a projectile.

CONCEPT C. A player must be in a desirable position in relation to the object to be projected.

CONCEPT D. Creating Force: The production and transfer of force depend upon mass, speed, and the striking surface used.

Sub-concept D-1. Increasing the mass used to produce force increases the force produced.

Sub-concept D-2. Increasing the speed of the implement or the body segment imparting force increases the force produced.

Sub-concept D-3. Increasing the range of movement of the body segment or the implement imparting force increases the

distance through which speed can be developed, as well as the force imparted to the object.

Sub-concept D-4. Setting the body in motion prior to contact with an object, or to the release of an object, builds greater force which in turn is transferred to the object. However, at the instant of contact or release, the body should be stabilized.

Sub-concept D-5. A follow-through allows for greater force to be transferred to an object.

Sub-concept D-6. Stabilizing the body segments involved in an action allows for greater force to be imparted to the object.

Sub-concept D-7. A firm striking surface allows for greater force to be imparted to the object.

Because of body structure, the greatest possible range when using the leg as a lever is derived from a forward-backward movement. This movement (a kicking action) involves the extension of the hip joint, flexion of the knee and possibly some lower trunk rotation during the backswing to achieve the greatest range to build speed and thus force. As the leg is swung forward to contact the ball, the hip is flexed and the knee extended. The action is a sequential movement with the hip joint being stabilized and the knee extending very quickly at the instant of ball contact. A strong follow-through insures that the speed of the foot is not decreased before contact with the ball. Additional momentum can be built by taking a few running steps before contacting the ball.

In addition to contributing to speed, rotation of the trunk and sequential movement also contribute to mass or weight in producing force. A third action, the transfer of body weight, occurs as one kicks and then runs to be in position to play the ball again. The total body moves forward over the supporting foot and weight is eventually transferred onto the kicking leg and foot in the follow-through as the player moves in the direction force is applied.

Stability of the body during the kick is somewhat of a problem since the base of support, the foot, is small. It is imperative that the soccer player center his weight over the supporting foot, lower his center of gravity with a slight flexion of the knee, and use his arms to counterbalance when projecting the ball with one foot or leg. Achieving a spacial relationship with the ball which allows the kicking leg to be positioned below the hip during contact rather than reaching out into space also contributes to stability. Thus, the supporting foot should be positioned beside the ball at the instant of contact.

Due to anatomical limitations, building momentum through range of motion when striking the ball with body parts other than the foot is limited. It is important, then, that greater body mass be incorporated into creating force for these contacts. For example, when using the head or shoulder to contact the ball, a forceful extension of the knees projects the total body upward and forward involving greater mass in force production. The feet usually leave the ground (in a jump) upon contact with the ball, and the total body follows through in the direction in which the ball is projected.

The knee also can be used to contact the ball. Again, range of motion is limited but not to the extent of a head or shoulder volley.[2] Mass, too, is incorporated in the knee volley and the total body may leave the ground as force is applied in a forward-upward direction.

The fourth factor in determining the amount of force imparted to the ball upon contact is the amount of force transferred to the ball by the striking surface. A striking surface that is firm and stable will transfer more force to the ball than one that is soft and pliable. This also applies to the amount of force returned to a ball that rebounds from contact with the body. The parts of the body that provide a firm rebounding surface are the head, shoulders, and feet, providing that the neck, shoulders, and ankles are stabilized. The flexed anterior surface of the knee joint also provides a firm stable surface for the knee volley.

CONCEPT G. To receive an object which is moving through space a performer must slow or stop its motion by absorbing all or part of its force.

CONCEPT H. Three techniques help the performer to absorb force efficiently: (1) establishing a stable position; (2) utilizing the largest possible surface area; and (3) increasing the time or distance over which the force is received.

Sub-concept H-1. A stable position should be maintained as the force of an object is absorbed.

Sub-concept H-2. A large surface area reduces the force that is received by any one area of that surface.

Sub-concept H-3. Moving the receiving surface with the ball upon contact (giving with the ball) allows force to be absorbed over a greater time and distance.

Controlling the ball by absorbing its momentum may involve stopping the ball completely (motionlessness), known as the trap, or merely absorbing the force of the

2. A volley is the act of contacting a high bouncing or aerial ball with some part of the body and projecting it in an upward direction again.

ball to some degree, causing it to remain near the body (as in the block). The purpose of both of these tactics is to place the ball in an appropriate position to be redirected. Keeping the eyes on the ball and getting in line to receive the force of the ball near the center of gravity of the body are necessary for successful execution of both the block and the trap. If an oncoming ball is received near to the center of gravity of the body the less chance there is for the body to be pulled off balance due to the extension of a body part away from the center of gravity or due to the added weight or force of the ball. When positioning the body to receive the ball for a block or a trap, the player should position himself directly in line with the pathway of the ball.

The striking surface for the block should be large and pliable to allow force to be absorbed over a greater area. To absorb force over a greater time and distance the blocking surface gives with the ball, or moves with the ball upon contact. This absorption can involve the foot or leg (the inside of the thigh) moving backward with the ball while the supporting foot remains stationary. A block with the anterior surface of the trunk or upper thighs involves the total body moving backward with a small jump. Curling the trunk, which provides a concave surface for the ball to strike and roll down, increases the time and distance over which force is absorbed. The body surfaces most often used for blocking are the chest and upper thighs. Girls may prefer to cross the arms over the chest to protect the breasts when blocking with the chest area. This action is legal providing the arms are not lifted or moved in any fashion to give impetus to the ball. If the arms are not folded across the chest they should be extended to the sides of the body for balance. The inside of the leg and foot can also be used to block the ball; however,

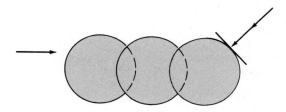

Figure 8.2. **Force to trap the ball is directed diagonally downward.**

this surface is smaller and less pliable. Securing the ball motionless against the ground is termed trapping. To counteract and stop the momentum of the ball, force must be applied diagonally downward and opposite to the direction of the approaching ball (fig. 8.2).

Again, the larger and flatter the contacting surface the greater are the chances for applying force through the center of gravity of the ball. If force is applied off-center, the ball will pop out of the trap in the direction of least resistance. The parts of the body suitable for trapping are the soles of the feet, front of both legs, inside of both legs and the front or inside of one leg.

Whether an oncoming ball is played with a trap or a block depends somewhat upon the ability of the individual. The block is a faster technique and is more desirable if opponents are in a position to attempt to gain possession of the ball. The trap affords greater control and might be the best choice for a beginner or the best choice for handling forceful spinning balls. The height at which the ball is traveling from the ground is obviously another factor to be considered.

CONCEPT F. Sending the ball to a receiver who is moving requires directing the ball to an open space ahead of him.

MOVING THE BODY AND AN OBJECT THROUGH SPACE

The concepts and discussion in chapter 5, pages 81–82 concerning dribbling apply to dribbling the ball in soccer.

CONCEPT I. Since the purpose of the dribble is to maintain possession of the ball while moving through space, the amount and direction of force applied to the ball must be controlled.

CONCEPT J. The ability to dribble with alternating hands or feet provides maximum flexibility in controlling the ball and its direction.

The ability to dribble with both the inside and outside of both feet in soccer lends itself to even greater flexibility in changing direction.

CONCEPT K. In order to reach the desired goal in the shortest possible time, the dribbler must move in a direct pathway; however, intervening opponents and other variables on occasion cause the dribbler to maneuver in flexible, non-direct pathways.

CONCEPT L. Although there is a distinct rhythmic pattern involved in dribbling, the tempo may increase or decrease as a pattern of play evolves.

CONCEPT M. Although the dribbler must focus his eyes on the ball during contact, he must also survey the playing area in order to be able to change tactics as the situation demands.

MOVING THE BODY THROUGH SPACE

CONCEPT A. Moving the body with control involves a conscious manipulation of the center of gravity in relation to the base of support, either to maintain stability or to initiate locomotor movement, as the situation demands.

Sub-concept A-1. Staying ready to move allows a player to get a faster start in order to outmaneuver the opponent, to gain possession of the ball, or to get into a desirable position to project an object.

Sub-concept A-2. Enlarging the base of support in the direction of the force allows a player to start, stop, and change direction quickly.

Sub-concept A-3. Running in a forward direction is the quickest way to cover a distance of some magnitude.

Sub-concept A-4. Sliding sideways or in a diagonally forward or backward direction is often a more efficient manner of moving the body through space if the distance to be covered is minimal and if the body needs to remain facing the immediate objective.

Sub-concept A-5. Recovering quickly after the execution of a skill involves reassuming the ready position and relocating oneself in space in the home position, or some other advantageous position, in order to stay alert and ready to react again.

Sub-concept A-6. Propelling the body through space requires a firm reacting surface and sufficient friction between the reacting surface and the base of support.

The soccer player must be alert to play on the field and continually maneuver into a desirable position in relation to the ball, teammates and opponents. Thus, he faces the direction of play, assumes a slight forward-back stride, and transfers his weight to the balls of the feet in a position of readiness. From this position the player may move sideward with a sliding action or sprint forward to cover a greater distance more quickly. The sliding action is possibly more of a defensive technique as the player maneuvers to close spaces through which the opponent and/or ball might pass. Although one finds the forward line and half-backs sprinting more often as they attempt to stay abreast of play, defensive backs should also sprint to meet a long pass or shot at the goal in order to reverse play before the opponents close in. Although all movements should be deliberate and purposeful, starting, stopping and changing directions become second nature to a soccer player who stays alert to the play as it evolves on the field. Appropriate footwear and favorable field conditions contribute to the efficiency of locomotor movements and the safety of the soccer player as he moves over the space of the field. After each maneuver the player should immediately recover and resume a waiting position of readiness.

CONCEPT B. Creating and absorbing force to control the movement of the body through space may involve all of the body or only parts of the body, in unison or in sequence; however, the relaxation of noncontributing muscle groups is imperative for smooth, efficient movement.

Sub-concept B-2. Absorbing the force of a landing or fall over a greater time and distance increases stability and decreases the chance of injury.

The possibility of tripping and/or falling is constantly present as players share the space of the field, accelerate, decelerate and change directions quickly. Although beginners probably lose their balance more frequently, the ability to absorb the momentum of a loss of balance safely and to recover to a balanced position on the feet quickly is important to all soccer players. Quite often a rolling action is incorporated deliberately to absorb force over a greater time and distance and to reestablish a position up on the feet.

Sub-concept B-3. Relaxing noncontributing muscle groups leads to smooth, efficient movement and thus to the proficiency of the performance.

Staying loose as one stays ready is not only important for the conservation of energy but also contributes to a smooth, coordinated initiation of locomotion or execution of the movement itself, whether it be movement of the body through space or the manipulation of the ball through space. Probably a feeling of confidence (the affective domain), the feeling that one can execute the right movement at the right time, makes the greatest contribution to the ability of the player to stay loose.

SAMPLE LESSON, GUIDED DISCOVERY METHOD

The following are a few sample problems in which the student explores alternatives and makes decisions as to which techniques are more desirable in each situation. The cognitive understandings that evolve from the experiences contribute to an understanding of major concepts while the movement techniques employed lead quite naturally into several specific soccer skills (kick, pass, block, and trap). The questions must be clearly and carefully constructed to lead the student to the predetermined solution (that solution predetermined by the teacher). Due to the need to have students scattered over a wide area and in order to allow students to work at their own pace, the problems should be mimeographed. The

LESSON

PREDETERMINED SOLUTIONS

Major Ideas:

Any surface of the foot may be used to send and receive the ball; however, the characteristics of the surface and the direction in which the body is facing will influence the choice of surface to be used.

Selected Facts:

1. A large, flat surface affords more control, since one is more likely to apply force through the center of gravity of the ball.
2. The top surface of the foot with toes pointed down is the best surface for sending the ball forward; the lateral surfaces (inside and outside of the foot) for sending it diagonally forward or sideward; and the heel for sending it backward.

SAMPLE PROBLEMS

Problems:

A. Working with a partner and keeping the ball low (rolling or at least at knee level), experiment to discover how many different surfaces of the foot can be used to send and receive the ball. Stop the ball each time before sending it back to your partner.
   1. Try all parts of the foot; top, bottom, inside, etc.
   2. Can you name the parts or surfaces?
   3. Do some parts give you more control over the ball than others?
   4. Try sending and receiving with your non-dominant foot (the one you do not automatically use).
   5. Can the same surfaces be used to both send and receive?
   6. List the parts that were most easily used and which gave you the most control.
   7. List the parts that were awkward.
   8. Do the surfaces most easily used have any characteristics in common (characteristics possibly not found in the awkward surfaces)?
B. Again sending and receiving with a partner, change the direction the body is facing in relation to your target (your partner).
   1. Face him squarely and send and receive. What part(s) of the foot is best used to send and receive from this position?
   2. Face directly away from him and send and receive. What part(s) of the foot is best used to send and receive from this position?
   3. Turn one side of your body toward your partner to send and receive. What part(s) of the foot is best used to send and receive from this position?

4. Turn to face diagonally away from your partner (a slight angle) and send and receive. What part(s) of the foot is best used to send and receive from this position?

5. Can you agree that the direction the body is facing in relation to the target will influence the choice of part(s) of the foot used to send and receive the ball?

The class should discuss the previous problems and concepts.

C. Send and receive again with your partner using the surfaces of the foot that give you the most control. Rather than trapping the ball to the ground when you receive, contact it with a light touch, causing it to rebound slightly but remain near the body.

1. Which surfaces keep the ball in front of the body in a good position to be sent?

2. What is the best position for the receiving surface in relation to the pathway of the ball?

3. How do your eyes help you make a controlled contact with the ball?[3]

Discuss problem C. Problem C involves two contacts with the ball, one to receive and one to send. Problems that follow can lead to:

(While stationary with partner)
a. one contact to send and receive;
b. three contacts: one to receive, one to position the ball, and one to send.

(Moving through space with a partner and a ball)
a. one contact to receive and send;
b. two contacts: one to receive and one to send;
c. three contacts (or more): one to receive, one to position the ball, and one to send.

3. This question stresses the need for objective focus, i.e., keeping the eyes on the ball when receiving.

total class may be gathered together periodically for discussion.

These problems lead the student to explore the alternatives or choices he has upon receiving the ball. Shall he pass it with the same contact he receives it? What are the advantages of this one-touch contact? What are the disadvantages? Or, shall he use one contact to impede the progress of the ball and a second contact to pass the ball on? What are the disadvantages of a two-touch maneuver? Or shall the player maintain possession of the ball and dribble?

Discovering the selected facts to gain an understanding of the concepts often necessitates deliberate effort on the part of the students and restricts their movements to a limited space. This can lead to boredom if pursued for too long a time. Each class period should include situations in which the students move in space with the ball and a partner (in small groups), using the concepts discovered in the first part of the period. For example, a lesson exploring the concepts of force can terminate in a practice session of dribbling and driving for the goal.

The combination of skills becomes more complex and game-like as the students progress in their ability to control the ball and their bodies in space.

INDIVIDUAL BALL HANDLING TECHNIQUES

The success of a soccer team is dependent not only upon teamwork but also upon the ability of each individual to control the ball, receive the ball, maintain possession of the ball, and gain possession of the ball from the opponent. Some of the techniques may be considered offensive techniques, while others are defensive. There are a variety of ways to classify these soccer skills. This section will classify them under two broad headings: "Controlling the Ball with the Feet," and "Controlling the Ball with Other Body Parts." The conventional skills of soccer can be learned while exploring the movement possibilities under these two broad categories.

Controlling the ball with the feet includes creating and applying force to the ball (kicking and volleying), stopping the momentum of the ball in order to control and redirect it (trapping), and gaining possession of the ball from the opponent (tackling).

Controlling the ball with body parts other than the feet includes creating and applying force to the ball (volleying), absorbing the force of the ball (blocking and picking up passes), and the goalkeeper's privileges of catching and punting, throwing, or drop-kicking.

Controlling the Ball with the Feet

Creating and applying force to the ball with the feet can be accomplished by using a variety of techniques for a variety of purposes. These actions are given specific titles which are descriptive of the techniques and/or the purpose of the play on the ball. Included in this section is an analysis of the dribble, the place kick, the volley with the foot, kicking with the heel, passing and shooting for goal. Each analysis is outlined according to the parts of the body used (body awareness) and the elements of movement (space, force, time, and flow). To envision the total technique one must read the total analysis.

THE DRIBBLE

The dribble is the technique of moving the ball along the ground while maintaining possession of it (fig. 8.3).

Body Awareness

1. It is desirable to dribble with both feet, alternating contacts with each foot.
2. The inside of the foot with the leg rotated outward is the easiest portion to use when traveling in a straight line.
3. Contacting the ball with the outside of the foot, or alternating contacts with the inside of one foot and the outside of the other, will move the ball in a curved pathway.

Space

1. The ball should be kept close to the feet, ten to twelve inches away, to maintain possession and control and to be in a position to change directions quickly.
2. One should dribble in a straight line (with a forward direction) to cover space more quickly.
3. One may need to dribble in a curved or zigzag pathway in order to evade opponents.
4. The dribbler should keep his eyes on the ball during contact, but should also look up to survey the playing field in order to change his pathway as the situation demands.

Figure 8.3. Dribbling with the inside of alternate feet using a kick, step-step-step; kick, step-step-step pattern

Force

1. In the dribble there is a very light application of force—a mere tapping of the ball.

2. Because the desired force is light, the backswing and follow-through of the kicking foot are almost nonexistent.

Time

1. There is a distinct rhythmic pattern when dribbling. The pattern most often used is a kick, step-step-step; kick, step-step-step; etc. One may also hop on the supporting foot when contacting the ball.

2. The player should adjust the speed of the ball and his steps so that the supporting foot is placed beside the ball as the kicking foot makes contact.

3. The player should be able to change the timing and rhythm of the dribble, increasing and decreasing speed in order to feint and outwit the opponent.

Flow

1. The dribble consists of a continuous sequence of movements that involves running and kicking while remaining on balance.

2. The center of gravity of the body is continuously shifted over the moving base (the feet) without stopping the movement.

3. The follow-through of the kick is either onto the kicking foot or taken onto the supporting foot with a hop.

4. The dribbling action involves a continuous flow of movement of both the ball and the body in the desired direction.

THE PLACE KICK

A place kick is a contact with the ball while it is in a stationary position on the ground. The kickoff, free kick, corner kick, goal kick and penalty kick are place kicks. The purpose of the place kick may be to send the ball a great distance with a great deal of speed or it may be to send it to some specific target, a person or goal. Although force may be important, one cannot discount direction and vice versa. The purpose of the kick will determine what part of the foot is used to contact the ball and how much force is applied (fig. 8.4).

Body Awareness

1. The part of the foot that will give the kick the most force is the instep (the top of the foot with toes pointed down).

Figure 8.4. **Place kick. A short preliminary run builds greater momentum.**

2. The player may kick with the inside or outside of the foot in order to deceive opponents; however, force is sacrificed for deception.

Space

1. Generally the supporting foot is placed alongside the ball when kicking.

2. Placing the supporting foot a little behind the ball will cause the ball to be lofted due to an application of force below the center of gravity of the ball.

3. The player should keep his eyes on the ball for the contact.

4. All comments concerning direction listed under "Major Concepts," pages 196–197, apply to place kicks.

Force

1. Due to the possibility of a greater backswing and follow-through, the instep kick will allow more force to be applied to the ball.

2. The inside of the foot rates second in being forceful, providing the body is well stabilized when kicking.

3. The kick with the outside of the foot is weak in force production due to an awkward backswing.

4. If force is the objective of the kick, one should precede the kick with several running steps to build momentum.

Time

1. It is of great importance that the movements are timed so that the body is stable at the instant of impact.

Flow

1. The momentum built by the preceding running steps should flow into the action of the kick and generally the follow-through will flow into a run or a ready position to allow the player to play the ball again.

VOLLEY WITH THE FOOT

The volley can be distinguished from the kick in that the ball is contacted before it strikes the ground. The kick is a contact with the ball traveling along the ground. The volley is a contact with an aerial ball (a ball traveling in the air) and generally the ball is sent back into the air as opposed to toward the ground (fig. 8.5).

Body Awareness

1. Any part of the foot may be used to contact and redirect the ball; however, a large, flat surface makes it easier to control the ball.

2. The inside and top of the foot (instep) are used most often; however, the outside of the foot may also be used.

3. A player should learn to use either foot equally well in volleying the ball.

Space

1. The part of the foot that is to contact the ball should be in line with the trajectory of the ball and angled in the desired direction to project the ball.

Force

1. If the ball is coming with sufficient force one need only present a firm, flat rebounding surface.

2. If the player intends to add to the force of the rebound the contacting surface or foot should be moving in the intended direction of the rebound. Again, the instep and inside of the foot are best for creating force because of a greater backswing. The outside of the foot has a shorter and more awkward backswing.

Time

1. The player must time the contact with the ball so that it is contacted knee-high or lower. It is extremely difficult to maintain balance and contact the ball with the foot if the ball is contacted much higher than the knee. If the ball is higher some other part of the body should be used to contact the ball—possibly the knee.

Flow

1. The sequence of movements involves getting into position behind the ball, shifting the weight to the supporting foot, contact-

Figure 8.5. **Volley with the foot**

ing the ball and following through into a position to be ready to play the ball again.

KICKING WITH THE HEEL

This type of kick is an exception rather than a rule. It might be used to save a ball from going out of bounds or to send the ball in the opposite direction after pursuing and overtaking the ball. This technique is utilized due to the position of the opponents.

Body Awareness

1. The back of the heel is used with the toe turned up and the knee flexed.

Space

1. Once the player has overtaken the ball, the supporting foot must be placed ahead of and alongside the pathway of the ball. In order to keep from stepping on the ball, players should be cautious not to leap into the ball's exact pathway.

2. The kicking foot must travel above the ball and come back down in front of the ball to contact it just about when it is alongside the supporting foot.

Force

1. Most of the force is generated from a flexion and extension of the hip joint, with the backswing being greater than the follow-through.

Time

1. The player must judge the speed of the ball and time the leap over the ball in order to contact it when it is alongside the supporting foot.

Flow

1. The sequence of movements is run-leap-kick (kicking in a backward direction).
2. After kicking the player pivots to follow the path of the ball and get into an advantageous position to play the ball again.

PASSING

Passing is the technique of sending the ball to a teammate. Although the foot is generally used to pass the ball, one may also pass the ball with a volley. Passing is essential for teamwork. A team that masters the techniques of passing stays in control of the ball.

Body Awareness

1. Different parts of the foot may be used to pass the ball, depending upon the force and direction desired.
2. Different parts of the body may be used to volley the ball in order to pass it to a teammate, depending upon the level at which the ball is approaching.

Space

1. If the ball is to progress downfield the players must use triangulr (diagonal) passes rather than square passes.
2. A short square pass can be used for deception at the beginning or end of a long diagonal pass (fig. 8.6).

3. When passing to a moving teammate the passer must pass to the space in front of the moving player.
4. Long passes (passes that must cover a great distance) are more easily intercepted than short ones.

Force

1. A ball with some force travels faster and is less likely to be intercepted.
2. Too much force on the ball makes it difficult for the receiver to handle the ball.

Time

1. The player must time the pass (i.e., kick it at the right time with the correct amount of force and speed) to get the ball to the intended spot at the same time the intended receiver arrives there.

Flow

1. There is a sequence of movements as the player passes and moves into position to play the ball again.
2. Unless the pass is made from a place kick there is also a sequence of movements of the ball and player prior to the pass (for example, dribble and pass, trap and pass, block and pass, etc.).

TRAPPING

Stopping the momentum of the ball in order to control and redirect it is known as trapping. Although an intended trap may turn out to be a block, the trap can be distinguished from other foot and leg contacts with the ball in that the momentum of the ball is stopped completely and the ball is trapped against the ground by some part of the leg or foot. Trapping and then redirecting the ball is more time-consuming than blocking and then redirecting the ball; however, it does provide more control of the ball

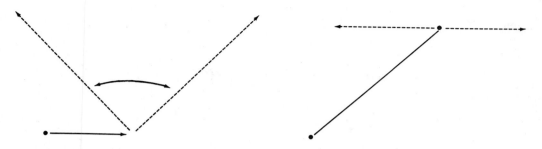

Figure 8.6. **Short square passes used for deception while progressing the ball downfield with the diagonal pass**

and should be used by beginners, especially on balls that have a great deal of "English" (spin).

Body Awareness

Several parts of the foot and leg, alone or in combination, may be used to trap the ball. However, due to anatomical structure, certain parts of the foot and leg lend themselves more readily to a good trap. The parts more easily used are:

    a. the sole of the foot (fig. 8.7)
    b. the front of one leg (fig. 8.8)
    c. the inside of one leg (fig. 8.9)
    d. the front of both legs (fig. 8.10)

Space

1. The part of the leg or foot that is to trap the ball should be directly in line with the pathway of the approaching ball.

2. The trapping surface applies force diagonally downward onto the ball as it enters the trap.

3. The space or shape of the pocket in which the ball is trapped is closed in the back so the ball cannot pass on through and open large enough in the front so the ball can pass into the trap.

    a. The position for the foot trap is with the total foot off the ground but not higher than the circumference of the ball. The toes of the foot face diagonally upward.

    b. The trap using the front of both legs also presents a slanting surface which comes down onto the ball as it enters the trap. This trap has a slow recovery due to the precarious position of the body.

    c. The one-leg trap (the front of the leg or inside of the leg) is a very stable and sure trap since the foot of the trapping leg is placed in a trailing position to the foot of the supporting leg, making a pocket for the ball.

Force

1. The force of the trap must be strong enough to dissipate the momentum of the ball and press it to the ground.

2. The bulk of the body's weight should be maintained over the supporting leg and foot rather than shifted over the ball. This is especially true in traps using one leg or foot because of the danger of falling and the disadvantage of a slow recovery.

3. More weight is transferred over the ball in the two-leg trap, using the front of the legs.

Figure 8.7. **Trap with the sole of the foot; weight must be balanced over the supporting leg.**

Figure 8.9. **Trap with the inside of one leg**

Figure 8.8. **Trap with the front of one leg**

Figure 8.10. **Trap with the front of both legs**

Time

1. The player must time the application of force so that the ball does not rebound from a closed trap or from the back wall of a trap that doesn't close soon enough.

2. The faster the ball is moving the faster the trap must move.

3. The trap that is the quickest both to employ and recover from is the sole-of-the-foot trap.

4. The trap that is the slowest in recovery is the front-of-two-legs trap, due to the great amount of body weight shited over the ball.

Flow

The sequence of movements involved in the trap is: (a) getting in line and ready to trap; (b) the trap itself; (c) recovery; (d) the dribble or pass.

After trapping, the ball must be put in position to play again either with a dribble, pass or shot for goal. The recovery involves this action. Generally the weight is shifted back to the supporting leg, while the foot of the trapping leg nudges the ball with a light force to put it out in front of the player so he can dribble, pass or shoot for goal.

TACKLING

Tackling is the name given to the technique of taking the ball away from the opponent by using the feet. Several specific methods of tackling are identified by the position the tackler uses in approaching the opponent and how he manipulates the ball during the tackle. Ideally the tackler should gain possession of the ball and direct it to his team's advantage. In reality this does not always occur and some tacklers do not actually gain possession of the ball. However, the attempt to gain possession of the ball may spoil the opponent's play and thus be termed a spoiling tackle. Both similarities and differences of various tackling techniques are noted in the following analysis.

Body Awareness

1. Various parts of the foot are used, depending on where the tackler is in relation to the opponent and the ball and whether the tackler intends to gain possession of the ball or merely spoil the play.

2. The *front tackle* is a contact with the ball with the sole of the foot and is very much like the sole-of-the-foot trap.

3. In the *side tackle* the player may contact the ball only with the outside of the foot to spoil the play. However, if the tackler is to gain possession of the ball he will contact the ball with both the inside and outside of the foot (or feet) as he dribbles around the opponent.

4. The inside or top of the foot is used in the *hook tackle*. The foot is used to reach, hook and draw the ball away from the opponent (fig. 8.11).

5. The *split tackle* is generally a spoiling tackle with the foot used to jab the ball away from the opponent. The sole of the foot reaches in from the side in this tackle.

Figure 8.11. **Hook tackle**

Space

1. The tackle is executed by a *reach* with the tackling leg and foot while the body leans in the opposite direction to maintain balance (a counterbalance) and to avoid contact with the opponent.

2. The tackler should strive to make contact with the ball while it is farthest from his opponent's feet in order to be more successful in securing the ball and to avoid tripping the opponent.

3. The *front tackle* is executed directly in front of the opponent and in line with the pathway of the ball. This tackle is most successful if the opponent is not keeping the dribble in close to the body.

4. The *split and hook tackles* are executed from in front (facing the opponent) and to the side of the opponent with the tackling leg reaching out to the side.

5. The *side tackle* is an attempt to gain possession of the ball when traveling alongside an opponent (both dribbler and tackler are moving in the same direction).

Force

1. The force with which one plays the ball is not a major factor; however, the force must be great enough to overcome the

momentum of the ball and change its direction. Unfortunately, beginners may apply too much force and only spoil the play rather than gain possession of the ball.

2. The force of gravity can work to the disadvantage of the tackler if he reaches too far and puts himself in an off-balance position, resulting in a slow recovery.

Time

1. The timing of the tackle should be exact in that the tackler preferably makes contact with the ball when it is farthest from the opponent's feet. If the ball is in contact with the opponent's feet, body contact may result with possible injury to the ankles and knees.

2. The tackle is a quick move. The tackler reaches, plays the ball, and quickly gets out of the pathway of the opponent.

3. After tackling and gaining possession of the ball the tackler must quickly get the ball away in order to avoid being tackled in return.

Flow

1. Except for the split tackle, the flow of the movement is continuous as the tackler moves into position, reaches to contact the ball and recovers to either play the ball or get into position to play the ball again.

2. In the split tackle movement is stopped as the tackler drops to one knee and reaches with the tackling leg to jab at the ball.

Controlling the Ball with Other Body Parts

In soccer one generally thinks in terms of playing the ball with the feet. Except for the goalkeeper in the penalty area, a player cannot use the hands or arms to play the ball unless they are held in contact with the body. However, other parts of the body may be used to legally contact the ball.

When teaching beginners one should stress keeping the ball low for safety reasons. As students become more adept in handling the ball (controlling direction and force), they can learn to direct the ball at a higher level more safely. Although one may strive in the game to keep the ball low there will be times when the ball will rise in the air and be difficult if not impossible to play with the feet. One will also encounter balls coming at a high level from the throw-in, the punt, the dropkick, or the throw from the goalkeeper as he clears the ball from the goal. The part of the body used to contact the ball will be partially determined by the level at which the ball is approaching and the intent of the player upon contacting the ball.

THE VOLLEY

The act of using a body part to redirect an aerial ball is called a volley. The volley with the foot was discussed earlier. This section includes a discussion of the use of other parts of the body in a volley.

Body Awareness

1. In order to return some of the force of the ball to the ball upon contact (the rebound), the contacting surface should be firm, hard and stable.

2. The level at which the ball is traveling will determine to some degree which part of the body is used to contact the ball.

3. The head can be used to volley a ball that is dropping from a high level (fig. 8.12).

4. The shoulder is a firm surface with which to volley a ball at a medium-high level (fig. 8.13).

5. The flexed knee can also be used effectively as a volleying surface (fig. 8.14).

Figure 8.12. **A forceful extension of the knees drives the body upward for the head volley.**

Figure 8.13. **Volley with the shoulder**

Figure 8.14. **Volley with the knee**

Space

1. The body part used to volley should be placed directly in line with the pathway of the approaching ball.

2. The direction or pathway the ball takes after the contact will depend upon the angle at which the ball strikes the rebounding surface. One may alter this direction or angle of rebound by altering the angle of the surface used to contact the ball.

3. The flatter and larger the rebounding surface, the more able one is to redirect and apply force through the center of gravity of the ball in line with the desired direction.

Force

1. If the ball is traveling with a great deal of momentum, one may only need to present a firm rebounding surface and return the majority of momentum of the ball through the rebound.

2. If one must add to the rebound force of the ball, the ball should be met with a moving body part—moving in the direction of the intended rebound pathway.

3. Muscles must be firm or contracted and contacting body parts stabilized in order to present a firm rebounding surface.

4. The action or movement used to create force will be different depending upon the body part used to meet the ball.

    a. When one meets the ball with the head or shoulder, force is created by crouching (flexing the knees, hips, etc.) and then forcefully extending to meet the ball. One pushes away from the ground to create force.

b. Meeting the ball with the knee involves a forceful flexion of the hip with the flexed knee leading the movement.

c. The more speed the striking surface has on contact, the more force will be imparted to the ball.

Time

1. The earlier or quicker one meets the ball, the less time the opponents have to intercept or to get into position to play the ball.

2. One must judge the speed of the ball and time his movements to contact the ball at the right time in space with the body on balance.

Flow

1. The striking surface must follow through in the direction of the intended flight.

a. When using the knee volley, the knee follows through carrying the total body forward, sometimes to the extent that the supporting foot hops to stay on balance.

b. The total body extends upward when using the head or shoulder on the ball; the feet actually leave the ground in a jumping action.

2. The sequence of movements for the volley involves getting into position, gathering the body in preparation for the contact, the actual contact, then the follow-through and recovery into a ready position.

THE BLOCK

The act of meeting an aerial ball with some part of the body and impeding its progress by absorbing the force of the ball upon contact is called blocking (fig. 8.15).

Body Awareness

1. To aid in absorbing the force of the ball upon contact, the contacting surface should be soft and pliable as opposed to rigid or hard.

2. The level at which the ball is traveling will determine to some degree which part of the body is used to block the ball.

3. The chest (possibly with the arms folded across), the abdomen, the front of the thighs, or the inside of the thigh of one leg can be used successfully in the block. The inside of one foot can also be used.

Space

1. The body part used to block should be placed directly in line with the pathway of the approaching ball.

2. Upon contact the body part moves with the ball (quite often backwards) in the same direction in which the ball is moving in order to absorb the force.

3. If the abdomen or chest is used to block the ball the upper trunk is flexed to present a concave surface for the ball to strike and roll down.

Force

1. The main objective of the block is to absorb the forward momentum (the force) of the ball and to allow gravity to pull the ball to the ground in front of the blocker. This places the ball in a good position to be redirected by the blocker.

2. The greater the distance and time over which the force of the ball is absorbed, the less chance there is for rebound. When blocking with the trunk or front of the thighs, a concave striking surface is presented; however, one can still move with the force (i.e., the ball) in order to increase the time of absorption.

3. The greater the force, the more the player must give with the ball.

Time

1. One must time the movements of the body so that the contacting surface gives immediately upon contact with the ball.

2. The time needed for the block is somewhat dictated by the force of the ball; however, one can learn to recover quickly and play the ball.

3. There is a definite timing or rhythm to the action of blocking, recovering and passing.

Flow

1. The sequence of movements for the block is moving into position, contacting the ball and then recovering into a position to play the ball (generally as a pass).

2. Blocking the ball with the trunk or upper thighs involves a jump backwards at the same time the body is taking a curved shape in order to allow the ball to hit and roll down the front of the body. One must then land from the jump, shift the weight to one supporting leg and play the ball.

3. Blocking with the inside of the leg or foot involves the contact, a transfer of weight onto the contacting foot, and then back to the supporting leg as the blocker maneuvers the body into a position to play the ball.

THE PUNT AND DROPKICK

The punt and dropkick can be used only by the goalkeeper in soccer due to the need to contact the ball with the hands prior to kicking. These two techniques, along with the throw, are used to clear the ball from the goal by sending it high over the heads of the potential scorers and to the offensive forward line of one's own team.[4] An analysis of the movement patterns of these two techniques reveals many similarities. Both

Figure 8.15. **The total body gives when using the abdomen to block the ball.**

similarities and differences are noted in the following.

Similarities: punt and dropkick

Body Awareness

The ball is contacted with the top of the foot (the instep) after being dropped in front of the body from the hands.

Space

1. The ball is dropped well away from the body to allow the leg to swing through a wide range.

2. The ball is contacted below and behind its center of gravity in order to send it up and forward.

Force

1. Momentum is built by transferring the weight forward onto the supporting leg in preparation for contact.

2. The hip is extended and the knee flexed on the backswing in order to increase the range of motion.

---

4. Throwing is covered more specifically in the chapter on softball.

3. The hip is flexed and stabilized and the knee forcefully extended at the instant of contact.

4. The leg follows through in the direction that the ball is projected.

Flow

1. The preparation, motion and recovery is one smooth, continuous motion.

2. The recovery may involve a slight hop on the supporting foot to maintain balance.

Differences: punt and dropkick

Space

1. In the punt the ball is contacted just before it strikes the ground, as it descends from the hands (fig. 8.16).

2. In the dropkick the ball strikes the ground and is contacted with the instep immediately as it rebounds (fig. 8.17).

Time

1. The rhythmic pattern for the punt is one-and, two; drop-step, kick.

2. The rhythmic pattern for the dropkick is one-and, two-and; drop-step, bounce-kick.

MAJOR CONCEPTS RELATED TO STRATEGY

Soccer is a goal-oriented team sport. Thus, it has many strategy concepts in common with other sports in this category. (See chapter five, pages 84–87). Again, for ease of reference the major concepts and sub-concepts from chapter five that are applicable to soccer are identified with the same letter and letter-number designation used in chapter five.

Player Positions and Responsibilities

CONCEPT N. Proper use of personnel, based on each player's strengths and limitations, is of paramount importance when molding a team.

Sub-concept N-1. Each player on a team must assume specific responsibilities for the position he is playing.

The *forward line* is identified as the left wing, left inner, center forward, right inner and right wing as they assume their positions facing the opponents' goal. The wings and inners are also identified as outside and inside forwards. Their main job is to move the ball down their opponents' half of the field and into the goal. When play is on their own half of the field or near their own goal they station themselves a little beyond the perimeter of the penalty area waiting for a clearing kick. Forward line players need both stamina and speed, for the area of the field they cover ranges from their opponents' goal back to the perimeter of the penalty area of their own half of the field.

The *halfbacks*—left half, center half, and the right half—perform a double duty. Although they are considered to be defensive players, they play an offensive game by backing up the forward line.[5] Defensively they mark, tackle, and cover spaces.[6] The right and left halfbacks mark the opposing wings, while the center halfback marks the opposing center forward.[7] They clear the ball from their own goal area, sending it to their forwards to begin the attack. The area of the field they cover ranges from their own goal line up to the perimenter of the

5. Backing up is discussed in chapter 5, page 85.
6. For a discussion of marking, see page 220; tackling, page 211; and covering spaces, page 220.
7. The left halfback marks the right wing. The right halfback marks the left wing.

Figure 8.16. **The punt**

Figure 8.17. **The dropkick**

penalty area on the opponents' half of the field.

The *fullbacks,* left and right, are the last line of defense before the goalie. Although primarily defensive players, they can take part in the offensive game by backing up if they are speedy enough to interchange and play in a diagonal position in relation to each other and the ball.[8] As strictly defensive players they may choose as a pattern of play one in front of the other in line with the ball, or side by side deep in their own territory. Even a speedy fullback in the process of backing up will not advance much beyond the center of the field. The fullbacks mark the opposing inners on their side of the field.

The *goalkeeper* is the last line of defense and is the only player who has the privilege of touching the ball with his hands. As the ball approaches he may kick, catch, or pick the ball up. If he elects to control the ball with his hands he then has the option of clearing the ball from the goal with a throw, punt, or dropkick. The goalkeeper may build momentum prior to the punt, dropkick, or throw by taking no more than four steps with the ball in his hands. He may also combine a dribble or bounce/catch with the throw, punt or drop kick.

It is imperative that the goalkeeper stay within the penalty area for two reasons: he has special privileges within this area only, and he is the last line of defense. As the last line of defense he should always stay between the ball and the goal, positioned to block the greatest number of angles from which goals may be scored. He coordinates the defense by calling for the ball when it is to his team's advantage for him to clear the ball from the goal.

The other backs can facilitate the job of the goalkeeper by marking their offensive player and not crowding the ball. When play becomes congested in front of the goal it becomes difficult for the goalkeeper to see the ball and/or read the play. The goalkeeper is not permitted to hold the ball and deliberately delay the game. The ball should be cleared from the goal with a forceful action projecting it toward the sideline to a speedy wing. Clearing toward the sideline also places the ball in a position for fewer angles at the goal should the opponents intercept the ball.

A common line-up or opening formation to begin play is depicted in figure 8.18. Sys-

8. For a discussion of the interchange, see page 221.

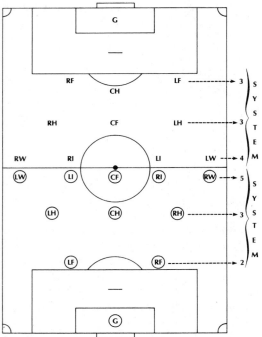

Figure 8.18. **The 3-3-4 and 2-3-5 system of positioning for the kickoff**

tems of play are most easily described by numbers which indicate the number of players in each of the three basic positions (fullbacks, halfbacks and forwards). The system of play in figure 8.18 could be described as a 3-3-4 system. A system of play utilizing five forwards, three halfbacks and two fullbacks would be a 2-3-5 system. Still another system is the 4-2-4. No one system is ideal in all instances. The system employed by a team needs to be flexible enough to take advantage of specific player strengths and weaknesses and to adjust to changing team strategies of both teammates and opponents.

Offense

CONCEPT O. In goal-oriented and field sports a system of offense is essential if a team is to be successful. The prime purposes of an offensive system are to build upon the strengths of the players, to shift the balance of power away from the defense, and to capitalize on defensive weaknesses.

Sub-concept O-1. If and when a player decides that maintaining possession of the ball will gain ground more successfully, the player must be able to dribble, dodge, and feint effectively.

Sub-concept O-2. Effective passing involves spatial patterns based on positioning of teammates and opponents.

Sub-concept O-3. Creating spaces is basic to sound team strategy.

In order to score the forwards of the team are constantly moving into a position to receive a pass or moving to pull the defense out of position in order to create spaces for a teammate to move into or for the ball to be passed through. *Angle passing,* or passing the ball diagonally forward toward the opponents' goal, is the quickest way to maneuver the ball downfield. To facilitate angle passing, two supporting teammates should move to form a triangle with the player with the ball rather than maintain a straight line formation. In addition to providing two options for angle passes, if the defense trails to mark the opponents, spaces for long passes may become available. However, periodically, a square pass is desirable. Although *square passes,* passes parallel with the end line, do not advance the ball in the desired direction they can be effective in avoiding the opponent, especially before or after a long pass. Nevertheless, overuse of a flat formation and square passes reduces passing possibilities, limits forward progress and increases the chances of interception. Players should practice forceful passes aimed at a space in front of the intended receiver in order to allow the receiver to take the pass in stride.

Although a passing game promotes teamwork and is a much faster game than a dribbling game, there are instances when a player must or should maintain possession of the ball and dribble. If a player is progressing with the ball using a dribble and is not being challenged by opponents, he should continue to dribble. If pass receivers are not open or a player finds himself ahead of his own forward line he must employ the dribble. Although a player should *draw* (feint in one direction and pass in another direction) and then pass before being tackled, he may need to *dodge* his opponent if no receivers are open. When using a dodge the player feints to cause the opponent to be off-balance and then moves around him while maintaining possession of the ball.

Another successful tactic used by the offense is that of diagonal runs with an interchange of positions. If the defense is employing a zone system of defense this forces the defenders to react to different players rather than become accustomed to the specific characteristics of just one opponent. Secondly, when two opponents enter the territory of a defender he must choose to challenge or mark one of the opponents if play is near his goal. Should he choose the one who is moving to create a diversion rather than to receive the ball a space may open for a possible shot at the goal.

Sub-concept O-4. In order to score it is necessary to place the ball in a strategic position in relation to the goal.

Sub-concept O-5. Shooting for a goal involves individual and team strategy.

Sub-concept O-6. Rushing the goal insures follow-up to a shot at the goal.

As the ball nears the opponents' goal it should be *centered* or passed across in front of the goal to place it in a position for another forward to *shoot* for a goal. The attempt for a goal should be deliberate and not just a kick in the general direction of the goal. Attempts for the goal that are slow moving or are shot from too far out are easily intercepted and cleared by the defense. As the shot is made the forwards should *rush* toward the goal in an attempt to score on a follow-up shot, should the first shot be deflected.

Another tactic a player having possession of the ball may employ is the *body block*. This involves placing one's body between the opponent and the ball. This tactic is used most often on the dodge, prior to sending a pass, or immediately after receiving a pass. There is no body contact during the body block. A player who employs a body block without having possession of the ball is called for obstruction. The penalty for obstruction is an indirect free kick for the opponents.

As the offensive team moves across into the opponents' half of the field they must be constantly alert to their position on the field in relation to the ball and their opponents in order to avoid being ruled offsides. A player is in an offsides position when he gains an advantage by being ahead of the ball when it is last contacted by one of his teammates and there are less than two defensive players between him and the opponents' end line. The defense is awarded an indirect free kick on the spot when an offensive player is offsides. This rule eliminates the possibility of positioning a forward near the goal and clearing the ball downfield to him. Therefore, the offense must move forward quickly with the ball.

Defense

CONCEPT P. Individual defensive techniques are for the purpose of closing spaces through which a ball can be passed or inhibiting the progress of a player or ball, thereby preventing the opponents from maintaining possession of the ball and/or scoring.

Sub-concept P-1. Defensive play depends on guarding techniques which enable the player to anticipate movement, to intercept passes, to tackle, or block.

Sub-concept P-2. Covering is a technique for closing spaces through which long passes might be sent.

The position of a defensive player should be either that of marking an opponent or covering a space. *Marking* is positioning oneself near enough to an opponent to intercept a pass or to tackle if that player receives a pass. Whether the back is in a marking position or a covering position depends upon the field position of the ball. The backs on the side of the field opposite the ball are positioned to cover spaces. *Covering* is closing those spaces through which long passes might be sent.

Covering is a technique also employed by the forwards when their team is on the defensive. This is their main contribution to the defense and is especially necessary on the goal kick, free kick, and throw-in. Forwards may also be defensive in tackling back immediately after they have lost the ball to the opposing tacker. This tactic by the forwards, hopefully, restricts penetrating moves and gains time for the defense to mobilize into central defense positions. However, the forwards should "pull off" once the backs become positioned; otherwise an interchange is initiated. Inners quite often assist the defense when the ball is in

the opponents' half of the field and their fullbacks are playing a strictly defensive game.

Sub-concept P-3. The defense should advance to tackle or guard immediately when the ball enters its territory.

Sub-concept P-4. Clearing the ball involves a fast defensive maneuver because the ball must be moved quickly away from the goal.

Backs should be proficient in tackling an opponent to gain possession of the ball. The defense should advance to tackle immediately once the ball has moved into their territory. If the tackle is not successful they will at least have hurried the offensive pass or shot. If the offense evades a tackler with a dodge an adjacent defensive back should quickly move into position to tackle again or back up his teammate. The defense must move constantly to keep themselves positioned between the ball and the goal. Once the defensive backs gain possession of the ball they should strive to pass quickly to their forwards, especally when deep in their own territory. This quick action can be advantageous in that it catches the opposing defensive backs in poor positions to mark and cover. When *clearing the ball* from the goal area the backs should never kick the ball across in front of the goal, but should use a forceful kick toward the nearest sideline and their wing.

CONCEPT Q. A system of defense is essential if a team is to be successful. The prime purposes of the defense are to prevent the opponents from scoring and to capitalize on offensive weaknesses.

Sub-concept Q-1. Team strategies follow a particular planned defensive pattern based on man-to-man defense or a spatial pattern (zone) defense.

Playing one's own position and man-to-man marking with covering spaces is the simplest system of team play to use when learning the game. However, in order to take advantage of each situation as the ball moves from place to place on the field and as a team is first offensive and then defensive, players must be able to *interchange* positions and duties. One instance in which an interchange of position and duties would be desirable is on the throw-in. The right halfback and center halfback move toward the sideline to mark the left wing and left inner respectively. The left halfback moves toward the center of the field to cover and tackle if necessary. Logically, the player with the ball should be tackled by the nearest defender. This action sometimes initiates an interchange between a forward and back. When a dribbler evades a tackler and another back moves in to tackle, the situation lends itself to an interchange. An offensive forward may move out of his territory as he dodges and dribbles or runs to be in position to receive a pass. The teammate whose territory he has invaded moves to interchange places with him. A man-to-man marking defense may be ineffective if the opponents are interchanging. Likewise, a straight line or flat defense formation has weaknesses. Once an attacker has penetrated the line of defense he has gained quite an advantage. A defensive formation of interlocking triangles provides better coverage in that it allows defenders to cover each other as well as spaces through which the ball or an offensive player might move. The defensive triangles should become tighter and concentrate in an area in front of the goal as the ball gets closer to the goal. This shifting zone defense with a strong back-up is a most effective system of defense.

SPECIFIC GAME SITUATIONS

Beside putting the ball into play with a kickoff at the beginning of each playing period and after a score, fouls, violations and out-of-bounds balls make it necessary to put the ball into play in various ways during the game. In a majority of instances—the *kickoff, free kick, goal kick, corner kick* and *penalty kick*—the ball is put into play by a place kick awarded to the opponents of the violators. According to N.A.G.W.S. rules these situations, with the exception of the goal kick and penalty kick, have three regulations in common: (1) all players other than the player putting the ball into play must be five yards away; (2) the player taking the kick cannot play the ball again until another player has contacted it; and (3) the impetus given the ball on the kick must cause it to travel at least the distance of its circumference. The *throw-in, drop ball* and *penalty kick* each have unique regulations which are discussed later.

The potential for scoring obviously lies with the team in control of the ball. The task for the offense then is to remain in control of the ball. The defense, on the other hand, defends their goal against the offensive team and also attempts to gain control of the ball. The suggestions which follow indicate both offensive and defensive strategy to be used with various game situations within the regulations of the N.A.G.W.S. rules.

KICKOFF

A place kick from the center of the field is the method of putting the ball into play at the beginning of each playing period and after a goal has been scored. In addition to the regulations stated previously, the ball must be projected in the direction of the opponents' goal. All players must be in their own half of the field and all opponents outside the center circle. The center forward

Key

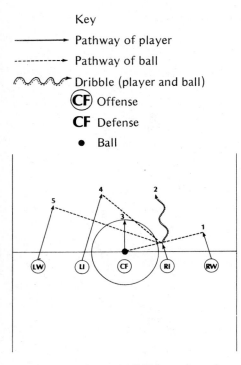

——————▶ Pathway of player

----------▶ Pathway of ball

〰〰〰〰 Dribble (player and ball)

(CF) Offense

CF Defense

● Ball

Figure 8.19. **Five possibilities after the kickoff. The pattern can be reversed if the left inner receives the ball from the kickoff.**

who takes the kick should strive to pass the ball to a teammate rather than kick the ball deep into the opponents' territory and risk putting his team on the defensive. The possible recipients of the kickoff pass are the inners and wings. If the ball is received by the right inner he may pass the ball on to the wing on his side of the field, or pass it across the field to either the inner or wing on the left side of the field, or he may pass it back to the center forward. He may also elect to retain possession of the ball and dribble (fig. 8.19).

If the forward line maintains possession of the ball there are five options available to any front-line player receiving that first pass. Obviously certain options are more de-

sirable. For example, short passes are less likely to be intercepted than long passes. The recipient of the kickoff pass must quickly survey the field, note the location of opponents, look for open spaces and available receivers, and then play the ball in a manner that best fits the situation at that moment.

The defensive team must remain outside the center circle until the ball is kicked. They then move forward and attempt to intercept the kickoff pass. If this maneuver fails, the forward line of the defensive team should move on through to allow their backs to mark or tackle their respective players. Beginning players, due to their eagerness to gain possession of the ball, many times move out of position on the kickoff and immediately begin to crowd the ball. The defensive forward line quite often attempts to tackle and play defensively rather than moving on through, allowing their defensive backs to do their job. The incorporation of a "learning regulation" by the teacher can help to alleviate this condition and encourage position and team play. Such a regulation might be that a forward line player can tackle another forward line player just once (i.e., tackle back), and then, if not successful in obtaining the ball, must move on through.

FREE KICK

The free kick is awarded to the opponents of the team which violates the regulations governing play or commits a personal foul within the field of play other than contact fouls by the defensive team within their own penalty area. The free kick is a place kick taken usually by a halfback on the spot the infringement occurred. Having a halfback take the free kick places the forward line in the best position to receive a pass. There is no whistle from the umpire to begin play; therefore, an offensive team should mobilize quickly and take the free kick in an at-

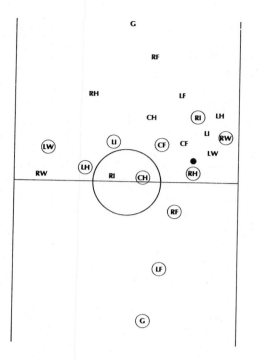

Figure 8.20. **Free kick**

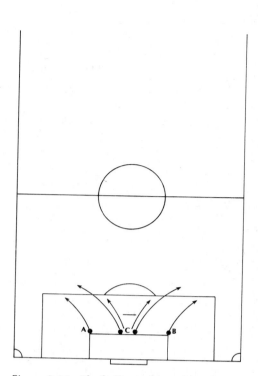

Figure 8.21. **The ball may be projected in a variety of directions from points C.**

tempt to catch the defense off-guard. The defense should stay alert. Backs should mark those forwards most likely to receive the pass and the remainder of the defensive team should cover those spaces through which long passes might be sent. A score may be made from a direct free kick awarded for fouls involving contact. A score can be made from an indirect free kick after the ball has touched another player. An indirect free kick is awarded to opponents of the negligent player for fouls with no contact (fig. 8.20).

GOAL KICK

The goal kick is a place kick taken anywhere in the same half of the penalty area as side of end line the ball went over. Although any player may take the kick, the ball is usu-

ally put into play by a defensive back. The goal kick is awarded as a result of the attacking team sending the ball out of bounds over the end line or crossbar. The intent of the kick is to clear the ball from the goal area and to send it well downfield to the forward line. The ball should never be kicked across in front of the goal but cleared toward the sidelines and the wings. Therefore, a ball positioned to the extreme right or left indicates to the opponents in which direction the ball will be kicked (fig. 8.21).

If the ball is positioned at point C (fig. 8.21), it may be sent in either direction away from the goal. The backs of the team taking the defense kick should be in marking and covering positions ready to tackle should the

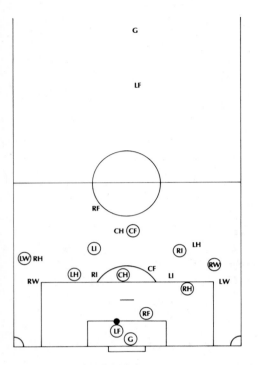

Figure 8.22. **Goal kick**

clearing action fail. The forward line of the offensive team should be downfield, ready to receive the ball and begin the attack.

The forwards of the team that is now defensive should cover spaces and attempt to intercept the clearing kick. The backs of this same team should be downfield in positions to mark and cover (fig. 8.22).

CORNER KICK

A corner kick is awarded the offensive team when the defense sends the ball out of bounds over the end line or over the crossbar, or when a player kicks the ball into his own goal from a free kick. The ball is put in play by a wing with a place kick from any spot within the quarter circle of the nearest corner. The forwards of the offensive team may be stationed anywhere on the field of play and should be located in a position to

receive the pass and to shoot for a goal. The total offensive team is shifted toward the side of the field from which the corner kick is being taken. The kick should be forceful and well-placed in order to send it to a teammate who can try for a goal or pass to another forward in a better position to score.

The defensive backs, too, have shifted their strength to the side from which the corner kick is being taken. (Note the position of the center halfback in relation to the goalie in figure 8.23. He would be on the other side of the goalkeeper if the kick were being taken on the other side of the field.) The defensive backs attempt to intercept or tackle while their forwards wait downfield for a clearing kick.

PENALTY KICK

The penalty kick is a place kick, taken on the penalty kick mark, awarded to the attacking team for fouls involving contact committed by the defending team within their own penalty area.[9] Any forward of the attacking team may take the kick; however, it is most often taken by the center forward. All players except the forward taking the kick and the goalkeeper defending the goal must be out of the penalty area and restraining line but within the field of play. The goalkeeper stands on the goal line until the ball is kicked. The kick must be an attempt to score. The player taking the kick must wait for the umpire's whistle and all players may move into the penalty area only after the ball is kicked. The defending forward line is downfield waiting for a clearing kick. The halfbacks of the attacking team take positions between the two lines of forwards in readiness to back up their own forward

9. Consult a current rule book for other violations for which a penalty kick is awarded.

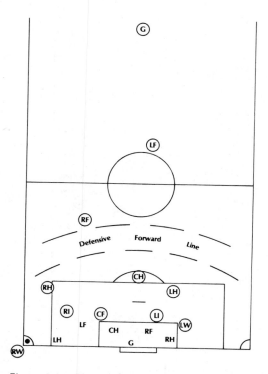

Figure 8.23. **Corner kick**

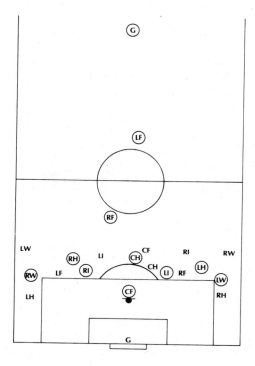

Figure 8.24. **Penalty kick**

line or tackle their opposing forwards should the ball be cleared from the penalty area (fig. 8.24).

THROW-IN

A throw-in is awarded to a team when their opponents have sent the ball out of bounds over the sideline. The ball is put in play with a throwing action at the spot from which it left the field. No opponent can be closer than ten yards from the spot of the throw-in until the ball is thrown. A halfback usually puts the ball in play; however, a wing occasionally takes the throw-in deep in his own territory. Again, there is no whistle to begin play and the attacking team can possibly gain an advantage by mobilizing quickly. As the offense shifts toward the sideline the defensive backs on that side of the field should be marking the opposing forwards.[10]

The offensive forwards should be ahead of the ball in an attempt to create spaces through which the ball can be passed. The defensive forward line attempts to intercept the pass and to cover spaces. The player throwing the ball in should aim for the feet of the intended receiver. A ball traveling close to the ground is easier to receive and control, while a high bouncing ball is slow moving and more difficult to control. A quick pass back to the thrower once he has entered the field can confuse the defense and possibly create spaces through which the ball can be passed (fig. 8.25).

10. Beginners may need to be cautioned against crowding into that area of the field.

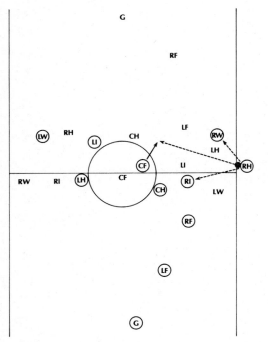

Figure 8.25. **Throw-in**

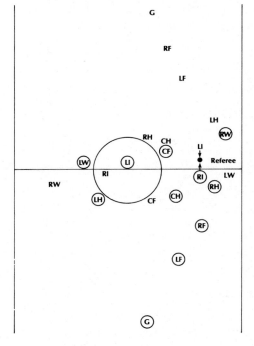

Figure 8.26. **Drop ball**

DROP BALL

The drop ball is used to resume play after three different instances during the game: (1) when opponents foul simultaneously; (2) when the ball is sent out of bounds (over the end line or sideline) by opponents simultaneously; and (3) to resume play after any temporary suspension of the game. The referee holds the ball waist high and drops it between two opposing players who are facing each other's goal. The players involved in the drop ball can contact the ball only after it rebounds from the ground. This is the only instance where the players involved in the play may dribble the ball or touch it again before it is contacted by another player (fig. 8.26).

REFERENCES

Callaghan, John. *Soccer*. Pacific Palisades, Calif.: Goodyear Publishing Co., 1969.

DiClement, Frank F. *Soccer Illustrated for Coaches and Players*. 2d ed. New York: The Ronald Press Co., 1968.

Moffat, Bobby. *The Basic Soccer Guide*. Mountain View, Calif.: World Publications, 1975.

Mott, Jane A. *Soccer and Speedball for Women*. Wm. C. Brown Company Publishers, 1973.

National Association for Girls and Women in Sport. *Soccer*. Washington, D.C.: American Alliance for Health, Physical Education and Recreation, (Current Edition).

Paterson, Ann, and West, Eula Lee. *Team Sports for Girls*. 2d ed. New York: Ronald

Press Co., 1971. (Contains information on speedball and speed-a-way.)

Rote, Kyle, Jr., and Kane, Basil. *Kyle Rote, Jr.'s Complete Book of Soccer.* New York: Simon and Schuster, 1978.

Wade, Allen. *The F. A. Guide to Training and Coaching.* London, England: Morrison and Gibb Ltd, 1967.

PART IV. □ FIELD SPORTS

A day for toil, an hour for sport.
Ralph Waldo Emerson

9.   Softball

INTRODUCTION

Although softball is the only activity classified as a Field Sport in this book, it shares some of the commonalities in strategy ascribed to the Goal-Oriented Sports (p. 91, Goal-Oriented and Field Sports). Chapter five summarizes as well the basic movement concepts used in softball as the players move about the diamond (p. 71, Moving the Body through Space), as they throw or hit the ball (p. 75, Moving An Object through Space), and as they field the softball (p. 80), Receiving an Object Moving through Space).

The background necessary for understanding these commonalities in chapter five is to be found in chapters two, three and four.

Softball is a very popular recreational activity and therefore nearly everyone has had some experience in playing it. It can be played and enjoyed on almost any skill level. Since it is so commonly played, the typical physical educator finds such a diversity of skill in his class that the resolution to individualize learning so that everyone experiences challenge and success is seemingly insurmountable. Attention to the suggestions made in chapter three, The Role of Methodology, and to the section on Individualizing Instruction in the chapter on softball which follows ought to prove helpful in this regard. Hints for personalizing the learning environment ought to be at least partially applicable to all sports; therefore, a perusal of the Individualizing Instruction section in any of the activity chapters might be beneficial.

In sum, softball is a universally popular activity, played at all levels of excellence. If it is true, however, that as skill increases interest becomes more long-lived, attention to personalizing and individualizing the learning of such skill ought to guarantee that the sport becomes a lifetime activity. Indeed, even among the elderly, it often is a refreshing recreational pursuit.

9

Softball

INTRODUCTION

Softball, a team game adapted from baseball, is played by two teams of nine players each. The playing area, its dimensions, and the position of the defensive players on the area are diagrammed in figure 9.1. As with baseball, each team is comprised of nine players; unlike baseball, a team has only seven innings in which to score more runs than its opponents. In case of a tie, extra innings are played until a winner emerges. Each team plays one-half of an inning as the offensive or "at bat" team, the other half as the defensive or "in the field" team. While on offense a team attempts to score by securing walks or hits which allow its members one or more bases. When a player goes completely around the bases, a run is scored. The defensive team, meanwhile, is attempting to put the offensive team out by striking out the batter, by catching fly balls, by throwing a batted ball to a base before the batter reaches it, or by tagging a runner before he reaches a base. A team is allowed three outs before it must trade places with the team in the field.

Since this is by necessity a brief and very general description of the game, the current rules guide should be consulted for all the rules necessary to play an official game and for a more comprehensive look at the total game. The most frequently used terms in softball are defined on pages 233–234.

In the past few years a variation of softball, called slow-pitch softball, has become quite popular. The game is generally a more active one because, as its name implies, the pitched ball must be delivered more slowly and with a perceptible arch; thus, it is hit much more frequently. Consequently all players on the team have many more opportunities to use their respective defensive

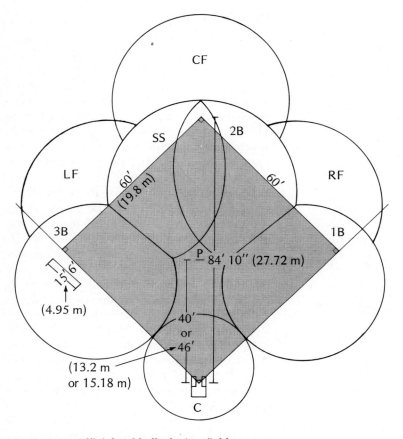

Figure 9.1. **Official softball playing field showing area to be covered by each player**

skills. The basic differences in slow-pitch softball are:

1. The team is comprised of ten players; the extra person is a shortfielder.

2. The pitch must be delivered more slowly than in regular softball and with a perceptible arch.

3. Bunting is illegal.

4. No base stealing is permitted.

5. The strike zone is a bit larger (from the knee to shoulder).

VALUES

Baseball is often referred to as America's national pastime. As a modification of baseball, softball is perhaps no less popular. It is played by both sexes, together and separately, and at diverse age and skill levels. As a recreational activity, it is played on the streets, at picnics, on the beaches, and in highly organized competitive leagues. The official rules are easily adaptable to extant situations and handicapping is commonly used to equate playing abilities.

Perhaps the game's greatest virtue lies in its catharsis value. It is a medium through which one can relax and release pent-up tensions while participating in a joyful activity. It satisfies a basic urge to compete and yet the skill level need not be so sophisticated that it excludes many persons.

ELEMENTS OF MOVEMENT

Softball is a spatial game. In fact, the official playing dimensions are such that the need to move skillfully and efficiently in a large general space is manifest. Likewise, the need for skilled movement in a smaller personal space is also apparent. The third baseman, for example, cannot play his position effectively if the shortstop constantly moves into his playing area.

Softball is a game of force. A great deal of force is required to hit the ball far enough for a home run or to throw the ball from short center field to the catcher. The absorption of force is also paramount in softball. As examples, a sharply hit ball to the shortstop needs to be fielded by giving with the ball if fumbling is to be avoided, and the catcher should draw the ball into his body as he catches a swiftly pitched ball.

Time, likewise, is an essential element in softball. The game is played around time constructs called innings. Timing is of paramount importance in the efficient execution of all skills. For example, a base runner may not leave the base until the pitcher releases the ball; if a batter wishes to hit to the opposite field he must time his swing so that the bat contacts the ball later than normally.

Softball is a game of flowing movement. A well-executed double play is poetry in motion, one skillful movement built on top of another from the time the shortstop fields the ball until it rests in the first baseman's mitt. Another easily seen example of flowing, sequential movement is the windup of the pitcher, followed by a smooth release of the ball, and a vigorous follow-through of the entire body.

SAFETY FACTORS

To develop safety-consciousness in softball, three areas should be considered: the playing field, equipment, and clothing.

The playing field should be level and free from obstructions; there should be plenty of room behind home plate and the foul lines so that foul balls may be fielded safely. Generally the entire field, with the exception of the base paths, is grass-covered. The bases, as well as home plate and the pitching rubber, should be securely fastened into the ground.

The playing equipment consists of a twelve-inch, smoothly seamed, leather-covered ball, bats with safety grips, and gloves or mitts. The rules dictate the maximum length and weight of bats, as well as allowing only the catcher and first baseman to wear mitts. In addition, the catcher must wear a mask and a chest protector.

Loose-fitting clothing, allowing for freedom of movement, should be worn. If sliding is taught, the players should probably not wear shorts. Regular tennis shoes or canvas-topped shoes with rubber cleats are proper. They should fit well and be securely laced.

It is imperative that players be taught not to throw the bat after hitting the ball. In addition, all players should remain a safe distance away from the batter's box. No bats or other equipment should be left in or near the batter's box or base paths.

TERMINOLOGY

Base on balls: a base is awarded when the batter is thrown four balls outside the strike zone.

Battery: the pitcher and the catcher.

Double: a two-base hit.

Double play: a play in which two base runners are put out.

Error: a fumble or misplayed ball by the defense which allows the runner to reach a base safely or to take extra bases.

Fair ball: any batted ball which lands in safe territory or is touched by a defensive player who is in safe territory.

Force-out: a play in which the base runner is put out because he lost the right to the base he was occupying by virture of the batter becoming a base runner.

Foul ball: any batted ball that settles or is touched by a fielder in foul territory, or one which lands outside the baselines beyond first or third base.

Foul tip: a batted ball which goes directly from the bat to the catcher's mitt and is held.

Hot corner: the area around and including third base.

Infield fly: a fairly hit ball, other than a bunt or a line drive, that in the opinion of the umpire could easily be caught by an infielder. If an infield fly occurs before there are two outs and if first and second bases or first, second and third bases are occupied, the batter is out.

Inning: the time construct of the game in which the teams alternately play offense and defense and in which each team has three outs.

Keystone corner: the area around and including second base.

Overthrow: a ball which, on a throw to first, third or home plate in an effort to put out a runner, goes into foul territory.

Passed ball: a pitched ball which the catcher should have caught.

Sacrifice: a ball which is bunted when there are less than two outs for the express purpose of advancing runners on base to the next base. The bunter is usually put out on the play. A *sacrifice fly* serves the same purpose.

Single: a one-base hit.

Strike zone: that area over home plate between the batter's armpits and the top of his knees.

Tagging: a play in which a defensive player, with the ball in his hand, touches a runner before he can reach the base. The runner is out.

Texas leaguer: a fly ball that neither the infield players nor the outfield players can catch.

Triple: a three-base hit.

Wild pitch: a poorly pitched ball that the catcher cannot catch or control with reasonable effort.

MAJOR CONCEPTS

The common major concepts from chapter five which apply to softball are listed as follows, together with a general discussion and examples of their applicability to the game of softball.

MOVING THE BODY THROUGH SPACE

CONCEPT A. Moving the body with control involves a conscious manipulation of the center of gravity in relation to the base of support, either to maintain stability or to initiate locomotor movement, as the situation demands.

Sub-concept A-1. Staying ready to move allows a player to get a faster start in order to outmaneuver the opponent, to gain possession of the ball, or to get into a desirable position to project an object.

Sub-concept A-2. Enlarging the base of support in the direction of the force allows a player to start, stop, and change directions quickly.

Sub-concept A-3. Running in a forward direction is the quickest way to cover a distance of some magnitude.

Sub-concept A-5. Recovering quickly after the execution of a skill involves reassuming the ready position and relocating oneself in space in the home position, or some other advantageous position, in order to stay alert and ready to react again.

Sub-concept A-6. Propelling the body through space requires a firm reacting surface and sufficient friction between the reacting surface and the base of support.

Perhaps the most easily seen application of these concepts and sub-concepts is that of fielding (catching) a ground ball preparatory to throwing to a base in an attempt to retire the runner (see "Individual Skills," page 238). Generally, the fielder must be in a ready position as he waits for the batter to hit the ball. Should the ball come toward him, he should run directly or diagonally forward to field it. He must catch and throw the ball almost in the same motion; therefore, his base of support must be enlarged as he steps into the throw. After the throw he should stay alert for any possible continuation of the play which may re-involve him. Obviously, the playing surface on occasion dictates a different or less efficient action. For example, if the field is wet it is harder to achieve maximum friction for propelling the body as it moves to meet the ball.

CONCEPT B. Creating and absorbing force to control the movement of the body through space may involve all of the body or only parts of the body, in unison or in sequence; however, the relaxation of noncontributing muscle groups is imperative for smooth, efficient movement.

Sub-concept B-1. A smooth transfer of momentum from one part of the body to another part, or to the total body, results in sustained movement, while an explosive transfer of momentum increases the speed and/or magnitude of the resulting movement.

Sub-concept B-2. Absorbing the force of a landing or fall over a greater time and distance increases stability and decreases the chance of injury.

Sub-concept B-3. Relaxing noncontributing muscle groups leads to smooth, efficient movement and thus to the proficiency of the performance.

Sliding is one of the more difficult skills to master in softball; a well-executed slide takes into account all the concepts listed. Momentum is transferred, via a jump, from the arms and legs to the total body. As the foot contacts the base, it must absorb some of the force of the rapidly moving body by giving with the contact. Force is absorbed as well by the bent leg as it becomes the sliding surface. If noncontributing muscles are not relaxed, the foot and leg remain stiff and injury is apt to occur.

Batting is another example of the necessity to transfer motion from one part of the body to the total body if efficiency in the skill is to be achieved (see page 244).

MOVING AN OBJECT THROUGH SPACE

CONCEPT C. A player must be in a desirable position in relation to the object to be projected.

The object to be projected, the softball, is struck by an implement, the bat. The batter must so position himself that the ball can be reached with the bat; however, the batter cannot allow himself to get too close to the ball. If he does, the pitch comes in on the wrists and if the ball is contacted, an inefficient hit results.

CONCEPT D. Creating force: The production and transfer of force depend upon mass, speed, and the striking surface used.

Sub-concept D-1. Increasing the mass used to produce force increases the force produced.

Sub-concept D-2. Increasing the speed of the implement or the body segment imparting force increases the force produced.

Sub-concept D-3. Increasing the range of movement of the body segment or the implement imparting force increases the distance through which speed can be developed, as well as the force imparted to the object.

Sub-concept D-4. Setting the body in motion prior to contact with an object, or to the release of an object, builds greater force which in turn is transferred to the object. However, at the instant of contact or release, the body should be stabilized.

Sub-concept D-5. A follow-through allows for greater force to be transferred to an object.

Sub-concept D-6. Stabilizing the body segments involvd in an action allows for greater force to be imparted to the object.

Sub-concept D-7. A firm striking surface allows for greater force to be imparted to the object.

The skill of batting is inextricably interwoven around all of these concepts. For a detailed account of this skill, see pages 244–247.

CONCEPT E. Directing force: The direction in which an object moves is determined by the point at which force is applied in relation to the object's center of gravity.

Sub-concept E-1. Applying force directly through the center of gravity of an object results in a straight trajectory; an off-center application of force produces a curved trajectory.

Sub-concept E-2. Keeping one's eyes on the object (i.e., objective focus or tracking) facilitates the application of force in line with the intended direction of flight or the absorption of force when slowing or stopping an object. However, if the performer is throwing at a target, he must focus on the target rather than on the projectile.

Sub-concept E-4. External forces such as gravity, air resistance, and friction alter the flight of a projectile.

Pitching, fielding a ground ball, and batting are each examples of some of these concepts in action. A pitcher often grips the ball in such a manner that spin can be applied to it, thus making it more difficult to hit. In fielding a ground ball, an infielder watches the ball until it is in the glove and then shifts his vision to the base to which he intends to throw. If a batted ball is hit sharply into the air, gravity affects its flight almost immediately and little distance is achieved. Even a ball which seems to be traveling a great distance can get "hung up" in air currents and thus have its potential distance cut significantly.

CONCEPT F. Sending the ball to a receiver wo is moving requires directing the ball to an open space ahead of him.

When a baseman is pulled off his base to field a ball, he expects one of his teammates to cover for him. As the teammate runs toward the base, the fielder must throw the ball ahead of him so that he need not break his running stride in order to catch it.

CONCEPT G. To receive an object which is moving through space a performer must slow or stop its motion by absorbing all or part of its force.

It is often said of a fielder who fumbles the ball that he tried to catch and throw it at the same time. Although it is true that the motion of the catch should flow smoothly into the motion of the throw, the momentum of the batted ball must be stopped before it can be thrown.

CONCEPT H. Three techniques help the performer to absorb force efficiently: (1) establishing a stable position; (2) utilizing the largest possible surface area; and (3) increasing the time or distance over which the force is received.

Sub-concept H-1. A stable position should be maintained as the force of an object is absorbed.

Sub-concept H-2. A large surface area reduces the force that is received by any one area of that surface.

Sub-concept H-3. Moving the receiving surface with the ball upon contact (giving with the ball) allows force to be absorbed oer a greater time and distance.

Fielding a very sharply hit ground ball efficiently requires attention to Concepts G and H. Unless the fielder's body is stabilized, not only is a fumble apt to occur, but the likelihood of being able to throw the ball successfully is minimized.

There is a larger surface area to absorb force in a mitt than in a glove. Only the first baseman and catcher are allowed to wear mitts, since they must catch balls that are thrown with greater force.

To execute a successful bunt, the bat must be kept in contact with the ball as long as possible. This type of giving with the ball is similar to the action of a fielder who meets a ground ball in a large forward-backward stride position and allows his weight to transfer to the back foot and leg as the ball comes into his glove.

STRATEGY

CONCEPT N. Proper use of personnel, based on each player's strengths and limitations, is of paramount importance when molding a team.

Sub-concept N-1. Each player on a team must assume specific responsibilities for the position he is playing.

These concepts are so obviously true for any team sport that it seems unnecessary to point out any specific application for softball. Nevertheless, such things as the physical abilities desirable when playing specific positions, the determination of a batting order, and the theory of backing up all play a great part in overall team efficiency.

CONCEPT O. In goal-oriented and field sports a system of offense is essential if a team is to be successful. The prime purposes of an offensive system are to build upon the strengths of the players, to shift the balance of power away from the defense, and to capitalize on defensive weaknesses.

Sub-concept O-2. Effective passing involves spatial patterns based on positioning of teammates and opponents.

The offensive system in softball is predicated upon using offensive strengths to good advantage while at the same time taking advantage of any defensive shortcomings in order to win. For example, if there is a weak fielder in left field, all batters should try to hit the ball to left field.

An example of sub-concept O-2 is the double-play throwing pattern.

CONCEPT P. Individual defensive techniques are for the purpose of closing spaces through which a ball can be passed or inhibiting the progress of a player or ball, thereby preventing the opponents from maintaining possession of the ball and/or scoring.

Sub-concept P-1. Defensive play depends on guarding techniques which enable the player to anticipate movement, to intercept passes, to tackle, or block.

Sub-concept P-2. Covering is a technique for closing spaces through which long passes might be sent.

Although some of the terminology in these concepts is not used in softball, the concept itself is meaningful if certain words are substituted (for example, "hits" for "passes").

Both infielders and outfielders often shift from their normal playing area when certain opponents come up to bat.

Players should anticipate steals and bunts and position themselves accordingly.

SAFETY

CONCEPT U. An affective attitude based on a cognitive understanding of the dangers inherent in an activity is necessary if one is to perform safely.

Sub-concept U-1. Providing a safe environment for participation contributes to the development of desirable affective attitudes toward the activity.

Sub-concept U-2. Educating the participants to use the environment wisely contributes not only to personal safety but enhances the total climate of the classroom.

As mentioned earlier, such factors as the condition of the playing field, appropriate costumes, and proper care of equipment are essential in softball. The teacher can make and enforce regulations concerning such things, but such enforcement may not contribute to a desired affective *attitude*. Therefore, the teacher must attempt to *educate* about safety as well as to enforce safety standards.

INDIVIDUAL SKILLS

CONCEPT. Any system of offensive or defensive play is only as good as the ability of the individual players to execute properly the fundamental skills involved.

The individual skills necessary to play softball well are those basic to many other activities—running, throwing and catching. In addition, hitting (striking with an implement) is essential. The mechanics of each of these skills, with the exception of throwing, are analyzed in detail elsewhere in this book. Therefore, throwing is discussed at length as the next topic, followed by a brief treatment of the specific application to softball of running, catching and striking.

Throwing

Basically there are only three different types of throws—overhand, underhand and sidearm—and each of them is used extensively in softball, although one of them, the underhand, is generally used by only one player, the pitcher. The factors which affect speed, direction and distance are the same regardless of the throwing pattern used.

Such factors are examined in chapter four, "Mechanical Principles of Movement," and touched upon again in chapter five, "Common Concepts."

OVERHAND

The overhand throw is used when speed and distance are important. Therefore, it is essential that every player learn the technique as well as possible.

Body Awareness

Initially, the body squarely faces the target. The ball is held in a tripod grip, using the first two fingers and the thumb. The distance the arm is taken back varies according to the position being played and the necessity for power and speed. For example, the catcher who needs to get a throw away very quickly takes the ball back to ear level. The outfielder may take the ball back higher and farther. Regardless, the body is rotated to the right and the thrower should step toward the target with the left foot (assuming the player is a right-handed thrower), rotate his torso forward, and follow the twist of the shoulder with a whip-like motion of the arm and hand. The ball is released just prior to completing the arm extension. The wrist snap, from hyperextension to flexion during release, is extremely important if distance and power are to be achieved. On the follow-through, the arm swings down and across the body as a step is taken on the right foot.

Space

Personal space must be fairly large for a powerful throw. There must be a direct, unobstructed pathway to the target. In some cases, such as when the second baseman throws to first base to complete a double play, the thrower must move laterally immediately after the throw to avoid contact with an oncoming base runner.

Force

The amount of force needed is determined by the necessary speed and distance the ball must travel. Generally, the overarm throw requires a significant amount of force, thus dictating the windup preparatory to throwing.

Time

Time is dictated by external conditions, but in a game situation it is usually essential to get the ball away quickly.

Flow

Movement flows from taking the arm back as the trunk rotates to the rear, to stepping forward on the opposite foot, to an uncoiling of the body through shoulder to elbow, wrist and fingers. The follow-through is in the direction of the throw, but circumstances on occasion dictate a modified follow-through, spatially.

UNDERHAND

The underhand throw must be used by the pitcher. About the only other time this pattern is used in softball is when the fielder is quite close to the teammate to whom he must throw. The largest single advantage of the underhand throw lies in its accuracy. Speed is sacrificed and this is the reason the rules dictate that all pitches must be underhand ones.

Body Awareness

The ball, controlled by the fingertips, is pushed out away from the body to a complete extension of the arm as it moves down and back. The top of the backswing is at shoulder height and there is a very slight rotation of the torso during the backswing. A forward step is taken on the left foot as the arm starts forward. The exact point of release varies according to the objective, but it usually occurs just after maximum vertical extension of the arm. The follow-through of the arm is a complete extension in the direction of the target and a step onto the right foot in the same direction.

Space

Personal space, in the case of the pitcher, is not limited except by the rules which dictate that he must start with his feet on the pitcher's plate, that at release his hand must be below the hip with the wrist not farther from the body than the elbow, and that he must not take more than one step on the follow-through. In the case of a fielder, personal space is somewhat smaller, since a teammate is often quite close.

Force

The force varies, from a great amount when the pitcher delivers a fast ball, to a small amount when a fielder lightly tosses to a teammate.

Time

The pitcher must deliver the ball within twenty seconds after he assumes the pitching position. For a fielder attempting to make an out by tossing to a teammate ahead of the base runner, the time is significantly reduced.

Flow

The pitching movement is a sequential flow from the ball held in both hands in front of the body, to a complete backward extension of the pitching arm, to a step forward on the opposite foot as the pitching arm comes vertically down and forward, to a release of the ball, to a step forward in the direction of the throw.

SIDEARM

Sidearm throws in softball are generally restricted to fielders who, after fielding a ground ball, must get the throw away in a hurry and thus do not have time to assume an erect position in order to use an overhand throw.

Body Awareness

The tripod grip is used and the backswing is a somewhat limited one, below shoulder level, parallel to the ground. A whip-like motion is used to release the ball, with the ball rolling off the fingertips at the last second. Since the body is generally a bit off-balance and the throwing arm is restricted by a horizontal backswing, accuracy may be diminished. The follow-through is a shift of weight from rear to forward foot, with the throwing arm leading the body around to face the target.

Space

Generally, space is limited only by the fielder's position in relation to the ground and, on occasion, to another player.

Force

A great amount of force can be generated on this throw since more muscles are used and a longer backswing is possible.

Time

The sidearm throw is usually dictated initially by a necessity for speed.

Flow

Flow is from running to either side to field the ball, to planting the left foot as the backswing is begun, to a complete extension of the arm and a wrist snap as the ball is released, to a step onto the right foot as the right arm leads the body in a turn toward the target.

PITCHING

The rules restrict the pitcher to using only underhand throws to the batter. The mechanics for such throws are generally as described previously for the underhand throw. However, the windup prior to the pitch may be a "windmill," wherein the ball is brought forward and up and then continues in a full circle around the shoulder joint, arm extended, until the point of release is reached. The rules restrict the windup to only one circular motion. The obvious advantage to the windmill type of windup is increased momentum. The grip on the ball is determined by the type of ball the pitcher wishes to throw, whether a curve, fast ball, drop, rise, or change-of-pace ball. Various types and degrees of spin can also be put on the ball which cause the ball to react differently, as discussed in chapter four.

Fast ball

The fast ball is the pitcher's "bread-and-butter" pitch and it should be mastered to some extent before experimenting with other types.

The tripod grip is used. As the ball leaves from the extreme ends of the fingertips, the palm is turned to the left.

In-curve

The tripod grip is used, but the wrist is snapped to the right as the ball rolls off the fingers between the thumb and first finger. The resultant left-to-right spin makes the ball curve in on the batter.

Out-curve

The method in the out-curve is the same as that for the in-curve, with the exception that the wrist is snapped right-to-left, resulting in the ball curving away (out) from a right-handed batter.

Rise

The tripod grip is used in the rise, but the thumb is under the ball. The back of the hand (the knuckle) faces the batter as the hand comes forward for the release. The wrist is snapped upward to add backspin.

Drop

The thumb and three fingers grip the ball. As the hand comes forward, the palm faces the batter. The ball rolls off the fingertips as the wrist moves toward hyperextension.

Change-of-pace

The ball is held in the palm by all five fingers. It leaves from the palm rather than the fingertips.

Pitching in the slow-pitch game

In the slow-pitch game, the pitch must be underhanded at a slow to moderate speed and with an arc between three and ten feet at its highest point. The strategy is to make the batter hit the ball as it comes down from the arc; if successful, most of the balls hit will be grounders.

Fielding

All of the analyses of catching as discussed elsewhere (e.g., chapter six, "Basketball") apply in softball as well. Two additional factors come into play in softball as the skill of catching is incorporated into fielding: the wearing of a glove or mitt on the catching hand, and the catching of a ball which has been projected by an implement, the bat.

Insofar as mere catching is concerned, the addition of a glove on the catching hand means only that there is a larger surface area in which to control the ball as force is

Figure 9.2. **Ready position**

Figure 9.3. **Ready position**

absorbed. Therefore, there is less likelihood of a fumble. The position of the hands, i.e., fingers pointing up or down according to the height of the ball, is the same as if a glove were not used.

DEFENSIVE READY POSITION

The defensive ready position is basically the same for outfielders and infielders. As such, it should be mastered by all players since it is considered the best position to assume when the batter steps into the box regardless of other factors, such as base runners and number of outs.

Body Awareness

In the ready position the fielder bends the knees with the weight balanced over the balls of the feet, which are spread shoulder-distance apart. The hands are on the knees and the eyes are focused on the batter. (Outfielders may not put their hands on the knees, but they should assume a crouched position; see figure 9.2.) As the pitch is made, the infielder's hands drop close to the ground (fig. 9.3). This is the most efficient placement of the hands in case of a hard-hit grounder, since it is easier to come up on a high bouncing ball than it is to go down on a low bouncing one. (Outfielders do not drop their hands as close to the ground as infielders, but they do let them hang down.) As soon as the ball is hit, the fielder moves as is discussed under "Infield Play" and "Outfield Play."

Space

Space is generally not a factor in that both general and personal space are not restricted to any significant degree. There are, of course, exceptions, as when, for example, a pop fly is hit to the right side of the infield and the second baseman, first baseman, pitcher, and even catcher converge into that area.

Force

The absorption of force, especially with infielders, is of prime importance in order not to fumble the hit ball. Creating and directing force enters the picture when the ball is thrown, as discussed in the following.

Time

Timing is important in two instances: the fielder must be in a ready position before the pitch is made; and there is little time available when attempting to put out a base runner.

Flow

The initial ready stance flows smoothly from a "get set" (hands on knees) to "get ready" (hands dropped) to "go" (going to meet the ball).

INFIELD PLAY

In addition to making ordinary outs, infielders are involved in double plays, pick-offs and run-downs. Regardless of the ultimate action, the ready position is taken and from then on factors such as if and to where the ball is hit, the number of outs, and the number and position of base runners dictate the succeeding play.

If a fast ground ball is hit to a specific fielder, he should advance to meet the ball and, with his hands well out in front of his body, he should watch the ball until it is firmly caught in his glove. If possible, his body should be squarely behind the oncoming ball so that it acts as a barrier in case the ball is missed. Quite often the catch must be followed immediately by a throw; thus, the fielder needs to so position his body that there is a smooth flow of movement from the catch to the throw. This involves, in addition, assuming a forward-backward stride position and allowing the momentum of the ball to be absorbed into the backswing of the subsequent throw. If time permits, it is desirable to "crow-hop" before throwing. A crow-hop is simply a hop on the right foot followed by a step on the left as the throw is made. This maneuver gives the fielder time to grip the ball properly and make a more forceful and more accurate throw.

OUTFIELD PLAY

It is imperative that an outfielder watch the ball come off the bat if he is to get a jump on it. In case of a fly ball, the fielder must make an instantaneous decision on which direction to run, how far and how fast. He should catch the ball, if possible, on his throwing side and at shoulder height with the back of his glove toward his body ("backhanding" the ball). This allows him to place his throwing hand on the ball immediately should the necessity arise to throw to a base ahead of a base runner who advances after the ball is caught. If the catch must be made below shoulder level, it should be made palm up in order for a rapid transfer of the ball to the throwing hand.

Ground balls hit to the outfield should be played much the same way as an infielder plays them. It is advisable to drop the knee on the throwing side to the ground to act as a backstop in case the ball is missed. If there is a runner on base who is advancing, the outfielder should move in to meet the ball. If there is no runner, the outfielder can generally afford to wait for the ball to come to him and thus be more assured of an efficient catch.

Hitting

Hitting is the most important offensive skill in softball, since without effective hitting, it is virtually impossible to score any runs. To a great extent, offensive strategy revolves around not only hitting the ball, but also the ability to place hits in strategic positions according to such factors as base runners and the number of outs. However, before one can be concerned with the strategy of hitting, the fundamentals of the skill must be learned.

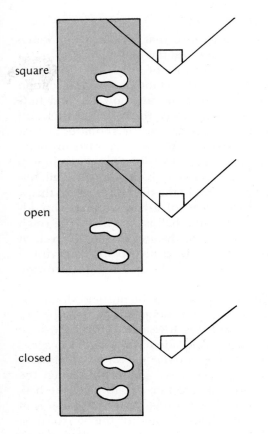

square

open

closed

Figure 9.4. **Stances**

FUNDAMENTALS OF HITTING

Baseball announcers and sportswriters often refer to natural hitters and their prowess with the bat. Unfortunately, even if there is such a phenomenon as a natural hitter, one comes along infrequently. Therefore, the need for all players to be aware of the various components of the skill is self-evident. The more one understands the basic mechanics, the more productive the practice of the skills becomes.

GRIP

The position of the hands on the bat varies from placing them at the extreme end (which permits a longer lever, and thus greater power) to choking up as high as four to six inches from the end (which permits greater control, but sacrifices power), to a position somewhere between the two extremes. Regardless of the position of the hands, the grip is basically the same.

Body Awareness

The bat, held by the fingers not the palms of the hands, is gripped firmly but not to the extent that tension is produced. The right hand is the top hand and it is held very close to the left hand. The backs of the hands form almost a square, with the second knuckle of the top hand directly above the base knuckles of the bottom hand.

STANCE

There are many variations of the stance, all dependent in part on where the hitter wishes to place the ball. The basic stance should be understood and used before any experimentation with it is conducted.

Body Awareness

In a square stance the front of the feet are on an imaginary line drawn parallel to the inside edge of home plate, the feet are shoulder-distance apart, and the weight is balanced over flexed knees and the balls of the feet. The torso can be flexed slightly at the waist, but the shoulders and hips should be parallel to the ground. The bat is held in a position that approaches the horizontal, with the front elbow up and well away from the body and the rear elbow pointing almost straight down. The hands are held somewhere between chest and shoulder level and both wrists are cocked. The eyes are focused on the ball and the head must remain motionless.

Space

The hitter must be within the confines of the batter's box. It is advisable to plant the rear foot near the back edge of the box. The distance the batter stands from the plate is determined by his reach. He must be able to extend the bat at least one to two inches beyond the farthest corner of home plate.

Time

The batter must be ready to take his stride toward the ball as soon as it is delivered.

STRIDE

The stride is nothing more than shifting the weight and stepping into the ball.

Body Awareness

As the ball leaves the pitcher's hands, the batter shifts his weight over the rear foot. The front foot comes slightly off the ground and the position in which it is again planted is determined by the pitch. If the pitch is wide, the front foot moves more directly toward the plate; if it is inside, the front foot moves toward the pitcher. The length of the stride is relatively short. The weight shifts forward, with the head, shoulders and hips maintaining a nearly level position as the striding foot is planted.

Space

The batter may not step out of the box until the ball is contacted.

Force

The body is ready to exert whatever force is necessary as discussed in the following, under "Swing and Follow-through."

Time and Flow

The stride is a relatively unhurried, smooth, continuous, fluid motion.

SWING AND FOLLOW-THROUGH

All of the basic fundamentals discussed are useless if the batter cannot hit the ball. The actual contact of the ball is part of the *swing* and the effectiveness of the hit, as well as its placement, is somewhat dependent on the *follow-through.*

Body Awareness

The swing must be fairly fast and very accurate. The bat should be pulled around by the front hand to a point where, on contact with the ball, it is parallel to the ground and in front of the body. Theoretically the ball is driven through the center of the diamond from such a contact point. The contact point must be changed if one wishes to pull the ball or hit to the opposite field (see "Place Hitting"). As the ball is contacted, the wrists are rolled over or unlocked.

Prior to contact, as the bat is pulled around in front of the body the hips rotate toward the pitcher and the body weight is transferred over the front leg. As a continuance of the contact and the rolling of the wrists, the bat is brought around well behind the opposite shoulder while the body continues to rotate toward the pitcher until the rear foot is well forward. the initial step toward first base is taken on the rear foot.

Space

The batter must stay within the confines of the batter's box until after the ball is contacted.

Force

The force required on the swing is dependent upon where the batter is attempting to hit the ball. Obviously, hitting for the fences necessitates maximum force, while hitting behind the runner breaking for second base requires a great deal less force.

Time

The swing must be timed with the pitch. A fast ball requires a quicker swing than a change-up.

Flow

There is a sequential and continuous flow of movement from the point at which the forward arm commences the swing until the completion of the follow-through.

PLACE HITTING

Novice players are content with the fact that they can hit the ball successfully. As their skill level increases, they ought to start working on the ability to place hits strategically. The *stance* and *swing,* as described, are basically those used when one wants to hit straightaway, or through the center of the diamond. In addition, a player should be able to pull the ball and hit to the opposite field.

Pulling the ball

Most right-handed hitters pull the ball into left field. This is a natural consequence of meeting the ball *well out* in front of the plate and completing the follow-through well behind the opposite shoulder. The ball is contacted just a bit sooner than on a straightaway hit and the follow-through is longer and thus more complete. Quite often, too, an open stance is used.

Hitting to the opposite field

The ball must be contacted late if it is to go to the opposite field (e.g., right field for a right-handed hitter). In addition, the follow-through is cut short. In some cases, a closed stance is used.

BUNTING

Bunting is a specialized form of place hitting which is most often used to advance base runners in a sacrifice play. A fast runner can also use the bunt in an attempt to secure a base hit.

Body Awareness

The bunter should assume the regular stance in order not to telegraph his intention to bunt. As soon as the pitcher releases the ball the batter should pivot and squarely face the pitcher in a somewhat crouched position. The right hand should slide up the bat to a position near the trademark; the lower hand grips the end of the bat firmly; and the bat is held stationary just below the shoulders. The hitter should attempt to hit the ball above its center in order to avoid a pop-up. (A bunt should never be attempted on a poor pitch unless the batter was signalled to do so as part of the sacrifice strategy). As contact is made, the bat gives with the ball, in much the same motion as catching the ball. There is just enough follow-through to push the ball down the desired base path. The initial step toward first base is really a part of the follow-through and it must be taken very quickly.

Space

The batter may not leave the confines of the batter's box until contact with the ball is made. Since the ball does not travel far, there is apt to be a congestion of players along the baseline: pitcher, catcher, and first baseman. The batter may not interfere with their attempt to field the ball.

Force

Very little batting force is required, but the runner must speedily generate a forceful movement of the body toward first base.

Time

The timing of the bunt is crucial. The stance must not be altered until the ball is released; as the ball is released, the stance and swing must be completed very quickly.

Flow

The entire act of bunting, including the initial steps toward first base, is broken down into two sequential movements: the first is the altering of the stance and the swing to get the bat into the proper position to wait for the ball; the second is the contact of the ball, the follow-through, and the break toward first base.

Figure 9.5. **Bunt**

Running

The skill of running, so obviously essential in softball, is analyzed in detail in chapter seventeen, "Track and Field." Therefore, the discussion of running in this section is limited to its unique application to base-running and to sliding.

BASERUNNING

In order to be an effective base runner, the player should be cognizant of the following hints and adept at putting them into practice.

It is essential for a hitter to break toward first as fast as possible. For the right-handed batter, this involves starting the run on the right foot as the left hand drops the bat; for the left-handed hitter, a cross-over step with the left foot is taken as the right hand drops the bat.

When the ball is hit to the infield and it is essential to get to first base speedily, the runner focuses his eyes on the base, runs in a straight line directly to it, and steps on it as he crosses over, still at full speed.

If the ball is hit to the outfield, the runner follows a path which is slightly outside the baseline until he is ten to twelve feet from the bag. He then angles back toward first and touches the inside corner of the base with the foot nearest the bag as he proceeds toward second following the same general procedure.

The base runner who must surrender a base should make certain that the batted ball is on the ground before proceeding very far away from the base. In case of a caught fly ball, it is imperative to return to the base quickly to avoid a double play.

If coaches are used at first and third bases, the runner must look at them for appropriate signals.

It is essential always to be aware of the game situation: how many outs there are, what the batter is going to attempt to do, etc.

Since the runner may not leave the base until the pitcher releases the ball, an attempt to steal should be tried only under ideal conditions.

The base runner should be constantly ready to move.

SLIDING

Sliding is not employed as often in softball as it is in baseball. It definitely is an advanced skill and how much stress is placed

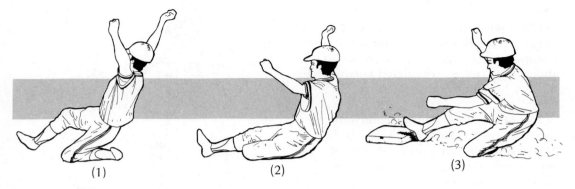

Figure 9.6. **Sliding**

on it in an instructional situation is a matter of choice. If taught, all necessary safety precautions should be followed. Sliding has three main purposes: to avoid being tagged out by coming in under the throw; to avoid over-running second or third base; and, finally, to break up a double play. (The last reason is more applicable to baseball than to softball.)

There are several different types of slides: bent-leg or sit-up, hook, and headfirst. The only one described here is the straight-in bent-leg, the easiest one to master.

Body Awareness

The left foot is the push-off or takeoff foot. As the runner approaches the base at full speed, and at about ten feet from it, he takes off on the left foot and throws his right foot toward the base. The left leg bends at the knee and is held under the right leg at approximately a ninety-degree angle to the base. The force of the slide is absorbed on the upper left leg and even on the buttocks if the slider leans back. The right foot contacts the base with the knee flexed to absorb the shock. The left leg is used to assume an upright running position immediately should conditions warrant. During the en-

tire slide the arms are out at the sides for balance.

Space

The space is limited in that the foot must touch the base. If a slide is used, it must be started approximately ten feet from the base. It is of little use to slide at a closer distance.

Force

The projection of the body horizontally through the air toward the base requires a great amount of force. Therefore, the take-off must be an explosive one. The absorption of force is equally as important lest injuries occur.

Time

Speed is essential.

Flow

There is no break in the total sliding pattern from a run at top speed, to the takeoff and slide, to contact with the base, and possibly to the resumption of the run. Any discontinuity of motion slows the body and thus defeats the purpose of the slide.

MAJOR CONCEPTS RELATED TO STRATEGY

Since softball is a team game, it stands to reason that attention must be paid to positioning players according to their prowess in individual skills as well as to the fundamental strategies into which such skills are interwoven.

Player Positions and Responsibilities

CONCEPT N. Proper use of personnel, based on each player's strengths and limitations, is of paramount importance when molding a team.

Sub-concept N-1. Each player on a team must assume specific responsibilities for the position he is playing.

Each of the nine positions on the team requires a unique skill, to some degree, as well as varying levels of ability in general skills. The following is a brief description of each position, according to the official number of the position.

1. Pitcher

The pitcher must place the ball over the plate *consistently*. The greater the number of pitches in his repertoire, the better. However, it is far better that he *control* only one or two types than throw many variations erratically.

2. Catcher

The catcher, to be effective, must master two skills, catching and throwing. His ability to throw must be better than average since it is his responsibility to get the ball to the base ahead of a base runner who is attempting to steal. He must be quick as well. The catcher is usually the quarterback of the team; therefore, he should understand the game thoroughly and possess leadership traits.

3. First baseman

The first baseman probably catches more often than any other player except the catcher. The necessity for good hands or a "good glove" is therefore obvious. Since the balls thrown to him by the other infielders are often off-target, he should be able to stretch in a variety of poses to catch the ball. Likewise, he must be able to throw quickly and accurately to all bases.

4. Second baseman

The second baseman must be an adroit fielder and he must possess quick reflexes which enable him to throw the ball rapidly as part of a double play combination. He must be quick and agile, and he must possess a sound knowledge of defensive strategy.

5. Third baseman

The third baseman also needs to be a very capable fielder. He must possess a slightly stronger throwing arm than the second baseman, since the throw from third base to first is a long one. He must be extremely quick and be able to field and throw on the run.

6. Shortstop

The best fielder usually plays shortstop since the majority of infield ground balls are hit to his area. He is the key to a good defense. He should possess an even stronger throwing arm than the third baseman. He should be very fast since he is responsible for an exceptionally large fielding area.

7. Left fielder

The left fielder needs to be able to field both ground balls and fly balls well. Of all the fielders the one with the weakest throwing arm can be placed in this position.

8. Center fielder

The center fielder must be the fastest of the three fielders since he has more territory to cover and since more hit balls come into his area. He must be able to run very fast and he needs a strong and accurate throwing arm.

9. Right fielder

In addition to the ability to run and to field well, the right fielder needs the strongest throwing arm of all the outfielders because of the distance from his position to third base. He needs to be able to get rid of the ball very quickly and his throws need to be accurate.

Offensive Strategy

CONCEPT O. In goal-oriented and field sports a system of offense is essential if a team is to be successful. The prime purposes of an offensive system are to build upon the strengths of the players, to shift the balance of power away from the defense, and to capitalize on defensive weaknesses.

The entire offense in softball has but one goal, to score runs. Effective hitting is, therefore, the most important part of offensive strategy. Baserunning, including stealing bases, is also very important. Since this topic is discussed generally under "Running" in this chapter, it is not presented here.

BATTING ORDER

Although every player should be adept at hitting all types of pitches, such a situation just does not exist. Therefore, the necessity to take advantage of a team's hitting strengths by careful placement of individuals in the batting order is apparent. The following is a brief description of how such an order might logically be constructed.

The lead-off batter should be one who gets on base often. A good eye, the ability to draw a walk, is more essential than the ability always to get a hit.

The second batter should be a good hitter, especially to right field when a runner is on first.

The third and fourth batters are the strongest hitters on the team. If there is a difference in their ability, the fourth batter or cleanup man should be the better long-ball hitter. Both should be fast and good base runners.

The fifth batter should also possess power, since many times he is in a position to drive in runs.

Batter number six should be a good hitter. Since often he is the first player to bat in an inning he, like the lead-off batter, should have the ability consistently to get on base.

The seventh through ninth batters in the rotation are the weakest hitters on the team. There is a strong precedent to place the pitcher in the ninth position; however, if the pitcher is a good hitter his talents should not be overlooked.

PLACEMENT IN HITTING

Placement in hitting is also an extremely important offensive strategy. Some consider this skill to be a greater factor in the slow-pitch game. In slow-pitch it is essential to be able to hit behind the runner since the runner may not leave the base until the pitched ball reaches home plate or is hit by the batter. The skill of place hitting is described on page 246.

Defensive Strategy

CONCEPT Q. A system of defense is essential if a team is to be successful. The pime purposes of the defense are to prevent the opponents from scoring and to capitalize on offensive weaknesses.

All of the players on a team are involved to some degree in defensive strategy. Consequently, each player must always be aware of three basic conditions:

1. *What* the game situation is.
2. *Where* he should *play* in such a situation.
3. *Where* to *throw the ball* if it comes to him.[1]

A thorough cognitive understanding of the game is essential if a player is to play intelligently. (The player who has such comprehension is often referred to as a "heady" ballplayer.) However, knowledge of the game without commensurate physical skill is of little consequence on the playing field. Conversely, the skill is of little avail if the player does not know where to station himself or where to throw the ball. The complete ball player must try to master both aspects of the game. Additionally, of course, the importance of such affective attitudes as playing one's best and subjecting one's individual talent to the good of the team cannot be overlooked.

The knowledge of where to play, as well as where to throw the ball, is probably best taught in specific play situations such as those covered in the next section.

Specific Game Situations

In softball, special play situations usually revolve around the number and position of base runners, the number of outs, and the ability of the specific offensive and defensive player(s) involved. For the purposes of this chapter a limited number of such situations are discussed under offense and defense.

OFFENSE

Offensive play situations are built mainly around place hitting, the sacrifice play, stealing bases, and the hit-and-run play.

Place hitting

The techniques of place hitting are discussed in the section on "Hitting" in this chapter. Some specific play situations which call for place hitting are as follows.

When there is a runner on third base with less than two outs, the batter should attempt to hit deep to left field. In the case of a fly ball which has been caught, even though the runner must tag third after the catch, the chances of a run being scored are enhanced by the distance the fielder must throw and the fact that the left fielder generally has the weakest throwing arm of all the fielders.

When there is a runner on second with less than two outs, the batter should hit deep to right field because of the great distance the fielder must throw to third base.

Sacrifice

Both of the previous situations are also examples of possible sacrifice flys. Usually, however, a sacrifice connotes bunting with the idea that the runner can advance since, by the time the first or third baseman can get to the ball, it is too late to throw to the base toward which the runner is advancing.

When there is a runner on first, or runners on first and second, and less than two outs, the batter should try to bunt the ball down the first or third baseline. The runner or runners lead off with the pitch and as soon as they see that the ball is batted on the ground they run as fast as possible to the next base. A runner often uses a slide into the base, particularly if he thinks he can break up a double play.

Hit-and-run

Hit-and-run plays are prearranged by some signal given by the coaches. Both the batter and the base runner must constantly

1. Virgil Ledbetter, *Coaching Baseball* (Dubuque, Iowa: Wm. C. Brown Company Publishers, 1964), p. 81.

watch for such signals. (The use of signals is not discussed in this book. Signalling is a traditional part of baseball and softball, and any book which deals exclusively with the sport can be consulted for details.)

When there is a runner on first, and less than two outs, the pitcher is "behind" the batter and must, therefore, throw a strike. The runner breaks for second with the pitch and the batter *must* try to contact the ball. If no contact is made, the runner may be thrown out by the catcher. The batter should attempt to hit behind the runner (i.e., to right field), another example of place hitting. This play is particularly effective when the count is three-one, since if the next ball is not in the strike zone, the runner automtically is awarded second base.

Stealing bases

Stealing is a great offensive threat in softball even though no lead-offs are permitted. To be successful, the runner must leave the base *with* the pitch and run as rapidly as possible to the next base. Since the runner must be tagged to be put out, a slide is often used in the hopes of coming in under the throw or even of jarring the ball loose from the baseman's glove.

DEFENSE

Defensive play situations are, of course, often dictated by what the offense does. Thus there are rather general defensive maneuvers to employ against the sacrifice, hit-and-run, and steals. In addition, the defense can take the initiative by attempting double plays, by employing cutoffs and relays, and by backing up.

Backing up

Backing up is a technique of covering a player in case of a fumbled ball or an overthrow. In figure 9.7, arrows are used to indicate where players should back up other players. In both figures 9.7 and 9.8 a ground ball is hit to right field, but in figure 9.8 there is a runner on base who may attempt to go to third on the hit. In figure 9.9 the batter hits a ball to the second baseman, with a runner on first. All players who may become involved in the play are backed up: the first baseman, by the catcher; the second baseman, by the right fielder; the shortstop, by the center fielder; and the third baseman, by the pitcher. The three situations diagrammed are representative, although there are, of course, many more play situations which routinely call for one player to back up another player.

Cutoffs

A cutoff man is used when there is at least one runner on base, less than two outs, and the batter hits a safe ball to the outfield. In such a situation the fielder should attempt to get the ball to the base to which the lead runner is advancing. Normally only the first and third basemen are used as cutoff men. The cutoff man should align himself directly between the player fielding the ball and the base in advance of the runner. In this position he can act as a target for the fielder as well. The fielder should throw low and hard to the cutoff man, who positions himself near enough so that the ball, if it passes him at shoulder height, ought to take one bounce into the baseman's glove (or catcher's mitt). If the third baseman or catcher wants the ball to come on through he says nothing. If he realizes that the ball is arriving too late to put the lead runner out, he yells, "Cut it." The cutoff man then takes the ball and tries to put out another advancing player. Figure 9.10 shows one such situation. With runners on first and second, the batter hits a safe ball to the left fielder. The shortstop immediately covers third and the third baseman positions himself as the cut-

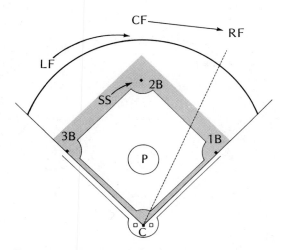

Figure 9.7. **No one is on base. Batter hits a grounder to right field.**

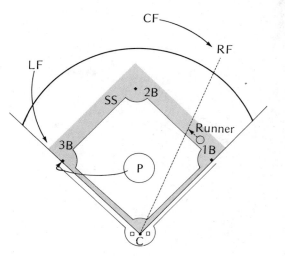

Figure 9.8. **Grounder hit to right field with a runner on first base**

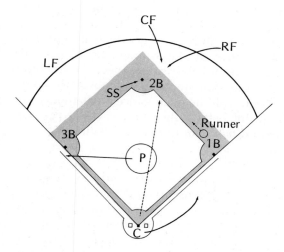

Figure 9.9. **With a runner on first, a grounder is hit to the second baseman.**

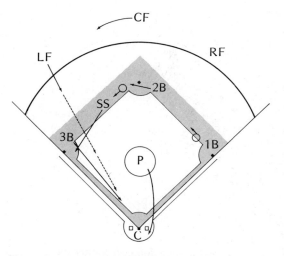

Figure 9.10. **Cutoff play; there are runners on first and second.**

off man in case the runner on second tries to take more than one base.

Relays

When the ball is hit deep to the outfield for extra bases the second baseman or short-stop runs out toward the fielder to act as a relay man in getting the ball to the appropriate base. The shortstop relays all balls hit on his side of second base; the second baseman relays all balls on his side of second. The relay man should align himself directly between the fielder and the base and ap-

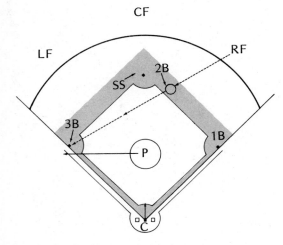

Figure 9.11. **Relay; ball is hit deep to right field.**

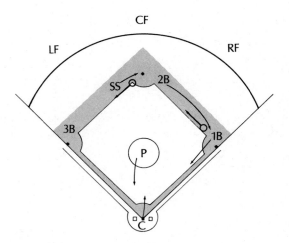

Figure 9.13. **Sacrifice defense; runners on first and second**

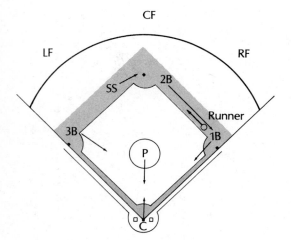

Figure 9.12. **Sacrifice defense; runner on first base**

proximately equal distance from both, as diagrammed in figure 9.11.

Hit-and-run

Since the hit-and-run is supposedly a surprise offensive move, the only truly effective defensive weapon is to anticipate the play and be ready for it. If the catcher suspects a hit-and-run is upcoming, he can call for a pitch-out and hope to get the ball to second in advance of the runner. If the second baseman and shortstop expect the hit-and-run, the shortstop usually moves to cover second with the pitch. Since the batter's goal is to hit behind the runner, this frees the second baseman to field the ball.

Sacrifice

With a runner on first and less than two outs, the defense should anticipate a sacrifice bunt and position themselves accordingly. Figure 9.12 shows that with a runner on first the pitcher, the catcher, the first baseman, and the third baseman all charge the ball. If there are runners on both first and second, the pitcher charges the third baseline, leaving the third baseman free to cover third (fig. 9.13).

Stealing bases

As previously mentioned, stealing is not employed as much in softball as in baseball. However, it is an effective offensive ma-

DIAGNOSTIC CHECKLIST—SOFTBALL SKILLS

Date: _____ Rater: _____

	G = GOOD			F = FAIR			P = POOR		
	Player:			Player:			Player:		
	G	F	P	G	F	P	G	F	P
THROWING									
1. Leads with elbow									
2. Eyes on target									
3. Steps toward target									
4. Wrist snap, whip action of arm									
5. Follow-through									
FIELDING									
1. Ready position									
2. Goes to meet ball									
3. Moves well, right									
4. Moves well, left									
5. Good hands									
6. Gets rid of ball quickly									
7. Catches fly balls correctly									
8. Strong, accurate arm									
9. Hustles									
10. Throws to correct spot									
BATTING									
1. Comfortable, balanced stance									
2. Short stride									
3. Quiet head, follows ball									
4. Hip and shoulder rotation									
5. Easy, level swing									
6. Quick wrists									
7. Follow-through									
8. Protects strike zone									
9. Bunting technique									
10. Aggressive batter									
RUNNING									
1. Runs bases correctly									
2. Good slider									
3. Gets jump on ball									
4. Runs out every hit									
5. Aggressive runner									
THINKS SOFTBALL!!									

COMMENTS:

Adapted from Don Edwards, *Baseball Coach's Complete Handbook* (West Nyack, N.Y.: Parker Publishing Co., 1966), p. 6.

Figure 9.14. **Diagnostic checklist**

neuver and thus a defense should be set up for it. Since second base is the base most often stolen, the second baseman and shortstop should have a clear-cut understanding as to who is to cover the base. Usually these two players have some system of signalling this information to each other. Once the pitch is made, the fielder who is to cover the base edges toward it. He cannot advance too far away from his position until he is sure that the ball is not going to be hit in his direction. One of the players, probably the second baseman, should yell to the catcher as soon as the runner breaks so that he can quickly get his throw off to second.

INDIVIDUALIZING INSTRUCTION

Softball can be a very boring game if there is a great disparity in skill levels. Therefore, on occasion, it behooves the instructor to modify the rules in order to make the game more interesting and enjoyable. Modifications might include such variations as: required slow pitches; a greater or fewer number of balls or strikes for outs; a greater or fewer number of outs before a side is retired; or using a sixteen-inch ball.

Figure 9.14 presents a diagnostic checklist, a form of peer or instructor evaluation, which is often quite meaningful to the individual. For further reference, several books on the general topic of tests and measurements in physical education discuss all sorts of tests for specific sports, including self-testing activities.

The use of videotape is unsurpassed for showing the student exactly how he hits, runs and catches. Although videotape recorders are quite expensive, their use seems to be increasing. Often athletic departments own such recorders and are willing to loan them to qualified personnel.

Finally, attention is again called to the sample lesson plans and sample exploration problems elsewhere in this book as well as to the suggestions in chapter three for individualizing instruction.

REFERENCES

Aaron, Hank. *Hitting the Aaron Way*. Englewood Cliffs, N.J.: Prentice-Hall, 1974.

Allen, Ethan. *Baseball Play and Strategy*. New York: Ronald Press Co., 1969.

Edwards, Don. *Baseball Coach's Complete Handbook*. Englewood Cliffs, N.J.: Parker Publishing Co., 1966.

Joyce, Joan and Anquillare, John. *Winning Softball*. Chicago: Contemporary Books, 1975.

Kneer, Marian E., and McCord, Charles. *Softball: Slow and Fast Pitch*. Dubuque, Iowa: Wm. C. Brown Company Publishers, 1976.

Ledbetter, Virgil. *Coaching Baseball*. Dubuque, Iowa: Wm. C. Brown Company Publishers, 1964.

Litwhiler, Danny. *Baseball Coach's Guide to Drills and Skills*. Englewood Cliffs, N.J.: Prentice-Hall, 1963.

National Association for Girls and Women in Sport. *Softball Guide*. Washington, D.C.: A.A.H.P.E.R. Press, (current edition).

Neal, Patsy. *Coaching Methods for Women*. Reading, Mass.: Addison-Wesley Publishing Co., 1978.

Walsh, Loren. *Contemporary Softball*. Chicago: Contemporary Books, 1978.

———. *Inside Softball*. Chicago: Contemporary Books, 1977.

Watts, Lew. *The Fine Art of Baseball*. Englewood Cliffs, N.J.: Prentice-Hall, 1973.

PART V. □ NET SPORTS

By sports like these are all their cares beguiled.

Oliver Goldsmith

10. Badminton
11. Tennis
12. Volleyball

INTRODUCTION

Badminton, tennis and volleyball are three net sports which are described in greater detail in the chapters which follow. Although each sport is unique in terms of specific skills, strategy and equipment, all share basic commonalities. The background for understanding these commonalities is presented in chapters two, three, and four. Each sport is played on a court with a net separating the opposing players. Each sport involves the fundamental skill of striking in which the player endeavors to hit an object to an open space on the opponent's court while covering the space of his own court. Each sport provides an opportunity for excitement and challenge to performers of all skill levels.

The focus of badminton, tennis and volleyball is on striking a moving object using either an implement (racket) or a body part (forearm, hand). A description of the various applications of space, force, time, and flow is included in each chapter. Chapter five summarizes the basic concepts used in these sports as the performer moves his body through space (p. 71), sends an object through space (p. 76), and receives a moving object (p. 80).

Specific points of strategy differ among the three sports, yet for all the sports the performer must be concerned with his position in relation to the boundaries (p. 88), a means of sharing his court space with a partner or with five teammates (p. 88) and techniques to capitalize upon weaknesses in the opponent's defense in order to score points (p. 88). These commonalities in strategy are also described in chapter five.

Instruction in badminton, tennis and volleyball should be directed at providing an atmosphere in which the learner is challenged yet successful. The learner should be actively involved in the learning process as he perfects old skills and learns new techniques, as he increases his understanding of the mechanics and strategy involved, and as he develops an awareness of, and an appreciation for, the activity. In each sport the performer must have sufficient skill to be able to keep the ball (or shuttlecock) in motion if enjoyment is to ensue. The instructor must recognize that the students with whom he works will differ in many ways—in skill level, in motivation, in speed of learning, in previous experience, etc. Thus, the learning environment should be a flexible one which provides opportunities for students to select from a range of tasks and to modify practice situations so that each situation is challenging yet affords success. Suggestions in terms of methodology have already been given in chapter three and additional ideas are enumerated in each of the following chapters.

Badminton, tennis and volleyball are grouped together as net sports to assist in understanding the common elements of these activities. The detail provided in each of the following chapters also aids in understanding the unique aspects of each activity.

10

Badminton

INTRODUCTION

Badminton is a space game. A racket is used to project a shuttlecock over a net five feet, one inch high into the space of the opponent's court.[1] The space on the playing court is diagrammed in figures 10.1 and 10.2. The space on either side of the net constitutes a player's territory and may be covered alone, as in singles, or shared with another, as in doubles. While covering the space of his own court a player endeavors to direct the shuttlecock to an open space on the opponent's court.

To be successful a player must be able to use space to his advantage. He must be capable of moving through space to reach a desirable position from which to contact the shuttlecock. He must be able to strike at a low level as in an underhand swing, a high level as in an overhand swing, or a medium level as in a sidearm swing. In striking he must be aware of how far he can reach with an implement in his hand.

Badminton is a game refined by rules. Play is begun by contacting the shuttlecock below the level of the waist and directing it across the net into the diagonally opposite serving court. Points are earned when the receiving side is unable to legally return the shuttlecock. Only the serving side may earn points. Play continues until one opponent reaches game score. For women this consists of eleven points in singles and fifteen points in doubles. Men's doubles and singles may be arranged at either fifteen or twenty-one points.

Badminton is a game of force. A player must be capable of producing and directing force. Since the racket is very light, force is achieved primarily through speed rather than mass. Thus, badminton becomes a

---

1. The net is five feet, one inch high at the posts and five feet high in the center.

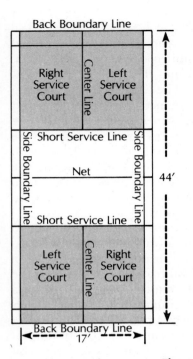

Figure 10.1 **Singles court. The shaded areas represent the right and left service courts. Note that the side alleys are not used in singles.**

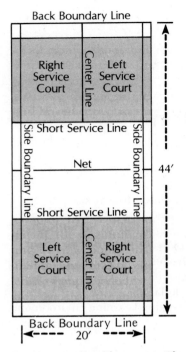

Figure 10.2. **Doubles court. The shaded areas represent the right and left service courts. Note that the back boundary line changes after the serve.**

game in which wrist action is used to move the racket very rapidly. Since the shuttlecock is also very light, air resistance affects its flight and influences the distance achieved.

Badminton is a game of time. The element of time is extremely important in badminton. A player must time his actions in order to contact the shuttlecock at the moment of peak force. He also must be aware that air resistance slows the flight of the shuttlecock and necessitates timing which is different from that used in activities in which a ball is struck. It is embarrassing to swing and miss only to realize that air resistance has been the culprit. Timing also necessitates that a player moves quickly to gain a desirable po-

sition from which to hit the shuttlecock and that the shuttlecock is hit as soon as possible to decrease the time an opponent has to prepare for the return.

Badminton is a game of flow. The flow is smooth and continuous as a player moves to hit the shuttlecock, contacts it, and then immediately returns to home position. Most strokes utilize a follow-through and thus require a smooth flowing action.

Badminton is a game enjoyed by individuals of all ages and all abilities. It is well-adapted as a leisure time activity. The cost of equipment and the facilities needed help to make it a suitable sport for individuals of different ages and abilities. Equipment costs range from the relatively inexpensive backyard set for the novice to the more refined and precision pieces of equipment for the experienced. The space needed for a court can be found in an indoor facility such as a gymnasium or an outdoor area such as a park or a backyard. The challenge afforded attracts both men and women, boys and girls, the recreational player, and the avid enthusiast. Singles, doubles, and mixed doubles provide a variety of different challenges for the participant.

The skill level of the badminton enthusiast may vary from that of the light-hearted picnic game to the serious and physically demanding encounter of tournament play. Many communities have badminton clubs affiliated with the American Badminton Association in which competition is conducted through local, district, and national tournaments. International competition is also prevalent, with the International Badminton Federation governing the sport.

Whether badminton is played by the novice or the expert, certain understandings are basic to successful play. These understandings are discussed in this chapter.

EQUIPMENT

Badminton rackets (fig. 10.3) usually weigh between 4½ and 5 ounces. A racket should be selected which feels good to the performer and allows for a great deal of whip, or quick movement. Rackets are made of wood, metal, or a wood frame with a steel shaft. Nylon or gut is used for the strings. Generally, nylon is cheaper and more durable. Regardless of the substance used, the material should be strung tightly to allow greater reaction force to be returned to the shuttlecock. Racket handles vary in circumference from 3½ to 4½ inches. A size should be selected which feels comfortable to the performer. The racket grip should be of a material such as perforated leather, which prevents the hand from slipping. To pre-

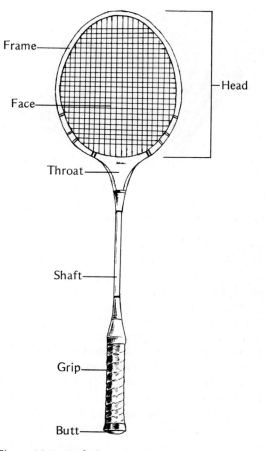

Figure 10.3. **Badminton racket**

vent warping, a wooden racket when not in use should be kept in a press with pressure applied equally to all portions of the frame.

Shuttlecocks (fig. 10.4) are made of plastic, nylon, or feathers, with either a rubber or cork base. A plastic or nylon shuttlecock is more durable and less expensive but its flight is not as true as that of the feather shuttlecock. The feather shuttlecock has a smoother surface and greater weight and thus is not as greatly influenced by air resistance. It is made of a cork base and fourteen

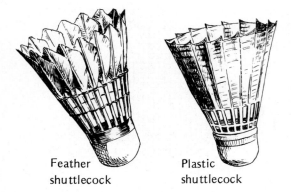

Feather
shuttlecock

Plastic
shuttlecock

Figure 10.4. **Badminton shuttlecocks:
feather shuttlecock, plastic shuttlecock**

to sixteen goose feathers, which are either rounded or pointed at the ends. Due to a more streamlined shape the pointed-end shuttlecock will travel farther. Feather shuttlecocks vary in weight from seventy-three grains (slow speed) to eighty-five grains (fast speed). Regardless of the conditions under which badminton is played, the shuttlecock should function at the same speed. To assure consistency it is necessary to select the weight of the shuttlecock according to the playing conditions. In instances of increased temperature and altitude the shuttlecock will fly faster. Thus, a lower-grain shuttlecock is used to assure a speed consistent with normal conditions. Under normal playing conditions a seventy-nine- or eighty-grain shuttlecock is used.

Since the feather shuttlecock is extremely delicate, care should be taken in its use and storage. To keep from damaging feathers, players should never begin play with an overhand motion, push the shuttlecock along the floor, or use it against a wall in a practice situation. Between each play the feathers should be smoothed and the moisture from one's breath blown onto the shuttlecock to prolong its life. To prevent the feathers from becoming brittle and

breaking, these shuttlecocks should be stored in a cool, moist place.

MAJOR CONCEPTS RELATED TO STROKES

Badminton is a game which requires moving an object through space. The fundamental skill of striking with an implement is used to propel the object, a shuttlecock. Force must be imparted quickly to the shuttlecock to prevent an illegal hit in which the shuttlecock rests momentarily on the racket. The basic strokes used to impart force include those in which maximum force is imparted—the clear and drive and smash; those in which minimal force is imparted—the drop and hairpin net; and those in which either maximum or mimimal force is used to start the shuttlecock in play—the short serve and the long, high serve.[2] Regardless of the stroke, certain concepts are basic to all. These concepts are identified in the pages which follow. Discussion within this chapter is devoted only to those concepts in which the application is unique to badminton; concepts and sub-concepts designated with letters and numbers are discussed more fully in chapter five.

CONCEPT A. Moving the body with control involves a conscious manipulation of the center of gravity in relation to the base of support, either to maintain stability or to initiate locomotor movement, as the situation demands.

Sub-concept A-1. Staying ready to move allows a player to get a faster start in order to outmaneuver the opponent, to

2. The terms maximum and minimal force both relate to producing sufficient force to enable the shuttlecock to clear the net. However, maximum force identifies the production of the greatest force possible while minimal force refers to a limited force which allows the shuttlecock to just clear the net.

gain possession of the ball, or to get into a desirable position to project an object.

Sub-concept A-2. Enlarging the base of support in the direction of the force allows a player to start, stop, and change directions quickly.

Sub-concept A-4. Sliding sideways or in a diagonally forward or backward direction is often a more efficient manner of moving the body through space if the distance to be covered is minimal and if the body needs to remain facing the immediate objective.

Sub-concept A-5. Recovering quickly after the execution of a skill involves reassuming the ready position and relocating oneself in space in the home position, or some other advantageous position, in order to stay alert and ready to react again.

Badminton is a game of starting, stopping, and changing direction as one moves to cover the space of his territory and to reach the proper position in which to contact the shuttlecock. The ready position, as described on page 72, allows for a quick initiation of movement. When not hitting the shuttlecock, a bouncing or dancing action is used to allow quick movement to any area of the court. As noted on page 73, a sliding motion may be used to move quickly, to allow for changing direction, and to maintain balance. If preferred, small steps may be used instead of the slide. As the shuttlecock is hit, the player's position should be established to provide a stable foundation for the action.

After each stroke a player returns to his home position. The exact location of this position is an individual matter depending upon the player's ability to move forward, backward, right, or left. Generally home position is located near the center of the territory the player must cover in order to facilitate movement to all corners of this territory.[3]

CONCEPT C. A player must be in a desirable position in relation to the object to be projected.

CONCEPT D. Creating force: The production and transfer of force depend upon mass, speed, and the striking surface used.

Sub-concept D-1. Increasing the mass used to produce force increases the force produced.

Sub-concept D-2. Increasing the speed of the implement or the body segment imparting force increases the force produced.

Wrist action is the key to force production and deception in badminton. A vigorous snap of the wrist is used to move the racket very quickly through space and produce maximum force. Lesser wrist action is used to produce miminal force. Thus, a player can deceive an opponent by using similar preliminary actions and varying the amount of wrist action used. To utilize the wrist to greatest advantage a proper grip of the racket must be maintained and the wrist kept floppy and relaxed. To increase the range of motion of the racket and to prepare for the production of force, the wrist is extended or cocked during the backswing. At the moment of contact with the shuttlecock it is vigorously flexed, causing the racket head to move very quickly (fig. 10.5). In observing the action it appears as if the wrist is leading the racket head until the moment of contact with the shuttlecock. A swishing

---

3. In singles, players often prefer a home position which is slightly behind the center of the court since it is easier and faster to move forward than backward.

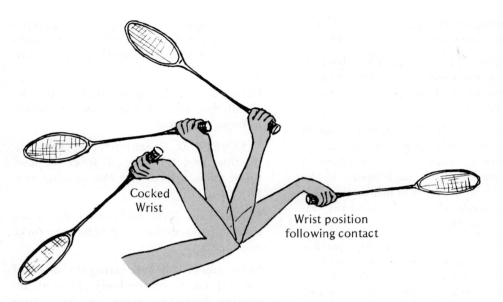

Cocked Wrist

Wrist position following contact

Figure 10.5. **Action of the wrist in the production of force**

sound results from the rapid movement of the racket. Proper use of the wrist in badminton feels the same as the use of the wrist in cracking a whip or fly casting.

Sub-concept D-3. Increasing the range of movement of the body segment or the implement imparting force increases the distance through which speed can be developed, as well as the force imparted to the object.

Sub-concept D-5. A follow-through allows for greater force to be transferred to an object.

Sub-concept D-6. Stabilizing the body segments involved in an action allows for greater force to be imparted to the object.

To allow for maximum force to be imparted, a player's position should be stable when contacting the shuttlecock. Beginners are often tempted to jump to reach a shuttlecock approaching at a high level.

Jumping decreases the stability of the player's position as well as interferes with timing; thus, it should be avoided. Instead of jumping, the player should move quickly to achieve a desirable position before hitting the shuttlecock.

CONCEPT. The flight of a projectile is dependent upon the direction the implement is moved prior to contact, the angle of the face of the implement at contact, and the air resistance present.

As discussed in chapter 4, "Mechanical Principles of Movement," (p. 56) an object that is struck moves in a line tangent to the point of contact in the striking arc. In badminton the striking arc may describe an underhand, sidearm, or overhand pathway. The direction the shuttlecock moves before being altered by air resistance is determined by the point in the arc at which it is contacted and the angle of the racket face at contact. Figure 10.6 shows the different directions possible due to different points of contact and the different angles of the racket face as it moves in the striking arc.

Sub-concept. Contacting an object with a flat striking surface facilitates achieving the direction desired.

When contacting the shuttlecock, the racket face must be flat to the direction of the intended hit if the desired flight is to be achieved. A correct grip and a proper swing of the racket arm are both essential to assure a flat racket face.

The grip used should be a comfortable one which allows for maximum wrist action and maintaining a flat racket face. To prevent restricting the action of the wrist the grip should be firm but not tight, with the racket being controlled by the fingers rather than the palm of the hand. In a stroke which requires maximum force the butt end of the racket may actually leave the heel of the hand as the fingers control the action. To maintain a flat racket face and allow for maximum wrist action, a forehand grip is used for shuttlecocks approaching on the racket side of the body, while a backhand grip is used for those on the non-racket side.

To obtain the correct forehand grip (fig. 10.7) the player should grip the throat of the racket with his non-dominant hand and hold the racket so that its face is perpendicular to the ground. The dominant hand "shakes hands" with the racket. The fingers grip the handle so that the V between the thumb and forefinger is on the top bevel of the racket and the butt end of the handle is near the heel of the hand.

To change to a backhand grip (fig. 10.8) the hand is moved counterclockwise until the V is on the top left bevel. The knuckle of the forefinger is now on the top bevel. The thumb may encircle the handle or extend along the back bevel.

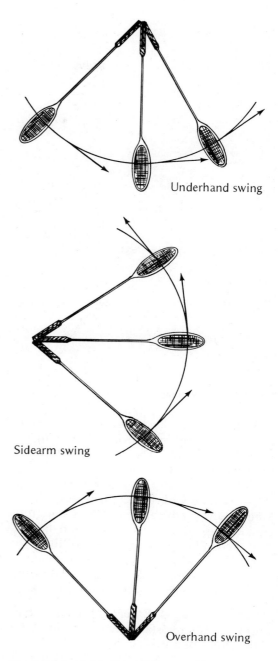

Underhand swing

Sidearm swing

Overhand swing

Figure 10.6. **Achieving different directions due to different points of contact in the arc of the swing**

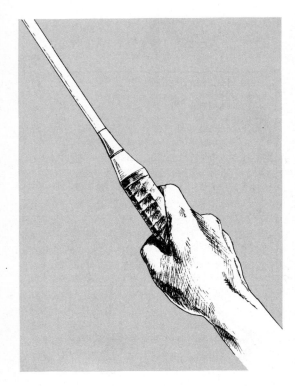

Figure 10.7. **Forehand grip**

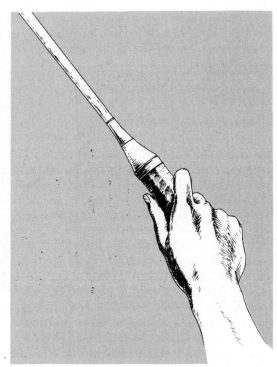

Figure 10.8. **Backhand grip**

Both grips may be adjusted to fit the comfort of the player by spreading or closing the fingers. However, the position of the V should not be altered. The player should be certain that his grip does not violate any of the mechanics of force production. The longest lever possible is desired and thus choking up on the handle should be discouraged. The range of motion of the lever arm is important; the forefinger should encircle the racket rather than extending up the handle, which would limit wrist action.

Sub-concept E-4. External forces such as gravity, air resistance, and friction alter the flight of a projectile.

Due to its light weight, shape, and the nature of its surface, air resistance has a greater effect on a shuttlecock than upon an object such as a tennis ball. The effect of air resistance is greater upon a plastic or nylon shuttlecock than upon the feather shuttlecock due to their more irregular surface area and lighter weight. With either shuttlecock air resistance slows its flight and causes an almost vertical drop. As the effect of air resistance increases, the path of the shuttlecock shows greater deviation from a parabola.

FUNDAMENTAL STROKES

Badminton is a game of force and direction. In endeavoring to earn points the shuttlecock is hit with varying degrees of force and directed to different areas of the opponent's court. A variety of strokes are

used to direct the shuttlecock to an undefended area of the opponent's court or to
force him to move to create open spaces.
These strokes are identified according to
both the force imparted and the trajectory
achieved. Maximum force may be imparted
to send the shuttlecock deep into the court
or sharply downward; minimal force may be
utilized to send the shuttlecock low over the
net and short into the court.

The basic badminton strokes utilize either
an overhand, underhand, or sidearm swing
executed from the racket or non-racket side
of a player's body. The height of the shuttlecock in relation to the player's body dictates
the swing to be used. A shuttlecock at a high
level is met with an overhand swing; one at a
low level with an underhand swing; while
one at a medium level requires a sidearm
swing. The position of the shuttlecock relative to the racket or non-racket side of the
body determines the side of the racket face
used. To contact a shuttlecock on the racket
side of the body the palm of the racket hand
faces the net and thus the palm side of the
racket is used. Beginners, especially, when
using an underhand swing on the racket
side of the body often incorrectly use the
back-of-the-hand side of the racket face and
thereby sacrifice control. To contact a
shuttlecock on the non-racket side of the
body the opposite or back-of-the-hand side
of the racket face is used.

Regardless of whether an overhand,
underhand, or sidearm swing is used to deceive the opponent, the player should disguise the degree of force to be imparted and
the intended placement of the shuttlecock.
The discussion which follows is limited to
the fundamental badminton strokes. These
strokes are categorized according to the
pathway of the swing to focus attention
upon strokes in which deception is possible.
The actions common to all strokes are sum-
marized. The similarity among strokes
should be noted and it should be recognized
that different strokes are the result of variations in force and placement.

Similarities Among Strokes

Body Awareness

1. The racket is used as an extension of
the arm. The player must be aware of how
far he can reach with a fully or partially extended racket arm.

2. The shuttlecock is contacted at the
center of a flat racket face.

3. The grip used for each stroke is determined by the location of the shuttlecock
in relation to the body. The forehand grip is
used for all strokes on the racket side, while
the backhand grip is used for those on the
non-racket side.

Space

1. A forward-back stride position utilizing the principle of opposition enlarges the
base of support in the direction of force and
allows for a transfer of weight into the
swing.

    a. For a stroke executed on the racket
       side of the body, the foot opposite
       the striking arm (the left foot for a
       right-handed player) is forward to
       allow full rotation of the racket arm
       and a forward transfer of weight
       (fig. 10.14, p. 275).

    b. For a stroke executed on the non-
       racket side of the body, the racket is
       moved across the body to contact the
       shuttlecock. The foot on the same
       side as the racket arm (the right foot
       for a right-handed player) is forward
       to allow maximum rotation and a
       forward transfer of body weight
       (fig. 10.15, p. 275).

2. The shuttlecock is contacted with an extended arm from a position in front of the body to allow for varying degrees of force to be imparted and a variety of trajectories to be achieved. Contact in front of the body enables the racket face to be positioned in a variety of different angles to achieve a trajectory that is high and deep, sharply downward, or low over the net. As the shuttlecock moves to a position that is directly overhead or alongside the player, it is contacted earlier in the arc of the swing, thus restricting the possible angles of the racket face and limiting the range of motion of the racket arm. Due to the angle of the racket face, an overhand stroke contacted behind the head will achieve height at the expense of distance and provide an easy return for the opponent.

3. An overhand swing should be used in preference to an underhand swing. Generally an underhand swing is considered defensive in nature and is to be avoided, as it results in an upward trajectory and allows greater time for the opponent to get into position. The overhand swing is considered offensive and desirable, as the shuttlecock can be directed downward and the time the opponent has to prepare for his return is reduced.

Force

1. The force imparted to the shuttlecock should be disguised for as long as possible. Thus the preliminary movements for various strokes should be similar until the application of force.

2. Force is increased by increasing the range of motion, speed, and body mass.

3. Rotation of the shoulder of the racket arm away from the net (for strokes on the racket side of the body) or toward the net (for strokes on the non-racket side of the body) allows for a greater backswing.

a. As the racket is swung away from the net, weight is shifted onto the back foot.

b. For strokes executed on the non-racket side of the body, the elbow of the racket arm is bent and points at the shuttlecock during the backswing (fig. 10.15, p. 275).

c. The wrist is relaxed and cocked.

4. Weight is transferred to the forward foot as the racket is swung forward to meet the shuttlecock.

5. The shuttlecock is contacted with the racket arm fully extended to increase the length of the lever arm.

6. The degree of wrist action used is the major variable in force production. The wrist may be flexed quickly and vigorously at contact to produce maximum force or it may be restrained just before contact to deceive the opponent and produce less force.

7. A follow-through is utilized to assure that the intended force is imparted to the shuttlecock.[4]

Flow

Except in the hairpin net stroke, the backswing, contact, and follow-through of all strokes form one smooth, continuous motion. The player moves to contact the shuttlecock and following contact quickly returns to a ready position in the center of the area he is to cover.

Overhand Strokes

The clear, drop and smash are the basic overhand strokes. The clear travels high over the net and deep into the opponent's court. It is used to move the opponent back

4. In some strokes only a limited follow-through is used due to the player's proximity to the net. It is illegal for the racket to touch the net. The hairpin net stroke does not use a follow-through, as minimal force is imparted and the player must immediately prepare for the opponent's return.

or to allow time to regain one's own court position. Since it travels both high and deep, it provides greater air time than other strokes. The drop, as its name implies, falls just over the net into the opponent's court. It is a valuable stroke to use when the opponent has been moved deep into his court. The smash, a forcefully hit shuttlecock angled sharply downward over the net, is used to put away a weak return by the opponent. All of these strokes can be executed from the racket or non-racket side of the body and should look similar until the application of force.[5] Both the clear and drop can be executed with either an underhand or overhand swing.

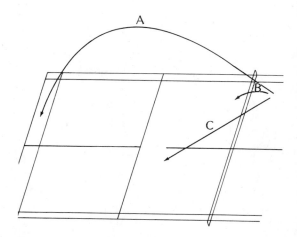

Figure 10.9. **Flights of the: (A) clear; (B) drop; (C) smash**

OVERHAND CLEAR

Space

1. Player assumes a forward-back stride position.*
2. The shuttlecock is contacted from a position overhead and in front of the player's body. The shuttlecock should be contacted at the highest reach possible with the racket arm fully extended.*
3. The racket face is angled slightly upward to direct the shuttlecock high and deep. If the upward angle of the racket is too great the shuttlecock will travel high but not deep.

Force

1. The shoulder of the racket arm is rotated away from the net (for a stroke on the racket side of the body) or toward the net (for a stroke on the non-racket side of the body) to increase the range of motion.*

   a. As the racket is swung away from the net, weight is shifted to the back foot.

   b. In the backswing the racket is dropped behind the shoulder as if

scratching the back to increase the range of motion.

   c. The wrist is relaxed and cocked.

2. As the racket is swung forward, weight is transferred onto the forward foot to increase the mass utilized to produce force.*
3. The shuttlecock is contacted with a vigorous snap of the wrist. The racket is "thrown" at the shuttlecock and a swishing sound is heard.
4. A follow-through is used to assure that the intended force is imparted.*

Time

Contact is timed so that the shuttlecock is hit at the point of highest reach and at the moment of peak force.

Flow

The flow is smooth and continuous. The player returns to an area central to the territory he is to cover and immediately resumes the ready position.*

5. An asterisk is used in the discussion of overhand, underhand, and sidearm strokes to identify actions that are similar for all strokes and are discussed in greater detail under "Similarities Among Strokes."

Figure 10.10. **The overhand clear (the basic pattern for the overhand swing)**

OVERHAND DROP

Space

1. A forward-back stride position is used.*

2. The shuttlecock is contacted from a position that is overhead but further in front of the body than that used for the clear. The racket arm is fully extended at the moment of contact so that the opponent cannot read the intention of the hit.

3. The angle of the racket face is dependent upon the player's position in relation to the net.

   a. If the drop is executed from close to the net, the racket face is angled down.

   b. As the player moves farther from the net, the downward angle of the racket face is decreased to allow the shuttlecock to clear the net.

Force

1. Force is controlled entirely through the action of the wrist. At the moment of contact the speed of the wrist is checked and a gentle action substituted for the vigorous wrist action of the clear and smash.

2. The preliminary actions are similar to the clear and smash in order to deceive the opponent (refer to "Overhand Clear," p. 269).

3. A slight follow-through is used as the speed of the lever arm is intentionally decreased prior to contact.

Time

Timing is not as essential as in the clear and smash, since minimal force is applied to the shuttlecock. For deception purposes contact is timed so that the shuttlecock is hit with the racket arm fully extended.

Flow

The flow is smooth. The player immediately resumes a central position and prepares for the opponent's return.*

SMASH

Space

1. A forward-back stride position is used.*
2. The shuttlecock is contacted when overhead and in front of the body as in the clear. The shuttlecock should be contacted at the highest point possible with the racket arm fully extended.*
3. The racket face is angled downward to direct the shuttlecock sharply down into the opponent's court. The effectiveness of the smash decreases as the player is positioned further from the net. As the distance from the net increases the shuttlecock cannot be angled as sharply downward and greater time is provided for a return by the opponent.

Force

Refer to the overhand clear.

Time

Refer to the overhand clear.

Flow

Refer to the overhand clear.

Underhand Strokes

Although the racket is swung at a different level, the underhand swing utilizes space, force, time, and flow in the same manner as the overhand swing (refer to "Similarities Among Strokes," p. 267). The clear, drop, hairpin net and serve can all be executed as underhand strokes. The discussion which follows focuses upon the serve and the hairpin net, since the clear and drop should be executed with an overhand motion whenever possible. However, in emergency situations an underhand swing may be utilized for a clear or drop by applying the mechanics discussed under "Similarities Among Strokes."

Figure 10.11. **For a legal serve the shuttlecock must be contacted below the level of the waist. The racket head must be lower than the hand holding the racket.**

The serve is used to initiate play. The rules require that the shuttlecock be contacted below the level of the waist with the racket head lower than the racket hand at contact (fig. 10.11). The server must be standing within the serving court and some part of both feet must remain in a stationary position in contact with the ground. Thus, stepping into the stroke is prohibited. The serve is directed into the diagonally opposite service court.

The long, high serve and the short serve are effective for beginning play. As with other strokes, they differ only in force and placement (fig. 10.12). Similar preliminary movements should be used with each to deceive the opponent.

The long, high serve is directed high over the net and deep into the service court. Its

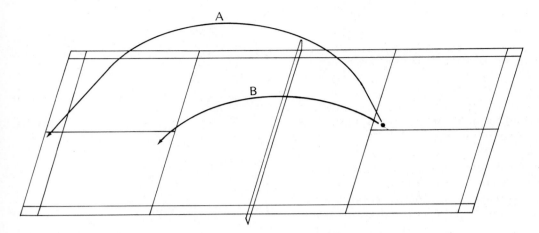

Figure 10.12. **Flights of the: (A) long, high serve and (B) short serve**

execution is similar to an underhand clear. To be successful the shuttlecock must travel at a height greater than the opponent can reach with an extended racket. The long, high serve is used primarily in singles to force the opponent deep into his court.

The short serve is used primarily in doubles. Since two players defend the space of a doubles court, little advantage is gained by forcing one away from the net. Instead the shuttlecock travels low over the net to a corner of the service court near the short service line, forcing the receiver to return it with an underhand or defensive swing.

For both serves the base of the shuttlecock is held between the thumb and index finger of the non-racket hand, dropped and contacted at about knee level ahead of the body. Beginners sometimes swing too quickly and miss the shuttlecock completely. Since air resistance slows its flight, correct timing can be achieved by coordinating actions to the phrase "drop *and* swing," rather than "drop-swing."

LONG, HIGH SERVE

Space

1. The player assumes a position a few steps to the right or left of the centerline and about a racket's distance from the short service line. This position allows him to move quickly to a central location on the court following the serve. Also, the shuttlecock does not have to travel as great a distance before crossing the net as it would if the server stood deeper in the court.

2. The player utilizes a forward-back stride position adhering to the principle of opposition.*

3. The non-racket hand holds the shuttlecock and is extended at arm's reach diagonally across the body to a position in front of the racket arm. The shuttlecock is dropped (not tossed) to initiate the serving action.

4. At contact the racket face is angled slightly upward to direct the shuttlecock high and deep.

Force

Force is increased by increasing the range of motion, mass and speed of the lever arm. All of the actions previously identified

Figure 10.13. **The long, high serve (the basic pattern for an underhand swing)**

under force in the "Similarities Among Strokes" section should be utilized with an underhand swing. Weight may be shifted forward, but the rules dictate that a step may not be taken.

Time

Contact is timed so that the shuttlecock is hit at the moment of peak force and at the instant the racket face is angled slightly upward. Swinging too soon results in either missing the shuttlecock or in a flight that is high but not deep. Swinging too late results in the shuttlecock failing to clear the net.

Flow

The backswing, contact, and follow-through form a smooth and continuous motion. Following contact the player moves to the home position, ready for the following play.

SHORT SERVE

Space

1. Refer to "Long, High Serve," points one through three.
2. The racket face is not angled as sharply upward as in the long, high serve, due to the lower trajectory desired.
3. To facilitate achieving a flat trajectory, some players use a slightly sidearm swing. However, care should be taken that the service rules are not violated.

Force

1. For deception the actions are similar to the long, high serve until the moment force is imparted.
2. Just prior to contact the speed of the wrist is checked and the shuttlecock is gently hit or guided over the net.
3. In the follow-through the racket face is pointed downward toward the area of the court to which the serve was directed.

Time

Contact is timed so that it occurs at the instant the racket face is correctly positioned.

Flow

As in the long, high serve, the flow is smooth. Following contact the player moves to the home position.

HAIRPIN NET

The hairpin net is an underhand stroke used to return a shuttlecock that falls perpendicularly and close to the net. Often it is the only possible return for a well-executed drop. The shuttlecock travels in a pathway which resembles a hairpin. It is contacted as near to the top of the net as possible, just clears the net and falls perpendicularly down the other side. It may be executed from either the racket or non-racket side of the body.

Space

1. The player is positioned several feet from the net in front of the short service line.

2. The shuttlecock should be contacted as close to the top of the net as possible to allow for a quick return.

3. The racket face is flat and angled upward to allow the shuttlecock to skim the net and drop. A shuttlecock directed too high into the air provides an opportunity for a smash by the opponent.

Force

The swing is limited to apply minimal force to the shuttlecock.

    a. Due to lack of time, very little backswing is used.

    b. The wrist is slightly cocked in preparation for the hit and the shuttlecock is gently stroked and guided across the net.

    c. A follow-through is not used, as little force is imparted and the player may not touch the net with his racket.

Time

The shuttlecock should be hit as soon as possible.

Flow

The flow is bound, since a follow-through is not used.

Sidearm Strokes

A sidearm swing utilizes the same mechanics of space, force, time, and flow as the overhand and underhand swings. These are identified under "Similarities Among Strokes," page 267. The swing is used to hit a shuttlecock that is right or left of the body at a height between the shoulders and waist. The grip used is dependent upon whether the shuttlecock is on the racket or non-racket side of the body.

The basic *sidearm* stroke is the drive. It is a technique used primarily in doubles play to return the shuttlecock low over the net to various parts of the opponent's court. It may be directed deep into the court or midcourt, straight down the sideline or crosscourt.

DRIVE

Space

1. A forward-back stride position is used.*

2. The shuttlecock is contacted to the side and in front of the body with the racket arm fully extended.

3. The racket face is flat and almost perpendicular to the ground to allow a flight that is low over the net.

Figure 10.14. **Forehand drive**

Figure 10.15. **Backhand drive**

Force

1. Trunk rotation is used to allow a long backswing. The player's shoulder is perpendicular with the net at the instant of contact. Generally time does not allow the player to turn more than his shoulder to the net in preparation for this stroke.*

    a. Forehand drive: (1) as the backswing is initiated, the shoulder of the racket arm is rotated away from the net; (2) in the backswing the elbow of the racket arm is bent and points at the ground, the wrist is cocked and the racket is moved behind the head to a position between the shoulder blades.

    b. Backhand drive: (1) as the backswing is initiated, the shoulder of the racket arm is rotated toward the net; (2) in the backswing the elbow of the racket arm is bent and points at the shuttlecock. The racket hand is moved to a position near the non-racket shoulder.

2. During the backswing, weight is shifted onto the back foot.*

3. The wrist is relaxed and cocked at the end of the backswing.*

4. As the racket swings forward, weight is transferred to the forward foot.*

5. The arm is fully extended and the wrist snapped as the shuttlecock is contacted.

6. The movement of the racket is continued in a follow-through.*

Time

The action is timed so that the shuttlecock is contacted with an extended arm at the moment of peak force.

Flow

The swing is smooth and continuous. The player quickly returns to a central location on the court and resumes the ready position.

MAJOR CONCEPTS RELATED TO STRATEGY

Whether the competition involves singles, doubles, or mixed doubles, a well-played game of badminton is both physically and mentally demanding. The successful badminton player is one who has the physical stamina to react quickly and skillfully to each position of the shuttlecock. He is able to move to his right or left, forward and back, in order to cover the space of his court. He has control of his body as he moves to reach the shuttlecock, imparts force, and immediately returns to the ready position in the center of the territory he is covering. He is mentally alert in his endeavor to outwit the opponent. The winning player is the thinking player. He is able to use space, force, time, and flow to his advantage. By varying the force imparted and the placement of the shuttlecock, he forces his opponent to move throughout the space of his court. He is quick to capitalize upon any error or weakness.

The concepts basic to badminton strategy are discussed in the pages which follow. The reader is referred to chapter five (p. 87) for an elementary discussion of these concepts. The discussion which follows is limited to applications of concepts from chapter five to badminton and sub-concepts not found in chapter five. Discussion is directed toward giving the beginning player an understanding of how points may be earned through mental as well as physical acuity. The mental challenge provided by badminton should be apparent as the player utilizes these concepts, is flexible enough to vary his game if he is not experiencing success, and is constantly alert to the situation at hand.

CONCEPT R. The player should be aware of his position within the playing area.

CONCEPT T. Creating spaces and sending the ball (or shuttlecock) to open spaces of the court or to weaknesses in the opponent's defense are basic to scoring.

A successful offense is one which places the opponent at greatest disadvantge. This may be accomplished by directing the shuttlecock to an undefended area of the court or to an apparent weakness in the opponent's game. The concepts appearing earlier in this chapter are basic to a successful offense. The player must be able to control his body as he moves in space as well as control the object he is projecting through space (Concepts A and Concept, pp. 262, 264). He must be able to use an underhand, overhand, or sidearm swing to produce varying degrees of force. He must utilize correct footwork to establish a desirable spatial relationship with the shuttlecock prior to contact (Concept C).

A quick point or loss of service often results from a hit which forces the opponent to move and thus creates open spaces. Generally the corners of the court are the most vulnerable areas and placement to these areas forces the opponent to move the greatest distance. A down-the-line shot forces the opponent to move forward or back, while the crosscourt return necessitates moving a greater distance.

In singles the task of moving the opponent is much easier, since only one player covers the space of the court. The long narrow boundaries of the singles court are used to advantage by forcing the opponent to move primarily forward and back. The long, high serve, clear, drop, and hairpin net are valuable aids in this endeavor. The smash is reserved as the stroke used to end the play. It is used with discrimination, as it leaves the player in an off-balance position and is tiring if used excessively.

Since two players cover the space of the doubles court, the attacking team must attempt to create spaces by moving both players out of position or by causing confusion between the two. The short serve, drive, hairpin net, and smash are valuable tools in this strategy.

Regardless of the strokes used to move the opponent, the pattern should be varied to catch the opponent unaware. As previously mentioned, an overhand as opposed to an underhand swing should be used whenever possible.

Sub-concept. The serve should allow the server to regain the offensive quickly.

The serve is a defensive hit, since the rules dictate that it must be executed from a level below the waist. To allow the server to regain the offensive quickly it must be strategically placed. Generally, for beginning players a serve directed to the non-racket corner of the receiving court results in a weak return that the server can utilize to his advantage. However, as the skill level improves, a serve directed to the non-racket corner when it is the outside corner of the receiving court allows the opponent a greater angle of return and places the server at a disadvantage. The server must then be prepared to defend against the down-the-line or crosscourt return. To decrease the possible angle of return, the serve must be directed to the inside corner of the receiving court.

The server should avoid directing the shuttlecock to the center of the receiving court. This placement forces little movement of the opponent from home position and often enables the receiver to utilize a smash return. To be successful a long, high serve must have sufficient height and depth so that it cannot be received by the opponent from a central position in the court. This serve is used primarily in singles to force the opponent deep into the court. The short serve, used mostly in doubles to force an underhand return, must travel low over the net and short into the receiving court if it is to be effective and prevent a smash by the receiver.

Sub-concept. The placement and force to be utilized with each hit should be disguised for as long as possible in order to deceive the opponent.

As previously noted, the preliminary motions for all underhand, overhand, or sidearm strokes should be similar until the point of contact with the shuttlecock. Placement can be varied by changing the force to be imparted or varying the angle of the racket face at contact. Thus, a sidearm stroke such as the drive can be directed crosscourt by contacting the shuttlecock earlier or later in the arc of the swing. It can be directed down the line by contacting it directly opposite and ahead of the player (fig. 10.6, p. 265). By varying the degree of wrist action applied the drive can be sent deep into the court or mid-court.[6] The opponent should not be able to detect the degree of force to be produced; the speed of the racket arm should be the same regardless of the force to be imparted. At the moment of contact, the wrist is either restrained or vigorously flexed.

If a player uses similar preliminary movements the opponent is prevented from anticipating whether an underhand swing will produce a clear or drop or whether an overhand swing will result in a clear, drop, or smash. Likewise, by using similar motions the server is able to disguise his intention of sending the shuttlecock high and deep or low and short.

CONCEPT S. Individual, partner, or team play is based on a particular plan of spatial arrangement.

Since the playing areas (figures 10.1 and 10.2 p. 260) as well as the number of players differ in singles and doubles, the demands on the player correspondingly change. Singles play requires agile footwork and physical stamina, as one player must cover the entire space of the court. In doubles two players work together to defend the space of their court, thereby decreasing the physical demands on each player while increasing the need to harmonize efforts to assure adequate court·coverage.

Whether a singles or a doubles game is played, the player must achieve a court position which facilitates converting a serve or hit from the opponent into a play to his advantage. Basic to receiving the serve is a ready position which allows quick movement forward or backward. A forward-back stride position is utilized with both feet stationary until the shuttlecock is contacted.[7] Weight may be shifted in the direction from which the shuttlecock is anticipated to allow for a faster start.

Following the serve, the player should return to a home position that is central to the territory he is to cover (sub-concept A-5, p. 263). In singles this position is one which affords quick movement to any area of the court. Thus, it is located midway between the sidelines and slightly behind the center of the court.[8] In doubles the home position becomes the center of the territory the player is to cover. In both instances the home position may be adapted to fit the strengths of the player while protecting any weaknesses in his game. Following each play a player must return to home position in order to assure complete court coverage.

Sub-concept. When sharing the space of the court with a partner, a formation should be utilized which allows: (1) the space of the court to be covered; (2) each player's territory to be well-defined; (3) a clear vision of the play; and (4) both players to be actively involved.

Many different techniques may be used to share the space of the doubles court with a partner after the serve. To be effective a system of doubles play should comply with the characteristics described in this sub-concept. The entire space of the court must be cov-

6. The mid-court drive is reserved for doubles play.
7. Official rules dictate that when receiving the serve some portion of both feet must be in contact with the ground in a stationary position until the shuttlecock is contacted.
8. Since it is easier and faster to move forward than backward, most singles players prefer a home position which is slightly behind the center of the court.

ered to prevent the opponents from utilizing open areas to score points. Each player must be certain of the territory he is to cover so that confusion is avoided and an area is not left open by mistake. Both players must be able to see the shuttlecock as it is in play. If one player's position blocks the vision of his partner, trouble is certain to ensue. For doubles to be played as the mental and physical battle it is intended to be, both players must be alert and react to the position of the shuttlecock on each play. Doubles can quickly become dull and unexciting for beginners if one player retires from the action and lets his partner do the work. Frequently beginners do not experience the excitement and challenge of doubles because they utilize a system of court coverage which places the burden on one partner. While this partner is actively involved, the other soon establishes a set position with his feet planted to the floor and becomes a spectator. Players may select from several different systems of covering the court. If information is desired on the up-and-back or side-by-side systems, the resources listed at the end of this chapter should be consulted. The diagonal system is described in the information which follows, as it adheres to all of the characteristics of good court coverage and keeps both partners actively involved in each play.

The basic idea of the *diagonal system* is that the space of the court is shared most effectively when partners stay on a diagonal with one another. When one moves to hit the shuttlecock, the other reacts by changing his position to maintain a diagonal relationship and assure complete court coverage. Figure 10.16 depicts this relationship.

Until beginners become accustomed to working with a specific partner, it is best to establish territories for each player to cover by dividing the court from the front left corner to the back right corner (fig. 10.17). The player on the right covers the entire net area and right sideline, while the player on the left is responsible for the entire back line and the left sideline. A shuttlecock approaching the dividing line should be returned by the player who can contact it from his racket side. The players' initial positions following the serve should allow movement to all areas of the territory to be covered. Thus, they are positioned in a central location on a slight diagonal. The player covering the net area is a few steps forward; the player covering the back line is a few steps back.

As the shuttlecock is directed into their court, both players react quickly. The one in whose territory it is placed moves to return the shuttlecock while his partner reacts by adjusting his position to maintain the diagonal relationship discussed. After the shuttlecock is contacted both players return to home position. As this system of play is being learned, it is valuable to have partners constantly talking to one another, calling for shots, and informing each other of changes in position.

As partners grasp the basic idea of reacting to one another's position, modifications can be made to fit their style of play. The territories to be covered can be modified to eliminate any problem they might encounter. A switch in territories may be used if one player, due to the position of the shuttlecock, is closer to his partner's home position than to his own (fig. 10.18). In this instance "Switch!" is called and each player returns to his partner's home position and defends his partner's territory. Following a point or loss of service they resume their original home positions.

When the idea of reacting to the movement of the partner who is hitting the shuttlecock is utilized, the diagonal system

Figure 10.16. **Diagonal system. As one player moves to hit the shuttlecock, his partner moves to maintain a diagonal relationship and assures complete court coverage.**

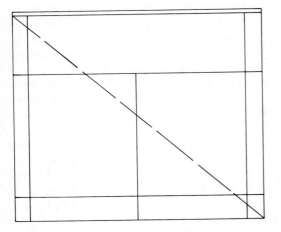

Figure 10.17. **Diagonal system (division of the court into playing territories)**

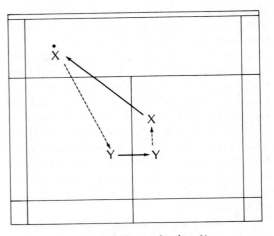

Figure 10.18. **Switch in territories. X returns to Y's home position; Y returns to X's home position.**

fulfills all of the characteristics of good court coverage. The space of the court is always covered as one partner adjusts his position to allow movement to any potential open space. Playing territories are well defined and confusion should not result if the court is divided as discussed previously. Clear vision is always provided as players maintain a diagonal relationship. When the shuttlecock is contacted by the player responsible for the net area, the back player avoids a position directly behind this player so that his vision is not obstructed.

Probably the greatest advantage of this system is that both players are actively involved and continuously moving. The problem of planted feet is eliminated and doubles becomes an exciting and challenging game.

PROVIDING A CHALLENGING LEARNING ENVIRONMENT

Unfortunately, in many learning situations the individual is not motivated to use the understandings (cognitive domain) he has digested and the skills (psychomotor domain) he has developed. To generate enthusiasm for badminton, to develop an appreciation of the mental and physical challenges it affords and to foster the desire to pursue it as a leisure activity (affective domain), a stimulating learning environment must be provided. The suggestions which follow are directed toward providing such an environment. They are intended only as examples and are by no means all-inclusive.

THE SKILL CARD

A skill card encourages meaningful practice prior to instruction. A sample skill card is included in figure 10.19. The items on the card may be changed as the skill level warrants. However, due to the limited space often available, and the inability of beginners to control the flight of the shuttlecock, it is wise to select skills which can be completed individually and which allow several players to share the space of a court or practice area. Individuals utilizing the card should focus upon those skills with which they need greatest practice. The potential for using skill cards to enrich the learning environment has already been discussed in chapter three, "The Role of Methodology," page 35.

To be successful at skills one and two (fig. 10.19) the individual must develop the hand-eye coordination essential for badminton play. A forehand grip should be utilized for both practices.

The wall volley in skill three provides excellent practice in the mechanics essential for a successful badminton player. Both wrist action and agile footwork must be utilized in this practice situation. (Players should be careful to use only nylon or plastic shuttlecocks.)

Practice on serves (skills four and five, fig. 10.19) provides the opportunity to develop a hit which will allow the server to regain the offensive quickly (sub-concept, p. 277). Often beginners are careless and serve directly to the opponent's position, initiating a sequence of plays which merely keeps the shuttlecock in the air rather than forcing the opponent to move. Standards should be established to measure a successful serve. It may be required that the long, high serve land within the back alley of the diagonally opposite serving court or that the short serve travel within a racket's distance of the top of the net and land within a racket's distance of the short service line.[9]

THE INDIRECT APPROACH

The indirect approach challenges each individual and allows each to progress at a rate commensurate with his ability. A sample indirect lesson has been included here.

Focus of the lesson

Maximum force is to be produced in the clear.

Method of teaching

Guided discovery is the teaching method used.

9. The back alley is the space between the back service line in doubles and the back boundary line following the serve.

	Skill 1	Skill 2	Skill 3	Skill 4	Skill 5
BADMINTON SKILL CARD			Name _____		
Date	Number of consecutive hits into the air using the palm side of the racket face	Number of consecutive hits into the air alternating sides of the racket face	Number of consecutive overhand hits against the wall	Number of legal long, high serves ———————— Number attempted	Number of legal short serves ———————— Number attempted

Figure 10.19

Grouping of students

Each student selects a partner. Partners move to opposite sides of the net. In instances in which court space is limited, players can be spaced near the net standards so that more players may be accommodated on each court.

Previous instruction

Prior to this lesson the students have learned the forehand and backhand grips and discussed the importance of wrist action and the effect of air resistance upon the flight of a shuttlecock.

DIRECTIONS FOR STUDENTS

1. Select a partner and find a space on one of the courts in which to work. Partners should be on opposite sides of the net. We are going to explore the production of maximum force in badminton. One player starts the shuttlecock in play in any manner desired and sends it as high and deep over the net as possible. His partner returns the shuttlecock, directing it high and deep. Play continues in this manner for as long as possible. Think about the actions you are using to produce maximum force to send the shuttlecock high and deep.
   A. Practice with your partner.
   B. Discussion: Which grip did you utilize as you contacted the shuttlecock? (Students should recognize that the forehand grip is used for shuttlecocks approaching on the racket side of the body and the backhand grip is used for shuttlecocks on the non-racket side.)

2. As you continue to send the shuttlecock as high and deep as possible, listen as you contact it. Does your racket make any noise? Should it?
   A. Practice with your partner.
   B. Discussion: Did you hear any noise as you contacted the shuttlecock? What does a swishing sound indicate? (Students should understand that for maximum force to be produced the racket arm must be moved very quickly. If wrist action is used to increase the speed of the racket arm, a swishing sound is heard.)

3. Now see if you can detect the effect that a backswing has on the force produced. Using either an overhand swing or an underhand swing, send the shuttlecock high and deep. Try to accomplish this by using a very small backswing. Then try to use the largest backswing possible. Remember to listen for the swishing sound. Do you hear a greater swish when you use a large or small backswing? Which backswing allowed you to send the shuttlecock the greatest distance? Why did it?
   A. Practice with your partner.
   B. Discussion: With which backswing were you most successful in imparting maximum force (i.e., sending the shuttlecock high and deep)? Why? (Discussion should focus upon the range of motion of the lever arm. Students should realize that a larger backswing provides a greater distance in which to develop the speed of the lever arm. For an overhand stroke the racket should be brought behind the head and between the shoulder blades as if scratching the back.)

4. Again direct the shuttlecock as high and deep as possible. Try to use just an overhand swing. See if you can determine where in relation to your body the shuttlecock was contacted for hits which went high and deep. Did you contact the shuttlecock in front of your body, directly overhead, or behind your body? Watch your partner. Where do you see him contacting the shuttlecock? Was the point of contact different for hits which did *not* go both high and deep?
   A. Practice with your partner.
   B. Discussion:
   (1.) Show where, in relation to your body, the shuttlecock should be contacted if it is to be directed high and deep. What occurs if you contact it more behind your body? Does this change the angle of the racket face and the flight achieved? What will you have to do if the shuttlecock is not coming to the position you have just indicated? (Students should recognize that the shuttlecock must be contacted as soon as possible while overhead and in front of the body. The arm should be fully extended at contact, as a longer lever allows greater force to be produced. Good footwork allows a player to reach the shuttlecock while it is still at a high level and in front of the body.)
   (2.) As you've been practicing, you have used both overhand and underhand swings to impart maximum force. Which swing should you strive to

use? Why? (Students should recognize that an overhand swing is offensive while an underhand swing is defensive.)

(3.) We have just learned the clear. It is one of the basic badminton strokes used to direct the shuttlecock high over the net and deep into the opponent's court. When might the clear be of value in a game situation? (Students should recognize that the clear is used to push the opponent away from the net and to allow time to regain one's court position.)

(4.) The clear requires the production of maximum force. Identify all of the actions which contribute to producing maximum force. (Students should recognize the importance of: (a) contacting the shuttlecock as soon as possible with a fully extended racket arm; (b) increasing range of motion through a large backswing; and (c) increasing the speed of the racket arm by using wrist action.)

Note: At this point a practice situation for the clear is advisable. The practice should be modified for those who are experiencing difficulty and made more challenging for those who are successful. As students are able to execute the clear, they may progress to exploring the production of minimal force (the drop) in order to hit to an open space.

THE SINGLES GAME

The opportunity to play singles challenges a player, since he must cover the space of his court alone and any weaknesses in his game cannot be protected by a partner. Beginners often have difficulty recognizing the importance of good footwork and placement of the shuttlecock to an open space. Exposure to the singles game emphasizes the importance of these elements of badminton play. Although space limitations often make singles difficult, wise planning will allow all players to be actively involved and to benefit from the experience. In instances in which court space is not sufficient to allow all players to play singles, the following suggestions may be of benefit.

1. Play half-court singles. Two singles games may be played on each court by dividing the playing territory in half at the centerline. If additional players are still available, one may be assigned to each half-court and rotate into the game as soon as an error is made. To provide a competitive situation an extra player may replace the player who committed the error. However, this is often the individual who needs additional practice. Thus it may be desirable to replace the player who successfully completed the play rather than the one who committed the error. In either instance, this practice situation provides a quick and frequent means of rotation and keeps all players actively involved and alert.

2. Allow two players to challenge one, using the boundaries appropriate for doubles on one side and singles on the other. Players should rotate positions frequently so each has the opportunity of covering the space of the court alone. This situation provides practice for both singles and doubles.

3. Establish the game length according to a time limit (such as five minutes) or a modified number of points (such as five points). As two players play sin-

EVALUATION OF GAME PLAY

Name of Evaluator: _____   Name of Player: _____

Directions: Read the following list. Observe one player for several minutes and then complete the items below. If an item is well-executed indicate a + in the space provided. If additional work is needed, indicate a − and specifically describe the weakness to be corrected. At the end of the playing time share your results with the player evaluated.

Space

_____ 1. The space of the court is covered well. _____
_____

_____ 2. The shuttlecock is contacted while in front of the body. _____
_____

_____ 3. An overhand swing is used whenever possible. _____
_____

_____ 4. The shuttlecock is directed to an open space. _____
_____

_____ 5. The player *quickly* resumes home position after contacting the shuttlecock.
_____

_____ 6. The player *quickly* resumes ready position following each play. _____
_____

Force

_____ 7. Wrist action is used to produce force. _____
_____

_____ 8. A variety of strokes are used to vary the force imparted. _____
_____

_____ 9. The long, high serve is directed to the back alley. _____
_____

_____ 10. The short serve is directed within a racket's distance of the short service line.
_____

Player's greatest strength:

Player's greatest weakness:

Figure 10.20

gles, two others can serve as coaches, each one focusing upon one of the players. At the end of the playing time responsibilities are exchanged. To guide the coaches in their responsibilities a check sheet such as the one indicated in figure 10.20 may be utilized.

REFERENCES

Bloss, Margaret Varner. *Badminton.* 3rd ed. Dubuque, Iowa: Wm. C. Brown Company Publishers, 1975.

Broer, Marion R. *Individual Sports for Women.* 5th ed. Philadelphia: W. B. Saunders Co., 1971.

National Association for Girls and Women in Sport. *Tennis-Badminton-Squash Guide.* Washington, D.C.: American Alliance for Health, Physical Education, and Recreation. (Current edition).

Pelton, Barry C. *Badminton.* Englewood Cliffs, N.J.: Prentice-Hall, 1971.

Poole, James. *Badminton.* 2nd ed. Pacific Palisades, Calif.: Goodyear Publishing Co., 1973.

United States Badminton Association. "Official Badminton Playing Rules." Swartz Creek, Mich.: The Association (P.O. Box 237), current edition.

11

Tennis

INTRODUCTION

The game of tennis should be considered a physically challenging as well as a mentally stimulated one. Learning the "how" along with the "why" of tennis can and should be an exciting experience for beginners. Advanced players often become intrigued with the application of basic movement principles and analyze their game in light of this knowledge.

The mechanics of the swing, the challenge of the body meeting an oncoming ball in space, and the thrill of well-placed shots can assume more meaning to players when they thoroughly understand and apply the principles of movement.

Tennis is a spatial game, played on a court limited by specific boundaries. The object of the game is for one player, or two players in a doubles game, to contact the ball and send it across the net to a specified spot in such a way that an opponent (or opponents) cannot return the ball after one bounce. The singles court is long and narrow, while the doubles court is wider because two 4½ feet alleys are added on both sides of the court (fig. 11.1).

Successful tennis players develop a keen sense of perceptual awareness as to where they are at all times within the spatial dimensions of the court. Some players refer to this sensory awareness as "court consciousness"; it is this sense that dictates to the player the type of stroke to use and the amount of backswing and force that is necessary from each particular position in the court. the strategic placement of shots involves a continuous flow of feedback information as to spatial awareness.

Tennis is a perceptual game involving visual, auditory, and kinesthetic sensory mechanisms. The ability to perceive a moving ball, track it through space and make the final decision as to where it should be contacted depends on acute vision as well as

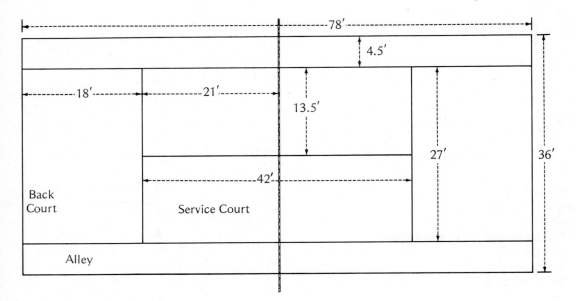

Figure 11.1. **Tennis court**

perceptual judgment. Listening to the sound when the racket contacts the ball provides feedback information. Kinesthetic awareness as to sensations involved with body movements, the racket, and the movement of body parts in space requires keen perceptual judgments.

Because tennis involves the relationship between a player and the ball, the following questions are important in that they refer to major perceptual concepts.

    a. How far does the arm reach in space in order to contact the ball?
    b. How close to the ball does one move to allow for the bounce?
    c. On the service, how far overhead does one toss the ball?
    d. How should the grip feel for the forehand and backhand drives?

Tennis is a game of form, and few sport skills are as aesthetically beautiful as well-executed tennis drives or serves. When a player is able to move skillfully and rhythmically into the proper position, contact the ball with a smooth, powerful, accurate stroke, and deliver a strategically placed shot to win a point, he has mastered movement patterns that display efficient, effective, even beautiful form. The player's footwork and body control should exemplify grace and poise and reflect an understanding of movement principles in action. A combination of knowledge, attitude and performance results in good form that is effective in play.

Tennis is a game of controlled force that follows all the principles of a leverage system. As in all striking patterns, the tennis swing is an example of a third class lever (see chapter four, "Mechanical Principles of Movement") and each player must learn how much force is necessary to increase or decrease the speed of the racket head. Whether to lengthen or shorten the lever arm which affects the force and the speed of the ball is a perceptual judgment that is based on training and playing.

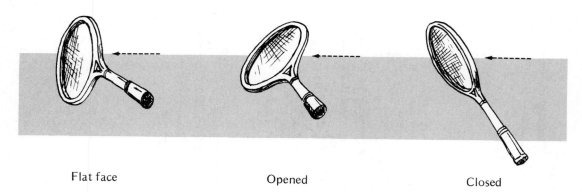

Flat face   Opened   Closed

Figure 11.2. **Racket positions indicate ball spin**

Tennis is a game of angles, and strategy depends on the player's knowledge and ability to handle these angles. Depending on the player's position on the court, the height of the player, the strength of the player and his opponent, each shot must be executed with a specific purpose in mind which will dictate the angle of the shot. The racket face as it contacts the ball determines the angle of the ball flight, which in turn determines the distance and the direction of the ball.

The angle of rebound of the ball from the court is pertinent and requires careful study of ball spin. A beginning tennis player first works toward accuracy and consistency in striking the ball. Learning to contact the ball and to control body position takes first priority. Beginning players usually attempt to strike the ball with a flat racket face, producing no spin (fig. 11.2). If and when the player decides to put a spin on the ball, he needs to study the mechanics of changing the angle of the racket face so that force is applied away from the center of the ball (refer to the discussion of ball spin in chapter four, "Mechanical Principles of Movement").

The grip will determine the angle of the face of the racket at contact with the ball. The Eastern forehand is the most universally taught forehand grip. The spreading of the fingers is important in keeping the wrist in a strong position. The V formed by the first finger and thumb rests on top of the racket. If the hand were opened, it would be perpendicular to the court. The grip is said to be a handshake position. The Eastern backhand grip is also commonly used and necessitates turning the hand and wrist toward the body so that the knuckle of the index finger is rotated on top of the handle, with the thumb placed diagonally across the back or wrapped around the handle. The player should feel pressure on the last three fingers and thumb and not on the flat, palm side of the hand. The thumb should never lie along the back of the racket. the continental grip can be used for forehands and backhands. The hand assumes a position halfway between the Eastern forehand and Eastern backhand grips (fig. 11.13).

Tennis is a game of style. In tennis the player is entitled to choices between styles of equipment and playing apparel.

Racket

The size of the grip, weight and balance of a tennis racket should fit the individual player. The only fairly uniform specification is the length of the racket (twenty-seven

Eastern forehand   Eastern backhand   Continental grip

Figure 11.3. **Grips**

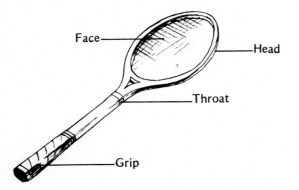

Figure 11.4. **Racket parts**

inches) and the distance across the racket face (nine inches) (fig. 11.4). Grips vary to fit the size of the player's hands and increase by ⅛ inch; the smallest is usually 4¼ inches and the largest is 5 inches. A grip that feels comfortable and doesn't turn excessively is desirable. Generally, women prefer grips of 4¼ to 4½ inches and men prefer grips of 4⅝ to 4¾ inches. Consideration for the

smaller size of youngsters' hands should be made and a small grip should be chosen for them.

Racket weight varies from 11½ ounces to 15 ounces, with girls and women preferring 12 to 13¾ ounces, and men and boys 14 to 15 ounces. Younger players may prefer rackets weighing 12 to 12½ ounces.

Balance may vary too. Some players especially prefer a heavy head to increase momentum. Some, especially net players, prefer a lighter head to gain better control. The style preference is the individual's choice to make.

Style also enters the picture when selection is based on the type of frame and strings. Traditionally, frames have been constructed of fine wooden pieces put together under pressure and heat. Lamination, usually of ash, gives the appearance of forming one solid piece of wood. A hardwood, often maple or beech, on the outer edge and throat of the racket makes the racket stronger. The grip is usually constructed of basswood or Molacca but covered with leather, plastic or rubber. Recently, racket frames have assumed a new style of construction. Steel, aluminum, and fiberglass have entered the range of choices.

Rackets are strung with gut or nylon strings. Gut is more expensive and is more resilient, but it is not moisture-proof. Continued dampness will cause strings to swell to the breaking point. Nylon is moisture-proof, but since it is elastic there may be difficulty in maintaining tension. For average players, fifteen-gauge nylon string is recommended. For tournament players, sixteen-gauge gut string is recommended. Seventeen-gauge string is the thinnest and has the highest resiliency, but it is the least durable.

The amount of tension used when stringing rackets is fifty to sixty pounds for the average player and up to seventy pounds for highly skilled players. The greater the tension, the more difficult the control factor is.

Rackets should be stored in a press with equal pressure on all sides. A waterproof cover should protect the racket when it is not in use. If the racket does become wet or damp, it should be wiped immediately with a soft cloth. The frame can be waxed to help preserve it.

Tennis apparel

You can choose the style of your clothes, all right,
But if you want to "play cool," the color is white.
Who knows for sure—in the future it seems
We might see colors introduced to the scene.

Heavy absorbent socks are recommended for comfort. The number of styles in tennis shoes have increased until many types are offered for selection. However, shoes with large perforations in the soles are frowned upon, as they can damage court surfaces.

Balls

Tennis balls should be fresh and should remain in the can until ready to play. Dead balls result from dampness or a loss of the fuzzy outer covering; these balls should be discarded.

Balls properly inflated with gas or compressed air must meet United States Lawn Tennis Association (U.S.L.T.A.) specifications. Recently developed balls are longer-wearing due to the new rubber compounds used.

Tennis has a unique scoring system. Zero score is referred to as love; the first point equals fifteen; the second point equals thirty; the third point equals forty. A player must win four points by a margin of two. A score of forty to forty is deuce and one player must win two consecutive points to win the game. If the server wins the first point, the score is "advantage in" or "ad in"; if the receiver wins the first point following deuce, the score is "advantage out" or "ad out."

MAJOR CONCEPTS

The ability of a player to make contact with a moving ball depends on perceptual judgments related to *vision, space,* and *kinesthetic awareness.* Although a tennis player seldom stops to analyze what happens at the moment his racket touches the ball or what has been involved in leading up to the moment of contact, he nevertheless has been combining many actions all based on sound movement principles.

The tennis player must be able to track the ball visually, anticipate the path of its trajectory, judge the ball's speed as he moves to intercept the ball and return it to a strategic spot in his opponent's court. Although experienced players perform these tasks automatically, the beginner should be made aware of several factors involved with visual perception.

Tracking a ball involves the ability of the player to detect the ball and isolate it from its background. In a learning session and in all practice sessions thereafter, the background should include all objects from which the player must isolate the ball. Reminding the player to keep his eye on the ball should facilitate figure-ground perception and enable him to learn to track the ball prior to making decisions.

Visual acuity is necessary for the player to perceive the exact location of the ball in space. Peripheral vision, depth perception, and twenty/twenty vision all enhance the opportunity for precision.

Tracking a moving ball also involves spatial perception. In learning to track balls in space, the beginning player may find it helpful to drop a ball beside him and catch it with his hand. The racket should be put aside for the moment. Practice in dropping and catching helps orient the player to ball movement. Dropping with the left hand and catching with the right hand in a swinging movement from the side simulates the path the racket takes in a tennis swing. Dropping and catching can be accomplished on both sides of the body. On one side the open palm of the hand makes contact in a handshake position and on the other side of the body the open palm must be turned over so that the back of the hand points toward the body. The palm of either hand always moves toward the net. Prior to teaching the serve it is helpful to instruct the player to throw the ball into the air with the left hand and catch it high over the head with a fully extended arm and a follow-through past the left shoulder. Mentally placing the ball in space at its exact position is the most difficult part of the serve. Many beginners lack an exact awareness of space above their heads. Sometimes the ball barely goes one foot into the air, while the player thinks he has placed it two to three feet above him.

The following concepts are discussed more fully in chapter five.

CONCEPT A. Moving the body with control involves a conscious manipulation of the center of gravity in relation to the base of support, either to maintain stability or to initiate locomotor movement, as the situation demands.

Sub-concept A-1. Staying ready to move allows a player to get a faster start in order to outmaneuver the opponent, to gain possession of the ball, or to get into a desirable position to project an object.

In tennis the *ready position* is assumed between every stroke unless the game is moving so fast that no time is available. The weight is carried on the balls of the feet so that movement forward or to either side can be accomplished immediately.

Sub-concept A-2. Enlarging the base of support in the direction of the force allows a player to start, stop, and change directions quickly.

As the stroke is executed, and at the contact moment, the knees remain flexed, enabling weight to be transferred to the forward foot effectively.

Sub-concept A-3. Running in a forward direction is the quickest way to cover a distance of some magnitude.

Sub-concept A-4. Sliding sideways or in a diagonally foward or backward direction is often a more efficient manner of moving the body through space if the

distance to be covered is minimal and if the body needs to remain facing the immediate objective.

Small sliding steps are used and sometimes longer strides are used in getting to the net. Diagonal steps are also used, but in all types of running steps, the last step turns into the pivot enabling the body to turn and the arm to swing.

Sub-concept A-5. Recovering quickly after the execution of a skill involves resuming the ready position and relocating oneself in space in the home position or some other advantageous position, in order to stay alert and ready to react again.

Sub-concept A-6. Propelling the body through space requires a firm reacting surface and sufficient friction between the reacting surface and the base of support.

The surface of a tennis court may be clay, grass, cement, composition, asphalt, Tartan, or any of the newer compositions. Each type of surface presents a different friction problem. In some cases high degrees of heat may affect the surface and cause it to become softer, thus complicating running, stopping, and starting.

CONCEPT B. Creating and absorbing force to control the movement of the body through space may involve all of the body or only parts of the body, in unison or in sequence; however, the relaxation of noncontributing muscle groups is imperative for smooth, efficient movement.

Sub-concept B-1. A smooth transfer of momentum from one part of the body to another part, or to the total body, results in sustained movement, while an explo-

sive transfer of momentum increases the speed and/or magnitude of the resulting movement.

In the tennis swing momentum begins with the back foot and moves up the leg to the hips. When the body rotates, momentum shifts from the shoulders to the forearms and to the firm wrist holding the striking surface, the racket. The sequential movement flows smoothly from one lever to the next when the movement is at peak speed.

Sub-concept B-3. Relaxing noncontributing muscle groups leads to smooth, efficient movement and thus to the proficiency of the performance.

Allowing movement speed to dissipate before transferring to the next sequential level produces a jerky type of movement. On the other hand, if the movement speed transfers too quickly, jerky movement also occurs. Relaxation of muscle groups not in use allows for a smoother transfer to take place.

CONCEPT C. A player must be in a desirable position in relation to the object to be projected.

The length of the tennis racket added to the length of the extended arm determines how far away the player is from the ball.

Spatial awareness helps the player to make a judgment as to his position. A pivot on the foot toward the ball enables the player to turn and be ready to swing.

CONCEPT D. Creating force: The production and transfer of force depend upon mass, speed, and the striking surface used.

Sub-concept D-1. Increasing the mass used to produce force increases the force produced.

Sub-concept D-2. Increasing the speed of the implement or the body segment imparting force increases the force produced.

Sub-concept D-3. Increasing the range of movement of the body segment or the implement imparting force increases the distance through which speed can be developed, as well as the force imparted to the object.

Sub-concept D-4. Setting the body in motion prior to contact with an object, or to the release of an object, builds greater force which in turn is transferred to the object. However, at the instant of contact or release, the body should be stabilized.

Sub-concept D-5. A follow-through allows for greater force to be transferred to the object.

In a tennis swing the follow-through enables the player to maintain balance following contact, since all effort is directed to the moment of contact. Follow-through also allows the body parts to slow down gradually, thus protecting the parts from abrupt action.

Sub-concept D-6. Stabilizing the body segments involved in an action allows for greater force to be imparted to the object.

Tennis players should move into position very quickly, but just prior to contact both feet should be on the ground with the foot toward the ball already pivoted into position to receive the transfer of weight. Lowering the knees slightly helps add to the stability.

Sub-concept D-7. A firm striking surface allows for greater force to be imparted to the object.

CONCEPT E. Directing force: The direction in which an object moves is determined by the point at which force is applied in relation to the object's center of gravity.

Sub-concept E-1. Applying force directly through the center of gravity of an object results in a straight trajectory; an off-center application of force produces a curved trajectory.

The angle of the racket face at ball contact helps determine the trajectory path of the ball (fig. 11.5).

In most sports when an object is propelled through space, a forty-five-degree angle is recommended for maximum distance. In tennis, however, spatial dimensions do not require maximum distance. Velocity or speed of the ball is the desirable objective, not distance, and most tennis strokes require less than a forty-five-degree angle.

In order to contact the ball with an angle that is less than forty-five degrees and yet diagonally upward enough to send the ball over the net, there must be both vertical force and horizontal force applied. The greater the horizontal force is, the closer to the net the ball will be as it clears. Just enough vertical force is required so that the pull of gravity will not affect the ball until *after* it clears the net. The path of all balls following contact forms a parabola because gravity pulls the ball to earth after the other forces have been dissipated.

Sub-concept E-2. Keeping one's eyes on the object (i.e., objective focus or tracking) facilitates the application of force in line with the intended direction of flight or the absorption of force when slowing or stopping an object. However, if the performer is throwing at a target, he must focus on the target rather than on the projectile.

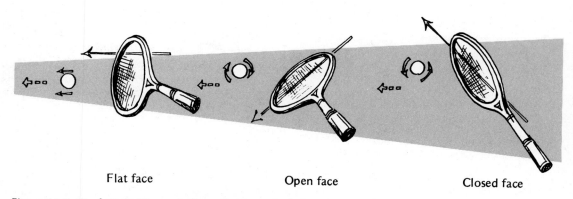

Flat face   Open face   Closed face

Figure 11.5. **Racket position—stroke and rebound action**

Tennis is a perceptual game and effective visual tracking is imperative. Tracking the ball right to the racket and then directing focus to the intended target area helps score points.

Sub-concept E-3. Contacting an object with a large, flat surface facilitates applying force directly through the center of gravity in the direction desired.

In a tennis swing the racket is moving fastest at the center of the swing. The contact point should occur after the racket has entered the center area of the arc.

To gain additional momentum, the mass of the striking implement should be considered. The greater the mass is, the greater the striking force is. In tennis this principle is modified slightly because the racket face is of standard size; however, the balance and weight of the racket may vary according to choice. A highly skilled player usually prefers a racket that is heavy in the head to provide more weight when contact is made. Beginners usually lack speed and control with a heavier racket head.

The middle of the arc inscribed by the racket head or the contact point should occur during the flat portion of the arc. The longer the racket can follow a flattened arc prior to contact, the greater the racket's

momentum will be in the desired direction of ball flight (fig. 11.6).

Sub-concept E-4. External forces such as gravity, air resistance, and friction alter the flight of a projectile.

In tennis several forces are acting on the ball, including movement of the racket, horizontal force, and vertical force. The height of a player will determine how far above the straight horizontal path is hit. Most girls need to hit slightly upward on their drive in order to clear the net.

Due to the dimensions of the tennis court, most tennis strokes require less than a forty-five-degree trajectory path to cover the distance required. The vertical force should be just enough to allow the ball to clear the net.

When all these forces are acting on the ball, the speed, direction and distance will be a result of a combination of all of them. Usually the path of the racket exerts the greatest influence because the racket is heavier than the ball. The body behind the racket is the central unit and can therefore exert more momentum than the ball.

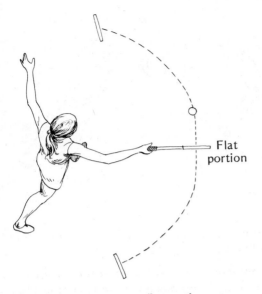

Figure 11.6. **Swing arc—flat portion**

BASIC SKILLS

Forehand and Backhand Drives

The forehand and backhand drives are the basic strokes in tennis and serve as the background upon which to build additional strokes. The striking pattern resembles throwing pattern, for the production of force is similar. The basic forehand drive is similar to the sidearm throw.

How a player executes a tennis drive depends on *how* he utilizes space, time, force and flow.

Space

1. A player must learn to judge how close to an approaching ball he can get in order to contact it with a forceful swing. After a ball bounces, it will travel approximately five feet before it is contacted. Beginners have a tendency to move too close to the ball.

2. A spatial judgment is involved in reaching for the ball, for a ball is struck approximately three feet away from the body

to allow for the arm to extend comfortably while holding a two-foot length of racket.

3. The ball is struck to either side of the body; the pivot facilitates turning the body to the side, allowing the arm to complete a full backswing. The words "turn and swing" denote a change in spatial direction from the ready position.

4. The backswing can follow either a straight path or a circular pathway, but the straight backswing, parallel to the court, is easier for beginners and is most often recommended (fig. 11.7). The racket head is kept level with or higher than the wrist but still lower than the point of contact. The spatial path of the backswing is a slightly upward arc. At the peak of the backswing the hand extends backward, forming an angle of approximately forty-five degrees to sixty degrees (fig. 11.7).

5. The ball is contacted slightly ahead of the front foot at about waist level with the racket head, which is perpendicular to the court (fig. 11.8).

6. Following contact the path of the racket continues in the flattened portion of the swing and finishes in an upward direction to about eye level.

7. The angle or space between the hand and wrist as it flexes is approximately thirty degrees (fig. 11.9).

8. The turn of the body in the backhand drive is greater than in the forehand, as the body must coil into position with the racket arm well away from the net so that the entire body may execute the forward swing of the racket.

Time

1. By the time the approaching ball crosses the net, the backswing should be completed. As the ball bounces, the foreswing begins ("... and swing").

Forehand

Backhand

Figure 11.7. **Backswing**

2. The backswing, the grip change, and the pivot are simultaneous.

3. The greater the force desired, the longer the backswing is and the more time must be allowed for that preparatory swing.

4. The foreswing must be timed so that the racket is moving fastest at the moment of contact—in the center of the flat portion of the swing. The words "... and *swing*" provide the rhythmic timing if acceleration occurs on the word "swing."

5. Following contact, the racket head speed decelerates; it does *not* stop. The follow-through should continue toward the net as long as possible to insure a longer flattened area for the contact point. To put top spin on the ball, the racket face should close on the follow-through (fig. 11.10).

Force

1. Learning where to place the feet for the maximum production of force is important. A forward stride with the front foot pointing diagonally forward and the back foot perpendicular to the first foot is usually preferred.

2. Stepping into the swing means stepping with the front foot moving toward the net, *not* toward the ball.

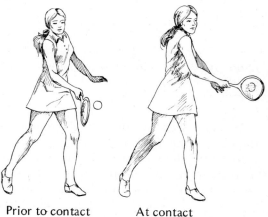
Prior to contact   At contact

Figure 11.8. **Swing**

3. Turning and swinging allows the whole body to be used in stroking the ball.

4. As the player steps into the swing, the front knee should bend.

5. Reaching for the ball will assure a comfortably extended arm and a faster moving racket head.

6. On the backhand, there is a roll over the racket which enables the wrist to remain straight and firm with slight cocking.

Figure 11.9. **Racket angle change**

Figure 11.10. **Follow-through on forehand wth top spin**

7. At the point of contact on the backhand drive, the shoulders are almost perpendicular with the net.

Flow

1. The words ". . . and swing" provide the timing for the flow of movement. On the word "and" the foot pivots to the side as the body turns and the weight shifts to that foot while the hand completes the backswing.

2. On the word "swing," sequential movement begins from the court level and ends with the racket striking the ball.

3. Movement flows smoothly from one body segment to the next when each segment has reached its peak of speed.

4. The flow of movement starts with the larger, more powerful muscles, and moves finally to the smaller, more controllable muscles. The larger muscles supply power; the small muscles supply direction and accuracy.

5. Flow of movement should continue beyond the point of contact and end with the player facing the net in a ready position.

6. It is the flow of movement from the swing angle that produces topspin. The flow of movement rolls up and over the ball after contact.

Body Awareness

A beautifully executed tennis drive has to be a natural movement sensed kinesthetically within the body. Bending the knees and allowing the body to turn while coiling up for release of the force is an action that must be sensed throughout the entire body. The uncoiling of the powerful muscles to initiate the flow of movement, the turning of the hips and trunk as the racket swings through to contact the ball, and finally the follow-through as the ball flies across the net are felt within all body segments.

1. The body must be aware of how it feels to reach for the ball with an extended arm.

2. At the peak of the backswing, the player must be aware of the poised muscles ready to spring into action.

3. The speed of the movement should become a conscious phenomenon.

4. The firmness of the wrist and forearm at the moment of contact should be sensed,

and there should be perceptual awareness of the sound as the racket contacts the ball.

5. An awareness of the entire body moving into the stroke should be sensed.

6. A return to the state of readiness as a position is taken with the body poised, weight forward, muscles on alert.

The Serve

The service in tennis puts the ball into play from behind the baseline and is based on an overarm throwing pattern. While the free hand lifts the ball into the air, the racket arm drops over the shoulder and then reaches high for the tossed ball at the top of its flight, directing it into the service court diagonally across the net. The Eastern forehand grip is used by most beginners.

Space

1. The position for the serve is with the non-racket side toward the net with the front foot at about a forty-five-degree angle with the baseline and the back foot parallel (fig. 11.11).

2. The ball is lifted from waist level to a height as high as the extended racket can reach. The hand should follow the ball toss. The arms lifts the ball; the ball is not tossed by wrist action. The ball is released above the shoulder, and the arm at full extension is in front of the face in line with the nose.

3. The path of the backswing follows a downward movement with the edge of the racket leading past the leg and knees and then a circular path to about shoulder height behind the body, with elbow bent. The wrist cocks to drop the racket head over the back (fig. 11.12).

4. From a position with the butt of the racket pointing upward, the elbow and wrist

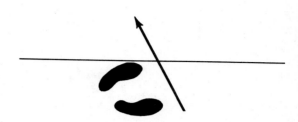

Figure 11.11. **Position of feet on serve**

extend upward to contact the ball at a point over the racket shoulder (fig. 11.13).

5. Following contact, the path of the racket swings down and across the front of the body on the non-racket side.

6. A step is taken with the racket-side foot in the direction of the court as momentum carries the body forward.

Time

1. The arm lifts the ball at the same time the racket drops down into the backswing. The hands move apart at the same time in opposite directions.

2. The service foreswing begins as the ball reaches the top of its flight.

3. The rhythm of the service accompanies the words "down, back, and swing."

4. The final step occurs as the racket swings across the body on the follow-through (fig. 11.14).

Force

1. Sufficient force is produced and released by virtue of the continuous length of the backswing and foreswing over a great distance.

2. The snap of the wrist, which changes the direction of the momentum from back to forward, facilitates the final spurt of speed of the racket head (fig. 11.14).

3. Final force and speed are produced by a shortening of the lever (by bending the elbow) during the final sequence of movement.

Starting Postion   Backswing .   Ball Release

Figure 11.12. **Ball lift in service**

Figure 11.13. **Drop of racket when ball is at its peak**

4. Rotation of the body facilitates the sequential timing of the body segments to account for the force of the foreswing (fig. 11.15).

5. The ball toss must be high enough to allow for the full extension of the racket arm so that the racket is moving at its fastest speed.

Flow

1. The flow of movement is down, back and swing, without any long hesitations. Sometimes there is a slight pause when the racket drops behind the shoulder before the snap.

2. Within the arc of the serve there is a flattened portion in which the ball should be contacted. If the ball is contacted prior to the flat portion of the arc, the ball's flight

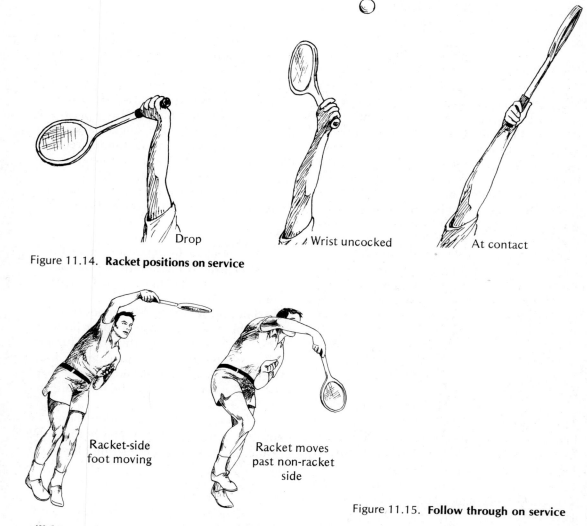

Figure 11.14. **Racket positions on service**

Drop

Wrist uncocked

At contact

Racket-side
foot moving

Racket moves
past non-racket
side

Figure 11.15. **Follow through on service**

will be upward, and if it is contacted after the flat portion, the flight will be downward.

Body Awareness

1. There is a feeling of building up force and speed during the serve as the body weight rocks from the forward foot to the back foot and then returns to the forward foot.

2. The twist of the body as it turns into the serve at the time of the snap provides a sensation of throwing the racket at the ball.

3. The stance provides the basis for a feeling of extreme stability.

4. The service in tennis provides an awareness of the body's leverage system in action probably more than any other skill, especially at the moment of contact with the arm in full extension. An awareness of space

above the head must be developed, as well as a feeling of where in that space the ball must be placed.

The Volley

The volley is a stroke used before the ball bounces, usually hit about six feet from the net, and projected downward from above the net. The volley is usually an offensive stroke that can be placed accurately. Sometimes a volley projected upwards or hit from below the net is considered a defensive shot. The grip is the same as that for the forehand and the backhand, although many players use a grip that is halfway between the two in order to save time.

Most players use the word "punch" to describe the volley, for the action is a short, forceful strike. There is no time for the lengthy backswing, as it is not necessary to produce speed. The idea is to assume a very stable position so that the racket and body are able to meet the force of the approaching ball.

Space

1. The beginning player should stand fairly close to the net so the ball does not bounce. If the player is back farther, he is too far away to handle the ball before it bounces; however, the first volley is sometimes taken at mid-court position. More advanced players can handle volleys in the backcourt.

2. The ball should be contacted well in front of the body.

3. Depending on *where* the player contacts the ball, he must change the racket face: high ball, flat racket; waist-level ball, racket parallel to the court; below the net, the racket rolls up and over the open face (fig. 11.16).

Time

1. Because the volley is a stroke requiring little or no backswing, little time is needed for execution of the stroke. It is a quick movement.

2. The timing requires a punching type of movement which is short and abrupt.

3. If the approaching ball is a slow one, there is more time for a longer backswing.

4. Careful judgment in timing requires the player to be in a position to contact the ball before it bounces (fig. 11.17).

5. If the approaching ball is a slow one, there is more time for a longer backswing.

Force

1. To shorten the lever and gain force, the player usually chokes up on the racket.

2. A very stable, slightly forward stride position is taken.

3. Since most of the force comes from the approaching ball, the player must hold the racket firmly and meet the ball squarely. (See Newton's third law in chapter four, "Mechanical Principles in Movement.")

4. A step forward helps the punching action.

5. The pivot and body rotation should be kept to a minimum. If the player turns, he can handle volleys on either side effectively (fig. 11.17).

Flow

1. The body is stabilized to meet the oncoming force; the flow of movement results from very few body segments being called into action.

2. The sequential movement in the volley occurs quickly in a short burst of movement in an abrupt punching action.

Body Awareness

1. To execute a volley well the player must be kinesthetically aware of his body position.

High forehand
volley

Low volley

Backhand volley

Figure 11.16. **Volley**

2. Spatial awareness is imperative to achieve good court position.

3. Visual tracking must be accurate and keen due to the reduction of time.

4. A posture of readiness and expectation is necessary to facilitate quick reactions.

5. The racket is held a bit lower and more forward than for the drive.

6. The necessity for modifications in a player's movement must be sensed and perceived, for he needs to react with force and placement rather than to think about speed and distance.

7. The stability a player senses enables him to use his entire body for force from a quick spurt of power. He has no time to wind up in order to develop force and speed.

The Half-Volley

When a player is caught at mid-court or in no-man's-land and does not want to retreat to the baseline, he uses a stroke called the half-volley. The ball is hit immediately after the bounce and long before it reaches the apex of the ball's arc. Not much force is

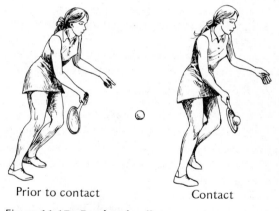

Prior to contact

Contact

Figure 11.17. **Forehand volley**

needed, as the ball is hit on the rise and it will go up and over the net because of the angle of the racket face rather than the force of the swing.

Space

1. The half-volley is usually executed in the backcourt when the player is unable to return to the baseline or to rush the net.

2. The ball is contacted as close to the ground as possible. The ball should not rise more than a few inches off the court before it comes in contact with the racket.

3. The racket is placed directly behind the spot where the ball is anticipated to bounce.

4. The point of impact is in front of the player.

Time

1. The shortage of time and the speed of the oncoming ball eliminate the necessity of a backswing.

2. The ball is contacted immediately after it contacts the court.

Force

1. Force is produced primarily from the speed of the oncoming ball as it rebounds from the court and then provides force for the return.

2. Control is achieved by the wrist action, which brings the racket forward and over the ball.

Flow

1. The flow of movement results from a firm wrist as the ball hits the racket face. The turnover of the wrist brings the racket over the ball.

2. The sequence of movement is a placing (rather than swinging) of the racket behind the ball at its point of rebound, followed by a gentle wrist flip to control the trajectory of the ball.

Body Awareness

1. The arm feels stretched as it reaches to place the racket behind the ball.

2. The feeling of flipping the ball is sensed, as this stroke demands more wrist action than the ground strokes.

3. Of particular importance is the ability to perceive the appropriate location for positioning the racket before contact.

The Lob

The lob is a stroke used to send the ball high into the air, landing in the backcourt near the baseline. It is generally considered an invaluable defensive stroke when the player is caught out of position and needs time. It is used when an opponent rushes the net, or used to change the pace of a hard-driving game. There are many instances when the lob may be considered an offensive weapon. If the lob falls short, the opponent will probably return a smash.

The same grips are employed for the forehand and backhand drives as for the forehand and backhand lobs. The basic swing is the same except that, in the lob, the open face of the racket lifts the ball into a high arc. Because less force is required, the backswing is shortened. (Refer to the basic principles of the forehand and the backhand drives.)

The Smash

The basic principles of movement that apply to the serve also apply to the smash. The basic differences are in court positioning (space) and visual tracking (timing). While the serve is executed behind the baseline, the smash may be executed from almost anywhere on the court. A very fine sense of timing must be developed because in the smash the approaching ball has varying speed and directionality as opposed to the consistent serve toss.

The smash is a hard, forceful stroke that is meant to score a point on the opponent's short lob. It is an overhead stroke that is similar to the last part of the serve—the snap from behind the shoulder to a full extension of the arm (fig. 11.18).

Drop of racket   Prior to contact   Follow through

Figure 11.18. **Overhead smash**

The player moves under the ball and slightly behind it. Keen perceptual judgment is necessary, so contact can be made when a full extension can reach and send it down at an angle. Timing is important, as most beginners rush into a smash and hit too hard. Half the speed of the serve will suffice.

MAJOR CONCEPTS RELATED TO STRATEGY

Singles

Most beginners are concerned with returning the ball across the net, but even in the beginning stages the player should start to think in terms of the target with every stroke. An early awareness of spatial concepts as discussed previously often helps the beginner to orient himself to tennis strategy.

The following basic concepts, organized as to space, time, and force, should help the beginner to think, feel, and move more effectively. Eventually, the player should be able to plan two or three shots ahead.

Space

CONCEPT R. The player should be aware of his position within the playing area.

1. The singles player must become conscious of spatial court positions by always noting the location of the baseline, service line, net, and sidelines. An awareness of being deep in mid-court, behind the baseline, or up close to the net should become familiar, comfortable position perceptions to the player.

2. Care should be taken not to position oneself in "no-man's-land," located approximately near the service court line, unless a player can use volleys or half-volleys suc-

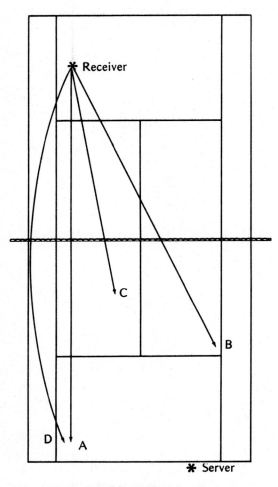

Figure 11.19. **Possible service returns**

tected part of the court are good possibilities.

6. When receiving, the player should position himself according to the opponent's skill. If the serve is deep and fast, he should stand just at the baseline or behind it. If the serve is shallow, he can move up between the center mark and the sideline.

7. After a return the player should move into a ready position near the baseline.

8. Possible returns for the receiver deal with spatial relationships: (fig. 11.19)

> A. a return deep to the baseline on the weak side of the opponent (usually the backhand side);
> B. a crosscourt return to pull the opponent out of position;
> C. a short shot to pull opponent into "no-man's-land";
> D. a lob to change the pace established prior to the serve

9. Moving to the net should be encouraged following any good, well-placed shot. A player should be prepared to direct shots into the corners, to the sidelines or the feet of the opponent.

Time

1. A player, when moving to the net position, moves quickly, but not so quickly that he takes his eyes off the opponent, the return, and the ball. He should be set in a stable position when ready to volley.

2. Changing the pace of the game is good strategy—from a hard-driving return to a lob or drop shot just over the net. Smash strokes are good to change the pace and score points.

Force

1. A strong, fast service is an important offensive stroke. A second serve should also

cessfully. In this position the beginning player is up too far for the ball to bounce and is back too far for a good volley.

3. When serving, a player should stand as close as possible to the center service mark.

4. Following a good, strong serve, the server should go to the net position, hesitating just long enough to note the opponent's return. The return dictates the final court position.

5. When serving, placement in the corners, to a weak side, or to an open, unpro-

be strong. If it is "patty-caked," it ceases to be an offensive stroke.

2. Knowing how to handle serves is good strategy. Slow serves should be returned with the regular, grooved backswing. If a fast serve is delivered, the backswing is shortened or met in mid-air, and the rebound force will carry the ball over the net.

Doubles

CONCEPT S. Individual, partner, or team play is based on a particular plan of spatial arrangement.

Beginners are often asked to play doubles before they feel adequately comfortable with the basic strokes. Many play net positions before they have mastered the volley. If beginners are encouraged from the start to follow a good shot to the net and are encouraged to be target conscious and court conscious, this awareness will prepare them for doubles play.

Doubles can become a couple's game, since there are four players on the court and there is more space in the court (see diagram of the court, figure 11.1. There are, however, basic concepts to be mastered for successful doubles' play.

CONCEPT T. Creating spaces and sending the ball (or shuttlecock) to open spaces of the court or to weaknesses in the opponent's defense are basic to scoring.

Space

1. Position on the court is the most important consideration in doubles. The partners who can control the net and drive the opponents to their own baseline will be successful.

2. Spacing of the partners while in service should be as follows. The server starts play from a spot about halfway between the

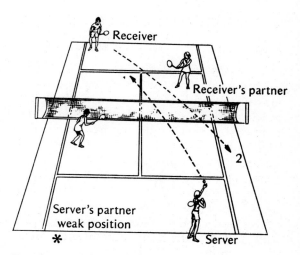

Figure 11.20. **A doubles court and positions of partners**

center mark and the sideline; the server's partner stands behind the baseline, midway between the center mark and sideline if the server is weak. The server's partner should stand arm's length from the net if the server is strong.

3. The serve should be placed in an area that requires a backhand return, which is probably a weaker stroke.

4. The receiving partners should place themselves in front of the baseline, always modifying their positions according to the strengths and weaknesses of the server.

5. The best target area for the return of a service is crosscourt, away from the player at the net. (See figure 11.20.)

6. When possible, opponents should be forced to the sidelines or into an up-back position. Vulnerable space then opens up between them, and shots should be placed in that space.

7. The target area when opponents are deep to the baseline is right at their feet or in the alleys.

INDIVIDUALIZING INSTRUCTION

INTRODUCTION, THE FIRST PERSONALIZED EXPERIENCE

Tennis is a sport in which an individual makes contact with an object while both are moving. Skills are based on a time-space relationship which allows force to be utilized effectively. A player, therefore, should move within a framework involving a cognitive (knowledge), affective (feeling), psychomotor (performance) combination movement sense. Knowing where the body moves and how it moves to make contact with the ball is the foundation of movement with meaning.

METHOD

Through movement tasks, the teacher leads players to an awareness of movement patterns resulting in a successful experience at each step in the learning process. Questions in the form of challenges or tasks are presented, with time allowed for the player to experiment and draw conclusions before progressing to the next step in the process.

Because the process is a personalized experience, the progress may be swift or slow, depending on the age level and previous experience of the student. A keen perception on the teacher's part should reflect the length of time spent on each phase. The students actually set the pace and, depending on their reactions and responses, the teacher follows their lead but maintains the progress toward the objectives set for the activities. The instructor guides and leads students to discover for themselves movement patterns that make sense.

OBJECTIVES TO BE EXPERIENCED

The student learns:

1. To move in space, being aware of what can be performed in *personal* space and in *general* space;
2. To become oriented within that spatial awareness to a time-space relationship in making contact with a moving ball;
3. To establish hand-eye coordination in a variety of perceptual-motor tasks, leading to an ability to track a moving ball and make contact;
4. To feel kinesthetically body movements necessary to complete the task of moving into position and then successfully contacting the ball;
5. To experience a rhythmic pattern developed by the player's awareness of time-space relationships: "drop and swing" to "back and swing";
6. To experience a shift of weight in order to utilize effective leverage action to gain speed and range of motion as well as force.

FORMAT

Questions are presented in numbered sequence. Possible answers are included in parentheses.

The format of wording or the sequence of questions will probably never be the same in any two classes. With this method, many directions can be pursued, all leading to the same objective.

Students are positioned at random on the courts facing the nets and the instructor.

DIRECTIONS FOR STUDENTS

A. Movement Tasks without a Racket

1. Can you throw the ball into the air with one hand and catch it with the other hand?
2. What was the motion of your hand as it caught the ball? (in a downward, scooping motion; in an upward motion; from the side)
3. Can you use a catching motion that is different from the last one?
4. What facilitates catching the ball? (body position; tracking the ball)

   Note: The instructor should use the words "Track the ball" rather than the phrase "Keep your eye on the ball." The latter is so overused, students don't pay any attention to it.

5. See if you can throw the ball high into the air with one hand and as it comes down, swing the free hand from the *side* and catch it at hip level, keeping the arm straight.
   a. If you missed the ball *why* did you miss it? (misjudged spatial position of ball; didn't actually track the ball; was too close to the ball)
   b. How far away from the ball do you have to position yourself so that the arm remains straight? Experiment to find out.
   c. What adjustments do you have to make to keep a straight arm? (move the body; shift weight; turn the body)
6. Try bouncing the ball with one hand and catching it from the side.
7. Do you have a follow-through across the body after you catch the ball?
8. As you bounce the ball, this time try to direct it to the same side of the catching hand.
   a. What movement do you have to make in order to bounce it to the side and catch it?
   b. Does turning the back foot to the side help?
   c. Where does the palm face?
9. Experiment by bouncing the ball at different spots around the side and decide at which spot it is easier for the catching hand to swing through and catch the ball.
   a. What enables the arm to go back farther so that the body can turn? (you turn the foot toward the ball)
   b. At what angle does the foot receive the weight last? (diagonally; partly toward the net)
10. Have you decided the best spot for the ball to be dropped, the spot that allows for the most effective swing and body movement? (in front of the forward foot; off the forward foot; toward the net)
11. In order to step into the swing and shift weight, what is the position of the forward foot? Experiment. How would you describe your body position? (side to net; stepping forward; facing net; didn't turn and swing)
12. Can you *feel* the weight shift?

13. At what precise part of the swing does it shift?
14. Can you fit a rhythmic pattern to the movement?
    a. "drop and swing"
    b. "turn and swing"
        (1) Where is your catching arm on "and"? (at the peak of the back-swing; on the way back)
        (2) Does the movement become faster as you say the words ". . . and swing"? Why?
15. Can you drop the ball on the other side of the body and still catch it?
    a. What adjustments have to be made in body position?
    b. In order to move the hand and palm toward the net, what movement is necessary for the arm and hand?
16. Where should the ball be dropped in relation to the body?

B. Racket in hand. With either a paddle or a full-size racket, repeat the same sequences.

C. Partner play. When that pattern is mastered, stand facing a partner who will drop balls on the spot you desire.
    1. How far away do you have to stand to allow for full arm extension?
    2. Is the path of the ball going up or coming down when you contact it?
    3. What adjustment do you have to make to catch the ball before it drops too low?
    4. At the moment of contact, what is the angle of the wrist and hand? Is the wrist firm?
    5. What is the position of the forward leg and knee at contact?

D. Three people. Have a third person observe and supply feedback information on the following questions.
    1. What is the path of the racket on the backswing?
    2. Does it go straight back, horizontally to the court?
    3. Is the movement slightly up or down?
    4. In the arc of the swing is there a flattened portion before contacting the ball?
    5. What happens to the arc on the follow-through? Does it go up or down as it swings across the body?

E. Conceptualization
    1. What principles of movement become apparent in the exploration of the swing?

    Answers might be:
    a. The longer the lever, the more speed and range of motion are possible.
    b. By lowering the center of gravity, better balance is achieved.
    c. When the body shifts weight, more force is used.
    d. By tracking the ball carefully, contact is made more effectively.
    e. The angle of the face of the racket determines where the ball goes.

f. The wrist has to be firm and square at the time of the impact, or at contact with the ball.

g. The total body is brought into play when all goes well.

2. What did you feel kinesthetically? What type of movement did you feel in the following body parts—hips, feet, knees, arms, hand, wrist, entire body?

F. Discussion

1. Objectives are reviewed in terms of the principles of movement used.

2. Time-space-force relationships are applied cognitively.

3. Movement is more effective and efficient when knowledge, feeling and performance are combined. What is the role feeling plays in self-satisfaction or success?

REFERENCES

Broer, Marion R. *Efficiency of Human Movement.* 3d ed. Philadelphia: W. B. Saunders Co., 1973.

————. *Individual Sports for Women.* 5th ed. Philadelphia: W. B. Saunders Co., 1971.

Gallwey, Timothy. *The Inner Game of Tennis.* New York: Random House, 1974.

Jensen, Clayne R., and Schultyz, Gordon. *Applied Kinesiology.* New York: McGraw-Hill Book Co., 1977.

Johnson, Joan, and Xanthos, Paul. *Tennis.* 2d ed. Dubuque, Iowa: Wm. C. Brown Company Publishers, 1971.

Kenfield, John F. *Teaching and Coaching Tennis.* 2d ed. Dubuque, Iowa: Wm. C. Brown Company Publishers, 1976.

Leighton, Jim. *Inside Tennis: Techniques of Winning.* Englewood Cliffs, N.J.: Prentice-Hall, Inc., 1977.

Murphy, Bill, and Murphy, Chet. *Tennis for Beginners.* New York: Ronald Press Co., 1966.

Murphy, Chet. *Advanced Tennis.* Dubuque, Iowa: Wm. C. Brown Company Publishers, 1971.

Pelten, Barry. *Tennis.* Pacific Palisades, Calif.: Goodyear Publishing Co., 1973.

Plagenhoef, Stanley. *Fundamentals of Tennis.* Englewood Cliffs, N.J.: Prentice-Hall, Inc., 1970.

Well, Katharine. *Kinesiology.* Philadelphia: W. B. Saunders Co., 1966.

12

Volleyball

INTRODUCTION

Volleyball is a space game. The space needed for an official game is eighteen meters (fifty nine feet) by nine meters (twenty nine feet, six inches). This space is shared by twelve players, six on each team. A net 2.24 meters (7 feet 4⅛ inches) high for women and 2.43 meters (7 feet 11⅝ inches) high for men separates the playing space into two courts, one occupied by each team. The purpose of the game is to send the ball over the net in such a manner that it cannot be returned by the opposing team.

The players on a team are identified according to their spatial relationships on the court (fig. 12.1). Each player must be able to move effectively within his self-space as he executes skills at high, medium, and low levels; be capable of utilizing space to position himself in relation to the ball; and be able to share court space effectively with five teammates.

Volleyball is a game defined by rules. Play is begun with a serve executed by the right back from a position behind the end line. After the serve a team is allowed three contacts to return the ball over the net. Points are earned when the receiving team is unable to return the ball legally. Only the serving team may earn points. A fault by the serving team ends their term of service and the receiving team is given the ball to serve. Prior to beginning a term of service, team members rotate in a clockwise direction (fig. 12.2). The team to first reach fifteen points is declared the winner. However, a team must be ahead by two points to win.

Volleyball is a game of force. The volleyball player must utilize his body efficiently in creating, directing, and absorbing force. He must be capable of creating maximum force to send the ball quickly downward over the net, controlled force to pass to a teammate, or minimum force to deceive the opponents

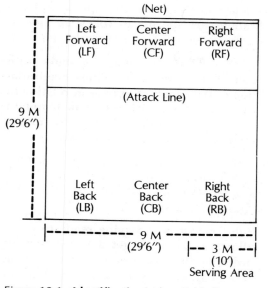

Figure 12.1. **Identification of volleyball players according to spatial relationships**

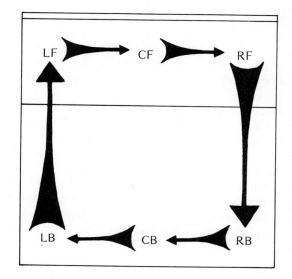

Figure 12.2. **Rotation**

and lightly tap the ball over the net. To earn points he must be able to control the direction of the ball as he passes to a teammate or hits to an open space on the opponents' court. The player must also be able to absorb the force of a fast serve or a powerful hit over the net and convert it into a ball that is playable by his teammates.

Volleyball is a game of time. Timing is essential as a team works together to maneuver the ball into the best position for a successful play and as each player executes individual skills. A team member who waits too long to back up the hit over the net or fails to move quickly enough to cover his court position weakens the entire team. For a successful team effort all players must react simultaneously and in harmony.

A player must be able to time his movements to the task to be completed. The advantage of a running approach in the hit over the net is sacrificed if the player completes the approach too soon and must wait for the ball. Likewise, the advantage of

using the muscles of the legs to produce force in an overhand volley is negated if the player extends from a crouched position only to find the ball is too high to reach. In each instance, the player must be able to coordinate his movements with the demands of the skill being executed.

Volleyball is a game of flow. A smooth and continuous flow of movement should be evident on a volleyball court as all players move to react to the ball and utilize the space of their court to the best advantage. Each player presents a graceful picture as he completes a well-timed, well-executed skill. His movement flows from one body part to another. Each muscle functions in sequence as a previous muscle has completed its task. Each fundamental movement is linked to another as the player moves to play the ball, contacts the ball, and prepares for the following play.

Volleyball is a game that presents a many-faceted opportunity to the player. The opportunity to respond physically to the demands of the game and to compete against an opponent is obvious. Less apparent is the opportunity to become more aware of one's own reactions as a participant in the game. How does it feel to participate? Is it a satisfying experience? Is it an experience that challenges mentally as well as physically? Is it an experience that allows freedom to exhibit uniqueness as an individual while contributing to the goals of the team? Is it an experience that one desires to repeat?

Successful participation in volleyball is dependent upon certain understandings, attitudes, and motor responses, all of which are discussed in this chapter.

MAJOR CONCEPTS RELATED TO BALL HANDLING TECHNIQUES

The fundamental skill used to play the ball in volleyball is the strike. The rules allow the ball to be struck by any body part above the waist. However, to be legal, the contact must be a quick action. If the ball is allowed to rest even momentarily on the striking surface, the action becomes an illegal hit. The basic ball handling techniques are the serve, the overhand volley, the forearm pass, the spike, and the block. Variations are possible in each of these techniques, depending upon the purpose of the hit. The hit may be intended to put the ball into play, to pass to a teammate, to set for the hit over the net, or to direct the ball over the net. Regardless of the intent, certain concepts are common to all volleyball techniques. The player is concerned with moving his body with control and moving the ball with control. Concepts related to these areas are included in the following pages. Since many of these concepts have already been discussed in chapter five, they are only listed here. The student should refer again to chapter five for additional explanation. In instances in which the concepts and/or applications are specific to volleyball, discussion has been included in this chapter.

CONCEPT A. Moving the body with control involves a conscious manipulation of the center of gravity in relation to the base of support, either to maintain stability or to initiate locomotor movement, as the situation demands.

A volleyball player is concerned with moving with control as he maintains a ready position, moves to play the ball, establishes his position, and contacts the ball.

Sub-concept A-1. Staying ready to move allows a player to get a faster start in order to outmaneuver the opponent, to gain possession of the ball, or to get into a desirable position to project an object.

CONCEPT C. A player must be in a desirable position in relation to the object to be projected.

CONCEPT D. Creating force: The production and transfer of force depend upon mass, speed, and the striking surface used.

Sub-concept D-1. Increasing the mass used to produce force increases the force produced.

Mass is increased by using the large, strong muscles of the legs in addition to the muscles of the upper trunk and arms. Thus, as a player contacts the ball in a forearm pass or an overhand volley, he extends from a crouched position to utilize the muscles of the legs.

Sub-concept D-3. Increasing the range of movement of the body segment or the implement imparting force increases the distance through which speed can be developed, as well as the force imparted to the object.

Sub-concept D-5. A follow-through allows for greater force to be transferred to an object.

Sub-concept D-6. Stabilizing the body segments involved in an action allows for greater force to be imparted to the object.

To increase stability when contacting the ball, a player moves to receive the ball directly in front of his body. In this position it becomes easier to maintain the center of gravity over the base of support (p. 48, chapter 4). Once in position behind the ball, a well-balanced stance is assumed. The player utilizes a forward-back stride position to provide a base of support which is enlarged in the direction of the force that is to be received or imparted. The knees are flexed to lower the center of gravity. This position must be firmly established prior to contacting the ball in order to provide a stable base and a firm foundation for the body parts which must move.

Sub-concept D-7. A firm striking surface allows for greater force to be imparted to the object.

CONCEPT E. Directing force: The direction in which an object moves is determined by the point at which force is applied in relation to the object's center of gravity.

Sub-concept E-1. Applying force directly through the center of gravity of an object results in a straight trajectory; an off-center application of force produces a curved trajectory.

Sub-concept E-3. Contacting an object with a large, flat surface facilitates applying force directly through the center of gravity in the direction desired.

The desirability of a large, flat striking surface has already been discussed in chapter five. In selecting the striking surface to be used in a volleyball skill the performer should realize that the fist presents an uneven surface area and its use should be avoided. The more irregular the striking surface, the more chance there is for the ball to be contacted with one small surface and to be projected in an undesired direction. For this reason, when executing certain volleyball techniques, a flat surface such as provided by the forearms or the heel of the hand is used in preference to the irregular surface produced by the knuckles of a closed fist.

CONCEPT H. Three techniques help the performer to absorb force efficiently: (1) establishing a stable position; (2) utilizing the largest possible surface area; and (3) increasing the time or distance over which the force is received.

In volleyball, force should be absorbed only when it allows for increased control without resulting in an illegal hit. Since the rules dictate that the ball may not rest on any body part, force is absorbed only by giving with the ball and increasing the surface area over which it is received. Absorption of force is desired when receiving a spinning or floating ball or one moving with great speed. Unless a player is able to control the spin, a spinning ball will rebound in the direction of the spin rather than in the direction desired by the player. When receiving a ball moving with great speed, such as a serve or spike, the player must absorb some of its force before redirecting it in order to prevent an uncontrolled return. In these instances a forearm pass is used to provide a large, firm striking surface. The arms and legs give, or move down and away from the ball, to allow for the legal and efficient absorption of force.

Figure 12.3. **Overhand volley**

BASIC BALL HANDLING TECHNIQUES

The basic ball handling techniques include: (1) a means of starting the ball in play, the serve; (2) a method of receiving and redirecting force, the overhand volley and the forearm pass; (3) an offensive technique for hitting the ball over the net, the spike, dink, and offensive volley; and (4) a means of defending against the hit over the net, the block.

Overhand Volley

The overhand volley (fig. 12.3) is a fundamental technique used to redirect a ball which is approaching at a high or medium-high level into the best position to be played by a teammate. It is a hit that is used as a pass to a teammate or a set for a spike, a hit that is high enough (generally ten to fifteen feet) to allow time for a teammate to move into position to play it.

Body Awareness

The fleshy portion of the first and second joint of all ten fingers provide a large, flat, and legal surface with which to contact the ball.

Space

1. The player is positioned in line with the ball and moves so that his body faces the direction of the pass.

2. A forward-back stride position is assumed to enlarge the base of support in the direction of the force.

3. The knees are flexed to lower the center of gravity and to allow use of the leg muscles.

4. The hands are positioned at eye level with fingers spread, thumbs almost parallel with the floor and palms slightly facing to allow all ten fingers to contact the ball. The wrists are hyperextended, elbows positioned away from the body, arms at shoulder level (fig. 12.4).

Force

1. Force is produced by the quick extension of the arms and legs, which allows the player to utilize the muscles of the arms and legs to increase the mass used to produce force. The player's feet remain in contact with the ground to provide a stable base upon which to operate and to assure that the force produced by the body is utilized in the volley.

2. Force is applied under and through the ball's center of gravity to prevent spin and to provide an upward trajectory. When contacting the ball, the wrists straighten and fingers and elbows extend.

3. The player hits through the ball and continues the motion of his arms in the intended direction of flight in a follow-through to prevent deceleration of the arms prior to contact.

Time

Contact is timed so that the ball is hit at the moment of peak force as the arms and legs extend.

Figure 12.4. Hand position for the overhand volley

Flow

The action is completed as one smooth and continuous motion.

THE OVERHAND VOLLEY AS A SET

With a basic understanding of the overhand volley, a player is able to utilize the volley as a set for the hit over the net. Generally, a set is high (ten to fifteen feet) and placed near the net (one to two feet). If the opponents are expecting a forward set, the player can project the ball backward over his head rather than forward as expected. In the back set (fig. 12.5) the body arches backward, and the arms extend in an upward and backward direction with the palms of the hands facing up and back.

If the opponents are expecting a high set, the force imparted to the ball can be limited to reduce the height achieved and to allow a

Figure 12.5. **Back set**

quick hit over the net. In the set, space and force relationships can be varied to keep the opponent off-guard.

Forearm Pass

The forearm pass (fig. 12.6) is used to receive the hit over the net, to play a ball traveling at a low level and to play a fast moving, spinning or floating ball which might result in an illegal hit if an overhand volley was used. Ideally the pass should have both height and direction. It should be high enough (ten to fifteen feet) to allow the receiver time to establish his position and it should be directed accurately toward its intended target.

Body Awareness

The inside of the two forearms or the inside of the wrists is used to present a large, firm, and flat striking surface. One arm may be used, but only as an emergency measure, since the size of the striking surface is reduced.

Space

1. The player is positioned in line with the ball in order to receive the force of the ball in line with the body's center of gravity.

2. A forward-back stride position is used to enlarge the base of support in the direction of the force.

3. The knees are bent to lower the center of gravity and to place the player in position to hit a low ball.

4. The striking surface is flat and positioned to allow the ball to rebound forward and upward. Two different techniques may be used to achieve a flat striking surface. (Fig. 12.7).

   a. One hand is placed in the palm of the other with the thumb of the bottom hand overlapped. The wrists are hyperextended until the thumbs point downward. The arms are fully extended and the elbows straight to provide a flat hitting surface. The ball is contacted with the inside of the forearms.

   b. The heels of the hands are placed together. One hand is closed in a fist with the fingers of the other hand covering it. The heels of the hands remain together while the wrists are rotated outward. The wrists are hyperextended until the thumbs point downward. The arms are fully extended and the elbows straight. The ball is contacted with the inside of the wrists.

Force

1. Generally a ball that is played with the forearm pass is traveling with enough force so that force should be redirected rather than created.[1]

1. In a one-arm pass the player lunges for the ball, moving the forearm down and under the ball while maintaining a firm striking surface.

Figure 12.6. **Forearm pass**

2. When the ball approaches with a great amount of force, it is necessary to absorb some of the force before redirecting it. To absorb force the legs bend and the arms move as a straight unit from the shoulders, giving with the ball on contact.

3. The striking surface is firm at contact to prevent an illegal hit.

4. Force is applied under and through the ball's center of gravity to provide an upward trajectory.

5. The follow-through is with the total body moving up and through the ball.

Time

The player must time his movements in order to establish a well-balanced position in which to contact the ball; i.e., he should be in a position which neither crowds the ball nor causes him to reach for the ball.

Flow

The entire movement is smooth and continuous.

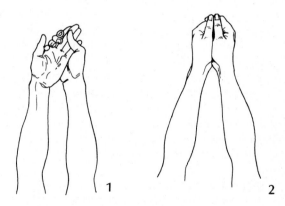

Figure 12.7. **Position of hands and forearms for the forearm pass**

Hit Over the Net

A team's offensive pattern culminates in a hit over the net that should be difficult for the opponents to return due to speed, placement, or spin. The hit may be a spike, dink, or offensive volley. To deceive the opponents, execution of each is similar until the application of force. For each, the performer must be aware of body parts used, his position in space, and the efficient production of force.

Body Awareness

The hit over the net is generally a one-handed hit to allow the body to rotate and the striking arm to produce the greatest force.

Space

1. The performer must be aware of his position in space; his distance from the net; the height of the striking arm in relation to the net; and his position in relation to the ball.
2. The player is positioned away from the net five to twelve feet and facing the net.
3. A running approach and a two-foot jump are used to achieve a position above the level of the net with the striking arm in line with and arm's distance from the ball.[2] The approach should consist of as many steps (at least three) as needed to achieve the proper relationship with the ball and net. A two-foot takeoff is used to achieve the greatest push against the ground (Newton's law of action-reaction). The point at which the jump is initiated must be judged by the player. He must be aware of how high he can jump and how close to the net he can be without committing a centerline or net violation.
4. The player lands from the jump on both feet, his base of support enlarged, the whole body giving to absorb the shock of landing.
5. The player immediately assumes a ready position in preparation for the next play of the ball.

Force

1. Whether the hit is a spike, dink, or offensive volley, the player's preliminary motions should be identical to prevent telegraphing the hit to the opponents.

2. The spike, dink and offensive volley differ in the degree of force desired and the point at which force is applied.
3. A basic throwing motion of the striking arm is used to produce force.

    a. Force increases as the range of motion of the striking arm is increased. Rotation of the striking arm away from the net and use of a backswing increase the range of motion and the distance through which force is produced.

    b. Force increases as the speed of the striking arm increases. A quick extension of the elbow and a snap of the wrist as the ball is contacted increase the speed of the striking arm and the force imparted.

Time

1. The running approach is begun once the ball has been contacted by the set player and its direction can be determined.[3]
2. The approach and jump are timed to allow contact with the ball above the level of the net and at the peak of the jump.

Flow

The approach, jump, and contact are one smooth, continuous motion.

On-Hand Spike

A spike is a well-placed, forceful hit that is angled sharply downward over the net (fig. 12.8). It is the key offensive measure, designed to place the ball so the opponents are unable to return it. A spike may be an on-hand spike or an off-hand spike. The on-

---

2. Beginners who are not able to coordinate the running approach, jump, and contact can execute the jump and hit over the net from a stationary position.
3. Using the forearm pass-set-hit pattern of play (p. 329), the serve is received with a forearm pass; the second hit is executed by the center forward (key setter) and is a set for the third hit (the hit over the net).

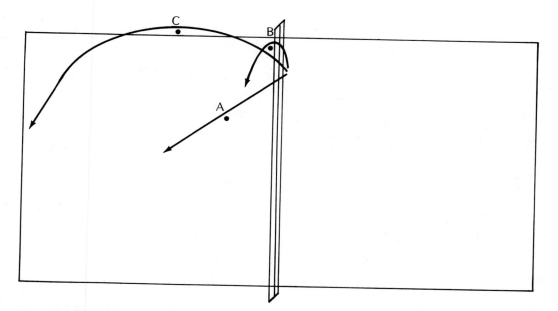

Figure 12.8. **Flights of: (A) spike; (B) dink; (C) offensive volley**

hand spike is executed when the ball is set from the spiking arm side of the spiker's body. A right-handed player executes an on-hand spike when the ball is set from his right. The off-hand spike, a more difficult skill, is utilized when the ball is set from the opposite side and must cross the player's body before being hit. A right-handed player executes an off-hand spike when the ball is set from his left.

Body Awareness

The heel and fingers of a relaxed, open hand are used to contact the ball.

Space

Refer to hit over the net.

Force

1. To assure the greatest force, the approach, jump, and contact must be completed as one sequential movement.

2. The range of motion and the speed of the striking arm are increased to increase the force produced. The striking arm is rotated away from the net, elbow flexed, the hand near the ear. The elbow leads the quick forward extension of the arm. The wrist is cocked, and snaps as the ball is contacted. (A relaxed hand is essential to allow for faster wrist action.)

3. The ball is contacted above and through its center of gravity, resulting in a sharply downward trajectory.

4. If possible, the striking arm continues its motion in a follow-through. On occasion the follow-through is limited to prevent touching the net.

Time

Refer to hit over the net.

Flow

Refer to hit over the net.

Figure 12.9. **On-hand spike**

Off-Hand Spike

In the off-hand spike the ball is set from the nonstriking side of the spiker's body. The running approach, force production, and timing in the off-hand spike are similar to those of the on-hand spike. However, in the off-hand spike, prior to the spiking action, the player must allow the ball to cross his body to reach a position in front of the striking arm. To do this it may be necessary for the spiker to move more toward the center of the court before approaching the net. Also, it may be necessary for the player setting the ball to direct it more toward the sideline to facilitate the ball crossing the player's body.

Spike Variations

Spike variations result from changes in space and force elements. For example, a change-of-pace spike can be executed by changing the height of the set or the force of the spike. A short set that is directed close to the net and only slightly (one to two feet) above the net will allow the spiker to execute a quick spike, contacting the ball before the opponents have had time to prepare their defense. A less forceful spike of a well-placed set will often destroy the opponents' defense and cause the ball to roll down the arm of a surprised blocker or fall short of a possible receiver.

DINK. If the opponents are expecting a spike and have moved into position to block, a dink can be utilized effectively to confuse the defense. The dink is also a valuable technique when the ball has been poorly set and cannot be spiked. It is a light hit that is placed over the hands of the opposing front row players and drops short of the back row players (fig. 12.8).

Body Awareness

The ball is contacted with the fleshy portion of the first and second joint of the fingers of one hand. The fingers are spread and stiff to provide a large, firm hitting surface.

Space

To deceive the opponents, the running approach and preliminary motions for the dink are similar to the spike until force is applied to the ball. (Refer to hit over the net.)

Force

1. The force of the striking arm is restrained and a light hit is substituted for the force of the spike.

2. The wrist of the striking arm remains firm at contact. Force is produced primarily by the extension of the elbow.

3. The ball is contacted under and through its center of gravity to provide sufficient arch to pass over the hands of the opposing front row players. If the dink is to be successful, the ball must not be contacted too far under its center of gravity, which would result in a high trajectory and allow the defense time to position themselves to play the ball.

Time

Except for purposes of deception, the timing of a dink is not as critical as in the spike and the player may contact the ball at the peak of his jump or while ascending or descending. (Refer to hit over the net.)

Flow

Refer to hit over the net.

OFFENSIVE VOLLEY. An offensive volley is a hit that is more forceful than the dink and is directed deep in the court to any open area (fig. 12.8). It is utilized when the opposing back row players have moved forward, leaving the territory near the back line unprotected, or when a set has been unsuccessful and cannot be spiked.

Body Awareness

The offensive volley may be a one-handed hit using the heel and fingers of an open hand or it may be a two-handed hit similar in execution to an overhand volley.

Space

In order to deceive the opponents, the running approach and preliminary movements are similar to the spike. (Refer to hit over the net.)

However, the player establishes his position and keeps both feet on the ground as he contacts the ball. The one-handed hit is contacted directly overhead or slightly behind the body while the two-handed hit is contacted in the same position as the overhand volley.

Force

1. The force of the striking arm is restrained and the ball is directed to an open space on the opponents' court.

2. In a one-handed hit the wrist snaps strongly as the heel of the hand and fingers contact the ball. In a two-handed hit the action is similar to the overhand volley.

3. The ball should be contacted slightly below its center of gravity to allow a flight over the net. It should have sufficient force to be directed to the designated court area.

Time

Timing is not as critical as in the spike since the player contacts the ball from a stationary position.

Flow

The player moves to the net and establishes his position. The striking action is completed as one smooth and continuous motion.

Hit Variations for Balls Below Net Level

A player will not always receive a set from a teammate that allows him to use an overhand motion to place the ball over the net. However, the player who has control of his body and a basic understanding of efficient movement will be able to convert a poor pass into a successful hit over the net.

The alert player who receives a pass below net level can use an underhand motion to direct the ball over the hands of opposing front row players to any open space on the court. The heel of a firm hand with the wrist hyperextended or the forearm is used to contact the ball. However, it must be realized that this is an emergency measure reserved for a third hit that must go over the net. Due to the low level of the ball, the trajectory of its flight will provide the opponents with time to prepare for their return.

On occasion a player executing a third hit will find his back to the net without sufficient time to change positions. To play the ball over the net in a legal manner, he may utilize a back pass (fig. 12.10). To direct the ball in a backward direction over his head and over the net he must get under the ball, arch his back, and move his forearms in an upward and backward direction as they contact the ball. To be successful he must be aware of his position in relation to the net, the amount of force to be produced and the portion of the ball to which it should be applied.

Block

The block (fig. 12.11) is a skill used to defend against the spike. One or more players attempt to block the path of the spiked ball in order to direct it back over the net or to reduce its speed and deflect it to a teammate. The block can be an individual effort or a multiple-player effort. Although a multiple-player block is the best defense against a skilled spiker, beginners should first focus attention on the individual or one-player block. (The multiple-player block is discussed on page 334.)

Body Awareness

The fingers of the hands are slightly flexed and spread to present a large striking surface for redirecting the ball quickly into the opponents' court.

Space

1. The blocking player must align himself in the space directly opposite the spiker's spiking hand and the ball.

2. The blocker must be positioned a sufficient distance from the net (generally one to two feet) to prevent touching the net or stepping over the centerline.

3. The blocker must be able to jump and achieve a level that allows him to reach above and over the net. The arms are extended overhead and forward to increase the blocker's reach. The hands are positioned above and slightly over the net, parallel to each other and perpendicular to the floor. The hands are just far enough apart to enlarge the striking surface, but close enough to prevent the ball from passing through.

Force

1. The major source of force in the block is the force of the spiked ball. The blocker is primarily concerned with redirecting this force to the advantage of his teammates.

Figure 12.10. **Back pass**

2. The ball rebounds from the blocker's hands. Impetus may be added by moving the hands toward the ball.

Time

1. To perform a successful block, the blocker must reach a position directly opposite the ball at the same instance the spiker contacts the ball. The earlier the blocker is positioned at the net, the better able he is to adjust to a short set for the spiker.

2. Just after the spiker has initiated his jump, the blocker jumps so that the ball is contacted at the peak of his jump.

Flow

The blocker moves to the net, waits, and then jumps to block. The flow is smooth and continuous from the moment of the jump through the contact.

Figure 12.11. **One-player block**

Serve

The serve is the technique used to put the ball into play. It becomes a valuable offensive technique when it is difficult for the opponents to receive. To increase the difficulty of a controlled return, the serve should travel low over the net with either great force or an unpredictable flight. Since only the serving team is able to score points, it is important that each player develop a serve that can be utilized to get the ball into play legally and consistently. There are a variety of serves from which a player may choose, including the underhand, overhand, overhand floater, and roundhouse; however, only the underhand serve and the floater serve are discussed in detail. Regardless of the serve used, certain elements are common.

Body Awareness

A large, flat, firm striking surface is desired.

Space

The level at which the player contacts the ball determines whether an underhand, sidearm, or overhand motion is used.

Force

1. The point at which force is applied in relation to the center of gravity of the ball determines whether the ball moves in a straight, curved, or irregular pathway.

    a. A serve which curves to the server's left (a left spin) is contacted through the right side of the ball.

    b. A serve which curves to the server's right (a right spin) is contacted through the left side of the ball.

    c. A serve which drops quickly (top spin) is contacted above the center of gravity.

    d. A serve which floats is contacted through the center of gravity (a follow-through is not used).

2. The force of the serve can be varied to deceive the opponents. Maximum force can be achieved by a transfer of body weight, trunk rotation, and a fast action of the striking arm. Minimum force can be achieved by a slow movement of the striking arm. However, for purposes of deception the speed of the striking arm for all serves should be consistent until the moment of contact, at which time the speed can be restrained or continued.

Time

1. When a ball toss is used, contact must be synchronized with the position of the ball in order to apply force in the direction desired.

2. If maximum force is desired, contact must be at the moment of peak force.

UNDERHAND SERVE

The underhand serve (fig. 12.12) is one of the easiest serves to execute. It is also one of the easiest to receive, due to the length of time the ball is in the air. Therefore, it has limited use.

Body Awareness

The heel of an open hand provides a large, flat striking surface.

Space

1. The ball is contacted at waist level or lower.

2. A forward-back stride position is assumed, utilizing the principle of opposition.[4]

3. The ball is held in the nonstriking hand and is contacted with an underhand swing after it has been released or tossed. The ball is positioned diagonally across the body in line with the striking arm. The upper trunk is bent forward from the waist and the holding hand extended to allow for a point of contact that is not too far under the ball.

Force

1. Rotation of the striking arm away from the net, a backswing, transfer of body weight from the back to the forward foot, and a follow-through in the intended direction of flight are used to produce force.

2. The ball is contacted under and through its center of gravity unless spin is desired.

3. Forward momentum is continued as the player moves quickly into the playing court after the serve.

1. Refer to chapter four, page 48 for a discussion of the principle of opposition.

Figure 12.12. **Underhand serve**

Time

Contact is timed so that the ball is hit at the moment of its release from the nonstriking hand.

Flow

The entire movement is smooth and continuous.

FLOATER SERVE

The floater serve (fig. 12.13) is difficult to receive due to its floating action. The ball lacks spin but responds to air currents by dipping, curving, and dropping. Its erratic flight makes it difficult to judge and receive.

Body Awareness

An open hand is used to contact the ball.

Space

1. The feet are in a forward-back stride position, utilizing the principle of opposition.

2. The serve is contacted at a point of full extension. The striking hand begins slightly above ear level.

3. The ball is held in the nonstriking arm and is lifted and released two to three feet above and in front of the shoulder of the striking arm. (A minimum of air time is desired to reduce chances of error.)

Force

1. The speed of the striking arm, rotation of the striking-arm shoulder away from the net, and transfer of body weight from the back to the forward foot are used to produce force. The bent elbow of the striking arm moves behind the body until the hand is even with the shoulder. The hand and forearm extend back and the elbow leads the throwing motion of the arm.

2. The ball is contacted slightly below the center of gravity with an open hand. The heel of the hand is used to gain force. The wrist remains stiff.

3. Following contact there is no follow-through.[5]

4. The player's forward momentum is continued as he moves quickly into the playing court after the serve.

Time

The lift and release of the ball by the nonstriking hand must be coordinated with the striking action.

---

5. Players who do not achieve a floating action may have used a follow-through or failed to keep the wrist stiff at contact.

Figure 12.13. **Floater serve**

Flow

The arm movement is stopped (bound) as the ball is contacted.

MAJOR CONCEPTS RELATED TO STRATEGY

Volleyball is a team game. Regardless of the skill level of individual players, six players must unite their efforts and work successfully together as a unit. The ball handling skills previously described are valuable only as they are combined into a team effort to play the ball across the net in the most effective manner.

Just as the individual player is concerned with space, force, time, and flow as he executes individual ball handling skills, the team is concerned with these same elements as it builds a strong offense or defense. The team is concerned with utilizing the space of its court and the abilities of its players to the best advantage in producing the strongest offense or defense possible. In utilizing a three-hit attack the ball is maneuvered in space into the best position for it to be played over the net. Each player must be aware of the force to be imparted to the ball in order to allow for a successful play to a teammate.

As a team, all actions must be synchronized to present a united, well-timed attack or defense. Each player must know when to move as well as where to move. As one player spikes the ball, the other players must react and cover the spiker. Timing is of the essence. If one player does not move at the correct instant, a court space is left open, the entire team is weakened, and a point may be lost.

In observing a team that works together to present a strong offense or defense, a continuous flow of movement is evident. All players are actively involved in each play. The action is continuous and purposeful. It is not an action of six individual players but an action that represents the oneness or unity of six players.

Basic to transforming six individuals into the collective unit known as a team is an understanding of the concepts of both offensive and defensive play. These concepts are described in the pages which follow. It is assumed that the reader is already familiar with the basic discussion of these concepts found in chapter five. The discussion which follows is limited to applications unique to volleyball and subconcepts not included in chapter five.

CONCEPT R. The player should be aware of his position within the playing area.

As discussed in chapter five, page 88, the player must be aware of his position in relation to the boundary lines and net. In addition, in a team sport in which the space of one's court is shared with several others, one must be aware of his proximity to other players. To cover the space of the court effectively, care must be taken to prevent teammates from moving to play the same ball or from assuming a position too close together. Failure to be aware of teammates' positions merely leads to confusion and ineffective team play.

CONCEPT T. Creating spaces and sending the ball (or shuttlecock) to open spaces of the court or to weaknesses in the opponents' defense are basic to scoring.

The hit over the net, whether a serve to initiate play or the third hit of the offense, should be directed to an open space on the opponents' court or to the weakest area of their defense. During the progress of the game the back row often shifts forward, leaving an open space near the end line. In other instances the space between the front and back rows often becomes a vulnerable area for a well-placed hit. Any serve or hit over the net should take advantage of a weakness in the opponents' positions or a weakness on the part of any player. Success often results from hitting to the territory covered by the weakest player or to an area left unprotected because players are standing too close or too far from the net. For the offense to be successful it must be alert to the positions of the defense and quick to convert any weakness into its gain.

Sub-concept. In general, the ball should be directed high into the air to a teammate and low over the net to the opponents.

When passing or setting within the space of one's own court the ball should have sufficient air time to allow a teammate to move into position. Generally, a high set or pass is desired to allow this time. However, in advanced play a short, quick set is sometimes used to confuse the opponents and reduce the time they have to establish their defense. Although air time is reduced in such a set, the spiker is prepared to react quickly and a successful hit is not sacrificed.

A hit directed over the net should be low to reduce the time the opponents have to prepare to receive the ball. The effectiveness of a spike, dink or offensive volley increases as their air time is reduced. A dink or offensive volley that is directed too high over the net allows the opponents time to move into position to receive the ball and negates the purpose of the hit.

Forearm Pass-Set-Hit Pattern

Sub-concept. The forearm pass-set-hit pattern is an offensive technique basic to volleyball.

The first hit completed by a team (generally a forearm pass to prevent an illegal hit) converts the serve or hit from the opponents into a pass to a teammate. The second hit sets the ball for the third hit—a hit over the net that the opponents are unable to return. In beginning strategy it is generally accepted that the first hit should be directed to the center forward, the player designated as the key set player. The center forward then sets the ball to a position near the net on either his right or left side. The right or left forward, designated as a spiker, sends the ball over the net, usually with a spike.

CONCEPT S. Individual, partner, or team play is based on a particular plan of spatial arrangement.

Team Formation

Receiving the serve initiates a team's offense. Generally, the serve is received with a forearm pass to prevent an illegal hit. The center forward never receives the serve, as he is the key set player and responsible for the second hit. The formation that a team selects to use to receive the serve should have certain characteristics: all court space should be covered; the playing territories of individual players should be well-defined; and all players should have a clear, unobstructed view of the net and the opposing team. The W formation and the crescent formation, when utilized with the interchange, meet all of these criteria.[6]

In the W formation the five players who are to receive the serve are positioned in a W (fig. 12.12). The left forward is positioned near the sideline so that any ball passing the shoulder closest to the sideline is out of bounds. The right forward is positioned six to eight feet from his sideline, since any ball directed to the right sideline will be in the air a longer time, and allow the right forward time to adjust his position accordingly.

The side forwards move forward, slightly to the right (left forward and right forward), or left (right forward), but never backwards. The two side back row players are positioned in relation to the back line so that any ball that is over their heads will be out of bounds. To provide a clear view of the net they stand several feet from the sidelines. The right back is positioned farther from the sideline due to the air time required for a ball to reach that sideline. Together the side backs are responsible for the entire back area of the court. The center back establishes his position in relation to the other four players to cover the remaining open space in the center of the court. The center forward, as the key set player, is positioned in the center of the court near the net. Figure 12.15 shows the players' responsibilities in the W formation.

After the serve the right forward and right back shift slightly toward the sideline since the path of the ball returned by the opponents is unknown and all court space must be covered. Figure 12.16 illustrates the W formation following the serve. (Note the slightly different arrangement between figures 12.14 and 12.16.)

The second formation frequently used to receive the serve is the crescent formation. The crescent differs from the W formation in the positioning of the center back player and the territories covered by the respective players. In the crescent formation, the center back stands at the center of the crescent, closer to the back line than in the W formation. Playing responsibilities are divided into lanes with each player covering his particular lane. Figure 12.17 shows the crescent formation and the players' territories. The key set player is playing the center forward position.

6. The interchange is a means of placing a player in the best court position according to his particular talents. It is discussed on page 332.

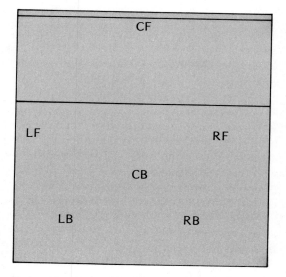

Figure 12.14. **W formation to receive serve**

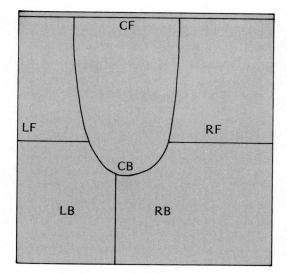

Figure 12.15. **Playing territories in the W formation**

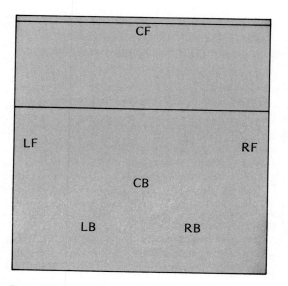

Figure 12.16. **W formation following the serve**

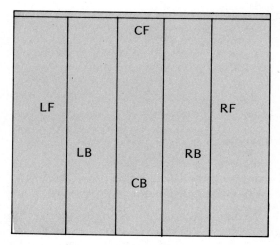

Figure 12.17. **Playing territories in the crescent formation**

The crescent formation allows players to judge balls that will be out of bounds, and to move forward to receive the serve with a forearm pass. However, the greatest weakness of the crescent formation is that each player's territory extends from the net to the back line.

In either the W or crescent formation the key set player has the responsibility of setting the ball for the spiker. He should make every effort to receive the pass from the player receiving the serve. In emergencies, when the pass is poorly directed and another player is in a better position to play the ball, this player should call for the ball and complete the pass. The key set player is positioned with his side angled toward the net so he may face the direction of the player completing the first hit. In beginning strategy the setter then sets the ball to the spiker he is facing. As the setter becomes more skilled, he is able to vary the offense by utilizing either a forward or a backward set. The direction of the set then becomes dependent upon whether the right forward or the left forward is the better spiker, the position of the opposing blockers, and the location of the ball.

Interchange

Sub-concept. An interchange of positions allows for players to be placed in position according to their strengths.

Fundamental to a sound offense is the utilization of the talents of individual players to best advantage. In instances in which all players are equally adept at both spiking and setting, a 6−0 offense may be used. Each player then becomes a spiker or a setter as the situation demands. However, when players are more skillful as either setters or spikers the 4−2 offense may be more appropriate. Two players are designated as setters, while the other players specialize as spikers.

To facilitate utilization of players as either spikers or setters an interchange of positions is often desirable. An interchange is a means of placing a player in a better court position according to his abilities. Thus a set player who is rotated from the center forward position may interchange positions with the new center forward, who may be more capable as a spiker. The interchange is initiated as soon as the ball has been served. The players remain in their new positions until the ball is dead. They then return to their original rotation order. In positioning players for the interchange care must be taken to assure that prior to the serve the players are positioned in their correct rotation order and that their feet do not overlap.

Figure 12.18 shows the correct positioning of a left forward and center forward for the interchange when the W formation is used. Upon contact of the serve the left forward moves to the center forward position. Prior to the serve, the left forward is closest to the sideline and to the net so that both feet are closer to the sideline than the center forward's feet, thus preventing an overlap. Figure 12.19 illustrates the crescent formation when an interchange is performed to allow the key set player to play the center forward position.

The effectiveness of the interchange is increased by the wise selection of starting positions. A team that has four spikers and two setters should assume a starting position that places the setters in diagonally opposite positions. The two strongest spikers should also be placed in diagonally opposite positions. Thus, as the players rotate, one setter and one strong spiker are always at the net.

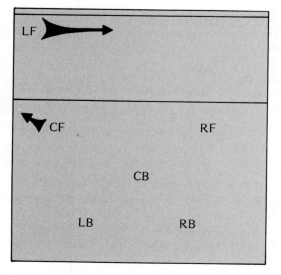

Figure 12.18. **Left forward and center forward interchange in the W formation**

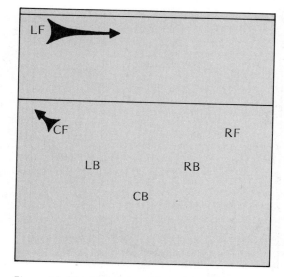

Figure 12.19. **Left forward and center forward interchange in the crescent formation**

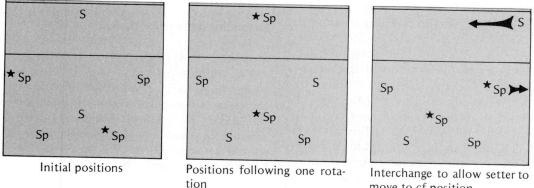

Initial positions

Positions following one rotation

Interchange to allow setter to move to cf position

Figure 12.20. **Selection of starting positions to assure that one strong spiker and one setter are always in the front row (S, setter; sp, spiker; *Sp, strong spiker).**

Through use of the interchange it is then possible to have a setter always move to the center forward position and a strong spiker move to a position for either an on-hand or off-hand spike. Figure 12.20 shows this relationship.

Circling the Ball

Sub-concept. Each player reacts to the position of the ball by circling the ball.

Besides always being alert to the position of the ball, each player must also react to each movement of the ball. As the ball

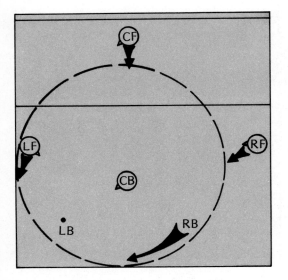

Figure 12.21. **Circling ball received by left back**

moves from position to position in a three-hit game, each player must be prepared for the possibility that the ball might come to him. As a teammate receives a hit over the net from the opponents, the remaining five players react to the position of the ball by circling the receiver. In this manner all players are ready to assist in case the ball handler has difficulty in playing the ball. Players may move closer to or farther from the ball handler in their attempt to circle the ball. However, they should be certain not to move so close as to distract the player or leave an open space on their court. A player close to the play should turn to face the play and pull away slightly so he is in a better position to play a poorly directed ball. A player positioned far from the ball handler needs to move closer if he is to be of assistance. For example, if the hit over the net is received by the left back deep in the playing court, the center back faces the left back; the right back moves to cover behind the left back; the left forward angles his body toward the

play and possibly moves closer; and the right forward moves in slightly from the right sideline. The key set player anticipates that the left back might have difficulty passing the ball to him and moves slightly closer to the left back. Figure 12.21 illustrates this relationship.

Sub-concept. The defensive team must be prepared to cover the space of its court against a spike or a less forceful hit over the net.

To cover the space of their court when receiving the hit over the net the defending team must read the intentions of the spiker. If the set is good and the player looks as though he will spike, the defense immediately prepares to block and cover the block. However, if it appears that the ball will not be spiked, the defense moves away from the net and prepares for a free ball. In either instance, the defense must be alert and ready to move.

Defending against the Spike

MULTIPLE–PLAYER BLOCK

The defending team uses a multiple-player block as its primary defense against the spike. A two-player block is used to force the spiker to avoid the block by hitting around or over it. The defending team should be prepared to execute a two-player block on every spike by the offense. The block increases the difficulty of the spiker's task, is psychologically unnerving to the spiker, and provides the defense with a ready response to the spike. The block is used to return the spiked ball over the net, or to deflect it to a teammate. The execution of the two-player block is similar to the one-player block described under "Basic Ball Handling Techniques," page 324, with the exception of the larger hitting surface provided by four hands rather than two.

Body Awareness

The hands of the two players are positioned close together to present a large surface with which to redirect the ball. (fig. 12.22)

Space

1. The center forward joins the front row player directly opposite the spiker to form the block.

2. Both players move into position, jump simultaneously and extend a wall of four firm hands. The outside blocker is positioned directly opposite the ball. His outside hand is turned inward to allow a rebound into the opponent's court rather than out of bounds. The inside blocker is positioned next to the outside blocker to form a surface of four hands, which are kept close to prevent the ball from passing through the block.

Force

The ball rebounds from the blocker's hands. Impetus may be added by moving the hands toward the ball.

Time

The blocking players must synchronize their movements and jump so that the ball is contacted at the peak of the jump.

Flow

The flow is smooth and continuous from the jump through the contact.

COVERING THE BLOCK

As players move to block a spike, the remaining players on the team must move to cover the court in case the ball is deflected off the block, directed around the block, or converted into a dink or an offensive volley.

Figure 12.22. **Two-player block**

All players move to circle the block (fig. 12.23).

1. The center back is responsible for all dinks. He moves to a position on the attack line that is directly behind the two blockers and begins to move forward as the spiker contacts the ball. He assumes a low position.

2. The side back behind the block is responsible for receiving spikes hit down the line. He moves to a position directly behind the two blockers and deep enough so that spikes which are too high to receive with a forearm pass will land out of bounds.

3. The side back away from the block moves to cover long, angled spikes. He moves to a position between the blockers and the corner of the court prepared to move to his right or left.

4. The side forward not involved in the block moves to cover sharply angled spikes. He moves to a position near the attack line and the sideline.

Defense against the Free Ball

Occasionally the spiker receives a poorly directed set that he is unable to spike. An alert defense will recognize the poor set as a sign of a weak hit over the net. A ball that is not spiked or a weak return over the net is called a free ball. The defending team responds to a free ball by assuming their basic

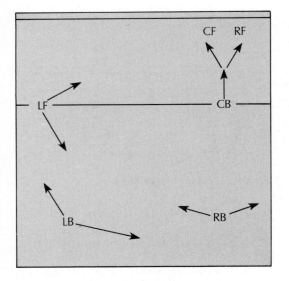

Figure 12.23. **Covering a block by the center forward and right forward**

W or crescent formation. The formation is shifted toward the center of the court since most free balls land there (fig. 12.24).

As soon as a defending player recognizes that the ball will not be spiked over the net, he yells "Free ball!" to signal his teammates to be prepared for a weak return. A sound defense is quick to convert the reception of a free ball into the beginning of an offensive play.

Covering the Spike

Sub-concept. The spiking team must support the spiker by covering all possible spaces for a spike that is returned.

The spiking team can anticipate several outcomes from a spiked ball. A point can be scored; the ball may be blocked; or an opposing player may receive the hit with a forearm pass. Regardless of what occurs, the spiking team must be prepared for a return of the ball. If the opponents deflect the spike or receive it with a forearm pass, the spiking team reacts by moving to block or to receive a free ball. If the ball is returned over the net by the opponent's block, the spiking team covers the spiker. A ball that is blocked may rebound just over the spiker's hands or deep into the court. To cover all possible paths of the ball the center forward, the center back, and the back row player on the side of the spike move close to the spiker, prepared to receive any ball just beyond his reach. Since a blocked ball traveling deep into the court will have greater air time, the two side players away from the spike are able to cover the remainder of the court. The first player to contact the ball passes it high into the air to the key set player (fig. 12.25).

INDIVIDUALIZING INSTRUCTION

The procedure for developing positive attitudes, feelings, and appreciations through volleyball is discussed in the following portion of this chapter. Included is a section concerned with adapting and arranging the content material to increase the effectiveness of teaching. The sample skill card included in this section can serve as a guide to developing skill cards for more advanced skills as well as skills for other sports. Table 12.1, "Development of the Total Individual through Volleyball," gives a progression of movement experiences related to developing the specific psychomotor skills needed to play the game of volleyball. The techniques of organization and the cognitive concepts included on the chart make it useful as a resource for developing lessons. Finally, one sample lesson, using an indirect approach to teaching, is included as a guide for the teacher who is inexperienced in using indirect methods. The section which follows is an extension of "The Role of Methodology," chapter three, as it applies specifically to volleyball.

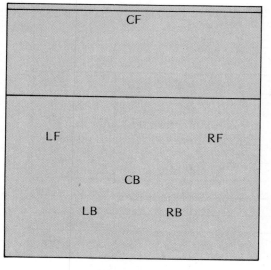

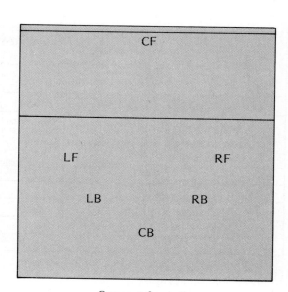

W formation

Crescent formation

Figure 12.24. **Position of the defense for a free ball**

ADAPTING AND ARRANGING CONTENT TO INCREASE THE EFFECTIVENESS OF TEACHING

In preparing a unit on volleyball, the instructor should:

1. Adapt the equipment to suit the needs of individuals. Large, lightweight balls should be provided for students who fear the ball or who hurt their hands upon contact with the ball due to poor techniques. For these students, a beach ball can be temporarily substituted for the volleyball.

2. Provide for successful experiences when students first encounter a new or difficult skill. For example, beginning students could be allowed to practice the serve from a position closer to the net than the baseline, or the net might be lowered for students' first experiences with the third hit, etc. At this time success is most important.

3. Space skill practices so that one body part is not overused. Variety should be planned so that the arms do not become ex-

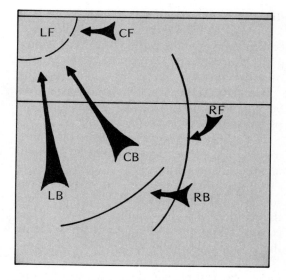

Figure 12.25. **Covering a spike by the left forward**

		1	2	3	4	5	6

INDIVIDUAL VOLLEYBALL SKILL CARD

Name _____

Class Time _____

Date Attempted	Consecutive Legal Wall Volleys	Overhand Volley from Partner's Toss	Forearm Pass to Partner from Toss	Serve (Type)	Receiving the Serve with a Forearm Pass	Hit Over Net
	1	2	3	4	5	6
		# Succeeded # Tried	# Succeeded # Tried	# Succeeded # Tried	# Succeeded # Tried	# Succeeded # Tried

Figure 12.26. **Volleyball skill card**

cessively sore or tired due to serve or forearm pass practice.

4. Intersperse game play with practice drills as soon as students' skills warrant.

5. Have students catch a poorly directed ball during practice rather than play it illegally. This helps to prevent the development of bad habits.

6. Have students catch a ball that has been illegally hit during skill practice to emphasize the need to contact legally.

7. Periodically require a three-hit game to emphasize the development of proper technique and teamwork.

8. Introduce the serve after players have sufficient skill to receive it. This prevents the game from developing into a serving contest. (Note the placement of the serve in the skill progression chart.)

9. Present rules as the need arises during game play rather than devoting one or more class periods entirely to rules.

10. Limit teams to six players to allow players to experience the challenge and excitement of volleyball. Extra players should be rotated in from the sidelines (refer to illustration, page 343).

11. Use a skill card to focus practice time upon the needs of each individual and to record the progress of each. A sample skill card is shown in figure 12.26. Except for the first activity, practice is done with a partner or in small groups and can involve reciprocal teaching. The skills listed on the card should serve only as suggestions. They measure mainly quantity of performance—the number of successful contacts over the number of attempts. They can be modified to measure both quantity and quality as students progress in their ability to control the ball. For example, the serve may also be judged by where it lands in the court. The third hit may be a spike, dink, or offensive volley and can also be rated according to placement. The choice of tasks on the skill card should reflect the skill level of the students.

TABLE 12.1
DEVELOPMENT OF THE TOTAL INDIVIDUAL THROUGH VOLLEYBALL

The chart which follows identifies a sample progression for teaching beginning volleyball students. It focuses upon the skills to be taught (psychomotor domain), suggestions for teaching to enhance learning (affective domain), and the knowledges to be gained (cognitive domain). Reading down the psychomotor domain column (left-hand column) shows the skill progression. Reading across the three columns shows the suggested teaching procedures and the understandings corresponding to each skill. In reading across the chart, corresponding information is identified by the same letter.

Psychomotor Domain (motor skills)	Affective Domain (attitudes, feelings, appreciations and values)	Cognitive Domain (knowledges)
Through carefully planned movement experiences the student progresses in the ability to control his body while performing purposeful movements. The movement skills which follow are specific to volleyball and the development of efficient and effective movement patterns.	Through student-centered methods of organization and techniques of teaching that are geared to individuals, the student develops certain positive attitudes and feelings about himself, his peers, the teacher, and the content area. Through an interaction with his peers in working toward a common goal the student develops concepts concerning fair play and teamwork. The techniques of organization which follow are only briefly outlined. For a more detailed outline refer to "The Role of Methodology," pages 34–40.	Through an application of the mechanical principles of movement to the skills of volleyball, the student develops concepts about how these laws affect his movements. Through practice in solving problems using movement and cognition the student progresses in the ability to: a. identify a problem b. gather facts c. explore alternatives d. make decisions e. apply known concepts to new movement patterns (i.e., solve problems). The knowledges listed below are basic to volleyball.

I. Components of Fitness

(The students engage in:)	(Organization:)	(The students need to understand:)
A. Discussing the components of fitness needed for volleyball. B. Exercising to strengthen fingers and wrists.	A. Students are grouped together for discussion. B. Students are scattered in space to experiment with conditioning exercises. (Students assume the responsibility for their own conditioning in relation to their own needs.)	A, B. That conditioning is unique to the individual and should be developed individually. That lack of finger and wrist strength is generally evident in beginning volleyball players. That employing the overload principle (increasing the intensity of the exercise through speed or weight) will develop strength. That actual participation in volleyball will develop the components of fitness needed to play volleyball.

II. Overhand Volley

(The students engage in:)   (Organization:)   (The students need to understand:)

Activities leading to the overhand volley.

A. Throwing and catching the ball, projecting it straight up toward the ceiling and to a partner, using first an underhand motion and then an overhand motion (two hands).

B. Throwing and catching overhand with just a few body parts, continually adding body parts until the total body is used.

C. Throwing and catching using all the concepts learned thus far, and experimenting with and without a follow-through.

D. Throwing and catching overhand, directing the ball toward the ceiling using a controlled force, and varying the position of the feet.

E. Throwing and catching using all the concepts learned thus far, and experimenting with the size of the surface contacting the ball.

F. Demonstrating, observing and discussing all material covered thus far.

Activities applying A through F to the overhand volley.

G. Throwing and volleying: one partner throws and the other uses the overhand volley to return the ball. The thrower catches the ball in a good volley position. (The procedure is then reversed.)

H. Working on a continuous volley between partners.

I. Working on a continuous volley in groups of four.

A–E. Students are scattered in space, working with a partner and sharing a ball.

1. Students choose where in space they will work and with whom they will work.

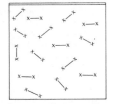

Partners working scattered in space.

2. Students decide with their partners which is the best height to throw the ball and why.

3. Students decide on a goal concerning how high the volley should be and then strive to reach this self-imposed goal.

F. Students are grouped together for discussion.
1. Students are involved in discussion.
2. All ideas are accepted and explored.
3. Variations of individual style are analyzed.

G, H. Students are scattered in space working with a partner and sharing a ball.
1. The teacher encourages reciprocal teaching between partners.
2. The teacher moves through the teaching station giving encouragement, help, and praise where it is needed.

I. Students combine to form their own groups.

A. That in order to contact a moving object (ball) a player must keep his eyes on the object (objective focus).

That in order to watch the ball while hitting it with an overhand motion, the trunk should be inclined slightly backwards (hyperextended).

That contact with the ball using an underhand motion with an open hand is illegal.

B. That the ball should be projected high into the air to allow a teammate time to establish his position.
1. The more force applied to the ball, the higher it will go.
2. The amount of force produced increases with an increase in the number of muscles used.

C. That a follow-through is utilized to assure that the intended force is applied to the ball.

D. That a forward-back stride helps one to maintain stability.

E. That a large hitting surface is desirable to apply force in the intended direction.

F. That to project the ball forward and upward in a straight pathway, force must be applied behind, below, and directly through the center of gravity of the ball.

That when playing the ball a player should be directly in line with the ball, contacting it in front of his body.

The student should choose the drill which focuses upon any problem he is experiencing.

Students (with the guidance of the teacher) are given the opportunity to decide when to move on to a more difficult drill.

Stationary
Partners

Groups of three
(must move more
quickly)

Groups of four
(move to the end
of opposite line)

Wall Volley

Changing Direction
(practice for the set)
(reverse directions)

Teamwork
(call the ball, choose the
correct technique)

Drill formations for the overhand volley

IV. Forearm Pass

(The students engage in:)	(Organization:)	(The students need to understand:)
A. Contacting a tossed ball at a level below the waist using a forearm pass. B. Experimenting with various hand positions to alter the striking surface for the forearm pass. C. Experimenting with body position, stance, and follow-through. D. Experimenting with altering the angle of the rebound surface and applying concepts of direction learned earlier. E. Working on forearm passes with a partner. One partner throws and the other uses the forearm pass to return the ball.	A–D. Students are scattered in space working with a partner and sharing a ball. E. All concepts learned previously (when practicing the forearm pass in individual, partner, or small group drills) are stressed. Note: The techniques of organization and the progression of movement experiences are similar for the overhand volley and the forearm pass. The drill formations shown on page 341 of this chart can be used to practice the forearm pass.	A. That when the ball is received at a level below the waist the body must assume a crouched position in order to get low enough to project the ball in an upward direction. That in order to contact a moving object (ball), a player must keep his eyes on the object (objective focus). B. That the inside of both forearms is the most desirable surface to use for the forearm pass, since this presents a large, flat, firm surface. C. That when playing the ball a player should be directly in line with the ball, contacting it in front of his body. That a forward-back stride helps one to maintain stability. That if one needs to create force it is created with an extension of the knees. Wrist, forearm, and shoulder movements are kept to a minimum. That the follow-through (if necessary) is with the total body moving in the direction in which the ball is sent. D. That to project the ball forward and upward in a straight pathway, force must be applied behind, below, and directly through the center of gravity of the ball. That the angle of the arms can be changed to alter the angle of rebound of the ball.

(The students engage in:)	(Organization:)	(The students need to understand:)

(The students engage in:)

A. Keeping the ball in play with a circle rally using either the overhand volley or the forearm pass.
1. Calling for the ball.
2. Counting the number of consecutive legal contacts completed by the group.

B. Learning a basic formation for covering the space of the court effectively.

C. Learning to rotate (chalkboard is used for clarification).

Trying the rotation on the court (optional).

D. Playing a game.

E. Discussing strengths and weaknesses.

(Organization:)

A. Students are given the opportunity to choose their own partners and to combine to form groups of six.

Groups should remain the same for several periods.

Groups may set their own goal for the number of consecutive volleys.

B, C. Students are grouped around the chalkboard.

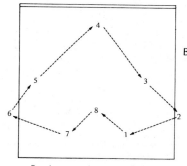

Rotating extra players into the game

D. The same groups formed earlier in the circle rally are used.

Concepts learned in the circle rally are stressed.

Students may call a time-out to solve any team problem.

Students are informed of rules as the need arises.

E. Students are grouped around the chalkboard for discussion and analysis of their game.

(The students need to understand:)

A. That they must react quickly to choose the correct technique to play the ball.

That feet must be constantly moving, or ready to move, to allow a player to get into position quickly enough to play the ball.

Note: All the concepts listed under the volley and forearm pass also apply.

That cooperation and communication are imperative to good teamwork.

B, C. That the formation covers those spaces where most of the balls will land.

That the formation places the majority of players in the back two-thirds of the court since one can move forward more quickly than backward.

That the formation places the players so that the boundaries of the court are well-defined and easily judged.

That the formation does not cause any player's view to be obstructed.

That the territories covered by each player are well-defined.

D. That volleyball is a *team game* and all members of the team must cooperate toward a common goal.

That rules are necessary for everyone to be given an equal opportunity in a competitive situation.

E. That the team and individual team members must learn to analyze their own weaknesses if they are to find ways to overcome them.

VI. Individual Skill Improvement

(The students engage in:)	(Organization:)	(The students need to understand:)

A. Discussing drills that may be used to improve skill.
 	
B. Using individual skill cards to guide practice. (See sample skill card page 338.)
	A. Students are grouped around the chalkboard for explanation (and possible demonstration) of drills that may be used to improve play. Emphasis is placed upon skills developed by each drill.
	
	B. Students are scattered in the space of the teaching station working on the drill of their choice.
	  1. For ease of organization the teacher may need to specify certain spaces for certain drills.
	  2. Students have individual skill cards on which to evaluate their progress. Work on the skill card may continue periodically for several weeks.
	  3. Students are given the opportunity to evaluate themselves. Reciprocal teaching (evaluation) occurs in the partner and group skills included on skill card.
		A. That one must understand what and how to practice if he is to improve.
		
		B. That skill practice must be individualized to be meaningful and beneficial to each student.

VII. Serve (Leading to Floater Serve)

(The students engage in:)	(Organization:)	(The students need to understand:)

A. Hitting a ball to a partner with an open hand. The ball is contacted above the level of the shoulder of the striking arm. The ball is lifted into this position with the nonstriking hand.	A. Students are scattered in space working with a partner and sharing a ball.
	  1. Partners begin practicing with only a short distance between them.
	  2. Partners increase the distance between them as their skill warrants.
	  3. Partners progress to serving over the net and continue to move farther apart until they reach the baseline.
		A. That the serve is a means of putting the ball into play.
		
		That an effective serve is well placed.
		
		That an effective serve travels low over the net.
		
		That in order to contact a moving object (the ball) a player must keep his eyes on the object (objective focus).
		
		That the direction the ball is to travel is determined by the point at which force is applied in relation to the center of gravity of the ball.
		
		That a large hitting surface is desired to apply force in the intended direction.

(The students engage in:)   (Organization:)   (The students need to understand:)

That the magnitude of the force produced and imparted to the ball is increased as the speed of elbow extension is increased.

That utilizing the principle of opposition and trunk rotation increases the force produced.

VIII. Hit over the Net

(The students engage in:)   (Organization:)   (The students need to understand:)

A–I. Tossing the ball for another student to send over the net.
1. Setting the ball rather than tossing.
2. Passing and setting prior to the hit over the net.

A–I. Students work with a partner using a wall, a curtain or the net.

Students work in small groups over the net.

Each 0 player has his own ball. 0 passes ball to X. X sets the ball. 0 moves forward for the hit over the net, hits the ball and then retrieves it before going to the end of the line.

Drill formation for a hit over the net

Note: Game play should be interspersed with practice drills, etc. Rules should be learned as the need for them arises in the game.

A. That the hit over the net is generally one-handed.

B. That the hit over the net should have speed or placement and preferably both.

C. That the force imparted to the ball may be produced in several ways.
1. A running approach builds momentum to be transferred to the ball.
2. Rotation of the trunk and striking arm away from the net increases the range of motion of the striking arm and the mass used to produce force.
3. A snap of the wrist as the ball is contacted increases the speed of the striking hand.

D. That a running approach utilizing a jump with a two-foot takeoff results in a higher jump.

E. That the pathway (trajectory) of the ball is determined by the point of contact in relation to the center of gravity of the ball.
1. The ball may travel sharply downward over the net (spike).
2. The ball may travel over the heads of the opposing front row players and drop short of the back row players (dink).
3. The ball may travel deep into the opposing team's court (offensive volley).

(The students engage in:)   (Organization:)   (The students need to understand:)

F. That the student should be aware of the level of the ball in relation to the level of the net as the ball is contacted.
   1. If the ball is contacted above the level of the top of the net, an overhand throwing motion may be used to angle it sharply downward over the net (spike).
   2. If the ball is contacted below the level of the top of the net, an underhand motion may be used to impart force in an upward and forward direction.

G. That it is illegal for a player to touch the net or completely cross the centerline while the ball is in play.

H. That the preliminary action for the hit over the net should be the same for the dink, offensive volley and spike in order to deceive the opponents.

I. That a player who is caught with his back to the net may legally play the ball over the net with a back pass.

IX. Block

(The students engage in:)   (Organization:)   (The students need to understand:)

A. Standing at the net and jumping to block the spike.
   1. Alone (one-player block);
   2. With a partner (two-player block).

A. One or two blockers are added to the drill used for the hit over the net.

Drill formation for the block

A. That the block is a skill (an individual or multiple-player effort) used to return a spike or to deflect it to a teammate.

That the block must be aligned directly opposite the spike.

That the block requires a large, firm surface from which the ball can rebound. The force of the ball is returned to the ball.

That the blocker(s) jumps just after the spiker leaves the floor.

X. Serve

A. The underhand serve.

The floater serve.

The sidearm serve.

Note: The serve introduced earlier leads to the hit over the net and the floater serve. The other serves taught depend upon the skill level of the students. It is hoped that the student is exposed to a variety of techniques and then chooses that technique which will provide him with success. The student should constantly strive to develop and perfect a more effective serve.

A. Students serve over the net from both ends of the court. It may be necessary to begin practice close to the net and move farther from the net as skill warrants.
 1. All students are serving at the same time. They retrieve a ball and serve again. All balls are used.
 2. The teacher moves among the students giving individual help.
 3. Periodically, students move in close for observation and analysis.

A. That there are many different ways a player can serve (underhand, overhand, etc.).

That a player must keep his eyes on the ball (objective focus).

That the direction the ball is to travel is determined by the point at which force is applied in relation to the center of gravity of the ball.

That a ball hit through the center of gravity will travel in a straight line, whereas a ball hit away from its center of gravity will spin and travel in a curved pathway.

That a large, firm, flat surface should be used to apply force to the ball.

That force may be produced in several ways.
 1. Trunk rotation (utilizing the principle of opposition) can increase the range of motion and the speed of the striking arm.
 2. A transfer of weight from the back foot to the forward foot increases the mass used to produce force.

(The students engage in:)	(Organization:)	(The students need to understand:)

A. Activities which include:
  1. Problem-solving situations to discover specific concepts;
  2. Gamelike drills to apply these concepts;
  3. Actual games applying all concepts previously learned.

Note: Offensive and defensive patterns may be as elementary or as advanced as skill warrants.

A. Students are grouped together periodically for discussion and analysis (using the chalkboard) and working as teams on the court.

Teams should be established.

Example of activity working on the block and covering the block

A. That volleyball is a team game and that the team must work together utilizing players' individual talents in order to be successful.

That the three-hit game (forearm pass-set-hit) is the basic offensive technique used to play the ball over the net with a forceful hit.
  1. The key set player is the center forward.
  2. The key spikers are the right and left forwards.
  3. The interchange is used after the serve since it places a good setter in the center forward position and good spikers in the left and right forward positions.

That a team should position itself on the court in a starting position that best utilizes individual talents.

That all players must be alert and move on the court to circle the ball when it is on their side of the net.
  1. Covering the spiker means circling the spiker to cover all possible trajectories of a returned ball.
  2. Covering the block means circling the blocker(s) to cover all possible trajectories of the ball.

That a multiple-player block is the best defense against the spike.

That the basic court formation (W or crescent) is the best defense against a free ball (a weak hit over the net).

SAMPLE LESSON: THE INDIRECT APPROACH AS APPLIED TO THE OVERHAND VOLLEY

This lesson is intended as one of the first activity lessons for beginning students in volleyball. Through guided discovery the teacher leads the student to discover how to apply force and direction to control the trajectory of an overhand volley. The concepts encountered in this lesson are transferred, applied and reinforced in later lessons developing other volleyball skills. The suggested techniques of organization may need to be altered to suit the facilities; however, all space and equipment should be utilized to the fullest extent. The exact organization and specific cognitive outcomes for this lesson are contained in the preceding chart, pages 340–341.

The time it takes to teach this lesson will vary with different groups. The teacher progresses at a speed to suit his students' needs. A class that has had some experience in volleyball may find the problems too elementary. They may move very quickly through these problems; the teacher may need to develop a lesson more in accord with their level of development.

The attention given to detail in this plan is for the benefit of the teacher who is unfamiliar with guided discovery. As a teacher becomes experienced with indirect teaching, lesson plans become less detailed and the dialogue during the lesson becomes more natural.

There are many ways to approach a unit in volleyball, even many ways to teach the overhand volley using indirect teaching methods. This lesson is concerned with the application of the mechanical principles to the overhand volley. Among the desired outcomes is efficient, effective movement with understanding.

Introduction

The verbal introduction to the lesson includes an emphasis on using the first two joints of the fingers on the ball rather than the palms of the hands.

Organization

Partners are scattered in the space of the teaching station. Each set of partners has one ball.

DIRECTIONS FOR STUDENTS

STATEMENT OF MAIN PROBLEMS AND SUBPROBLEMS

A. Choose a partner, get a ball for the two of you and find a space in which to work (not too far apart) and begin throwing the ball back and forth.
  1. Can you limit your throwing and catching to using both hands?
  2. Using both hands, can you throw with an underhand motion?
  3. Using both hands, can you throw with an overhand motion?
  4. Using two hands, pass the ball to your partner with a high arc. The ball should travel toward the ceiling before it drops toward your partner. (The teacher may clarify why he limits the throw to a high arc. This is a desirable characteristic of both the forearm pass and overhand volley.)
    a. Can you do this with an underhand motion?
    b. Can you do this with an overhand motion?
  5. Think about where on the ball you are applying force to cause it to go up and to your partner. (Students may discuss with their partners where force must be applied. They should realize that force is applied under and behind the ball to cause it to go up and forward to their partner.)

B. Continuing to use a high pass, can you start the pass from different levels?
1. Using an underhand motion, can you start the pass at knee level—hip level—waist level—chest level—nose level?
   a. Is there some point at which the underhand pass becomes awkward and ineffective?
2. Using an overhand motion, can you start the pass at nose level—chest level—waist level—etc.?
   a. Is there some point at which the overhand pass becomes awkward and ineffective? (Students may again discuss the problem with their partners. The point at which both the overhand and underhand will become awkward is somewhere between the chest and the waist. The students may decide that to play a ball at this level one would have to crouch and play it with an overhand action.)
C. Continuing to throw the ball with a high arc and using the appropriate technique (an underhand motion to send the ball from a low level, an overhand motion to send the ball from a high level), try to kinesthetically feel if there is a difference in the angle of the trunk for an overhand and an underhand throw.
1. Can you see a difference in the angle of the body of your partner as he throws using first an underhand and then an overhand motion?
2. Can you feel the difference in the position of your own body as you throw? (Students should both feel and see that the trunk is inclined forward for the underhand throw and backward for the overhand throw.)

Note: If there is difficulty in solving this problem, the teacher may need to structure another problem. (Stand perfectly straight as you throw with first an underhand and then an overhand motion. Does this position feel natural or does your body want to move? How does it want to move?)

OBSERVATION–DEMONSTRATION

Students can be brought in close for a demonstration-observation clarifying what they have just experienced and learned. This is also an excellent opportunity to introduce the next section of the lesson, focusing upon how to get force and direction.

D. Let's concentrate next on how we produce force to project the ball up and forward to our partners. Using the overhand motion and sending the ball from shoulder level or higher, try to project the ball up and forward to your partner using just the fingers and wrists to produce force. The remainder of the body should not move and only the first two joints of the fingers should contact the ball.
1. Now try adding force produced by the arms and shoulders.
2. Now project the ball as high as you can, using any number of body parts to apply force to the ball. (Students quickly realize that the entire body is used to produce force and that knee extension is important.)

E. Again throwing and catching in good volley position, stop the motion of the body the instant the ball is released. Try to apply as much force as you can, but stop the action of the body immediately upon releasing the ball.
1. Now throw and catch allowing the body to extend and the arms to follow in the direction the ball is released (use a follow-through).
2. Can you feel a difference when you use a follow-through and when you don't? Which feels better?
3. Can you see a difference in your partner's actions when he uses a follow-through and when he doesn't?
4. Is it possible to produce more force when using a follow-through or when not using a follow-through? (Students should realize that the follow-through is necessary if the intended force is to be applied to the ball.)

F. Continue throwing the ball back and forth with controlled force.
1. Can you vary the height that the ball travels by varying the amount of force you apply to the ball? Be sure to throw with control.
   a. Can you make the ball travel very high?
   b. Can you make the ball travel medium-high?
   c. Can you make the ball travel low?
2. Which of the three balls was easier to catch?
   a. The one that traveled very high?
   b. The one that traveled medium-high?
   c. The one that traveled low?
3. Why was it easier to catch? (Students should realize that the pass must be high enough to allow the partner enough time to get under it. A higher pass allows more time. The students should be allowed to set a goal for how high the ball should go—for example, as high as the basketball hoop or some marking on the wall.)

G. Continue using an overhand motion to throw the ball, but now throw the ball from the same position in which you catch it. Remember, only the first two joints of the fingers contact the ball. Let's experiment with throwing and catching the ball from different levels in relation to the body to determine if there is one level in which it is easiest to achieve height and control while keeping your eyes on the ball.
1. Try sending and receiving the ball from the level of the chest.
   a. Can you keep your eyes on the ball?
   b. Can you easily send the ball in an upward-forward direction from this position?
2. Try sending and receiving the ball from over your head.
   a. Can you keep your eyes on the ball?
   b. Can you easily send the ball in an upward-forward direction from this position?

3. Try sending and receiving the ball from the level of your forehead.
   a. Can you keep your eyes on the ball?
   b. Can you easily send the ball in an upward-forward direction from this position? (The students should realize that sending and receiving from forehead level puts them in the best position in which to watch the ball and project it in an upward-forward direction. The teaching phrase becomes, "Look through the triangle formed by the thumbs and fore-fingers.")
H. The position of the hands, arms, and trunk that you have been using to throw and catch the ball is the beginning of a good position to use for the overhand volley. Let's experiment with different positions of the feet. Throw and catch the ball, keeping the feet very close together.
   1. Place the feet apart sideways while you throw and catch.
   2. Now try one foot ahead of the other.
   3. Try the other foot in the forward position.
   4. Try these various positions and apply a great deal of force to the ball.
   5. Try these various positions and apply a small amount of force to the ball.
   6. Which foot position helps you to apply more force to the ball and also helps you to be better balanced in both throwing and catching? (Students should understand that the forward-back stride position helps to produce greater force to apply to the ball and helps the player to maintain a balanced position.)
I. Let's experiment with the size of the surface applying force to the ball. Using all the concepts and techniques you have just learned, throw and catch the ball in a good volley position, using just the thumbs and index finger to apply force.
   1. Now use the thumb, index, and middle fingers to apply force.
   2. Add the ring fingers.
   3. Now add the little fingers. Use all ten fingers to apply force. Remember that the ball may not touch the palms of the hands.
   4. Try keeping the fingers close together as you throw and catch.
   5. Now spread them apart in the shape of a triangle.

OBSERVATION–DEMONSTRATION

The points that need to be clarified are:
1. The center of gravity of a round mass (the ball) is the exact center.
2. If one wants to send the ball forward and upward in a straight line he must apply force behind, below, and directly through the center of gravity.
3. One is more likely to apply force through the center of gravity in the desired direction when using a large surface to apply force.

*Application of all problems to
the overhand volley*

The teacher explains that the overhand volley is one of the basic volleyball skills used to convert a ball approaching at a high or medium level into a pass or set for a spike. The ball may not rest upon the hands as in throwing but must receive immediate impetus from the fingers. The students should be able to identify the key ideas just learned which apply to the overhand volley.

1. The base of support is enlarged in the direction of the force (forward-back stride position).
2. Force is increased by:
   a. Increasing mass (utilizing the muscles of the legs in a crouched position);
   b. Using a follow-through.
3. The hitting surface should be large, with the first two joints of all ten fingers contacting the ball. (The ball may not rest on the fingers.)
4. The ball should be played at forehead level.
5. The ball should be directed high into the air to give a teammate time to get into position for the play which follows.

In the preceding part of the lesson the teacher's main concern was the progression of problems and an awareness of the students' movement responses. He should, however, roam among the students offering suggestions to individuals as needed.

The portion of the lesson described below is for skill practice. The progression leading to the overhand volley is as follows.

1. Partners *throw* and catch using good volley techniques with control.
2. One partner throws and the other uses an *overhand volley* to return the ball. The thrower catches the ball in a good volley position.
3. Partners switch positions and repeat number two above.
4. If both partners show good control with the single overhand volley they should try a continuous volley.
5. Couples combine into groups of four and work on a continuous volley.

Note: If the student cannot get into position to volley the ball correctly, he should catch the ball and start again rather than play the ball illegally.

During this portion of the lesson the teacher can truly gear the material to the individuals. He can move among the students and spend time helping those students who need special attention. He can allow students to progress at their own rate through the five problems listed. Some students may even work on a few of the drills listed on page 341.

REFERENCES

Keller, Val. *Level I Technical Module.* San Francisco, Calif.: U.S.V.B.A. Publications, 1977.

Keller, Val. *Point, Game and Match!* San Francisco, Calif.: U.S.V.B.A. Publications, 1977.

National Association for Girls and Women in Sport. *Volleyball Guide.* Washington, D.C.: American Alliance for Health, Physical Education, and Recreation. (Current edition.)

Peppler, Mary Jo. *Inside Volleyball for Women.* Chicago: Henry Regnery Company, 1977.

Scates, Allen E., and Ward, Jane. *Volleyball.* 2nd ed. Boston, Mass.: Allyn & Bacon, 1975.

Scates, Allen E. *Winning Volleyball Fundamentals, Tactics and Strategy.* 2nd ed. Boston, Mass.: Allyn & Bacon, 1976.

Schaafsma, Frances, and Heck, Ann. *Volleyball for Coaches and Teachers.* Dubuque, Iowa: Wm. C. Brown Company Publishers, 1971.

Slaymaker, Thomas, and Brown, Virginia H. *Power Volleyball.* 2nd ed. Philadelphia: W. B. Saunders Co., 1976.

Tennant, Mark. *Volleyball Team Play.* Vanier Ontario, Canada: Canadian Volleyball Assoc., 1975.

United States Volleyball Association. *Official Guide & Rule Book.* San Francisco, Calif.: U.S.V.B.A. Publications (557 Fourth St.), current edition.

PART VI. □ INDIVIDUAL SPORTS

True sportsmen ... delight in the pursuit.
—Alexander Pope

INTRODUCTION

The term *individual sports* describes a category of sport in which a participant need not interact with another person. This does not negate the possibility of players working together, or a collection of individuals becoming a team due to affiliation with the same organization (school or club). The fact that the participant can work alone may be the most obvious commonality of this total group of sports; indeed, the differences are much more obvious than the similarities. The individual sports included in this text are archery, golf, gymnastics, swimming, and track and field.

Both commonalities and differences are evident in the movement patterns and in the application of biomechanical principals to the skills of the individual sports. Swimming differs from the other sports in this group in that the medium in which movement occurs is water; thus, the principles of buoyancy and propulsion apply only to swimming. Although archery, golf, gymnastics and track and field occur on land, the designated space and equipment requirements sufficiently alter the movement patterns to make the techniques of each sport distinctly different. This does not mean that the biomechanical principles discussed in chapter four do not apply to these sport techniques. However, due to the uniqueness of the environment (medium, space and equipment) and of the resulting movement patterns, the general application of principles through major concepts (chapter five) is limited. The common concepts, where applicable, are cited (e.g., Golf, pp. 396–404). The common major concepts and subconcepts are again identified throughout the sport chapters by the same letter-number designations as in chapter five (A, A-1, A-2, etc.). The majority of concepts and subconcepts in the individual sports are unique to each sport; thus they have no letter-number designation, but they are italicized (e.g., Archery). Occasionally both common and unique concepts and subconcepts are included for each sport (e.g., Golf, pp. 396–404, Gymnastics, pp. 427–431, Track and Field, pp. 519–533).

The number of events and/or movement techniques possible in several of the individual sports require the teacher to give special attention to ordering the learning materials. However, the diversity of content also makes possible the matching of individual students to content and/or event. A discussion of techniques and tools to individualize and personalize learning is included in chapter three, The Role of Methodology. Specific application of these ideas is included throughout the individual sport chapters as sample tools and lessons.

The problems that ensue due to diversity of content and individuality of students are not insurmountable. Such situations do require extra effort in planning and organizing the learning environment. The offering of *individual sports* in the school program is well worth the extra effort since many of these sports become life time activities for the adult.

13

Archery

INTRODUCTION

Archery is a space activity. An arrow is propelled into space so that it will hit a target a given distance away. The space needed for archery varies according to the event. In target archery, arrows are propelled toward a target of concentric circles placed 10 to 100 yards away. In clout shooting the target is flat on the ground at a distance of 120 to 180 yards. For flight shooting the arrow is propelled the greatest distance possible. Field archery presents a shooting distance unknown to the archer, varying from twenty feet to eighty yards.

The space needed for archery can be found in indoor or outdoor facilities. Many communities have commercial indoor ranges. In some localities, public parks have outdoor targets with an area clear for shooting. A gymnasium provides sufficient indoor space for shooting, while school athletic fields provide the area needed outdoors. A shooting range can even be safely organized in the space available in one's backyard or basement. Thus, archery is an activity in which participation can occur in small or large spaces, indoor or outdoor areas.

Archery is an activity requiring force. The archer must be able to produce and direct force. The bow is the piece of equipment used to impart force to the arrow. The muscular effort of the archer bends the bow. As the bow is released from its bent position, force is imparted to the arrow. Sufficient force must be transferred from the bow to the arrow to allow the arrow to reach its intended destination. Force is directed through the actions in the shooting sequence completed by the archer.

Archery is an activity for everyone. Men, women, boys, girls, the handicapped, the highly skilled or the less skilled can derive satisfaction from archery. Participation can occur in a number of different forms. Archery provides the opportunity to shoot at a target, to hunt, to fish, to play golf, to compete against oneself or to compete against others.[1] Those who enjoy the activity quickly become involved. Involvement for some means joining a local archery club or working to achieve individual goals in terms of score or form. For others it includes making or repairing equipment, individual practice, or tournament participation. Archery as a recreational activity provides a fascinating adventure for many.

MAJOR CONCEPTS

Certain concepts are basic to archery regardless of the event in which participation occurs. These concepts are described in the pages which follow and serve as the foundation for the shooting sequence. Due to the uniqueness of archery these concepts have not been previously discussed in chapter five.

Equipment

CONCEPT. Equipment unique to archery is used to propel an arrow toward a target.

An archer can spend a relatively small sum of money to purchase the equipment essential for shooting or he can devote large sums of money to purchase or make archery tackle. The tackle used usually increases in complexity and expense as the archer becomes more skillful or a more avid follower of the sport. However, the essential tackle— a bow, arrows, an arm guard, and a finger tab or shooting glove—can be relatively inexpensive. The archer should be concerned with how to select this tackle, prepare it for use, and use it safely.

BOWS

The bow (fig. 13.1) is the piece of equipment used to impart force to the arrow. The force produced is dependent upon the weight of the bow, its construction, and the actions of the archer. Presently bows are constructed of fiberglass and wood. The best bow available is a composite bow, in which the main body is wood with a thin layer of fiberglass on the face and back. A recurve bow, due to its design, provides additional leverage, and thus increases the potential for imparting force to the arrow. During the draw the curves at the ends of the bow open to create additional leverage.

Selecting a bow

The weight of the bow refers to the force it takes to draw the string a specified distance. Most bows are measured at a twenty-eight-inch draw. Thus, if one draws a twenty-five-pound bow twenty-eight inches, it takes twenty-five pounds of force. However, if the bow is drawn a lesser distance due to a shorter arrow length, lesser force is required. Likewise, if one uses an arrow longer than twenty-eight inches, greater force is needed to reach a full draw. Bows vary in weight from 10 pounds to over 100 pounds, with the heavier bows being used for big game hunting. It is extremely important that the archer select a bow which is appropriate for his strength. It is wisest to begin shooting with a bow the archer can handle rather than to over-bow oneself and select a heavier bow. A lighter bow allows the archer to concentrate on developing

1. Archery golf is similar to golf in that the objective for each hole is to use the fewest number of shots to hit a target (a four-inch ball balanced on top of a wire support). The archer begins from behind the tee marker, shooting toward the target. For each of the following shots the archer moves to a position directly behind the point of the arrow which just landed. Shooting continues in this manner until the ball has been hit.

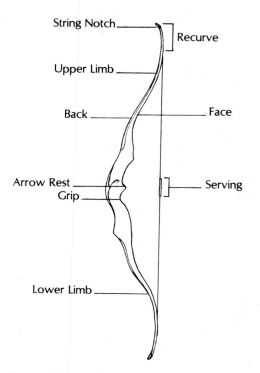

Figure 13.1. **Bow**

Figure 13.2. **Mechanical bow bracer. Note that the archer is in a low position and the arm reaches over the string.**

sound shooting technique. As skill increases, the archer should change to a heavier bow.

A twenty-pound bow should be used by most beginning college students.[2] On occasion, a student may be better suited to a seventeen-pound bow. As he exhibits the strength to utilize correct form, he should change to a heavier bow.

Most bowstrings are made of dacron. The number of strands of dacron depends upon the poundage of the bow. Strings are manufactured according to bow length and weight. An eight-strand string is recommended for a twenty-pound bow, while a sixteen-strand string is used with a sixty-pound bow. The serving placed at the nocking point and loop ends of the string protects the string from the friction created by the bow notches, the archer's string fingers, and the arrow nock.

Preparing the bow for shooting

Bracing the bow is the act of preparing the bow for shooting. The string is placed in the notches of both ends of the bow, transforming the bow into a slightly bent position possessing potential energy. A variety of methods may be selected to brace the bow. Regardless of the method selected, the archer must consider how he can utilize the strength he has to produce a bend in the bow while allowing one hand to remain free to guide the string into the upper notch. Safety must also be foremost in his mind. He must begin with the string secure in the lower notch and position his body out of the pathway of the bow in case it should slip. The archer may rely totally on his muscles to bend the bow or he may use a mechanical bow bracer (fig. 13.2). This is a commercial device which allows the archer to bend the bow with a minimum of effort.

2. Ten-, fifteen-, or twenty-pound bows may be more appropriate for younger students. In all instances bows should be selected in accord with the strength of the archers using them. In class situations it is wise to have bows available which are heavier or lighter than the standard used by that age group. Thus, it is possible to provide bows appropriate for all of the individuals within the class and to allow students to progress to heavier bows as they are able.

Figure 13.3. **Step-through method of bracing the bow**

The step-through method (fig. 13.3) is one of several ways to brace a bow. The archer assumes a side stride position. The upper limb of the bow is held by the dominant hand and the bow is placed diagonally in front of the archer's body with the face of the bow up. The curve of the lower limb is placed over the ankle of the outside foot. The position of the lower limb should be adjusted until comfortable. With the free hand, the archer separates the string from the bow. With his inside leg he steps between the bow and the bowstring and raises the bow until he feels the handle directly behind the upper thigh. The stepping leg is slightly bent. The dominant hand is moved to a position just below the string loop. The fingers are open and the heel of the hand is against the bow. The archer is now ready to use leverage to bend the bow. The heel of the outside foot is lifted to prevent twisting of the bow limb.[3] The stepping leg straightens and pushes back against the bow while the heel of the dominant hand pushes the upper limb forward to achieve a bend in the bow. With the free hand the archer slips the string into place and slowly relaxes. He then checks to see that the string is secure in both notches of the bow. Throughout the entire procedure it is important that the archer keeps his head away from the bow. To unstring the bow the procedure is reversed.

Using the bow safely

Prior to shooting a bow the archer should be sure that the bow is safe to use. He should check to see that the bow is not cracked or splintered, that the string or serving is not frayed, and that it is correctly braced with the string secure in both notches. He should never draw and release a bow without an arrow, as this can damage the limbs. However, it is possible to draw to anchor position and slowly let the string down.

ARROWS

The object propelled in archery is an arrow (fig. 13.4). Arrow shafts are made of wood, fiberglass, or aluminum. For wooden shafts Port Orford cedar is recommended. The fiberglass arrow is more expensive but also more accurate and durable. Temperature and moisture do not affect this arrow and it is very difficult to break or bend. The most accurate of all arrows is the aluminum arrow. It is also the most expensive and recommended for use only by the highly skilled.

Fletching refers to the feathers or plastic vanes placed on the arrow to stabilize its flight. In a three-feather arrow, the feather placed perpendicular to the slit in the arrow nock is the index feather. Generally it is of different color than the other two feathers.

The *crest* is the colored band on the shaft of the arrow. It aids the archer in identifying his arrows.

3. Incorrect placement of the bow against the ankle or thigh will result in pressure exerted against the edge of the limb of the bow and a twisting of the limb.

Selecting arrows

Arrows should be long enough for the archer and matched to the weight of the bow. With matched arrows the flight is truer and the accuracy of shooting increased.

Arrow length is measured from the back of the point to the bottom of the slit in the nock (fig. 13.4). It is extremely important that an archer use arrows of proper length. For safety reasons a beginner should start with arrows one or two inches longer than needed. An arrow that is too short should never be used. As the beginner becomes consistent in his form, he should be fit with arrows of proper length to increase his efficiency in shooting.

Several methods exist for selecting arrow lengths. One of the most accurate is to use a bow constructed specifically for this purpose. An arrow marked in one-inch intervals is attached to the string of a light bow. As the string is drawn, the arrow moves back through a guide attached to the bow. When the archer is at full draw using a proper anchor, the mark on the arrow which is lined up with the back of the bow is noted.[4] This indicates the length arrow appropriate for the archer.

Another method of measuring arrow length involves placing a yardstick against the sternum of the archer. The archer then extends both arms forward (not stretching or reaching) with the palms of the hands against both sides of the yardstick. The point at which the fingertips touch the yardstick indicates the correct length for the archer.

In a third method the archer places the nock of the arrow against his sternum. Both arms are extended with the palms of the hands along the shaft of the arrow. The arrow should extend one to two inches beyond the archer's fingertips. Again, it is important that the archer merely extends his

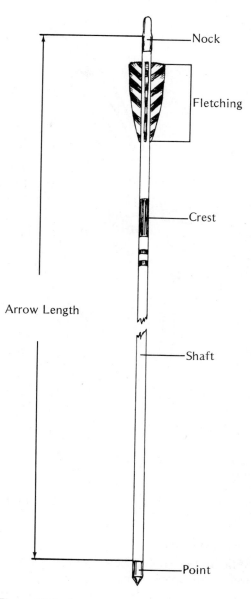

Figure 13.4. **Arrow**

4. The anchor is the spatial relationship achieved between the string, string hand and face with each draw. Refer to page 370 for additional information.

it is to be shot, and a bow loaded with an arrow should never be pointed at anyone. To avoid crushing the feathers, arrows should be carried near the point with the shafts and feathers separated.

Retrieving arrows

Once arrows have been shot the archer must retrieve them in a manner which is both safe to the archer and not damaging to the arrows. If an outside shooting range is used, all arrows in the grass should be retrieved as the archer walks to the target. If the fletching is embedded in the grass, the arrow is pulled through the grass point-first to prevent damaging the fletching. Otherwise arrows are removed nock-first.

When removing arrows from the target (fig. 13.5), the area in front of the target and in line with the arrows should be clear of people. The archer should stand to the side of the target and place the back of the hand closest to the target against the target to prevent damaging the face or pulling the target over. The index and middle fingers of the hand are separated on each side of the arrow. The hand farthest from the target should grip the arrow shaft as close to the target as possible and pull the arrow from the target at the same angle at which it entered. If deeply embedded, the arrow must be twisted a few times and then removed from the target. If the fletching of the arrow is embedded in the target, the arrow should be pulled through the target rather than removed nock-first.

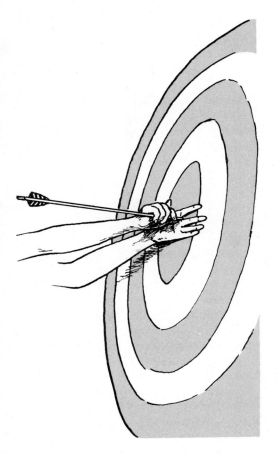

Figure 13.5. **Removing arrows from the target**

arms and does not stretch or reach more than is normal.

Using arrows safely

The archer should be certain that his arrows are of proper length and in good condition. The fletching, nock, and point should be secure and not damaged. A cracked or splintered arrow cannot be safely repaired and should be destroyed or cut to a shorter length. Due to the potential for injury an arrow should never be drawn unless

ARM GUARD AND FINGER TAB OR SHOOTING GLOVE

An arm guard (fig. 13.6) and a finger tab or shooting glove (fig. 13.7) are two other essential pieces of archery equipment. Archers should always wear an arm guard on the forearm of the bow arm for protection

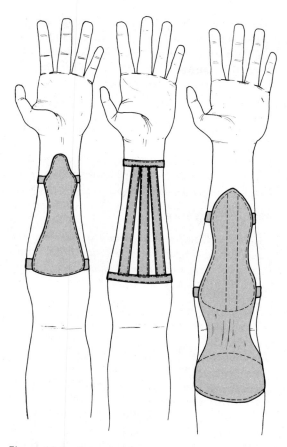

Figure 13.6. **Arm guards**

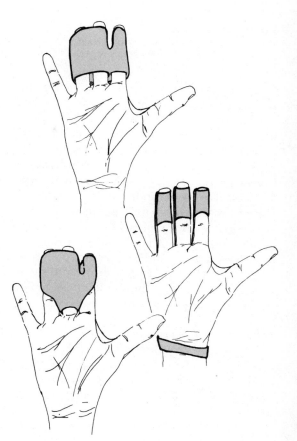

Figure 13.7. **Finger tabs and shooting glove**

against string contact.[5] Arm guards are manufactured in a variety of shapes, sizes, and materials. Plastic and leather are two of the most common materials used. Regardless of the material, the arm guard should be thick enough to provide the needed protection.

Finger protection is also essential to provide a smooth release and to protect the fingers of the string hand from becoming irritated or blistered due to the friction created by the string.[6] A finger tab or shooting glove is used for these purposes. The tab is made of a pliable material (cordovan leather or calfskin), one, two, or three layers thick. Ex-

cess material should be trimmed from the tab so that it fits the archer. It should be just large enough to provide protection for the string fingers. Shooting gloves of cordovan or elk skin provide greater protection, as they cover each of the string fingers. However, often they are not as pliable as the finger tab.

5. "Bow arm" refers to the arm of the hand which holds the bow.
6. "String hand" refers to the hand which grasps the string.

Safety

CONCEPT. All actions used to propel the arrow must contribute to safe participation.

Due to the nature of archery tackle, the potential for injury is great if one is careless. Common sense and proper use of equipment are the best guarantees of safe participation. Prior to shooting the archer must consider all of the factors which will assure his own safety as well as the safety of other archers. The suggestions following are directed toward eliminating potential hazards. It would be advantageous for all archers to establish safety regulations appropriate for their shooting situation, keeping in mind their personal safety in using equipment, and safety related to the shooting range and using this range with others.

PERSONAL SAFETY

1. The clothing worn should provide freedom of movement and yet not be so loose as to get caught in the string. All jewelry should be removed prior to shooting.

2. An arm guard and a finger tab or shooting glove should always be used to provide protection for the archer.

3. Equipment should be used in the manner for which it was designed (refer to pages 360 and 362).

SHOOTING RANGE

1. The target area should be clear of people. No one should be standing in the line of fire or behind the targets.

2. All archers should assume the same shooting line, shoot, and then retrieve at the same time. In group situations it is wise to assign one archer as a field captain to signal when shooting may begin, when it should stop, and when arrows may be retrieved. As archers finish shooting they should step be-

hind the shooting line to assist the field captain in determining when to halt shooting.

3. When nocking the arrow (loading the bow) the point of the arrow should be directed toward the ground or the targets and away from other archers.

4. An arrow that falls in front of the shooting line should be considered shot unless the archer can retrieve it with his bow from where he is shooting. Under no circumstances should anyone step in front of the shooting line once shooting has begun.

Shooting Sequence

CONCEPT. Space: Archery is a space activity in which a proper spatial relationship must be achieved among archer, bow, arrow, and target.

If an arrow is to be propelled so that it will hit a target, it must be positioned in relation to the target. The bow as the piece of equipment used to propel the arrow and the archer as the individual using this piece of equipment must be in correct spatial alignment with the target. The actions of the shooting sequence allow the archer to achieve the proper alignment among bow, arrow, and target. The description of these steps is included under "The Shooting Sequence," pages 367–377.

Sub-concept. The archer must be kinesthetically aware of the position of his body parts in space in relation to the bow, arrow, and target.

To achieve a proper spatial alignment between archer, bow, arrow, and target, the archer must be aware of his actions and the affect each has on the bow and arrow. An arrow that achieves the desired destination indicates a successful shot, but the archer should also kinesthetically feel that it was a successful shot. He should be aware that his body parts were positioned correctly, and that the proper muscles were used to produce force. Each of the steps in the shooting sequence, when executed correctly, should present to the archer a kinesthetic picture of the shooting sequence—a physical awareness that each action was completed properly.

CONCEPT. Force: Archery is a force activity requiring sufficient force to be transferred from the bow to the arrow in order to propel the arrow to its intended destination.

As a bow is bent, it produces potential energy. At the moment of release the potential energy is converted to kinetic energy, which is imparted to the arrow. For efficient shooting the archer must produce the maximum force which he is capable of achieving efficiently and safely. Failure to impart sufficient force to the arrow results in the arrow falling short of its target.

Sub-concept. Force increases as the bow is bent to the greatest degree which is efficient *and* safe.

Increasing the bend in the bow increases potential energy to be converted to kinetic energy and thus increases the force produced. However, it is unsafe to bend the bow to the extent that it is overdrawn and might break. Therefore, the bow should be bent to the greatest extent which is both efficient and safe.

Sub-concept. Only the muscles which increase the efficiency of the shooting procedure should be utilized in the production of force.

As in most sport activities, beginning archers have a tendency to use more muscles than necessary, resulting in inefficiency and wasted effort. In archery, this tires the archer, increases the possibility of error, and makes it difficult to maintain the greatest bend in the bow. The upper back muscles (rhomboids and trapezius) are the major muscles used to bend the bow. Excessive use of the finger or lower arm muscles decreases both the efficiency and accuracy of the shooting procedure.

CONCEPT. Precision: Archery is a precision activity requiring preciseness and consistency in the archer's actions.

Sub-concept. The archer must be able to duplicate his exact actions with each arrow shot.

A successful archer is a consistent archer. Even before the archer has perfected his form, it is essential that he be consistent in his shooting if any flaws in performance are to be discovered. Once the archer utilizes correct technique he must be able to repeat his exact actions with each shot. A slight deviation in form can mean a major deviation in placement of the arrow on the target.

Sub-concept. Precision is measured in terms of arrow placement on the target and a scoring system unique to archery.

The difference between consistency and inconsistency is apparent in the placement of arrows on the target and the score achieved. The archer who is consistent achieves a grouping of arrows in close proximity, whereas the inconsistent archer scatters his arrows across the target face. Scores begin to improve and to be more indicative of shooting skill as consistency increases. The score received for six arrows grouped in the center of the target is much higher than that for six arrows scattered to different areas.

Rules

CONCEPT. Rules have been established to standardize shooting procedures and the methods of scoring.

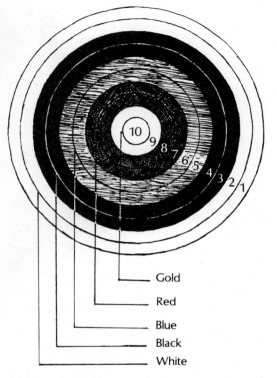

Figure 13.8. **Target face colors and point values**

Gold

Red

Blue

Black

White

Name	*Cindy Weaver*	
Round	*Columbia*	*Nov. 16*

Distance __50__

						Hits	Score
9	9	7	7	5	5	6	42
7	5	5	5	3	1	6	26
7	7	7	5	5	5	6	36
7	5	3	3	0	0	4	18
						22	122

Distance __40__

9	9	9	7	7	0	5	41
7	7	7	7	5	5	6	38
9	9	7	5	3	3	6	36
9	9	9	5	1	1	6	34
						23	149

Distance __30__

7	7	7	7	7	1	6	36
9	9	9	9	5	5	6	46
9	9	7	5	5	3	6	38
9	7	7	7	7	5	6	42
						24	162
					Totals	69	433

Figure 13.9. **Procedure for recording scores**

How does an archer know if he has been successful? Obviously, he can see the placement of the arrows on the target. But if he desires to compare his present performance with past performances or to compete against other archers there must be some assurance that shooting conditions have been similar and the means used to evaluate success consistent. Thus, rules have been established to standardize shooting and scoring procedures.

SCORING

The scoring face consists of five concentric circles of different colors. Each circle is divided by a thin line into two equal scoring areas. The entire target consists of ten different scoring areas.

Only those arrows which land within this area count as hits. Figure 13.8 shows the point value for each of the scoring areas.

Figure 13.9 shows the correct procedure for recording scores.

1. Scores are recorded in descending order rather than in the order shot.

2. An arrow hitting the petticoat (the area beyond the outside ring) is recorded as a miss.

3. An arrow that touches two colors or touches the dividing line within a color receives the higher value.

4. An arrow which is witnessed and rebounds from the target or passes through the target counts seven points.

GENERAL RULES

1. All archers must straddle a common shooting line.

2. Only six arrows are shot. Six consecutive arrows shot by one archer are referred to as an end. If a greater number of arrows are shot, only the lowest six are scored.

3. If an archer drops an arrow in front of the shooting line and cannot retrieve it with his bow from the position in which he is shooting, the arrow is considered shot.

4. In the event of an arrow hanging across the target, the individual in charge of shooting should be notified and the shooting halted until the arrow is placed securely in the target where it hit. This prevents the arrow from being hit by another arrow.

5. A *round* is a given number of arrows shot at more than one distance. The longest distance is shot first. For example, a Columbia Round consists of twenty-four arrows shot from fifty meters, twenty-four from forty meters, and twenty-four from thirty meters. The fifty-meter distance is shot first. The thirty-meter distance is shot last.

THE SHOOTING SEQUENCE

Once the archer has secured the necessary equipment and is aware of the safety factors which must be followed he is ready to begin shooting. He is now concerned with the actions to be completed which allow him to propel the arrow. These actions are identified in Table 13.1 and are based upon the space, force, and precision concepts previously discussed.

STANCE

The stance is the position assumed by the archer in order to achieve proper alignment with the target, to assure that body parts are out of the pathway of the string and to pro-

TABLE 13.1
STEPS IN SHOOTING SEQUENCE AS RELATED TO SPACE, FORCE, AND PRECISION CONCEPTS

Steps in Shooting Sequence	Space Awareness	Force Production	Precision
1. Stance	X		X
2. Grip	X		X
3. Nock	X		X
4. Draw		X	X
5. Anchor	X	X	X
6. Aim	X		X
7. Release		X	X
8. After-hold	X		X

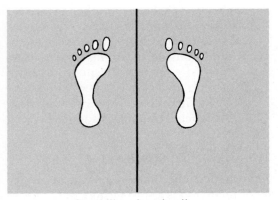

Straddling shooting line

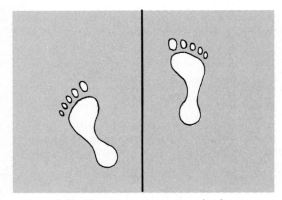

Adjusting stance to remove body from pathway of string. The foot closest to the target is moved diagonally backward.

Figure 13.10. **Stance**

vide an effective position for the production of force.

The archer straddles the shooting line.[7] The shoulder of the bow arm (for a right-handed archer, the left shoulder; for a left-handed archer, the right shoulder) is closest to the target. When extended at a right angle from the body to the target, the bow arm should be in line with the center of the target. The body is erect in good posture with feet, hips, and shoulders forming a line

perpendicular to the ground. The head is turned to look over the shoulder at the target. If, due to body build, this position does not allow freedom from the pathway of the string, the body should be adjusted by moving the foot closest to the target diagonally backward until the shoulder and bow arm are removed from the string's pathway.

The position assumed should be stable to allow for maximum force production. The archer's base of support should be large enough to assure stability and his center of gravity should be centered over the base of support.

The bow arm when extended toward the target is positioned so that the forearm is rotated away from the pathway of the string (fig. 13.11). The elbow is straight to aid the archer in achieving the greatest bend in the bow and to withstand the resistance provided by the bow.

GRIP

The hand is positioned on the bow to assure proper alignment between the bow arm and the bow and to aid in the efficient production of force.

A relaxed grip is used to aid the archer in utilizing only those muscles which contribute to the efficient production of force. The thumb and index finger loosely encircle the bow and slightly overlap. The pressure of the bow is felt along the lifeline of the hand (fig. 13.12). The remaining three fingers are not involved in gripping the bow and should be completely void of tension.

NOCK

Nocking the arrow is the act of placing the arrow on the bowstring in preparation for shooting. Nocking is important in achieving

7. In field archery both feet are behind the shooting line.

a proper and consistent spacial relationship between the bow and the arrow.

The bow is held in a position perpendicular to the body and parallel with the ground. The index feather or vane is placed perpendicular to the string and the nock of the arrow is slipped onto the string. It is essential that the arrow is nocked consistently in the same place. To aid in consistency a nocking point may be placed on the string.[8] Tape, dental floss, or a commercial device may be used to build up a portion of the string to serve as a nocking point. The nock of the arrow is placed directly below this point.

DRAW

The draw is the act of moving the string to anchor position, bending the bow and gaining the greatest potential energy from the bow. To achieve force, the bow should be bent to the greatest degree which is efficient and safe. Only those muscles which contribute to the task should be utilized.

Proper placement of the fingers on the string is extremely important if an efficient draw is to occur. A Boy Scout salute is assumed, with the thumb and little finger touching in order to remove these fingers from the drawing action. The string is placed in the first joint of the first three fingers of the string hand. The arrow is between the index and middle fingers. The string hand is used as a "dead hook" on the string. It is void of tension and the fingers are spaced away from the nock of the arrow to prevent pressure on the arrow. The back of the hand and the wrist are flat and

8. To determine placement of the nocking point a bow square or a ruler can be used. The bow should be braced with the ruler lightly touching the arrow rest and extending toward the string, making a right angle with the string. The base of the nocking point is placed ⅛ inch above the intersection of the bottom edge of the ruler and the string. The arrow is nocked directly below this point.

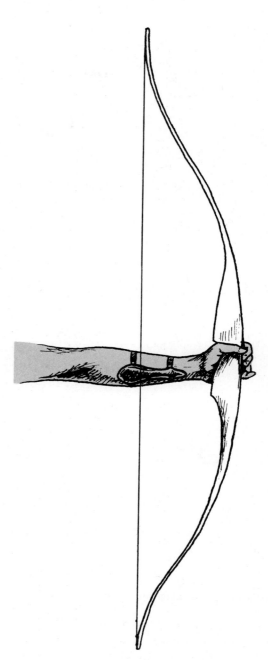

Figure 13.11. **Position of the bow arm**

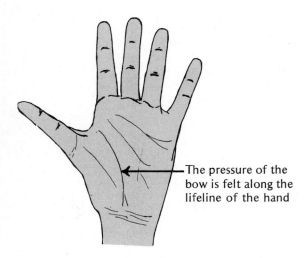

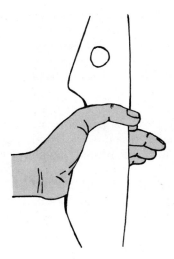

The pressure of the bow is felt along the lifeline of the hand

Figure 13.12. **Gripping the bow**

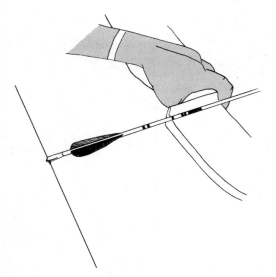

Figure 13.13. **Nocking the arrow**

muscles of the upper back (rhomboids and trapezius) as the major source of force, the string is smoothly pulled until the anchor position is reached.

For efficient production of force in the draw, the archer must rely upon the back muscles rather than the finger, wrist, or arm muscles. Kinesthetically, the archer should feel as if he is squeezing his shoulder blades together. An extended position of the bow arm and use of the back muscles helps the archer to achieve and maintain the greatest bend in the bow.

ANCHOR

The anchor is the spatial relationship achieved between the string, string hand and face with each draw. The anchor is essential for consistency in shooting.

A consistent anchor assures that the same bend in the bow and thus the same force is produced with each draw and that each arrow is released from the same position in

relaxed, as they do not contribute to the production of force.

In the draw, the bow is moved to a position perpendicular to the ground. A correct bow arm position is assumed. Using the

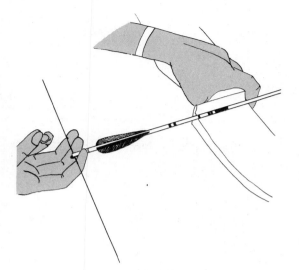

Figure 13.14. **Gripping the string**

Figure 13.15. **The draw**

relation to the archer. A low anchor or a high anchor may be used.[9]

In the low anchor (fig. 13.17) the string bisects the archer's face and is drawn tight against the tip of the nose and the center of the chin. The string hand remains flat, with the index finger positioned directly under and in contact with the jawbone.

In the high anchor (fig. 13.18) the string hand is flat, with the top edge of the index finger tight against the cheekbone and the tip of the index finger at the edge of the lip. The "horseshoe" of the hand formed by the index finger and thumb is hooked on the back of the jawbone.

Due to the difference in string-hand position in the two anchors, the trajectory of the arrow is different. The low anchor allows for greater trajectory and thus greater distance is achieved.

In either anchor it is essential that the archer continue to use the back muscles to draw the string tight against the anchor point and that he consistently achieve the same anchor point. To achieve consistency

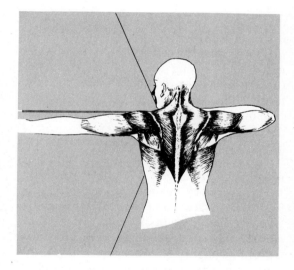

Figure 13.16. **The muscles of the upper back are used as the major source of force.**

9. The low anchor is commonly used in target archery technique. The high anchor is commonly used in the instinctive, field, and hunting techniques.

Figure 13.17. **The low anchor**

Figure 13.18. **The high anchor**

the archer must be kinesthetically aware of the position of his string hand in relation to his face. The position of the head does not change during the anchor. It remains turned to look over the shoulder at the target. The string hand remains flat and free of tension.

AIM

Aiming is the method used to align the arrow with the target.

Since archery involves propelling a projectile into space, all of the factors which influence the flight of a projectile must be considered. Due to gravity, the arrow will travel in a slight arc. At close distances, the velocity of the arrow is much greater than gravitational acceleration and thus its flight is only slightly arched. However, as the shooting distance increases, the arc in the flight also increases. When shooting great distances such as in clout or flight shooting, the angle of projection should not exceed forty-five degrees.[10] The effect of air resistance should also be considered by the

archer, as this alters the relationship between the archer and the target.[11]

Two popular methods of aiming are the sight method and the pre-draw-gap method. The archer should select the method best suited to his ability and his purpose. Regardless of the method used, the archer should continue to utilize the back muscles to maintain the bend in the bow throughout the aiming procedure. He must hold his position during the aim until his bow arm is relatively steady and he is able to maintain the position of the point of the arrow or the sight pin. To be successful with either aiming method the archer must be consistent in his form.

Bow sight method

A bow sight (fig. 13.19) is a mechanical device which is placed on the back or face of the bow and assists the archer in achieving the proper relationship between arrow and target. A commercial device may be pur-

10. Refer to page 64, chapter four, "Projectiles."
11. Refer to page 42, chapter four, "Motion and Factors Affecting Motion."

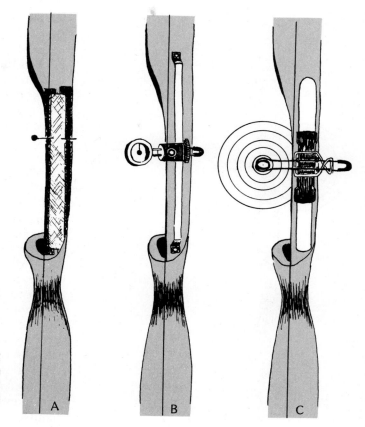

Figure 13.19. **Bow sights. Example C illustrates archer's view of target when sight is properly aligned. Note that string is aligned with the center of the bow.**

A   B   C

chased or a simple sight constructed by inserting a stick pin into adhesive tape placed on the bow. Adjusting the sight assists the archer in compensating for differences due to shooting distance, wind, and gravity.

To facilitate using a sight the archer should be aware of eye dominance. Most archers are right-handed and right-eyed or left-handed and left-eyed, but some are crossed hand-eye dominant, such as right-handed and left-eyed. Unless he is aware of this condition, it becomes difficult for the archer to achieve the proper alignment between target and arrow and the arrow usually flies right or left of the desired mark. To test for eye dominance, the archer should sight the index finger of his dominant hand on a distant object with both eyes open. One eye should then be closed to see if the finger remains pointed on the object. The same procedure is completed with the other eye closed. With the dominant eye open the finger will continue to point at the object. An archer who has crossed hand-eye dominance may continue to shoot with his dominant arm and compensate for this difference in his method of aiming, or if he is a beginner, he may learn to shoot with his non-dominant arm.

In using a bow sight, the sight should extend from the same side of the bow as the

Figure 13.20. **An archer who is right-handed but has a dominant left eye should see the sight pin to the left of the center of the target.**

arrow. The eye closest to the target is closed. (In instances where the archer is crossed hand-eye dominant, the dominant eye may be the eye closed.) The eye farthest from the target is used to align the sight pin with the center of the desired target. The sight pin, rather than the point of the arrow, is used as the basis for the aiming procedure. To compensate for crossed hand-eye dominance, the archer should align the sight with the right or left edge of the center of the target (fig. 13.20).[12] For example, an archer

who is right-handed but has a dominant left eye should align the sight pin with the left edge of the center of the target (the left edge as the archer faces the target). As success in shooting is achieved, the archer marks the desired setting for that particular distance on the sight or on a piece of tape placed on the bow for that purpose.

To approximate where to first set the sight pin the archer should measure the distance between his eye and chin and place the sight pin this distance above the arrow rest.[13] If the sight needs to be adjusted due to incorrect trajectory and/or alignment, the archer should consider the effect that moving the sight has upon the bow. Raising the sight will lower the bow; lowering the sight will raise the bow. Pushing the sight pin closer to the bow for a right-handed archer will move the bow to the left, while extending the sight pin will move the bow to the right.[14] Since arrows which are flying high indicate that the bow is positioned too high in relation to the target, the sight pin must be raised to lower the bow. Likewise, arrows which are traveling to the right for a right-handed archer indicate that the bow is positioned too far to the right. To move the bow to the left, the sight pin is pushed in closer to the bow. To achieve the proper relationship between arrow and target the archer should always *move the sight in the direction of the error.* However, before adjusting a sight the archer should be certain that the sight, rather than his form, is the cause of the difficulty.

12. The distance the sight pin is placed away from the center of the target is dependent upon the archer's vision. For some archers only slight adjustment may be needed. For others it may be necessary to sight the pin further to the right or left of the center of the target.
13. Refer to the indirect lesson on adjusting a sight, page 382.
14. For a left-handed archer, pushing the sight pin closer to the bow will move the bow to the right, while extending the sight pin will move the bow to the left.

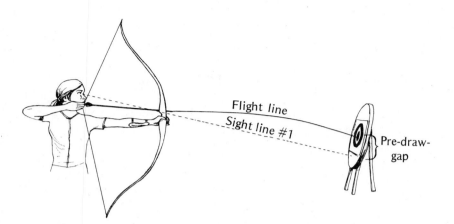

Figure 13.21. **The archer's eye and the point of the arrow are not on the same level which necessitates aiming a certain distance above or below the desired destination of the arrow.**

Pre-draw-gap method

The pre-draw-gap method is an instinctive method of aiming in which the relationship between the arrow and target is estimated by the archer in terms of a certain size gap. In instinctive shooting both eyes are open and used to sight the point of the arrow in relation to the target. Since the archer's eyes are not on the same level with the point of the arrow, the arrow will not travel to the destination sighted except at point-blank range.[15] Thus, a gap exists between the archer's eye and the point of the arrow (fig. 13.21) and necessitates aiming a certain distance above or below the desired destination for the arrow.

Aiming occurs prior to the draw to allow the archer full concentration on the target as he releases. Before drawing the archer sights the point of the arrow on the bottom of the gap. The size of the gap is based upon the archer's distance from the target. For distances of less than thirty yards the size of the gap changes very little. As shooting distance increases beyond thirty yards the size of the gap decreases. For short distances, the gap is sighted below the center of the

target. As the archer moves further from the target, the size of the gap decreases until at point-blank range the archer aims directly in the center of the target. For distances beyond point-blank range the gap extends above the center of the target. Thus, aiming is a process of determining the proper size of the gap for any specific shooting distance.[16]

Once the archer has sighted the point of the arrow on the bottom of the gap, his eyes shift to the center of the target, he draws to high anchor, and releases (fig. 13.22). The archer must be careful not to change the position of his bow arm after aiming has been completed.

Arrows that are landing above or below the center of the target indicate an incorrect gap. A gap that has been sighted below the

15. Point-blank range refers to the shooting distance at which an archer can aim in the center of the target and the arrow will hit the center of the target.
16. For additional information on determining the size of the gap, refer to Marion R. Broer, *Individual Sports for Women*, 5th ed. (Philadelphia: W. B. Saunders Co., 1971), p. 43.

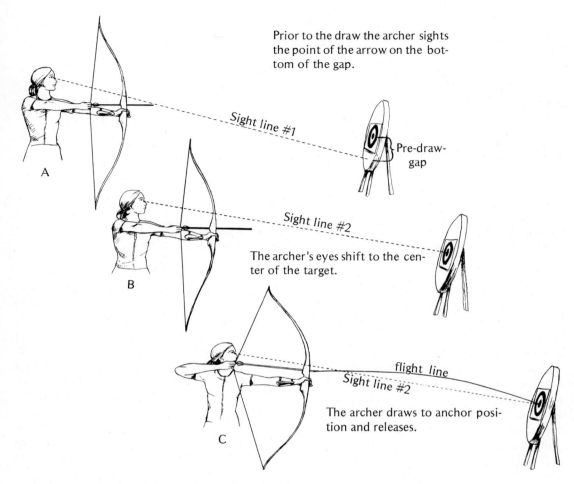

Prior to the draw the archer sights the point of the arrow on the bottom of the gap.

Sight line #1

Pre-draw-gap

A

Sight line #2

The archer's eyes shift to the center of the target.

B

flight line

Sight line #2

The archer draws to anchor position and releases.

C

Figure 13.22. **Pre-draw-gap method of aiming**

center of the target should be decreased in size for arrows flying low, while increased in size for arrows flying high.

RELEASE

The release is the act of letting go of the string, transferring the force of the bow to the arrow. The release should be smooth to allow maximum force to be imparted to the arrow. A live release is desired.

Correct timing of the release is essential if maximum force is to be imparted. The release occurs after the correct spatial arrangement has been achieved between archer and string with a proper anchor, after the arrow has been aligned with the target through aiming, and after the greatest force has been produced by continued contraction of back muscles and a tight anchor. In the release, the fingers of the string hand relax and the string rolls off the fingers. If the archer has maintained a flat string hand and strong contraction of the back muscles, a live release will occur. The string hand will recoil, lightly brushing the archer's neck. This is the string-hand follow-through, an unconscious reaction to the release of the string (fig. 13.23). The bow hand remains relaxed with the bow at the draw level and reacting naturally.

AFTER–HOLD

The after-hold is the final step in the shooting sequence. Following the release of the arrow the archer holds his position until he has had time to analyze his form. The archer should analyze form in terms of the concepts basic to archery.

Space

The proper spatial relationship should be achieved between archer, bow, arrow, and target.

1. The archer should have good posture, with feet, hips, and shoulders in line with the target.

2. The string hand should remain at the archer's neck, indicating a proper anchor and release.

3. The eye closest to the target remains closed if target archery technique is used.

4. The bow arm should remain at the proper level in relation to the target.

Force

The bow is bent to the greatest degree which is both efficient and safe.

1. The bow arm should be fully extended toward the target.

2. The archer should feel the contraction of the back muscles throughout the shooting sequence.

Figure 13.23. **String-hand follow-through**

3. The archer should also feel the string pressed tightly against the anchor point, indicating a full draw.

4. The archer's string hand should finish touching his neck, indicating a live release. This is an unconscious rather than a forced action.

The proper muscles must be used in the shooting sequence.

1. The archer's stance is relaxed, the shoulders down and back.

2. Tension should be felt primarily in the back muscles.

3. The string hand is kept flat and free of tension.

Precision

1. Total concentration must be devoted to the shot.

2. The archer should be able to duplicate his exact actions with each succeeding shot.

COMMON PROBLEMS

Several problems may appear as the archer strives to have all arrows hit the center of the target. If arrows are not reaching the desired destination, the archer must re-evaluate his actions to discover the fundamental space, force, and precision concepts which have been violated.[17]

Space

A proper spatial relationship must be achieved among archer, bow, arrow, and target.

1. Nock: Incorrect placement of the nock of the arrow in relation to the bowstring will affect the flight of the arrow. Nocking too low sends the arrow high. Nocking too high sends the arrow low.

2. Grip: Pinching the arrow nock or an incorrect spacing of the string fingers, causing pressure to be exerted against the nock of the arrow, will cause the arrow to fall off the arrow rest. Failure to keep the string equally aligned on all three string fingers (and particularly allowing the string to slip off the third finger) will send the arrow high.

3. Anchor: Failure to achieve the proper relationship between string hand and face will alter the flight of the arrow. The archer should feel the index finger of the string hand against the cheek or under the chin, depending upon the anchor used. Opening the mouth when anchoring changes the position of the string hand. In target archery this lowers the anchor point, causing the arrow to fly high.

4. Aim: Faulty alignment may be due to an incorrect sight setting or gap size. Factors such as wind resistance and eye dominance should also be considered when aiming. Adjustment should be made in the sight setting or placement of the gap.

Force

Force increases as the bow is bent to the greatest degree which is efficient and safe. Arrows flying low may be indicative of insufficient force production caused by a failure to achieve or maintain sufficient bend in the bow.

1. Draw: Failure to utilize a full draw prevents the string from being drawn to anchor position and reduces the bend in the bow. A flexed position of the bow arm prevents the archer from gaining the greatest bend in the bow.

2. Anchor: Failure to maintain strong contraction of the back muscles until the release prevents a tight anchor and allows forward movement of the string hand, thereby reducing the bend in the bow.

3. Release: Failure to utilize a live release indicates that maximum force was not imparted to the arrow.

Only the muscles which increase the efficiency of the shooting procedure should be utilized in the production of force. Unnecessary use of muscles decreases the efficiency of the shooting process, tires the archer, and often causes directional errors in the flight of the arrow.

1. A hyperextended bow-arm position causes arrows to fly left and often results in a string bruise on the bow arm.

2. Incorrect use of the shoulder muscles as indicated by a hunching of the bow-arm shoulder results in arrow flight to the left and often results in the string contacting the shoulder. The shoulders should be drawn down and back to facilitate use of the back muscles.

3. Tension in the string hand results in plucking the string or throwing the string fingers out from the anchor position. The string hand should remain flat and the wrist

17. It is not the intention of this text to identify the cause and correction for each of the problems possible. Rather, it is desired that the reader recognize the relationship between problems experienced and the fundamental space, force, and precision concepts which have been violated. For a detailed discussion of specific errors, their causes and corrections, the reader is referred to the references listed at the end of the chapter.

straight throughout the entire shooting sequence.

4. Jerking the string hand back before the release sends the arrow high. The string hand should be free of tension and the follow-through should be a natural rather than forced movement.

Precision

The archer must be able to duplicate his exact actions with each arrow shot. Scattering arrows over the target indicates inconsistency in the shooting technique. Arrows that are grouped in close proximity indicate consistency in form.

SUGGESTIONS FOR INCREASING THE EFFECTIVENESS OF INSTRUCTION

If archery is to foster involvement satisfaction and challenge, the learning experience must be one which is stimulating, rewarding, and affords opportunity for success. The archer should experience success in his execution of the shooting fundamentals; he should understand the concepts basic to archery; but possibly most important, he should develop a positive attitude toward archery. The activity should provide personal satisfaction and a challenge appropriate to his abilities. In planning the learning situation the instructor should strive to meet the needs of the individuals within the class and to foster a favorable learning climate. The suggestions which follow should serve only as a guide for the reader in his endeavor to provide a meaningful and pleasurable learning experience.[18]

The instructor should:

1. Prepare the bows for use. The bows should be braced before class starts for the first few periods of shooting. This will allow more shooting time during the class and more time for the instructor to give individual help.

2. Provide a safe learning environment. The bowstring must be prevented from bruising the archer's bow arm from the first arrow released to the last. A bruise on the arm can also bruise feelings toward archery. It is possible to purchase or make an extended arm guard which gives protection from the forearm to above the elbow.

3. Provide the opportunity to quickly experience success. Beginners should be placed close to the target as they release their first arrows. A ten- to twenty-foot shooting distance, depending upon the size of the target, will allow archers of all ages to experience success.

4. Provide a challenge suitable to each individual. Where facilities and equipment allow, target face size and shooting distances should be varied to provide a challenge suitable to the skill levels within the class. If moveable targets are used, they can be arranged at different distances with all class members utilizing the same shooting line (fig. 13.24). Commercial target archery faces range in size from sixteen inches to forty-eight inches. Several different sizes can be used to challenge both the highly and less skilled.

5. Involve students in the decision-making process. Students should be given the freedom to set their own goals according to their interest. For example, instead of all competing in a tournament, some may prefer to continue to perfect form or to learn a different archery event such as field archery. It is possible to have individual practice, instruction in field technique, and a tournament occurring simultaneously.

18. Ideas taken from this material also appear in an article written by one of the authors (Bonnie Neuman, "An Individualized Approach to Archery Instruction," D.G.W.S. *Archery-Riding Guide*, Washington, D.C.: American Association for Health, Physical Education & Recreation, 1972, pp. 52–57).

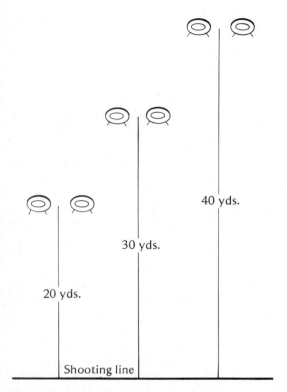

40 yds.

30 yds.

20 yds.

Shooting line

Figure 13.24. **Target arrangement for a class situation with individuals of differing abilities**

6. Allow for students to be actively involved throughout the class period. Reciprocal teaching provides for such involvement. Students work in partners. Instructions should be directed to the partner who assists the archer as observer, corrector, and reinforcer.

Use of the partners arrangement provides immediate feedback for the archer. An alert partner can detect an error and help the archer to eliminate it. It is not necessary to wait until the instructor is free to observe and assist each archer. As he works with an archer, observing and correcting weaknesses, the partner's own understandings of archery are enhanced.

To be successful, emphasis must be placed upon the partner rather than the archer; the partner should be made aware of what to look for and how to correct common problems which may occur. The partner is given a specific focus. For example, he may concentrate on the archer's anchor position for several ends of arrows, assuring that a correct, tight anchor is used prior to release. It may be necessary for him just to reinforce that the anchor is correct, or he may need to increase the archer's awareness of a flaw in performance. The instructor is then free to move among the partners, giving assistance as needed to each partner, who in turn helps the archer. The instructor must continually provide direction for the partner; explain, and re-explain items to observe; and comment upon the success of the partner.

As students increase in their abilities to observe and correct, the responsibilities given may increase in complexity. Partners may be given a skill card to complete. A skill card pertaining to the essentials in the shooting sequence can be used to focus attention on problems in performance and to note improvement (fig. 13.25).

7. Use an individual skill card to allow students to progress at their own rate and to measure their own improvement.[19] The items listed on the skill card should correspond with the focus for the class. A sample skill card has been shown in Figure 13.26.

8. Increase understandings through an indirect approach to archery instruction. The student is provided with problems to explore. Due to the nature of archery it is essential that the problems can be solved while adhering to safety regulations. Within the limitations imposed by safety, the student can explore the concepts related to archery to increase his awareness and understanding of the "why" behind the actions he

19. Refer to page 35, chapter 3.

TARGET ARCHERY FORM EVALUATION

Archer: _____   Evaluator: _____

Directions: Indicate with a plus (+) each step correctly executed. Indicate with a minus (−) each error in form and describe the error in the comments column.

	Date / / / / /					Comments

Stance
    Proper body alignment with target
    Good posture						

Nock Arrow directly below nocking point						

Draw
    Use of back muscles
    String hand flat
    Full draw achieved						

Anchor
    Consistent
    Tight
    Index finger under chin; string bi-
        sects nose and chin						

Aim
    Eye closest to target closed
    Position held until bow arm is steady						

Release
    Live release
    Fingers void of tension						

After-hold Archer analyzes before relaxing						

Figure 13.25

INDIVIDUAL SKILL CARD—TARGET ARCHERY

Name _____

Directions: Record the date you were first able to complete each of the items below for one end of arrows. If you were able to complete the item for more than one end of arrows, record the number of ends in the adjacent column. When items one and two have been completed, move to the long shooting distance.

		Date Completed	Number of Ends
Short Distance[1]	1. Three arrows grouped on target face.[2]		
	2. All arrows hit scoring area.		
Long Distance	3. Three arrows grouped on target face.		
	4. All arrows hit scoring area.		
	5. All arrows land on or within black ring.		
	6. All arrows land on or within blue ring.		
	7. All arrows grouped on target face.		
	8. All arrows land within red or gold rings.		

[1]The lengths of the shooting distances should be decided by the instructor. Refer to numbers 3 and 4 (p. 379).

[2]The proximity of arrows needed for a grouping may be decided by the class or the instructor. One measure might be the ability of the archer to place both hands around the arrows.

Figure 13.26

is performing. The mechanics of a bow sight and the production of force (as examples which follow) are just two of the many areas which can be explored by the student with the guidance of the instructor. For the experience to be meaningful, the questions to be explored must be probing.

EXPLORATION OF THE MECHANICS OF USING A BOW SIGHT

Understandings developed

The student should understand: (1) the effect that moving the sight pin has upon the position of the bow; (2) the mechanics of adjusting a sight.

Previous progress of students

Students have practiced all of the fundamentals in the shooting sequence. Sight settings have been approximated by measuring the distance between the eye and the chin and setting the sight this distance above the arrow rest. The focus of previous lessons has been on achieving a grouping of arrows rather than on hitting any specific part of the target.

Technique of organization

Students work in partners. Each student is given written directions.

Time needed will vary from approximately ten to twenty minutes, depending upon the individuals within the class. Class time is minimized as the second problem is completed outside of class after fundamental understandings have been gained. Suffi-

cient time should be provided to allow each student to proceed at his own rate. As students finish the first problem, they should begin to shoot while others continue to work on the problem.

WRITTEN INFORMATION FOR STUDENTS

Several methods of aiming may be used by an archer. In class, when shooting target archery, we shall concentrate on aiming with the use of a sight. As we shoot at different distances we shall find the best sight setting for each distance, and mark it on the tape near the sight. Then as we change shooting distances it is only necessary to move the sight to the predetermined point, rather than to experiment each time to find the best setting.

The sight pin or the circle end of the mechanical sight should extend from the same side of the bow as the arrow.

Indicate whether you are a right- or left-handed archer: _____

Directions: One partner observes as the other partner performs the following. Then change places so that the observer becomes the archer and complete the actions a second time.

I. The effect that moving a sight pin has upon the position of the bow.
   A. Place the sight pin approximately three inches above the arrow rest. (If you are right-handed, the sight pin should extend from the left side of the bow as it is held in draw position. If you are left-handed, it should extend from the right side.) Sight so that the sight pin is in the gold of the target.
   B. Maintain this bow-arm position while your partner *lowers* the sight pin one inch. Now focus the sight pin in the gold.

   Discovery: When the sight pin is lowered, the bow is _____ .

   C. Place the sight pin two inches above the arrow rest. Sight so that the sight pin is in the gold of the target.
   D. Maintain this bow-arm position while your partner *raises* the sight pin one inch. Now focus the sight pin in the gold.

   Discovery: When the sight pin is raised, the bow is _____ .

   E. Place the sight pin so that it extends ½ inch from the bow. Sight so that the sight pin is in the gold of the target.

F. Maintain this position while your partner pushes the sight pin so that it barely extends from the bow. Now focus the sight pin in the gold.

Discovery: When the sight pin is pushed in so that it is closer to the bow, the bow is moved _____ .

G. Place the sight pin so that it extends ½ inch from the bow. Sight so that the sight pin is in the gold of the target.

H. Maintain this bow-arm position while your partner pulls the sight pin so that it *extends* one inch from the bow. Now focus the sight pin in the gold.

Discovery: When the sight pin is pulled out so that it extends farther from the bow, the bow is moved _____ .

II. Use of a sight pin when shooting at different distances.
   A. As an archer moves farther from the target, his bow must be _____ (raised or lowered) if the arrows are to land in the gold. To cause this action on the bow, the sight pin should be _____ (raised or lowered).
   B. As an archer moves closer to the target, his bow must be _____ (raised or lowered) if the arrows are to land in the gold. To cause this action on the bow, the sight pin should be _____ (raised or lowered).

   Discovery: As an archer moves closer to the target, his sight pin is _____ . As he moves farther from the target, his sight pin is _____ . The degree to which the sight is raised or lowered is dependent upon the size of the distance moved.

III. Adjusting the sight. (Complete the following questions outside of class using the information you have discovered here. Turn in your answers at the beginning of the next class period.)
   A. If an archer achieves a grouping of arrows that is not in the gold, his form is consistent and his sight probably needs to be changed. If an archer's arrows are consistently going low on the target and his form is not at fault, it may be assumed that the position of his bow in relation to the target is at fault.
      1. Is his bow positioned too high, or too low? _____
      2. Should his bow be raised or lowered to correct the problem? _____
      3. What direction should the sight pin be moved to cause the bow to move in the direction you have just indicated? _____
      4. When arrows are going low on the target, the sight pin should be _____ to correct the problem.
      5. Targets *A* and *B* show two different groupings of arrows. For which target would the sight pin have to be moved the greatest amount to correct the problem? _____

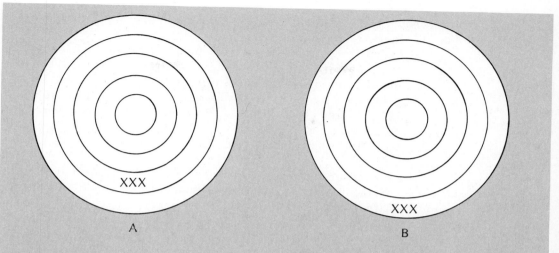

A   B

B. If an archer's arrows are consistently going high on the target and his form is not at fault, it may be assumed that the position of his bow in relation to the target is at fault.
   1. Is his bow positioned too high, or too low? _____
   2. Should his bow be raised or lowered to correct the problem? _____
   3. In what direction should the sight pin be moved to cause the bow to move in the direction you have indicated? _____
   4. When arrows are going high on the target, the sight pin should be _____ to correct the problem. The degree to which the pin is moved depends upon how high above the gold the arrows are landing.

C. If an archer's arrows are consistently going to the left of the gold and his form is not at fault, it may be assumed that the position of his bow in relation to the target is at fault.
   1. Is his bow positioned too far to the right or too far to the left? _____
   2. Should his bow be moved to the right or to the left to correct the problem? _____
   3. In what direction should the sight pin be moved to cause the bow to move in the direction you have indicated? _____
   4. When arrows are going to the left of the gold, the sight pin should be _____ to correct the problem. The degree to which the pin is moved depends upon how far to the left the arrows are landing.

D. If an archer's arrows are consistently going to the right of the gold and his form is not at fault, it may be assumed that the position of his bow in relation to the target is at fault.
   1. Is his bow positioned too far to the right or too far to the left? _____
   2. Should his bow be moved to the right or to the left to correct the problem? _____

3. In what direction should the sight pin be moved to cause the bow to move in the direction you have indicated? _____

4. When arrows are going to the right of the target, the sight pin should be _____ to correct the problem. The degree to which the pin is moved depends upon how far to the right the arrows are landing.

E. In summarizing the preceding, we have found that when arrows are going high, the sight pin should be _____ ; when the arrows are going low, it should be _____ ; when arrows are going to the left it should be _____ ; and when arrows are going to the right it should be _____ .

Summarize how a sight setting is corrected. You should be able to do this in *one sentence*. Remember that a sight setting should be corrected only after a grouping of arrows has been achieved.

Discovery: _____

_____

_____

_____

FORCE PRODUCTION AND THE FLIGHT OF AN ARROW

Understandings developed

The student should understand: (1) the effect that the degree to which the bow is bent has upon the force imparted to an arrow; (2) the effect of a full draw upon the force imparted to an arrow; (3) the execution of a live release and its effect on the force produced.

Previous progress of students

Students have practiced all of the fundamentals in the shooting sequence. Focus on previous lessons has been upon anchor position, use of back muscles, and the mechanics of a bow sight.

Technique of organization

Students work in partners. Each student is given written directions.

Class time required to complete problems

Depending upon the skill of the students, approximately forty to sixty minutes of class time is needed. Provisions should be made to allow students who complete the problems to practice while others finish the problems.

Safety

All students assume the same shooting line, shoot, and then retrieve as a group.

WRITTEN INFORMATION FOR STUDENTS

The flight of an arrow is dependent upon both internal force (supplied by the contraction of the archer's muscles and external force (such as gravity and air resistance).

Internal force is the force produced by the archer through muscular contraction. Through the contraction of the muscles (primarily the upper back muscles—rhomboids and trapezius) the archer bends the bow. As the bow string is released, the energy of the bow is transmitted to the arrow to propel it into space.

Directions:

1. Work with a partner. One partner observes as the other partner completes sections IA–ID. Then change places so that the observer becomes the archer and completes IA–ID a second time. Follow this procedure in completing all problems. Do *not* change the position of your sight during the completion of the problems.

2. Be sure that all comments pertaining to the archer's form are marked on the *archer's sheet.*

3. If at any time your results to the problems do not appear to be logical, indicate your results, identify what you feel should have occurred, and explain the possible causes for the difference.

I. Determining the effect that the degree to which the bow is bent has upon the force imparted to the arrow.

A. Shoot at the same distance you have been shooting. Do not change your sight setting for any of the items which follow.

B. Shoot three arrows using correct form. Continue to shoot three arrows until your partner indicates that the proper form has been used. Do *not* attempt item C until your partner's approval has been received.

Partner: Check the following items when each has been completed for three consecutive arrows.

———1. Draw. (Upper back muscles are used to the fullest. If in doubt, place a hand between archer's shoulder blades as he draws.)

Comments:

———2. Anchor:
   a. The index finger of string hand is directly under his chin.
   b. The string *touches* the center of his nose and chin.
   c. The string hand is flat, void of tension. (The archer should present a straight line from the joint of the fingers to the elbow. Be sure that neither wrist nor knuckles are bent.)

Comments:

_____3. Aim. (The eye closest to the target is closed.)

_____4. Release. (The fingers of the string hand are relaxed; the string rolls off the fingers.)

Comments:

_____5. After-hold. (The archer holds and analyzes his form.)

C. On the target to the right, mark with an X the placement of the three arrows just shot.

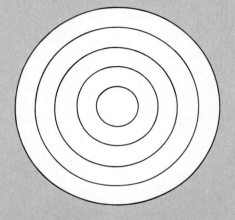

1. Was the archer's form consistent?
2. How do you know?

D. For the next three arrows to be shot, adjust the position of your anchor so that the *wrist* of the string hand rather than the index finger is under the chin. The fingers should extend forward from the chin and the string should not touch the chin but be several inches in front of it.

Partner: It is essential that you check that the anchor described is used and that the form used is consistent with that for the first three arrows. Have the archer shoot until this is accomplished and then check the spaces which follow.

_____1. Form is consistent with the first three arrows except for anchor. (If form is not consistent, you will have difficulty answering the following questions.)

_____2. The wrist rather than the index finger is under the chin for anchor.

E. On the target shown (IC) mark with a zero (0) the position of the three arrows just shot.

1. Did the first three arrows (X) or the last three arrows (0) land higher on the target? _____

2. Was the bow bent to a greater or lesser extent when shooting the arrows that landed higher on the target? (It may be necessary for you to repeat steps IA–ID with your partner, concentrating on the degree to which the bow is bent.) _____

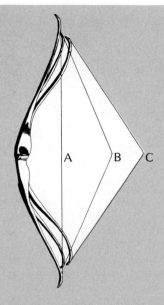

3. Which letter shown indicates the draw which would produce the most force? _____

Discovery: The force imparted to an arrow increases as the bow is bent to a _____ (lesser or greater) extent. Remember it is not safe to bend the bow to the extent that the arrow is overdrawn.

If you believe that your form was not consistent and the previous answers are not accurate, identify what you believe should have occurred.

II. Determining the effect that a full draw has upon the force imparted to an arrow.
   A. Continue shooting at the same distance. Do *not* change your sight for any of the items which follow.
   B. Shoot three arrows using correct form. Have your partner indicate here that proper form was used. Partners should refer to the characteristics listed previously.
   _____ Draw
   _____ Anchor
   _____ Aim
   _____ Release
   _____ After-hold

C. On the target shown, mark the placement of these arrows with an X.

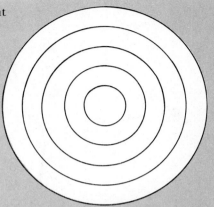

D. For the next three arrows to be shot, concentrate on maintaining a strong contraction of the back muscles until the arrow hits the target.
   1. The archer continues to use the back muscles to keep the string tight against his nose and chin during the aiming process. Until the release he feels as if he is drawing the string through his chin.

      Partner: Be sure that archer does not overdraw. It is essential that the string is drawn to the center of the chin and not overdrawn to the side of the face.

   2. The archer is in a straight line from the elbow of the string hand to the tip of the arrow.
   3. A *string-hand follow-through* occurs naturally after the release if tension in the back muscles was maintained. Following the release the string hand is relaxed and brushes the neck, indicating the use of a *live release*. In a *dead release* the string hand remains at anchor position following the release.
E. On the target shown (IIC) mark the placement of these arrows with a zero (0).

   Partner:
   1. Did the archer maintain strong tension in the back muscles until the arrow hit the target?
      _____a. Was the string kept tight against the face until the release?
      _____b. Was the archer in a straight line from the tip of the arrow to the elbow?
      _____c. Did a string-hand follow-through occur?
   2. Did the archer use a live release or a dead release? How do you know?
F. Did the first three arrows (X) or the second three arrows (0) land higher on the target? _____
   1. Assuming that correct form was used, this indicates that _____ (X arrows or 0 arrows) received the greater force.

2. Since these arrows received the greater force, it can be assumed that the bow was bent to a _____ (lesser or greater) extent when shooting these arrows.

   If no difference was found in the placement of the arrows or if your results do not appear to be logical, indicate what should have occurred and why it did not.

G. We have just learned that the force imparted to an arrow increases as the bow is bent to a _____ (lesser or greater) extent.
   1. Identify the *three* major actions the archer must complete in order to achieve the greatest possible force.

   a. _____

   b. _____

   c. _____

REFERENCES

Barrett, Jean A. *Archery.* 2nd ed. Pacific Palisades, Calif.: Goodyear Publishing Co., 1973.

Broer, Marion R. *Individual Sports for Women.* 5th ed. Philadelphia: W. B. Saunders Co., 1971.

Haugen, Arnold O., and Metcalf, Harlan G. *Field Archery and Bowhunting.* New York: The Ronald Press Co., 1963.

Klann, Margaret L. *Target Archery.* Reading, Mass.: Addison-Wesley Publishing Co., 1970.

McKinney, Wayne C. *Archery.* 3d ed. Dubuque, Iowa: Wm. C. Brown Company Publishers, 1975.

Miller, Myrtle K. *Archery Training Guide.* Teela Wooket Archery Camp, 1968.

National Archery Association. *The Archer's Handbook: United States, International and Olympic Archery.* Lancaster, Penn.: The Association (1951 Geraldson Dr.), current edition.

National Association for Girls and Women in Sport. *Archery-Fencing Guide,* Washington, D.C.: American Alliance for Health, Physical Education, and Recreation. (Current edition).

Pszczola, Lorraine. *Archery.* 2nd ed. Philadelphia: W. B. Saunders Co., 1976.

Smith, Julian W. *Archery: A Planning Guide for Group and Individual Instruction.* Washington, D.C.: American Association for Health, Physical Education & Recreation, 1975.

14

Golf

INTRODUCTION

Golf is one of America's most popular sports and fortunately it can be enjoyed throughout a lifetime by everyone. Learning the skills early and understanding the movement principles that are basic to building an effective swing may pay rich dividends to the golfer.

A golf swing can be analyzed to the point that the complexity would confuse most beginners; however, all students of golf should understand a few basic concepts that account for the mechanics of a personalized swing. An educated golf swing becomes the basis for meaning.

Golf is a swinging game and therein lies its attraction, for each player must build a swing that is unique to him. Each time a player swings a club, he tries to make it as near perfect as possible so that he can reach the desired target. Becoming *swing* conscious and not ball conscious is the first step toward becoming successful at golf.

Golf is a game of mechanical principles based on cause and effect, for the swing is based on scientific laws of physics that control the path and trajectory of the ball. Speed, accuracy and distance become the major objectives in golf, all of which are based on a complete understanding of why and how the body moves.

Golf is a game of squares. The square-to-square method of swinging a golf club has evolved as the simplest, most effective method yet devised to make the best use of the improved golf equipment today. It is a transition from a throwing swing to a pulling swing and is a result of the introduction of less flexible steel shafts. Steel shafts require a different type of swing in order to develop greater speed while increasing accuracy.

The fundamental concept of the square-to-square method is that a square club face at impact looks down the target line and delivers a drive that flies straight. The square club face at address and the square club head at impact supply the name for the square-to-square method. This author recommends the square-to-square method as the most logical, sound method of teaching golf to beginners.

Basically what the square-to-square method involves is: a grip that places the thumb of the target hand, the left hand, on top of the handle, or at a one o'clock position; a straight-line relationship between the back of the left hand, wrist and lower forearm; a maintenance of this position at address, takeaway, top of the backswing, downswing and at impact; no additional manipulation of wrists or hands; a more upright plane for the swing; a full shoulder turn and minimal hip turn; a downswing led by dynamic pulling of the legs and lower body; a square club face at impact and into the follow-through.

After the basic swinging sensation is appreciated by the beginner, he is ready to learn golf by the square-to-square method.

Golf is a game of kinesthetic awareness; for every stroke, whether the stroke is a wood or an iron shot, it has its own sense of feel and timing. Each body segment involved in the golf swing *feels* the sensation of movement; feedback from that sensory information dictates the swing. Consciousness of muscular movement should be developed into a keen sense. Each time a player makes the conscious mental effort to feel the handle of the club swinging, he is developing a sense of swing through feeling and thinking. Swinging the top of the club with the forearms prevents overuse of the wrists and hands.

Golf is a mental game that demands the power of concentration—keeping the head still, keeping the knees easy are essential. Research *has* demonstrated that mental

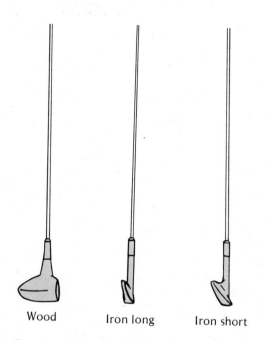

| Wood | Iron long | Iron short |

Figure 14.1. **Angle of clubs**

learning is effective in golf. Golfers should *think* swing, not imitate it unconsciously.

Golf is a game of angles, since each club is engineered so that the face of the club delivers a trajectory path suited to reaching the specific distance desired (fig. 14.1).

Golf is an extremely personal game, for form is an individual matter. Movement patterns based on mechanical, anatomical and kinesiological evidence are essential, but the style of form will be unique to each player. The skill of each student is determined by physical characteristics, motor abilities, physiological components of fitness, perceptual abilities and his emotional makeup. It is difficult to put people into a mold when teaching golf skills. The rate of learning is personal and different for each individual. Telling a beginner to imitate a golf pro's swing is probably a very poor teaching

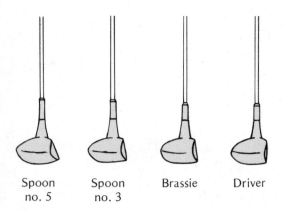

| Spoon
no. 5 | Spoon
no. 3 | Brassie | Driver |

Figure 14.2. **Set of woods**

technique. Demonstrations might prove helpful, but of more importance is the development of each individual's kinesthetic awareness of how a golf swing feels to him. The golf swing is rhythmical and is based upon good sequential timing. The smooth swing that is relaxed and yet hits the ball a "country mile" is the dream of every golfer. Tension and stress seem to have an adverse effect that ruins the sequential timing of the effective golf swing.

Golf is a game that uses unique equipment. The names of the clubs are unique; the woods are called driver (number one wood), brassie (number two wood), and spoon (numbers three and four woods). Some clubs are made of well-seasoned persimmon wood and some are made of iron. The woods are longer and have various sizes of heads—hence their various names. The length of a wood is from forty-one to forty-three inches; it can weigh twelve to sixteen ounces. Weight is important and should be fitted to the player's swing. A matched set of clubs is one in which every club has approximately the same swinging weight. A matched set of woods satisfies the angle needs for all distances (fig. 14.2).

Golf is a game in which the low score wins. Par is the standard of excellence determined for each hole and representing perfect play. Par for men and women is different.

Men: up to 250 yards, par 3
251–450 yards, par 4
451–600 yards, par 5
601 yards and over, par 6

Women: up to 210 yards, par 3
211–400 yards, par 4
401–575 yards, par 5
576 yards and over, par 6

One stroke over par is called a *bogie.* One stroke under par is called a *birdie.* Two strokes under par is called an *eagle.*

Score cards show the number of the hole, the yardage, the par and then reserve a place for the player's score. Handicap scores based on the difficulty of each hole are shown on the right side of the score card. The first handicap hole is the most difficult to par, so players would receive strokes on that hole first.

Handicap is a figure determined by a percentage of the difference between par and the player's average score. For example, *A* has a handicap of six; *B* has a handicap of nine. In a match, *A* would receive three strokes from *B,* one *stroke* on the hole listed with 1 in the handicap column, one stroke on the hole with 2 in the handicap column, and one stroke on the hole with 3 in the handicap column.

Golf is an outdoor game played on a large acreage specifically designed as a golf course.

Beginners should be helped to appreciate and respect the investment that owners and players have in a golf course. Each player owns part of the great out-of-doors while he is playing on a golf course. Each course is designed with a different pattern in the arrangement of the holes, but the enormous care of courses is the same. The fairway, greens, rough, water and sand hazards require constant attention. Each player should acquaint himself with the basic rules of the golf course.

Most golf courses consist of a total of eighteen holes. The first nine, or front nine, is referred to as "going out" and the second nine is the back nine or "coming in." Some courses have only nine holes instead of eighteen. In this case the nine holes are played twice, since eighteen holes comprise a regulation game of golf.

Most courses range from 5,000 yards to 7,200 yards when the yardage for all holes is totaled. Par is usually about 72. Most courses that are regulation courses of eighteen holes have four 3-par holes, four 5-par holes, and the rest are 4-par holes. The golf course is designed in such a manner that successive congestion is avoided at any of the holes.

Golf is a game of etiquette, sportsmanship and, courtesy. Before any player steps foot on a golf course, he should become acquainted with basic rules concerning the tee, fairway and green.

FAIRWAY ETIQUETTE AND RULES

1. As the players walk up the fairway, the first ball they meet should be played as the next shot. A person is said to be "away" when his shot is farthest from the pin.

2. Other players stop and remain still while a player hits his ball.

3. If a ball is lost, the player takes his shot from a spot as close as possible to the spot where the ball was lost and adds one penalty stroke to his score.

4. A ball that goes out of bounds adds penalty for stroke and distance. A stroke is added for bringing it in from out of bounds and dropping it in bounds. Another stroke is added when it is hit.

5. In order to avoid delay, players who are slow or who are hunting balls should wave the following foursome through.

6. All players must be off the green before another player takes an approach shot.

7. A player should call out "Fore!" if the ball looks as if it might hit another player.

8. A player should replace all divots carefully so the grass will not be destroyed.

GREENS ETIQUETTE AND RULES

1. Placing golf bags on the side towards the next tee avoids walking across the green following play, enabling the next foursome to approach immediately.

2. The flag is placed, not dropped, off the edge of the green.

3. All marks left by the ball shoul be repaired. The green should be left smooth by each foursome.

4. The ball farthest from the cup is always played first.

5. Players should never stand or walk across the line of flight of a ball; cleat marks can spoil a putt. It is courteous to step across the line of flight. A player should avoid casting shadows, as they can be disturbing to others.

6. A player may pick up any loose debris between his ball and the cup, but he may not press, smooth or push the ground to improve a line of flight.

7. The first player to hole his ball should be the one to go pick up the flag, hold it low, and place it back in the cup as soon as the last player sinks his putt. Replacing the flag becomes the signal to the next foursome to approach.

8. Players should leave the green immediately and go to the next tee to discuss their scores, etc.

MAJOR CONCEPTS

The student must develop early a concept of the full golf swing, which resembles all other swinging movements in sports. Word concepts that convey the meaning of the swinging action are arc, circle, plane, square-to-square, timing, and sequential body movement.

The golf swing is an action one feels; it is movement with meaning when feeling and thinking produce a swing that is mechanically correct and when the ball hits the target. The word "target" is not used nearly often enough when teaching golf. For years teachers have been telling the player to watch the ball; this puts too much emphasis and concentration on the ball. Instead of thinking of the ball, a player should think of the target where the ball must go. Good players actually see the ball in flight toward the target and this seems to help them swing more smoothly through the ball.

Introduction to the square-to-square method and concepts provides the basic fundamentals necessary for the development of an effective golf swing.

The square-to-square relationship is a simple one, for fewer body parts are moving, thus providing less chance for error. The hands and club head as a unit move into the proper position for a powerful, square impact. The club head faces the intended line to the target squarely; it moves along the target line over a greater distance. This method emphasizes and generates a strong left side in not allowing the right side to take over and dissipate club head speed before impact.

The square-to-square method provides greatest control because there is less manipulation of the club with the hands and wrist. The hands, wrists, and forearms act as a unit.

The descriptions of the golf swing in this chapter refer to the square-to-square method of instruction since it is the most feasible method to teach to beginners.

CONCEPT C. A player must be in a desirable position in relation to the object to be projected.

Preparation for the golf swing starts when all body parts are mechanically ready in the address position. The alignment and posture of the body at address directly determines how the golfer swings the club.

The following five sub-concepts are unique to golf and are included in order to clarify the position of all body parts. These sub-concepts are not discussed in chapter five.

Sub-concept. Hands: Because the hands supply the only contact with the club, the force and speed built up in the body flow through the hands to the club.

The anatomical structure of the hands, their size and strength, oftentimes dictates the grip that will be used to grasp the club.

The major goal of the square-to-square swing is to position the club head to the ball so that the impact is absolutely square; the club head should be looking down the target line in a square position. If the club head is facing either to the right or left, the shot will *not reach the desired target.*

The grip must allow the back of the left hand, wrist and lower forearm to face down the intended target line during impact; they also must be positioned squarely to the target.

The grip must enable the player to swing the club head quickly through the ball. The grip encourages a player to swing on a relatively upright plane. It must prevent a fanning open of the club face. Finally, the grip must allow a firm hold for control of the club throughout the swing.

Figure 14.3. **Grips**

Three grips are recommended by golf professionals and teachers to accommodate differences in structure of hands, the only variance being the placement of the little finger of the right hand (fig. 14.3).

The overlap grip is the most acceptable because the hands work closer together as a unit and there is greater sensitivity to feeling the club. The position of the thumb is important, as is the position of the last three fingers of the left hand, where grip pressure is felt. Pressure with the thumb and forefinger of the left hand and all fingers of the right hand should be only firm enough to avoid letting the club slip. Tension should be felt in the muscles of the underside of the left arm (fig. 14.4).

Each player should become extremely perceptive of the *appearance* of his hands on the shaft rather than the feel of the position, as the feel is awkward at first to most people.

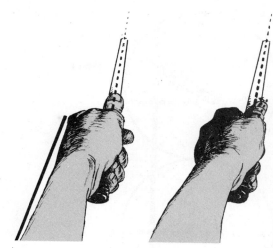

Figure 14.4. **Positions of left hand**

Sub-concept. Feet: The stance forms the stable, balanced foundation which allows good body movement.

The feet are placed so that a line can be drawn across the toes and point in the direction of the target (fig. 14.5).

Most golfers prefer a square stance, for it is a natural position, and if the stance is changed, it should be a slight change. The square-to-square method emphasizes a square right foot and the target foot toeing out slightly to a two o'clock position.

The width between the feet can vary with the personal desires of the golfer and to fit the purpose of the swing. In long drives for maximum distance, the feet should be placed shoulder-width apart to allow for a solid base that will help the body to maintain balance in a wide arc swing. If the shot requires short distance, a narrow stance is all that is necessary.

Placement of the ball should fit the swing pattern and since the center of the arc of the swing is approximately opposite the left foot, that is where the ball should be placed.

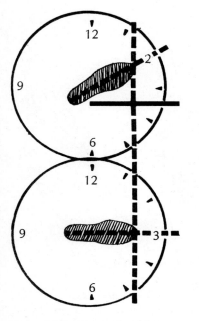

Figure 14.5. **Stance for drive**

The weight of the body has already shifted to the left foot by the time of contact.

Most golfers place the ball opposite the inside of the left heel for almost all shots. For iron shots the stance is narrowed, and the arc of the swing will naturally fall closer to the center.

Sub-concept. Body Position: In the address position the body must be balanced, allow freedom of movement of the hands and arms, and be free of tension and muscle tightness.

The knees should be easy or slightly flexed, lowering the center of gravity over a stable base of support in readiness for engaging the powerful muscles of the legs and hips. The address position must allow for a balanced swing in a sufficiently upright plane to maintain the square impact (fig. 14.6).

The golf swing resembles a pendulum and the shoulders and arms must be free to swing. The body must bend forward at the hips to allow the club head to reach the ball. Elbows should point down and in toward the sides, into proper positon for the arms to swing freely in conjunction with the body turn. The back is straight; the shoulder alignment should be square (fig. 14.7). The golf swing then can become a relaxed swinging motion, allowing a full shoulder turn and a minimal hip turn. The modern trend is toward lesser hip turn for more efficient utilization of the tremendous potential power of the body's large muscles.

Sub-concept. The Pelvic Girdle: The center of gravity is located at the pelvis and controls the shift of weight built up during the backswing by the amount of rotation involved.

The rotation of the body or pelvic girdle to the rear foot during the backswing is affected by the amount of rotation involved. Excessive swiveling of the hips tends to cause the shoulders and upper body to swivel also. This forces a flatter swing pattern than is desirable. The square-to-square method encourages the correct setup in relation to the ball and if it is done properly, the hip turn will also be properly executed.

Sub-concept. The Head: The golf swing is a movement around an axis of rotation, the spine, with the head as a pivot point.

The head, when held constant, helps the body to turn around its axis.

CONCEPT D. Creating Force: The production and transfer of force depend upon mass, speed, and the striking surface used.

Sub-concept D-1. Increasing the mass used to produce force increases the force produced.

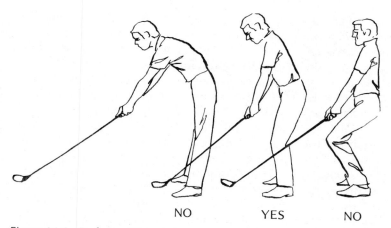

NO   YES   NO

Figure 14.6. **Body position posture**

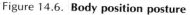

Figure 14.7. **Body position**

Figure 14.8. **Address**

The lower the number of the club used, the larger is the mass, thus producing more force for longer distance shots. The driver (number one wood) has the largest amount of mass.

Sub-concept D-2. Increasing the speed of the implement or the body segment imparting force increases the force produced.

The longer the club, the faster the club head moves, thus imparting additional speed and force.

Sub-concept D-3. Increasing the range of movement of the body segment or the implement imparting force increases the distance through which speed can be developed, as well as the force imparted to the object.

The fuller shoulder turn in the golf swing provides the range of movement necessary to provide force. If the left arm does not remain fairly straight on the backswing, the arms will allow the body to rotate too much. If the club head is allowed to drop below the horizontal line at the top of the backswing, then valuable extra time and energy must be expended to raise the club head against gravity to start the downswing.

In a golf swing, the square position of the hands, wrists and forearms provides the final velocity to the swing. The modern trend in golf instruction is to emphasize swinging the handle of the club with the forearms. The idea of the hands, wrists and forearms forming a unit that moves at one time eliminates opening or closing the club face with the hands and wrists and eliminates throwing the club head into the ground behind the ball or over the top of it with hands and wrists.

Hands and wrists directly influence the club head, either beneficially or adversely. The forearms directly affect the top of the club. Moving them together affects the swing path and the impact.

Whether or not to teach and emphasize cocking the wrists on the backswing is a controversial matter; however, most golf experts have been advocating a square-to-square movement in which, instead of pronating the club face, the left wrist remains square through the ball. Cocking the wrists is not emphasized because there is a tendency for beginners to overswing. Many golf professionals contend that the only type of wrist action needed or desired is that which lifts and lowers the club.

If the grip is proper, a hinging of the wrists will occur at the base of the thumbs, producing wrinkles. This wrist action gives the swing height and leverage and lowers the club head to the ball during the downswing. Modern golf critics say that a backward-forward hinging at the back of the wrists delivers not only a very minimal source of power, it represents the worst feature of the "old" golf swing, misdirecting the head of the club (fig. 14.9). Granted, distance comes from the speed at which the club is moving, but vertical unhinging lowers the club head so that this speed can be applied to the ball. This does not mean that the rolling of the forearms in the downswing is underestimated. The rolling of the arms gradually turns the handle of the club so that the club face squares to the target line during impact and then continues to turn to the left. If the hands and wrists take over from the arms, they independently flip the club head and can distort the square impact.

Jorgensen has found that greatest speed results when the hands are slightly ahead of the still-cocked wrists.[1] When the uncocking catches up with the hands, the club head is moving at its greatest speed.

All the force produced in effective sequential movement transfers *if* the wrists and hands are firm at impact. A firm grip on the club prevents recoil of the club head at the important moment of contact and insures that *all* of the force will be transferred to the ball (fig. 14.10).

The knees, remaining in an easy, slightly flexed position, allow the body to rotate effectively for transfer of weight. If the right knee is stiffened or hyperextended, the entire arc of the swing changes its path. With the knee in a locked position, the transfer of weight, if any, becomes a less efficient movement pattern.

Emphasizing the easy knee position facilitates the left heel remaining on the ground or coming off the ground just slightly. Many golf experts advocate this solid position,

1. Theodore Jorgensen, Jr., "On the Dynamics of the Swing of a Golf Club," *American Journal of Physics* 38 (May 1970):649.

Figure 14.9. **Wrist action**

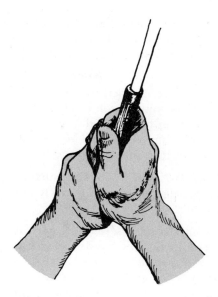

Figure 14.10. **Grip**

with heel remaining on the ground, as more effective for weight transfer. Some professionals maintain that women, in order to gain force, automatically rise up on their toes. Whether the left heel remains on the ground or not is a decision to be made by each individual, according to personal preference.

Sub-concept D-4. Setting the body in motion prior to contact with an object, or to the release of an object, builds greater force which in turn is transferred to the object. However, at the instant of contact or release, the body should be stabilized.

In golf, the movement prior to beginning the backswing, often a small movement, is called the waggle. Moving the forearms and hands behind the club prior to initiating the backswing appears to facilitate the preparatory set in a manner that might reduce tension, increase tension, or help with

alignment, depending on the individual player. Mechanically there is no reason why a waggle is necessary to introduce movement for the backswing, yet the majority of golfers appear to develop their own individualistic waggle.

The soles of golf shoes are equipped with cleats so that a solid base is provided upon which the body rotates. Utilizing Newton's law of action and reaction (see chapter four) there will be a counter-reaction from the ground to supply the force necessary for efficient body movement.

Sub-concept D-5. A follow-through allows for greater force to be transferred to an object.

In golf, the club head follows the swing arc as far as the arms will permit. The body completes its rotation with the left side dominant and a relaxed right side. The head and eyes remain down looking at the spot behind the ball until well after the ball has been contacted.

Sub-concept D-6. Stabilizing the body segments involved in an action allows for greater force to be imparted to the object.

At the moment of contact, the entire left side of the body becomes a solid wall against which the force can be directed. (See Newton's second law, chapter four.) The feet are firmly planted to give support to the body.

Sub-concept D-7. A firm striking surface allows for greater force to be imparted to the object.

Golf grips have been described earlier. At the moment of impact, the hands are as firm as possible. The grip should allow the hands to work together for additional strength.

CONCEPT E. Directing force: The direction in which an object moves is determined by the point at which force is applied in relation to the object's center of gravity.

Sub-concept E-1. Applying force directly through the center of gravity of an object results in a straight trajectory; an off-center application of force produces a curved trajectory.

The law of centrifugal force plays a major role in the downswing to the point of contact and immediately after contact. The force by which a body tends to move outward from the center of a curvature is called centrifugal force. Thus, any object being whirled in a circle and released at some point continues in the direction it was traveling as a tangent of the circle at the point of release.

In golf the club head is swinging about a radius and releases its force at a point on the arc which dictates direction. The objective of the swing is to produce an arc that places the point of contact at a spot where the hands, wrists and forearms are moving in such a way that the ball will take off in the proper direction and allow speed to be fully utilized for desired distance (fig. 14.11).

A ball travels in the direction in which the resultant force is applied. The angle of the face of the club applies force at a point below the horizontal axis in proportion to the degree of loft from the perpendicular. At impact resultant force is a combination of a horizontal force and a vertical force supplied by the face of the club, the point on the arc where impact occurs, and the path of the swing. The club face supplies the loft and the basic swing pattern should not be changed.

The more vertical the club face, the more distance and less height will be obtained; for maximum distance, a vertical club face should be chosen—woods one, two, or three. As less distance and more height are needed, the clubs with open faces should be selected. Harvey states that generally, the lower the ball is contacted, the greater the backspin (fig. 14.12). On clubs with sharper loft the grooves are closer, making contact time less and backspin less.[2]

The path of the club on the downswing helps to determine the direction of the flight of the ball.

For years golf instructors have emphasized a swing that is inside out and have warned against an outside-in swing. This has confused beginners because they have a tendency to exaggerate, producing a hook (a ball that gives curve to the left). The square-to-square concept should ensure the correct swing path. It is wise for an instructor to refer to the line of intended flight (the target line) and then show the influence of the path of the swing in relation to the line

2. T. D. Harvey, "How Spin Controls Flight," *Golfing* 18 (1954):20–23.

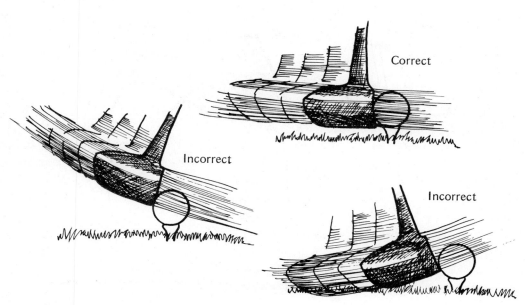

Correct

Incorrect

Incorrect

Figure 14.11. **Resultant force**

of flight. The golf ball will move only in the direction of the club face as it contacts the ball (fig. 14.13).

> **Sub-concept E-2. Keeping one's eyes on the object (i.e., objective focus or tracking) facilitates the application of force in line with the intended direction of flight or the absorption of force when slowing or stopping the object. However, if the performer is throwing at a target, he must focus on the target rather than on the projectile.**

> **Sub-concept E-3. Contacting an object with a large, flat surface facilitates applying force directly through the center of gravity in the direction desired.**

Club head speed *squarely* applied (through the center of gravity) governs distance. This concept is the basis for the square-to-square method.

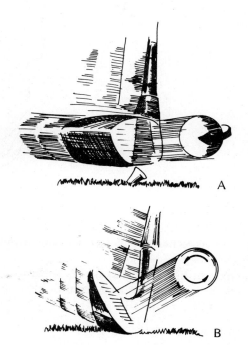

A

B

Figure 14.12. **Ball spin**

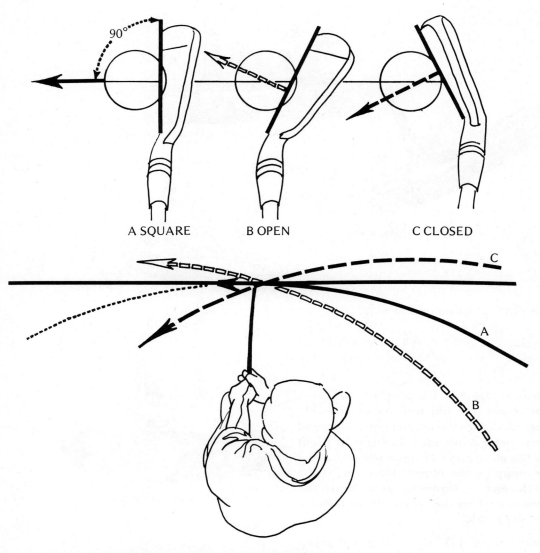

Figure 14.13. **Direction of club face and path of club head**

Sub-concept E-4. External forces such as gravity, air resistance, and friction alter the flight of a projectile.

Air resistance increases rapidly as speed increases, so it can become a factor affecting the flight of the golf ball. Because of the speed and distance desired from a golf shot, the angle of the ball's projection must be much lower than the oft-quoted forty-five-degree angle. The horizontal force should be exaggerated and can overcome any air resistance. Due to the small size of the golf ball, and due to its weight, air resistance usually does not present a major problem unless wind is present.

BASIC GOLF SKILLS

The strokes discussed are the full swing or the drive, the short iron shot, the pitch shot or approach shot, the chip, and the putt.

The Drive

The drive can be analyzed with so much detail that it becomes extremely complex. The elements of space, time, force, flow and body awareness will be used to study the drive in four positions: the takeaway or backswing, the top of the backswing, the downswing into the hitting area, and the follow-through. The address position was described in discussion relating to basic concepts (Concept C and the three sub-concepts following it).

TAKEAWAY

Space

The position of the body and the club head in space during the takeaway or backswing is important. Personal space is the area through which the club head travels in its arc. The path of the club head remains low to the ground, and the left hand and arm push the club head back and out along the portion of the target line that continues behind the ball.

Directions to push or pull the club head back are sometimes used to prevent the pattern of lifting the club straight up. In space, the body moves on planes; for example, it is the turning of the shoulders on a tilted plane (see figure 14.14) that forces the club head to begin moving inside the line and upward. Tilting the shoulders—lowering the left shoulder and the resultant raising of the right shoulder—causes the club head to move. If the club is *lifted*, the right hand and arm will automatically do much of the lifting and will move the club out of the proper

Figure 14.14. **Takeaway**

plane and the left arm will probably bend. The shoulders and arms form a triangle (fig. 14.14) that moves as a unit.

If the shoulders do not tilt, the player may be swaying his upper body laterally away from the target when taking the club straight back. Bending from the waist will prevent swaying and will enable the shoulders to move properly.

Time

The beginning of the backswing is fairly slow and deliberate; too rapid a backswing may throw the golfer off balance.

Force and Flow

The triangle (shoulders, arms and hands) moves back as a unit. A slight squeezing of the last three fingers of the target hand (the left hand) occurs at the very start of the takeaway and it is almost imperceptible. It is this squeezing action, sometimes referred to as "curling under," that contracts the muscles on the underside of the forearm. It is this move that establishes the proper position of the target hand and forearm at takeaway. Curling the fingers under establishes the straight-line square relationship between the back of the left hand and lower forearm and sets up the dominant left side for the remainder of the swing. The curling under of the last three fingers of the target hand can be incorporated into the waggle, the movement of the club head backward and forward behind the ball.

The knees remain slightly flexed to give freedom for the hips to turn. It is absolutely essential that the nontarget knee (the right knee for most golfers) remain flexed, for if it straightens, the hips will swivel into a much fuller turn than is desirable.

The left arm remains firm and extended to give length to the lever.

Body Awareness

The first goal is to feel left-side dominance by feeling the correct muscles contract on the underside of the left forearm when the last three fingers of the left hand are squeezed.

The second goal is to feel the relationship of the back of the left hand and back of the lower forearm. The straight line is continuous with no break at the wrist.

The proper takeaway will not feel natural at first because the normally weak side (the left side) must dominate the usually stronger side. New muscles will be brought into use and some soreness can occur.

TOP OF THE BACKSWING

Space

The arc of the swing should be side, vertical and extended through space, the entire length of the fully extended left arm holding the club.

The club shaft in the square-to-square method should be vertical to the ground. If it becomes horizontal, then the left shoulder has not been properly lowered.

The club head will move inside the target line only as the shoulders begin to turn.

The head occupies the same space as at the address position (fig. 14.15).

Time

An upright swing plane will ease the burden placed on the left side.

The backswing is rather slow and controlled.

There may be a slight hesitation at the top of the backswing.

Force

The shoulders are fully turned; the hips are turned minimally. The ideal minimum hip turn is due largely to retaining a slight bend in the right knee throughout the backswing, thus preventing any swiveling of the hips.

The left wrist should be firm and straight, forming a continuous line between the back of the left hand and lower forearm. The left arm is fully extended and straight.

The weight is transferred, shifted to the nontarget foot with a little weight on the toe or inner border of the target foot. The target foot should remain on the ground, preferably.

The knees remain flexed so that full use can be made of the larger muscles in the back and legs.

Flow

Movement has followed a sequential pattern until the entire backswing position is difficult to maintain because of the strain placed on the left side since the left arm has remained firm and straight.

The line across the shoulders, when fully turned, should point to the ground. If the line points to the ball position, the shoulder turn is superb. Bending at the waist ninety degrees (see fig. 14.16) will allow the shoulder to turn on a sufficiently upright plane.

SQUARE

Figure 14.15. **Top of backswing**

The hip turn is slight and the pelvic girdle remains over the base of support. To check the flow of movement, the player can drop a line from the belt buckle. If it falls outside the feet, he has swayed. If it falls between the feet, he has kept his center of gravity over the base of support and has maintained a balanced backswing.

90°

Figure 14.16. **Angle of body at top of backswing**

Body Awareness

There should be a feeling of a gradual buildup of tension across the back and down the left arm, side and thigh. The left arm should feel the pull of extension. The knees should remain relaxed, flexed and lowered. The right hand and side should feel relaxed, as they were at address.

The head should remain over the center of the spine, which is in the axis. The right elbow is close to the body. Pressure on the inside of the right foot should increase and should not move to the outside of the foot.

The body should feel like a tightly coiled spring that is about to snap. A player must resist the temptation to give in to the muscle tension he is experiencing. He should not collapse the back of the left wrist, loosen the right hand or rush into the downswing.

DOWNSWING INTO HITTING POSITION

Space

The club head moves from its vertical point into a wide, downward arc. The goal is

Figure 14.17. **Downswing** Figure 14.18. **Impact**

to pull the club head down and along the target line for as great a distance as possible in the impact area. As it moves through the impact zone the club face is square to the ball (fig. 14.17).

Time

There is an instinctive reaction of unwinding by letting go of everything into a quick downward movement. First, there is a lateral shifting of the lower left side (below the thigh) to the left. The legs continue to drive forward to the left, pulling the shoulders, arms and club downward. Even though the lower left side starts, the shoulders will unwind almost at the same time. Once the downswing pattern is started, nothing can be altered. There isn't time to reroute the swing.

Force and Flow

The downswing is the unwinding of the body to produce force (fig. 14.18).

A lateral movement of the lower left quadrant puts the downswing into a *pulling* pattern with the lower left side pulling the club. The head and shoulders must not be

allowed to shift laterally. The lateral shift is made with the left knee still flexed and *leading* the left hip. If the hip leads, the leg has a tendency to stiffen, causing the hips to spin instead of shift. Such an action can throw the club head outside the target line.

The left arm should be pulling hard enough to keep the right hand and arm from overpowering the left side.

The left wrist should remain firm, connecting the left hand and forearm in the straight-line impact relationship. The firm impact position should be maintained until *past* impact. The left wrist cannot be allowed to collapse when the resistance of the ball is encountered.

Body Awareness

The golfer feels the pulling of the club down and through to initiate the downswing and then is aware of a firm left wrist.

The player must feel the lateral shifting of the lower left side to the left and the forward drive with his legs.

FOLLOW–THROUGH

Space

The path of the club head completes the arc of the swing, with the club head traveling low and long until the left arm folds as the right arm extends. If the shoulders are turned in a sufficiently upright plane and if left side control has been maintained, the hands will automatically finish in a high position.

Time

There is a decelerating of the swing as the club head finishes high over the target shoulder.

Force

There is a deceleration of force after the club head has contacted the ball and swung through the ball. The left wrist should remain firm into the follow-through.

Flow

The sequential movement pattern is complete when movement has flowed completely to the left side (fig. 14.19).

Body Awareness

There is a feeling of turning toward the target while up higher on the non-target foot.

Weight transfers to the left foot with the right foot pushing off. The head remains down and has not moved. The head then comes up as the right shoulder continues to a position underneath the chin. The hips turn almost ninety degrees, with arms and hands ending up clear around the shoulder.

The Iron Shots

Following the wood shots on the drives, the remaining shots are considered as the short game and consist of hitting irons numbered one through nine. The long irons are numbers one, two, and three; the medium irons are numbers four, five, and six; the short irons are numbers seven, eight, and nine. All of these irons use the same basic swing as that for the drives except that the emphasis shifts to accuracy instead of distance. Because distance is not the objective, the backswing is shortened; the less distance required, the shorter the backswing. The triangle (shoulders, arms and hands) moves as a unit and many times the action is like that of a pendulum—just the arms are used and the remainder of the body is not involved.

In playing irons, the player should stand closer to the ball than in the drive because

Figure 14.19. **Follow-through**

the shaft of an iron is shorter than a wood; the swing becomes more upright.

The player chooses a short iron with an open face if a sharp loft is required and a medium or long iron if a lower, longer shot is required, but all iron shots are struck on the downward swing imparting some amount of backspin.

A clear mental picture of each iron shot is necessary before selecting the proper club to use; this is one of the secrets of a strong, short game. Until the player decides how far and how high the ball should fly, where it should land, and how much it should roll, he should not address the ball.

Many players use the same favorite club for every shot. By using the wrong club for a particular shot, a needless variable is introduced. A club with too much loft may affect the mental image and then a de-lofting compensatory action may become incorporated into the stroke. Picturing the shot and then selecting the club that matches the picture is a major concept to be used in iron shots.

Short Iron Shot

The ability of a golfer to put the ball on the green from a distance of 100 to 125 yards provides him with the control and accuracy that produce low scores. The short iron shot is a major stroke that does not require distance or power, but does involve control of the club head.

The short irons, the seven, eight, and nine, should be used usually at distances of less than 125 yards. Better accuracy and consistency are obtained by hitting an easy eight iron than a hard nine iron.

The short irons are used to get out of trouble, sand, rough and water. Basically the swing is the same as that for the drive, but modifications are made because the clubs are shorter and have more loft to the face.

Space

The space between the golfer and the ball is less for the short irons than for a drive. The club is shorter, so the player must stand closer.

The stance is usually an open one, but it can be square. The open stance necessitates the left foot being drawn slightly back from the line of flight, turning the body toward the target.

The ball was placed off the left heel for the drive; however, for the short irons, it is placed closer to the center of the stance.

The club follows a path in space that goes no higher than shoulder height at the top of the backswing.

Time

The timing for the short irons is the same as that for the drive except the backswing is shorter; a player should swing back and through.

Force

The hands lead the club head slightly in the address position.

The shot is not a power shot; the hands, wrists and forearms as a unit go back only to the point at which the hands are at shoulder level.

Firm wrists create a leverage action that results in a square impact and utilizes the speed created by the arms and the club. At impact, the hands are slightly ahead of the ball, creating a straight line from the club through the left arm to the left shoulder.

Flow

The body must be in a perfectly balanced position with the head remaining still so that sequential movement can flow around it.

On the follow-through, the club head follows a line out as far as possible toward the target. The swinging motion should carry as far as the arms will allow. This flow of movement causes the arms to pull upward and around, helping the hips and shoulders to turn.

The hands should finish high.

Body Awareness

The position of the body on the short iron shots is turned slightly toward the target. On the iron shots it is imperative that the player be relaxed and comfortable in the address position.

The hands are held close to the body with the grip about one inch from the top of the shaft.

The head is over the ball because the club is shorter, which causes the player to stand closer to the ball. On the iron shots, the head should be kept down until the ball has left the club. The body pivot is slight.

THE PITCH SHOT

There are just two principles to follow on the pitch shot: the ball must go high into the air and the player must hit down on the ball. The shot lands with little or no roll. Height and backspin result when a seven, eight, or nine iron is used because of the steep loft. When the ball is contacted squarely, the loft of the club will cause the ball to rebound perpendicularly to the club face.

The pitch shot is a control shot taken from not more than fifty yards. It can be used to clear a sand trap or water hazard. Because there is so much backspin on the ball, it sometimes actually jumps backwards (fig. 14.20).

Space

The feet should be close together and slightly open. The ball is played off the right foot.

The backswing is short and the hands and arms travel only to hip level.

The direction of the downswing is that of hitting down and through the ball.

Time

The backswing is short and the timing is rhythmic with the words "down" and "through" emphasized. Timing is smooth, with emphasis on the word "through."

Force and Flow

When the wrists and forearms remain firm on the backswing, the square-to-square sequence becomes easier.

The swing should be pendular in nature, created by the movement of the arm-shoulder triangle being maintained throughout the swing.

The pendular swing applied to short irons (the seven, eight, and nine) will give greater loft and less roll. Backspin is caused when at contact the ball slides up the lofted club.

Figure 14.20. **Pitch shot**

Selecting a medium iron (the four, five, or six) and using the pendular swing will give the ball slight loft and greater roll; this is called a pitch-and-run shot.

To decide on the amount of backswing needed, a player can compare the movement to the hand tossing a ball a short distance, for both actions are similar.

There is very little body pivot on the pitch shot.

The ball is hit first and then the turf. (Taking a divot is difficult for some players. Whether a divot should be taken remains a controversial issue.)

Body Awareness

There must be a feeling of control instead of power and distance in the address position. The feeling of hitting down and

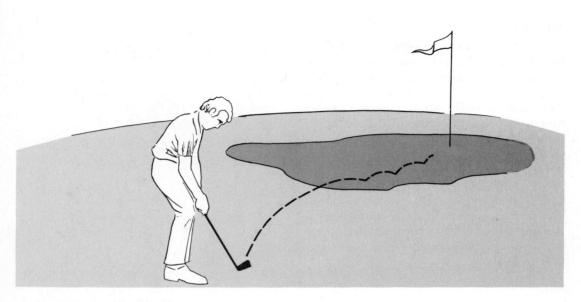

Figure 14.21. **Chip shot**

through is difficult both for beginners and experienced players.

CHIP SHOT

The chip shot is a control shot that is used from a distance of about forty-five feet to just a few feet from the pin. It is a shot that travels in the air about one-third of the distance and rolls two-thirds of the way toward the pin. Often this shot is taken from the apron of the green. A middle iron (the four, five, or six) should be used for better control and if farther away, a six or seven iron is used. Experienced players sometimes use a wedge or the nine iron. The objective is a chip and a putt so the shot ends up near the pin (fig. 14.21).

Space

The stance is open with the ball played off the right foot or from the middle of the stance.

A short space is used for the path of the backswing and follow-through. Spatial awareness is a must in this shot.

Time

There is a very smooth, well-timed short backswing. It must not be jerky or awkward.

Force

The left arm remains straight and the club acts as an extension of the arm. The square-to-square method is effective on the chip shot because wrists remain stabilized.

The club should not be carried any more than knee-high on the backswing or on the follow-through.

There is very little body movement in this shot. Weight is usually stabilized by putting the majority of the weight on the left foot.

What force there is gives the player a feeling of pushing the ball.

Flow

The method most accepted on the chip shot is the pendular swing with both hands locked; there is no break or wrist cock on the backswing or the follow-through.

The hands lead the club head slightly at address and are maintained in this position throughout the stroke. All of the work is done by using the club as an extension of the arms.

Some golfers prefer the hinge method, in which the wrists break in the backswing and in the follow-through. The wrists do all the work. Because the wrists have to break, they have to re-break as they come into the ball. This creates a weaker stroke, as beginners have a tendency to try to loft the ball by giving the right hand a little flip. Advanced players have developed more of a feel and can control their hands more effectively.

Body Awareness

There must be awareness of short distances. Most beginners cannot achieve the feeling of where the club head is in relation to the body. They usually over-swing on the chip shot.

The right arm stays close to the body and there is minimal body movement. There must be an acceptance through kinesthetic awareness that the body does little so that the club head is allowed to swing as a pendulum and strike the ball.

The hands should develop a keen sense of feeling for smooth timing and gentle strokes.

PUTTING

Putting is the easiest aspect of golf to learn but the most difficult one to master. The putt, chip and short iron shots make up 80 percent of the game. Putting is approximately 50 percent of the game, and yet golfers generally spend less time practicing putting than any other part of the game.

Each putt varies because of distance, slope, roll, speed, and the condition of the green. Psychology also plays a part and some golfers are "psyched out" before they ever get to the putt. Confidence in oneself is important in putting. A player must develop a positive approach. Needed first is a mental resolution, a total commitment to a particular line and then the determination to putt it. Knowing the exact style to use is important—a tap or a stroking action with wrists and forearms in one piece. Too many players try to jab, coax, steer or drag the putt.

Putting is extremely individualistic and golfers develop personalized grips, stances and body positions. As long as the player is comfortable and relaxed and he allows the club head to contact the ball squarely, he can develop his own good putting style.

Space

The golfer should be close to the ball with his head directly over the ball.

His feet should be close together with his weight evenly distributed.

Spatial awareness accounts for sound judgment in putting. Ability to judge distances takes experience.

Spatial judgment is knowing where the club head is in space on the backswing and on the follow-through.

Time

Putting requires a smooth swing even though there is little or almost no backswing. The stroke must be even and well-timed.

Force

Long putts require more force than do short putts, in which a minimal amount of force is applied.

The body should be well balanced with the knees flexed, thus lowering the center of gravity.

The head remains motionless, looking up only when the ball stops rolling.

The hands control the blade as it comes into the ball.

Flow

In the pendular swing, the arms hang free and swing freely from the shoulders. The arm-shoulder triangle *strokes* the ball with a follow-through in the same position.

In the method where the wrists break, the hands *tap* the ball with little follow-through.

Body Awareness

In order to acquire a more sensitive feel on the club, the reverse overlapping grip is recommended. In the reverse overlap grip, both thumbs extend down the shaft. The club is held mostly by the fingers of the right hand and the palm of the left hand. As in all shots, the back of the left hand points toward the target, i.e., the cup. The index finger of the left hand is placed over the right fingers to hold the club steady.

The body should be well balanced with the knees flexed, lowering the center of gravity.

Relaxation is a must in putting. If sufficient tension in the hips develops, it might cause an unbalanced position and result in a change in the position of the club head as it contacts the ball.

There must be a keen sensitivity developed in the hands as they control the blade of the putter as it comes into the ball.

TROUBLE

Every golfer gets into trouble; it is part of the game and getting out of trouble presents one of the real challenges in golf. Knowledge, practice, common sense and sometimes sheer physical strength are required in meeting the challenge.

Troublesome Lies

Rough or deep grass requires a clean stroke that is a descending blow. Backspin is best applied by an iron that is opened a few degrees at address. The grip must remain firm to apply a punching type of stroke (fig. 14.22).

Anything coming between the ball and the club face at impact reduces backspin, thereby reducing control over the shot. Sweeping the club head back and through takes in too much grass. Striking down and through the ball is desirable.

The basic bunker shots are generally the result of three situations:

    a. the lie is good and ball is close to the green.
    b. the lie is bad; the ball is close to a sand ledge or buried.
    c. the distance is great.

The first shot, when the lie is good, requires an explosion or blast shot. The ball itself is never contacted; the sand behind the ball is struck. The distance behind the ball varies between two and four inches; generally, the less sand taken, the farther the ball must travel. Swinging at the ball is a mistake; instead, skimming the club head through the sand behind the ball and floating it out is preferred.

Space

The ball is positioned opposite the left heel.

Force

The feet and shoulders are in an open position; the left side is pulled back from the target line.

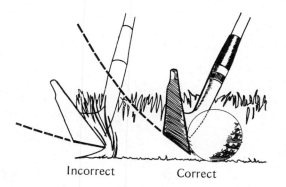

Incorrect   Correct

Figure 14.22. **Getting out of the rough**

Time

The backswing is short, requiring little time, but is rhythmic. The words "down and through" set the timing.

Flow

The club is swung smoothly along the open shoulder line.

Body Awareness

There is no deliberate turn of the shoulder; knees are flexed and the upper body is relaxed.

The second shot, when the ball is partly or completely buried in the sand, requires a swing that is well down and under the ball (fig. 14.23). The easiest way to accomplish this is to close the club face so that its sharp leading edge will knife through the sand when the stroke is swung sharply down behind the ball.

The third type of bunker shot is that in which distance is necessary. In this case the ball is hit first, the sand second. To ensure that the ball is hit first, it is necessary to play the ball farther back in the stance than normal, which has the effect of decreasing the loft of whatever club is chosen. The club, even when de-lofted, should carry the ball clear of the lip of the bunker.

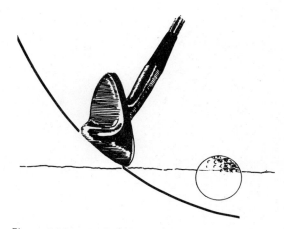

Figure 14.23. **Buried shot**

To Cope with a Slope

Downhill lie

To hit down the slope, it is necessary to assume a slightly open stance perpendicular to the slope, which places most of the weight on the left side and the hands ahead of the ball. The ball is played near the right foot. The right knee is flexed (fig. 14.24).

The backswing consists of a fast pickup of the club and then a striking action down the slope, down and through. It is best to use well-lofted clubs. If there is a solid contact, the ball will travel lower and farther than from a level lie. The tendency is to slice, so the arm should be to the left of target.

Uphill lie

The non-target shoulder is lower than usual as a perpendicular stance is assumed. The swing is parallel to the slope. Hints include aiming to the right of the target (hooking is common) and using more club than normal, to increase height (fig. 14.25).

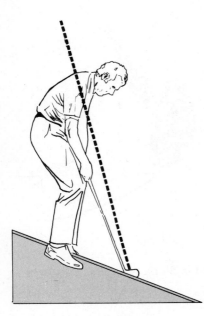

Figure 14.24. **Downhill lies**

Figure 14.25. **Uphill lies**

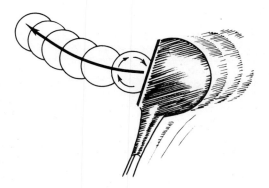

Figure 14.26. **Slice (open face)**

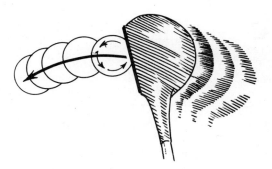

Figure 14.27. **Hook-closed face**

High ball

A ball higher than the player's feet requires a flatter swing, a more erect address position and more space between the player and the ball. A hook is common, so one should aim to the right of the target. It often helps to use a shorter club. Stance is opened slightly and the ball is near the right foot.

Low ball

A ball lower than the player's feet requires the player to bend over farther in order to reach the ball. The player must stand closer to the ball and swing in a more upright plane. Body turn is restricted, so the swing is all hands and arm. A slice is common, so aim is to the left of the target. A longer club is often useful.

Flight Problems

The major golf problems result because the club face does not meet the ball squarely at impact. A grip must be found that enables the club head to return the face *squarely* to the ball. If the club face is open, closed, to the left, or to the right of the target line, problems will prevail.

Because approximately 80 percent of all golfers slice, that swing should be analyzed in detail. Usually slicers tend to swing with the shoulders rather than the club head.

The club face is open to the swing path, causing the ball to finish to the right of the target (fig. 14.26).

Slicers must avoid compensating for the open club face. They often resort to aiming the club face left at the address. Because this compensation places the ball too far forward, it forces the shoulders to be aligned to the left of the target.

The position of the ball in the stance and the compensatory position of the shoulders force the grip to slide, thus weakening the ability to return a square club face to the ball at impact. The slicer usually pulls the club on the backswing to the inside, which opens the club face. From the top of the backswing, the downswing usually is thrown outwards toward the target line, approaching the ball steeply across the target line outside-in; a slice results.

The hook ranks with the disaster shots in golf alongside the shank. The true hook starts to the right of target, then bends or curves to the left. If it flies straight to the left or starts left and then flies farther left, the shot is a pull or a pulled hook (fig. 14.27). They do *not* stem from the same action that produces a *true* hook—in fact, just the opposite.

TABLE 14.1
FLIGHT PROBLEMS

Fault	Club face	Swing Path of Club	Ball Flight	Correction
Push	Open; face matches swing line	Inside out	Straight right	Square club face to target line
Pushed slice	Open; faces right	Outside-in	Starts right, curves farther right	Square club face to target line
Hook	Closed; to the left	Inside out	Starts right, curves wide left	Square club face to target line
Pull	Face matches swing line	Outside-in	Straight left	Square club face to target line
Banana slice	Open; to the right	Outside-in	Starts left, curves hard right	Square club face to target line
Pulled hook	Closed; to the left	Outside-in	Starts left, curves farther left	Square club face to target line
Faded slice (Tail away)	Open; to the right	Right of proper swing line	Starts straight, curves right at end	Square club face to target line
Faded hook (Fall away)	Closed; left of swing line	Left of proper swing line	Starts straight, fades at end to left	Square club face to target line

The true hook results from the club face meeting the ball on an inside-outside path with the face closed to that path. Often the closed face results from the arms, wrists, and club head swinging too freely. The square-to-square line relationship of the wrist and forearm would prevent the closing of the club face.

To compensate, the golfer aims to the right of the target at address, then sets the ball too far back in the stance, which sets the shoulders to the right. This positioning forces the grip to change and strengthen or close. From the top of the backswing, the golfer cannot swing with the legs and hips first because his grip has robbed him of proper timing and it forces the wrists to roll over too fast. The club thus travels in a very shallow arc, from inside to outside the target line.

BASIC SWING FAULTS

Faults that involve actions other than flight paths are the topped shot, fat shot and shank.

TOPPING

A faulty swing pattern accounts for topping the ball. Even though many golfers think topping results from raising the head too quickly or lifting the body on the backswing, most "tops" are simply expressing a steep outside-in, slice or pull pattern. It is well-established that correct grip and arm action allow the club to return to a square position at impact. At the point in the backswing where the wrists are cocked, the radius maintained by a straight left arm is decreased. If, in the downswing, the wrists do not uncock sufficiently to reestablish the radius, the ball is likely to be topped or hit "thin." Using the arms on the downswing in a strong pulling motion establishes a path in which the club head can return squarely to the ball.

FAT SHOTS

Hitting the ground behind the ball results in a fat shot, a fault often due to bad posture causing a loss of balance. Weight forward on the toes throws the downswing forward so that the player actually is falling into the shot or is forced to dip his shoulder to meet the ball.

An additional reason for fat shots can be hitting too easily with the hands and wrists before the hips have cleared the way. Those who hit hook shots are also prone to hitting fat shots because the arc of their swing is too wide. The player should correct the downswing leg-hip movement and perhaps deliberately restrict wrist action so that the hands and wrists hit *later*.

SHANKING

Perhaps the worst disaster in golf is the shank; in fact, the word is not used anywhere near a golf course for fear the idea will become planted in the golfer's mind. It is a shot veering directly to the sharp right and incurring the addition of two strokes— one for the shanked shot and the next one to return to the target from a point farther away.

A shank is caused by hitting the ball with the neck or the shank of the club. The face of the club does not contact the ball. A highly exaggerated outside-in swing coupled with very little pivot and a very loose, quick wrist action often causes the shanked shot.

To correct this shot the basic swing must be analyzed. Starting the backswing in one piece with the triangle moving as a unit is the first correction to consider. A solid left wrist with little wrist action usually corrects the shank.

Sometimes a novice will attempt to cut a shot by opening up the face of the club at address, deliberately hitting with an outside-in swing. Hitting cut shots is a job for the experts, not beginners. Only after much experience would a player attempt to alter swings. If a shank results, it can discourage a newcomer to the game. Unfortunately, the shank can appear at any time and has a tendency to come and go.

A PERSONALIZED EXPERIENCE

INTRODUCTION

The first experience with golf should be to feel the dynamics of the swing. Depending on the block of time available, all components of the swing (the body parts and the role they play in the swing) can be introduced by providing specific movement tasks.

No balls are used at first, for full concentration should be on feeling the swing pattern.

METHOD

The questions asked do not have to be asked in the order given here. Depending on the answers, the order will probably be entirely different. The direction the instructor takes depends on the response of the class. Objectives are to be kept in mind. The sophistication of the questions and answers depend on the grade or age level of the students.

The grip may have to be taught by a rather direct method since it is complex and needs explanation. Independent experimentation may lead to a comfortable incorrect grip.

It is important to establish early the terminology to be used throughout the teaching-learning process. The words target, nontarget, swing line, target line, square-to-square, triangle, straight-line relationship, etc., should be used consistently.

OBJECTIVES

The objectives include that the student learn:

To feel the rhythm of a swing pattern;

To feel the shift of weight to the non-target foot and back to the target foot;

To establish the feeling of the triangle (shoulders, arms, hands) moving as a unit, keeping the left arm firm;

To experiment with posture and body position at address in order to establish a balanced position;

To swing with a wide shoulder turn and a minimal hip turn;

To become aware of the flexed position of the knees on the backswing and throughout a swing;

To use the proper grip in a free and easy swing.

EXPLORATION

Questions are presented. (Possible answers are included within parentheses in the following lesson for the teacher's use.)

DIRECTIONS FOR STUDENTS

1. Using a wand, a broom handle or a golf club, swing it from one side to the other across the body.
   a. How many swinging-type movements can you name? (any throwing pattern: softball, baseball, tennis, bowling, field hockey)
   b. Are there any similarities in the way the body moves? (weight shifts to back foot, body turns to build momentum, balance is important)
   c. Can you swing this time by moving your shoulders, arms and hands as if they were a triangle? (See figure 14.14, page 405.)
2. Swing with the club held at the apex of the triangle. Repeat; remember, it is a unit moving.
   a. As you swing:
      (1) What adjustments in body position do you make?
      (2) If the club head has to swing through the grass, what body adjustments can be made? (keep knees flexed throughout, left shoulder turns in toward the ball)
   b. In order for the arms and hands to swing freely in the triangle, what seems to be the best posture to assume? (lean over, bend from the waist, keep back straight, extend posterior in back)

3. Experiment by moving your feet from a position together to a position far apart. Each time the feet move, swing and then decide which width provides the best balanced position for a swing. (Probably shoulder-width apart will be the most common answer; the players can practice by swinging a towel or by using a partner to feel the movement pattern for the following.)
   a. If we want to follow the principle that the longer the lever, the more speed and range of motion will be generated, how can we adjust our swing? (by keeping the arms straight, keeping the left arm straight, by keeping the left arm firm on backswing and right arm firm on follow-through)
   b. Does keeping the left arm firm throughout the swing force changes in any other body parts? (knees want to straighten, the upper part of the body lifts up, the upper body moves to the right, the hands slip as the club goes back)
   c. How does it feel to keep the left arm firm? (feels strained, feels stretched, the arm wants to bend and give in)
   d. If the club is swung only as far as the firm left arm permits, how can the shoulders move to help? (shoulders tilt so that left one moves under the chin)

   (The players can practice by swinging a towel or by using partners to feel the movement pattern.)
4. Let's try a grip that will help the hands work together. Which part of the hands must be facing the target squarely? (back of the left hand, target hand, palm of the right hand, nontarget hand)
5. Try holding the palms of the hands together straight out in front of you at the apex of the triangle. Now can you lower the triangle and place the hands on both sides of the club handle?
6. Place the left thumb on top or at a one o'clock position and curl the last three fingers upward around the handle. Place the right thumb at the eleven o'clock position and place the middle two fingers on the club. Place the little finger in the groove between the forefinger and middle finger of the left hand.
   a. Have you maintained the straight-line relationship of the left hand and forearm? That relationship should be maintained throughout the swing.
   b. Can you lift the club up and down in front of you so that wrinkles appear at the base of the thumb? (See fig. 10.10, p. 249.)
   c. Can you swing the club with the new grip; does it feel comfortable at first? Try not to let the grip slip. What happens to the grip at the top of the backswing?
   d. Can you feel a rhythm to the swing?
   e. Which is more effective, a slower takeaway or a fast takeaway?
   f. When is there a speeding up of the swing? (after the top of the backswing is reached)
   g. Can you supply words to fit the timing? ("back and through," "and swing," "back—and swing")

CONCEPTUALIZATION AND DISCUSSION

1. What principles of movement are represented by a proper swing pattern?
2. How can force be used most effectively?
3. What is the time-space relationship represented in the golf swing?
4. What specific body movements did you experience or feel?
5. What body movements contributed to an effective swing?

Typical Answers:
Triangle; moving as a unit
Keeping left arm firm
Keeping knees flexed
Posture: bend at waist, keep back straight
Left shoulder moves under chin
Grip feels uncomfortable
Straight line between forearm and left hand
Feet shoulder-width apart
Shift of weight to nontarget foot and back to target foot

Following this beginning personalized experience, each principle can be explored in depth.

REFERENCES

Aultman, Richard. *The Square-to-Square Golf Swing.* New York: Bantam Books, 1970.

Bowling, Maurine. *Tested Ways of Teaching Golf Classes.* Dubuque, Iowa: Wm. C. Brown Company Publishers, 1964.

Broer, Marion R. *Efficiency of Human Movement.* 3d ed. Philadelphia: W. B. Saunders Co., 1973.

————. *Individual Sports for Women.* 5th ed. Philadelphia: W. B. Saunders Co., 1971.

Cochran, Alastair, and Stobbs, John. *The Search for the Perfect Swing.* Philadelphia: J. B. Lippincott Co., 1968.

Crogen, Corrine. *Golf Fundamentals.* Palo Alto, Calif.: National Press Books, 1964.

Harvey, T. D. "How Spin Controls Flight." *Golfing* 18 (1954):20–23.

Jacobs, John. *Practical Golf.* New York: New York Times, 1972.

Jorgensen, Theodore, Jr. "On the Dynamics of the Swing of a Golf Club." *American Journal of Physics* 38 (May 1970):649.

Nance, Virginia L., and Davis, Elwood C. *Golf.* 2d ed. Dubuque, Iowa: Wm. C. Brown Company Publishers, 1975.

Nicklaus, Jack. *Golf My Way.* New York: Simon and Schuster, 1974.

Rehling, Conrad. *Golf for the Physical Education Teacher and Coach.* Dubuque, Iowa: Wm. C. Brown Company Publishers, 1954.

15

Gymnastics

INTRODUCTION

In no other sport are the elements of movement incroporated into moving the body in more unusual and beautiful ways than in gymnastics. The unique characteristics of each piece of apparatus lend themselves to movements specific to each. The gymnast defies gravity on the narrow balance beam as she travels, pivots, balances and rolls in sequence. The horizontal and uneven bars lend themselves to hanging, swinging and rotating as the gymnast travels through the space below, above and between the bars. A combination of dance, balancing and tumbling is the basis for the floor exercise. The use of music in the floor exercise for women allows the gymnast to feel, interpret, and project those feelings as she leaps, jumps, turns and rotates through the space provided. In side and long horse vaulting the body is projected in flight in a variety of body postures or shapes. The multiple variations and combinations of the elements of movement—force, flow, time and space—lend themselves to the possibility of an ultimate variety of movements, each unique to the performer and the apparatus.

The gymnastic program of the Olympics consists of four events for women (floor exercise, side horse vaulting, balance beam and uneven parallel bars) and six events for men (floor exercise, long horse vaulting, parallel bars, horizontal bar, side horse and rings). However, many other activities and apparatus are utilized to provide varying experiences in gymnastics for the novice. Some of these events are unique in their own right and are used in competition other than the Olympics. Still others are used for demonstrations or merely because they provide challenge and satisfaction for the performer. These activities include individual and doubles tumbling (mat work), rebound tumbling (trampolines of various sizes), double balancing and pyramid building, and rope climbing. In a search to provide more and varied opportunities in gymnastics one may find women performing on some of the apparatus traditionally used only by men. The still rings are used to develop skill in gripping, hanging, and inverting the body in a variety of positions. The horizontal and parallel bars are used to learn basic skills that are later performed on the uneven bars. In fact, if an uneven parallel bar is not available, girls can be challenged on the even parallel bars and perform with success. Although each activity is in some way unique, the commonality of movement in the variety of activities unifies the study of gymnastics under several broad categories.

A detailed analysis of all the movement possibilities of each activity would fill volumes. In fact, single volumes are published dealing with only one aspect of gymnastics, and they in themselves do not exhaust all the available material for that activity. This one chapter is not nearly so ambitious. It attempts to categorize the skills of gymnastics under several broad topics according to commonalities. The development of concepts and supporting facts within categories, coupled with an application of the biomechanical principles to these commonalities, leads to greater understanding and facility in teaching and learning provided transfer occurs. This chapter is not intended for the coach but for the teacher; therefore, the activities touched upon are those most appropriate for class instruction in the secondary school in light of the facilities usually found in the gymnasium, the level of ability of the students, and their growing interest in more conventional skills of gymnastics.

The exclusion of basic movement per se and educational gymnastics (English ap-proach) from this chapter is not a reflection of their lack of value as preliminary to the level of skill development proposed in this chapter.[1,2] Certainly the experiences and understandings gained in basic movement and educational gymnastics enhance the student's opportunity for achievement of conventional gymnastic skills. However, the authors view basic movement as a content area appropriate to elementary school with educational gymnastics as an outgrowth of basic movement. Educational gymnastics is an intermediate phase between basic movement and conventional gymnastics in which the student continues to solve movement problems creatively, although with greater sophistication. Indeed, conventional skills of gymnastics may and will be evident in the movement solutions of some students involved in both basic movement and educational gymnastics. This chapter is intended to begin at that point when students desire to learn the conventional skills. However, it presupposes the student has had experiences in the two preliminary units and depicts this relationship and continuity through the use of movement terminology and classification of skills. If the students have not had these prior experiences they can be incorporated as an introduction to any of the three groups into which gymnastic skills have been classified for the purpose of this chapter (static balancing, transferring body weight with step-like actions, and rotation of the total body). The creative movement solutions that result from such introductions provide the opportunity for alerting the students to the very same concepts and biomechanical principles that apply to conventional skills of this nature. For exam-

1. Bonnie Cherp Gilliom, *Basic Movement Education for Children, Rationale and Teaching Units* (Reading, Mass.: Addison-Wesley Publishing Co., 1970).
2. E. Mauldon and J. Layson, *Teaching Gymnastics and Body Control* (London: Macdonald and Evans, 1975).

ple, movement problems that involve students in transferring their weight from hands to feet (or to other body parts) in step-like motions along the floor or up onto and down from apparatus lead to the conventional skills of vaulting, mounting and dismounting from apparatus, cartwheels, limbers, etc. Transferring weight by rocking and rolling leads to rolls on mats or apparatus as well as other types of rotations on apparatus. A sample introductory lesson for rotation of the total body is included on page 000. This sample shows one way in which the teacher might review (or introduce for the first time) the preliminary experiences encountered in basic movement and educational gymnastics. However appropriate these introductions might be, it is not the purpose of this chapter (or unit of study at this level) to be dominated by creative movement solutions.

The question arises as to which method of teaching would serve best to achieve the desired outcomes of specific gymnastic skills. Obviously, a direct method would be most efficient in terms of time. Safety, too, might best be served by a direct method with specific spotting techniques being taught. Task and reciprocal methods of organization which allow students to work at their own level in a skill progression provide for individualization. However, direct methods of teaching need not be the sole method used in conventional gymnastics. Those conventional skills that can be learned safely without a spot can be taught through guided discovery. A skeleton outline of movement problems leading to the round-off and cartwheel is included on page 000 as an example. In other instances the teacher can pose problems for students to experiment and discover variations in ways to begin and/or end certain skills once the primary movement is mastered (for example, varia-

tions in rolls, pages 485–86). Problem solving to create new movements, transitions, or variations of a more difficult nature should only be attempted after the performer and spotters understand the dangers inherent in that type of movement and know how to devise progressions and spotting techniques to provide for safety with achievement. The cognitive (conceptual) approach in the arrangement of material in this chapter is intended to serve as a base for such an understanding. Secondly, a cognitive approach facilitates the job of the teacher by allowing him to plan lessons around concepts related to one type of movement and still provide for individualization by allowing students to progress when ready for more difficult skills of this same movement type. For example, while some students may need several class periods to work on rolling on the mats, with variations and progressions, others may move quickly through these progressions and be ready for rolls on the apparatus following the first lesson. A sample outline of a lesson on rolling which progresses to rolling in a forward direction on mats with variations, on the balance beam, on the even parallel bars, and rotating over one bar of the unevens to a stand on the mat is included on pages 483–85. Individuality can continue to be fostered through progression throughout the unit and even in the termination of a unit by allowing students to create their own compositions.

The major concepts derived from the human movements unique to gymnastics (balancing, rotating, etc.) *are not* included in chapter five due to the diversity and magnitude of the material. Thus, the major concepts in this chapter relate essentially to gymnastics and particularly to the types of movement under discussion. However, the foundation for the biomechanical principles cited in this chapter is found in the information located in chapter four.

Analyses of the concepts and skills discussed in this chapter are grouped under three main headings: "Static Balancing," "Transferring Body Weight with Step-like Actions," and "Rotation of the Total Body." The purpose of grouping skills according to commonalities rather than by specific skills is two-fold: (1) to show the relationship among skills on the different apparatus that involve the same movement pattern; and (2) to encourage the teacher to present concepts with the teaching of the basic skills and to allow the students to progress at their own speed as they experience and apply these same concepts in more advanced work. The variations included after the analyses of many of the skills require a greater than average degree of proficiency. Specific spotting techniques are also included after the analysis of each skill.

The last section of this chapter is concerned with individualizing gymnastics. Included in this section is a sample of "tools" that could be used in a gymnastics unit to individualize learning and allow each student to progress at his own rate.

TERMINOLOGY

Terms often have different connotations in different areas of the country. Before delving into the main body of this chapter the reader should become aware of various terms and their interpretation according to the authors. Also included in this list are some basic body positions and basic hand positions used in gymnastics.

Abduct: to move a limb of the body in a sideward direction away from the midline of the body.

Arch (open): a term used mainly to describe the trunk of the body. Open or arched denotes extension or hyperextension as opposed to flexion. In basic movement the open body would be straight and narrow as opposed to rounded or twisted; the range would be large or long as opposed to small or short.

Cast: a movement on the horizontal and uneven bars in which the body is piked and then pushed backward and upward in an open position away from the bar. This action is used to place the body into a position above the bars in order to build momentum as gravity pulls the body downward.

Free leg: that leg which may be positioned in a variety of ways; it is free in that it is not used for support.

Grips: there are three basic grips on the horizontal and uneven bars: (a) the forward or over-grip with the fingers curled forward over the bar; (b) reverse or under-grip which is the opposite or reverse of the forward grip; (c) the mixed grip, with one hand positioned in an over-grip, the other hand in a reverse grip.

Half-kneel, half-squat: a position used in spotting in which the spotter is at a low level to lift if necessary and is still able to come to a stand quickly if the need should arise.

Hurdle: a preliminary movement used to build momentum. The hurdle for vaulting is discussed on page 451; the hurdle which precedes a rotating movement is discussed on page 475.

Kinesthetic awareness: a muscular awareness of the position of the body or body parts in space.

Long hang (horizontal and uneven bars): the body hangs fully extended, hands gripping the high bar.

Long sitting hang: (uneven bars) weight is supported by the hands on the high bar, hips on the low bar; the body is flexed only slightly at the hips.

Mount: a transfer of weight from the floor (a low surface) to an elevated surface (the apparatus) with the purpose of staying up on the elevated surface.

Pike: the hips are flexed, legs straight (the nose and knees are brought closer together). The body may be free of support, balanced on a single body part or a combination of body parts.

Prone: the anterior or front surface of the body faces the supporting surface. The body is horizontal, face down.

Shape: the body form or the position of the body in space at any given time. The basic movement terminology to describe shape— rounded, straight and narrow, etc.—becomes more specific in gymnastics (i.e., tuck, squat, open or arched, pike, straddle, etc.).

Side stride support: the body faces in a line of direction perpendicular to the length of the apparatus. Weight is supported mainly by the hands. One leg is positioned in front of apparatus, the other leg on the opposite side. (The position is the same as a forward-back stride would be if the feet were on the floor.)

Squat: the lower extremities are flexed, heels brought to the buttocks, upper trunk open or extended.

Straddle: a position of the legs in which each leg is abducted laterally. The body may be free of support or balanced on any single body part or combination of body parts.

Supine: the posterior or back surface of the body faces the supporting surface. The body is horizontal, face up.

Takeoff board: an inclined surface used to gain a slight advantage in height for vaulting and mounting the apparatus. See page 451.

Trailing leg: the leg of the foot which is last to leave the mat. The trailing leg follows behind the lead leg.

Tuck: a position in which all parts of the body are brought close to the center of the body, with the chin on chest, posterior surface rounded.

Whipping leg or lead leg: the leg that builds momentum with a swing and leads the movement into the inverted position or up onto a surface.

SAFETY

CONCEPT U. An affective attitude based on a cognitive understanding of the dangers inherent in an activity is necessary if one is to perform safely.

Sub-concept U-1. Providing a safe environment for participation contributes to the development of desirable affective attitudes toward the activity.

A safe environment includes equipment in good condition, properly assembled and padded, and with heights adjusted to the capabilities of the students. Equipment should be checked periodically to be certain the hardware has not worked loose. Attachments to the ceiling and/or floor should be checked for security. Straps, ropes and/or cables of suspended apparatus should also be checked for wear. Rips and tears in padded surfaces should be mended to eliminate the possibility of the performer catching a finger or toe in the torn surface. Wooden surfaces should be kept free of a build-up of chalk (carbonate of magnesium) and checked often for splinters or cracks that would indicate the wood has become fatigued (brittle).

Once the equipment has been positioned and secured, mats should be used to pad the area below and around the base of the apparatus. When several small mats are used they should be butted rather than overlapped if possible. A performer can easily injure an ankle when dismounting on the uneven surface of an overlapped mat. Most equipment companies now sell fitted mats—mats cut and sewn to order. Figure 15.1 illustrates parallel bars with the base

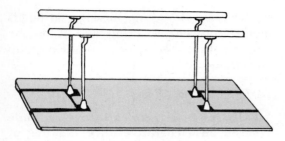

Figure 15.1. **Parallel bars with the base covered by a fitted mat**

covered by a fitted mat. Although the initial cost may seem prohibitive, the security of having the base well-covered and the freeing of the smaller mats for the tumbling station makes the expenditure worthwhile. For example, one may use four or five eight-by-ten mats to adequately pad the area below and around the balance beam. With a fitted mat possibly only one eight-by-ten mat would be necessary on the dismount area in addition to the fitted mat. This then would free the other mats to be used at a tumbling station. In tumbling when mats are placed end-to-end to form a continuous mat for a series of skills or when placed together to form one large matted area, they should again be butted. They may also require being taped together to keep them from sliding apart as the performer travels from mat to mat.

The height of the equipment should be adjusted to meet the capabilities of the students. Quite often regulation height for competition is too high for the novice. Lowering the equipment helps the novice to overcome fear, makes it easier to spot the beginner, and provides the novice with successful experiences as he progresses in skill and gains confidence. Nothing succeeds like success in motivating the student to want to learn more.

The arrangement and spacing of the equipment pieces in relation to each other

and to the available space should also be considered. The trampoline must have clearance above the bed. The vaulting station should be located so that there is a minimum of traffic across the approachway. All equipment must be placed well away from walls and other obstructions found in the gymnasium. The spacing of the equipment must allow for students to move through the environment without interfering with those students working at different stations. Quite often traffic patterns must be established. It is most important that students are aware of traffic patterns, especially if the organization is such that students are allowed to move from station to station at will. Training students to set up, dismantle, and adjust the equipment makes them more aware of what is necessary for a safe environment.

Sub-concept U-2. Educating the participants to use the environment wisely contributes not only to personal safety but enhances the total climate of the classroom.

If students are to work safely in gymnastics they need to be knowledgeable concerning the content of gymnastics. An understanding of movement techniques and related biomechanical principles enables the students to assist each other by spotting (aiding a colleague in his performance) and enlightens them concerning movement progressions. Mastering simple techniques before progressing to the more difficult moves develops control of the body and builds self-confidence in the performer. Lead-up activities on mats or lowered equipment and part-learning is the basis for safe performance of more complex skills.[3] Needless to say, the performer must be cognizant of his

3. Part-learning refers to learning some part of the skill in isolation, just as part-teaching is opposed to whole-teaching.

own capabilities and limitations and choose his activities accordingly.

Competent spotters whom the performer trusts aid the progress of the novice. That they are competent implies a knowledge of the skill to be attempted and an awareness of the points of stress, and a knowledge of the performer and his capabilities and limitations. The spotter then stations himself in a position to merely touch as a means of instilling confidence or to carry the performer through the movement should the need arise. At all times the spotter must protect the head, neck, and back of the performer. Although one spotter, or even two, cannot always carry the total weight of the performer, they must protect the vital areas. Such protection involves easing the performer down to the mat (breaking his fall) and, if possible, adjusting his body position to allow a landing on the feet or less vital, well-padded areas, such as the hips. A more detailed analysis of spotting techniques is included in each section for the various activities and/or for specific movement skills when necessary.

STATIC BALANCING (INCLUDING MAJOR CONCEPTS)

Static balances are still positions in which the gymnast displays his skill in balancing by assuming various body shapes while using a small or unlikely body part as a base of support. The most beautiful and spectacular static balances are those balances executed on the balance beam, which is a little less than four inches wide. Pyramid building, although employing a wider base, is none less challenging as students problem-solve for more unusual ways to balance each other at higher and higher levels. The basic concepts and skills of balancing are best learned individually at a low level and on a padded surface—a mat. It is here the student learns to employ the principles of stability as he develops the kinesthetic feeling and muscular control to stabilize his body on various bases of support.

The principles of stability as discussed in the following material refer only to static balancing. However, the force of gravity is always present and balance principles must not be violated if one is to remain on balance while performing dynamic movements. The reader will find mention of these same principles periodically through the text of this chapter.

CONCEPT. An understanding of the principles of stability aids the performer in developing the techniques and muscular control to perform static balances.

Sub-concept. Lowering the center of gravity and enlarging the base of support in the direction of force contributes to stability.

The line of gravity must fall within the base of support if balance is to be maintained. However, the nearer to the center of the base the line of gravity falls, the greater the distance one may move in all directions before stability is lost by the line of gravity falling outside the base.[4] The gymnast then needs to center his weight by distributing it equally on all points or edges of the base of support. For example, in the headstand, if weight is equally balanced on the head and both hands, the position is most stable. However, if the body weight is shifted toward the head (or hands) only a slight movement in that direction will pull the line of gravity outside the base and cause the performer to come down out of the headstand position.

4. Refer to chapter 4, page 47.

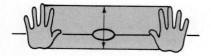

Figure 15.2. **Positioning the hands and head in a straight line in the headstand provides a very narrow base in a forward-backward direction.**

Enlarging the base of support increases stability; however, the performer must be cognizant of the direction in which force is to be exerted before deciding on the size and direction of the enlargement. A larger base allows a greater range of movement while maintaining the line of gravity within the base. The components of the base of support for the headstand (the head and hands) can be placed in a variety of positions in relation to each other. All three points could be placed in a straight line. This provides a wide base in a sideward direction but a very narrow base in a forward-backward direction. Enlarging the base further to the side will not make this base more stable. However, moving the head to a position forward of the hands enlarges the base in the direction in which it was previously narrow and allows for a greater range of movement in all directions before the line of gravity falls outside the base. Besides, moving into the headstand requires that force be exerted in a forward-backward direction as the trunk tilts forward and inverts and/or the legs whip to invert the trunk. Thus, placing the head forward of the hands provides the body with a counterforce to check or to stop the forward momentum created by the trunk and legs. In doubles balancing and pyramid building the base should be enlarged in the direction from which the top man is mounting to counteract the thrust and weight of the mounter.

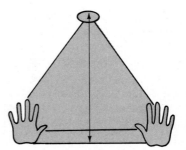

Figure 15.3. **Positioning the hands and head to form a triangle provides a wider base in the direction in which force is exerted (forward-backward).**

If force or weight is to be supported directly over the base (directly downward) there is a limit to how wide the base can become and still be sturdy. If the base gets much wider than the body it is supporting, a lateral component of force is introduced which reduces the amount of force the base can exert upward to counteract the weight or force pushing downward. Therefore, when supporting or balancing on the hands or feet, or on the hands and knees together (as in doubles balancing and pyramid building), the width of the base should not much exceed the width of the shoulders or hips.

A balanced position with a low center of gravity is more stable than one with a high center of gravity, providing the base remains the same. An object or body with a low center of gravity can tip much farther before the line of gravity falls outside the base than can an object with the same sized base but a higher center of gravity. One utilizes this principle when the tripod is taught prior to the headstand. A gymnast employs this principle in many other instances. A quick flexion of the knees on the balance beam or the flexion of the elbows in the handstand is an effort to maintain or regain stability by lowering the center of gravity. A wise beginner uses this principle as he learns to balance in body shapes that have a low center of gravity before attempting balances that require a high center of gravity.

Sub-concept. Positioning various body parts to counterbalance each other and focusing the eyes on some stable object contributes to the ability of the performer to maintain balance.

When a body part moves away from the center of the body the line of gravity moves in that direction. If the body is to remain on balance without changing the base of support, some other body part must move in the opposite direction to counterbalance or pull the center of gravity back over the base. This principle in action is seen most often in static poses on the balance beam (fig. 15.4). One example is the arabasque or front scale in which the inclination of the trunk in a forward direction counterbalances the extension of the leg in a backward direction. The gyrations of arms, legs and trunk of a beginner on the balance beam as she begins to lose her balance are efforts at counterbalancing. However, because these movements are quick and somewhat involuntary, they many times cause the beginner to overbalance rather than counterbalance and she finds a new base of support down on the mat.

Focusing the eyes on some stable object while trying to balance in an unfamiliar postion helps orient the body as to its position in space and contributes to stability. One does not realize how necessary the eyes are for stability until he has tried balancing on a small base of support (even one foot) with the eyes closed. However, just keeping the eyes open may not be enough. A concentrated effort at focusing the eyes on one specific spot contributes to stability in all feats of balance, both static and dynamic. A good example of the necessity of employing this principle in dynamic balance is on the

Figure 15.4. **Front scale (arabesque). Note the counterbalance of the limbs and upper trunk to keep the line of gravity within the small base of one foot.**

trampoline as the body is projected into the air, free of all support.

Individual Inverted Balances on the Mat

Tripod

The tripod is a three-point balance with a low center of gravity. It is quite often used as a preliminary balance to learning the headstand.

1. *Starting position:* The performer assumes a hand-knee position on the mat with hands placed approximately shoulder-width apart. The front and top of the head is then placed forward of the hands to form a triangle.

2. *Force to move into position:* The performer raises his knees and walks the feet toward the head until the hips are directly over the shoulders. He then places one knee

Figure 15.5. **The tripod is a preliminary balance before extending the legs into the headstand position. The lower center of gravity in the tripod makes balance easier to maintain than in the headstand.**

at a time on each of the elbows and carefully removes his feet from the mat.

3. *Body parts supporting weight:* The head and the two hands support the weight equally.

4. *Body shape:* The total body is inverted at a low level with the elbows, hips and knees flexed (fig. 15.5).

5. *Spot:* The spotter checks to see that the hands and head are placed correctly and then spots the hips to keep them located over the base.

Headstand

The headstand is a three-point balance with a high center of gravity.

1. *Starting position:* (a) In the tripod extension method one assumes the tripod position and then very carefully remove the knees from the elbows and extend the legs toward the ceiling. (b) A second method of starting is to assume a front-back stance at a medium level and then place the head and hands to form the triangular base.

2. *Force to move into position:* (a) The tripod extension method keeps all movements within the base of support, which contributes to stability. However, it takes more strength in the body extensors than does the following method. (b) This second method

Figure 15.6. **Headstand. One should try to reach for the ceiling with the toes.**

takes less strength since the back leg is used as a whip to build rotatory momentum to invert the body. However, one must be careful not to over-whip, and thus overbalance. The forward foot pushes off the mat and follows the lead leg into a position above the trunk.

3. *Body parts supporting weight:* The body weight shifts toward the head as the performer moves into position. Once the body is positioned, weight is shifted back so that all three points—the head and two hands—support the weight equally.

4. *Body shape:* The trunk and legs are extended toward the ceiling. The performer should have the feeling of stretching the toes to touch the ceiling. All segments are aligned above the base, as in an upright standing posture in reverse (fig. 15.6).

5. *Spot:* The spotter stands to the side of the performer and uses the inside of one thigh to support the back. The spotter's hands are then free to grasp the knees and assist the legs and hips into the proper position.

6. *Variations of movements out of the headstand:* (a) the procedure for extension is re-

versed and the return is to the tripod position; (b) one foot is dropped to the mat, followed by a walk back down (the reverse of a kick up); (c) an overbalance toward the posterior (back) surface and a roll-out forward.

Tip-up

The tip-up is a two-point balance with a low center of gravity and a narrow base in a forward-backward direction. The main difference between the tip-up and tripod is that the head is not used as a base of support; only the hands are used.

1. *Starting position:* The performer assumes a squat position with the hands placed approximately shoulder-width apart on the mat and the knees placed on the outside of the elbows.

2. *Force to move into position:* The performer begins to tilt forward, keeping the neck hyper-extended (the head up). If the chin is pulled to the chest the body will become round, overbalance, and roll forward. The tilt brings the knees or inside of the thighs against the elbows or upper arms. One should tilt carefully and only enough to bring the line of gravity over the small base of the hands. The toes are carefully removed from the mat once this position is reached.

3. *Body parts supporting weight:* Only the hands support the weight, which makes the base narrow in a forward-backward direction. If the fingers are pointing forward they can be curled slightly to allow the fingertips to press against the mat to counteract an overbalance in a forward direction.

4. *Body shape:* The trunk is somewhat horizontal as opposed to vertical, with the head up. The elbows, hips and knees are flexed, keeping the body in a compact shape at a low level (fig. 15.7).

5. *Spot:* The spotter assumes a low position (half-kneel and half-squat) and places

Figure 15.7. **Tip-up. The body tilts slowly into a balanced position on two hands at a low level.**

one hand on the shoulder and the other hand under the back of the thigh. The hand on the thigh can help to lift and position the hips while the hand on the shoulder counteracts an overbalance forward. The performer should be cautioned to tuck the head and roll out if he cannot control an overbalance in a forward direction.

Handstand

The handstand is a two-point balance with a high center of gravity and a narrow base in a forward-backward direction.

1. *Starting position:* The performer assumes a front-back stance and leans forward to place the hands on the mat approximately shoulder-width apart, fingers spread and pointing forward. The shoulders should be aligned directly over the hands with the head up.

2. *Force to move into position:* The force is the same as the second method of getting into the headstand—one leg kick up.

3. *Body parts supporting weight:* The body parts supporting the weight are the same as those for the tip-up.

4. *Body shape:* The arms, shoulders, trunk and legs are extended. Again, one should have the feeling of stretching. All segments of the body are aligned one on top of the other—shoulders over hands, hips over

Figure 15.8. Handstand. The shoulders and hips are in line above the hands. The performer reaches for the ceiling with the toes.

shoulders, and toes stretching for the ceiling (fig. 15.8).

5. *Spot:* The spotter stands on the kicking leg side of the performer. The inside of one leg can be used against one shoulder to keep it from moving forward beyond the hands. The spotter's hands are free to grasp the knee(s) and to assist the legs and hips into alignment above the shoulders. The spotter pulls upward on the legs of the performer to help him gain an awareness of stretch.

6. *Progressions:* Once the performer is certain his arms will hold his weight he may begin the handstand from a standing position. The arms are whipped down to their position on the mat at the same time the leg is whipped upward. This action, along with a transfer of weight from the back foot to the forward foot, creates greater rotatory momentum.

7. *Variations of getting into the handstand are:* (a) a cartwheel into a handstand; (b) a

back pike roll into a handstand, commonly called a back extension; (c) a press from a headstand into a handstand; (d) a slight dive, pike and extension; (e) a slow press from a pike position into extension.

8. *Variations in movements out of the handstand are:* (a) one foot is dropped to the mat, followed by a walk back down (the reverse of a kick-up); (b) an overbalance toward the dorsal surface. The arms are bent, head tucked (chin to chest), followed by a touch down on the back of the head and shoulders and a roll-out; (c) an overbalance toward the ventral surface, a body arch and a chest roll down; (d) an overbalance toward the dorsal surface and an arch-over, with one or both feet placed on the mat for a walk-over or limber (p. 477); (e) a slow descent into a headstand.

Static Positions on the Balance Beam

Including static poses in an exercise on the balance beam adds to the value of the routine or composition by contributing to the variety of movements, causing a change of pace or rhythm, and increasing the point value for difficulty if the static position is of sufficient worth. There is a multitude of static positions possible on the balance beam. Balances may be at a high, low, or medium level. Any body part—the feet, one foot, the hands, a shoulder, the seat, etc.— or any combination of parts may be used as the base of support. The shape of the body may be straight and narrow, curved, angular or any combination of shapes. In any one balance the arms, legs, head or trunk may be varied to convey a different mood. The gymnast should precede and succeed the static position with appropriate movements to depict flow and rhythm. And last but not least, the gymnast must be master of her own body to defy gravity and maintain her position on the narrow surface of the balance beam. Therefore, it is imperative that the gymnast employ the principles of balance previously mentioned.

Before beginning work on a beam at standard height, many of the static positions can be practiced on a line on the floor or a low balance beam. This also contributes to safety in that one does not have so far to come down if there is a loss of balance and it is much easier for a spotter to aid the balancer at this lower level. An initial experience of merely climbing up onto the high beam and then dismounting with a jump helps to acquaint the novice with descending and landing from a greater height.

The following is a description of three simple balances that can be easily mastered. They differ in their base of support and the height of the center of gravity from the base of support.

Front scale

The front scale is a balanced position on one foot with the arms and upper trunk leaning forward to counterbalance the extension of the non-supporting leg in a backward direction (fig. 15.4, p. 431).

1. *Procedure:* Facing the beam lengthwise, one assumes a forward-back stride position with the foot that is most comfortable to balance on forward. The eyes are focused on the end of the beam or at some spot on the far wall in front.[5] The back foot is slowly raised and the trunk tilted forward to counterbalance. The trunk is extended or even hyper-extended as the eyes maintain contact with the predetermined focal point. The leg may be raised to various levels in back depending upon the ability of the performer. However, if the leg is raised quite high, one will find that the hips shift backward in relation to the supporting foot due to the greater mass of the upper trunk moving forward.

Figure 15.9. **Knee scale**

2. *Spot:* The spotter stands to the side and extends a helping hand. A beginner may grasp and maintain contact with the spotter throughout the movement. A more confident performer may attempt the balance alone and only grasp the helping hand if stability is threatened. If the performer loses her balance and begins to come off the beam, the spotter should not attempt to hold her on by grasping her trunk or legs, but merely support her hand on the way down. The position of a front scale lends itself well to a jump to the mat.

Knee scale

The knee scale is a balanced position with both hands and the knee, foot and lower portion of one leg as a base of support. The free leg is extended back and up with the trunk and neck hyperextended (fig. 15.9).

1. *Procedure:* The beginner moves into this balance from a low position on the

5. Although physiologically the eyes will have to adjust less if the focal point is approximately twenty feet away, a beginner is better able to tell where the beam is in relation to her own body if she focuses her eyes on the end of it.

Figure 15.10. **V-seat. The hands may grasp the top and sides of the beam or the fingers may grasp below the beam with the heels of the hands against the sides of the beam.**

beam, such as a squat or straddle seat. The hands are positioned below the shoulders with the thumbs and the base of the thumb portion of the palm on top of the beam. The thumbs are side by side with the fingers spread down along the sides of the beam. The supporting knee is placed directly under the hip and the foot extended to allow the lower leg to make contact with the beam. The free leg is extended back and up, trunk hyper-extended, and head up with eyes focused on some predetermined spot.

2. *Spot:* The spotter is stationed on the side of the supporting leg. (This allows the performer to reach for the mat with the free leg should she overbalance toward that side.) One hand supports the upper arm and the other can support either the trunk or extended leg in order to keep the line of gravity over the beam.

V-Seat

The V-seat is a balanced position in which the gymnast sits lengthwise on the beam

with the hips piked and legs raised to form a V shape with the trunk (fig. 15.10).

1. *Procedure:* The performer assumes a straddle seat facing toward the end of the beam. The hands are placed behind the trunk, thumbs together and on top with the fingers extending down alongside the beam for lateral stability. Some individuals prefer to grasp below the beam to use the hands to pull as well as balance. The trunk tilts backwards as the hips are piked and the legs raised to a position above the horizontal. Beginners may flex the knees to the chest and then extend the legs after the trunk is in position. This action takes a little less effort, as it is easier to raise a shorter lever against gravity. If the performer is quite comfortable and well-balanced she may release the hands and balance only on the seat.

2. *Spot:* The spotter stands to the side of the performer, grasps the upper arm to stabilize the shoulders, and supports the legs under the thighs with the other hand.

Static Positions on the Still-Rings

The term still-rings implies that the performer attempts to maintain the rings in a relatively stationary position as he elevates, rotates and supports the body in various static positions. Although the proficient gymnast works above and below (supports and hangs) the level of his hands on the rings the beginner works mainly from a hanging position below the level of the hands. In fact, the height of the rings may need to be lowered to the level of the shoulders for the novice who is working on static positions and be raised to a height just beyond the performer's grasp as he progresses to working on rotating dismounts. Lowering the rings accommodates both the performer and the spotter. The lowered height makes it easier for the performer to elevate or rotate his body to a support from a stand on the mat while it facilitates the job of the spotter who must reach to support and position the performer's body.

We have all marveled at the strength and control of the proficient performer who presses a handstand, lowers to an L-support and terminates the sequence in the famous iron-cross. Although this may be the dream of the novice, he must begin work with static positions that are less demanding in terms of strength and balance. As in other apparatus, where static positions are evident, the principles of stability must not be violated if one is to maintain static positions while working on the rings. The task is a bit more difficult on the rings since a sudden shift of body weight causes the rings to swing a little. Nevertheless, the line of gravity of the body must fall between the rings (e.g. within the base of support) if one is to maintain balance. Violation of this principle causes the performer to rotate (or fall out) into a hanging position below the rings. Counterbalance is used as body parts extend forward and backward beyond the narrow base of the hand grasp on the rings and the performer may assume a position with a lower center of gravity when stability is threatened. The principles of stability must be applied to work on the rings, however, strength and kinesthetic awareness are necessary requisites. The following are three skills appropriate for the novice in that they require minimum strength yet provide the opportunity for the performer to develop kinesthetic awareness and apply the principles of stability.

Inverted pike hang

The inverted pike hang is a simple inverted static position the performer might assume if stability is threatened while executing more difficult feats of balance. The low center of gravity of the inverted pike hang enhances stability, however, the

Figure 15.11. **Inverted pike hang**

legs and head must counterbalance the hips to maintain the static position (fig. 15.11).

1. *Procedure:* The following analysis describes the procedures for moving into an inverted pike hang by rotating backwards from a standing position between the rings. The performer grasps the rings with palms facing toward the body. Momentum to rotate backward into the inverted position is generated in the same manner as that of the hip circle mount on the low bar (p. 000). As the hips and legs rotate up and over the trunk, the elbows straighten to lower the body into a comfortable hanging position. Bent elbows during the rotation shorten the radius of rotation to facilitate moving into the position with less effort (e.g. requires less force and strength). A tight pike position with the legs close to the face lowers the center of gravity. The location of the hips in counterbalancing the legs and head varies with individuals due to differences in body build and subsequent distribution of body mass.

2. *Spot:* The spotter stations himself to the side of the performer. One of his tasks is

Figure 15.12. **Inverted open hang**

to ensure that the performer maintains his grasp on the rings. Thus, he may support some part of the performer's body weight in a variety of ways. His second task is to help the performer rotate into the inverted position. This is accomplished by supporting and lifting the hips. And last, he may need to help the performer adjust his pike position to find that point of counterbalance between hips, legs and head. Two spotters may be necessary for some students.

Inverted open hang

As the name implies the body is inverted while hanging in a stretched (open or arched) position. The center of gravity is higher in the open position than in the piked position. Thus, a greater kinesthetic awareness and more muscle control is needed to maintain the line of gravity of the body between the rings (fig. 15.12).

1. *Procedure:* From the pike hang the performer extends the hips as the feet travel upward toward the ceiling. The hips and shoulders move toward an imaginary center line between the rings (line of gravity of the body) as the feet move upward. Once the open position is achieved the feeling should be that of *stretch* as in the headstand and handstand. A more proficient student may hyperextend the neck to compliment the openess of the body. A less proficient student may need to keep the chin on the chest in order to see the position of the feet if kinesthetic awareness is lacking.

2. *Spot:* The tasks of the spotter(s) are the same as for the pike hang. The performer should be cautioned to quickly lower the hips and legs into the pike position if stability is threatened in the open position. However, the spotters may need to catch the body if the performer lacks control and/or support and direct the body into the pike position.

Bird's nest

The name bird's nest possibly was devised to describe this skill since it looks somewhat like the nest of the Baltimore oriole, a bird which hangs its nest from the limb of a tree. The bird's nest involves the hands and feet in the rings while the body is arched and hanging below the supporting rings (fig. 15.13).

1. *Procedure:* The performer first assumes an inverted pike hang. The knees are then bent to place or hook one foot in each of the rings. The body is now in a tight tuck position. To move into the bird's nest position the hips are extended and the anterior surface of the body is forced forward and downward as the back is hyperextended or arched. Some describe the action as "turning inside out."

2. *Spot:* The spot checks to be sure the feet are securely hooked in the rings and then supports the mid-section of the trunk as the performer "turns inside out." Maintaining stability is not a problem due to four body parts as a base of support. However,

one must be careful that the performer does not rotate into the arched position with too much vigor for the feet or hands may be jerked from their contact with the rings.

There are many more static positions possible on the rings. One might consult the selected references (p. 494) for more conventional skills. However, once the student understands how to apply the principles of stability to work on the rings and can work safely, he might problem solve to discover other body parts to use as bases of support as he hangs and supports on the rings.

Doubles Balancing and Pyramid Building

When an individual adds an external weight to the body the center of gravity of the supporting body is displaced in the direction of the added weight. If the supporting body is to remain on balance the performer must change his base of support by enlarging it or adjust the position of his body (counterbalance) to have the new line of gravity fall within the base of support. This is the principle that applies when two people or several people use their bodies to build a balanced structure of some specific shape or form. The number and combination of possibilities is only limited by the imagination. However, many multiple balances have been recorded and identified, such as the angel balance, the knee-shoulder stand, the table balance and the typical squash pyramid. These, plus others, are usually found in the older or earlier books on tumbling or gymnastics. The following material is not an attempt to pick and choose from that which has been recorded, but an attempt to stimulate the imagintion of the student to create and construct that which is possible. The lesson is both appropriate and exciting for any grade level from late elementary through college, since there are

Figure 15.13. **Bird's nest**

no predetermined standards and all students work within their own level of ability; the proficient are not held back and the less skilled do not fail. This lesson is written in detail to convey the objectives (motor, cognitive and affective) which the lesson is intended to develop. It is not offered as a model, but only as a sample. The cognitive knowledges (the principles of stability) explored could be expanded, condensed, or deleted entirely and others substituted in their place. The main problems and sub-problemse could be changed. The grouping of individuals could be altered. With each fluctuation and with each group of students the motor solutions can be different.

Lesson on Balancing
Major Idea

The body can assume different balanced positions, both alone and with others; however, all are governed by the principles of stability.

Objectives
A. Cognitive (related to the principles of stability)
   1. One is more stable with many bases of support or a large base of support.
   2. One becomes less stable as the hips or center of gravity move further (or higher) from the base of support.
   3. The eyes can help one balance if they are focused on one spot.
   4. When one individual supports another, the center of gravity of the supporting person moves in the direction of the person being supported.
   5. A doubles balance with both trunks horizontal has a relatively low center of gravity.
   6. A doubles balance with the trunk of the base horizontal and the trunk of the top vertical has a higher center of gravity than when both trunks are horizontal.
   7. A doubles balance with both trunks vertical has a higher center of gravity than either of the two balances mentioned previously (numbers five and six).
B. Motor (the student progresses in his ability)
   1. to balance on a single small base of support with his hips at different levels.
   2. to use various parts of the body as a base when supporting the partial or total weight of another individ-ual. (This applies to the base partner.)
   3. to use various parts of the body to support a partner partially or totally. (This applies to the base partner.)
   4. to balance on various parts of the body while being supported partially or totally by another person. (This applies to the top partner.)
   5. to combine single, double and possibly triple balances to form various pyramids (i.e., air patterns).
C. Affective (Motivation, attitudes, and appreciations) (the student needs to become:)
   1. able to interact with his peers in a give and take process to make a decision and/or find a solution.
   2. able to work with a group toward a common goal.
   3. a contributing member of a group.
   4. self-disciplined and self-directed in his own skill development.
   5. success-oriented in his own movement, which enhances his self-image and motivates the student.
   6. appreciative of the movements the human body can perform and receptive to his own limitations and the limitations of others.

Procedure

Each individual warms up in his own way in a scattered formation. The teacher might alert the student to the types of movements that will be encountered in the lesson in order to guide the student in his warm-up.

INDIVIDUAL WORK

Problems

A. Find a buddy to help you carry a mat and place it on some spot on the gymnasium floor. Remember to use space well and keep the mats well-spaced. Once you have your mat placed, work individually and assume a balanced position on the mat with as many body parts supporting you as possible.

You are not working as partners yet; you are only sharing a mat. Get into a balanced position with many bases of support—as many body parts as possible touching that mat.

1. Think about falling out of this position. It is possible to lose balance and fall out of this position?
2. If I can make you lose your balance with a slight shove, you have not found your most balanced position. (The teacher may roam through the group and push students off balance if they have not assumed a low balance with many parts of the body touching the mat.)
3. Now remove one body part from the floor, i.e., remove one base of support.
4. Now remove another.
5. Remove still another base of support.
6. Continue to remove one body part at a time until you are balancing on just one base of support.
7. Hold that position on one base of support. (The teacher may again roam through the group and push students off balance.) Is it easier or more difficult to hold this position compared to your original position with many bases of support?
8. Relax.

What conclusions can we draw concerning the number of bases of support and the ease of balancing? (Balance is more stable with many bases of support, or, as the bases of support decrease, balance becomes less stable.)

B. Still working alone, find a balanced position on two or three bases of support and make a mental note of the location of your hips.

1. Find two different bases of support and again be aware of where your hips are located.
2. Can you find still another two or three bases of support? Again, be aware of where your hips are located.
3. Now balance on your hands and feet but keep the hips at a very low level, close to those bases of support.

4. Balance on this same base and raise your hips farther from the floor or from those bases of support.
5. Raise your hips even higher—as far from the floor as possible. (The teacher may again roam through the group and tip students off balance.)

When was it easier to balance, with hips high in the air or close to the floor? What conclusion can be drawn from this? (Balance becomes less stable as the hips or center of gravity moves farther from the base of support. The lower the center of gravity, the more stable the body.)

C. Still working alone, find one base of support on which to balance. Can you extend or stretch all other limbs of the body while balanced on this one support?
1. Can you find a different single base of support and again stretch all limbs (the arms and legs) of the body?
2. Experiment; try to find other single bases of support with all limbs extended.
3. Choose your most stable position on one base, extend all limbs and hold. (The teacher may need to limit students to balancing on one foot.)
4. Now close your eyes and hold.
5. Again assume this position with eyes open. Turn your head and look to the right, to the left, at the ceiling, etc.
6. Again assume this position and find that spot to look at which will help you balance.

What conclusions can you draw from these experiences? (Your eyes can help you balance if you focus on one spot directly ahead. Maintain eye contact with that spot.)

PARTNER WORK

We have just experimented with three of the principles of balance. There are many more principles of balance; however, these three are rather basic. We are now going to balance with a partner. Keep these three principles in mind and be aware of the ways in which they apply as two people work together balancing.

One may not always be able to reverse the base and the top due to body build and weight; however, on certain balances you will be able to reverse positions. You be the judge as to when you can reverse positions.

Problems
A. Can both partners maintain contact with the mat and yet have one partner (the base) support some part of the other partner's weight?
1. Can you find another way to do this?
2. Can one partner use his hands as a base of support while the other stays on his feet?

3. Can you find other bases of support as one partner supports some part of the weight of the other?

B. Partners, can you find some way to support and balance with the top partner having no contact with the floor? Can you find a way to support and balance when the top partner is supported completely by the base?
   1. Can you find another way to solve this problem?
   2. Base, if your stomach is facing the mat, can you change and support with your back to the mat, or vice versa?
   3. Top partner, can you be supported and balanced with first your stomach to the ceiling and then your back to the ceiling?
   4. Base, establish a stable contact with the mat and support the top partner in a vertical position.
      a. Top, can you extend your body and limbs in an open position?
      b. Top, can you bend at the hips and balance in a piked position?
   5. Base, if you have been in a position facing the ceiling, or the floor, can you reverse your position and can the top partner solve these same problems?
   6. a. Can you balance in a position with both trunks in a horizontal position?
      b. Can you balance with the trunk of the base partner horizontal and the trunk of the top partner vertical?
      c. Can you balance with both trunks in a vertical position?

Gather around the chalkboard for discussion.

Discussion

1. While acting as base, did you find it easier to balance your partner while on your hands and knees with your stomach facing the floor or your back facing the floor? Why? (The back as a base of support is rounded; it tends to roll. With four bases, the hands and knees, each of the bases can exert force separately to counteract a shift of weight.)
2. Did you find it easier to balance with both bodies horizontal, both bodies vertical, or one body horizontal and one vertical? Why? Draw these balances with lines and locate the center of gravity of the two people together (see figure).

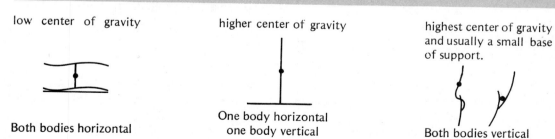

low center of gravity

Both bodies horizontal

higher center of gravity

One body horizontal
one body vertical

highest center of gravity
and usually a small base
of support.

Both bodies vertical

PYRAMID BUILDING

Problems

A. Partners, join with two other sets of partners near you to make a group of six. Use your mats as needed—group them. The problem is to build a group of balances using six people. You may use single balances, double balances, or, if you would like to try a triple balance, you may. Remember to apply the principles of balance that you have discovered.

(The teacher might need to stimulate the groups with some suggestions.)

1. Can you group your balances so that the air patterns you make look like those in the figure?

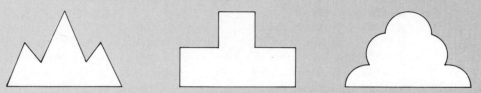

2. Once you have decided on the structure, send some person of your group to draw the air pattern on the chalk board.

Demonstrations may come at any time during the lesson when appropriate and certainly at the end of the lesson to view the final product.

TRANSFERRING BODY WEIGHT WITH STEP-LIKE ACTIONS (INCLUDING MAJOR CONCEPTS)

CONCEPT. Transferring body weight with step-like actions, while maintaining balance over changing or moving bases of support, involves the body in linear or curvilinear movements which are both purposeful and aesthetic.

Into this group fall all the locomotor movements used in gymnastics. The even locomotor movements of walk or step, run, hop, leap and jump, are combined in a variety of ways to form different rhythmic patterns. Although these locomotor movements are commonly considered transitional moves, when performed with style on the beam and in floor exercise they add to the diversity and aesthetic value of the composition.

The run is used most often to build momentum. Momentum may be necessary for the purpose of clearing the apparatus in vaulting, mounting the beam or the bars, or carrying the body through a difficult rotatory movement in floor exercise.

Quite often the mount itself up onto the beam or bars is step-like in nature as the weight is transferred from one foot to the other foot, or from the feet to the hands and sometimes back to the feet again. All vaulting skills are also a transfer of weight in step-like actions.

Included in this section is a discussion of the locomotor movements on the beam, the more basic vaulting actions, and the mounts of beam and bars that are step-like in nature.[6]

6. Rotatory mounts on the bars are included in the section "Rotation of the Total Body," page 460.

Locomotor Movements on the Balance Beam

Sub-concept. Locomotor movements on the balance beam involve a transfer of weight using the feet as a base of support; eye focus, firm trunk muscles and arm movements aid in balancing.

The locomotor movements referred to here are those in which the feet are used as the base of support. The manner in which the feet are used to create and receive weight identifies each movement pattern. However, the use of the body as a whole in contributing to the movement is common to all the locomotor movements.

Good posture aids in balancing as the firm trunk muscles hold the body in alignment. Firm abdominal and back muscles hold the trunk erect. The head is held high with a kinesthetic feeling of stretch. The body must stay centered over the moving feet. The tightening of the trunk muscles aids in balancing in that there is less sway which would tend to pull the line of gravity beyond the narrow width of the beam.

The use of the arms in a balance beam composition is both functional and aesthetical. One performs the locomotor movements with more than the feet. Besides the trunk of the body depicting height and confidence, the arms help to convey a mood or attitude. Although beginners prefer to hold the arms in one position as they concentrate on balancing and moving, they soon develop enough confidence to move the arms in a manner to complement the foot movements. These arm movements add to the rhythm and flow of the routine. The movements of the arms may also be functional. The arms may lift to gain height on the leaps and jumps, or be used to counterbalance the legs or trunk by moving in the opposite direction. It is also imperative that the arms are used in opposition to the legs on the leap to keep the body moving directly forward over the length of the beam.

Focusing the eyes on some stable object while moving along the surface of the beam orients the body as to its position in space and contributes to stability. To maintain orientation with the surface of the beam, beginners find that focusing their eyes on the end of the balance beam is the best focal point. The head is held erect and only the eyes are cast down. Tilting the head forward pulls the line of gravity toward the front edge of the base, gives an unpleasing appearance and an impression that the performer lacks confidence. When jumping and leaping the focus may need to be on the surface of the beam just ahead of where the feet (or foot) will land. Again, the head is held erect and only the eyes are cast down.

The following is a description of the locomotor movements which have an even rhythmic pattern. These five movements form the basis for all locomotor movements done on the beam. They are varied and combined to form uneven rhythmic patterns and many recognizable dance steps.

Walk

The walk is the simplest locomotor movement for a beginner since the pace is moderate and one base of support (the foot) is always in contact with the supporting surface (the beam). The toes are pointed as the foot reaches for the beam, with the ball of the foot contacting first. The walk may be varied by changing its speed, direction and level.

Run

Adding a slight suspension in the air to a very fast walk develops into a run. There is just a slight lean of the trunk in a forward direction. The leg is extended as it is swung forward to contact the beam with the ball of the foot. If the run is light and fast, the heel may never contact the beam.

Leap

The leap is developed by stretching one running step to cover a greater distance and using arm lift to attain a greater height. This allows for longer suspension in the air. The arms are used in opposition and the eyes focus on a spot in front of where the foot will land.

Hop

The hop is a takeoff on one foot and a landing on that same foot. Again the ball of the foot is used to push off and land. One can vary the tempo, direction and height of the hop. It is usually combined with other locomotor movements to depict different rhythmic patterns.

Jump

The jump, like the leap, is an explosive movement. The pattern for the jump is a one- or two-foot takeoff with the landing always on two feet. The purpose may be to depict height or cover distance. The center of gravity remains over the feet to project the body up and is moved slightly forward of the feet to cover distance forward. The arms are used to lift the body in the desired direction. Variations in the jump are commonly identified by the shape of the body or the position of the legs (tuck, straddle, split, stag, etc.).

Side Horse with Pommels

Sub-concept. Side horse work requires strength and stability for the body weight is transferred from one hand to the other as the legs and trunk swing around and over the apparatus and pass many times between the hands and the supporting surface.

Intermediate and advanced work on the side horse requires exceptional strength in the arms and shoulders in order to transfer weight and maintain the stability of a supporting position with the arms. The use of rhythmic flow to transfer momentum in a sequence of movements; however, can decrease the degree of necessary strength. The requisite of rhythmic flow may be the most important aspect of work for a beginner if he is to progress to more difficult skills. The following are a few very basic moves for the beginner. Combining the moves into a smooth sequence necessitates rhythmic flow.

Very little if any spot is needed for side horse work since a loss of balance generally results in a sitting position on the apparatus or a stand on the mat. Occasionally one may aid the performer in the execution of a move by supporting the performer's supporting arm and lifting the hips/legs to clear the apparatus. This type of aid is most helpful on a dismount since there is no subsequent move with which the spotter might interfere.

BASIC SUPPORTS

1. *Front Support:* The performer faces the broadside of the horse, grasps a pommel in each hand and jumps to a support on the hands with the front of the thighs against the apparatus. The resulting support is a front support (fig. 15.14). Although the front support may be used as a mount, it is also a position the performer assumes periodically in a sequence of movements.

2. *Rear Support:* The rear support is a support with a hand grasping each pommel, the back of the body facing the broad-

Figure 15.14. **Front support**

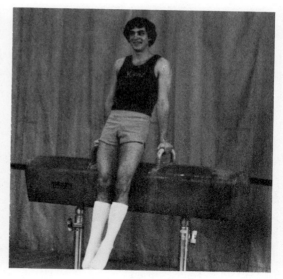

Figure 15.15. **Rear support**

side of the apparatus and the back of the thighs against the apparatus (fig. 15.15).

3. *L-Support:* The L-support is a support on the hands (on pommels) with the body in a sitting pike or L position (fig. 15.16). One may move into the L-support from a rear support or may squat through between the pommels from a front support to an L-support. One might also squat through to an L-support from a stand on the mat as a type of mount.

4. *Feint Position:* The feint position is used to locate the body in a desirable position to build momentum for circling or dismounting. From a front support, pass the left leg over the left end (neck) of the horse to a position with the legs straddling the left arm. The majority of weight is now over the left pommel (fig. 15.17). From this position a single-leg half-circle backwards with the left leg generates momentum to circle in a counterclockwise direction. Likewise a feint position over the right arm allows for greater momentum to be generated in a clockwise direction.

Figure 15.16. **L-support**

LEG CIRCLES

The term leg circles aptly describes the action of swinging the legs up over the horse and around the pommels. A leg circle may be a half-circle in which the legs travel in an 180° arc of a circle or a full-circle, 360°, which brings the legs back to their original

Figure 15.17. **Feint position**

position. Leg circles may be executed with only one leg (single-leg) or with both legs (double-leg). Thus, one might execute a single-leg half-circle, a single-leg full-circle, a double-leg half-circle and a double-leg full-circle. In addition, circles may be executed to the left (clockwise) or to the right (counterclockwise).

If the performer is to maintain a support position on the apparatus while swinging the legs, the line of gravity of the body must fall within the base of support made by the hands or hand. Another principle of stability states that if some body segment is moved away from the center of the body the center of gravity of the body moves in the direction of the displaced segment; and that if the base of support remains the same, then some other body segment must move in the opposite direction to counterbalance. These principles of stability are applied in side horse work. As the left leg circles, the body must lean to the right and shift the weight of the body over the right hand. In fact, there is an instant of total support on the right

hand as the leg passes under the left hand and over the left pommel. The same phenomena occurs to the left as the right leg circles. The lean is even more pronounced in double-leg circles due to the greater mass of both legs circling.

Momentum to begin the legs swinging and circling is achieved through muscular effort. Thus, a continuous motion with a smooth transfer of momentum conserves energy (Law of Inertia, p. 00). The appropriate degree of lean and a weight shift from hand to hand at the appropriate time facilitates the quality of rhythmic flow. No doubt proficiency in this technique requires practice. The novice, however, begins by learning the leg circles singly as described in the following section.

1. *Single-Leg Half-Circles:* The move is initiated from a front support. As the left leg is circled up and over the left side of the horse the weight shift and body lean is toward the right arm and hand. The left hand lifts off the left pommel momentarily as the left leg passes over the pommel. The left hand regrasps the pommel immediately as weight is shifted back to both hands and the body assumes a stride position supported over the saddle between the pommels. The left leg has described an arc of 180° (fig. 15.18). One would execute a half-circle backwards with the left leg to return to the starting position. However, instead of a half-circle backwards, one could execute a half-circle forward with the right leg to terminate in a rear support. In fact, a sequence of four half-circles, two forward and then two backwards without a pause in the rear support, can be used to develop rhythmic flow as the weight shifts from right to left to right to left. The performer must maintain straight strong arms when working on the side horse. If the elbows begin to bend, the

performer soon finds himself sitting on the apparatus or back on the landing mat in a standing position.

2. *Single-Leg Full-Circles:* In a full-circle the leg circles 360°. Beginning in a front support position, the left leg travels forward in a half-circle as described in the preceding section (single-leg half-circles). Rather than stop at 180° the left leg continues its clockwise direction, passes over the right pommel and under the right hand to its original position in a front support. A single-leg full-circle from a front support is executed with the right leg in a counterclockwise direction. Greater lean is necessary in the second phase of the full circle as the left leg circles backward over the right pommel and/or the right leg circles backward over the left pommel.

3. *Double-Leg Half-Circles:* The direction of movement and shift of weight is the same as that of the single-leg half-circles. The difference is that both legs circle as one unit to the left or to the right to terminate in a rear support.

4. *Double-Leg Full-Circles:* Again the direction of movement and the shift of weight is the same as that of the single-leg full-circles. The difference is that both legs circle as one unit in either a clockwise or counterclockwise direction to describe a full circle (360°).

MOUNTS AND DISMOUNTS

Few conventional mounts and dismounts are simple enough for the beginner. However, with a little innovative problem solving, the beginner can find a variety of ways to mount into one of the support positions described previously. The flank, rear and front vaulting actions (p. 000) lend themselves readily to dismounts from the side horse. The following is a description of a relatively simple dismount that utilizes a rear vault action.

Figure 15.18. **Single-leg half-circle**

1. *Single Rear Dismount:* The single rear dismount can be executed to the right over the croup or to the left over the neck of the side horse. A dismount to the left begins with a feint around the right arm and vice versa. The dismount described here is to the right. Begin with a feint around the left arm. Continue to support the weight over the left arm as both legs swing counterclockwise over the right pommel. The body rotates to assume a pike sitting position as the rear passes over the horse. The right arm, which released its grasp to allow the body to pass over, returns to the horse to add stability upon landing. The left arm (supporting arm) pushes off and is then extended to the side upon landing. The performer lands with his right side adjacent to the horse. This dismount can be initiated from a neck-pommel support or a pommel-croup support. That beginning position would be easier in that the rear would not need to pass over a pommel during the vaulting phase of the dismount.

Vaulting Over the Side Horse

Sub-concept. The vault is a transfer of body weight from the feet to the hands to the feet in a straight-line floor pattern with a curvilinear air pattern as the body takes any one of a number of postures (body shapes) and describes various air patterns as it passes up and over the apparatus.

The sequence of movements in vaulting can be divided into: (1) the approach run; (2) the hurdle and takeoff; (3) the pre-flight; (4) the contact with the horse; (5) the after-flight; and (6) the landing. A perfected vault is analyzed according to the appropriate and desirable characteristics of each of these component parts.

The *approach* should build sufficient momentum to carry the body through the other phases of the vault with ease and amplitude. The *hurdle* (a one-foot takeoff from the floor to a two-foot landing on the takeoff board) and *takeoff* convert forward momentum to upward momentum. During the *pre-flight* the body is free of support and traveling between the takeoff board and the apparatus. The weight is then transferred to the hands as they contact the horse. The *contact* should be quick and firm, contributing to the momentum for an extended after-flight. As the hands contact the horse, the body passes over the horse in the posture or shape of the vault being executed. The body is free of support again in the *after-flight* as it rights itself to touch down with the feet. The *landing* is soft and well-balanced as the ankles, knees and hips flex to absorb the force.

EQUIPMENT

Although regulation equipment is specified in competition, one can learn the techniques of vaulting on a variety of improvised pieces of apparatus. The regulation apparatus used for women's vaulting is the side horse without the pommels. A takeoff board and a padded landing area are the other two requisites for vaulting. However, when equipment is lacking one can improvise in a variety of ways. Mats can be placed over the balance beam and used to vault over. The buck, although not used for competitive vaulting, is much less expensive than the side horse and is quite appropriate for class work. A stage, an old trunk, a sturdy low table, as well as other stable objects can be used to learn the approach and mount leading to the vault.[7] The most desirable takeoff board is the Reuther board. (Note in figure 15.19 the S shape of the construction to cushion the impact of the takeoff on the shins.) More recent innovations in the construction of the Reuther board include steel coiled springs or inflated rubber tubes in place of the S-shaped wooden piece. However, again one can improvise with a homemade inclined ramp (fig. 15.20). Two five-by-ten tumbling mats, one on top of the other, make a suitable landing surface to help absorb force.

PROGRESSIONS

The sequence of movements in vaulting can be broken down into simple parts and practiced separately. Many preliminary movement experiences can be used to acquaint the student with the motor (movement) patterns used in vaulting. Merely transferring the body weight from the hands to the feet to the hands, etc. while traveling along the floor is a very simple movement related to the vaulting pattern. Placing the hands on a raised surface such as a bench and moving both feet simultaneously from one side of the bench to the other provides an experience in projecting the hips into a higher lever while supporting

7. Older gymnasiums which serve a dual purpose as an auditorium usually have a stage at one end.

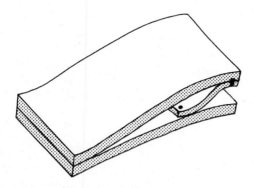

Figure 15.19. **Reuther board**

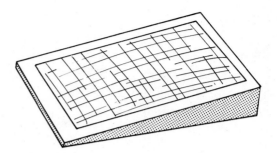

Figure 15.20. **Improvised takeoff board for vaulting. The top must be nonskid surface. Rubber matting is necessary on the floor or the base portions that touch the floor to keep the board from sliding.**

weight on the hands. The correct placement of the hands (shoulder-width apart, fingers pointing forward) should be practiced during these activities.

The approach, hurdle and takeoff can be practiced before attempting to vault over an obstacle. A short run (or a few steps) and a jump (one-foot takeoff, two-foot landing) constitute the approach and hurdle. The students can practice this pattern in any open area. The next step in progression would be to hurdle onto some predetermined spot. Once this is mastered the takeoff board is introduced and the student can practice the sequence of approach, hurdle and takeoff with the board using a mat on which to land.

The next step is to place the takeoff board in a position to mount the vaulting piece.[8] If adjustable, the vaulting apparatus should be lowered. This, along with placing the takeoff board relatively close to the apparatus, provides security and success for beginners. It is desirable to have students merely place their hands on the top of the vaulting apparatus and bounce on the takeoff board several times before trying the approach, hurdle and takeoff to mount the apparatus.

The amount of momentum needed to raise the body to a mount position on top of the apparatus is much less than that needed to vault over the apparatus. Therefore, the novice needs to use only a few slow running steps in the approach. Emphasis is on developing a smoothly flowing, controlled movement. The performer then concentrates on a soft balanced landing as he jumps from the apparatus to the landing mats.

The least difficult mount is a mount to a kneeling position because the hips (the center of gravity) are kept low. A mount to a squat position up on the apparatus requires one to raise the hips a little higher. This then logically leads to the conventional squat vault. The straddle and stoop vaults can also be learned in a similar progression by stopping the movement on top of the apparatus.[9] Many of the more difficult vaults can also be divided into parts to be mastered separately. For example, the latter half of the handspring vault can be learned by starting on top of the apparatus, kicking into a

8. Mount as it is used here means to stop the movement on top of the apparatus before continuing over to a landing on the other side.
9. The straddle and stoop vaults are described on page 453.

handstand and then arching or limbering off the apparatus. This action necessitates using the horse lengthwise.

TRANSFER OF EYE FOCUS

To assure stability and proper foot-hand contact with the apparatus, the eyes focus first on the takeoff board, second on the top of the apparatus, and finally on a spot out in front of the landing area. Beginners quite often contact the takeoff board in the wrong spot because they have failed to keep their eyes focused on the board until they have begun the hurdle. Contact should be six to eight inches back from the front edge of the takeoff board and at the top of the S-curve on the Reuther board. One minimizes the advantage of a takeoff board by contacting too far back on the board, while contacting too far forward can lead to injury if the feet slip off the front edge. Once the vaulter has begun the hurdle the eyes shift to the top of the apparatus. As the hands contact the apparatus the eye focus moves to a spot directly out in front (at approximately eye level) of the landing area. Again beginners must be cautioned against looking down at the landing mat. The forward tilt of the head causes the body to tilt forward. This action gives the vaulter the sensation of falling forward face-first and quite often terminates in a landing with the hands on the mat.

VAULTS IDENTIFIED BY BODY SHAPE

Vaults can be identified or named according to the posture or shape the body takes as it passes over the apparatus. The following movements are both progressions and conventional vaults identified by their common names. Identifying the progressions by name gives the less skilled student a sense of accomplishment as these movement sequences are mastered. The simplest vaults for a beginner are those in which the center of gravity is kept low and the arms and legs are used symmetrically. The following order is from simple to complex as the hips are raised higher and higher to mount or pass over the apparatus in the various body shapes.

Kneel, stand, jump-off

The vaulter approaches, hurdles and mounts to a balanced kneeling position. Once balance is assured he stands and jumps to the landing mat, absorbing the force of landing by flexing the ankles, knees and hips. This is a very simple progression that divides the vault into two parts, allowing the beginner to get the feel of the movement. The vaulter develops both control and confidence in this simple sequence of movements.

Courage vault

Again the vaulter stops in a balanced kneeling position on top of the apparatus. The dismount from this position is a whip action. The hips are flexed (the body is crouched with buttocks on heels while kneeling) and the arms are extended back and down behind the body. To build momentum the arms are whipped forward and up as the body extends. This action lifts the body forward and upward (fig. 15.21). As the legs clear the apparatus they extend downward for the landing on the mat.

Squat-on, squat vault

A mount to a squat position (feet between the hands) up on the apparatus requires that the hips be raised slightly higher than in the kneel-on. Again, one may dismount with a jump. When the vaulter has confidence and control and performs the squat-on with a light, quick jump-off, he is ready for the conventional squat vault. The spotter can encourage the vaulter with the phrase "up

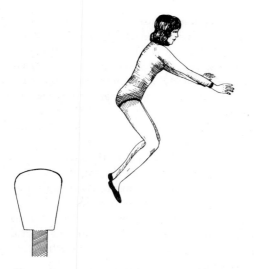

Figure 15.21. **The flight off the horse in the courage vault**

Figure 15.22. **After-flight of the stoop vault**

and over" to counteract the tendency to stop on top of the apparatus.

Straddle-on, straddle vault

The vaulter again approaches, hurdles, and places the hands shoulder-width apart on top of the apparatus. The legs are straddled (abducted) and the hips are raised high enough to allow the feet to clear the apparatus and come down on top. The knees are straight and the head must be kept looking forward. The wider the straddle of the legs, the less high the hips must be raised. Balance is less stable due to the narrow base in a forward-backward direction and a high center of gravity. One must employ the principle of counterbalance to remain on balance while stationary on top of the apparatus in this position. The upper trunk leans beyond the front edge of the apparatus to counteract the hips extending beyond the back edge of the apparatus. The straddle-on progression can only be used if the vaulting apparatus is long enough to

allow the feet to be placed in a wide straddle position outside the hands. The buck, due to its size, is not suitable for this progression. Again, when the vaulter performs the straddle-on progression with confidence and control he is ready for the straddle vault. Quite often one must remind the beginner to bring the feet together for the landing on the mat. The tendency is to maintain the straddle position for the landing, which places a lateral strain on the knees and ankles.

Stoop-on, stoop vault

The stoop vault is like the squat vault in that the feet pass between the hands. However, balance is less stable in the stoop vault than the straddle and squat vaults since the legs are kept straight and fully extended, raising the hips higher than in the straddle or squat positions. Again, one may use the progression of stopping on top of the apparatus before executing the conventional vault in one sequence of movements (fig. 15.22).

Wolf vault

The wolf vault is a combination of the straddle and squat vaults. One leg is straddled to the side and passes outside one arm

Figure 15.23. **Wolf vault. The left leg is tucked against the chest as in the squat vault.**

while the other leg is bent and passes between the arms (fig. 15.23). As in the straddle, the hands push off and are actually removed from the apparatus before the body passes over. Again, due to the straddle position of one leg the tendency is to land only on the leg that passed between the arms. The beginner must be reminded to bring the legs together and to land equally balanced on both feet.

VAULTS IDENTIFIED BY BODY SURFACE

Vaults may be identified or named according to the surface of the body that passes nearet to the apparatus. The following vaults—flank, front, and rear—imply that the side of the body, the anterior or front surface, and the posterior or rear surface, respectively, pass nearest to the apparatus in each of the three vaults. The flank vault may be the least difficult of the three in that the body remains facing forward throughout the total sequence of movements. Because the center of gravity is kept low it could fit

into a progression of vaults immediately after the squat vault. The center of gravity can also be kept low on the front and rear vaults; however, they involve a quarter-turn as the body passes over the apparatus. The rear vault also involves a transfer of weight from one arm to the other and the replacement of one hand on the apparatus for stability upon landing. In each of these vaults (flank, front, and rear) both legs stay together and pass to either the right or left of center over the apparatus. Although the vault can be mastered to both sides, a beginner will find he has a preferred direction to move the legs and should master that side first rather than trying to master both directions at once.

Flank vault

The approach, hurdle, and placement of the hands (shoulder-width apart) are the same as for the symmetrical vaults. As the hands touch the apparatus the hips and legs begin to swing to the preferred side. As the body passes over the apparatus the arm on the preferred side is removed and raised upward. Only the one remaining arm is supporting the body for a split second. The supporting arm pushes off and the landing is with the back to the apparatus.

Front vault

Again, the vaulter approaches and hurdles into a two-foot takeoff. As the hands contact the apparatus the head and shoulders turn to face the opposite direction from which the feet and legs will go. This causes the trunk to roll or rotate around the vertical axis of the body until the stomach faces the apparatus. The arm on the side of the body toward which the head was turned will carry the majority of the body weight and can remain on the apparatus during the landing for reasons of stability. The other hand is removed as the body passes over the apparatus and remains extended out to the side of the body for the landing. The performer lands on both feet with the side of the body of the supporting arm nearest the apparatus.

Rear vault

Again, the approach, hurdle, takeoff, and placement of hands are the same as for the symmetrical vaults. However, on the rear vault, as the shoulders begin to move over the hands, the head and shoulders rotate toward the side (left or right) or toward the direction in which the legs are extended. The body assumes a piked sitting position with the buttocks and back of the legs facing the apparatus. As this occurs the hand on the same side as the legs must be removed to allow the hips to pass over the apparatus. This same hand is then replaced on top of the apparatus as the other hand is removed to allow the hips to continue on over. The landing is with the side of the body to the apparatus, one hand on the apparatus and the other hand extended horizontally.

SPOTTING THE VAULTER

The main task of the spotter in vaulting is to support the shoulder girdle, thereby protecting the head and neck, and to assist the vaulter to a safe landing on the feet. To accomplish this the spotter or spotters are stationed on the landing side of the apparatus and off to one side of the center. The spotter turns partially toward the center of the apparatus in order to watch the approach and extends his base of support in the direction of the oncoming force, the vaulter. The near hand supports the wrist and lower arm of the vaulter while the far hand supports the upper arm once the vaulter's hands are placed on the apparatus. This location of the spot allows the spotter to keep the upper trunk from overbalancing

forward and to lift and pull to help the vaulter clear the apparatus if necessary. The forward-back stride of the feet provides for a quick step backward to travel with the vaulter on the after-flight and landing. On the vaults in which the leg or legs pass to one side over the apparatus (the wolf, flank, front and rear vaults) the spotter must be stationed on the side or end of the apparatus opposite the legs. If necessary the spotter can support the upper arm with the far hand and reach over the apparatus with the near hand to lift and assist the hips over the apparatus.

The spotter for the straddle vault must be stationed directly in line with the vaulter since the legs travel over both sides of the apparatus. He grasps both upper arms, lifts, pulls, and steps back to provide room for the vaulter to land.

The dismount for the courage vault must free the vaulter's arms to whip for the lift off the apparatus. The spotter may hold one hand of the vaulter, leaving the other free to whip, or he may only spot the waist area to catch the vaulter should the feet not clear the apparatus. In all the foregoing vaults the spotter may release the upper arms and spot the waist once he is certain the upper trunk is not going to overbalance forward. This frees the vaulter's arms to be extended upon landing, which aids him in making a balanced landing.

LOCATION OF TAKEOFF BOARD

The distance the takeoff board is located in relation to the apparatus varies with the proficiency of the vaulter. Beginners should have the takeoff board only an arm's reach from the apparatus. They need the security of having the hands placed on the apparatus immediately after the feet leave the takeoff board, if not before. As the vaulter develops confidence and skill the takeoff board is moved away from the apparatus. This then necessitates a speedier and longer approach run, which in turn contributes to a greater pre-flight and after-flight. This increase in momentum is necessary for success in executing the more difficult vaults and contributes to the quality of movement in all vaults.

Mounts and Dismounts for the Beam and Bars

Sub-concept. All mounting and dismounting moves involve a transfer of weight from one surface to another, as well as a transfer of weight from one body part to another.

This section is concerned only with those mounts and dismounts which are void of rotating movements.

Many of the movements described as vaulting progressions in the previous section are also appropriate as mounts for the balance beam. These progressions include the kneel, squat, straddle, stoop and the wolf vault position stopped and held on top of the horse or beam as a mount. The kneel-on can be modified to one knee and be followed by a pivot to a knee scale. These movements should be mastered first on the side horse since balance is less stable on the narrow beam and the padded vaulting apparatus is less likely to bruise the shins should the performer fail to reach the necessary height. The spotting techniques are the same as for vaulting and it is permissible to use a takeoff board. The takeoff board should be removed after the performer has mounted, since it becomes a hazard should the performer fall or need to jump down in that area.

The vaulting actions do not adapt as readily to the bars since movement should not be halted on the bars. Swinging, hanging and rotating movements should predominate a bar routine. Some of the vaulting actions can be used; however, the subsequent movement places these mounts into an intermediate or advanced category. One example of such a vaulting action would be a squat over the low bar, followed by an immediate catch to the high bar, cast, and rotation on the low bar. Another is a straddle-on, reverse grip, and rotation forward, followed by allowing the feet to come off at the peak of the swing and a glide kip to a support. Still another might be a stoop-on, sole circle, kip and catch to the high bar with a half-turn, cast and rotation on the low bar.

The jumps described under "Locomotor Movements on the Balance Beam" (p. 446) can all be used as dismounts from the beam. They are simple and safe and provide an opportunity for the beginner to work on controlling the body in flight and absorbing the force of the body upon landing.

Several of the vaulting actions can be used for dismounting from the bars. The squat, straddle and flank movements over the bar to a landing on the mat are most appropriate. These can be executed both over the low bar and the high bar. If initiated from a front support the body must employ the cast to place it in a position to go up and over the bar. However, the vaulting action over the high bar can be initiated from a stand on the low bar, facing the high bar. These dismounts should be mastered over the low bar before attempting them over the high bar.

The following section describes several basic mounts and dismounts for the beam and bars which have not been previously mentioned and fall into this category of step-like actions.

BALANCE BEAM MOUNTS

Straight arm support

The straight arm support is often used to pivot into a straddle seat.

1. *Starting position:* The performer faces the beam from the side and places the hands on top of the beam.

2. *Body parts receiving weight:* The weight is transferred from the feet to the hands and then onto the seat if one pivots to a straddle seat.

3. *Force and balance:* A slight push off the balls of the feet transfers the weight to the hands. The shoulders move forward beyond the hands to keep the weight centered over the beam. One leg is raised sideways as weight is transferred to the arm on the opposite side of the body for the pivot into a straddle seat.

4. *Spot:* The spotter (if needed) stands on the far side of the beam and supports the upper arm(s).

5. *Variations:*

   a. The approach may be started from a short run at a right angle to the beam.

   b. One leg may pass between the hands (in a squat position) to a side stride support across the beam.

   c. Both legs may squat through the hands to a rear support, hips partially resting on the beam.

   d. Both legs may squat through the hands to an L-support, or a pike V-seat support. The hips may or may not rest on the beam.

   e. Both legs may pass over the beam and outside the hands to a pike straddle support. The hands must be placed closer together and the hips do not touch the beam.

Modified step-on

1. *Starting position and approach:* The performer stands a few feet away from the beam and faces diagonally toward it. The preferred side of the body for whipping and supporting is toward the beam. The performer must gauge the distance to allow for a one-foot takeoff from the board.

2. *Body parts receiving weight:* Weight is transferred from the takeoff foot (foot farthest from the beam) to the opposite hand and foot as the performer steps up onto the beam. Thus, if the preferred side of the body for whipping and supporting is the right side, the performer will complete the mount supported by the right hand and foot.

3. *Force and balance:* The few approach steps build forward momentum which is transferred diagonally upward as the near leg whips up onto the beam. Weight is centered between the supporting hand and foot with the body in a semi-squat position.

4. *Spot:* Two spotters are used for beginners. One spot is located on the far side of the beam and grasps the upper arm and wrist of the supporting arm. The second spot grasps the free hand of the performer, approaches with her and supports as she steps up onto the beam.

5. *Variations:*

   a. The performer may immediately remove the hand and assume a squat pose on both feet or one foot.

   b. The performer may refrain from using the hand to support at all and merely step up onto the beam into a low or high static pose, or move right into some locomotor variation.

   c. Once the performer can mount without the hand support she may take the step-on mount to the end of the beam.

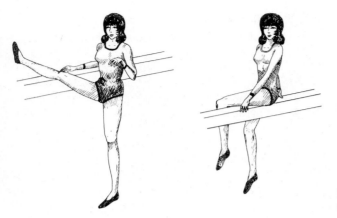

Figure 15.24. **Riding seat mount (fence vault mount)**

Riding seat mount

The riding seat mount is also known as the scissors seat or fence vault mount (fig. 15.24).

1. *Starting position and approach:* The starting position and approach are the same as for the modified step-on.

2. *Body parts receiving weight:* Weight is transferred from the far foot to the near hand (the supporting hand) and then to the seat as the legs assume a sidesaddle position on the far side of the beam.

3. *Force and balance:* The force and balance are the same as for the step-on mount with the exception of the weight being centered between the supporting arm and seat at the termination of the mount.

4. *Spot:* The spot is the same as for the step-on mount.

LOW BAR MOUNT (UNEVEN OR HORIZONTAL)

Front support mount

1. *Starting position:* The performer faces the bar and grasps it with an over-grip.

2. *Body parts receiving weight:* Weight is transferred from the feet to the hands with some part of the front of the thighs resting against the bar.

3. *Force and balance:* The force and balance are the same as for the straight arm support on the beam.

4. *Spot:* The spot is the same as for the straight arm support on the beam.

5. *Variations:* Variations are the same as those for the straight arm support on the beam. However, it is desirable to move from these positions into swinging or rotating movements very quickly when working on the bars.

DISMOUNT FROM THE BALANCE BEAM

Flank-off

1. *Starting position:* For a beginner this dismount may be initiated from a knee scale or a prone support (a push-up position).

2. *Body parts receiving weight:* From the support position on top of the beam weight is transferred to the hands still on top of the beam and then to the feet as they come down to the mat.

3. *Force and balance:* The extended leg of the knee scale or the preferred whipping leg of the prone support is dropped below the level of the beam and then whipped upward. The supporting foot pushes up away

Figure 15.25. **Flank-off dismount from a knee scale. The same dismounting movement can be initiated from a prone support (push-up position) or an English handstand.**

from the beam and rises to meet the whipping leg at the peak of its swing. This shifts the weight to the hands. The shoulders remain over the hands for the most stable support. The neck is hyperextended and the head is up. Besides the force being directed upward it must also be sideward in the direction the performer wants to dismount. The landing is on two feet with one side of the body nearest the beam. The near hand may remain on the beam for balance when landing (fig. 15.25).

4. *Spot:* The spotter stands on the opposite side of the beam from the intended dismounting side and faces the performer. The near hand supports the upper arm while the other hand guides the lower trunk (the waist or hips) to be certain the performer clears the beam to the side.

5. *Variations:* The same movement pattern can be initiated from a stand on the beam. The performer kicks into a semivertical English handstand and drops the feet to the mat beside the beam. Balance is more precarious in that the center of gravity passes through a much higher level.

DISMOUNT FROM LOW BARS (UNEVEN OR HORIZONTAL)

Cast back to a stand

1. *Starting position:* All casts on the uneven bars are initiated from a front support position. This particular dismount is started from a front support position on the low bar.

2. *Body parts receiving weight:* Weight is transferred from the hands on the bar to the feet on the mat.

3. *Force:* The legs are piked below the bar to place them in a position to build greater momentum by whipping through a greater distance. The elbows are flexed slightly to allow the legs to pike under the bar and then extended as they push the body back and away from the bar in conjunction with the leg whip. The body moves upward and backward in an *open position.* The landing is on two feet. If the momentum generated is great enough, the hands should release the bar and be used to balance upon landing.

4. *Spot:* The spotter (if needed) might support the upper arms, guide the body back away from the bar and/or help maintain balance during the landing.

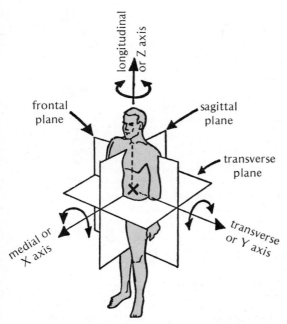

From Geoffrey Dyson, *The Mechanics of Athletics*, 5th ed. (London: University of London Press, 1970), p. 74. Reprinted with permission from Dover Publications, Inc.

Figure 15.26. **Center of gravity of the body (x) axes and planes passing through that point**

5. *Variations*

   a. If the purpose is to move away from the bar the performer moves in the manner described. However, if the cast is to build momentum to travel to the low bar (unevens), the performer maintains her grasp on the bar until the hips contact the low bar. The momentum built on the backswing carries her forward as gravity pulls her down. Upon meeting the low bar she does a back hip circle rotate.

   b. If the cast is used to raise the body above the bar in some way the shoulders move forward over the bar to center the weight as the legs whip backward and upward to raise the hips. This type of cast is used to build momentum for the backward hip circle (p. 474).

ROTATION OF THE TOTAL BODY (INCLUDING MAJOR CONCEPTS)

CONCEPT. Rotation of the total body in space involves movement around the center of gravity of the body and movement around one or more of the axes that pass through this point.

Figure 15.26 depicts the center of gravity of a human body, the axes that pass through this center point, and the planes in which these three axes are located. Rotation of the total body can be described with reference to these items.

In forward and backward rotating movements the body rotates around a horizontal axis and through the saggital plane. The forward and backward roll is an example of this type of rotation. When the body passes through the inverted position moving laterally, as in the cartwheel, it rotates around a horizontal axis and through the frontal plane. Pivots and turns are rotations around the vertical axis. More complex movement patterns may involve movement around two axes. A back flip (somi) with a half-twist is one example of rotation around two axes.

Rotation of the body occurs in a variety of ways in gymnastics and uses a variety of supporting surfaces. Nevertheless, the varieties can be grouped into six categories according to the supporting surface(s):

1. a transfer of weight during rotation onto adjacent body parts along the same supporting surface (rolling);
2. a transfer of weight during rotation from one body part to another and from one supporting surface to another (rotation or roll-like actions

up onto or down from a piece of apparatus—mount and dismount);

3. no transfer of body weight and no change in the supporting surface as some body part maintains contact with a supporting surface and rotates around it (rotating around a bar);
4. a transfer of weight during rotation along the same supporting surface, using the hands and feet as bases of support in step-like actions (cartwheel, handspring, etc.);
5. a transfer of weight during rotation from one supporting surface to another, using the hands and feet in step-like actions (the skills in category four are used for mounts and dismounts on apparatus);
6. a transfer of body weight from feet to feet with the body being free of all support during rotation (aerials).[10]

Sub-concept. The speed of rotation is determined first by the initial muscular force used to overbalance and secondly by the length of the radius of rotation.

The initial force can be a quick forceful action that moves the center of gravity beyond the edge of the base to initiate movement or it may include a preliminary movement to build momentum prior to overbalancing. A forceful extension of the legs in the forward roll is an example of the first method described. Preceding this forceful extension with a few running steps is an example of a preliminary movement used to build momentum prior to overbalancing. The cast that must precede the back hip circle around a bar is another example of a way to build momentum prior to the actual rotating movement.

During rotation the speed is controlled by the length of the radius. To increase the speed of rotation one should shorten the radius of the body or pull body parts into a compact shape. A novice applies this principle when learning the forward and backward roll on the mat. It is sometimes desirable to decrease the speed of rotation for greater control. This is accomplished by straightening the legs and rolling in somewhat of a piked position. This controlled roll is necessary when rolling on the balance beam, parallel bars, or when rotating around one bar. The rotation is stopped by opening the body and/or applying force in the opposite direction to counteract the momentum of the rotation.

Rolling

Rolling on a surface (mat, beam, or parallel bars) requires a careful transfer of weight onto adjacent body parts with these parts forming a curved shape. If these body parts receiving weight in the roll are not naturally next to each other they must be positioned near to each other in order to receive weight smoothly. The direction the roll takes will be determined by the direction the line of gravity is moved beyond the edge of the base. The force to overbalance is muscular action with gravity taking over to pull the body down and continuing the momentum of the roll. If the body is to move in a straight pathway, the initial force must be through the center of gravity and the supporting body parts must defy gravity equally at all times. The speed of the rotation is determined by both the initial force and the length of the radius of rotation, as described earlier.

10. This action, in which the body rotates free of all support (aerials), will not be covered in this chapter. Nevertheless, the same principles apply to these aerial movements.

ROLLING FORWARD

Tucking the head and leading with the hips allows for a smooth transfer of weight when rolling in a *forward direction.* Muscular force is needed to invert the trunk and move the hips beyond the front edge of the initial base of support. Pulling the chin to the chest helps to round the upper trunk in preparation for the roll. Allowing the hips, rather than the feet, to lead the movement as gravity pulls the body over helps to keep the lower trunk rounded for a smooth transfer of weight. Teaching phrases that could be used are "tuck your head" and "lead with your seat." The foregoing principles apply to all forward rolls regardless of the body parts used to receive weight or the apparatus upon which the roll is executed. The following is an analysis of specific movements on different pieces of apparatus. Because the analysis dwells on the movements specific to each apparatus it dwells on differences; the commonalities of the movement are not always repeated.

Forward roll, mats

1. *Starting position:* The body assumes a squat position with hands placed approximately shoulder-width apart on the mat.

2. *Body parts receiving weight:* Weight is transferred from feet to hands, to the curved posterior surface of the body, and again to the feet.

3. *Body shape:* The body is a curved shape with all parts tucked or hips piked.

4. *Force:* The initial force is a push from the feet. At the end of a pike roll the knees may be quickly flexed to build momentum to pull the body back up onto the feet.

5. *Spot:* The spotter assumes a crouch position near the performer. One hand is placed on the back of the head to keep the head tucked. The other hand is placed under the back of the thigh to help lift the hips. As the two spotting hands apply pressure they also keep the body rounded.

6. *Variations:* Problem-solving for variations in rolls are contained on pages 485–486.

Double forward roll, mats

1. *Starting position:* One partner is supine with legs raised to allow the second partner to grasp his ankles. The second partner stands with feet on either side of the bottom partner's head. Each grasps the ankles of his partner. The partner's feet are now used as the hands would be used in an individual forward roll.

2. *Body parts receiving weight:* Weight is transferred from the feet to posterior surface to the feet to posterior surface as the partners alternate bottom and top positions in rolling forward.

3. *Body shape:* Again, the shape of the two bodies is rounded. However, since the top partner during the rotation must clear the length of the trunk of the bottom partner, the bodies are somewhat piked rather than tucked.

4. *Force:* The initial force comes from the top partner overbalancing forward as he places his partner's feet on the mat close to the buttocks and begins the roll. The bottom partner aids the movement by sitting up and maintaining a grasp on the rolling partner's ankles to help pull him to his feet in preparation for his roll (fig. 15.27).

5. *Spot:* The spot must move with the roll, tucking the heads under if necessary. The other arm may be used under the midsection of the trunks to help carry the weight forward and keep the bodies rounded.

Figure 15.27. **Double roll; movement may be forward or backward.**

Forward roll, parallel bars

1. *Starting position:* The performer assumes a straddle seat across both bars, facing the end of the bars.

2. *Body parts receiving weight:* Weight is transferred from the thighs, to the hands, to the upper arms, and back to the thighs as the body is rotated forward in a rolling action along the surface of the bars. The width of the bars is adjusted to allow the padded deltoid muscle area of the upper arm to receive the weight through the inverted position. The arms are abducted at the shoulder joint to place the upper arms in positions to receive weight and to keep the body from sliding down between the bars.

3. *Body shape:* The back is rounded, the hips are piked and the legs are straddled. It is imperative that the hips lead the movement rather than the legs and that the hands re-grasp as the hips roll out. Otherwise the performer smacks his legs on the bars and ends in an open supine position on the bars.

4. *Force:* The initial force is a pulling action of the arms, dorsal trunk muscles and shoulders in an effort to invert the trunk. Beginners may have trouble in initiating this movement. If such is the case the feet can be hooked up over the bars in back and the top of the foot used in a pushing action as the legs straighten to invert and overbalance the hips (fig. 15.28).

1

2

3

Figure 15.28. **Forward roll on the parallel bars. Note the modification of the instep on top of the bar (picture 1) to provide the force to push the body into an overbalance forward. More proficient students pull with the trunk muscles to invert the trunk and overbalance forward; thus, the feet need not be placed over the top of the bars but are allowed to extend down in a straightleg straddle position.**

| 1 | 2 | 3 |

Figure 15.29. **A pike straddle forward roll on the mats is used as a preliminary movement to rolling on the parallel bars.**

5. *Spot:* The spotter keeps the performer from falling between the bars and aids in a smooth transfer of weight. (A word of caution when spotting on the parallel bars: the spotter should never extend the arms over the bars in a position where they might get caught between the performer's body and the bars.) One or two spotters can be used at the side of the bars. Standing a little ahead of the position of the performer the near hand (with palm facing ceiling) is used to keep the arms abducted. The far hand reaches *under* the bar to support the back on the roll-out. A third spotter may be stationed between the bars facing the performer. As the hips come over he reaches up, grasps the hips, tucks his head and guides the hips of the performer to a seat on his upper back.

6. *Preliminary movements:* The preliminary movements leading to the forward roll on the parallel bars are as follows:

   a. On the mats one may practice a controlled pike roll beginning with a straddle stand and ending with a straddle seat (fig. 15.29).

   b. One may also practice on a low set of parallel bars if there is a fear of height. A mat placed across one end of the bars can be used to receive the weight at the end of the roll. This eliminates the fear of falling through the bars and can be used as an aid especially for those students who fail to keep the legs straddled. A mat over the high bars can also take the place of the third spotter between the bars.

7. *Variations:*

   a. The hips can be shifted to one side to roll up to a seat on one bar.

b. The legs can be kept together, allowing the body to drop below the bars to an upper-arm support position.

c. The roll can be started from a swing rather than a straddle seat position.

d. The roll can be used as a mount with a two-foot takeoff from a Reuther board at the end of the bars.

Forward roll, balance beam

1. *Starting position:* The starting position must place the hips in a position to be moved above and beyond the hands in order to initiate the roll. With weight on the feet the body may be in a crouch, or standing pike position. The hands are placed on the top of the beam (thumbs together and fingers extending down the sides of the beam), ready to receive weight as the hips move forward.

2. *Body parts receiving weight:* Weight is transferred from the feet to the hands to the dorsal surface of the body as the hands grasp under the beam to slow the movement and then re-grasp near the small of the back to push the body into a straddle seat on the beam. The hands must grasp quickly under the beam as the shoulders receive weight in order to check the momentum of the roll.

3. *Force:* The initial force to move the hips beyond the front edge of the base (the hands) is supplied by straightening the legs and pushing off with the feet.

4. *Body shape and balance:* Since the top surface of the beam is slightly less than four inches, the pull of gravity creates a balance problem. The hips (the center of gravity of the body) must stay over the beam if the performer is to stay on the beam. This means the initial force must be in line with the top surface of the beam and the hands must support and pull equally to keep the trunk over the beam. Keeping the center of gravity of the body as low as possible will allow the body more lateral movement before the line of gravity falls outside the top surface of the beam. This is accomplished by keeping the body in a tight pike, which allows much of the dorsal surface to contact the beam before the feet are brought over. The pike position also slows rotation and keeps the trunk and leg muscles contracted to control those segments of the body. The roll is a controlled movement, not a relaxed, freely flowing movement.

5. *Spot:* The spot aids in keeping the hips over the beam and controls the speed of rolling out. The spotter stands alongside the beam facing the performer. He grasps on either side of the hips (he may lift to initiate the roll) and supports the hips as the performer rolls out. Once the hips contact the beam the spotter may transfer his spot to the trunk and upper arm to help the performer to a straddle sitting position.

6. *Variations:*
   a. The starting position may be varied. One may begin the roll from a squat, stand, lunge, front scale, needle scale, standing pike, etc.
   b. The ending position may be varied. One may end in a straddle seat, one-leg squat, knee and foot position, V-seat, side seat pose, etc.
   c. The forward roll may be used as a mount from the end of the beam or a mount from a diagonal approach to the middle of the beam.
   d. The forward roll may be used to terminate the English handstand.
   e. The forward roll can be executed without the aid of the hands.

ROLLING BACKWARD

Leading with the toes through the inverted position and applying force equally with both hands (sometimes pushing and sometimes pulling, depending upon the surface on which the roll is being executed) allows for a smooth transfer of weight when rolling in a *backward direction*. Rolling backwards is generally a little more difficult than rolling forward because the hips must be lifted against gravity. In the forward roll the legs push or the hips are positioned at a high level in order to facilitate overbalancing and allowing gravity to help one roll out. In the backward roll there might be a slight thrust from the hands or feet or a preliminary movement to build momentum; however, it becomes necessary for the abdominal muscles to curl the trunk into an inverted position. Again the chin is on the chest and the total dorsal surface is curved. As one rolls up into the inverted position the hands must apply force to maintain momentum and continue the rotation on over to the desired base. The feet lead the movement through the inverted position. The hands must apply force equally to keep the body moving in a straight pathway; otherwise, the performer falls off balance to the side.

Again, the length of the radius of rotation affects the effort needed to rotate. The same principles apply to the backward roll as were stated in the introduction for rolls (p. 460).

Backward roll, mats

1. *Starting position:* The performer assumes a low squat position with weight on the balls of the feet and fingertips touching the floor in front for balance.

2. *Body parts receiving weight:* The performer sits back onto the buttocks and continues to roll, transferring weight onto other body parts in the following sequential order: curved dorsal surface, shoulders, head, hands, and finally feet.

3. *Body shape:* The body is in a curved shape with all parts tucked or hips piked.

4. *Force:* The sit back builds momentum and then the hands push equally from a po-

Figure 15.30. **Backward roll on the mat. At this point the spotter may need to grasp the hips and lift the performer up and over to a position on the feet.**

sition equidistant on either side of the head to continue momentum on over to the desired base of support.

5. *Spot:* The spotter stands to the side and faces diagonally toward the direction of the performer. As the performer rolls up onto the shoulders, the spotter reaches to place one hand on either side of the hips and lifts or pulls the roller up and over. The spotter should *never push*. The purpose of the spot is to take pressure off the head and neck and to aid the rotation. Pushing adds pressure to these parts (fig. 15.30).

6. *Variations:* Problem-solving for variations in rolls are contained on page 485.

Double backward roll, mats

1. *Starting position:* The starting position is the same as that for the double forward roll.

2. *Body parts receiving weight:* The body parts receiving weight are the same as those for the double forward roll with the only difference being a reverse of direction (fig. 15.27, p. 463).

3. *Body shape:* The body shape is the same as in the double forward roll.

4. *Force:* The initial force comes from the top partner sitting down close to the head of the bottom partner and rolling back as he

pulls on the ankles of his partner. The bottom partner aids the movement by curling the lower trunk to invert his body and applying force against the mat with his hands on his partner's ankles. As the bottom partner begins to assume an upright position the first roller raises his legs by hip flexion to assist his partner into the upright position. The initial bottom partner is now the top man and is in position to sit and roll to continue the movement.

5. *Spot:* The spot is the same as that for the individual backward roll on the mats.

Backward roll, parallel bars

1. *Starting position:* The performer assumes a straddle seat across both bars facing the end of the bars. The hands grasp the bars behind the thighs.

2. *Body parts receiving weight:* Weight is transferred from the thighs (in the seat) to the hands, which grasp the bars *behind* the thighs, to the upper arms as the trunk passes through the inverted position. Weight is then transferred back to the thighs and hands as they re-grasp *in front* of the thighs in the roll back up to a straddle seat. The adjustment of the bars and the abduction of the arms are the same as for the forward roll on the bars. In fact, the body parts receiving weight are also the same with the only difference being the direction of the roll and the position of the hands on the bar at the beginning and end of the roll.

3. *Body shape:* The back is rounded, the hips are piked and the legs are straddled. The chin is kept on the chest until the hands re-grasp to push the body into an upright position. The toes lead the body through the inverted position.

4. *Force:* The initial force is a roll back onto the upper arms; however, the abdominal muscles and hip flexors must also contract to curl the lower trunk and bring the legs over. Once the hips begin to move the hands press against the bars to aid in overbalancing the hips in a backward direction. When the hips are overbalanced gravity aids in pulling them down to the bar as the hands re-grasp and push the upper trunk into an upright position.

5. *Spot:* The spotters should keep the performer from falling through between the bars and aid in keeping the body centered over the bars. The spotters are positioned outside the bars to spot the hips and shoulders. A lift on the hip area helps the performer to curl the lower trunk and the spot on the shoulders keeps the performer from adducting the arms and sliding through between the bars. The spotters must apply force equally on both shoulders to keep the roll centered over the bars. The performer should also be instructed to release and regrasp both hands at the same time. Failure to do this can cause the performer to roll diagonally and slide into a straddle position on one bar, rather than ending in a straddle position on both thighs centered over both bars.

6. *Preliminary movements:* The preliminary movements leading to the backward roll on the parallel bars are:

   a. On the mats one can practice a controlled pike roll beginning with a straddle seat and ending with a straddle stand.

   b. One may also practice on a low set of parallel bars if there is a fear of height.

7. *Variations:*

   a. The roll can be started from a sitting position on one bar.

   b. The legs can be kept together and dropped between the bars to end in a position with the hands supporting the body weight (straight arm support, pike support).

c. The roll can be started from a swing rather than a straddle seat.

d. The roll can be used as a mount when initiated from an upper arm support with the body standing or hanging between the bars.

Backward shoulder roll, balance beam

1. *Starting position:* The performer assumes a supine position with the body centered directly over the beam. The hand on the same side of the body as the shoulder to be used in the roll reaches to grasp under the beam opposite the head, which drops to the other side of the beam. The other hand may also grasp under the other side of the beam next to the head or may be used on top with the fingers extending down along the side of the beam to counterbalance the pull of the hand below the beam.

2. *Body parts receiving weight:* Weight is transferred from the dorsal surface as the body rolls up to the shoulder and then to the top of the foot and knee of one leg as the body assumes an upright position sitting on the lower leg. The hands receive some weight and maintain contact with the beam until the completion of the roll. Generally the leg used as the base of support for the termination of the roll is on the same side of the body as the shoulder used in the roll. For example, if the performer rolls over the right shoulder, she concludes the roll with the right leg on the beam (fig. 15.31).

3. *Force:* The initial force to curl the lower trunk and legs is flexion of the hips and abdominal muscles. The hand(s) on the bottom of the beam aids in curling the trunk by pulling. Once the hips are overbalanced backwards gravity aids in pulling the legs down. If both hands were placed below the beam at least one hand must now travel to the top of the beam to push the trunk upright. This production of force to roll backwards on the beam is very much like that of the backward roll on the parallel bars.

4. *Body shape and balance:* Just as in the forward head roll on the beam (p. 465), a tight piked position keeps the center of gravity low, slows rotation, and keeps the trunk and leg muscles contracted to control those segments of the body. The head, as it extends down alongside the beam, is in a good position to see the beam, which helps the performer to know where to place the foot. If the hands are used, one on top of the beam and one below the beam, they can work in opposition to counterbalance (push or pull as the need might be) in order to maintain the center of gravity over the beam. As the hands push the upper trunk away from the beam on the roll-out, the performer should lower the hips onto the heel of the supporting leg and allow the other leg to drop alongside and below the beam to lower the center of gravity. The inside of the thigh of this free leg can also be pressed against the side of the beam to help stabilize the body.

5. *Spot:* The spot aids in the rotation and balance by lifting and guiding the hips over the beam. The spotter stands alongside the beam facing the direction of the roll. He grasps the hips to lift and guide. Once the intended supporting leg makes contact with the beam he may transfer his spot to the trunk and upper arm to help push the upper trunk away from the beam into an upright position.

6. *Variations:*

a. The roll can be initiated from a straddle seat.

b. The ending position may be varied. One may end in a knee scale, a straddle seat, one-leg squat, etc.

c. The performer may begin a backward shoulder roll and extend the

Figure 15.31. **Backward shoulder roll on the balance beam. Lowering the hips to a seat on the heel and allowing the free leg to hang alongside the beam lowers the center of gravity, which provides greater stability for the novice.**

legs into a shoulder stand balance before rolling out.

d. One may begin a backward shoulder roll and pass through the shoulder balance position quickly and smoothly, coming down from this position with a chest roll—a fish flop on the beam.

Rotation around One Bar

LOW HORIZONTAL AND UNEVEN BARS

Rotating around a single bar is very much like rolling and yet has some unique characteristics in that the movement is not *on* but *around* the base of support with the possibility of no transfer of weight unless the movement is used as a travel from one bar to the other (unevens), a mount or a dismount.

> *Sub-concept. When rotating around one bar the performer works with gravity on the downswing and against gravity on the upswing.*

To initiate the rotation around the bar the performer may be working with gravity if the movement is started from a position above the bar, or working against gravity if the movement is initiated from below the bar. One would work both with gravity and against it if the movement makes a complete circle around the bar or if the movement is a swing down and back up again. Lengthening the lever (i.e., moving the body parts as far from the bar as possible and still maintaining contact with the bar) on the downswing builds greater momentum. Shortening the lever by flexing body parts and pulling closer to the bar on the upswing, against gravity, takes less effort (momentum). Beginners may need to apply both principles to be successful. More advanced performers maintain a longer lever throughout the rotation, which adds to the beauty of the movement.

The least complex forward rotating movement around a bar is a dismount that ends with a transfer of weight as the feet are placed on the mat.

Forward roll dismount

1. *Starting position:* Movement is started from a straight arm front support position with the hands in an over-grip (fingers in front, thumbs behind).

2. *Body parts as a base support:* The hands maintain a grip on the bar and rotate around the bar with the body. Weight is transferred to the feet as the body opens to a long hanging position below the bar. (The grip on a high bar may be forward or mixed, depending on the next movement intended if the roll is not a dismount.)

3. *Force:* One allows gravity to aid the movement by leaning or overbalancing on the bar in a forward direction. The performer can aid gravity by keeping the arms straight and the upper trunk extended. This produces a long lever which builds momentum as it travels downward. The momentum is then transferred to the hips and legs to lift and pull them off the bar. The arms flex to help lift the hips off the bar and then extend slowly to check the rotatory momentum. Beginners quite often curl the trunk toward the bar too soon, which decreases momentum and makes it difficult to lift the hips off the bar.

4. *Body shape:* The trunk is curled and the hips are piked as they lead the roll-out. The hip flexors and abdominal muscles control the speed with which the hips and legs descend.

5. *Spot:* The main task of the spotter is to check the speed of the roll-out by supporting the hips. If the performer has trouble lifting off the bar the spotter may need to lift on the shoulder of the inverted trunk or lift the thighs up and over the bar.

6. *Variations:*

   a. From a front support on the high bar facing the low bar, the body rotates forward to a long sitting hang on the low bar. The body is rotated with control and the legs lowered and placed on the low bar. An uncontrolled drop to the low bar can break the bar.

b. From a front support on the high bar facing away from the low bar, the body rotates forward to a long hang.

c. From a front support on either the high or low bar, the body rotates in a forward direction *around* the bar. One complete rotation brings the performer back into a front support position. This movement pattern is commonly known as a forward hip circle.

The least complex backward rotating movement around a bar is a mount which begins from a stance on the mat and terminates in a front support on the low bar. This movement is commonly called a hip pull-over mount or a hip circle mount.

Hip circle mount

1. *Starting position:* The performer stands facing the low bar and grasps it with an over-grip. The feet are placed in a forward-back stride with the strongest whip leg back.

2. *Body parts as a base of support:* The hands maintain a grip on the bar and rotate around the bar with the body. Weight is transferred from the feet to the hands and anterior surface of the pelvic girdle as the body rotates into a front support position.

3. *Force:* The whip leg produces angular motion as it kicks forward and upward for a spot above and behind the head as the arms pull the body toward the bar to shorten the radius of rotation. The trailing leg pushes off and joins the whip leg to drop behind the bar to counterbalance and aid the arms as they push the upper trunk into an upright position ending in a front support. The chin is kept on the chest and the trunk is rounded until the body opens above the bar as the thumbs grip to counteract the momentum of the rotation. Beginners quite often extend the arms and throw the head back as they kick, which makes rotation very

difficult, if not impossible, as the body drops away from the bar.

4. *Body shape:* The trunk is curled and the hips are piked as the feet lead the movement up over the bars. The rotation terminates in an open front support position (fig. 15.32).

5. *Spot:* The main task of the spotter is to aid in rotating the hips upward against gravity. The spotter stands on the opposite side of the bar from the performer and lifts in the hip area. As the legs drop behind the bar he may place one hand on the back of the thighs and the other hand on the upper arm to aid the performer into an upright position.

6. *Variations:*

a. This same movement may be used to travel from the low bar to the high bar of the uneven bars. The spotter aids rotation by pushing upward on the hips and shoulder and then grasps the ankle of the performer as the legs drop down behind the high bar.

b. The movement used as a mount may be initiated by a two-foot take-off. A good push with both feet, a strong pull by both arms, and a forceful sustained contraction of abdominal muscles is needed to rotate the body backwards from this position.

GRIP

Sub-concept. When rotating around the bar with no change in supporting surface, the direction of rotation will dictate the grip to be used.

When rotating around the bar with no change in supporting surface (i.e., the body has no supporting surface other than the one bar) the body must allow gravity to build momentum on the downswing to aid the performer in rotating back up onto the bar. (Review again "Rotation around One Bar,"

Figure 15.32. Hip circle mount on the uneven or horizontal bars. The arms pull the body close to the bar as the legs create the force to rotate around the bar to a front support.

page 470.) A simple guideline to use to determine the grip for these rotating movements is to use the thumb as a prehensile digit and point it in the direction of the rotation; the direction of rotation thus dictates the grip to be used. For example, when rotating backwards an over-grip would be used. This positions the bulk of the hand on the side of the bar opposite the direction of rotation, which affords a firmer grip. When rotating forward an under-grip or reverse grip should be used. The least complex movement of this nature is the swing down and up, or one-half knee circle backwards.

One-half knee circle backwards

1. *Starting position:* The body assumes a side stride position with a regular grip.

2. *Body parts as a base of support:* The hands and back of the forward knee maintain contact with the bar during rotation.

3. *Force:* The arms lift the body off the bar as the back leg whips backwards to pull the body into an off-balance position behind the bar. Keeping the arms extended and trunk open provides a long lever to build momentum on the downswing. As rotatory momentum is overcome by the force of gravity the body reverses direction and begins to travel back up. On the upswing gravity again overcomes rotatory momentum and muscular effort must be used to pull the body back up into a support above the bar. This is accomplished by pulling with the arms toward the bar (shortening the lever) and whipping the free leg backward to build angular momentum to aid the body in moving up over the bar again. This is a controlled, smoothly flowing movement as opposed to a relaxed, deadweight feeling. The kinesthetic feeling is that of stretching.

4. *Body shape:* The body is in somewhat of a sitting position (except for the free leg) on the downswing, trunk erect, and one hip flexed. On the upswing the body curls somewhat toward the bar as the arms pull.

5. *Spot:* The main task of the spotter is to aid the performer on the upswing and to eliminate a very natural fear of falling backwards. Verbal encouragement as well as maintaining contact with the performer on the downswing helps eliminate this fear. The spotter stands in front of the bar and reaches under to grasp the wrist of the performer. The grasp is with the back of the hand facing forward and the thumb pointing down. The other hand is placed on the front of the thigh on the free leg. The spotter grasps the front of the thigh and pushes back and up to help the performer regain a position on top of the bar. A second spotter stationed on the other side may assume the same grasp of the other wrist and insure that the forward knee stays bent around the bar. As the performer rotates back up onto the bar the spotter may need to support the upper arm.

6. *Variations:* The variation of continuing the rotation around the bar to an upright position leads to the full knee circle backwards. In the full knee circle backwards, both the starting positions and body parts used as a base of support are the same as in the one-half knee circle backwards. With regard to force, the performer may need to overbalance (move beyond the bar in a backward direction) with a little more thrust to generate enough momentum to rotate completely around the bar. The body shape is the same as in the one-half knee circle backwards. The spotter grasps the wrist with the near hand as described for the one-half knee circle backwards. However, the other hand does not spot the legs but catches the upper arm as the body rotates below the bar and aids the performer on the upswing by lifting.

Stride circle or mill circle forward

1. *Starting position:* The body assumes a side stride support (p. 427) with a reverse grip; the thumbs point in the direction of the rotation, forward.

2. *Body parts as a base of support:* The hands and front inside portion of the thigh of the back leg maintain contact with the bar during rotation.

3. *Force:* The arms lift the body off the bar as the front leg moves forward to pull the body into an off-balance position. Again, one must maintain a long lever to build sufficient momentum. A high lift off the bar and a strong step-like action of the forward leg add to the momentum of the downswing.

4. *Body shape:* The body must maintain an open, stretched position throughout the movement. The anterior surface of the body leads the movement with the head staying in line with the spine.

5. *Spot:* The spotting technique is the same as that of the full knee circle backwards The only difference is that the spotter stands behind the bar rather than in front, since the rotation is forward.

6. *Variations:* The stride circle or mill circle can be done backwards with the technique of spotting being exactly the same as that for the full knee circle backwards. The grip must be changed to a forward grip when rotating backwards.

Backward hip circle

1. *Starting position:* A straight arm front support position with the hands in an overgrip (p. 426) is used.

2. *Body parts as a base of support:* The hands maintain a grip on the bar and rotate around the bar with the body. The anterior surface of the pelvic girdle also maintains contact with the bar during rotation.

3. *Force:* The preliminary movement of casting is needed to build momentum for rotation. As the body returns to the bar from the cast the hips flex quickly (pike) to convert forward momentum to rotatory momentum. The higher the cast, the more momentum created. The arms pull constantly during rotation to keep the body close to the bar.

4. *Body shape:* The body pikes to push away, extends in the cast, and then pikes again to rotate around the bar. However, the body must remain open until the exact instant of contact with the bar or momentum is lost and the body drops away from the bar. Beginners quite often anticipate the action and pike before contacting the bar. Throwing the head backwards also causes the body to fall away from the bar. The head should be kept in line with the spine or even tilted a little forward.

5. *Spot:* The spotter stands in front of the bar, with one side to the bars. As the body begins the rotation he reaches below the bar to support the small of the back and back of the thighs to aid in the rotation. The spotter may then need to travel to the upper arm to stabilize the body in the front support.

6. *Variations:*

   a. Once the performer has mastered the hip circle on the low bar she may precede or build momentum for the rotation with a swinging long hang from the top bar. This action involves a transfer of the hands from the top bar to the bottom bar during rotation (unevens).

   b. The performer may then precede to a cast from the high bar to a hip circle on the low bar (unevens).

   c. The hip circle can be performed on the high bar.

   d. The hip circle can be worked into a mount or it may build momentum for a dismount (such as the Hecht dismount) from either the low or high bar.

Rotation with Step-like Actions

The extension skills of cartwheels, limbers and walk-overs, as well as the kipping actions such as the headspring, fall into this category. In each skill the body rotates around its own center of gravity as it rotates over moving bases of support, the hands and feet. The sequence of bases touching the floor is feet to hands (the hands and head in the headspring) to feet. The rotation may move in a forward, backward and sideward direction. If the body is flexed or hips are piked, the radius is shortened and rotation is faster. In the majority of these skills it is considered good form to extend the body for a slow, controlled movement. However, the kipping action in the headspring involves a piked body to gain an advantage in building rotatory momentum. This action will be discussed in greater detail under that skill. Besides the length of the radius affecting the speed of rotation, these skills have several other commonalities.

Sub-concept. The center of gravity must be centered and shifted over the moving bases of support in order to describe a straight line of movement in the desired direction.

This sub-concept implies that all bases must defy gravity equally on all sides to keep the line of gravity centered over the base. Both hands or both feet when used as the supporting base must push equally against the mat to keep the body from falling to the side. Force too must be applied directly through the center of gravity of the body to cause it to move in a straight line.

TRANSFERRING MOMENTUM

Sub-concept. The momentum created in one section of the body is transferred to another part of the body to sustain the rotation and bring the body back over onto the feet.

The initial rotatory force is created by the action of the arms moving downward to the mat and the whip of the leg(s) upward to invert the body. Placing the hands too far forward of the feet creates a diving action which restricts rotation rather than aids it. Once the hips have overbalanced, gravity aids the rotation downward. The hands also push against the mat by a forceful shoulder extension to aid the upper trunk in rotating back up over the feet.

PRELIMINARY MOVEMENTS TO BUILD MOMENTUM

Sub-concept. Setting the body in motion by a short run prior to takeoff builds linear momentum that is transferred to rotatory momentum at takeoff.

The termination of the run differs if the takeoff is on two feet as opposed to one foot. The two-foot takeoff is the same as the pattern described for vaulting (p. 451). The one-foot takeoff is also called a hurdle in some texts; a hopping action is involved on the whip leg (the back leg), with a high knee lift on the forward leg. As the forward leg comes down to meet the mat the back leg is whipped up behind. The hurdling action can also be used without the run. The performer must be certain of controlling and supporting the body through the inverted position before building momentum with a run and/or hurdle.

SPOTTING DURING ROTATION

Rotating the total body with step-like actions using the hands and feet as bases of support requires spotting which involves *supporting the back and aiding the rotation.* For movements in a forward direction one hand supports the small of the back and the other supports the shoulders to aid the upper trunk in rotating back up over the feet. In backward rotating movements one hand supports the small of the back and the second hand aids rotation by lifting under the hips or the thighs. In sideward rotation (such as a cartwheel) the hands support slightly during the beginning and end of the execution of the skill, but only guide the body through the inverted position.

The sample of skills described as follows are learned first on the mat; however, they can be adapted and used in a variety of ways on the apparatus. The cartwheel and walk-over can be executed on the balance beam. Because the supporting surface of the beam is narrow, the direction of movement must be in a straight line and over the beam if one is to stay on the beam. Using the cartwheel, walk-over, or limber as dismounts off the beam is much less difficult, since the body has much more time to rotate and right itself as it travels to the lower surface of the mat. The cartwheel can even be used as a mount up onto the beam; however, this is certainly an advanced move which requires a great deal of momentum to raise and rotate the body up onto the higher level of the beam. Preceding the handspring action with a two-foot takeoff and rotating over the side horse converts the handspring action into a vault. The action of a handstand arch-over is much like that of the limber and can be used as a dismount from the bars.

MATS

Cartwheel

The cartwheel is a rotatory movement in a sideward direction with the body extended and the legs straddled.

1. *Starting position:* The performer assumes a side stride position with weight on the foot away from the intended direction of movement. The arms are raised and ready to move sideward and downward to receive the weight to initiate rotation. Some performers prefer a forward-back stride, which necessitates a quarter-turn of the upper trunk before placing the hands on the mat.

2. *Body parts receiving weight:* Weight is transferred from one hand to the second hand and over onto the foot of the whipping leg and then the foot of the trailing leg. Each step is even and can be counted—one, two, three, four, or hand, hand, foot, foot.

3. *Body shape:* The body is fully extended, neck hyperextended and head up, with the legs in a wide straddle.

4. *Force:* The force is as described on page 475 (transferring momentum).

5. *Spot:* The spotter stands behind the performer and in a position to be directly behind him during the inverted position. The near hand supports the near hip of the performer, palm up so the performer rotates onto the hand. The far hand of the spotter crosses *over* the near hand and grasps the hip on the far side. The spotter may need to travel with the performer.

6. *Variations:*
   a. The cartwheel can be developed to either side.
   b. A quarter-turn is initiated during rotation and the feet are brought together to be snapped down to the mat. The performer is now facing in the direction from which he came. This is commonly known as a round-off.
   c. Another variation is the one-handed cartwheel using only the near or first hand down for support. (This would be the left hand when cartwheeling left and vice versa.)

d. Another variation is the one-handed cartwheel using only the far hand for support. (This would be the right hand when cartwheeling to the left and vice versa.)

e. Finally, an advanced variation is the aerial cartwheel with no hand support.

Limber or arch-over

The limber or arch-over is a forward rotating movement in which the trunk is hyperextended. Both hands contact the mat simultaneously to support the body through the inverted position and both feet contact the mat simultaneously to support the body as it returns to the upright position (fig. 15.33).

1. *Starting position:* The performer assumes a forward-back stride with weight on the back foot and arms raised and ready to move forward and downward to receive weight and initiate rotation.

2. *Body parts receiving weight:* Weight is transferred from both hands to both feet. The count is one, two; hands, feet.

3. *Body shape:* The body is extended during the inverted position and then the shoulders and back are hyperextended as the body rotates down during the second phase of the rotation.

4. *Force:* The force is as discussed on page 475 (transferring momentum).

5. *Spot:* The spotter stands to the whipping-leg side of the performer and grasps the knee to help invert the body. The spot then moves his hands to the small of the back and the shoulder as described on page 476.

6. *Variations:*

a. Once can use any method of getting into a handstand (p. 000) and then use the limber or arch-over to return to the upright position.

b. The movement may be reversed, beginning in a backbend and pullover

1	2	3	4	5

Figure 15.33. **Limber or arch-over. Smooth, continuous movement aids in the transfer of momentum to bring the body back up to a stand on the feet.**

backwards. The spot is the same as that for a back walk-over.

Backward walk-over

The back walk-over is a backward rotating movement initiated from one foot and terminated on one foot. The legs are positioned in a forward-back stride during the entire rotation.

1. *Starting position:* The performer assumes a forward-back stride with the weight on the back foot. The arms are positioned overhead, ready to move backward and downward to the mat in order to receive the body weight.

2. *Body parts receiving weight:* The body weight is transferred to both hands simultaneously and then on to the leading leg as it rotates down to the mat.

3. *Body shape:* The trunk and neck are hyperextended with the eyes looking for the mat. The body passes through the inverted position extended, feet in a forward-back stride. The hips flex to bring the feet back to the mat.

4. *Force:* Force is as discussed on page 475 (transferring momentum).

5. *Spot:* The spotter kneels or squats to the side of the performer. One hand is placed under the small of the back for support and the other hand is placed under the thigh of the leading leg to lift the hips up and over.

6. *Variations:* The legs may execute a switch kick as they pass through the inverted position.

Front walk-over

The front walk-over is a forward rotating movement with the same characteristics as the back walk-over.

1. *Starting position:* The starting position is the same as that for the limber.

2. *Body parts receiving weight:* The body parts receiving weight are the same as those of the back walk-over.

3. *Body shape:* The body shape is the same as in the limber, with the exception of the legs being positioned in a forward-back stride.

4. *Force:* Force is as discussed on page 475 (transferring momentum).

5. *Spot:* The spot is the same as in the limber.

6. *Variations:* Variations are the same as those of the back walk-over.

Forward handspring

The movement pattern of the forward handspring is very much like that of the limber. However, greater momentum is developed with a run and hurdle, which causes the body to rotate faster and pass through a slight period of suspension after passing the vertical position.

1. *Starting position:* The starting position is a run with a hurdle and a one-foot takeoff (p. 475, preliminary movement).

2. *Body parts receiving weight:* The body parts receiving weight are the same as those of the limber.

3. *Body shape:* The body is open and somewhat hyperextended. Less hyperextension is needed than in the limber because the greater momentum generated carries the body through the rotation. The head must stay back (neck hyperextended) until the hands leave the mat.

4. *Force:* Force is discussed on page 475.

5. *Spot:* The spotters stay on their feet and ready to move to be in a position beside the performer when he is inverted. The spot is on the small of the back and shoulder. Two spotters are desirable for equal support on both sides. (See page 476.)

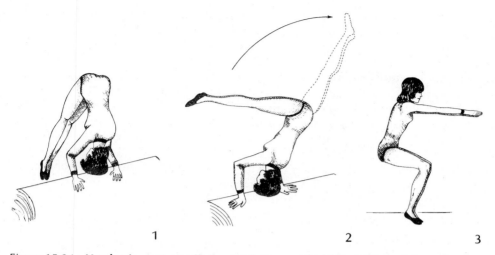

Figure 15.34. Headspring over a rolled mat. The toes trail and the hips overbalance to place the body in a deep pike in preparation for the kipping action, which brings the body to a balanced semisquat stand.

Headspring

The headspring is a forward rotating movement involving the head and hands as a base of support during the inverted position. This skill differs from the ones described previously in this category in that movement is commonly initiated from a two-foot takeoff and a kipping action is used to rotate the body to an upright position.

1. *Starting position:* The performer stands with feet together, bending forward to place the hands and head on the mat. The hands and head may more nearly approach a straight line than the tripod hands and head position (p. 430).

2. *Body parts receiving weight:* Body weight is transferred from the feet to the head and hands and then back to the feet.

3. *Body shape:* The body begins in a piked position, passes through an extended position and lands in either an extended position or crouched position. A beginner should flex upon landing (crouch) to absorb the force of the landing. A more proficient performer absorbs the force with the feet

and ankles as the body remains extended or open upon landing.

4. *Force:* The initial force is a push from the feet to overbalance the hips beyond the head—the performer must *lean*. A forceful whip (kipping action) of the legs as they describe a large arc in the air carries the body over and onto the feet. The hands also push vigorously against the mat to aid in rotating the trunk upright over the feet (fig. 15.34).

5. *Spot:* The spotter(s) assumes a low position (a crouch or kneel) to the side of the performer and adjacent to the spot in which the performer will be inverted. The near hand (palm up) grasps the performer's upper arm. The other hand is used under the small of the back. The spotter(s) supports and lifts to aid the performer in passing through a high arc in order to allow time and space for a landing in an open position.

6. *Variations:*
   a. The initial attempt at performing a headspring should be done on the raised surface of a rolled mat. This

provides the beginner with more time to get his feet back under his body for landing. The spotter sits in a straddle on the mat.

b. Movement can be initiated from a one-foot takeoff.

c. Headsprings can be done in succession down the mat, diving into each succeeding one immediately upon landing.

d. The movement pattern of the headspring can be executed over the side horse as a vault.

INDIVIDUALIZING INSTRUCTION

The varieties of human physiques and temperaments are never more evident than in a lesson in gymnastics. The ponderous and the slender, the strong and the weak, the confident and the shy, the enthusiastic and the lethargic all respond in their own way to the gymnastic unit. Some meet each new challenge with enthusiasm and confidence. Others hang back with feelings of frustration and fear. It becomes a task for the teacher to challenge each individual within his own limitations and provide successful experiences as the student progresses and develops at his own rate.

Too often the gymnastic unit each year is a repeat of material as the teacher strives to bring all students up to the same level of proficiency. The more proficient are held back and the less skilled are frustrated as the teacher tries to gear to the "average" student in the class. The traditional unit must be set aside and the methods of organization and teaching changed if one is to reach each individual student.[11] Included with the context of this chapter are suggestions for variations to allow the more proficient student to progress once he has the basic understanding and skill of the movement being

presented. Problem-solving lessons, too, can stimulate students to delve a little deeper into the content as they seek original solutions to the problems. A reciprocal organization of students within the class (i.e., the buddy system) for spotting and helping each other frees the teacher to move through the group to give help where it is most needed and allows students to progress at their own speed.

The following are samples of tools and techniques that can facilitate individualized instruction, allow students to progress at different rates and succeed at various levels of proficiency. The first is a sample checklist of the forward and backward roll progression. Once a student understands the concepts related to rolling and can control a roll on the mat he may prefer to take the rolling action to the apparatus. Others may prefer or need to continue on the mats. A sample outline of a lesson on rolling is included on page 483. Problem solving for variations in rolling adds interest as the student masters and refines the movements on the mats as well as the apparatus. Sample problems for roll variations on the mat follow the lesson on rolling. Numerous progressions and variations are possible if gymnastic skills are grouped according to commonalities with an application of related concepts.

Problem solving for balance beam mounts (p. 486) is one example of how a small group of students could work independently. Similar problems could be devised for other apparatus and content. Teaching the cartwheel through guided discovery (p. 487) ensures that all students develop the foundational movement pattern of a lateral step-like rotational movement. Likewise, progressions could be developed for

11. Chapter 3, "The Role of Methodology," treats this subject more fully.

other skills. Sample feedback checklists (p. 489) provide students with the tools to aid each other in mastering specific skills. Finally, culminating activities are discussed briefly (p. 491). Included are two examples of how a beam and uneven bar composition can be altered to both challenge the more proficient and yet provide the less proficient with success. These sample tools and techniques are but a few of the many innovations possible in gymnastics.

GYMNASTIC CHECKLIST

Name _____ Class _____

Rate: 5 to 1 (5 is high, 1 is low)

    5—excellent; controlled, no spot.

    4—good; controlled, light spot.

    3—fair; student is starting to develop control, spot needed for confidence and possibly safety.

    2—coming along; spot definitely needed for safety.

    1—student tried; spot was required to carry the student through the movement.

ROTATING MOVEMENTS: ROLLING

Mats

Skill	Rating (5–1)	Evaluator	Comments
1. Forward roll:			
a. squat to squat	_____	_____	_____
b. (suggested	_____	_____	_____
c. variations	_____	_____	_____
d. pg. 485.)	_____	_____	_____
2. Backward roll:			
a. squat to squat	_____	_____	_____
b.	_____	_____	_____
c.	_____	_____	_____
d.	_____	_____	_____
3. Double roll:			
a. forward	_____	_____	_____
b. backward	_____	_____	_____
4. Triple roll:			
a. forward	_____	_____	_____
b. backward	_____	_____	_____

Even Parallel Bars

1. Forward roll:
   a. low bars   _____   _____   _____
   b. regulation bars   _____   _____   _____

   Variations in starting position:
   a.   _____   _____   _____
   b.   _____   _____   _____
   c.   _____   _____   _____
   d.   _____   _____   _____
   etc.

   Variations in ending position:
   a.   _____   _____   _____
   b.   _____   _____   _____
   c.   _____   _____   _____
   d.   _____   _____   _____
   etc.
   (Suggested variations are located in the context of the chapter along with the analysis of the skill.)

2. Forward roll used as a mount:
   a.   _____   _____   _____

Skill	Rating (5–1)	Evaluator	Comments

3. Backward roll:
   a. low bars   _____   _____   _____
   b. regulation bars   _____   _____   _____

   Variations in starting position:
   a.   _____   _____   _____
   b.   _____   _____   _____
   etc.

   Variations in ending position:
   a.   _____   _____   _____
   b.   _____   _____   _____
   etc.

4. Backward roll used as a mount:
   a. _____ _____ _____

   Variations in starting and ending position:
   a. _____ _____ _____
   b. _____ _____ _____
   c. _____ _____ _____

Balance Beam

1. Forward head roll:
   a. squat to straddle seat

   Variations in starting position:
   a. _____ _____ _____
   b. _____ _____ _____
   c. _____ _____ _____
   d. _____ _____ _____
   etc.

   Variations in ending position:
   a. _____ _____ _____
   b. _____ _____ _____

Skill	*Rating (5–1)*	*Evaluator*	*Comments*

2. Forward shoulder roll:
   a. knee to
      straddle seat _____ _____
   etc.

3. Backward shoulder roll:
   a. _____ _____ _____
   b. _____ _____ _____
   etc.

4. Backward head roll:
   a. _____ _____ _____
   b. _____ _____ _____

SAMPLE OUTLINE OF A LESSON ON ROLLING

The following sample outline of a lesson is to serve as an example of how material in this chapter can be ordered conceptually to allow the teacher to build the lesson around several main concepts while allowing students to progress at their own rate through skills dependent upon an understanding of these concepts. The lesson begins with experiences to develop an understanding of body shapes (positions) and how certain body shapes and surfaces lend themselves to rolling, progresses to the forward roll on the mat (including variations), and terminates in forward rolls on the various apparatus. The methods used early in the lesson are a combination of problem solving and guided discovery. Direct teaching with demonstrations (the task method) is used to show specific techniques of execution and spotting of the conventional skills. The final organizational pattern is that of reciprocal aid in which couples or small groups of students move at will throughout the various equipment stations (mats and apparatus), working at their own level of proficiency. Thus, the teacher is free to move among the students to offer help as needed. The outline of the lesson is as follows. The type of motor activity the student experiences is identified by capital letters (A, B, C, etc.). The understandings that should evolve from these experiences are identified by numbers (1, 2, 3, etc.).

A. Exploration of the various shapes the body and/or body parts may assume along with identification of each by names commonly used in gymnastics (squat, tuck, open, pike, straddle)
   1. One may assume these shapes using various bases of support on both mats and apparatus as well as in the air, free of all support.
B. Rocking and rolling on mats in these various body shapes to determine which shapes and which body surfaces lend themselves to a smooth transfer of weight
   1. Rocking and rolling on a mat requires a careful transfer of weight onto adjacent body parts forming a curved shape.
C. Explanation, demonstration and practice of the conventional forward roll (in the tuck position) on the mat along with learning the spotting technique
   1. Tucking the head and leading with the hips allows for a smooth transfer of weight when rolling in a *forward direction*.
   2. Applying force directly through the center of gravity of the body (pushing equally with both feet) and defying gravity equally with both hands through the inverted position allows one to roll in a straight forward pathway.
D. Variations of the forward roll
   1. A forward roll can be executed from a variety of starting positions and terminate in a variety of ending positions with the arms and legs assuming various positions and functions, provided momentum is applied to overbalance the hips in a forward direction, the head is tucked, and the back is curved.
   2. The degree of initial thrust to overbalance, the length of the radius of rotation, and the muscular effort in defying gravity on the roll-out determine the speed of the rotation.
   Note: At this point the student may practice the controlled pike and pike straddle roll-out on the mats in preparation for rolling on the apparatus (beam and bars).
E. Explanation and demonstration of the forward roll on the various apparatus including the spotting technique.

The ideas encountered earlier in the lesson are again applied to the rolling action. It is imperative that the controlled pike roll-out position is stressed to slow rotation and maintain control when rolling on all apparatus. An explanation of the execution of the forward roll, spotting techniques, progressions from mat to apparatus, and possible variations of the rolls on the various apparatus is included on the following pages: (a) parallel bars, p. 464; (b) balance beam, p. 465; (c) horizontal and uneven bars, p. 470.

Task cards, visual aids, etc., may be available at each station to guide the students, who are now free to move at will from station to station. The teacher, too, is free to move among the students to spot, instruct, encourage, etc., as he is needed.

VARIATIONS: FORWARD ROLL

Perform a forward roll by varying the beginning and the ending position.
1. From a squat to a squat.
2. From a squat to a stand.
3. From a stand to a stand.

Choose your own starting position.
4. End in a low balance on one foot.
5. End by stepping forward to a medium balance on one leg.
6. End by stepping forward to a high balance on one leg.
7. End in a long sitting position.
8. End in a V-seat.
9. End on one knee and one foot.
10. Can you end on one knee and one foot and slide one leg forward into a split?
11. Can you begin in a pike position and end in a pike position?
12. Can you begin in a straddle position and end in a straddle position?

The roll itself can be varied.
13. Can you do a forward roll without using your hands?
14. Can you roll in a forward direction over one shoulder and end in various balance positions (such as one knee and one foot)?
    a. Do this with the hands.
    b. Do this without the hands.
15. Can you discover some variations of your own?

VARIATIONS: BACKWARD ROLL

Perform a backward roll by varying the beginning and the ending position.
1. From a squat to a squat.
2. From a squat to a stand.
3. From a stand to a stand.

Choose your own starting position.
4. End in a balance on two knees.
5. End in a balance on one knee (and two hands).
6. End in a straddle balanced position.
7. End in a pike position; a stand.
8. End in a split.

9. Can you begin in a straddle position and end in a straddle position?
10. Can you begin in a long sitting position and end in a pike?
11. Can you begin in a pike and end in a pike (i.e., stand, pike, sit, roll, pike, and stand)? Use your hands to cushion the pike sit to mat.
12. Can you roll backwards over one shoulder without using the hands, ending in a balance on your knees?
13. Can you discover some variations of your own?
14. Working lengthwise on the mats, combine variations. For example, squat, roll to straddle, roll to pike, stand, etc.

PROBLEM SOLVING FOR BALANCE BEAM MOUNTS

These problems should be attempted only after the student has been successful in executing the symmetrical vaults. Limitations are also incorporated into the lesson in order to standardize the spotting techniques. For all of these vaults a spotter should be stationed on the far side of the beam, facing the performer. The spotter's job is to support the upper arm(s) to keep the performer from tipping forward. A second spot can be stationed near the takeoff area to aid the performer in jumping back down to the mat should she fail to gain the necessary height and balance. The per-former must tell the spotters what she is attempting in order for the spotters to stay clear of her legs.

Limitations:

1. The beam is lowered to approximately waist height.
2. No takeoff board is necessary because of the lowered beam and for safety reasons.
3. The approach must be from a right angle, facing the beam broadside.
4. Hands must contact the beam first.
5. The performer must use a two-foot takeoff.

Problems

Can you mount to a position—
1. Sitting in a straddle on the beam?
2. With one knee on the beam?
3. With two knees on the beam?
4. With two feet on the beam? Can you vary this position by (a) the body being in a squat position; (b) the body being in a straddle position?
5. With one foot between the hands and the other foot outside the hands?

Have you come to realize these mounts have much in common with some vaults we have learned? You may need to go back to the horse (the vaulting apparatus) to practice some of these movements before trying any more on the beam.

Can you mount to a position—
6. With one leg on either side of the beam, facing broadside (called a side stride support)?
7. With both legs passing between the hands?
8. With a variation of number seven?
9. With both legs passing outside the hands and support only on the hands?
10. With the feet higher than the head?

DEVELOPING THE ROUND–OFF AND THE CARTWHEEL THROUGH GUIDED DISCOVERY

Preliminary experiences should include the following movement tasks.[12]

a. Movements are explored which give meaning to the term "step-like." (The present base of support leaves the supporting surface and weight is transferred to another base of support, or back to that same base, while weight is shifted over these changing bases.)

b. Tasks are included in which a variety of body parts, alone or in combination, receive and transfer weight in step-like actions.

c. Preliminary experiences should include movements in which the body travels symmetrically and/or asymmetrically (including twisting actions) in step-like actions.

d. All the elements of movement (their divisions and dimensions) are explored in step-like actions.

e. Movements are experienced in which the body travels along level surfaces as well as up onto, down from, and over apparatus (boxes or other obstacles) in step-like actions.

f. Experiences are included emphasizing that the hands and arms support best if placed about shoulder-width apart when taking weight.

g. Early experiences should emphasize that the position of the head will determine whether the body becomes rounded (with the chin on chest) and tends to roll or remains open (with the chin out, neck hyperextended) and moves in linear patterns.

h. Movement experiences are presented illustrating that when hips and legs are raised higher than the head in step-like motions it takes more effort and muscular control to remain on balance while moving.

Depending upon the level of ability of the group being taught, their sophistication and their appreciation of movement of the human body, one might begin with the activity of transferring weight from side to side over an ordinary bench. This activity should result in the student becoming aware of several of the items from the preceding list. In addition, because the skill toward which these experiences are moving is the round-off and the cartwheel, the teacher might pose problems related to taking off and landing on both feet, or one foot, or some combination (one-foot takeoff to two-foot

12. "Preliminary experiences" refers to basic movement, educational gymnastics or possibly experiences used as an introduction to this type of movement at the secondary level.

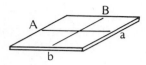

Figure 15.35

landing, etc.). Encouraging students to raise their hips and legs into higher levels, with control, also gives experience in movements necessary for the conventional round-off and cartwheel.

Progressing to mats, the teacher should continue to guide the students in exploring foot and leg actions of leaving the mat and coming back to the mat, including raising the hips and legs higher and higher. However, the feeling and movement change somewhat because now the head is at a lower level. A cross drawn on the mat can be useful in helping the student evaluate and strive for better hand and foot placement. To begin, the hands are placed on line *Aa* (see figure 15.35) while the feet travel through the air across line *Bb*. Eventually the hands and feet are both moving along line *Aa* with the inverted position occurring as the body crosses line *Bb*.

As the student becomes more proficient in this movement pattern the hands are pulled off the mat as the feet return to the mat on the landing. Exploring the alternative of beginning with the hands placed on the mat as opposed to standing and rotating the upper trunk and limbs downward to the mat reveals that greater momentum is built with a standing starting position. Students still having problems with generating enough momentum to carry the legs over in a high

extended position can be taught a hurdle (hop-step, p. 475) to build greater momentum. The aid of a spotter may not be necessary for some students; however, those who seem to have some fear of getting their hips and legs into a high level may feel more confident with a spotter and thus be more successful.

The student who has mastered the round-off and cartwheel in one direction (to the left, or to the right) might try these same movements in the other direction. Continued progress in using this movement pattern might include variations on the mat, including: (a) a one-handed cartwheel with only the near hand being placed on the mat; or (b) a one-handed cartwheel with only the far hand placed on the mat; or (c) no hands on the mat (an aerial cartwheel).

Taking this movement pattern to the apparatus, one can use the round-off and cartwheel as dismounts (most often from the beam; however, one might use the side horse as a progression leading to the beam, or a cartwheel on the beam itself). Obviously, some of these variations may need direct help from the teacher in explanation and spotting. However, students will achieve a higher level of proficiency if they understand what they need to do to control their body in a movement pattern and are guided through a progression of movements step-by-step. In addition, each student can work on variations within the progression. The more proficient can move ahead to be challenged with this same movement pattern at some more difficult spot in the progression.

FEEDBACK CHECKLISTS FOR IMPROVEMENT OF PERFORMANCE

The value of immediate and accurate feedback is well documented. The following checklists can serve as tools for immediate feedback. They may be used with a peer or used individually if one has the use of a video tape recorder. The simultaneous use of both a peer and the video tape to give feedback is most desirable.

BACKWARD SHOULDER ROLL (BEAM)

Good   *Needs Work*

(initial position)

——— ——— 1. Body is in a supine position on beam with body weight centered directly over beam. Muscles firm, toes pointed.

——— ——— 2. Head is off to one side of beam with hand on opposite side of body grasping below beam. Arm on same side of head may be above or below beam.

(rotation)

——— ——— 3. Legs raised with pike action from hips. Legs remain straight (knees extended).

——— ——— 4. Arms pull as trunk is curled. Trunk muscles firm to maintain center of gravity over beam.

——— ——— 5. Toes reach for beam behind head as hips come up and over. Keep center of gravity low. Do not extend legs and hips upward.

——— ——— 6. Top of foot touches beam and then knee of the same leg contacts beam. Hips descend to sit on heel of supporting leg while nonsupporting leg moves downward alongside of beam.

(ending position)

——— ——— 7. Hands (one above and one below, or both on top of beam) push chest away from beam as trunk assumes an upright sitting position.

——— ——— 8. Numbers 3–7 occur smoothly. Transfer of weight is continuous and controlled.

HANDSTAND (MATS)

Good   *Needs Work*

(initial position)

_____   _____   1. Hands flat on mat shoulder width apart with fingers spread and pointing forward.

_____   _____   2. Hands placed *close enough* to feet to facilitate rotation to an inverted position rather than *too far* which causes a "braking action."

_____   _____   3. Shoulders are positioned directly over hands.

_____   _____   4. Neck slightly hyperextended with eyes focused on a spot forward of hands.

(action)

_____   _____   5. Leg whip generates appropriate degree of momentum to invert and hold; or (circle one)
a. too much—leg passes beyond vertical position.
b. too little—leg does not reach vertical position.

(final position)

_____   _____   6. Shoulders over hands.

_____   _____   7. Neck slightly hyperextended.

_____   _____   8. Hips over shoulders and hands.

_____   _____   9. Heels over head.

_____   _____   10. "Toes reach for ceiling." Overall appearance is *stretched* rather than *sagged.*

_____   _____   11. Muscles of shoulders, trunk and legs firm to hold position with toes pointed for ceiling.

INVERTED HANGS FROM BACKWARD ROTATE (RINGS)

Note: Rings should be positioned approximately shoulder high for individuals.

Good   *Needs Work*

(backward rotate)

_____   _____   1. Leg force is directed to a point up and over the head rather than out in front.

Good	Needs Work	
————	————	2. Elbows remain flexed during rotation and only straighten as the hips rotate to a level above shoulders.

(pike hang)

Good	Needs Work	
————	————	3. Hips fully flexed to maintain a low center of gravity.
————	————	4. Hips extend behind rings on one side to counterbalance feet and leg extension on other side.
————	————	5. Chin on chest to aid kinesthetic awareness.
————	————	6. Toes pointed with all muscles firm to hold position.

(inverted hang)

Good	Needs Work	
————	————	7. Slow extension of hips to maintain center of gravity between rings, (e.g. as feet go upward toward vertical line of rings, hips also approach the line of the rings.)
————	————	8. Chin on chest to aid kinesthetic awareness.
————	————	9. Toes pointed with total body extended and firm to hold position.

Note: Lower carefully into pike position to dismount or go into bird's nest.

(bird's nest from inverted pike hang)

Good	Needs Work	
————	————	10. Able to maintain balance while assuming a tuck position to insert feet in rings.
————	————	11. Controlled arch out—turning out only as far as one can control.
————	————	12. Ankles ("cocked") dorsi flexed to maintain feet in rings.
————	————	13. Head back (neck hyperextended) during the bird's nest position.

CULMINATING ACTIVITIES IN GYMNASTICS

In most sport and game the student looks forward to becoming sufficiently proficient to engage in game play. Possibly game play in gymnastics is participating in a gymnastic meet. Indeed, with the current rapid growth of gymnastics, there are organizations and related competitive meets to serve the needs of gymnasts at a variety of levels of proficiency. Thus, a student who so desires can become affiliated with an organization that meets his needs for competition. There are others who may not desire the competitive experience yet would like to culminate their work in gymnastics in gymnastic-like activities. One characteristic depicted by gymnasts is the ability to combine skills into a sequence to form routines or compositions. Thus, a logical culminating activity for students in gymnastics is work on mastering routines or compositions.

Officially compositions are classified as compulsory or optional. If the teacher requires the same compulsory routines of all students he is assuming all students are working at the same level of proficiency. Seldom is this the situation. Optional routines better meet the needs of individ-

uals; however, the novice quite often is unsure of what to combine into a composition when given the choice. A composition requirement which has choices within limitations may meet the needs of both the novice and the more advanced student.

The following culminating activities for uneven bars and beam are examples of compositions that have choices within structure. Note that the difficulty increases from level one to level three. The choice of skills to include within the composition (routine) depends upon the range of proficiency within the class as well as the specific skills the total class has encountered in that particular instructional unit. Similar compositions can be devised for any of the events of gymnastics.

UNEVEN BAR COMPOSITIONS

The difficulty of the compositions increase with the addition of more difficult rotating movements and the substitution of a more difficult mount or dismount.

Level 1	Level 2	Level 3
	Add one additional rotating move (#2 or #9) and substitute in a more difficult mount (#1) or dismount (#10).	Add two additional rotating moves (#2 & #9) and substitute in a more difficult mount (#1) or dismount (#10).
1. Jump to straight arm support	1. Hip circle mount	1. Hip circle mount
2. (go to #3)	2. Back hip circle	2. Back or forward hip circle

3. One leg over to side stride support
4. Swing down and up (half knee circle backward)
5. Grasp high bar and pass leg forward to rear lying hang
6. Hip pull-over travel up to high bar (show open position)
7. Roll (forward) down to low bar or kip, drop, sit to low bar
8. Pass one leg back and grasp low bar (side stride support)

Level 1	Level 2	Level 3
9. (go to #10)	9. Mill circle (pass leg backward)	9. Mill circle (pass leg backward)
10. Single leg flank dismount	10. Choose one: a. Double leg flank dismount b. Straddle over dismount c. Squat through dismount	10. Penny drop

BALANCE BEAM COMPOSITIONS
(HEIGHT OF BEAM MAY BE MODIFIED)

	Level 1	Level 2	Level 3
		Substitute one roll (#2 or #4) as a more difficult move and a more difficult mount (#1) or dismount (#6). (2 substitutions)	Substitute three of the following more difficult moves: (1) two rolls (#2 & #4) and *one* mount (#1) or dismount (#6); (or) (2) one roll (#2 or #4) and both a mount (#1) and a dismount (#6). (3 substitutions)
Order of Skills			
1. Mount ————	1. Modified step-on	1. Squat or Straddle on	1. Squat or Straddle on
2. Locomotor —— movement forward	2. Using feet as base of support	2. Forward (head) roll	2. Forward (head) roll
3. Balance ————	3. High balance	3. High or low balance	3. High or low balance
4. Locomotor —— movement backward or sideward	4. Using feet as base of support	4. Backward (shoulder) roll	4. Backward (shoulder) roll

Order of Skills (Cont.)	Level 1	Level 2	Level 3
5. Pivot - - - -	5. Low pivot	5. High or low pivot	5. High or low pivot
6. Dismount - -	6. Knee scale flank-off	6. Roundoff (or cartwheel) off end of beam	6. Roundoff (or cartwheel) off end of beam

REFERENCES

Carter, Ernestine Russel. *Gymnastics for Girls and Women.* Englewood Cliffs, N.J.: Prentice-Hall, 1969.

Cochrane, Tuovi S. *International Gymnastics for Girls and Women.* Reading, Mass.: Addison-Wesley Publishing Co., 1969.

Cooper, Phyllis. *Feminine Gymnastics,* 2d ed. Minneapolis, Minn.: Burgess Publishing Co., 1973.

Dyson, Geoffrey. *The Mechanics of Athletics.* 7th ed. London: University of London Press, 1977.

Figley, Grace E., Mitchell, Heidie C. and Wright, Barbara L. *Elementary School Physical Education: An Educational Experience.* Dubuque, Iowa: Kendall/Hunt Publishing Company, 1977.

Gilliom, Bonnie Cherp. *Basic Movement Education for Children, Rationale and Teaching Units.* Reading, Mass.: Addison-Wesley Publishing Co., 1970.

Johnson, Barry L., and Garcia, Mary J. *Gymnastics for the Beginner: A Coeducational Approach.* New York: Appleton-Century-Crofts, 1976.

Johnson, Barry L., and Bondreaux, Patricia Duncan. *Basic Gymnastics for Girls and Women.* New York: Appleton-Century-Crofts, 1971.

Kjeldsen, Kitty. *Women's Gymnastics,* 2d ed. Boston, Mass.: Allyn & Bacon, 1975.

Loken, Newton C. and Willoughby, Robert. *Complete Book of Gymnastics,* 3d ed. Englewood Cliffs, N.J.: Prentice-Hall, 1977.

Maddux, Gordon T. *Men's Gymnastics.* Pacific Palisades, Calif.: Goodyear Publishing Company, Inc., 1970.

Mauldon, E., and Layson, J. *Teaching Gymnastics and Body Control.* London: Macdonald and Evans, 1975.

Ryser, Otto E. *A Manual for Tumbling and Apparatus Stunts,* 6d ed. Dubuque, Iowa: Wm. C. Brown Company Publishers, 1976.

Taylor, Bryce,; Bajim, Boris and Zivic, Tom. *Olympic Gymnastics for Men and Women.* Englewood Cliffs, New Jersey: Prentice-Hall, Inc., 1972.

Tonry. Don. *Gymnastics Illustrated.* Northbridge, Mass.: Gymnastic Aides, Box 475, 1972.

16

Swimming

INTRODUCTION

Swimming is an activity which has almost universal appeal and which provides a challenge, as well as a form of recreation, to nearly every person regardless of age, sex, physical condition or skill. Nearly all physical educators consistently rank swimming at the top of activities which contribute most to the majority of the objectives for the field.

Interest in swimming and in related aquatic activities is at an all-time high. This is attested to, in part, by the large number of boat owners, the increasing popularity of waterskiing and skin and scuba diving, the hundreds of thousands of backyard swimming pools, and the increasing number of municipal and school pools.

The progress in stroke development in the past century is fairly well documented, but it is not the purpose of this book to delve deeply into history of this sort. Regardless of history, the sport of swimming with its attendant activities is here to stay. More and more people are participating in it daily, and scientific advances in the understanding of the mechanics of swimming are unprecedented. Perhaps the most scholarly single treatise on the subject is that by Counsilman, and the reader who is truly interested in this aspect of swimming would be well-advised to pursue his work thoroughly.[1]

VALUES OF SWIMMING

The values of swimming are many and diverse. They range from prophylaxis to catharsis, and from a medium of self-expression to a medium for pure enjoyment. Everyone can enjoy swimming. There are no barriers of age, sex, strength, endurance or skill. Even the most unskilled person can find pleasure in merely splashing around in

---

1. James E. Counsilman, *The Science of Swimming* (Englewood Cliffs, N.J.: Prentice-Hall, Inc., 1968).

the water. Likewise, there is always a new challenge for the highly skilled individual.

ELEMENTS OF MOVEMENT

The elements of movement around which the concepts in this book are built—force, flow, time and space—are as important in swimming as in any other activity.

Force

Swimming is an activity requiring the judicious use of force. Two extreme examples of the use of force are: the arm pull in the butterfly stroke, when there is a tremendous amount of total force exerted; and the squeezing together of the legs in survival swimming, when there is just enough force engendered to lift the head slightly from the water. Regardless of the momentum needed, the swimmer must learn to deal effectively with force, including the kinesthetic awareness of how much force is being produced.

Flow

Swimming is perhaps one of the better examples of the continuity or sequential flow of movement. For example, in the elementary backstroke, a resting stroke that every swimmer should master early, the movements of the arms and the legs are synchronized in such a way that non-propulsive actions flow smoothly into propulsive actions which move the body in the desired direction.

Space

The space in swimming, both general and personal, is perhaps a bit different than in land activities. In most instructional situations, general space is defined by the size of the pool. In addition, especially in the case of the beginners, space is delimited to the shallow area which is often marked by the use of lifelines. Likewise, personal space is often quite limited, for safety reasons if for no other. Beginning swimmers should not be accidentally shoved or ducked; each individual should be aware of the boundaries of his personal space and not trespass into another's area.

Time

As in all other activities, time is important in swimming. Coordination, a component of skill which is dependent upon proper timing, is as vital in swimming as it is in, say, a tennis serve. The timing of breathing is not only important but can be a lifesaving factor. In addition, beginners often execute strokes to a count pattern.

HYGIENIC AND SAFETY FACTORS

Insofar as safety is concerned, many rules and regulations are dictated, some of them because of the unnatural medium in which swimming takes place. Inattention to such rules may endanger one's life. Some of these rules are discussed later in this chapter. In addition, there are several facets of swimming which may be categorized as safety precautions but which are not as potentially harmful if ignored.

Swimsuits should be brief and streamlined. They should fit tightly enough so that water cannot collect in them, resulting in a resistance factor. They should not be so tightly fitting as to be restrictive. Fast-drying synthetics are probably the best all-around fabrics for suits.

Generally, caps should be worn for several reasons. First, if a swimmer's hair is long, the cap keeps it in place and out of his eyes. Second, some filtration equipment is hard-pressed to take care of all the hair which accumulates if caps are not worn. Third, some individuals with ear problems are well-advised to wear caps, since they keep a great deal of water out of the ears.

The wearing of noseclips, except for synchronized swimming, should be avoided since they tend to become a crutch. A swimmer is well-advised to learn proper breath control in order to keep water out of the nose. The use of flotation devices also should be avoided except under the direction of the instructor because of the danger inherent in losing such a device.

Sanitary conditions in a pool are extremely important if the spread of disease is to be prevented. Certain chemicals are used in the water to offset bacteria, algae and the like. However, the individual swimmer's attention to personal sanitation is vital. He should shower thoroughly before entering the water and he should remove such things as Band-Aids, corn plasters, and chewing gum. Street shoes should never be worn on pool decks.

All swimmers tend to want to help other swimmers in distress. Lifesaving techniques are highly refined skills and unless one is thoroughly competent, he should not attempt to use them. It is more effective to yell for help or to run for assistance. One drowning is bad enough; two are inexcusable.

The remainder of this chapter is devoted to a discussion of major concepts important to swimming. A knowledge of them is essential to the person who is attempting to become a reasonably well-skilled swimmer, as well as to the teacher of swimming. In addition, sub-concepts are listed and discussed as they become fundamental to specific skills.

The stroke mechanics of five basic strokes are discussed in detail according to the elements of movement involved.

MAJOR CONCEPTS: MOVING THE BODY THROUGH WATER

Relaxation

CONCEPT. In order to become a proficient swimmer, one must be perfectly at home (i.e., relaxed) in the water. Relaxation depends to a great extent upon efficient breathing techniques and the ability to float.

When dealing with nonswimmers in particular, the teacher must give primary attention to the development of relaxation. Until the student feels somewhat comfortable in the water, his progress is minimal at best. Two very different types of factors contribute to relaxation: physiological and psychological.

The physiological factors in relaxation are related to such things as temperature of the water and air, and the biological principle of reciprocal inhibition as discussed in chapter five under "Moving the Body through Space." The importance of this principle to efficient movement cannot be emphasized too strongly.

The psychological implications of relaxation (the affective domain) are often overlooked, particularly by the neophyte teacher who is so skill-oriented that he wants to develop champion swimmers in a short period of time. All swimming teachers should be cognizant of one of Thorndike's laws of learning, the law of effect, which simply states that the learner repeats those experiences which are satisfying and avoids those which are not. Many nonswimmers at the teenage level and above verbalize, "I almost drowned once." It is unlikely that such an experience occurred; nevertheless, the statement indicates that an undesirable reaction to the water occurred and, factually based or not, the teacher must empathize with such a feeling and make an attempt psychologically to prepare the student for a pleasant experience.

As stated, two basic skills are essential before one can feel perfectly relaxed in the water: breathing and floating.

BREATHING

Sub-concept. Rhythmical breathing, in which a small amount of air is constantly being exchanged in the lungs, is vital to proficiency in swimming.

Many teachers of swimming engage in a kind of chicken-or-egg controversy about whether breathing or floating should be taught first. This decision is obviously a personal one on the part of the teacher. Both skills are extremely important and they can be taught almost simultaneously.

It is doubtful that swimmers, except perhaps at the very young age level, should be taught to hold their breath underwater. Such a practice serves only to defeat the objective of relaxation, since the act is an unnatural one and thus is tension-producing. Instead, swimmers should be taught to inhale a moderate amount of air through the mouth and exhale the same amount through the mouth and nose while underwater. It cannot be emphasized too strongly that the mouth should be partially open at all times. Whether one should be taught initially in rhythmical breathing to roll his head to the side or to lift it is debatable. Some strokes require rolling the head to the side (e.g., front crawl), while others require lifting it (e.g., breaststroke). Regardless of the movement pattern taught, variations in the technique can be taught as the need arises.

Initially, then, swimmers should stand in shallow water, bend forward at the waist and place their hands above the knees to help stabilize themselves. Then, either lifting the head slightly or rolling it to one side (always

the same side), they should inspire a small amount of air and immediately place their face in the water. As soon as the face is in the water, the exhalation process begins. This should be a slow and steady procedure, not forced, and should continue until the mouth is again lifted or rolled from the water. At this point, expiration of all inspired air should have occurred and the swimmer is again ready to inhale.

The biggest fault of beginning swimmers in this practice is the inhalation of too much air. Over-inhalation does not contribute to the amount of oxygen exchanged in the lungs; instead, it tends to contribute to the accumulation of unexpired air, which in the end is self-defeating since the lungs become full of stale air and thus further inspiration is impossible. The teacher, therefore, must experiment with methods to communicate the "feeling" of a sufficient amount of air. It is probably good practice with most beginners to overemphasize the small amount of air needed. "A bite of air" seems to be a meaningful phrase to many.

BUOYANCY

Sub-concept. A buoyant individual floats high in the water, displacing little water and creating little resistance, thus having less inertia to overcome.

Archimedes' principle states that a body immersed in water is buoyed up by a force equal to the weight of the volume of water displaced. The degree of buoyancy is directly proportional to the relationship between weight and volume, and the ability to float varies with different body types. Several factors contribute to this variance, among them bone size and density, vital (lung) capacity, adipose tissue, weight distribution, and muscular development.

Whereas in activities performed on land one must be conscious of the center of gravity of the body, in skills performed in the water one must be just as concerned with the *center of buoyancy.* The center of gravity tends to be near the hip region; however, because the chest area containing the lungs is very light in relation to its mass, the center of buoyancy is in the chest region.

Several factors, including the high percentage of bone and muscle tissue in the legs and a lesser amount of subcutaneous fat, tend to make males float less well than females (i.e., their center of gravity is lower in the water than their center of buoyancy). It stands to reason that the more buoyant person should learn to swim more easily, although there are many highly skilled swimmers whose ability to float is minimal. If the ability to float is to be an aid to becoming a proficient swimmer, the teacher must understand what needs to be done to overcome some of the delimiting factors listed.

The easiest float to master, and the one usually taught first since it tends to prove to the beginner that the water will support his weight, is the jellyfish float. It is extremely important in this first experience of being supported by the water for the student to be aware of the position of his body, the direction his body will move as his feet leave the bottom of the pool, and what he must do to regain the same relative position in space from where he started.

Jellyfish float

The student stands in water approximately waist-deep. The feet should be approximately shoulder-distance apart to insure a stable base. The student leans over, places both hands just above the knees, takes a bite of air, and puts his face in the water. The hands run down the front of the legs toward the ankles. As the ankles are approached, the feet leave the bottom and the body rolls forward until it is suspended in

Figure 16.1. **Jellyfish float**

the water. In order to regain a standing position, the hands are run back up to the knees, the feet are pressed to the bottom, and the head and shoulders are lifted. Both the general space and personal space for this skill should be as great as possible in order to prevent someone who may topple sideways from bumping another person. (See figure 16.1.)

Just as there is a controversy among swimming teachers about whether to teach breathing or floating as the first skill, there is a controversy about whether to teach the back float or the prone float after the jellyfish is mastered. Proponents of teaching breathing first will probably start with the prone float and vice versa.

Back float

For the next two floats, back and prone, it is probably advisable that students work with partners. It gives the beginner a sense of security to know that someone is standing by while, at the same time, the nonperforming partner can be designated an assistant "teacher" whose job it is to *analyze* what the swimmer is doing. In order to increase each individual's cognitive understanding of swimming, much attention must be given to precise explanations of the mechanics involved in particular skills. Assigning an in-

Figure 16.3. **Prone float**

Figure 16.2. **Back float**

dividual the task of helping in analyzation should ensure more serious attention to the application of cognitive understandings.

If working in pairs, one partner should stand behind the other, who has lowered his shoulders under the water by bending his knees. The floater then places his arms out to the sides at shoulder height, inhales and gently lays his head back in the water. (At this point, especially during the first few attempts, the partner may place a hand under the floater's head.) The floater's feet should leave the bottom of the pool but they need not come to the surface; in fact, most people float on their back in a semi-vertical position. The hips should be extended and the chest should be raised as high as possible.

Balanced float

Sub-concept. Buoyancy can be increased by bringing the center of balance close to the center of buoyancy and by increasing the volume of the body without increasing its weight.

If the feet tend to sink and thus pull the head under the water, the floater may "fin" slightly with his hands or even bring his arms back past shoulder height. The arms must always be under the water, however. If these techniques do not appreciably alter the sinking pattern, the floater must attempt to achieve a balanced position (the center of gravity located closer to the center of buoyancy) by arching the back, thus expanding the chest cavity to permit fuller breathing, and by bending the knees and drawing the feet closer to the torso.

To regain the standing position, the floater needs only to raise his head, drop his hips, and scoop the arms forward and up to the surface. Again, the partner may assist, if necessary, by a slight upward pressure of his hand on the back of the floater's head.

Prone float

Perhaps the simplest way to master the prone float, a relatively simple skill for everyone, is to assume the jellyfish float position, and then to let go of the ankles. The arms should float to the surface in a relatively horizontal position. Likewise, the legs should float to the surface, although not as high as the arms. To regain the standing position, the knees are drawn up to the chest, the hands placed on them, and the legs gently pushed to the bottom. As the body begins to roll back to a vertical position, the head should be lifted from the water.

After this skill is mastered, the jellyfish phase can be omitted. The student simply stoops down until the shoulders are under the water with the arms outstretched in front, inhales, places his face into the water, and gently pushes his feet from the bottom. In order to regain a standing position, the arms are pushed down through the water, and the head raised while the feet sink to the bottom.

Safety

CONCEPT U. An affective attitude based on a cognitive understanding of the dangers inherent in an activity is necessary if one is to perform safely.

Sub-concept U-1. Providing a safe environment for participation contributes to the development of desirable affective attitudes toward the activity.

Sub-concept U-2. Educating the participants to use the environment wisely contributes not only to personal safety but enhances the total climate of the classroom.

Recreational activities in and on the water are increasing in number annually. Various forms of boating, waterskiing, fishing, and skin and scuba diving are a few of the more popular but, strictly speaking, nonswimming water events in which a great number of people participate. The safety implications seem obvious; however, it is not unusual to see basic safety rules broken repeatedly. Some of the more important rules to be imparted to students are:

1. Never swim alone.
2. Never dive into water of unknown depth or description.
3. Always wear a life jacket when in a boat or when waterskiing.
4. Do not "horse around" in the water by pushing and ducking others.
5. Never swim immediately after eating a meal.
6. Skill should not be overestimated.
7. Do not run on pool decks.
8. Respect the water at all times!

SAFETY SKILLS

Sub-concept. Water, an unnatural medium, demands certain standards of safety not necessary in land activities; therefore, certain safety skills are essential to an effective swimmer and they should be mastered as quickly as possible after initial exposure to swimming instruction.

Swimming with the eyes open

Many swimming instructors insist that one cannot be completely relaxed in the water until he learns to keep his eyes open at all times, even when underwater. It seems obvious that this is mandatory for safety reasons as well. There may be some initial discomfort associated with this practice, especially in heavily chlorinated pools, but this tends to pass as the practice becomes an automatic one.

Perhaps the best way to teach this skill to beginning swimmers is to have them work in pairs. As one partner stands in shallow water with his hands on his knees, he places his face in the water and opens his eyes. (It seems to be almost an automatic reflex to close the eyes as they come in contact with the surface of the water as one goes under.) He then counts the number of fingers his partner is holding beneath him. He should understand that his vision, at least at first, will be a bit blurred; however, even in murky water such as in some lakes and rivers one can distinguish outlines and shapes. After the swimmer gets somewhat acclimated to this, he can practice simply submerging and looking around—at the lines on the bottom of the pool, at various colors in bathing suits, at the sides and ends of the pool, etc.

Bobbing

The skill of bobbing is basic in survival swimming, a more advanced safety technique discussed later in this section. Bobbing is not difficult, but since it involves alternate inspiration and expiration of air in a new medium, it should be practiced until such breathing becomes automatic.

Standing in chest-deep water, the student takes a quick bite of air, bends the knees and submerges, keeping the eyes completely open and the mouth partially open. All inspired air is gently but steadily exhaled. The student then breaks the surface of the water by straightening the knees, inhales again and repeats. The number of repetitions should be increased gradually until the technique is mastered. When mastered, it will seem almost as natural as normal breathing. The swimmer will learn, probably more through trial and error than anything else, not to swallow any water which may remain in his partially open mouth while he is underwater. Instead, he should eject it as he breaks the surface for another inspiration. Once bobbing is fairly well learned, the swimmer can combine it with jumping up and down in the shallow end of the pool, hanging onto the overflow trough, or moving about the pool in a vertical position, using any kick he wishes.

Finning and sculling

Almost invariably as the beginner floats on his back, he begins to try to propel himself by the use of his hands and arms. His initial action is usually similar to *finning,* a technique in which, as the arms are held somewhat close to the sides, the hands and wrists are alternately moved in and out from the body. Propulsion results mainly from pressing the water forward as the hands return to the sides. From this step, it is quite easy to progress to sculling, in which greater proportions of the arms are used in a figure-eight motion. The ability to fin and scull can be a lifesaving factor. For example, the novice swimmer who becomes overfatigued can, with minimal exertion, fin or scull just hard enough to keep his head above water.

Figure 16.4. **Turning over**

Turning over

Although turning over in the water is a very simple skill, the beginner may panic when the need to turn over arises unless he has been taught what to do. Such a need may arise, for example, when the person who is swimming in a prone position experiences difficulty in breathing.

When turning from the prone float to the back float, and vice versa, a nearly horizontal position should be maintained. The arm on the side of the desired turn is lowered diagonally across the body. As the head and shoulders are turned to that side, the elbow of the dropped arm leads in rolling the body over. Conversely, to roll from the back float to the prone float, the arms should be extended to the side. As the head and shoulders initiate the roll in the desired direction, the arm on that side is pulled across the body. It is sometimes helpful to cross the opposite arm and leg as well, but it is usually not necessary.

Treading water

The ability to tread water is an essential skill, especially to those who engage in boating and waterskiing. Tragic accidents can be averted when, for example, a water-skier

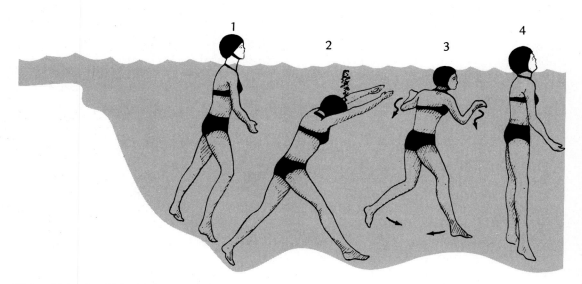

Figure 16.5. **Survival swimming**

who takes a tumble can tread water until the boat returns to him. Likewise, the distance swimmer who gets a cramp in his foot can "rub it out" while he treads water.

It is essential in treading water to keep only one's face above the water. Beginners tend to wear themselves out by attempting to raise the entire upper torso out of the water. If the swimmer is relaxed, he need only employ a slow sculling motion with his hands and arms while at the same time using an easy scissors or whip kick.

Treading water can be taught in shoulder-deep water, or it can be taught in deep water with the swimmer hanging onto the gutter with one hand. As he gains confidence, he should release his grip on the gutter and begin sculling with both hands.

Survival swimming

This method of saving oneself in the water should be taught to everyone who engages in water activity of any sort. Even nonswimmers and novice swimmers can save their own lives by employing this technique if they can stay calm and thus relaxed.

As in treading water, survival swimming (or "drownproofing") can first be practiced in shoulder-deep water. Or, depending on the ability of the learner, it can be taught in deep water. Assuming almost the prone float position, the swimmer should take a breath and let himself sink under the water. As he sinks he should move his arms out away from the body while his legs assume a wide forward stride position. The breath is slowly exhaled all the while the face is underwater. In order to regain the surface, he presses his arms on a diagonal to his side and gently brings his legs together. This combined motion should be enough to bring him to the surface so that he can raise his head and get another bite of air. The entire pattern is repeated over and over, in a fixed rhythm which is closely allied to a normal breathing pattern. When mastered, this practice can be continued for hours and has proven to be a lifesaving technique on many occasions.

Resistance

CONCEPT. For efficient swimming, resistance of the water to moving in the desired direction must be decreased; at the same time, resistance of the water to moving in the opposite direction must be increased if propulsion is to be maximal.

Resistance, sometimes called "drag," is a problem to all designers of moving vehicles if the speed of motion is important. Changing the shape of the body is not as easily accomplished as redesigning an automobile; in fact, it is virtually impossible. However, streamlining the body in the water in order to decrease resistance is possible and much of the progress in competitive swimming is due to this very factor. In fact, Counsilman states that the reduction of resistance is probably the greatest single factor in the improvement of stroke mechanics.[2]

One must not overlook the latter part of this concept (resistance must be increased if propulsion is to be maximal); however, this facet of resistance is discussed later under "Propulsion." The following concerns itself briefly with only the *negative* effects of resistance and what must be done to minimize such effects. (Detailed analyses of specific skills, such as the flutter kick, are also presented later.)

Swimmers must present the least amount of surface area possible in the direction of the intended movement. This dictates a total body position which is as horizontal as possible. Generally, then, one must be cognizant of the following facts.

1. The legs constitute a big part of the total surface of the body. Therefore, every effort should be made to reduce the tendency to drop them in the water. When it is necessary to drop all or part of the legs as in a dolphin kick, the time they are dropped should be as minimal as possible. The nega-

tive portion of the dropped position (drag) should be counterbalanced and, if possible, overbalanced by the time and force of the positive resistance (propulsion).

2. The position of the head is significant. In the front crawl, for example, a buried head offers greater resistance (drag) than a head carried partially at surface level or above. Obviously, if the head is carried too far out of the water, air resistance, in this case a negative factor, is increased.

3. As the hand enters the water the fingertips should lead to decrease drag.

4. The farther the arms are extended from the torso, the greater the negative resistance.

5. Air resistance is less than water resistance. Therefore, recovery of the arms out of the water reduces negative resistance.

6. Streamlining the body is just as essential in strokes performed on the side or back as it is in strokes performed in a prone position. How ineffective the sidestroke is if the body is not streamlined on the lateral plane!

In summary, the body should be streamlined and horizontal, carried high in the water, and all movements which do not create propulsion in the desired direction should be minimized.

Propulsion

CONCEPT. Propulsion, the force that moves the swimmer in the desired direction, is created by effective use of the arms and legs.

Propulsion depends upon resistance, but the resistance referred to here is positive in that it moves the swimmer in the desired direction. Therefore, the factors discussed in this section are in direct opposition to those discussed with regard to negative resistance.

2. Counsilman, *Science of Swimming*, p. 2.

Sub-concept. Every action has an equal and opposite reaction.

This action-reaction principle (Newton's third law of motion) is of utmost importance in swimming. Every action in swimming is propulsive in the opposite direction. The extent of the reaction is dependent upon the amount of force exerted. Forward pressure moves the body backward, while backward pressure moves it forward; downward pressure lifts the body, upward pressure sinks it; pressure to the left moves the body to the right, while pressure to the right moves it to the left. No doubt the neophyte swimmer has experienced this principle in action while he was learning floating and safety skills; however, he must understand it thoroughly and attempt to feel it in action (kinesthesia) as he learns kicks and pulls.

Sub-concept. Generally, the most direct and most forceful pressure should occur only during the middle portion of the movement which is intended to send the body in the opposite direction.

It should be apparent that violating this sub-concept brings about unnecessary movements in other directions, all of which make the stroke less effective. For example, in the front crawl, if the hand were to exert direct pressure the moment it hits the water, the body would be raised slightly due to downward pressure against the water. Likewise, raising the arms too high above the head in the elementary backstroke serves only to move the body to the right and left. Even though these may be counterbalancing movements, energy is wasted.[3]

Sub-concept. In order to obtain maximum force, the body must present as large a surface as possible to the water.

The position of the arm as it pulls through the water is of extreme importance.

For example, in the arm portion of the front crawl, dropping the elbow during the pull results in less water being pushed backward. Likewise, the position of the hand which seems to produce the most efficient movement in the same stroke is with the hand flat, not cupped, and with the fingers slightly spread.[4]

Sub-concept. An object has inertia to any change in its movement.

In compliance with Newton's first law, stroke mechanics should be so designed that the swimmer can travel at as even a speed as possible. Since it takes greater force to start an object moving than it does to keep it moving once movement has started, force should be used to propel the swimmer in the desired direction. If the swimmer alternately accelerates and decelerates, at least part of the force he produces must be used to overcome inertia. In order to obtain maximum stroke efficiency, once the body has started in motion, an even application of force must be produced.

Sub-concept. The resistance a body creates in the water increases with the square of the velocity.

As stated before, Newton's action-reaction law dictates that in order to move in one direction, positive resistance must be created in the opposite direction. The sub-concept cited here dictates, additionally, that the speed of the movement is directly proportional to the speed with which those body parts move that are applying the opposite force. However, as the speed of the moving parts increases, the energy expenditures in-

3. Marion R. Broer, *Efficiency of Human Movement*, 3d ed. (Philadelphia: W. B. Saunders Co., 1973).
4. Counsilman, *Science of Swimming*, p. 12.

crease disproportionately. It is obvious, then, that very rapid movements cannot be continued for a long period of time.

Sub-concept. The momentum of one part of the body can be transferred to another part of the body or to the total body.

Although this concept can be seen in many skills both in and out of the water (e.g., the swimmer who winds up the arms as a part of his racing dive, or the momentum created by the racket arm in the tennis serve), the best application in swimming skills is perhaps in the glide phase of resting strokes such as the elementary backstroke. The propulsive action of both the arms and legs tends to drive the body in the desired direction with considerable force. At the end of the power phase of the stroke, then, it is essential to streamline the body and let the built-up momentum carry the body along for several feet.

STROKE MECHANICS

In order to employ stroke mechanics properly, a cognitive understanding of the concepts discussed previously in this chapter is essential. Once they are understood, their proper application to actual skill techniques becomes easier.

There is not universal agreement among swimming teachers about the exact methodology to be employed when teaching strokes. The time-honored argument about the whole vs. the part method of teaching invariably arises with any discussion of teaching methods. It is not the intent of this chapter to settle the controversy. However, it should be noted that research on methodology tends to support the superiority of the whole method and a reexamination of chapter three, "The Role of Methodology," makes it quite apparent

that the authors of this book favor a problem-solving approach. Such an approach tends to be holistic. Much of the controversy centered around this entire problem could perhaps be resolved if everyone fully understood the theory (and the semantics) of "whole vs. part." A psychological comprehension of the whole can be instilled in the learner and subsequently parts (or "wholes") within wholes can be the focus of attention, but not to the point where parts of skills are practiced in isolation.

Regardless of the method that is to be employed, the remainder of this chapter is devoted to quite precise analyses of the more popular strokes. There are always variations of the suggested "correct" form, especially in competitive swimming. It is assumed that the strokes presented are being taught to beginners or novice swimmers. Coaches can build on this base, but it should be remembered that it is unwise ever to disregard the basic concepts presented earlier. Minor variations may, at some time, seem desirable. It is doubtful, however, if this would be true while teaching basic strokes.

Each stroke is discussed according to four parts: body awareness, force and flow, breath control and time. The dimension of space is not discussed, since both general and personal space tends to be the same for all strokes.

The order in which the strokes are taught is a matter of personal choice. The elementary backstroke is often taught first, since it is relatively easy to acquire a fair degree of skill with this stroke and thus self-confidence is built.

Front Crawl

The front crawl is possibly the most popular of all the swimming strokes, especially when one is trying to swim with some degree of speed. If the stroke is to be an efficient one, it must be done correctly.

Body Awareness

The body should be as flat in the water as possible, with the water line breaking somewhere between the hairline (or cap) level and the eyebrow level. It must be remembered that the higher the head is held, the lower the legs sink, thus creating negative resistance or drag.

Not only should the body be as streamlined as possible in the prone position, but the lateral body alignment must also be considered. For example, the legs should not be carried at an angle from the torso. Usually, attention to streamlining the prone position will also take care of the lateral plane. However, such things as rotating the head to breathe may cause lateral sway.

Force and Flow

Kick. The kick used in the front crawl is called the flutter kick and it is characterized by an alternate, parallel, up-and-down movement of the legs.

There is disagreement among authorities on swimming concerning whether propulsion or stabilization is the primary function of the flutter kick. Counsilman is an advocate of the latter; however, regardless of function, he urges attention to the mechanics of the kick.[5]

The kick should originate at the hip and the legs should be held fairly straight but not rigid. There is no knee bend on the upward thrust, but there can be from slight to considerable knee flexion on the downward drive. With beginners, it is probably best to emphasize the straight-but-relaxed leg concept and not try to differentiate between the thrust of the two legs. The primary propulsive movement comes from thrusting upward (action-reaction law), while perhaps the primary stabilizing movement comes from allowing the hips to roll as the shoulders roll, with no break in the leg action.

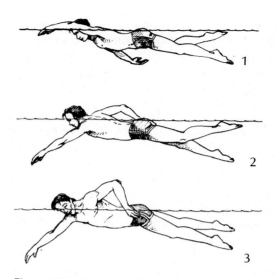

Figure 16.6. Front crawl

This causes a lateral thrust which in turn neutralizes any lateral movement caused by the arm recovery or by breathing. Again, it is questionable how much of this detail should be emphasized with the beginning swimmer. However, the instructor should not become unduly concerned if he sees a slight lateral kick during one phase of the complete stroke.

The kick should be from twelve to eighteen inches in depth and usually a six-beat kick is used. The latter is explained under "Time," pg. 508. The feet and toes should be extended; if the extension is sufficient, the toes will turn in, thus permitting greater thrust. Only the heels, if any part of the foot, should break the surface of the water. The concepts about resistance and action-reaction previously discussed show the futility of thrusting the feet and legs against the air.

Arm Stroke. The arm stroke in the front crawl consists of two phases, pull and recovery.

5. Counsilman, *Science of Swimming*, pp. 25–36.

The pull phase commences with the entry of the hand into the water, although the propulsive movement is not immediately started. Instead, the hand, held in a flat position, glides diagonally downward for a very short time before the catch is started. The swimmer should be instructed that his kinesthetic awareness will tell him when the propulsive effort commences to be effective, since he can *feel* the pressure building on his hands. The hand and forearm, with elbows up, should be pulled back close to the midline of the body. As the hand reaches a position approximately under the center of the torso, a slight rotation of the arm should occur which, in turn, causes the palm to face *very slightly* outward as the press continues through the hip.

The recovery phase begins with the lift of the arm above the water and with the elbow held high and the hand trailing. The elbow should remain high throughout the recovery. As the hand passes the shoulder, it should be approximately in line with the shoulder. From this point, the hand leads and the palm begins to face the water. The fingertips then enter the water and the propulsive phase begins. The arm should be relatively relaxed during the entire recovery phase and the rhythm of the stroke should not be broken.

Breath Control

For the front crawl stroke, breathing should be done only on one side and always on the same side. The head should be rotated to the side on the longitudinal axis, just far enough for the mouth to break the surface of the water, at least partially. The mouth can be pulled toward the ear by the use of facial muscles. As mentioned on page 000, only a small inspiration of air is necessary, after which the head immediately begins rolling back to a point *slightly beyond* the midpoint of the body. During this entire roll, until the mouth once again breaks the surface of the water, there is a gentle but steady exhalation of air through the mouth and nose. Depending upon the amount of air inspired and the position of the head just before the mouth breaks the water, it is sometimes wise to eject the remaining air forcefully at this point. This helps, too, to blow water out of the mouth, although the swimmer can learn to breathe over this water.

Time

Usually a swimmer in the prone position begins his kick first, then adds the arm portion of the stroke, and finally the breathing.

Assuming a six-beat flutter kick with inhalation to the right, the timing is as follows.

1. Just as the right arm finishes its pull with the elbow breaking the surface, the right leg begins its downward thrust, the left leg begins its upward thrust, and the mouth breaks the surface.

2. As the right hand breaks the surface, the swimmer inhales.

3. The downward thrust of the right leg and the upward thrust of the left leg end as the swimmer moves his right arm forward and completes the inhalation.

4. The recovery arm continues forward, the head begins to roll back toward the body's midline with continuous exhalation, and the right hand enters the water. (At this point, the left arm has completed approximately one-half of its pull.)

5. The cycle is repeated with the left arm. In a six-beat crawl there are, of course, three kicks to each arm stroke.

Back Crawl

The back crawl is the only stroke on the back used for speed; it was not a part of the competitive swimming scene until 1912. In spite of the fact that beginners in swimming may not be interested in competitive swimming, the back crawl should be taught to everyone.

Body Awareness

As in the front crawl, the body should be streamlined and carried relatively high in the water. However, in the back crawl the body should not be perfectly horizontal, since this would tend to raise the legs too high for effective kicking. The head should be back far enough so that the ears are underwater, but the chin should be tucked (flexed) slightly. The biggest fault with beginners is a tendency to "sit" in the water.

Force and Flow

Kick. The flutter kick is also used in the back crawl. The main differences in the kick for this stroke are as follows.

1. The kick is deeper—approximately eighteen to twenty-four inches below the surface.

2. The emphasis on the upbeat of each leg is even greater, since this is where the legs furnish the greatest propulsion.

3. The legs are kept fairly straight on the down kick. Although the knees bend considerably at the beginning of the kick, they extend fully at the end of the propulsive phase.

4. No part of the leg or foot should break the surface.

Arm Stroke. Just as in the front crawl, the arm should not be kept straight during the pull, although it is straight as the hand enters the water directly over the shoulder. The pull begins some six inches under the surface and the elbow begins to bend immediately. The pull at this point is not very deep in the water. The elbow bend reaches its maximum (around ninety degrees) as the hand passes the shoulder. In the remainder of the propulsive phase, the pull is backward

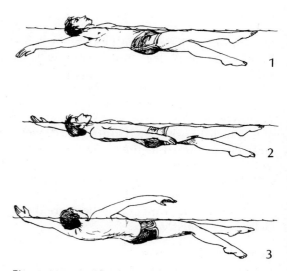

Figure 16.7. **Back crawl**

(toward the feet) and downward as the elbow straightens out.

The recovery portion of the arm stroke begins underwater by flexing the wrist or turning the palm toward the body in an effort to decrease drag. The recovery continues vertically up and toward the head with the arm held straight, but relaxed. When the recovery arm is well out of the water, the palm rotates outward away from the body. As a result, the little finger enters the water first; the thumb, last. Unlike the front crawl, the speed of the recovery arm and the pulling arm are practically identical.

Breath Control

Since the face is constantly out of the water, the swimmer can breathe at any time. However, he will have a more relaxed and efficient stroke if he breathes rhythmically with a complete inspiration and expiration of air for each arm cycle. For example, he can inspire as his right arm and hand breaks the surface of the water on the recovery and commence his exhalation as the same hand reenters the water.

Time

Assuming a six-beat flutter kick, the coordination of arms, legs and breathing is as follows.

1. As one arm enters the water preparatory to the pull, the other arm commences its recovery.

2. The opposite leg from the recovery arm starts upward at the same time as the recovery phase starts.

3. Inspiration commences as the preferred hand breaks the surface.

4. As with the front crawl, there are three kicks to each arm cycle.

Elementary Backstroke

The elementary backstroke is a resting stroke, one in which the glide is held for a much longer period of time than in the speed strokes. It is a valuable stroke for everyone to master, if for no other reason than safety. It is a very popular stroke for two reasons: it is not tiring and, since it is done on the back, breathing is relatively simple.

Body Awareness

The body position is practically identical to that in the back crawl. The arms are always held close to the sides of the body in the glide phase. At no time should any portion of the arms or legs break the surface.

Force and Flow

Kick. The kick can be either the whip or the wedge. The whip kick is discussed in detail on page 512. Therefore, only the wedge kick will be described here. The whip kick is more efficient than the wedge in terms of propulsion, but the wedge is a bit easier to master. Therefore, the choice of the kick again becomes a personal matter.

From a position with the legs together, the knees are drawn up, as they rotate outward, by flexing the hips while the heels are held together (count one). With no pause in the action, the legs and knees move diagonally outward (count two). Then the legs are forcibly squeezed together in the extended position (count three). This position is held for the glide phase of the stroke (count four).

Arm Stroke. From a position with the arms held close to the sides, both arms are drawn up at approximately shoulder level (count one). The hands and fingers point away from the body as the arms are extended diagonally outward slightly above shoulder level (count two). The arms are forcibly pulled back to the side of the body (count three). This position is held for the glide (count four).

Breath Control

Since the swimmer is on his back, he can breathe any time he wishes. However, just as in the back crawl, breathing rhythmically assists in the development of a more relaxed stroke. Inspiration, then, can be done on count one and expiration on counts two, three, and four.

Time

Since arm and leg actions, as well as a suggested breathing pattern, were described by count, all that is necessary is to synchronize the counts. Once movement is initiated, there is no pause in it until the body is again in the glide position. Therefore, since the arms have a bit farther to travel, they can, and probably should, start just a bit ahead of the legs on the first count.

Count one: The arms start moving up the side of the body. As they approach the vicinity of the armpits, the wedge kick commences.

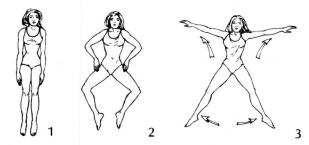

Figure 16.8. **Elementary backstroke**

Count two: The legs are extended diagonally outward and the arms somewhat diagonally upward.

Count three: The legs are squeezed forcibly together while at the same time the arms are pulled alongside the body.

Count four: The streamlined glide position is held until just before the momentum garnered from the propulsive action wanes. *It should not be held so long that inertia again sets in.*

Sidestroke

According to some historians, a version of the sidestroke was one of the first strokes that was known to man. It can be done on either side. However, beginners tend to practice it exclusively on one side and they thus find it difficult to do when they try it on the other side. Many people seem to be able to do the arm portion of the stroke reasonably well on either side, but they find it easier to do a reverse scissors kick on the nonpreferred side.

The sidestroke is also a resting stroke, but because it is a bit more difficult than the elementary backstroke, it is not nearly as popular. Then, too, it is difficult to maintain a floating position on the side and thus the glide is shortened. However, a modification of the stroke is used in lifesaving skills.

Body Awareness

The body should be streamlined in a side float position with the bottom arm extended forward just under the surface of the water and the head resting on it while the top arm, extended downward, rests on the body. The legs are together and straight. Neither the legs nor the bottom arm should ever break the surface of the water.

Force and Flow

Kick. The kick used in the sidestroke is called the scissors kick for rather obvious reasons. Both legs should be pulled up toward the hips with the knees bent (count one). The top leg then moves foward and the bottom leg back in a fully extended position (count two). The legs are then forcibly squeezed together in a horizontal plane until they just meet (count three). This position is held for the glide (count four).

Arm Stroke. The *lower arm* is pulled diagonally toward the chest with the elbow decidedly flexed in the latter part of the pull (count one). In the recovery phase of the lower arm stroke, the elbow drops and the fingers lead the arm back to its original position under the head (counts two and three). This position is held for the glide (count four).

The *upper arm* is bent at the elbow and the hand knifes through the water to a position in front of the chest (count one). Then the

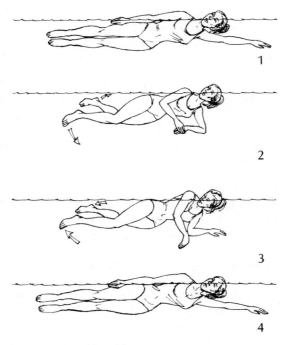

Figure 16.9. **Sidestroke**

palm is turned vertically to the chest and forcibly propelled back to the starting position, resting on the top of the thigh (counts two and three). The glide follows (count four).

Breath Control

Again, breathing is no real problem since the mouth is always out of the water. Nevertheless, rhythmical breathing is beneficial. A typical pattern is to inhale on count one and exhale on counts two, three, and four.

Time

Both the kick and the arm stroke are described by count. Therefore, one needs only to put the counts together, as follows (the section on force and flow provides greater detail).

Count one: Both legs are pulled toward the hips, the lower arm is pulled diagonally toward the chest, the top upper hand is knifed to a position in front of the chest and inhalation occurs.

Count two: The top leg is extended forward, the bottom leg backward; the lower arm begins the recovery phase while the upper arm begins the propulsive stage. Exhalation is commenced.

Count three: The legs are squeezed together, and the recovery portion of the lower arm finishes as the propulsive phase of the upper arm finishes. Exhalation continues.

Count four: A glide is held and air gently exhaled until momentum begins to wane. It is easy to determine when this occurs, since the body tends to roll on the front or back.

Breaststroke

The breaststroke, also a very old stroke, was the first one to be used competitively. It can be used either for resting or for speed. It is a stroke in which both arms work identically, as do both legs.

Body Awareness

The body is in a prone position with arms extended forward beyond the head and with the face in the water (i.e., a prone gliding position). The body should be as horizontal as possible with the legs just under the surface. Any marked drop of the hips causes negative resistance.

Force and Flow

Kick. The whip kick should be used for the breaststroke. Although the wedge kick can be used, research tends to prove that it is not nearly as efficient in terms of force and subsequent speed.

The feet are separated only slightly as the heels are brought up toward the buttocks by flexing the legs at the hips and knees (count one). With no pause, the knees and upper legs rotate slightly inward as the feet are pointed outward (count two). The legs now whip very forcibly together in a circular motion until complete extension is again obtained (count three). The amount of time the glide position is held (count four) varies with the purpose for which the stroke is being used.

Arm Stroke. The propulsive phase of the arm stroke comes on count one (after the hands are separated and allowed to sink a few inches under the surface), as the hands and forearms are pulled forcibly and diagonally downward and outward. During the latter part of the pull, the elbows should be bent so that greater positive resistance can be generated (count one). With no pause in the movement, the forearms and hands should be knifed in under the chin (count two) and then extended to the original position (count three). A glide is held on count four.

Breath Control

Since the pull of the arms tends to raise the shoulders, this is the point at which the breaststroker should inhale. He must be careful not to lift his head and shoulders too high, however; his chin probably should remain in the water as the head lifts. Conscious attention to this should prevent an over-lift. Immediately after the inspiration of air as the arms pull (count one), the head drops back into the water until it is nearly submerged. Expiration comes on counts two, three, and four.

Time

By putting together the counts described, the following stroke pattern develops.

Count one: The arms are pulled in the prescribed manner and air is inspired. The legs are motionless.

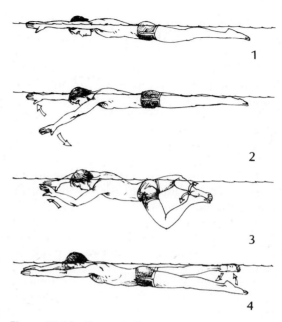

Figure 16.10. **Breaststroke**

Count two: The arms and legs both begin the recovery phase and expiration of air starts.

Count three: The arms extend to the original position as the propulsive phase of the kick occurs.

Count four: A glide is held. The phrase "pull and inhale, kick, glide" is meaningful to most beginners as they try to master this coordination.

INDIVIDUALIZING INSTRUCTION

Several environmental factors can be given attention each day before the swimmers enter the water to help them feel more relaxed.

1. Soft music can be played.
2. The temperature of the water should be warm, from eighty-two to eighty-four degrees.

3. The air temperature should also be warm, two to four degrees above water temperature.

4. Adequate mechanical ventilation should be used to remove the steamy atmosphere.

5. All surfaces should be immaculately clean.

6. The water should be clear and clean.

7. Adequate lifelines should be in place.

8. The instructor should encourage everyone to get into the water as soon as he enters the poolroom.

9. Brightly colored objects can be placed in the pool to be brought up from the bottom; this encourages underwater exploration.

In addition to environmental influences, the instructor can further individualize teaching as follows.

1. The opportunity to experience propulsion through the water should be provided the very first day the student is in the water. This may be nothing more than a prone glide, a glide with a kick, or some modification of the human stroke ("dog paddle"). Regardless, this opportunity should leave the student exhilarated, confident, and eager for the next lesson.

2. A challenge for each student according to his ability should be provided. There is no reason for making all members of the class progress at the same rate. If nothing else, this challenge can be extended during "free swim" times at the beginning and end of the formal lesson.

3. Students should be allowed to assist in decision making. For example, they might be asked which float they would prefer to learn after the jellyfish.

4. The buddy system should be used not only for safety reasons but for instructional purposes as well. If the partner is taught to look for certain errors, he can provide immediate feedback to the learner and together they can attempt to remedy the situation.

5. Exploratory problems should be provided. These can be mimeographed and handed out to individuals or partners, as the swimmers seem to be ready for them. For example, a problem might be posed regarding buoyancy (sample problem number one) or propulsion on the front crawl (sample problem number two). Obviously, the handling of papers and pencils in the water is a problem. This can be overcome by having the students read the problem as posted on a master sheet on a pool wall. The results can be verbalized. As long as the student recognizes what happens and why, the problems have served their purpose.

SAMPLE PROBLEM NUMBER ONE: BUOYANCY

You have now achieved a fair degree of skill in the three basic floats: jellyfish, prone and back. Experiment a bit and see what happens with the following.

DIRECTION	RESULT	WHY
a. Exhale all air before going into a jellyfish float		
b. On a back float, extend the head and neck backwards so that at least one-half of the face is under the water		
c. On a prone float, keep the arms at the sides		

SAMPLE PROBLEM NUMBER TWO: PROPULSION, FRONT CRAWL

DIRECTION	RESULT	WHY
a. While doing the flutter kick in a prone glide position, stiffen the knees and kick with a completely straight leg		
b. Emphasize only the down portion of the kick		
c. After the hand enters the water, pull the arm down and back as far away from the body as possible		

REFERENCES

American Association for Health, Physical Education & Recreation. *Knowledge and Understanding in Physical Education.* Washington, D.C.: National Education Association, 1969.

Broer, Marion R. *Efficiency of Human Movement.* 3d ed. Philadelphia: W. B. Saunders Co., 1973.

————. *Individual Sports for Women.* 5th ed. Philadelphia: W. B. Saunders Co., 1971.

Counsilman, James E. *The Science of Swimming.* Englewood Cliffs, N.J.: Prentice-Hall, Inc., 1968.

Frost, Reuben B. *Psychological Concepts Applied to Physical Education and Coaching.* Reading, Mass.: Addison-Wesley Publishing Co., 1971.

Vannier, Maryhelen, and Poindexter, Hally Beth, *Individual and Team Sports for Girls and Women.* Philadelphia: W. B. Saunders Co., 1976.

Vickers, Betty J., and Vincent, William J. *Swimming.* Dubuque, Iowa: Wm. C. Brown Company Publishers, 1976.

Wells, Katharine F. and Luttgens, Kathryn. *Kinesiology.* Philadelphia: W. B. Saunders Co., 1976.

17

Track and Field

INTRODUCTION

The natural movement patterns of man include locomotion of the body and manipulation of objects. Each day man uses these patterns as he adjusts and attempts to control his environment. These movement patterns are learned at an early age with little or no instruction. As the child moves in his environment he walks, runs, jumps, leaps, and throws. The purpose of the movement is quite often objective, and yet it is not unusual to see a child running for the joy of the movement and throwing or jumping merely to test himself in his environment. He is learning about his own capabilities and the factors in the environment that limit his movements. There is a limit to how fast he can run as well as to how high and how far he can jump or throw.

The child enters school usually with a sense of joy in moving and movement patterns somewhat established. It becomes the task of the teacher to foster this enjoyment of movement while refining the fundamental skills. The child has the potential to run faster, to jump and throw farther. Such potential can be developed through track and field activities which may be introduced into the curriculum with some modifications as early as the intermediate elementary school grades (fourth or fifth grade). Self-testing records and field days with the participants grouped according to ability can be used to motivate the elementary student to better his performance. Intramurals in track and field at the junior and senior high level can be used for the termination of a unit in the instructional program. Competition between classes, homerooms, grade levels, or a combination of these divisions involves a great many participants. And finally, the needs of the more highly motivated and skilled student can be met via a club or team that competes extramurally. However, the material in this chapter is intended for the teacher rather than the coach, and for the amateur as opposed to the highly skilled competitor. Thus, several events are analyzed which would not warrant inclusion with another emphasis.

A review of all track and field events reveals that they can be categorized under two components, *speed* and *distance*. The purpose of the track events, the races, is to move the body from one point (the starting line) to another point (the finish line) in the least amount of time; thus, *speed* is the objective. Obviously, the locomotor movement that allows one to move with the greatest amount of speed is the run. The races, however, are categorized according to the distance covered. Short distances are classified as sprints or dashes. Greater distances are classified as the middle- and long-distance races. The sprinter is challenged to an even greater degree when he must leap objects (hurdles) placed in his pathway. The race may be a multiple effort involving more than one person, such as a relay. In a relay the thrill of the team effort is heightened by the passing of the wand (baton) to a teammate as one member of the team finishes his leg of the race.

The component of distance is measured either horizontally or vertically in the field events. Horizontal distance is the goal in events where the body is projected across an area (such as in the standing long jump, running long jump, and triple jump). Vertical distance is the goal as the body is projected upward in jumping events (such as the high jump and pole vault). The throwing events involve the projection of an object: a ball, discus, shot, or javelin. In these events horizontal distance is the goal. All field events involve a short-distance run or preliminary movement to build momentum prior to the takeoff or release; thus, distance and speed become interdependent.

ELEMENTS OF MOVEMENT

The elements of movement, space, force, time, and flow, are evident in all track and field events. Although the use of *space* is limited by the regulations governing each event and certainly not shared except in passing the baton in the relay race, the spatial relationship of body parts and the kinesthetic awareness of body shape in space is of prime importance. The thrower must confine his movements to the space available for the preliminary movement to build momentum in order to project the discus and the shot. The hurdler must alter his movements to the space between each hurdle in order to cover the space in the least amount of time. The defined space is a limiting factor in track and field events and the challenge is to utilize the available space in an efficient manner in order to accomplish the goal.

The production and transfer of *force* is quite evident in all track and field events. The forceful extension of the leg(s) sends the performer bounding along the track or flying through the air in one of the jumps. The body twists and untwists as it generates and then imparts momentum to an object to send it flying through the air. Although the human body is limited anatomically, the body as a system of levers can be manipulated to produce explosive force in a variety of ways.

Time and force are interrelated. Timing is of the utmost importance in transferring momentum from one body part to another in sequential movement or in releasing an object at the exact instant peak force has been generated. The rate at which the feet contact the track partially determines how fast the runner covers distance. Each skill has a rhythmic pattern and an accent of execution which makes each event both explosive and fluent.

All aspects of the movement must *flow* together to make the whole movement pattern. The pattern may be repeated over and over as the sequential motion in the run. Or the total skill pattern may be a sequence of movements (a run to build momentum for the hop, step, jump of the triple jump or the long or high jump) linked together smoothly so that one action flows into the next with the absence of extraneous movements. The running and leaping action of the hurdler must flow together without a break in stride. The baton must be passed smoothly from one runner to the next in a relay race. The presence of flow in the movement adds to the proficiency of the performance.

The remainder of this chapter categorizes the events of track and field under two conventional headings: "Track Events" and "Field Events." The first portion of each of these two sections includes the application of major concepts from chapter five. Due to the amount and diversity of material in track and field, the presentation of supporting facts through the analysis of specific skill events is also organized conceptually rather than by the elements of movement (force, flow, time, space), as in the other activity chapters. Although the material in this chapter could be analyzed in the same manner, a conceptual analysis is more efficient. Frequent reference is made to the elements of movement throughout the discussion of the analyses. *Those concepts unique to specific skills are distinguished from the major concepts of chapter five in that there is no alphabetical or numerical designation.* A brief explanation of the regulations which govern each event follows each analysis. The final portion of the chapter, "Individualizing Instruction," includes a brief discussion of progressions in skill development and organizing a unit of instruction.

TERMINOLOGY

Accent of execution: that instant that the foot leaves the ground in the jumps or the projectile leaves the hand in the throws.

Body lean: the tilt of the body away from a vertical position; the forward angle of the body while running.

Buck or *bucking movement:* (1) jerky movements of the trunk involving forward trunk flexion when running. This action is quite often due to tension; (2) forward trunk lean and forward reach with the arm in hurdling. This movement is most evident in hurdlers with shorter legs or in the high hurdle races.

Check mark: markers of some type which are placed alongside the approach runway to develop and insure consistency in the approach.

Drive leg (foot): the leg with the foot in contact with the ground and in the act of exerting force to propel the body.

Free leg: the nonsupporting leg.

Free space: the distance or space gained by the reach of the arms (of both the passer and receiver) while passing the baton in the relay race.

Gather: (1) the act of getting ready both physically and mentally for the accent of execution (most often referred to in the field events); (2) the last five steps of the approach to throw the javelin.

Lead leg: the leg that crosses over the barrier first in the hurdles and high jump; the leg other than the takeoff leg; the lead leg leads the movement in the jumps.

Leg of the race: that portion of the total distance that one member of a relay team runs.

Medley: a type of relay in which the legs or distances run by the different members are of different lengths.

Meter: the meter equals 39.37 inches.

Pacing: distributing one's efforts by running at less than maximum acceleration over the distance of the race or various portions of that distance.

Plant: the action of placing the takeoff foot on the ground for the jumps or the forward foot in the throws. Plant implies stability or a stable point of resistance for the final thrust.
Scratch line: a line marked on the ground to improvise for a foul line in the field events.
Straightaway: that portion of the oval track that is straight as opposed to curved.
Style: slight deviations in the technique of various competitors due to differences in body build and competency.
Takeoff leg (foot): that leg or foot which leaves the ground last in the jumps; the drive leg; also the trailing leg in the hurdles.

TRACK EVENTS

The fundamental skill of running is the basis of all track events and is used also as a preliminary movement to build momentum for many of the field events. Thus, a beginner in track and field should concentrate first on developing an efficient running style. This style will differ slightly for each individual because of a difference in anthropometric measurements. Nevertheless, an efficient run cannot violate the biomechanical principles. The prime consideration in learning to run efficiently is to develop a powerful stride with all body parts complementing the action of the legs.

Major Concepts

Other than for the baton pass, the skills needed for the track events can be classified as *moving the body through space.* The major concepts from chapter five that apply are as follows.

CONCEPT A. Moving the body with control involves a conscious manipulation of the center of gravity in relation to the base of support, either to maintain stability or to initiate locomotor movement, as the situation demands.

Sub-concept A-1. Staying ready to move allows a player to get a faster start in order to outmaneuver the opponent, to gain possession of the ball, or to get into a desirable position to project an object.

Sub-concept A-2. Enlarging the base of support in the direction of the force allows a player to start, stop, and change directions quickly.

Sub-concept A-6. Propelling the body through space requires a firm reacting surface and sufficient friction between the reacting surface and the base of support.

The runner must be acutely aware of the position of the center of gravity in relation to the base of support in both the running posture (body lean) and the starting position. He not only stays ready to move, but he enlarges his base of support and positions his center of gravity in very specific ways (i.e., the low crouch starting position) in order to get a speedier start. The use of starting blocks provides the best reacting surface for the initial thrust during the start of the race. To receive full benefit from the driving leg, the surface upon which one is running must also provide equal reaction force. This requires a firm track which supplies sufficient friction between the shoes worn by the runner and the track. Students should not be permitted to dig holes in the track to use for starts in the absence of starting blocks, and any low spots or erosion of the track surface should be repaired in order to maintain the resisting surface. Ideally, track shoes provide the greatest friction; however, a flexible, lightweight tennis shoe with a rough bottom is sufficient for instructional classes.

CONCEPT B. Creating and absorbing force to control the movement of the body through space may involve all of the body or only parts of the body, in unison or in sequence; however, the relaxation of noncontributing muscle groups is imperative for smooth, efficient movement.

Sub-concept B-1. A smooth transfer of momentum from one part of the body to another part, or to the total body, results in sustained movement, while an explosive transfer of momentum increases the speed and/or magnitude of the resulting movement.

Sub-concept B-3. Relaxing noncontributing muscle groups leads to smooth, efficient movement and thus to the proficiency of the performance.

Although the initial start of a race involves an explosive transfer of momentum, in running, movement is sustained with a smooth transfer of momentum as the body moves as a total unit along the surface of the track. The most obvious movement of body parts is the movement of the arms and legs.

The legs provide the driving force while the arms complement the action of the legs by moving in opposition, which keeps the body focused forward. Any excessive lateral movement is wasted action. Such inefficient movement is most often caused by tension. Excessive tension is usually evident in the hands of the runner and can be seen in tightly clenched fists or rigidly extended fingers. Although evident in the hands, tension does not stay localized but travels to the neck and the trunk, wasting energy and causing fatigue. This eventually results in jerky, bucking movements rather than a smooth, fluid motion. A conscious effort at relaxing the neck, back, and arms while practicing helps alleviate unwanted tension.

The relaxation of those muscles not contributing to the running action is of vital importance in order to conserve energy and develop a flowing rhythm.

The importance of maximum acceleration for the sprints as well as the need for optimum acceleration with a conservation of energy (pacing) for middle- and long-distance races necessitate a closer examination of the running technique as the fundamental skill basic to all track events. The next section, "Running," is concerned with an analysis of techniques that must be mastered if the most efficient running style is to be developed.

Running: Striding Technique

CONCEPT. Although speed is the goal in track events, maximum acceleration and rate of stride should be stressed only after the development of technique.

The force to drive the body forward is created by the extension of the hip, knee, and ankle joints as the center of gravity of the body moves over and forward of the driving foot. The more powerful the extension of the joints, the greater the momentum created. This has the effect of projecting the body both faster and farther; however, developing a full comfortable stride takes precedence over speed. Beginners need to be reminded to drive with the back foot and to reach forward with the recovery foot in order to lengthen their stride, an unnatural reach, however, results in overstriding, that is, reaching too far forward and having the foot contact the ground with the center of gravity too far behind the contact point. Overstriding forces the body into an upward position, and checks or retards forward momentum somewhat, with the result that the body bobs up and down instead of moving smoothly forward.

Under-striding, although not as common an error, is inefficient in that the powerful extension of the joints is not utilized and too much time is spent with the foot contacting the track. Ideally, the time spent in contact with the track and the time spent suspended in the air should be almost equal with each stride.

Sub-concept. Body lean usually develops naturally and varies with the purpose of the run.

The center of gravity of the body must be forward of the driving foot if the body is to be moved in a forward direction. The amount of lean depends upon individual need and the type of race to be run. Sprinters lean forward to a greater degree than middle- and long-distance runners. There is also more evidence of up-and-down motion in middle- and long-distance runners. An over-exaggeration of body lean causes an inefficiency in the movement by restricting the knee lift needed for a full stride.

Sub-concept. All movement and effort should be concentrated in sending the body in a forward direction.

Any lateral movement of arms, legs, trunk or head is wasted motion and detracts from the energy that could be used to drive the body in a forward direction. The feet contact the ground with the toes pointed directly forward, thus allowing the ankle, knee and hip joints to be used efficiently in extension. The arms move forward and backward in opposition to the feet. The use of opposition counteracts the tendency of the trunk to rotate laterally as the legs are alternately extended forward. Although the hands may approach the midline of the body at the peak of the forward movement, they should not cross the midline. To correct lateral arm action the runner should concentrate on carrying the elbows close to the sides. Supi-nating the hands (thumbs outward, palms upward) helps to keep the elbows close to the trunk. The head is positioned naturally in line with the spinal column.

Sub-concept. In order for the arms to complement the speed of the legs they must be positioned to move rapidly.

Bending the elbow to approximately ninety degrees shortens the lever of the arm and allows the runner to move the shortened lever with greater speed and less effort. The pathway of the hand should describe an arc in the space between the shoulder and the hip. It is not unusual nor inefficient for the elbow to straighten a little as the arm moves backward. Although the arms do not drive the body forward, it is imperative that they move in opposition to the legs at the same rate of speed in order to balance the drive of the legs and keep the trunk facing forward.

Racing: Sprinting and Distance Races

Sprinting commonly connotes running at full speed over a short distance. The shortest distance might be a twenty-five- or fifty-yard dash used for younger children (the upper elementary or junior high school grades). High school and college girls usually run the 100 meter (100-yard) and 200 meter (220-yard) dashes. For men the 400 meter (440-yard) dash is classified as a sprint. Although it is certainly desirable to cover the distance at full speed and seasoned competitors can do this, the novice finds that in the longer sprinting distances he needs to pace himself. Since speed is the prime consideration, the runner must place his body in a starting position that allows him to overcome inertia and reach maximum acceleration in the shortest possible time; this is the rationale for the low crouch starting position.

STARTING THE RACE

CONCEPT. The advantages of the low crouch position for starting outweigh the disadvantages; thus, it is the most widely used position for beginning a sprint.

The greatest merit of the low crouch start is that it allows for a strong horizontal thrust by placing the center of gravity well in front of the feet. The two disadvantages are the need to place the hands on the ground for stability, which puts the shoulders in a low position, and the distance of the front foot from the starting line. The runner should keep the shoulders as high as possible by: (a) placing the hands only shoulder-width apart; (b) keeping the arms straight; and (c) making a high bridge with the fingers and the thumb.

The magnitude of the second disadvantage, the distance of the front foot from the starting line, is partially determined by the length of the runner's trunk and legs. However, with practice this distance can be lessened somewhat by leaning or pitching the body weight farther forward over the starting line.

Sub-concept. The distance between the front and back foot is used to identify three types of starts: elongated, medium, and bunch, each having certain advantages.

The *elongated* position allows for a well-balanced running position when coming out of the blocks but it lacks explosive power. The *bunch* start allows for the greatest explosive power but it lacks stability, especially in the set position. A compromise between these two extremes is found in the *medium* start, which combines the advantages of both the elongated and bunch starts and tends to minimize the disadvantages. Variations of the medium start are most often used (fig. 17.1).

Sub-concept. The spatial relationship of the feet and the hands in the low crouch starting position should allow the individual to be relatively comfortable.

Beginners quite often have a difficult time finding *any* crouch position that feels comfortable to them. The teacher may need to help them decide on some spacing with which to practice for a while until they become accustomed to the low position. The initial spacing should probably approach the elongated position rather than the bunch position. Some may even have trouble deciding which foot should be placed in the front block. To determine the power foot the runner should be pushed off balance in a forward direction while standing with feet together. The foot he steps out on to regain his balance should be the foot placed in the back block. Or, the runner may be asked to punt an imaginary football. He should kick with the same foot he stepped out on in the previous experiment. One then assumes the foot that remained on the ground is the power foot and should be placed in the front because the power foot remains in contact with the ground or block the longest. For right-handed people this is generally, but not necessarily, the left foot.

To find a desirable spacing, the runner should place the knee of the back leg alongside the front foot somewhere in the space between the arch and a spot two to three inches in front of the toes. The hands should be placed on the track under the shoulders with elbows extended and fingers and thumbs forming a bridge. The hips should then be raised to a position level with the shoulders in order to test the space arrangement in the set position. The hands may need to be placed farther from the front foot for greater stability in the set position. One should experiment a bit with the distance the hands and back foot are from the front foot until the most comfortable spacing is found. If the runner is using starting blocks, the distance from a line drawn in front of the fingers to the ball of the front foot is the distance the front block should be from the starting line. The distance between the balls of the feet is the span between the two starting blocks. One must be careful not to sacrifice too much power for comfort. The greater the distance between the hands and front foot, and between the two feet, the less flexion possible in the knee joints, resulting in a less forceful thrust for the start.

Sub-concept. The commands to start the race are for the purpose of placing the runner in a state of readiness (both physical and mental) to concentrate all efforts forward at the signal to go.

At the command, "Take your mark," the runner positions his hands and feet, or if starting blocks are available, he backs into them. The feet are positioned first and then the hands placed behind the starting line. Only the toe of the shoe touches the ground, with the soles firmly planted against the surface of the blocks. The knee of the back leg may rest on the ground as the runner relaxes a minute waiting for the next command.

At the command "Get set," the hips are raised and the weight is shifted forward. The head and neck should be in line with the trunk, with the eyes focused on a spot just a short distance in front of the starting line. A hyperextension of the neck to look down the track causes unwanted tension. At this point there should be such inward concentration on the drive that the sprinter automatically leaves the blocks with any loud noise.

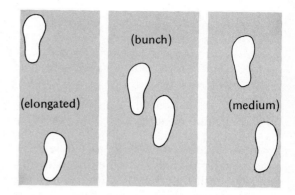

Figure 17.1. **The distance between the feet in the starting position identifies the starting position as: (a) elongated— greater than twenty inches between blocks or the balls of the feet; (b) bunch —the toe of the back foot is opposite the heel of the forward foot; (c) medium— sixteen to twenty inches between blocks or the balls of the feet.**

At the sound of the gun, or "Go," the sprinter drives hard from the blocks in a straight line. The length of the stride is less than full because of the exaggerated body lean which restricts the action of the legs. The body lean decreases and the length of the stride increases as the runner gains speed (fig. 17.2). If the runner tends to stumble in his first few strides, he needs to concentrate on raising his knees higher and moving his legs faster.

RUNNING THE RACE

CONCEPT. The length of the distance to be covered (e.g., a sprint or middle-distance race) and the condition and ability of the runner will determine whether he maintains maximum acceleration throughout the distance or paces himself for some portion of that distance.

Speed is the result of the length of stride and the rate at which the feet strike the

Figure 17.2. **The sprinting start: "Take your mark"; "Get set"; "Go"**

1   2   3

ground. When comparing the style of a sprinter and that of a middle-distance runner, one finds the sprinter with greater body lean, a longer stride, a more forceful drive (greater extension of back leg), and a more rapid rhythm. The body appears to be moving forward with a fluid motion. Since there is a limit to how rapidly the body can move, the chore of the sprinter is to find the style which gives him maximum acceleration and then develop the ability to maintain that maximum acceleration over the full distance of the race or dash.

The longer the distance to be run, the greater the necessity for a natural stride. It is in the middle- and long-distance races that the individual style of each runner becomes most evident. The stride is generally shorter than the sprinting stride and the foot sinks farther back to the heel before leaving the track surface. This provides a moment of relaxation which conserves much-needed energy, since endurance plays a large factor in these races. The driving leg (the back leg) is not extended as forcefully or perhaps even as fully, and the arms are carried in a much more relaxed manner than in the sprint. The body more nearly approaches an upright position and the knees are not carried through the recovery phase in as high a position (fig. 17.3).

A set pace must be developed if a runner cannot maintain maximum acceleration throughout the entire race. Pacing is distributing one's efforts by running at less than maximum acceleration over some portion of the distance to be covered. Although a seasoned competitor will run at full speed for the 200 meter (220-yard) race, the novice will find it necessary to pace himself. In the middle-distance races (the 400 meter or 440-yard and 800 meter or 880-yard), the novice should distribute his efforts by pacing. Pacing can be learned by timing the runner over different portions of the distance to be covered.[1] The most efficient use of body effort results when there is no great difference between the time it takes to run the first half and the time it takes to run the second half of the race. The split time should not vary more than a few seconds.

CONCEPT. Since maximum acceleration for the entire race is not a factor in the middle- and long-distance races, a low crouch start is not necessary.

A standing start is used in races other than the sprints. However, the same biomechanical principles are adhered to as the runner assumes a forward-back stride with arms in opposition, leans the body forward to place the center of gravity somewhat forward of the feet, and flexes the knees slightly to get a good forward thrust. Starting blocks and the low crouch start are not used for distance races beyond the 400 meter (440-yard) run.

1. Consult Ken Foreman and Virginia Husted, *Track and Field Techniques for Girls and Women* (Dubuque, Iowa: Wm. C. Brown Company Publishers, 1977), for a more detailed discussion of pacing.

Figure 17.3. **The natural stride of a long-distance runner**

CONCEPT. The runner must counteract the pull of centrifugal force when running the curve of the track.

The tendency for objects traveling in a circular pathway to be pulled off in a straight line (centrifugal force) must be counteracted when running the curves. Leaning the body toward the inside of the curve and pushing harder with the outside foot (the right foot, since all races are run counterclockwise) creates centripetal force to counteract the pull of centrifugal force. The right arm may also need to swing slightly across the body when running the curve. The runner can practice this technique by running in small circles on a surface, such as sand, which provides little reaction force. The runner should also travel along the inside edge of his respective lane to minimize the distance he must cover.

CONCEPT. The best strategy to use at the finish line is to run at full speed through the tape to some point beyond.

Quite often a novice anticipates stopping after the finish line and begins to slow down before he reaches the tape. An over-anxious runner may try leaping or thrusting the body forward to reach the tape. Such an effort quite often destroys balance and actually slows the runner. The accepted technique of thrusting the chest forward on the last stride can gain the runner a few inches; however, if improperly timed, it can be detrimental. The best technique for most runners, especially for the beginner, is to run through the tape.

REGULATIONS GOVERNING RACES

In conducting a race, the following rules must be applied:[2,3]

a. All races are run in a counterclockwise direction.
b. No part of the runner's body may touch the ground beyond the starting line after taking his mark.

2. All regulations listed in this chapter are taken from the *N.A.G.W.S. Track and Field Guide* (Washington, D.C.: American Alliance for Health, Physical Education & Recreation, 1972). For greater detail and certainly for competitive situations the current N.A.G.W.S. guidebook should be consulted.
3. For men, each state has its own atheltic association; however, all are affiliated with the National Federation of State High School Athletics Association, 7 South Dearborn Street, Chicago, Illinois 60603.

c. Two false starts disqualify a runner. A false start is any motion after "Get set" and prior to the signal "Go."

d. Competitors are timed (and finishes determined) according to when the torso crosses the finish line.

e. All races in the straightaway are run in lanes and all competitors must stay within their respective lanes. The same holds true for races run around curves if the starting positions are staggered.

Relay Racing

Relay races are, for many, the most exciting events of all track and field events. The relay combines the efforts of four runners as they attempt to move the baton over some specified distance at the fastest possible speed. Since the techniques of running have been previously learned, one must only develop the additional skill of passing the baton for the relay race. Relay racing then becomes a matter of strategy in placing the runners in a sequence in which their individual strengths will be advantageous to the team.

TYPES OF RELAYS

CONCEPT. Relay races are classified according to the direction and/or pathway described by the race and the distance traveled by each team member.

The *shuttle relay* is run back and forth between two parallel lines. The distance between the lines will vary with the ages and skills of the participants and may be as short as twenty-five yards for elementary school children (the fourth to sixth grade). The shuttle race can be adapted to the available space and can even be run in a gymnasium. If batons are not readily available the participants can tag the shoulder of their teammates as they finish their leg of the journey.

The tag on the shoulder is the technique used by boys in the shuttle hurdle relay. The baton-passing technique for the shuttle relay is a relatively simple technique. The baton is passed from the right hand of the passer to the right hand of the receiver in a vertical position (see figure 17.4 for mechanics of the pass). The receiver is waiting in a standing start position and the pass is accomplished with a forward thrusting motion.

In a *pursuit relay* the runners travel in the same direction around an oval track. Each contestant runs a specific distance or leg. If the legs are of different lengths, the relay is called a *medley*. The 800 meter (880-yard) medley is the most common for girls and it requires a combination of sprinters and middle-distance runners.[4] In the 800 meter (880-yard) medley one runner travels 400 meters (440 yards), another 200 meters (220 yards), and the other two team members 100 meters (110 yards) each. The advantage of this medley is that it allows each runner to run his specialty, providing the runners are chosen accordingly. The most common pursuit relay for high school girls is the 400 meter (440-yard) pursuit relay. Each runner sprints 100 meters (110 yards) and passes to the next runner within a 20 meter (twenty-two-yard) passing zone. Logically, the prerequisite for the 400 meter (440-yard) relay is the 100 meter (100-yard) dash.

PASSING THE BATON

Many relays are won or lost in the passing zone. A team of fast sprinters who pass the baton poorly can lose a relay race to a team of mediocre runners with smooth, efficient passes. Many variations in passing have been developed and the search continues as each team attempts to develop the technique that

4. The medley race for boys covers the distance of one mile 400-200-200-800 meters (440-220-220-880 yards).

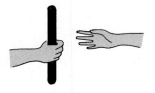

Figure 17.4. **The baton is passed in a vertical position in the shuttle relay.**

Figure 17.5. **Blind pass. The baton is thrust upward into a V-shaped pocket made by the thumb and index finger.**

Figure 17.6. **Blind pass. The baton is thrust downward into an upturned palm.**

best suits its individual characteristics. The major variations of passing the baton fall into three categories according to:

1. whether one or both teammates actually view the pass;
2. the direction the palm of the receiver is facing, which in turn alters the direction the baton is passed (upward, fig. 17.5 or downward, fig. 17.6);
3. the various combinations of using the right or left hand to pass and receive in the three passes of the relay. Different combinations of these variations can be employed to create a variety of techniques for passing the baton. Technically there are advantages and disadvantages in each of the variations in terms of speed or accuracy.

CONCEPT. A team sacrifices speed for accuracy when using a visual pass. Conversely, a blind pass sacrifices accuracy for speed.

In the visual pass both the receiver and passer see the pass take place; in the blind pass, only the passer views the procedure. Obviously, when both are looking at what is happening there is less chance to fumble or drop the baton. However, in order to view the procedure, the receiver must rotate the trunk, look over the shoulder and extend the arm backward to receive the baton. The resulting position does not lend itself to traveling at full speed (fig. 17.7).

In the blind pass the receiver runs facing forward. As the passer comes within range

the receiver extends one arm backward during the normal backswing and the baton is quickly placed in the hand by the passer during the regular upswing of his arm. Timing is of the essence and ideally the pass should take place within the normal stride, with both runners moving at nearly maximum acceleration.

The blind pass is most desirable in that it is speedier and the goal is to move the baton over the distance of the race as quickly as possible. The blind pass is commonly used in the 400 meter (440-yard) sprint relay since the passer should not be extremely fatigued. Responsibility for the success of the pass lies mainly with the passer, since the receiver is not looking back. Although the visual pass may be used for any relay, two instances justify the use of the visual pass: (1) the visual pass is safer in the medley when the passer has just run a long leg and is extremely tired; and (2) young runners or beginners often find the visual pass more

Figure 17.7. **Visual pass. Both passer and receiver view the exchange.**

comfortable during their initial encounter with relay racing.

CONCEPT. Passing the baton downward into an upturned palm minimizes the chances of dropping the baton, whereas passing the baton upward into an inverted pocket (the palm down or back) allows the receiving hand to remain in a more natural position.

The upturned palm is achieved by rotating the arm medially and extending the arm backwards with the wrist flexed (fig. 17.5). A second method involves rotating the trunk toward the receiving arm and rotating the arm laterally while reaching back. The second method is the technique commonly used for the visual pass (fig. 17.7). In both instances the thumb points toward the midline of the body and the surface of the palm of the hand approaches a horizontal plane due to the flexed wrist. The baton is slapped downward into the palm.

In the palm-down technique the receiving arm is stretched backward with the thumb and fingers making an inverted V pocket in which to receive the baton. The passer slaps the baton upward into this pocket. The inverted V pocket deviates less from the natural position of the hand in the arm swing than does the upturned palm. Re-

gardless of whether the palm is facing upward or downward, if the pass is blind both the passer and receiver strive to maintain maximum acceleration and pass and receive the baton with an exaggerated reach during the regular forward and backward movement of the arms.

CONCEPT. Passing the baton from the left hand of the passer to the right hand of the receiver in all three passes of the relay has the advantage of consistency, while alternating hands (left to right, right to left, etc.) can save time and work to the advantage of the receivers on the curve.

If the hand pass is consistent rather than alternate, the baton is commonly passed from the left hand of the passer to the right hand of the receiver. This necessitates the second and third runner transferring the baton to the left hand in order to pass it on. The baton is normally transferred immediately after it is received. Each time the baton is passed, whether it is passed from one person to another or transferred from one hand to another, a little time is lost and the chances of fumbling or dropping the baton increase. Therefore, the first runner should begin with the baton in the passing hand (left hand) and the last runner should finish the race with the baton in the hand with which he received it (right hand). The greatest advantage of this technique (left to right, passer to receiver) is its consistency. The order of the four runners can be changed if necessary (it is usually changed for reasons of strategy) because the passing technique is the same (left to right) throughout the race.

The use of alternate hands to pass and receive the baton eliminates the need of the second and third runner to transfer the baton to the left hand for the next pass. This saves time and eliminates two chances of dropping or fumbling the baton. In the alternate hand pass, the first runner begins with the baton in the right hand and the first pass is made right to left; the second pass, left to right; and the third pass, right to left, with the last runner keeping the baton in the left hand for the finish. With this pattern the first and third passes are from the right hand to the left hand, which allows the first receiver in the 400 meter (440-yard) relay to accelerate along the outside edge of the lane and then cut sharply into the straightaway after receiving the baton.

CONCEPT. To allow the reach in the pass to be directly forward and backward, and to eliminate the possibility of running into the receiver, the passer must run in a pathway to either side of the receiver instead of directly behind him.

If the pass is from the left hand to the right hand, the receiver accelerates along the inside edge of the lane. The passer approaches in a pathway near the outside edge of the lane. The hands should meet when the arms are stretched directly forward and backward. If the pass is from the left hand to the right hand the receiver is nearer the inside edge of the lane and the passer nearer the outside edge. Each runner attempts to diminish the distance traveled by

running the curves on the inside edge, cutting the corners, and moving to the outside or inside edge of the lane in a straight line when the passing pattern necessitates the maneuver.

CONCEPT. Regardless of the passing technique used, the runners attempt to run quickly and reach far during the pass in order to gain as much free space as possible.

Free space is that space through which the baton travels in the pass. If the runners are moving at full speed, the farther they reach to pass the baton the greater the distance of free space gained. In other words, free space is the distance gained in the pass with no expenditure of time.[5]

STARTING POSITION

CONCEPT. The 400 meter (440-yard) pursuit relay is a sprint which necessitates a crouch position for the start.

The mechanics of an efficient start are the same as those for the sprints, with the exception of holding the baton while using the hands for balance. The baton should be held by one or two of the fingers against the base of the thumb while the other fingers and thumb form the bridge.

MOLDING A RELAY TEAM

CONCEPT. The common errors of beginners can be eliminated and the proficiency of the passers can be developed through practice and communication.

It is not unusual for the novice receiver to stand motionless or even stop running to receive the pass. On the other hand, an over-

5. Fred Wilt and Tom Echer, *International Track and Field Coaching Encyclopedia* (West Nyack, N.Y.: Parker Publishing Co., 1970), p. 108.

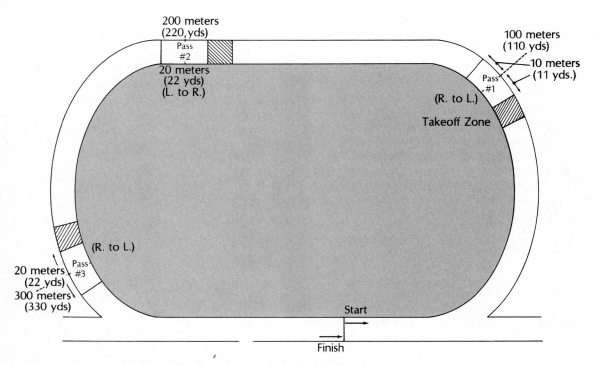

Figure 17.8. Lane marks for the 400 meter (440-yard) pursuit relay

anxious receiver may run away from the passer due to the inability to judge the speed or the fatigue of the passer. The pass must take place within a twenty-two-yard passing zone. (See figure 17.8 for marking the passing zones on the track for the 400 meter (440-yard) pursuit relay.) However, the receiver may begin to accelerate at a spot eleven yards prior to the beginning of the passing zone. This additional space, designated as the takeoff zone, provides the receiver more space in which to attempt to accelerate to maximum. However, the receiver must still judge the speed of the incoming passer in order to complete the pass in the last third of the passing zone. By experimenting the pair can develop a check mark, a spot marked on the track approximately five to seven yards before the eleven-

yard takeoff zone. As the incoming runner (the passer) crosses that spot the receiver should begin to accelerate from a semi-crouch position. Audible cues can also be used. The passer might call "Run!" as he crosses the check mark or "Reach!" when he is within range for the pass. Whatever techniques are used, concentrated practice is needed to develop a more efficient pass.

CONCEPT. The arrangement of runners in the relay should place each runner in the position where his individual strong points will be utilized to the maximum.

Some of the questions that must be answered are: Who is the best starter? Who runs the curves the best? The straightaways? Who is the fiercest competitor? Who can maintain acceleration the longest? Who runs best when ahead? When behind? Who are the best baton handlers? What passing-receiving combinations work best together?

Without a doubt the most important position is that of runner number one. He must be a good starter and be able to maintain acceleration over the longest distance, since he must run the distance of the first leg plus another seven yards to pass in the last one-third of the passing zone. The second and third runners travel equal distances; however, the second runner's leg is mainly the straightaway, while the third runner must contend with the curve. Because the fourth leg of the relay is most exciting a common misconception is that the fourth runner must be the fastest runner. In reality this leg is the shortest distance since the baton is received approximately 100 yards from the finish line. A fierce competitor, one who runs well when behind or ahead is needed for the last leg. Then, too, one must consider the passer-receiver combination that works best when the runners are positioned in the relay.

REGULATIONS GOVERNING RELAYS

The regulations governing relays include the following:

a. No competitor may run more than one leg of a relay.
b. The baton must be passed in the twenty meter passing zone.
c. If the baton is dropped during the exchange the passer must pick it up.
d. A baton dropped outside the passing zone is picked up by the runner who dropped it.
e. In the shuttle relay, all parts of the runner's body must be behind the restraining line until he is tagged or receives the baton.
f. All rules listed for running events, page 525, also apply to the relays.

Sprinting the Hurdles

The hurdling events are really sprinting races with the addition of imposed barriers the runner must clear. For some beginners, hurdles not only impose a physical but also a psychological barrier. Thus, a cautious, progressive approach to this event must be used.[6] A good hurdler needs speed, flexibility and courage. The hurdling events may vary in distance from fifty yards to 200 meters.[7] The number of hurdles encountered in any one event varies with the distance to be run. The longer the distance, the more hurdles, and the more strength and endurance needed to complete the race with maximum acceleration. In an instructional class one would begin with the fifty-yard, four-hurdle event and possibly progress to the seventy-yard, six-hurdle race. The standard heights of hurdles for women are two feet, six inches and two feet, nine inches; however, for elementary children and even for beginners one may start with a barrier as low as eighteen inches. Events for high school boys include a high (thirty-nine inches), 120-yard, ten-hurdle event and a low (thirty inches) 180-yard, eight-hurdle event.

DEVELOPING HURDLING TECHNIQUES

CONCEPT. *The hurdler achieves maximum speed by developing a hurdling style that causes the least disruption to his style and rhythm of sprinting.*

The movement over the hurdle is really a leap—not a jump, which is an exaggerated stride of the run. The leg that crosses first is designated as the lead leg and the other the takeoff leg or trailing leg. The momentum to clear the hurdle is obtained from the

6. Suggestions for progressions are included at the end of this chapter under "Individualizing Instruction."
7. A meter is equivalent to 39.37 inches; thus, 200 meters equals approximately 217 yards.

speed of the sprint as well as the forceful extension of the takeoff foot against the ground. The efficiency of the hurdle, like the efficiency of the sprint, is governed by biomechanical principles. Because of the similarities in the movements, the principles are the same. The arms must move in opposition and in time with the rhythm of the legs to maintain balance. The center of gravity is placed ahead of the driving leg by body lean. The weight is received and propelled from the ball of the foot with the foot pointing forward as it strikes the ground. There is an absence of lateral motion in all movements except the recovery of the trailing leg, which is abducted in order to clear the hurdle. The less one has to buck or exaggerate the stride over the hurdle, the less the sprinting rhythm is disturbed; thus, greater speed is achieved. Because of this, tall, long-legged individuals by nature of endowment make the best hurdlers. However, one must allow for variations in style due to variations in body build.

CONCEPT. A speedy, forceful leg action and a low trajectory of the center of gravity contributes to the efficiency of the hurdling movement.

As the sprinter approaches the hurdle, the lead leg is quickly raised in a forward-upward direction as the takeoff leg thrusts against the ground. This causes a stretched split position between the thighs. The path of the center of gravity cannot be altered after the takeoff foot leaves the ground; therefore, the center of gravity must be well in front of the driving foot during the thrust. A shortened stride immediately before takeoff can aid the hurdler into getting the center of gravity into this position. A dip or lean of the trunk in a forward-downward direction helps to keep the center of gravity forward as well as low. In fact, the chin may be as far forward as the knee of the lead leg

during clearance. The heel of the lead leg just clears the hurdle and then begins to descend. The center of gravity must be at least over and possibly ahead of the lead foot as it contacts the ground. Nevertheless, the sooner the lead leg reaches the ground the better. Slapping the lead foot to the ground or pulling the trailing leg through earlier forces the lead leg down. Thus, the takeoff leg trails for a split second after the thrust and then if the hurdler is truly skimming the crossbar, the trailing leg must be elevated, abducted and carried forward quickly in this horizontal position. The knee is pulled toward the chest to ensure a full stride with the next step. Upon clearing the first hurdle the eyes are focused on the next hurdle (fig. 17.9). Although it is desirable to keep the knee of the lead leg flexed slightly, shorter individuals may need to straighten this leg and lean the trunk forward to a greater degree in order to skim over the hurdle rather than lope up and over.

CONCEPT. The length of the stride, which is partially determined by the body build of the runner, determines the number of strides between hurdles.

The distance between the starting line and the first hurdle is 12 meters (39 feet, 4½ inches).[8] Generally seven, eight, or nine strides are needed to reach the takeoff point for the first hurdle. The faster the runner is moving, the farther back that takeoff point can be from the hurdle, due to greater horizontal velocity. The number of steps needed (seven, eight, or nine, etc.) is not nearly as important as the runner's ability to stride consistently and use the same number of

8. This distance applies to the fifty-yard, four-hurdle in or outdoor race only. The following discussion concerning distances and number of steps must be adjusted for other hurdle events due to a greater distance between hurdles and a greater distance from the starting blocks to the first hurdle.

Figure 17.9. **Clearing the hurdle**

strides each time. He must also assume a position in the starting blocks that will result in the preferred lead leg being in the correct position when he encounters that first hurdle. If an uneven number of strides (seven or nine) is needed to cover the distance (39 feet, 4½ inches), the lead leg must be placed in the front starting block. If an even number of steps are needed, the lead foot is placed in the back block. The number of strides between hurdles must be an uneven number if each hurdle is to be cleared with the same foot leading. The most desirable number of strides between hurdles is three; however, beginners may need to use five and youngsters may need as many as seven. Three strides to cover 8 meters (twenty-six feet, three inches) at first glance seems unrealistic. However, the return of the lead foot to the ground at the completion of the hurdle is not considered one of the three strides and one may cover as much as eight feet of this distance in the hurdling movement. The distance from the last hurdle to the finish line varies with the distance of the race and the number of hurdles. Beginners may need to be prompted to sprint across the finish line. Psychologically they may feel the race is over when they clear the last hurdle.

CONCEPT. Concentration on the first few strides out of the blocks and the first stride after the touchdown by the lead foot can remedy many of the common errors of beginners.

If the first few strides away from the blocks are too short, the hurdler has to stretch his last few strides to reach the desired takeoff spot or he must take off too far back from the hurdle. In both instances he will float over the hurdle rather than skim over. The floating action occurs when the body remains in the air for too long a time. If some stride must be shortened it should be the one just prior to the takeoff which forces the center of gravity to move well forward of the takeoff foot to provide more horizontal thrust. Overstriding and taking off too close to the hurdle also diminish horizontal thrust; the body is forced to go up and over the hurdle rather than forward and over. The first full stride by the trailing leg after clearing the hurdle can in turn alter the takeoff point for the next hurdle. Thus, concentrated practice on the crouch start and sprint over the first two hurdles can do much to develop hurdling techniques.

REGULATIONS GOVERNING HURDLES

The regulations governing hurdles include the following:

a. The hurdles are placed on the track with the base extended in the direction from which the runner will approach. In this position they will fall in the direction of the run if bumped by the runner and possibly avert an injury.
b. There is no penalty for knocking down any number of hurdles.
c. The legs must pass over and not alongside or around the hurdle.
d. The rules for running events also apply to the hurdling races.

FIELD EVENTS

The field events include both jumping (projecting the body through space) and throwing (projecting an object through space). The jumping events discussed in this chapter are the high jump, the running long jump, the standing long jump and the triple jump. The triple jump is used only in men's meets. Included in the discussion of throwing events are the discus, the shot, the javelin, and the ball throwing events. Although the shapes, sizes and weights of the objects projected vary greatly, all field events have four things in common:

1. a preliminary movement of some nature that builds momentum through range and speed;
2. an accent of execution (the takeoff or release) at the instant peak force is generated;
3. an angle of projection; and
4. a follow-through or absorption of force upon landing.

The next section includes a general discussion of major concepts from chapter five related to field events. An analysis of each concept as it applies to each event is discussed in greater detail under that specific event.

Major Concepts

PRELIMINARY MOVEMENT

Sub-concept D-4. Setting the body in motion prior to contact with an object, or to the release of an object, builds greater force which in turn is transferred to the object. However, at the instant of contact or release, the body should be stabilized.

In the majority of field events the preliminary movement is a sprint or an approach run.[9] An exception, the standing long jump, as the name implies, prohibits this locomotor movement; thus, nonlocomotor movements of swinging and rocking are used to build momentum. Two other variations in the preliminary movement are necessary for the shot and discus. The limitation of the circle in the shot and discus events as well as the nature of these two objects necessitate a preliminary movement unique to each of these events. Nevertheless, the purpose of the preliminary movement is to build momentum through speed to achieve greater distance during flight. The optimum amount of acceleration generated in the preliminary movement is dependent upon the event and the proficiency of the performer. The degree of acceleration should be that maximum amount the performer can achieve and transfer with control at the instant of release or takeoff.

ACCENT OF EXECUTION

CONCEPT B. Creating and absorbing force to control the movement of the

9. High jump, long jump, triple jump, javelin, and ball throwing events are included in this group.

body through space may involve all of the body or only parts of the body, in unison or in sequence; however, the relaxation of noncontributing muscle groups is imperative for smooth, efficient movement.

Sub-concept B-1. A smooth transfer of momentum from one part of the body to another part, or to the total body, results in sustained movement, while an explosive transfer of momentum increases the speed and/or magnitude of the resulting movement.

CONCEPT D. Creating force: The production and transfer of force depend upon mass, speed, and the striking surface used.

Sub-concept D-1. Increasing the mass used to produce force increases the force produced.

Sub-concept D-2. Increasing the speed of the implement or the body segment imparting force increases the force produced. ·

Sub-concept D-3. Increasing the range of movement of the body segment or the implement imparting force increases the distance through which speed can be developed, as well as the force imparted to the object.

Sub-concept D-6. Stabilizing the body segments involved in an action allows for greater force to be imparted to the object.

Prior to takeoff or release the body gathers horizontal velocity (developed in the preliminary movement), and combines it with vertical velocity to generate peak force in the desired direction. Vertical velocity is developed by a forceful extension of the leg(s) against the ground, aided by the arms, which are used to lift and balance the body in the jumps or transfer the momentum of the trunk and legs to the projectile in the throws. The gather then implies some degree of flexion of the joints of the body and rotation of the trunk, as well as some position of the arms which allows them to extend and/or reach explosively in the desired direction. The task becomes one of manipulating the body into this position with a minimum loss of horizontal velocity. A part of this act has been designated as the plant of the takeoff foot in the jumping events or the plant of the forward foot in the throwing events. The plant establishes a point of resistance for the final thrust by checking the momentum of the lower limbs and transferring that momentum to the upper body or that portion of the body which will lead the movement in the intended line of direction. Actually, the plant is a part of the gather, for as the foot is planted the leg flexes slightly both to absorb the force of the foot contacting the ground as well as to position joints for a forceful extension.

ANGLE OF PROJECTION

CONCEPT E. Directing force: The direction in which an object moves is determined by the point at which force is applied in relation to the object's center of gravity.

Sub-concept E-4. External forces such as gravity, air resistance and friction alter the flight of a projectile.

The optimal angle of projection varies with the different events. When horizontal distance is the objective, the desirable angle of release for the different projectiles varies with their velocity, aerodynamics due to their shape, and the height of release point in relation to the landing surface. A forty-five-degree angle is optimal when the horizontal and vertical velocities are equal, when the point of projection is equal to the landing surface, and when there is no interference from air resistance. Obviously these conditions are not present in the field events. Analysis reveals that the optimum angles of release in the field events are less than forty-five degrees. In addition to a different angle of projection for each event, there is a slight additional variation in the prescribed angle due to individual competencies. Dyson treats this subject comprehensively in *The Mechanics of Athletics*.[10]

ABSORBING FORCE AND FOLLOW–THROUGH

Sub-concept B-2. Absorbing the force of a landing or fall over a greater time and distance increases stability and decreases the chance of injury.

Sub-concept D-5. A follow-through allows for greater force to be transferred to an object.

The subsequent action after the release of the projectile and the projection of the body are different. For the throwing events the body must dissipate the momentum gradually while maintaining balance; thus, the follow-through. In the jumping events the body must absorb the impact of the landing. Upon landing the body limbs receiving the weight flex to absorb the force over a greater time and distance and to increase stability by lowering the center of gravity. The legs and hips flex in the long jumps, while the landing from the high jump may involve the flexion of the arms as the hands touch down first. The time and distance used to absorb force can be increased to an even greater degree by placing the hands down in front of the feet on the long jumps

and rolling onto the shoulder and back in the landing from the high jump.

At the instant of release in the throwing events, the total body is focused in the direction of projection. The arm continues to move in the arc described in the throwing action. The front foot acts as the brake; however, the momentum created may be so great that this position of the feet (in a forward-back stride) is not adequate to keep from fouling. Thus, a quick reversal of feet may be necessary in the follow-through. This involves transferring weight onto the back foot, which has now come forward. One also may find it necessary to hop several times after the reversal to maintain balance and absorb the force over a greater time. This reversal of feet should not be taught as a matter of fact but only introduced after the performer has delivered the projectile with enough momentum to necessitate a reversal to keep from fouling. Otherwise, a beginner who anticipates the reversal initiates the action too early and sacrifices momentum in the delivery.

High Jump

The sequence of movements for the high jump involves an approach run, takeoff, and flight across a horizontal bar supported by vertical uprights. The horizontal bar is light and easily displaced when bumped. The landing pit must be soft to absorb the force of the landing with no threat of injury regardless of what part of the body touches down first. Materials that have been used successfully in the pit are foam rubber and air-filled canvas.

The conventional techniques of high jumping can be divided into two broad categories: those techniques in which the

10. Geoffrey Dyson. *The Mechanics of Athletics.* 7th ed. (London: University of London Press, 1977), pp. 23–27, 217–234.

body maintains a vertical position, and those in which the body assumes a horizontal position. The scissors technique is the only style in which the trunk is kept in a vertical position. In all other styles the body assumes a horizontal position. The horizontal styles can be further identified according to which surface of the body passes closest to the bar during clearance. The choice of surface limits the proximity of the body's center of gravity to the top of the bar and thus determines the degree of efficiency of the technique. The choice of surface also determines which parts of the body receive the weight upon landing. The scissors jump, western roll, straddle roll, and Fosbury flop are compared in the following analysis. They are discussed in isolation only in those aspects in which they differ.

CONCEPT. The approach builds momentum through speed that is converted into vertical lift as the body gathers all forces at takeoff to project the body in an upward direction.

A short, deliberate approach run of seven to nine strides is desirable. The angle of approach is approximately forty-five degrees, with the point of takeoff being about an arm's length from the bar. As the takeoff foot is planted the center of gravity is behind the takeoff foot, the arms are back, and the whip leg is trailing. The body is gathering all forces for the vertical thrust. The arms and lead leg whip forward and upward as the takeoff leg pushes (extends) forcefully against the ground. At the instant of thrust the center of gravity is above the takeoff foot. Although the development of momentum through speed during the approach run is essential, an excess of speed can be a limiting factor if the legs are not quick and strong enough to develop vertical lift before the center of gravity travels for-

ward of the takeoff foot. The direction and force imparted to the center of gravity of the body is determined while the takeoff foot is still in contact with the ground. The trajectory of the center of gravity cannot be altered once the foot has left the ground.

CONCEPT. Although the pathway of the center of gravity cannot be altered after the foot leaves the ground, adjusting various segments of the body by applying the law of reaction allows trailing body segments to be raised.

Quite often the jumper clears the bar with the body and then displaces the crossbar with a trailing arm or leg. The trailing parts can be raised by utilizing the law of reaction; if the body parts that have cleared the bar are rotated upward and away from the bar, the trailing parts can be lifted upward and away from the bar.[11,12] This accounts for the popularity of the straddle roll, since it lends itself to a greater application of this principle.

CONCEPT. Different styles used to clear the bar vary in the amount of body mass between the top of the bar and the center of gravity, thus determining the height at which the bar can be cleared.

SCISSORS JUMP

In the scissors jump the body is kept vertical or nearly so with the buttocks and back of the legs passing next to the bar. In this style the whip leg, the one nearest to the bar, passes over the bar first. The takeoff leg (the leg farthest from the bar) trails in a scissoring action; thus the name, scissors jump. (Note in figure 17.12a the great amount of body mass between the top of the bar and the center of gravity of the body.) This style of high jump, although easy to master, is the

11. Dyson, *The Mechanics of Athletics,* pp. 109–113.
12. Tom Echer, *Track and Field Dynamics* (Los Altos, Calif.: Tafnews Press, 1974), pp. 72–77.

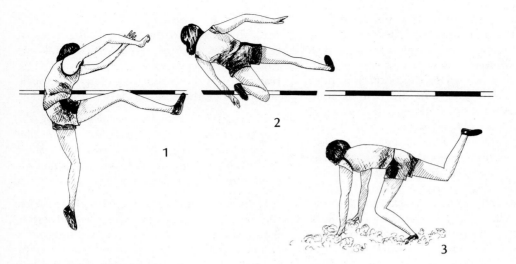

Figure 17.10. **Western roll**

least efficient of all the techniques used to clear the bar.

WESTERN ROLL

In this style the outside leg whips while the takeoff leg (the leg nearest the bar) thrusts against the ground and is then flexed and pulled close to the chest during bar clearance. The side of the body faces the bar during clearance and the head, arms and shoulders cross the bar first. The landing is on three points—two hands and the takeoff foot (fig. 17.10). The horizontal position of the body allows the center of gravity to pass much closer to the top of the bar than in the scissors jump; however, it still lacks efficiency when compared to the straddle roll (fig. 17.11).

STRADDLE ROLL

In the straddle roll the body rotates over the bar with the front of the body facing the bar. As in the western roll, the takeoff foot is nearest the bar on the approach; however, the whip leg becomes the lead leg and the takeoff leg trails. The inside arm is held close to the trunk as the outside arm and the knee of the lead leg reach over the bar. The arm, head, and shoulders clear the bar a little ahead of the knee of the lead leg and begin to drop. As the lead arm and leg clear the bar, they are rotated upward and away from the bar to facilitate the rotation of the trailing arm and leg upward and away from the bar. The body continues to rotate over the bar, which often results in a landing on the side of the body or the back. In the straddle dive, a variation of the straddle roll, the upper trunk and extremities are well ahead of the hips and legs in bar clearance, which allows them to drop sooner; the body is draped over the bar. The efficiency of this style of jumping is obvious when one compares the proximity of the center of gravity to the top of the bar (figs. 17.12c and 17.11).

FOSBURY FLOP

In the Fosbury flop the back of the body faces the bar during clearance. This style of high jump utilizes the same takeoff foot (the outside foot) as does the scissors style. The

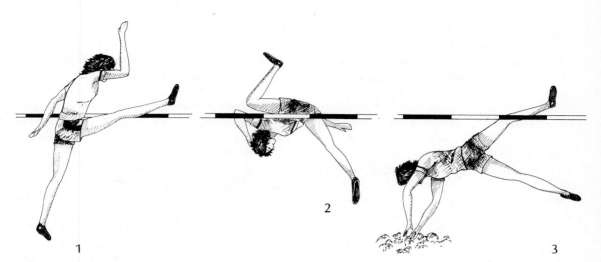

Figure 17.11. **Straddle roll**

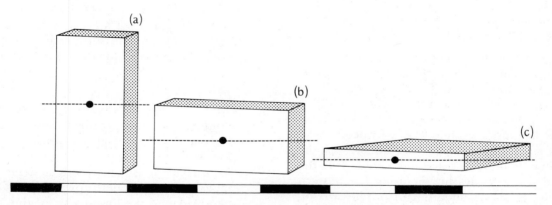

Figure 17.12. **The body is depicted as a box with its largest dimension as height, second largest dimension, width, and smallest dimension as depth. The proximity of the center of gravity of the box (body) to the top of the crossbar changes with various body positions.**

inside leg is swung up and across the body just before takeoff to aid in vertical lift and body rotation. The arms lift and then aid in counterbalancing the legs as the jumper dives backwards over the bar (the arms and legs may be symmetrical or asymmetrical, depending upon the individual). The upper body clears the bar and moves downward as

the body drapes over the bar. The jumper is dropping toward the pit head-first. In order to clear the bar with the legs, the hips flex once they have crossed the bar. This causes the hands and feet to be raised upward toward each other (in an action-reaction). This equal and opposite reaction, in addition to aiding in bar clearance, is imperative to positioning the body for a landing on the back. The landing pit must be foam rubber or air-filled canvas. The approach run is short, speedy and may take a variety of angles, including a circular pathway, to utilize centrifugal force. However, initial efforts in attempting this style are most successful if practiced from a stationary, two-foot takeoff with the back to the bar. Once the jumper masters the dive, followed by the quick flexion of the hips to assure a safe landing on the back, greater concentration can be given to the approach and takeoff.

CONCEPT. Greater height can be attained with the same amount of effort if the center of gravity is positioned close to the top of the bar; however, those styles which provide for this positioning also involve a precarious landing position.

This concept is depicted in figure 17.12. (Note that the center of gravity in the scissors style must be raised much higher if the hips are to clear the bar; see figure 17.12a.) In the western roll the side of the body faces the bar and the center of gravity need not be raised as high as in the scissors; or, with the same amount of force one could clear the bar a few inches higher using the western roll (fig. 16.12b and fig. 16.10). The proximity of the center of gravity to the crossbar is the greatest advantage of the horizontal lay-out position over the vertical body position. In the straddle lay-out, the center of gravity is still closer to the bar as the body faces the bar (figs. 17.12c and 17.11). In the Fosbury flop it is even closer, as the back faces the bar and the upper and lower body parts drape over the bar.

The landing position partially determines the attractiveness of each of these styles for the beginner. Obviously, the Fosbury flop has some inherent dangers in landing and should be reserved for intermediate and advanced students. The scissors jump, due to the landing on the feet, appeals to the beginner and is certainly advisable for use in the elementary program. The lack of a soft landing pit in a school setting may also limit the high jump event to only the scissors style. The western roll allows a fairly comfortable three-point landing on two hands and one foot, while the rotation of the body in the straddle roll may result in a landing on the side of the body and whip leg or even the back. In the past some variation of the straddle roll was used most often by competitors; however, the possibility of the attainment of greater height in the flop is appealing to the more serious jumpers.

REGULATIONS AND MEASUREMENTS GOVERNING THE HIGH JUMP

The regulations and measurements governing the high jump include the following:

a. The jumper must take off from one foot.
b. Knocking the crossbar off, or extending any part of the body beyond the plane of the uprights, counts as a failure.
c. Measurement is taken with a steel tape from the ground upward, perpendicular to the lowest part of the upper side of the crossbar.

Running Long Jump

The running long jump involves a sequence of movements that begins with an approach run, and flows into a one-foot takeoff, which in turn projects the body into flight with the purpose of covering the greatest possible horizontal distance before landing. The length of the approach varies with individual differences in developing speed. The takeoff board is normally four feet long, eight inches wide, and four inches thick. It is set flush with the ground with the edge nearest the landing pit being the foul line. The standard distance between the takeoff board and landing pit is fifteen feet; however, the distance should be shortened considerably for beginners in order to insure that the beginner lands in the soft pit. If the class must use a standard facility, the teacher might disregard the takeoff board and make a takeoff line closer to the landing pit. The distance is dictated only by the skill of the students using the facility.

Different styles of long jumping are distinguished according to the position or movements of the body during flight. Attention to this phase of the jump, although important in the final analysis, is unnecessary and possibly confusing for the beginner as he struggles with the techniques of approaching, taking off and landing. Thus, the following discussion dwells on an analysis of the basic concepts necessary for all styles and only briefly mentions the various styles as they relate to the efficiency of the landing.

THE APPROACH

CONCEPT. The ability to achieve repeatedly the most desirable takeoff position along with the development of appropriate horizontal velocity is dependent upon practice and attention to consistency in the approach.

The horizontal velocity developed in the approach combines with the takeoff thrust to carry the body forward and upward over a horizontal distance. However, maximum acceleration detracts from the efficiency of lift during takeoff. Therefore, the speed of the approach is most often described as maximum acceleration with control. The distance and number of strides used in the approach varies with each individual. A general rule of thumb states that the approach must be long enough to allow the jumper to develop appropriate acceleration and yet not so long as to tire him and waste energy needed for the takeoff. The number of strides used in the approach usually falls between seventeen and twenty-three. Once the number of strides has been established, the mark to begin the approach is found by starting at the takeoff board and striding in a reverse direction back along the runway. The runner must be consistent in the length of his strides as well as the number of strides if he is to contact the takeoff board with the appropriate foot each time. Check markers are placed along the runway to help the runner develop such consistency. For example, a jumper initiates his approach with a step onto the takeoff foot and terminates his approach with this same foot on the takeoff board. Thus, he has used an uneven number of strides to reach his destination (possibly nineteen strides). Using nineteen strides and placing one check mark four strides from the takeoff board and the other check mark at a point approximately halfway through the remaining distance, the check marks should coincide with the seventh and fifteenth stride. These strides will be taken on the takeoff foot. The exact placement of these check marks can be determined only through experimentation. Through practice, with the aid of check marks, one develops consistency in the length and the number of strides.

The technique of the approach is really a sprint; however, a standing start is normally used. The speed of the approach partially determines the amount of gather employed by the jumper in the last few strides before takeoff. Generally, fast sprinters employ less gather, while jumpers with a slower approach tend to gather more for the takeoff.

1   2   3   4

Figure 17.13. **Running long jump; takeoff and landing**

THE TAKEOFF

CONCEPT. The takeoff initiates vertical lift through the forceful extension of the takeoff leg, combined with the whip of the arms and free leg in an upward-forward direction.

Although the most desirable angle of projection of the center of gravity is considerably less than forty-five degrees, the beginner must concentrate first on developing vertical lift during takeoff.[13] Too often beginners tend to speed off the board, sacrificing vertical lift in their takeoff. During the later phase of the gather, the takeoff foot is planted on the takeoff board. As the center of gravity moves over the takeoff foot, the arms and free leg (flexed to increase velocity of movement) initiate the lift by moving in an upward-forward direction. A forceful extension of the takeoff leg completes the upward thrust and the body is airborne. The distance the body travels horizontally is determined by a combination of horizontal velocity, vertical thrust, and angle of takeoff, in addition to the ability of the jumper to keep his feet in the air as long as possible and still make an efficient landing.

THE LANDING

CONCEPT. The angle of the trunk and legs in the long sitting position immediately preceding

the touchdown influences the degree to which the legs can reach to gain distance and still maintain a balanced landing.

A balanced landing is one in which the heels touch down first; as the feet sink into the pit, the body flexes and rotates forward over the feet. The hands touchdown forward of the feet, if necessary. Regardless of the style during flight, the body position immediately preceding the touch down is a long sitting position. The beginner who disregards flight technique assumes the sitting position very soon after takeoff. Although the trajectory of the center of gravity of the body cannot be altered, distance can be gained by reaching forward with the legs in order to have them touch down well in front of the center of gravity. However, the danger lies in overextending, which results in an inability to carry the body forward upon landing and thus the buttocks mark the pit behind the heels. If the arms are thrust forward quickly the instant the heels touch down, they counteract the pull of gravity and aid in the rotation of the body forward over the feet. The jumper must find that position which allows him optimal reach with a balanced landing (fig. 17.13).

13. Dyson, *The Mechanics of Athletics*, p. 185.

Regulations and measurements of the long jumps are located after the triple jump (p. 545).

Standing Long Jump

The standing long jump is easier for beginners to master than the running long jump, since the body is used symmetrically; both legs thrust and both arms whip. Balance is less of a problem in takeoff since the feet must remain in contact with the takeoff surface during the period of building momentum. The jump may be initiated from behind a scratch line or from an elevated board.[14] An outdoor running long jump facility can be easily converted to a standing long jump facility by marking a scratch line or placing a takeoff board close enough to the pit to allow the jumper to land in the pit. Such a facility can also be easily improvised indoors using tumbling mats for a landing area.

As in the running long jump, the purpose of the standing long jump is to travel the greatest possible horizontal distance. Less horizontal velocity is achieved due to the standing start; thus the distance achieved in the standing long jump is much less than that of the running long jump. The technique of landing is much the same as that of the running long jump and the measurement of the jump is exactly the same. Consequently, the following discussion is concerned only with the techniques of building momentum and taking off.

CONCEPT. The momentum to project the body in the standing long jump is achieved by a forceful thrust of the legs against the takeoff surface, accompanied by a whip of the arms to aid in the lift.

Any swinging motion of the arms or rocking of the body is permissible and can aid in building momentum, providing the movement is smoothly coordinated and leaves the body in a desirable position for takeoff. The whip of the arms in an upward-forward direction initiates the takeoff. As the center of gravity moves forward of the feet, the legs extend forcefully with the balls of the feet and toes being the last to leave the takeoff surface. Since the horizontal and vertical thrust can be controlled (equalized) and the takeoff and landing surface are level, or nearly so, the most desirable angle of projection to gain the greatest horizontal distance is forty-five degrees (fig. 17.14.)[15] Regulations and measurements of the long jumps are located after the triple jump (p. 545).

Triple Jump

The triple, or hop-step-jump, as it is commonly called, is a most exciting and challenging event. Although it is officially a field event for men only, women and even children in the upper elementary grades can master the sequence of movements with little difficulty. Obviously the student must be able to execute the individual locomotor skills of the hop, leap, and jump (a one-foot takeoff, two-foot landing) before attempting to put them into a sequence. The initial effort at performing the sequence might prove more successful from a standing start. Nevertheless, it is not long before the student is eager to precede the sequence with a running approach in order to see just how far he can travel in this unusual sequence. With the running approach and two-foot landing the triple jump has much in common with the running long jump.[16] As in the running long jump, the triple jumper

14. A takeoff board, elevated four inches, is acceptable and the jumper may curl the toes over the front edge of the board providing they do not touch the ground or floor.
15. Dyson, *The Mechanics of Athletics,* p. 26.
16. Check the subsection "Running Long Jump" for a detailed analysis of the approach and landing.

Figure 17.14. **Standing long jump**

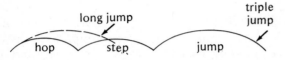
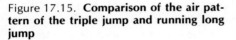

Figure 17.15. **Comparison of the air pattern of the triple jump and running long jump**

must find the right combination of horizontal velocity and vertical thrust, since overemphasis of one is detrimental to the other and thus causes a loss of distance. Because the long jump involves one single thrust, the direction is *upward and forward*. The triple jump, because of three power actions, has a focus of *forward and upward* (fig. 17.15).

CONCEPT. To ensure a smooth transfer of speed and power, the jumper must prepare for the power thrust of the next movement as he descends from the previous movement.

As the foot touches down between the hop-step and between the step-jump sequence, the ankle, knee and hip flex slightly to cushion the landing, but more importantly to coil the body for the spring into the subsequent movement. The trailing leg, which becomes the lead leg in the next movement, is carried under the body in a flexed position, ready to be driven forward and up-

ward to aid the thrusting leg. The arms are used for balance and lift and are carried in a variety of positions, depending upon the needs and style of the jumper. However, as the jumper descends the arms are behind the body ready to be thrust forward and upward to complement the power thrust of the leg.

CONCEPT. Although an accomplished triple jumper establishes his own rhythmic pattern in the sequence, the novice should concentrate on an even rhythmic pattern in his initial efforts.

Even the champions do not vary to a great degree from an even rhythmic pattern. Generally the hop (the first movement) or jump (the third movement) cover the greatest distance; however, the step or leap (the second movement) is not decidely shorter. Beginners quite often try to cover too much distance on the hop, causing an off-balance landing which is detrimental to the efficiency of the body and the distance gained in the next two movements. One should be a little conservative on the hop and strive for a longer step; however, the step cannot be so long that it markedly decreases the horizontal velocity needed for the jump. Figure 17.15 depicts a rhythmic pattern with the jump covering the greatest distance. Poor rhythm in the sequence might be solved by changing the takeoff leg.

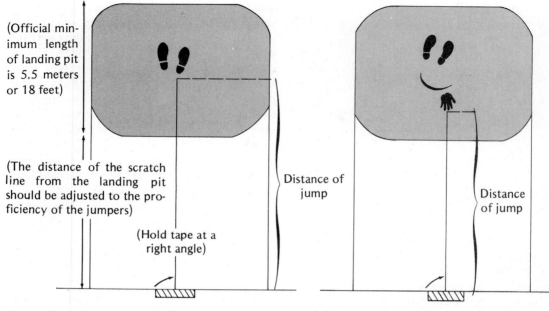

(Official min-imum length of landing pit is 5.5 meters or 18 feet)

(The distance of the scratch line from the landing pit should be adjusted to the pro-ficiency of the jumpers)

(Hold tape at a right angle)

Distance of jump

Distance of jump

Figure 17.16. **Long jump station and measurements**

Figure 17.17. **Measurement is taken to the nearest impression made by the jumper (in this instance, the hand).**

If one is accustomed to using the left leg as the takeoff leg in the running long jump, he should try beginning his hop on the right leg.

REGULATIONS AND MEASUREMENTS GOVERNING THE LONG JUMPS

Regulations governing the long jumps include the following:

a. The long jumps are measured along a line that describes a right angle with the takeoff board to the nearest impression the body (hopefully the heels; however, it might be the hands or buttocks) has made in the pit (figs. 17.16 and 17.17).

b. The pit is raked smooth after each jump.

c. No part of the jumper's body can touch the ground beyond the scratch line during the jump.

Putting the Shot

The restriction of a seven-foot-diameter putting circle (2.135 meters), the weight of the shot (six pounds for the novice; eight pounds for high school girls and junior high school boys; twelve pounds for high school boys), and the regulation that the shot must be thrust rather than thrown makes the action of putting unique. The complete putting action involves a glide across the back half of the circle, a plant of the left foot against the toe board at the front of the circle, an uncoiling of the trunk, and a forceful extension of the arm as momentum is transferred through the center of the shot. The total action must be smooth and sequential

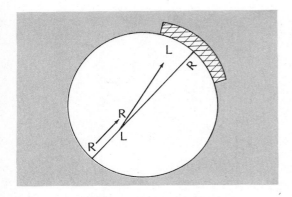

Figure 17.18. **Foot pattern across the circle for putting the shot**

or the momentum of the glide is lost. Due to the complexity of the gliding action and the lack of glamour in the event itself, beginners must experience a sense of accomplishment early or interest diminishes. For beginners, putting from a stationary stance and/or a modified movement across the circle provides early success. In fact, the novice may be challenged with a modified technique and continue to work to improve efficiency at this modified level. The more proficient student or potential competitor should progress to the glide. In the initial efforts at gliding, the support of a partner holding the putter's hands stabilizes the body and allows greater concentration on the leg action. This partial action is then combined smoothly with the thrusting action learned from a stance and becomes one sequential motion for putting the shot.

CONCEPT. A shot that is carried in a low horizontal pathway across the back half of the circle is in a good position to gather optimum momentum on the rotation and release.

In order to utilize the large heavy muscles of the legs and trunk, the body is flexed and rotated away from the intended direction of projection during the initial movement, the

glide. At the start, the student locates himself at the back half of the circle in a crouch position with weight carried mainly on the right foot.[17] The eyes remain focused on a spot behind the circle to discourage a premature uncoiling of the body during the glide. The shot is balanced in the hand at the base of the fingers with the thumb and little finger providing lateral stability. The shot is cradled against the neck or cheek and must be projected from a position in front of the shoulder. The left arm is carried in a position which is comfortable and which aids the putter in balancing. Movement backwards is initiated by a strong whip action of the left leg with a simultaneous slight extension of the right leg in order to take the weight (in the hips) backwards and allow the right foot to glide along the surface. The foot pattern and putting action are depicted in figures 17.18 and 17.19.

CONCEPT. The shot remains in a trailing position during the sequential extension and uncoiling of the legs and trunk and leaves the hand at the instant peak force is generated in the final extension of the arm.

After the whip action which initiates the glide, the left leg reaches forward and the foot is placed against or near the toe board at the front of the circle. The left leg acts as a brake and also a fulcrum as horizontal momentum is transferred upward and outward. As the right leg extends, the hips begin to rotate out, followed by the shoulder. The body is arched with the focus upward as the thrust drives through the center of the shot in an up-and-over catapulting action. The most desirable angle of projection is forty to forty-five degrees. The follow-through is with the total body focused in the

17. Analysis is for a right-handed person for all throwing events.

Figure 17.19. **Putting action**

1   2   3   4

direction of the projection. (See "Absorbing Force and Follow-through," page 536.)

REGULATIONS AND MEASUREMENTS GOVERNING THE SHOT

Regulations and measurements governing the shot include the following:

    a. The shot must be put from the shoulder by one hand only and shall not pass behind or below the shoulder during the attempt.

    b. No part of the body can touch the ground inside or outside of the circle nor the top of the toe board.

    c. After the put, the competitor must leave from the back half of the circle and not before the distance has been marked.

    d. The throw is measured from the spot where it first touched down back to the inside circumference of the circle along a line that would pass through the center of the circle if continued.

    e. The dimensions of the throwing circle, toe board and sector lines defin-ing the legal landing area are stan-dardized as depicted in figure 17.20.

Throwing the Discus

The restriction of an 8 foot, 2½ inch throwing circle and the shape of the discus (fig. 17.21) make this event the most unusual of the throwing events. The total action involves a turning movement of the body across the diameter of the circle to build centrifugal force, which is transferred to the discus as it rolls in a clockwise direction off the index finger. Speed in the turn is essential; however, balance is vital if the force generated is to be fully utilized. As in the other throws, a delivery from a stationary stance is learned first. The turn, too, may be modified for the beginner.

Beginners quite often have difficulty in releasing the discus in a clockwise direction off the index finger. Practice in rolling the discus out of the hand with an underhand motion helps to overcome this problem. Another difficulty encountered by the beginner is that of maintaining a firm grasp on

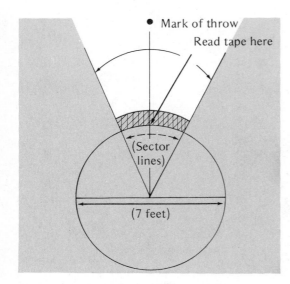

Figure 17.20. **Standard putting station showing the measurement of the put**

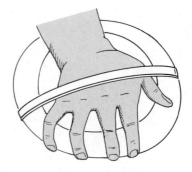

Figure 17.22. **Discus with strap to aid in securing the grip during practice of the turn**

Figure 17.21. **Discus**

Figure 17.23. **Gripping the discus with the wrist cocked slightly toward the little finger**

the discus while learning the turn. This can be helped by practicing the turn, omitting the release, with a discus that is strapped to the back of the hand (fig. 17.22). Eventually the centrifugal force generated by the turn holds the discus against the cushions of the fingers. In gripping the discus the palm of the hand is centered over or slightly behind the center of the discus (toward the little finger). The ends of the fingers are curled over the edge of the discus and the thumb rests on the top surface. The fingers may be spread evenly and exert equal pressure, or the index and middle finger may be placed close together, which allows those two fingers to exert greater pressure. A smaller

hand usually requires that the palm be centered and the fingers evenly spread. In either case a slight cock of the wrist toward the little finger keeps the discus from sliding out the back of the grip during the turn (fig. 17.23).

CONCEPT. Optimum speed with controlled balance during the turn across the circle is the key to building momentum in the discus throw.

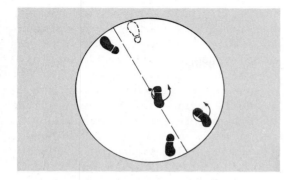

Figure 17.24. **Foot pattern across the circle during preliminary movement to build momentum prior to the release of the discus**

Figure 17.25. **Position of discus beginning the last quarter-turn prior to release**

To begin, the thrower assumes a comfortable stance at the back edge of the circle, facing away from the intended direction of flight. The feel or rhythm of the movement is initiated by several swings of the discus back to the right and then across the body to the left hand. The turn is initiated with the weight on the left foot. The hips move off balance toward the center of the circle as the body pivots on the ball of the left foot and the right foot reaches around to receive weight at about the center of the circle. The hips continue to lead as the body pivots on the ball of the right foot and the left foot reaches around and is planted to the left of an imaginary line bisecting the circle (fig. 17.24). Movement should describe a circular air pattern in a horizontal plane with a lift coming during the last quarter-turn before the release. The legs and hips are flexed to lower the center of gravity during the turn and to place the body in position to extend during the last quarter of the turn. The left leg acts as a brake as the right leg and hip drive rotatory momentum up into the release.

CONCEPT. The key to utilizing the centrifugal force generated during the turn is to keep the discus in a trailing position.

The rotation is begun with the discus in a trailing position. Thus, the feeling should be that of *pulling* the discus around as it hangs at the end of the arm. Little effort should be expended to carry the discus through a wide arc until the last quarter of the turn. At this point, as the left leg brakes and horizontal momentum is transferred upward, the discus travels in a wide arc (a straight arm is used) from a position behind the body, upward to shoulder level, where it is released (fig. 17.25).

REGULATIONS AND MEASUREMENTS GOVERNING THE DISCUS

Regulations and measurements governing the discus include the following:

a. A competitor cannot touch the ground inside or outside of the circle with any part of the body before the discus lands and he then must leave by the rear half of the circle.

b. The throw is measured from the spot where the discus first touched down back to the inside circumference of the circle along a line that, if

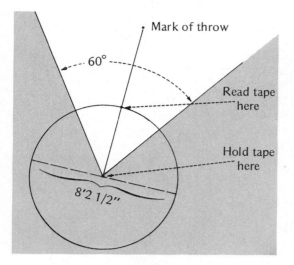

Figure 17.26. **Standard throwing station for the discus showing the measurement**

Mark of throw

60°

Read tape here

Hold tape here

8'2 1/2"

continued, would pass through the center of the throwing circle.

c. The dimensions of the throwing circle and the sector into which the discus must land are standardized as depicted in figure 17.26.

Throwing the Javelin

The sequence of movements for the javelin throw involves an approach (a preliminary run) to build horizontal speed, a gather to manipulate the body into a position to transfer maximum momentum to the javelin, and finally the release and follow-through. Due to the inherent dangers of the spear-like implement, authorities prohibit the javelin throw in high school events in many areas. Obviously, strict safety precautions must be enforced both at practice and during competition. The throwing space for the javelin should be located in a large open space well away from other events. Extra precaution can be taken by roping off the area around the throwing sector. If several

persons are practicing throws from a scratch line, a system of retrieving the javelins similar to that of retrieving arrows in archery must be established. The regulation throwing station is depicted in figure 17.27.

Breaking the total action into parts and allowing the beginner to release the javelin in his first practice session maintains interest and develops a sense of accomplishment. Thus, throwing the javelin from a stationary stance to a target that is not too far distant might logically be the first part the student practices. Next the five-step gather, combined with the release, could be practiced. A short approach run and finally the full approach completes the total action.

CONCEPT. The approach involves a run and a five-step gather to build and position the body to impart maximum velocity to the javelin.

A well-designed approach has an uneven number of strides (approximately fifteen) with the first step (check point one) taken on the same foot (the left foot for right-handed throwers) that begins the gather (check point two). Eventually, this foot is the forward foot at the instant of release (fig. 17.28). The approach is a gradual acceleration to achieve a speed that the thrower can control in order to transfer that momentum to the javelin.

Several styles of foot patterns have been used for the gather (the last five steps) over the past years. These include the hop, the glide, the rear cross-over and the front cross-over. The front cross-over is described in the following analysis. With an approach of fifteen strides, step number eleven begins the gather. On steps eleven, twelve, and thirteen the trunk rotates backwards to the right, which causes the feet to point diagonally to the right. Because of this rotation and the angle of the feet, step fourteen takes the form of a front cross-over step. Step fifteen is the plant or brake step that initiates the

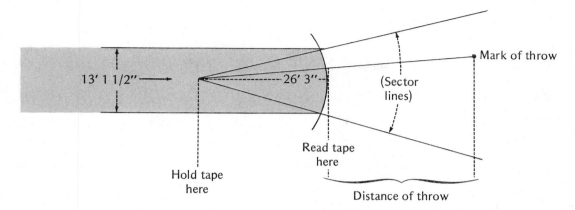

Figure 17.27. **Standardized throwing station for the javelin showing the measurement**

transfer of horizontal momentum to forward-upward momentum. Step fifteen
should be far enough back from the arc or
scratch line to allow for a reversal of feet on
the follow-through without fouling. (See
"Absorbing Force and Follow-through,"
page 536.)

*CONCEPT. The appropriate grip, carry and
gather allow momentum to be transferred
through the length of the shaft upon release.*

The javelin is positioned diagonally across
the palm of the hand with either the index
or middle finger hooked around the rear
edge of the binding or whipcord. The grip
of the thumb and remaining fingers stabilizes the javelin in the hands. The degree of
tension in the grip is only moderate during
the running portion of the approach and increases during the gather in preparation for
pulling the javelin forward just prior to release. The finger wrapped around the back
of the binding exerts the greatest pressure
during the forward movement.

During the approach the javelin is carried
above the shoulder, the point up or down
slightly, but pointing forward in the direc-

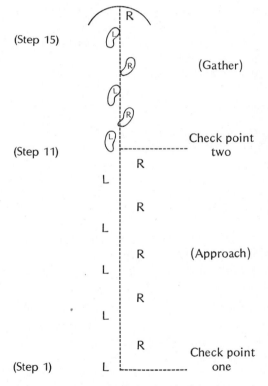

Figure 17.28. **Foot pattern of the approach and gather for the release of the
javelin**

Figure 17.29. **Gather and release of the javelin**

tion of the run. The total javelin may move forward and backward slightly with the rhythm of the run. With the beginning of trunk rotation for the gather, the javelin is pulled backwards with the thrower's arm fairly straight, so that the point of the javelin is located in line with the head. As the trunk uncoils the javelin is pulled through the space above the shoulder and released high above the right shoulder with a final whip-like action of elbow and wrist (fig. 17.29). A forty-five-degree angle of release is recommended for a wooden shaft, less than forty-five degrees for a steel shaft.[18]

REGULATIONS AND MEASUREMENTS GOVERNING THE JAVELIN

Regulations and measurements governing the javelin include the following:

a. The javelin must be thrown from one hand and the last contact of the body with the javelin must be with the grip.
b. The release must be overhand (over the shoulder or upper part of throwing arm) as opposed to an underhand sling.

c. The thrower cannot turn his back to the throwing sector at any time after preparing to throw.
d. Upon landing, the point of the javelin must touch the ground before any part of the shaft to be a legal throw.
e. Measurements are depicted in figure 17.27.

Ball Throwing Events

The softball and basketball throws are the two ball throwing events. These two are listed by the N.A.G.W.S. as official events for the upper elementary grades through high school and are substituted most often for the javelin throw when and where it is prohibited.[19] The throwing events lend themselves well to inclusion in class programs due to the availability of these types of balls. In addition, the approach and gather for the overhand throw serves as an introduction to the javelin, while the sidearm throw approaches the technique

18. J. Kenneth Doherty, *Shot, Discus, Javelin, Hammer.* 2d ed., Track and Field Movies on Paper, vol. 1. (Swarthmore, Pa.: J. Kenneth Doherty, 1967), p. 63.
19. There are no official ball throwing events for boys.

used to release the discus. As in other field events, the thrower attempts to develop speed through an approach and throwing position that allows the greatest practical range of motion in order to transfer maximum momentum to the ball upon release. Thus, the forward-back stride with opposition, trunk rotation and sequential uncoiling, must be stressed during the delivery. The plant before the gather comes into play as in other throwing events with the addition of an approach which can take a variety of forms, including that of a glide, hop, or cross-over step as described for the javelin.

CONCEPT. The size of the ball determines the grip and style of delivery for the different ball throwing events.

The *softball* is small enough to be gripped by the fingers and projected with an overhand pattern. The index and middle fingers are comfortably spaced over the top of the ball with the thumb and remaining fingers around the sides. The ball is cushioned against the pads of the fingers and rests at the base of the fingers rather than in the palm. As in the javelin throw, the arm folds and unfolds (the elbow flexes and extends) as the ball is brought forward. However, the action with the ball is a whip-like one as opposed to a pulling action with the javelin. To utilize the range of motion and speed, the elbow must be kept up and away from the body.

The larger size of the *basketball* necessitates a full hand span across the back of the ball, with the wrist cocked slightly to cradle the ball against the lower forearm. The non-throwing hand may be used to balance the ball on the backswing. To keep the ball balanced the elbow remains straight and the pattern of delivery describes an arc to the side of the body. The action is whip-like in nature with the shoulder as the fulcrum.

REGULATIONS AND MEASUREMENTS GOVERNING THE BALL THROWING EVENTS

The regulations and measurements governing the ball throwing events include the following:

a. The ball must be delivered from one hand.
b. The scratch line is ten feet long and all throws are measured from the spot the ball touched down to the center of this line.
c. The ball may be delivered from a stationary position or may be preceded by a locomotor approach.
d. The participant cannot step on or over the scratch line until the throw has been marked.

INDIVIDUALIZING INSTRUCTION

CONCEPT U. An affective attitude based on a cognitive understanding of the dangers inherent in an activity is necessary if one is to perform safely.

Sub-concept U-1. Providing a safe environment for participation contributes to the development of desirable affective attitudes toward the activity.

Sub-concept U-2. Educating the participants to use the environment wisely contributes not only to personal safety but enhances the total climate of the classroom.

Each student approaches the track and field unit with an individual outlook. Some are apprehensive about success or failure. Others approach with enthusiasm and confidence. Still others may have doubts concerning their ability to perform these activities without injury to themselves. It is thus a multifaceted problem for the instructor to develop a program that emulates safety while providing both challenge and a sense of accomplishment for all students. In addition, the nature of track and field activities as individual sports, which dictates the arrangement of scattered facilities, poses several other problems. Total class (mass) instruction becomes a necessity when material is new and/or safety is a factor. Yet mass instruction which provides limited involvement for the participants soon becomes boring and students lose interest. Thus, the initial introduction of students to the track and field program, as well as to specific events, must be carefully guided and carefully organized by the teacher.

A review of the previous sections of this chapter reveals that there are both concepts and skills common to many aspects of track and field. The techniques of running, establishing a takeoff foot and considering the angle of projection are three of the most common. They can be explored with total class involvement by using a large grassy area and improvising and substituting various equipment and situations. Even initial instruction in the various specific events can be treated in this manner.

The progression in which beginners are introduced to the various events can establish the foundation for an affective attitude based upon both cognitive understanding and psychomotor success. Logically, the running events, other than hurdling, are less novel to the beginner and therefore should be introduced first. Either the projection of objects into space (the throwing events) or the projection of the body into space (the jumping events) could come next. However, in both instances modifications provide for early success.

In the throwing events the initial effort might be with objects the student is accustomed to handling: the softball, soccer ball, and basketball. During the encounter with these less complex skills one can become aware of the need for a body position that allows the maximum transfer of momentum to the object upon release, and the desirability of a preliminary movement that allows the optimum amount of momentum to be transferred. Although the student should be aware of the total action in the more complex throwing events, a part-whole approach to learning the event lends itself to greater success and safety. Thus, the progression for learning these events would proceed from learning to release the object from a stationary position first, adding a short preliminary movement or modified movement next, and finally incorporating the run (or turn or glide) to complete the total sequential action.

The progression for the jumping events should follow along the same lines. The student can get the feel of the movement and the experience of landing without the speed generated in the preliminary movement. Techniques in which the performer lands on the feet should precede those in which other body parts receive weight upon landing. The standing long jump, running long jump, hop-step-jump, and scissors high jump have this characteristic. In addition, getting accustomed to the landing pits by walking, jumping and bouncing (in the high jump pit) in that area helps develop confidence in the facility to receive the body upon landing without sustaining injury. Willingness to try the high jump techniques that involve landing on body parts other than the feet will then follow. In the long jumps the distance between the takeoff point and the landing pit should be adjusted to the proficiency of the students to assure them that their landing will be in the soft landing pit.

However, the field event of high jumping and the track event of hurdling both involve the act of clearing an obstacle. Although both obstacles are easily displaced when bumped, the mere fact of their existence and mass creates a psychological barrier for some students. Two different kinds of modifications can help to overcome this fear: (1) the height of the hurdle or the bar can be adjusted (lowered for beginners); and (2) a flexible material (gauze, yarn, stretchy or elastic rope) can be substituted for the bar or the hurdle. Both of these modifications can be used simultaneously. Thus, the student is free to concentrate on executing the technique. As the technique is mastered, confidence is gained and the desire for greater challenge leads to the incorporation of the standard equipment.

Very careful preplanning is needed to keep students involved in all three learning domains (the cognitive, motor and affective). Once the student understands the goal and the techniques or processes needed to achieve that goal, he can go about working on his own with a partner or even in small groups at the various stations or facilities.

Task cards can help guide him in his endeavors and give him feedback on his progress. Goals may differ both in intensity and number through student choice with teacher direction. For example, a student may be exposed to all events. However, in his final choice of activities he may choose to strive for greater proficiency in those events in which he is most interested. Most often this choice coincides with his chances for success in that activity. Some direction and limitation of choices may need to be established by the instructor in order to foster new interests and broaden perspectives. Included at the end of this section is a sample student contract which provides for choices within limits. In the final analysis the teacher must accept the fact that not all students will develop proficiency in all areas; nor will they all desire to develop expertise. The meaning each individual finds in movement determines his involvement. Although the teacher helps each student to find meaning in movement, he should not impose his meaning upon students.

Individual Student Contract
Notice to Students:

Our class has just finished learning (or reviewing) the fundamental movement patterns and skill techniques (sometimes modified) for four track and four field events. The track events included the 100 yd. dash, the 440 yd. run, the 80 yd. hurdles and the 440 yd. pursuit relay. The field events included the running long jump, the high jump, the discus and the shot put. The next three weeks will be spent in practicing four events of your choice. You will then participate in your chosen four events during an intraclass meet the last week of the unit. Note that in the description of the events there are modifications to provide for your safety and to ensure some success even for the beginners in class.

Practice for the next three weeks should be done with a partner or small group. Partners should give each other immediate feedback on improving technique, aid in adjusting/positioning equipment and assist in measuring progress. Note that your best score for each event is to be recorded each practice session. Schedule your class time to include practice on at least two events per class period. Work safely and do warm-up appropriately for each event. Deposit your contract in the class folder for safekeeping at the end of each class period. Your chart of daily progress will be used to place you on teams for the intraclass meet.

Name _____ Date _____

Grade level (circle one) 9   10   11   12   (7   8)

Briefly describe any previous experiences you have had in track and field other than your classwork these last few weeks.

_____

_____

_____

_____

Events: You must choose to practice four events: two track events and two field events. Mark a √ in the space provided for the events of your choice.

Track Events

_____ 100 yd. dash   (You must use starting blocks.)

_____ 440 yd. run   (You may choose not to use starting blocks and can use a standing start if you prefer.)

_____ 80 yd. hurdles (You must use starting blocks. Stretch ropes positioned 24″ from the ground are to be substituted for regulation hurdles.)

_____ 440 yd. relay   (Practice with the group of four to which you have been assigned. Decide upon the type of pass to be used, order of running, etc.)

Field Events

_____ Running long jump (The take off line is just 5′ from the landing pit.)

_____ High jump (You may choose to use the scissor, western, or straddle style.)

_____ Discus (Preliminary movement is optional. Balls in rope bags with rope handles may be substituted for the discus.)

_____ Shot (Preliminary movement is optional. The small five pound medicine balls are to be used rather than the regulation shot.)

Record of Daily Progress

List of Events:

(Dates)	4/3	4/5	4/10	4/12	4/17	4/19	Intraclass Meet	
1. _____								Record your best time or distance for each practice session
2. _____								
3. _____								
4. _____								

REFERENCES

Amateur Athletic Union. *The A.A.U. Official Track and Field Handbook and Rules.* New York: Amateur Athletic Union, published yearly.

Doherty, Ken. *Track and Field Omnibook.* 2d ed. Los Altos, Calif.: Tafnews Press, 1976.

Dyson, Geoffrey. *The Mechanics of Athletics.* 7th ed. London: University of London Press, 1977.

Ecker, Tom. *Track and Field Dynamics.* 2d ed. Los Altos, Calif.: Tafnews Press, 1974.

Ecker, Tom. *Track and Field, Technique Through Dynamics.* Los Altos, Calif.: Tafnews Press, 1976.

Foremen, Ken, and Husted, Virginia. *Track and Field Techniques for Girls and Women.* 3d ed. Dubuque, Iowa: Wm. C. Brown Company Publishers, 1977.

National Association for Girls and Women in Sport. *Track and Field Guide,* Washington, D.C.: American Alliance for Health, Physical Education & Recreation, current edition.

National Federation of State High School Athletics Associations. *Track and Field Rules and Record Book.* 7 South Dearborne Street, Chicago, Illinois 60603.

Robison, Clarence F.; Jensen, Clayne R.; Sherald, James W.; and Hirschi, Willard M. *Modern Techniques of Track and Field.* Philadelphia: Lea and Febiger, 1974.

Thompson, Donnis Hazel. *Modern Track and Field for Girls and Women.* Boston, Mass.: Allyn and Bacon, Inc., 1973.

Wakefield, Francis, and Harkins, Dorothy. *Track and Field Fundamentals for Girls and Women.* St. Louis, Mo.: The C. V. Mosby Co., 1977.

Wilt, Fred, and Ecker, Tom. *International Track and Field Coaching Encyclopedia.* West Nyack, N.Y.: Parker Publishing Co., 1970.

INDEX